CLYMER®

HONDA

CB650 FOURS • 1979-1982

The world's finest publisher of mechanical how-to manuals

P.O. Box 12901, Overland Park, Kansas 66282-2901

FIRST EDITION
First Printing August, 1981
Second Printing January, 1982

SECOND EDITION
Updated by Ed Scott to include 1982 models
First Printing July, 1983
Second Printing June, 1985
Third Printing July, 1986
Fourth Printing December, 1987
Fifth Printing November, 1988
Sixth Printing April, 1990
Seventh Printing October, 1991
Eighth Printing December, 1992
Ninth Printing June, 1994
Tenth Printing March, 1996
Eleventh Printing November, 1997
Twelfth Printing September, 1999
Thirteenth Printing September, 2001
Fourteenth Printing April, 2004
Fifteenth Printing September, 2011

Printed in U.S.A.

ISBN-10: 0-89287-343-4

ISBN-13: 978-0-89287-343-2

Technical assistance from Brian Slark, San Juan Capistrano, California, Technical illustrations by Mitzi McCarthy.

TOOLS AND EQUIPMENT: K & L Supply Co. at www.klsupply.com.

COVER: Photographed by Michael Brown Photographic Productions, Los Angeles, California. Assisted by Tim Lunde. Motorcycle courtesy of Bill Krause Sportscycles, Inglewood, California. Helmet courtesy of Simpson Sports, Torrance, California. Sweater and gloves courtesy of Bates Industries, Long Beach, California.

Publisher Ron Rogers

EDITORIAL

Editorial Director
James Grooms

Editor
Steven Thomas

Associate Editor
Rick Arens

Authors
Michael Morlan
George Parise
Ed Scott
Ron Wright

Technical Illustrators
Steve Amos
Errol McCarthy
Mitzi McCarthy
Bob Meyer

SALES

Sales Manager–Marine
Jay Lipton

Sales Manager–Powersport/I&T
Matt Tusken

CUSTOMER SERVICE

Customer Service Manager
Terri Cannon

Customer Service Representatives
Dinah Bunnell
Suzanne Johnson
April LeBlond
Sherry Rudkin

PRODUCTION

Director of Production
Dylan Goodwin

Production Manager
Greg Araujo

Senior Production Editors
Darin Watson
Adriane Wineinger

Associate Production Editor
Ashley Bally

P.O. Box 12901, Overland Park, KS 66282-2901 • 800-262-1954 • 913-967-1719

More information available at *clymer.com*

CONTENTS

QUICK REFERENCE DATA

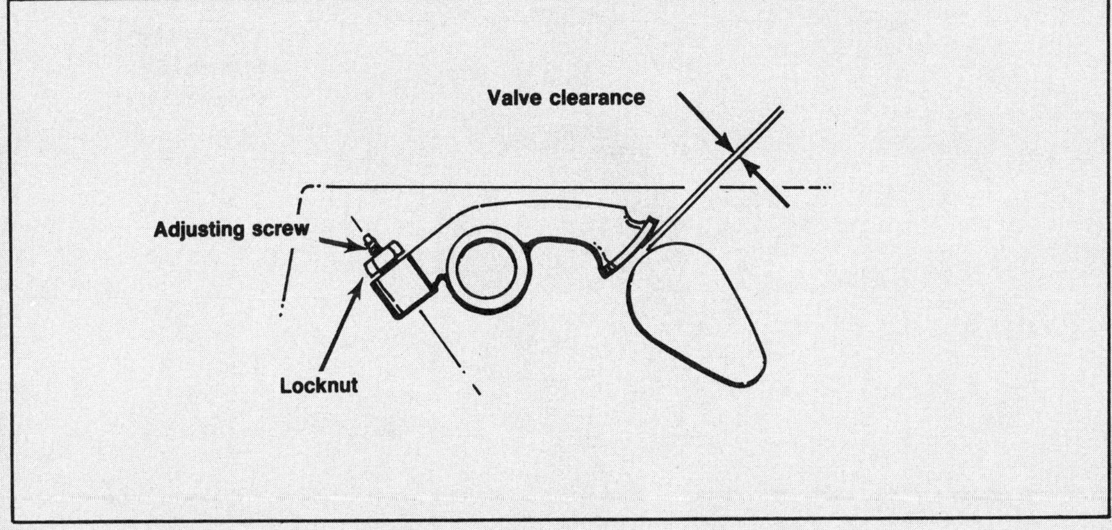

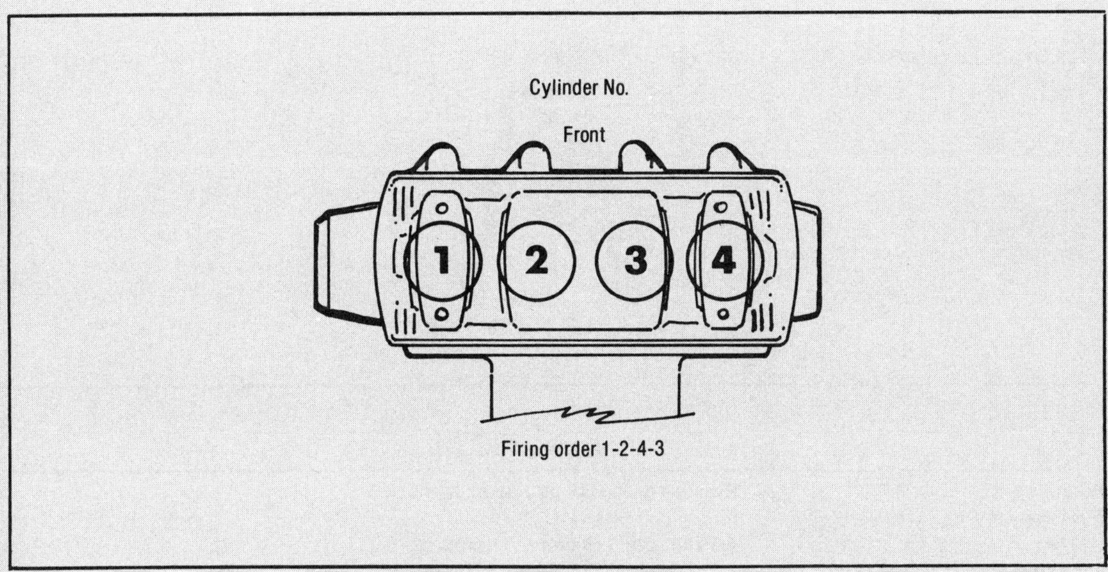

REPLACEMENT BULBS

	Wattage	Trade No.
Headlight		
1979-1980	12V 65/50W (sealed beam)	
1981-on	12V H4 Phillips No.12341/99 or equivalent (quartz bulb)	
Tail/brakelight	12V 8/27W	SAE No. 1157
Directionals		
Front	12V 23W	SAE No. 1034
Rear	12V 23 W	SAE No. 1073
Speedometer, tachometer illumination	12V 3.4W	SAE No. 57
Indicator lights (all)	12V 3.4W	SAE No. 57
Pilot (city)		
Used with regular headlight	12V 3W (Stanley)	
Used with quartz headlight	12V 4W (Stanley)	

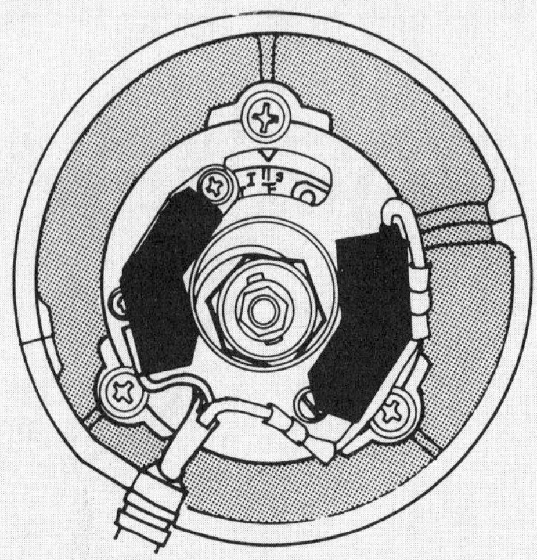

TIMING MARKS
Static 1.4 S-F
Dynamic 1.4F-1

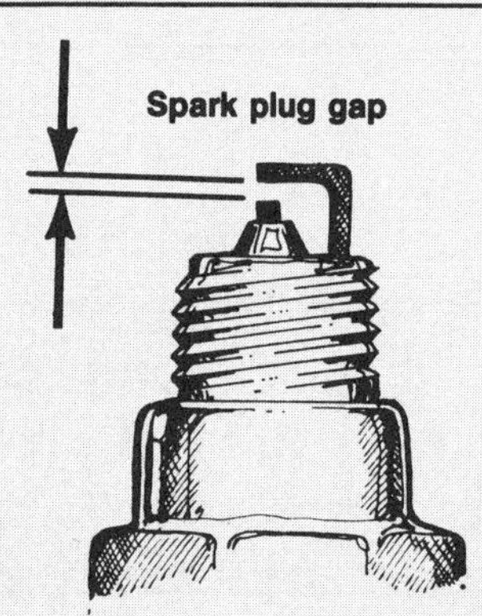

FLUIDS

Fuel type	Regular grade 91 octane or higher
Fuel capacity	
1979	4.8 U.S. gal. (18 liters, 3.9 Imp. gal.)
1980-on	3.5 U.S. gal. (13.5 liters, 3.0 Imp. gal.)
Oil capacity	
Oil drain	3.2 U.S. qt. (3.0 liters, 2.6 Imp. qt.)
Engine assembly	3.7 U.S. qt. (3.5 liters, 2.8 Imp. qt.)
Fork oil capacity @ drain*	
1979	5.0 oz. (150 cc)
1980	
Standard	5.3 oz. (155 cc)
Custom	6.5 oz. (190 cc)
1981	
Standard	6.5 oz. (190 cc)
Custom	7.6 oz. (225 cc)
1982	
Standard	10.2 oz. (320 cc)
Nighthawk	6.5 oz. (190 cc)

* Capacity of each fork leg.

TIRE INFLATION PRESSURE AND TIRE SIZE

Load	Air Pressure
Up to 200 lb. (90 kg)	
Front—all models	28 psi (2.0 kg/cm^2)
Rear	
Standard models	28 psi (2.0 kg/cm^2)
Custom models	28 psi (2.0 kg/cm^2)
Maximum load limit*	
Front—all models	28 psi (2.0 kg/cm^2)
Rear	
Standard models	36 psi (2.5 kg/cm^2)
Custom models	32 psi (2.25 kg/cm^2)
Front tire size	
Standard	3.50 H19 4PR
Custom	3.50 S19 4PR
Rear tire size	
Standard	4.50 H17 4PR
Custom	130/90-16 X 67S

*Maximum load limit includes total weight of motorcycle with accessories, rider(s) and luggage.

FRAME TORQUE SPECIFICATIONS

Item	Foot pounds (ft.-lb.)	Newton meters (N•m)
Front axle nut		
Standard Model and 1980 Custom	40-48	55-65
Front axle clamp nuts	13-18	18-25
Front axle		
Custom since 1981	40-48	55-65
Caliper mounting bolts	22-29	30-40
Brake system union bolts	18-25	25-35
Handlebar holder/fuse panel bolts	20-23	28-32
Fork bridge bolts		
Upper	7-9	9-13
Lower	22-29	30-40
Steering stem bolt	58-87	80-120
Fork cap bolt		
Non air assist	15-22	20-30
Air assist	11-22	15-30
Air assist forks air fittings		
Connector to right-hand fork leg cap bolt	3-5	4-7
Air hose to left-hand fork fork cap bolt	3-5	4-7
Air hose to right-hand connector	11-15	15-20
Rear axle nut	58-72	80-100
Rear swing arm pivot bolt nut	43-51	60-70
Shock absorbers		
Upper and lower mounting nut and bolt	22-29	20-40
Brake torque link bolt	13-18	18-25

ENGINE TORQUE SPECIFICATIONS

Item	Foot-pounds (ft.-lb.)	Newton meters (N•m)
Engine mounting bolts		
8 mm flange bolt	19-23	26-32
10 mm flange bolt	22-29	30-40
12 mm flange bolt	58-72	80-100
Cylinder head cover, breather cover and tachometer driven gear housing	6-9	8-12
Valve adjusting locknut	9-12	12-16
Spark plug	9-12	12-16
Cam chain tensioner bolt	7-10	10-14
Alternator bolt	36-43	50-60

TUNE-UP SUMMARY

Valve clearance (cold)	
Intake	**0.002 in. (0.05 mm)**
Exhaust	**0.003 in. (0.08 mm)**
Compression pressure (at sea level)	**170 ±28 psi (12.0 ± 2.0 kg/cm^2)**
Spark plug type	
1979-1981	
Standard heat range	
U.S.	**ND X24ES-U or NGK D8EA**
Canadian	**ND X24ESR-U or NGK DR8ES-L**
Cold weather*	
U.S.	**ND X22ES-U or NGK D7EA**
Canadian	**ND X22ESR-U or NGK DR7ES**
Extended high-speed riding	
U.S.	**ND X27ES-U or NGK DR9EA**
Canadian	**ND X27ESR-U or NGK DR8ES**
1982	
Standard heat range	**ND X24ESR-U or NGK DR8ES-L**
Cold weather*	**ND X22ESR-U or NGK DR7ES**
Extended high-speed riding	**ND X27ESR-U or NGK DR8ES**
Spark plug gap	**0.024-0.028 in. (0.6-0.7 mm)**
Spark plug torque	**9-12 ft.-lb. (12-16 N•m)**
Ignition timing	**"1.4 F-1" @ 1,050 ±100 rpm Advance timing mark "II" @ 2,725 rpm**
Idle speed	**1,050 ±100 rpm**
Firing order	**1-2-4-3**

*** Cold weather climate: below 41° F (5° C).**

DRIVE CHAIN REPLACEMENT NUMBERS

1979	**DID 50DK OR RK 50NK by 102 links**
1980	**DID 50HDK or RK 50NK by 104 links**
1981-on	
CB650SC	**DID 50V or RK 50 MO by 106 links**
Others	**DID 50V or RK 50MO by 104 links**

CLYMER®

HONDA

CB650 FOURS • 1979-1982

INTRODUCTION

This detailed, comprehensive manual covers Honda CB650 models, 1979-1982. The expert text gives complete information on maintenance, repair and overhaul. Hundreds of photos and drawings guide you through every step. The book includes all you need to know to keep your Honda running right.

Chapters One through Twelve contain general information on all models and specific information on 1979-1981 models. The Supplement at the end of the book contains specific information on 1982 models that differs from earlier years.

Where repairs are practical for the owner/mechanic, complete procedures are given. Equally important, difficult jobs are pointed out. Such operations are usually more economically performed by a dealer or independent garage.

A shop manual is a reference. You want to be able to find information fast. As in all Clymer books, this one is designed with this in mind. All chapters are thumb tabbed. Important items are indexed at the rear of the book. All the most frequently used specifications and capacities are summarized on the *Quick Reference* pages at the front of the book.

Keep the book handy. Carry it in your tool box. It will help you to better understand your Honda, lower repair and maintenance costs and generally improve your satisfaction with your bike.

CHAPTER ONE

GENERAL INFORMATION

The troubleshooting, maintenance, tune-up, and step-by-step repair procedures in this book are written specifically for the owner and home mechanic. The text is accompanied by helpful photos and diagrams to make the job as clear and correct as possible.

Troubleshooting, maintenance, tune-up, and repair are not difficult if you know what to do and what tools and equipment to use. Anyone of average intelligence, with some mechanical ability, and not afraid to get their hands dirty can perform most of the procedures in this book.

In some cases, a repair job may require tools or skills not reasonably expected of the home mechanic. These procedures are noted in each chapter and it is recommended that you take the job to your dealer, a competent mechanic, or a machine shop.

MANUAL ORGANIZATION

This chapter provides general information, safety and service hints. Also included are lists of recommended shop and emergency tools as well as a brief description of troubleshooting and tune-up equipment.

Chapter Two provides methods and suggestions for quick and accurate diagnosis and repair of problems. Troubleshooting procedures discuss typical symptoms and logical methods to pinpoint the trouble.

Chapter Three explains all periodic lubrication and routine maintenance necessary to keep your motorcycle running well. Chapter Three also includes recommended tune-up procedures, eliminating the need to constantly consult chapters on the various subassemblies.

Subsequent chapters cover specific systems such as the engine, transmission, and electrical system. Each of these chapters provides disassembly, inspection, repair, and assembly procedures in a simple step-by-step format. If a repair is impractical for the home mechanic it is indicated. In these cases it is usually faster and less expensive to have the repairs made by a dealer or competent repair shop. Essential specifications are included in the appropriate chapters.

When special tools are required to perform a task included in this manual, the tools are illustrated. It may be possible to borrow or rent these tools. The inventive mechanic may also be able to find a suitable substitute in his tool box, or to fabricate one.

The terms NOTE, CAUTION, and WARNING have specific meanings in this manual. A NOTE provides additional or explanatory information. A

CAUTION is used to emphasize areas where equipment damage could result if proper precautions are not taken. A WARNING is used to stress those areas where personal injury or death could result from negligence, in addition to possible mechanical damage.

SERVICE HINTS

Time, effort, and frustration will be saved and possible injury will be prevented if you observe the following practices.

Most of the service procedures covered are straightforward and can be performed by anyone reasonably handy with tools. It is suggested, however, that you consider your own capabilities carefully before attempting any operation involving major disassembly of the engine.

Some operations, for example, require the use of a press. It would be wiser to have these performed by a shop equipped for such work, rather than to try to do the job yourself with makeshift equipment. Other procedures require precision measurements. Unless you have the skills and equipment required, it would be better to have a qualified repair shop make the measurements for you.

Repairs go much faster and easier if the parts that will be worked on are clean before you begin. There are special cleaners for washing the engine and related parts. Brush or spray on the cleaning solution, let stand, then rinse it away with a garden hose. Clean all oily or greasy parts with cleaning solvent as you remove them.

WARNING

Never use gasoline as a cleaning agent. It presents an extreme fire hazard. Be sure to work in a well-ventilated area when using cleaning solvent. Keep a fire extinguisher, rated for gasoline fires, handy in any case.

Much of the labor charge for repairs made by dealers is for the removal and disassembly of other parts to reach the defective unit. It is frequently possible to perform the preliminary operations yourself and then take the defective unit in to the dealer for repair, at considerable savings.

Once you have decided to tackle the job yourself, make sure you locate the appropriate section in this manual, and read it entirely. Study the illustrations and text until you have a good idea of what is involved in completing the job satisfactorily. If special tools are required, make arrangements to get them before you start. Also, purchase any known defective parts prior to starting on the procedure. It is frustrating and time-consuming to get partially into a job and then be unable to complete it.

Simple wiring checks can be easily made at home, but knowledge of electronics is almost a necessity for performing tests with complicated electronic testing gear.

During disassembly of parts keep a few general cautions in mind. Force is rarely needed to get things apart. If parts are a tight fit, like a bearing in a case, there is usually a tool designed to separate them. Never use a screwdriver to pry apart parts with machined surfaces such as cylinder head or crankcase halves. You will mar the surfaces and end up with leaks.

Make diagrams wherever similar-appearing parts are found. You may think you can remember where everything came from — but mistakes are costly. There is also the possibility you may get sidetracked and not return to work for days or even weeks — in which interval, carefully laid out parts may have become disturbed.

Tag all similar internal parts for location, and mark all mating parts for position. Record number and thickness of any shims as they are removed. Small parts such as bolts can be identified by placing them in plastic sandwich bags that are sealed and labeled with masking tape.

Wiring should be tagged with masking tape and marked as each wire is removed. Again, do not rely on memory alone.

Disconnect battery ground cable before working near electrical connections and before disconnecting wires. Never run the engine with the battery disconnected; the alternator could be seriously damaged.

Protect finished surfaces from physical damage or corrosion. Keep gasoline and brake fluid off painted surfaces.

Frozen or very tight bolts and screws can often be loosened by soaking with penetrating oil like Liquid Wrench or WD-40, then sharply striking the bolt head a few times with a hammer and punch (or screwdriver for screws). Avoid heat unless absolutely necessary, since it may melt, warp, or remove the temper from many parts.

Avoid flames or sparks when working near a charging battery or flammable liquids, such as gasoline.

No parts, except those assembled with a press fit, require unusual force during assembly. If a part is hard to remove or install, find out why before proceeding.

Cover all openings after removing parts to keep dirt, small tools, etc., from falling in.

When assembling two parts, start all fasteners, then tighten evenly.

Wiring connections and brake shoes, drums, pads, and discs and contact surfaces in dry clutches should be kept clean and free of grease and oil.

When assembling parts, be sure all shims and washers are replaced exactly as they came out.

Whenever a rotating part butts against a stationary part, look for a shim or washer. Use new gaskets if there is any doubt about the condition of old ones. Generally, you should apply gasket cement to one mating surface only, so the parts may be easily disassembled in the future. A thin coat of oil on gaskets helps them seal effectively.

Heavy grease can be used to hold small parts in place if they tend to fall out during assembly. However, keep grease and oil away from electrical, clutch, and brake components.

High spots may be sanded off a piston with sandpaper, but emery cloth and oil do a much more professional job.

Carburetors are best cleaned by disassembling them and soaking the parts in a commercial carburetor cleaner. Never soak gaskets and rubber parts in these cleaners. Never use wire to clean out jets and air passages; they are easily damaged. Use compressed air to blow out the carburetor, but only if the float has been removed first.

Take your time and do the job right. Do not forget that a newly rebuilt engine must be broken in the same as a new one. Refer to your owner's manual for the proper break-in procedures.

SAFETY FIRST

Professional mechanics can work for years and never sustain a serious injury. If you observe a few rules of common sense and safety, you can enjoy many safe hours servicing your motorcycle. You could hurt yourself or damage the motorcycle if you ignore these rules.

1. Never use gasoline as a cleaning solvent.
2. Never smoke or use a torch in the vicinity of flammable liquids such as cleaning solvent in open containers.
3. Never smoke or use a torch in an area where batteries are being charged. Highly explosive hydrogen gas is formed during the charging process.
4. Use the proper sized wrenches to avoid damage to nuts and injury to yourself.
5. When loosening a tight or stuck nut, be guided by what would happen if the wrench should slip. Protect yourself accordingly.
6. Keep your work area clean and uncluttered.
7. Wear safety goggles during all operations involving drilling, grinding, or use of a cold chisel.
8. Never use worn tools.
9. Keep a fire extinguisher handy and be sure it is rated for gasoline (Class B) and electrical (Class C) fires.

EXPENDABLE SUPPLIES

Certain expendable supplies are necessary. These include grease, oil, gasket cement, wiping rags, cleaning solvent, and distilled water. Also, special locking compounds, silicone lubricants, and engine and carburetor cleaners may be useful. Cleaning solvent is available at most service stations and distilled water for the battery is available at supermarkets.

SHOP TOOLS

For complete servicing and repair you will need an assortment of ordinary hand tools (**Figure 1**).

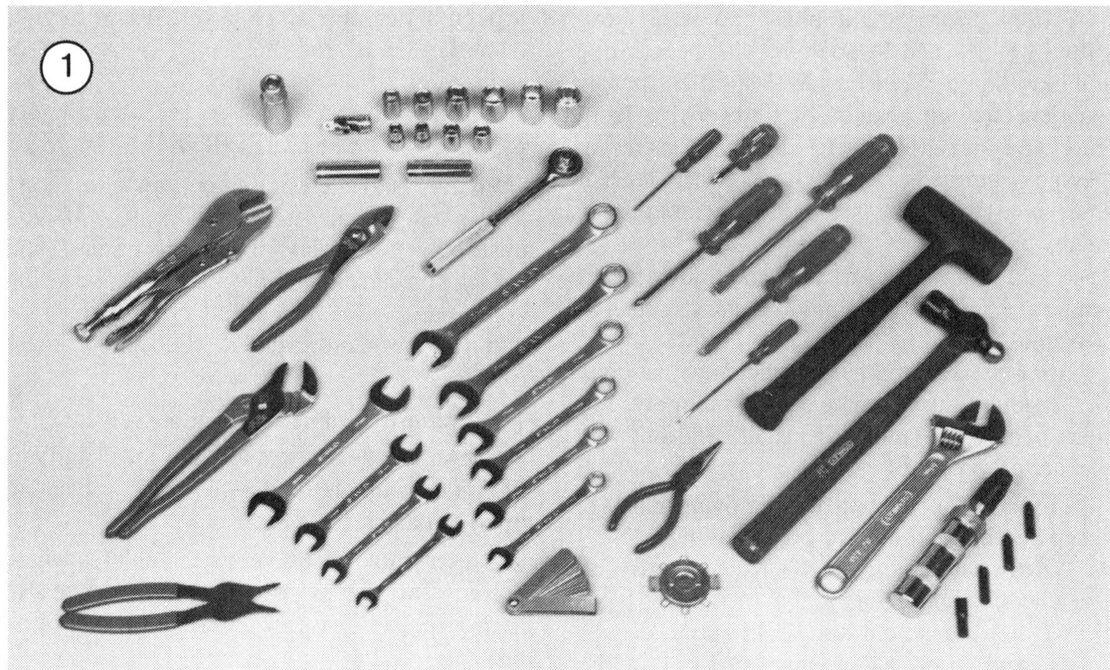

As a minimum, these include:

a. Combination wrenches
b. Sockets
c. Plastic mallet
d. Small hammer
e. Impact driver
f. Snap ring pliers
g. Gas pliers
h. Phillips screwdrivers
i. Slot (common) screwdrivers
j. Feeler gauges
k. Spark plug gauge
l. Spark plug wrench

Special tools required are shown in the chapters covering the particular repair in which they are used.

Engine tune-up and troubleshooting procedures require other special tools and equipment. These are described in detail in the following sections.

EMERGENCY TOOL KITS

Highway

A small emergency tool kit kept on the bike is handy for road emergencies which otherwise could leave you stranded. The tools and spares listed below and shown in **Figure 2** will let you handle most roadside repairs.

a. Motorcycle tool kit (original equipment)
b. Impact driver
c. Silver waterproof sealing tape (duct tape)
d. Hose clamps (3 sizes)
e. Silicone sealer
f. Lock 'N' Seal
g. Flashlight
h. Tire patch kit
i. Tire irons
j. Plastic pint bottle (for oil)
k. Waterless hand cleaner
l. Rags for clean up

Off-Road

A few simple tools and aids carried on the motorcycle can mean the difference between walking or riding back to camp or to where repairs can be made. See **Figure 3**.

A few essential spare parts carried in your truck or van can prevent a day or weekend of trail riding from being spoiled. See **Figure 4**.

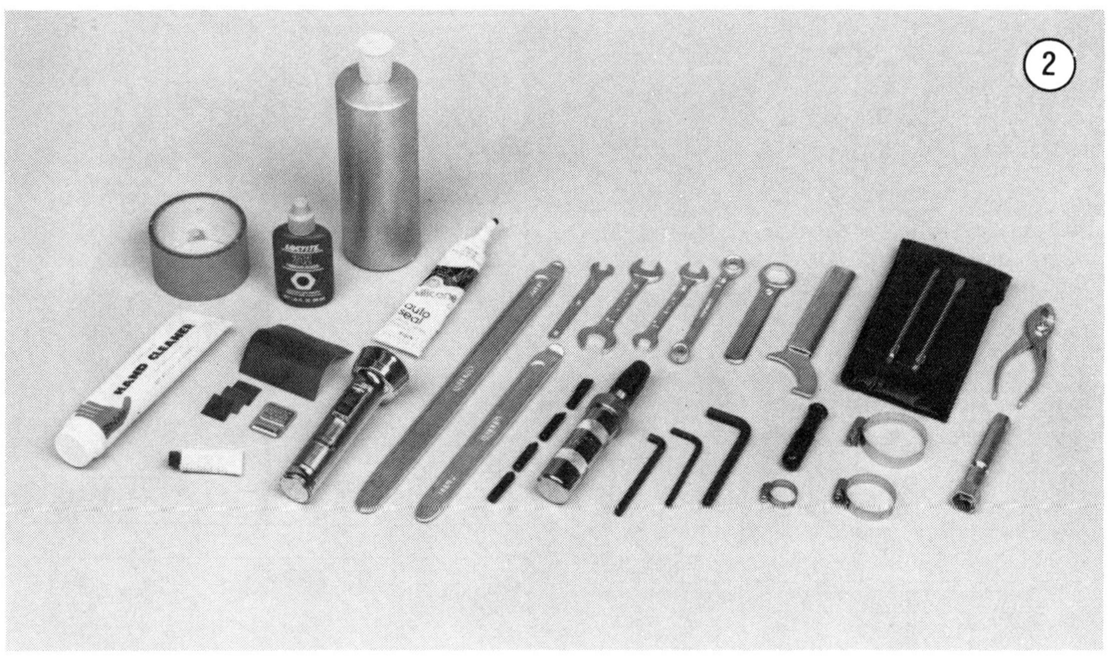

On the Motorcycle

a. Motorcycle tool kit (original equipment)
b. Drive chain master link
c. Tow line
d. Spark plug
e. Spark plug wrench
f. Shifter lever
g. Clutch/brake lever
h. Silver waterproof sealing tape (duct tape)
i. Loctite Lock 'N' Seal

In the Truck

a. Control cables (throttle, clutch, brake)
b. Silicone sealer
c. Tire patch kit
d. Tire irons
e. Tire pump
f. Impact driver
g. Oil

WARNING

Tools and spares should be carried on the motorcycle — not in clothing where a simple fall could result in serious injury from a sharp tool.

TROUBLESHOOTING AND TUNE-UP EQUIPMENT

Voltmeter, Ohmmeter, and Ammeter

For testing the ignition or electrical system, a good voltmeter is required. For motorcycle use, an instrument covering 0-20 volts is satisfactory. One which also has a 0-2 volt scale is necessary for testing relays, points, or individual contacts where voltage drops are much smaller. Accuracy should be ± ½ volt.

An ohmmeter measures electrical resistance. This instrument is useful for checking continuity (open and short circuits), and testing fuses and lights.

The ammeter measures electrical current. Ammeters for motorcycle use should cover 0-50 amperes and 0-250 amperes. These are useful for checking battery charging and starting current.

Several inexpensive VOM's (volt-ohm-milliammeter) combine all three instruments into one which fits easily in any tool box. See **Figure 5**. However, the ammeter ranges are usually too small for motorcycle work.

Hydrometer

The hydrometer gives a useful indication of battery condition and charge by measuring the

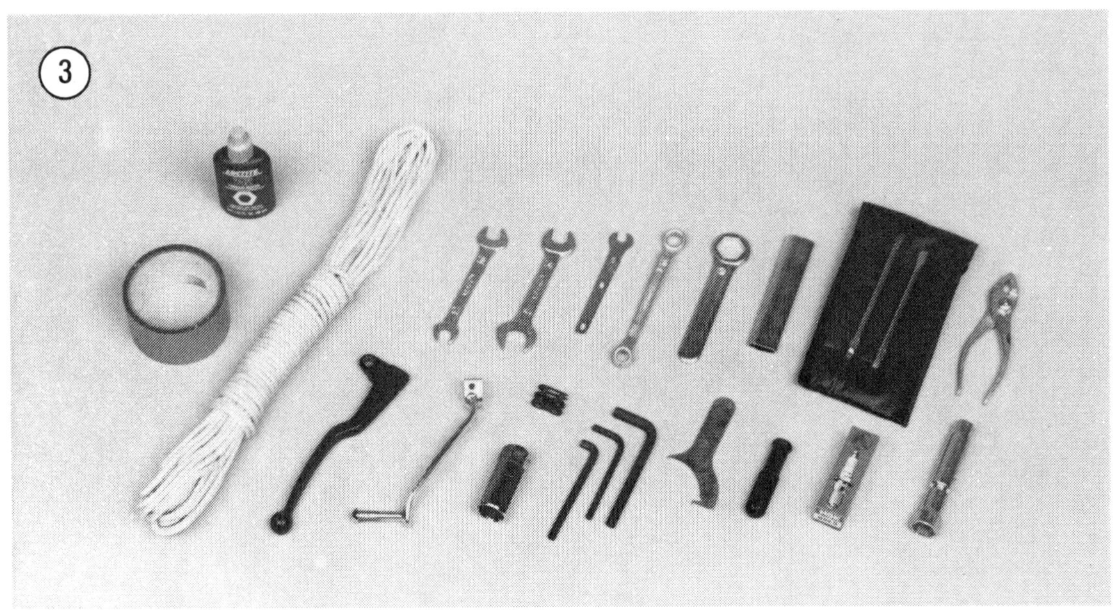

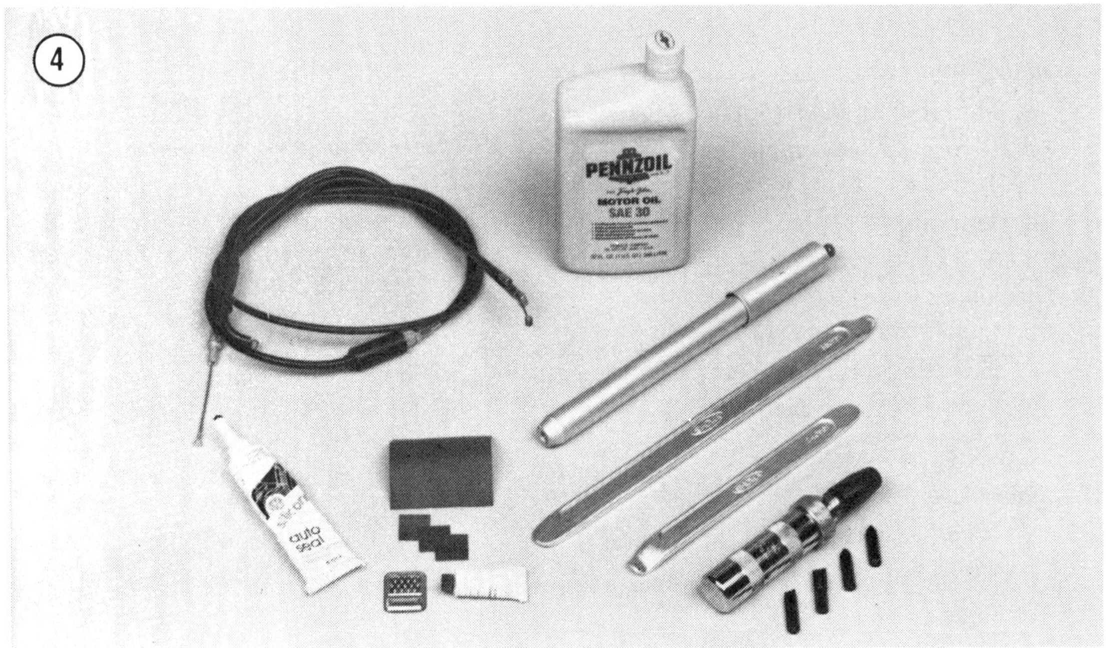

specific gravity of the electrolyte in each cell. See **Figure 6**. Complete details on use and interpretation of readings are provided in the electrical chapter.

Compression Tester

The compression tester measures the compression pressure built up in each cylinder. The results, when properly interpreted, can indicate general cylinder, ring, and valve condition. See **Figure 7**. Extension lines are available for hard-to-reach cylinders.

Dwell Meter (Contact Breaker Point Ignition Only)

A dwell meter measures the distance in degrees of cam rotation that the breaker points remain closed while the engine is running. Since

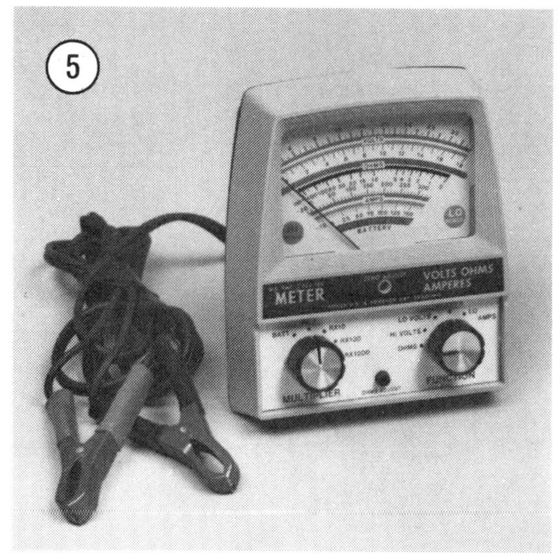

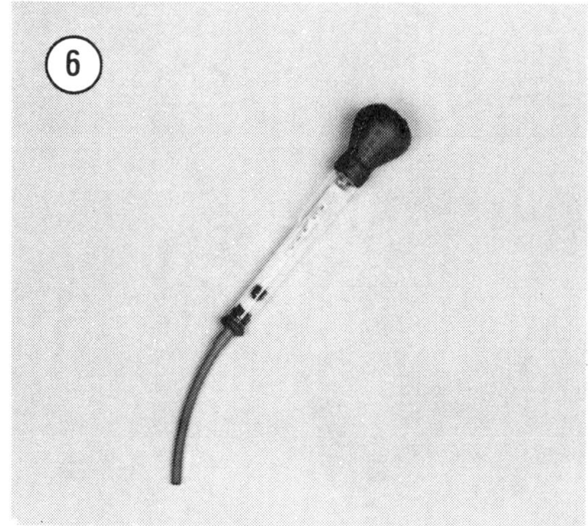

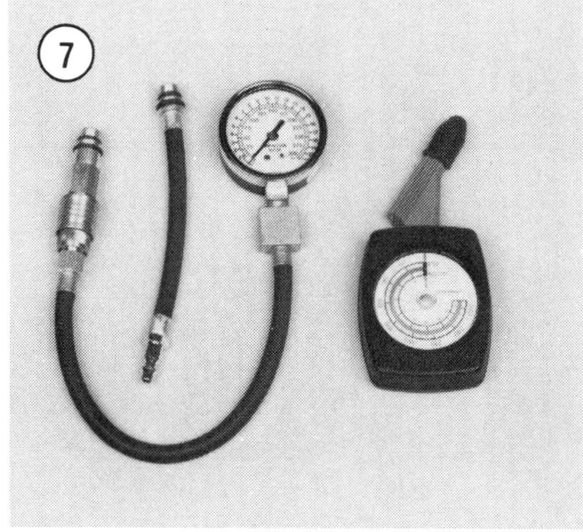

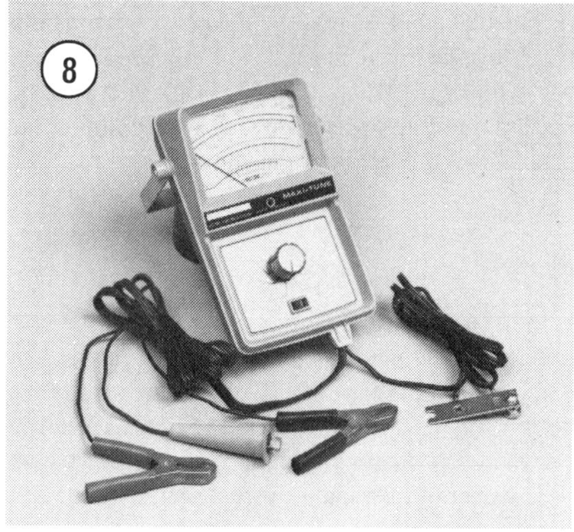

this angle is determined by breaker point gap, dwell angle is an accurate indication of breaker point gap.

Many tachometers intended for tuning and testing incorporate a dwell meter as well. See **Figure 8**. Follow the manufacturer's instructions to measure dwell.

Tachometer

A tachometer is necessary for tuning. See **Figure 8**. Ignition timing and carburetor adjustments must be performed at the specified idle speed. The best instrument for this purpose is one with a low range of 0-1,000 or 0-2,000 rpm for setting idle, and a high range of 0-4,000 or more for setting ignition timing at 3,000 rpm. Extended range (0-6,000 or 0-8,000 rpm) instruments lack accuracy at lower speeds. The instrument should be capable of detecting changes of 25 rpm on the low range.

NOTE: *The motorcycle's tachometer is not accurate enough for correct idle adjustment.*

Strobe Timing Light

This instrument is necessary for tuning, as it permits very accurate ignition timing. The light flashes at precisely the same instant that No. 1 cylinder fires, at which time the timing marks on the engine should align. Refer to Chapter Three for exact location of the timing marks for your engine.

Suitable lights range from inexpensive neon bulb types to powerful xenon strobe lights. See **Figure 9**. Neon timing lights are difficult to see and must be used in dimly lit areas. Xenon strobe timing lights can be used outside in bright sunlight.

Tune-up Kits

Many manufacturers offer kits that combine several useful instruments. Some come in a convenient carry case and are usually less expensive than purchasing one instrument at a time. **Figure 10** shows one of the kits that is available. The prices vary with the number of instruments included in the kit.

Manometer (Carburetor Synchronizer)

A manometer is essential for accurately synchronizing carburetors on multi-cylinder engines. The instrument detects intake pressure differences between carburetors and permits them to be adjusted equally. See **Figure 11**.

Fire Extinguisher

A fire extinguisher is a necessity when working on a vehicle. It should be rated for both *Class B* (flammable liquids — gasoline, oil, paint, etc.) and *Class C* (electrical — wiring, etc.) type fires. It should always be kept within reach. See **Figure 12**.

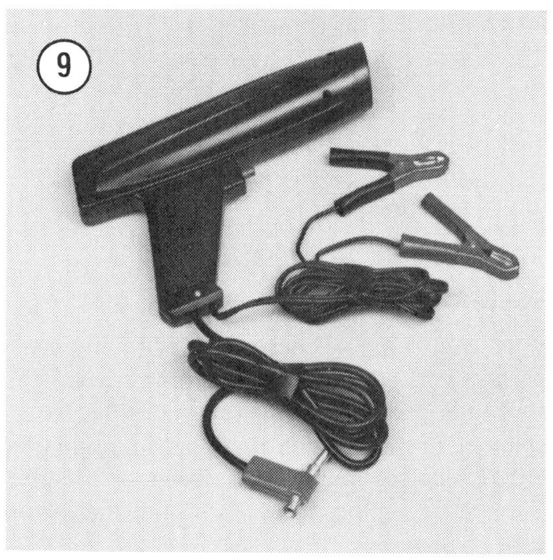

9

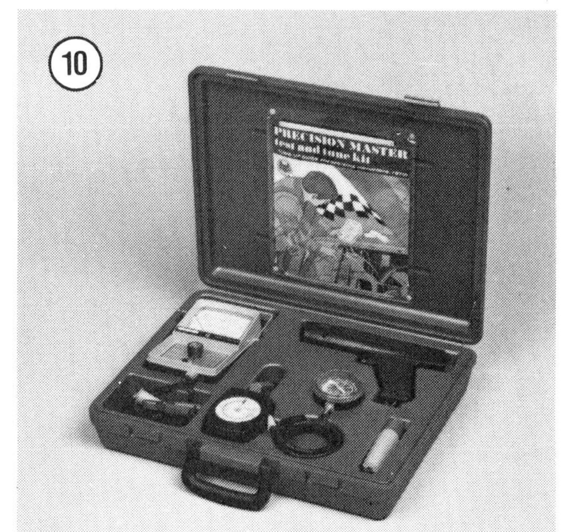

10

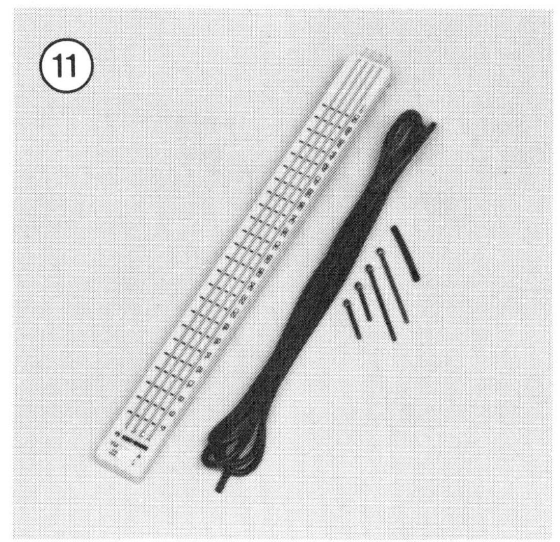

11

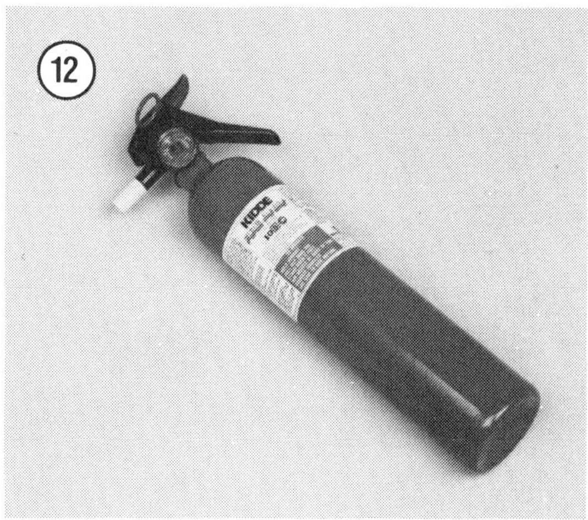

12

2

CHAPTER TWO

TROUBLESHOOTING

Troubleshooting motorcycle problems is relatively simple. To be effective and efficient, however, it must be done in a logical step-by-step manner. If it is not, a great deal of time may be wasted, good parts may be replaced unnecessarily, and the true problem may never be uncovered.

Always begin by defining the symptoms as closely as possible. Then, analyze the symptoms carefully so that you can make an intelligent guess at the probable cause. Next, test the probable cause and attempt to verify it; if it's not at fault, analyze the symptoms once again, this time eliminating the first probable cause. Continue on in this manner, a step at a time, until the problem is solved.

At first, this approach may seem to be time consuming, but you will soon discover that it's not nearly so wasteful as a hit-or-miss method that may never solve the problem. And just as important, the methodical approach to troubleshooting ensures that only those parts that are defective will be replaced.

The troubleshooting procedures in this chapter analyze typical symptoms and show logical methods for isolating and correcting trouble. They are not, however, the only methods; there may be several approaches to a given problem, but all good troubleshooting methods have one thing in common — a logical, systematic approach.

ENGINE

The entire engine must be considered when trouble arises that is experienced as poor performance or failure to start. The engine is more than a combustion chamber, piston, and crankshaft; it also includes a fuel delivery system, an ignition system, and an exhaust system.

Before beginning to troubleshoot any engine problems, it's important to understand an engine's operating requirements. First, it must have a correctly metered mixture of gasoline and air (**Figure 1**). Second, it must have an air-tight combustion chamber in which the mixture can be compressed. And finally, it requires a precisely timed spark to ignite the compressed mixture. If one or more is missing, the engine won't run, and if just one is deficient, the engine will run poorly at best.

Of the three requirements, the precisely timed spark — provided by the ignition system — is most likely to be the culprit, with gas/air mixture (carburetion) second, and poor compression the least likely.

STARTING DIFFICULTIES

Hard starting is probably the most common motorcycle ailment, with a wide range of problems likely. Before delving into a reluctant or non-starter, first determine what has changed

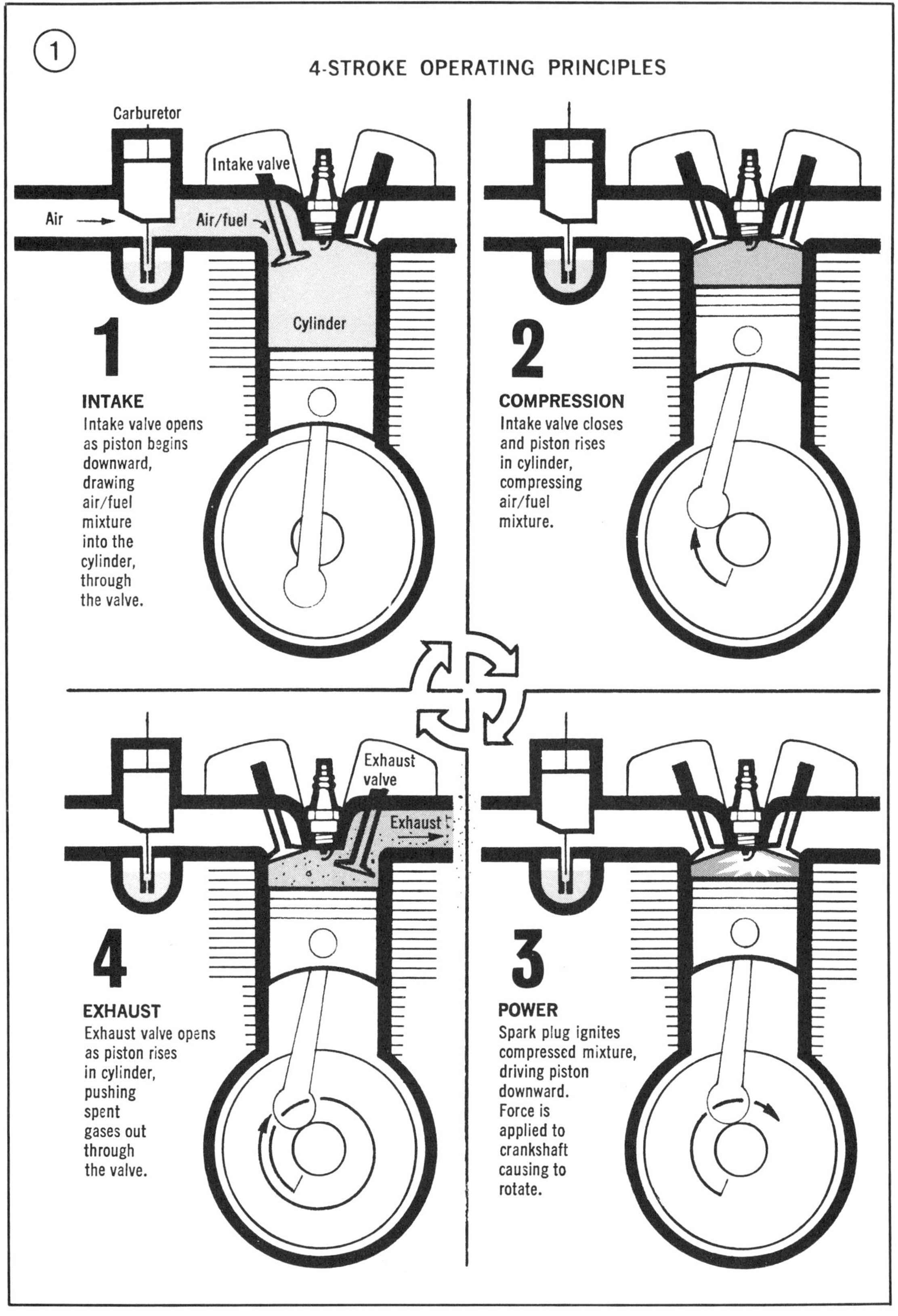
1
4-STROKE OPERATING PRINCIPLES
Carburetor
Intake valve
Air
Air/fuel
Cylinder
1
INTAKE
Intake valve opens as piston begins downward, drawing air/fuel mixture into the cylinder, through the valve.
2
COMPRESSION
Intake valve closes and piston rises in cylinder, compressing air/fuel mixture.
Exhaust valve
Exhaust
4
EXHAUST
Exhaust valve opens as piston rises in cylinder, pushing spent gases out through the valve.
3
POWER
Spark plug ignites compressed mixture, driving piston downward. Force is applied to crankshaft causing to rotate.

since the motorcycle last started easily. For instance, was the weather dry then and is it wet now? Has the motorcycle been sitting in the garage for a long time? Has it been ridden many miles since it was last fueled?

Has starting become increasingly more difficult? This alone could indicate a number of things that may be wrong but is usually associated with normal wear of ignition and engine components.

While it's not always possible to diagnose trouble simply from a change of conditions, this information can be helpful and at some future time may uncover a recurring problem.

Fuel Delivery

Although it is the second most likely cause of trouble, fuel delivery should be checked first simply because it is the easiest.

First, check the tank to make sure there is fuel in it. Then, disconnect the fuel hose at the carburetor, open the valve and check for flow (**Figure 2**). If fuel does not flow freely make sure the tank vent is clear. Next, check for blockage in the line or valve. Remove the valve and clean it as described in the fuel system chapter.

If fuel flows from the hose, reconnect it and remove the float bowl from the carburetor, open the valve and check for flow through the float needle valve. If it does not flow freely when the float is extended and then shut off when the flow is gently raised, clean the carburetor as described in the fuel system chapter.

When fuel delivery is satisfactory, go on to the ignition system.

Ignition

Remove the spark plug from the cylinder and check its condition. The appearance of the plug is a good indication of what's happening in the combustion chamber; for instance, if the plug is wet with gas, it's likely that engine is flooded. Compare the spark plug to **Figure 3**. Make certain the spark plug heat range is correct. A "cold" plug makes starting difficult.

After checking the spark plug, reconnect it to the high-tension lead and lay it on the cylinder head so it makes good contact (**Figure 4**). Then, with the ignition switched on, crank the engine several times and watch for a spark across the plug electrodes. A fat, blue spark should be visible. If there is no spark, or if the spark is weak, substitute a good plug for the old one and check again. If the spark has improved, the old plug is faulty. If there was no change, keep looking.

Make sure the ignition switch is not shorted to ground. Remove the spark plug cap from the end of the high-tension lead and hold the exposed end of the lead about ⅛ inch from the cylinder head. Crank the engine and watch for a spark arcing from the lead to the head. If it's satisfactory, the connection between the lead and the cap was faulty. If the spark hasn't improved, check the coil wire connections.

If the spark is still weak, remove the ignition cover and remove any dirt or moisture from the points or sensor. Check the point or air gap against the specifications in the *Quick Reference Data* at the beginning of the book.

If spark is still not satisfactory, a more serious problem exists than can be corrected with simple adjustments. Refer to the electrical system chapter for detailed information for correcting major ignition problems.

Compression

Compression — or the lack of it — is the least likely cause of starting trouble. However, if compression is unsatisfactory, more than a simple adjustment is required to correct it (see the engine chapter).

An accurate compression check reveals a lot about the condition of the engine. To perform this test you need a compression gauge (see Chapter One). The engine should be at operating temperature for a fully accurate test, but even a cold test will reveal if the starting problem is compression.

Remove the spark plug and screw in a compression gauge (**Figure 5**). With assistance, hold the throttle wide open and crank the engine several times, until the gauge ceases to rise. Normal compression should be 130-160 psi, but a reading as low as 100 psi is usually sufficient for the engine to start. If the reading is much lower than normal, remove the gauge and pour about a tablespoon of oil into the cylinder.

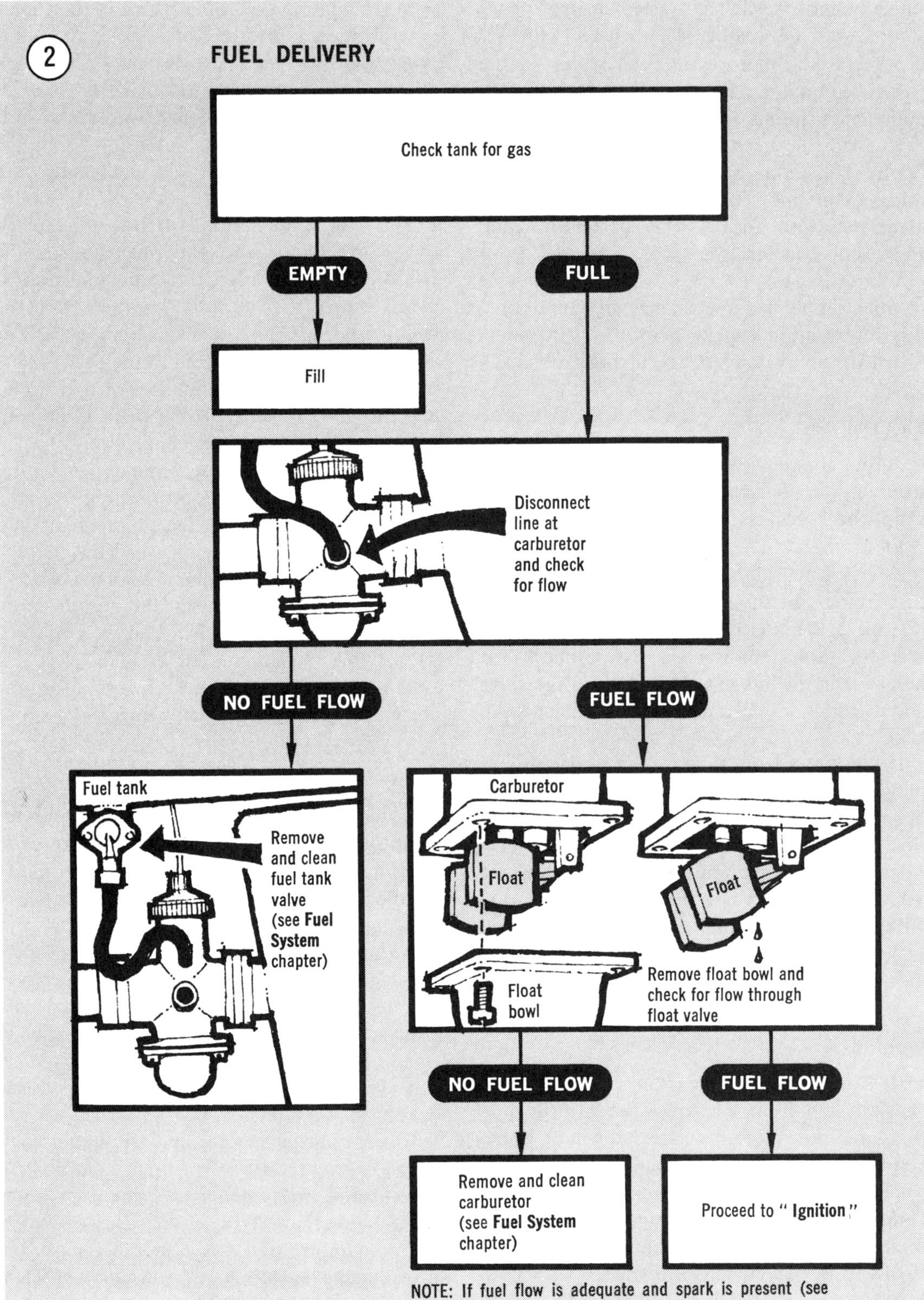
2
FUEL DELIVERY
Check tank for gas
EMPTY
FULL
Fill
Disconnect line at carburetor and check for flow
NO FUEL FLOW
FUEL FLOW
Fuel tank
Remove and clean fuel tank valve (see Fuel System chapter)
Carburetor
Float
Float
Float bowl
Remove float bowl and check for flow through float valve
NO FUEL FLOW
FUEL FLOW
Remove and clean carburetor (see Fuel System chapter)
Proceed to "Ignition"
NOTE: If fuel flow is adequate and spark is present (see Ignition which follows), increase fuel ratio with idle screw.

NORMAL
- Appearance—Firing tip has deposits of light gray to light tan.
- Can be cleaned, regapped and reused.

CARBON FOULED
- Appearance—Dull, dry black with fluffy carbon deposits on the insulator tip, electrode and exposed shell.
- Caused by—Fuel/air mixture too rich, plug heat range too cold, weak ignition system, dirty air cleaner, faulty automatic choke or excessive idling.
- Can be cleaned, regapped and reused.

OIL FOULED
- Appearance—Wet black deposits on insulator and exposed shell.
- Caused by—Excessive oil entering the combustion chamber through worn rings, pistons, valve guides or bearings.
- Replace with new plugs (use a hotter plug if engine is not repaired).

LEAD FOULED
- Appearance — Yellow insulator deposits (may sometimes be dark gray, black or tan in color) on the insulator tip.
- Caused by—Highly leaded gasoline.
- Replace with new plugs.

LEAD FOULED
- Appearance—Yellow glazed deposits indicating melted lead deposits due to hard acceleration.
- Caused by—Highly leaded gasoline.
- Replace with new plugs.

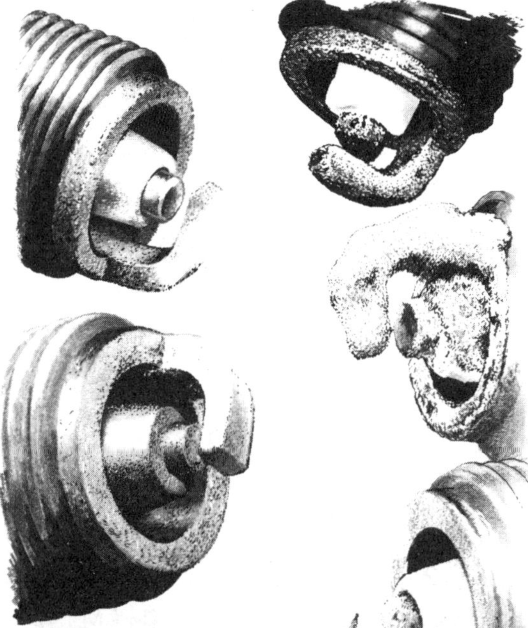

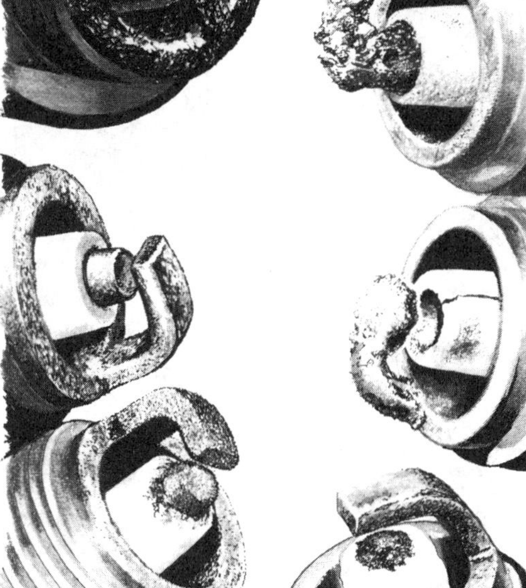

OIL AND LEAD FOULED
- Appearance—Glazed yellow deposits with a slight brownish tint on the insulator tip and ground electrode.
- Replace with new plugs.

FUEL ADDITIVE RESIDUE
- Appearance — Brown colored hardened ash deposits on the insulator tip and ground electrode.
- Caused by—Fuel and/or oil additives.
- Replace with new plugs.

WORN
- Appearance — Severely worn or eroded electrodes.
- Caused by—Normal wear or unusual oil and/or fuel additives.
- Replace with new plugs.

PREIGNITION
- Appearance — Melted ground electrode.
- Caused by—Overadvanced ignition timing, inoperative ignition advance mechanism, too low of a fuel octane rating, lean fuel/air mixture or carbon deposits in combustion chamber.

PREIGNITION
- Appearance—Melted center electrode.
- Caused by—Abnormal combustion due to overadvanced ignition timing or incorrect advance, too low of a fuel octane rating, lean fuel/air mixture, or carbon deposits in combustion chamber.
- Correct engine problem and replace with new plugs.

INCORRECT HEAT RANGE
- Appearance—Melted center electrode and white blistered insulator tip.
- Caused by—Incorrect plug heat range selection.
- Replace with new plugs.

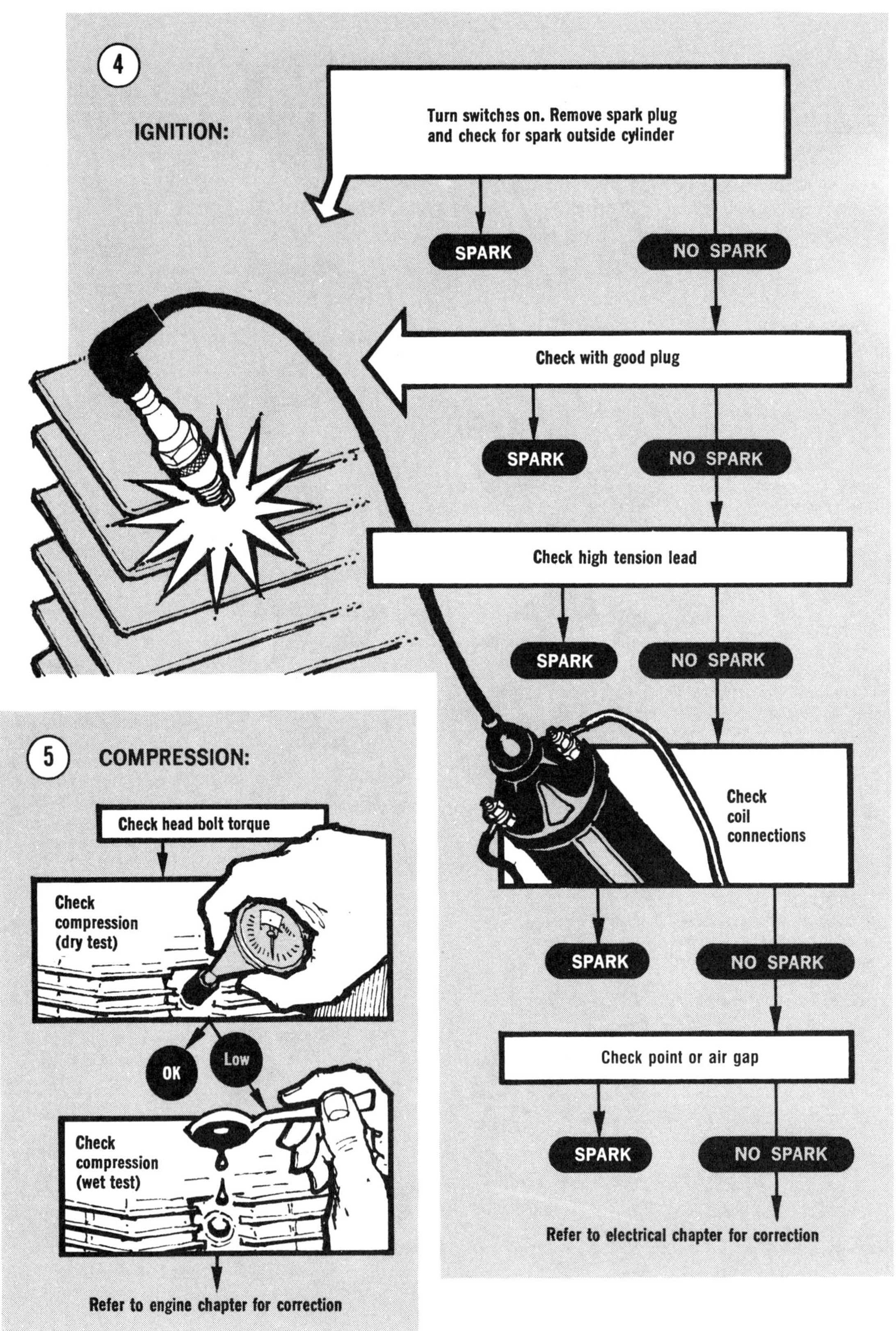
4
IGNITION:
Turn switches on. Remove spark plug and check for spark outside cylinder
SPARK
NO SPARK
Check with good plug
SPARK
NO SPARK
Check high tension lead
SPARK
NO SPARK
Check coil connections
SPARK
NO SPARK
Check point or air gap
SPARK
NO SPARK
Refer to electrical chapter for correction
5
COMPRESSION:
Check head bolt torque
Check compression (dry test)
OK
Low
Check compression (wet test)
Refer to engine chapter for correction

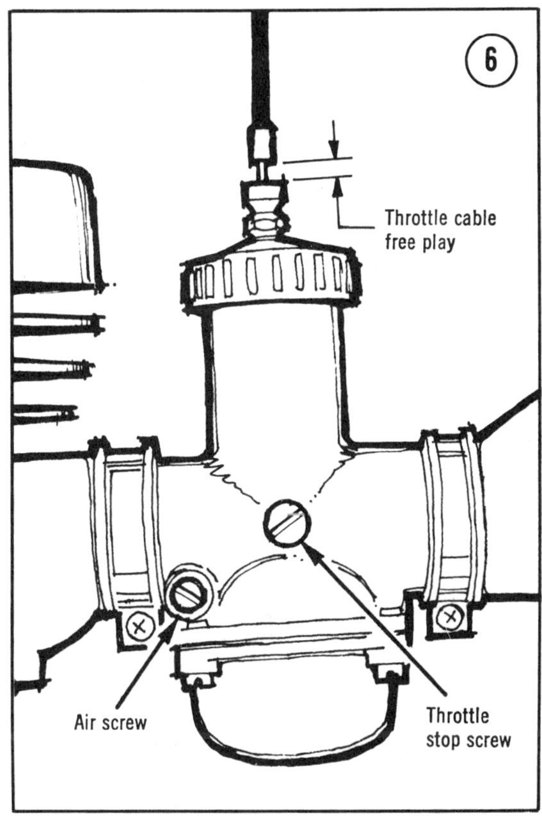

Crank the engine several times to distribute the oil and test the compression once again. If it is now significantly higher, the rings and bore are worn. If the compression did not change, the valves are not seating correctly. Adjust the valves and check again. If the compression is still low, refer to the engine chapter.

NOTE: *Low compression indicates a developing problem. The condition causing it should be corrected as soon as possible.*

POOR PERFORMANCE

Poor engine performance can be caused by any of a number of things related to carburetion, ignition, and the condition of the sliding and rotating components in the engine. In addition, components such as brakes, clutch, and transmission can cause problems that seem to be related to engine performance, even when the engine is in top running condition.

Poor Idling

Idling that is erratic, too high, or too low is most often caused by incorrect adjustment of the carburetor idle circuit. Also, a dirty air filter or an obstructed fuel tank vent can affect idle speed. Incorrect ignition timing or worn or faulty ignition components are also good possibilities.

First, make sure the air filter is clean and correctly installed. Then, adjust the throttle cable free play, the throttle stop screw, and the idle mixture air screw (**Figure 6**) as described in the routine maintenance chapter.

If idling is still poor, check the carburetor and manifold mounts for leaks; with the engine warmed up and running, spray WD-40 or a similar light lube around the flanges and joints of the carburetor and manifold (**Figure 7**). Listen for changes in engine speed. If a leak is present, the idle speed will drop as the lube "plugs" the leak and then pick up again as it is drawn into the engine. Tighten the nuts and clamps and test again. If a leak persists, check for a damaged gasket or a pinhole in the manifold. Minor leaks in manifold hoses can be repaired with silicone sealer, but if cracks or holes are extensive, the manifold should be replaced.

A worn throttle slide may cause erratic running and idling, but this is likely only after many thousands of miles of use. To check, remove the carburetor top and feel for back and forth movement of the slide in the bore; it should be barely perceptible. Inspect the slide for large worn areas and replace it if it is less than perfect (**Figure 8**).

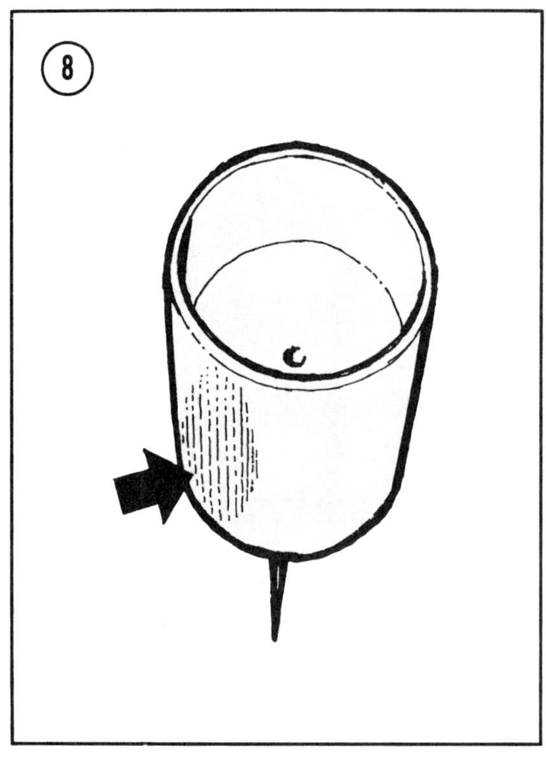

If the fuel system is satisfactory, check ignition timing and breaker point gap (air gap in electronic ignition). Check the condition of the system components as well. Ignition-caused idling problems such as erratic running can be the fault of marginal components. See the electrical system chapter for appropriate tests.

Rough Running or Misfiring

Misfiring (see **Figure 9**) is usually caused by an ignition problem. First, check all ignition connections (**Figure 10**). They should be clean, dry, and tight. Don't forget the kill switch; a loose connection can create an intermittent short.

10

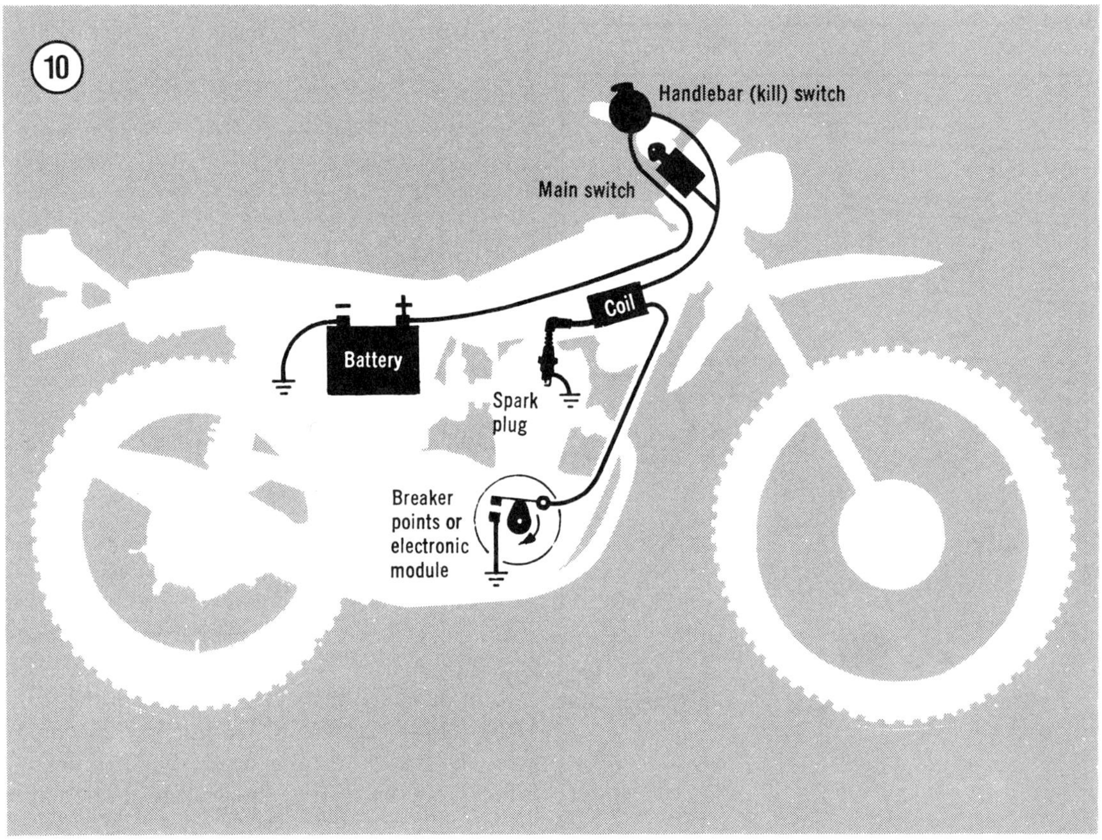

Handlebar (kill) switch

Main switch

Coil

Battery

Spark plug

Breaker points or electronic module

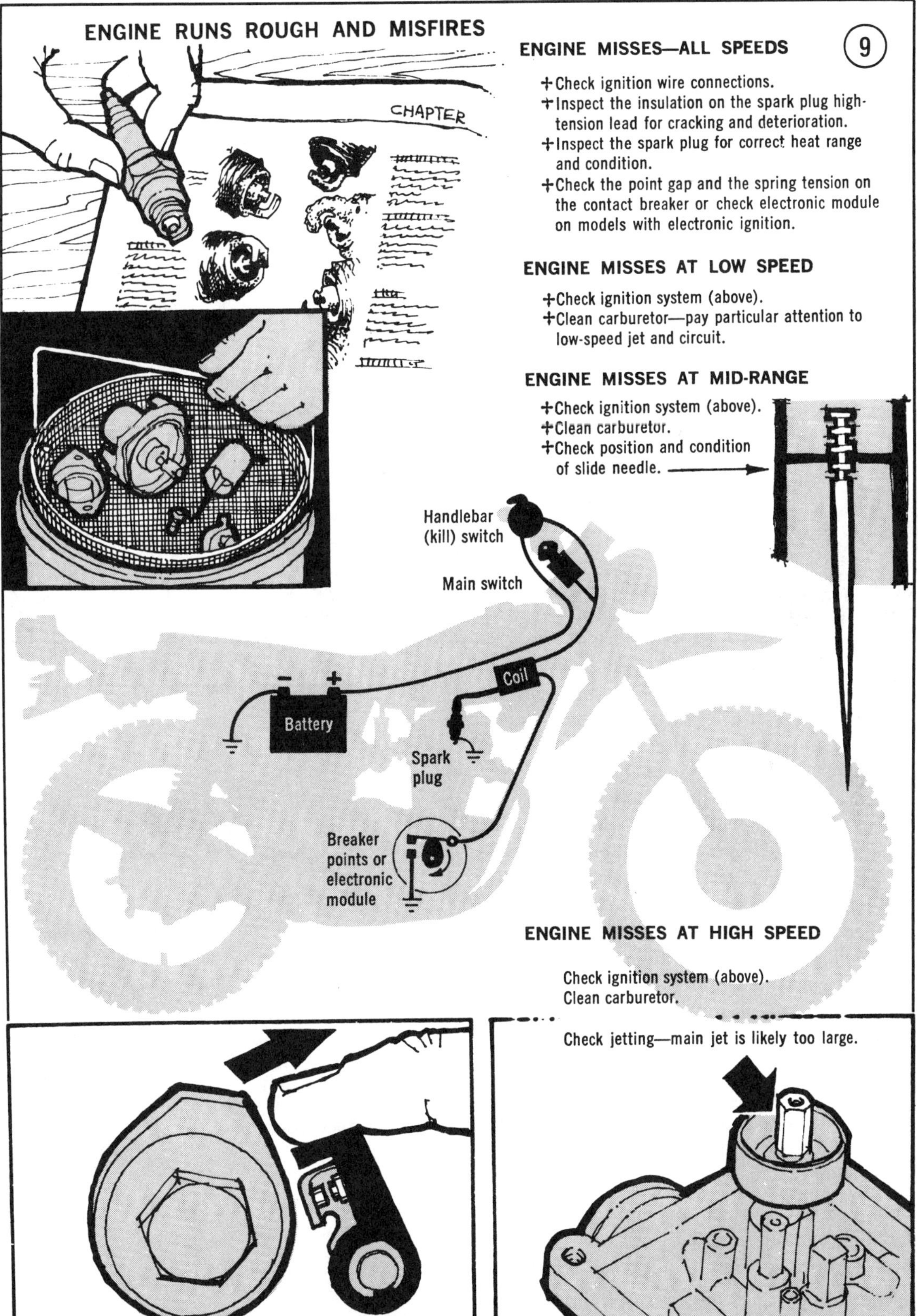
ENGINE RUNS ROUGH AND MISFIRES
CHAPTER
ENGINE MISSES—ALL SPEEDS
9
+Check ignition wire connections.
+Inspect the insulation on the spark plug high-tension lead for cracking and deterioration.
+Inspect the spark plug for correct heat range and condition.
+Check the point gap and the spring tension on the contact breaker or check electronic module on models with electronic ignition.
ENGINE MISSES AT LOW SPEED
+Check ignition system (above).
+Clean carburetor—pay particular attention to low-speed jet and circuit.
ENGINE MISSES AT MID-RANGE
+Check ignition system (above).
+Clean carburetor.
+Check position and condition of slide needle.
Handlebar (kill) switch
Main switch
Coil
Battery
Spark plug
Breaker points or electronic module
ENGINE MISSES AT HIGH SPEED
Check ignition system (above).
Clean carburetor.
Check jetting—main jet is likely too large.

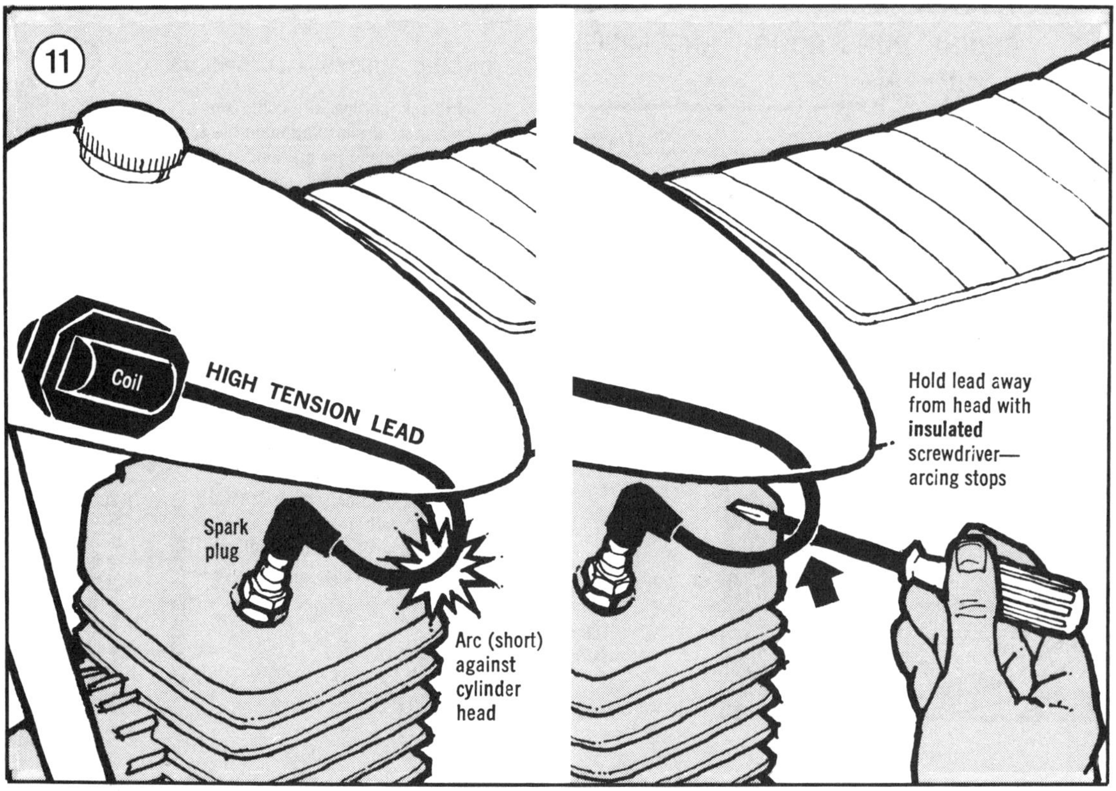

11

Coil
HIGH TENSION LEAD
Spark plug
Arc (short) against cylinder head
Hold lead away from head with **insulated** screwdriver—arcing stops

Check the insulation on the high-tension spark plug lead. If it is cracked or deteriorated it will allow the spark to short to ground when the engine is revved. This is easily seen at night. If arcing occurs, hold the affected area of the wire away from the metal to which it is arcing, using an insulated screwdriver (**Figure 11**), and see if the misfiring ceases. If it does, replace the high-tension lead. Also check the connection of the spark plug cap to the lead. If it is poor, the spark will break down at this point when the engine speed is increased.

The spark plug could also be poor. Test the system with a new plug.

Incorrect point gap or a weak contact breaker spring can cause misfiring. Check the gap and the alignment of the points. Push the moveable arm back and check for spring tension (**Figure 12**). It should feel stiff.

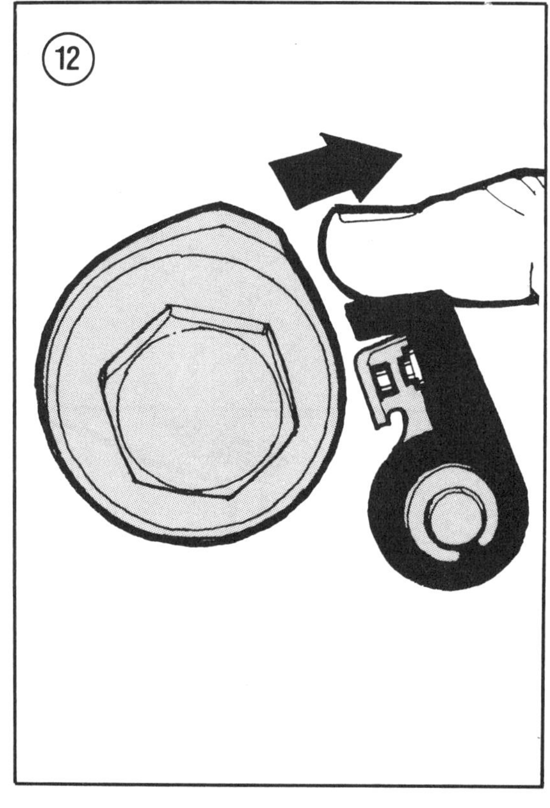

On models with electronic ignition, have the electronic module tested by a dealer or substitute a known good unit for a suspected one.

If misfiring occurs only at a certain point in engine speed, the problem may very likely be

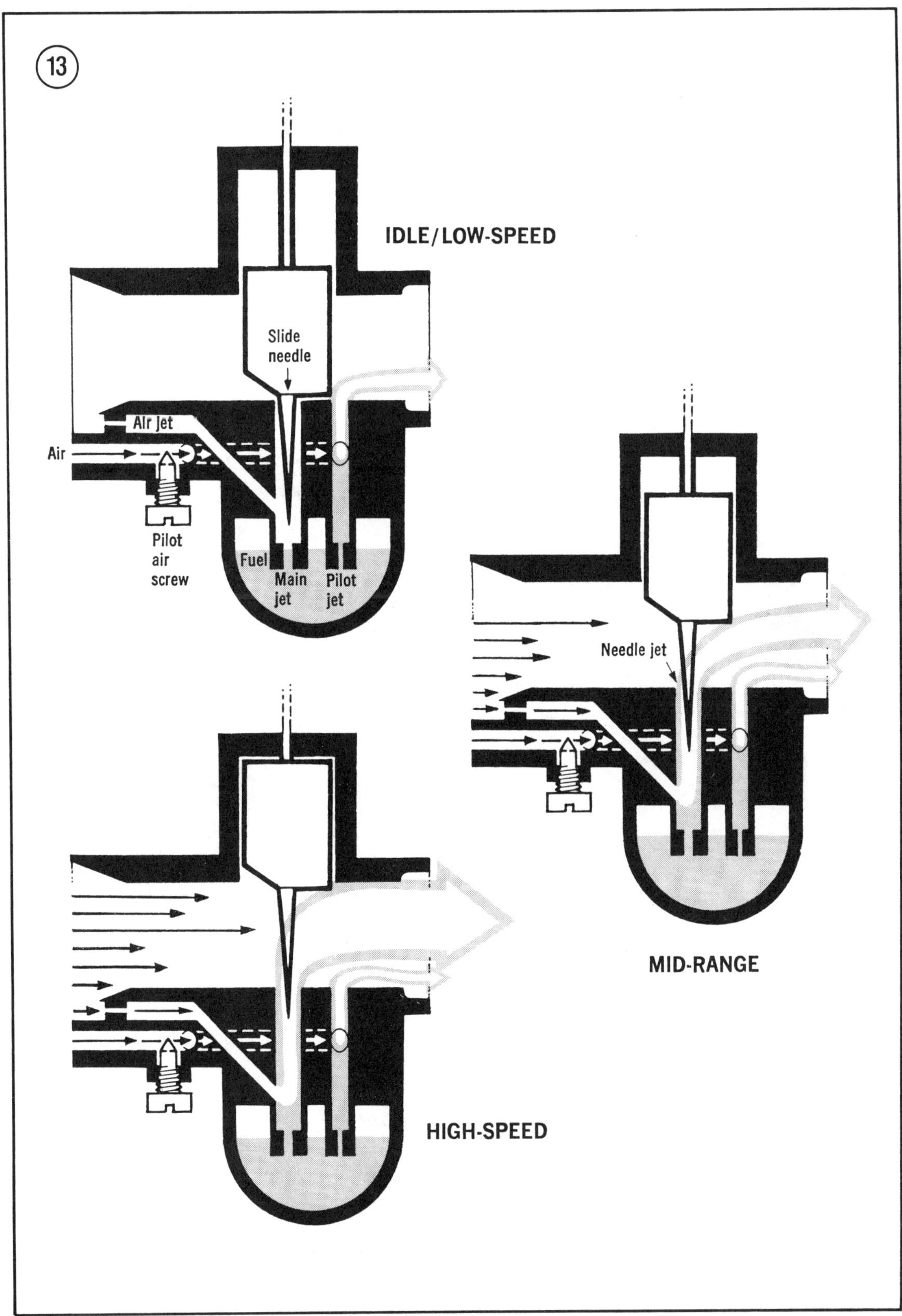
13
IDLE/LOW-SPEED
Slide needle
Air jet
Air
Pilot air screw
Fuel
Main jet
Pilot jet
Needle jet
MID-RANGE
HIGH-SPEED

2

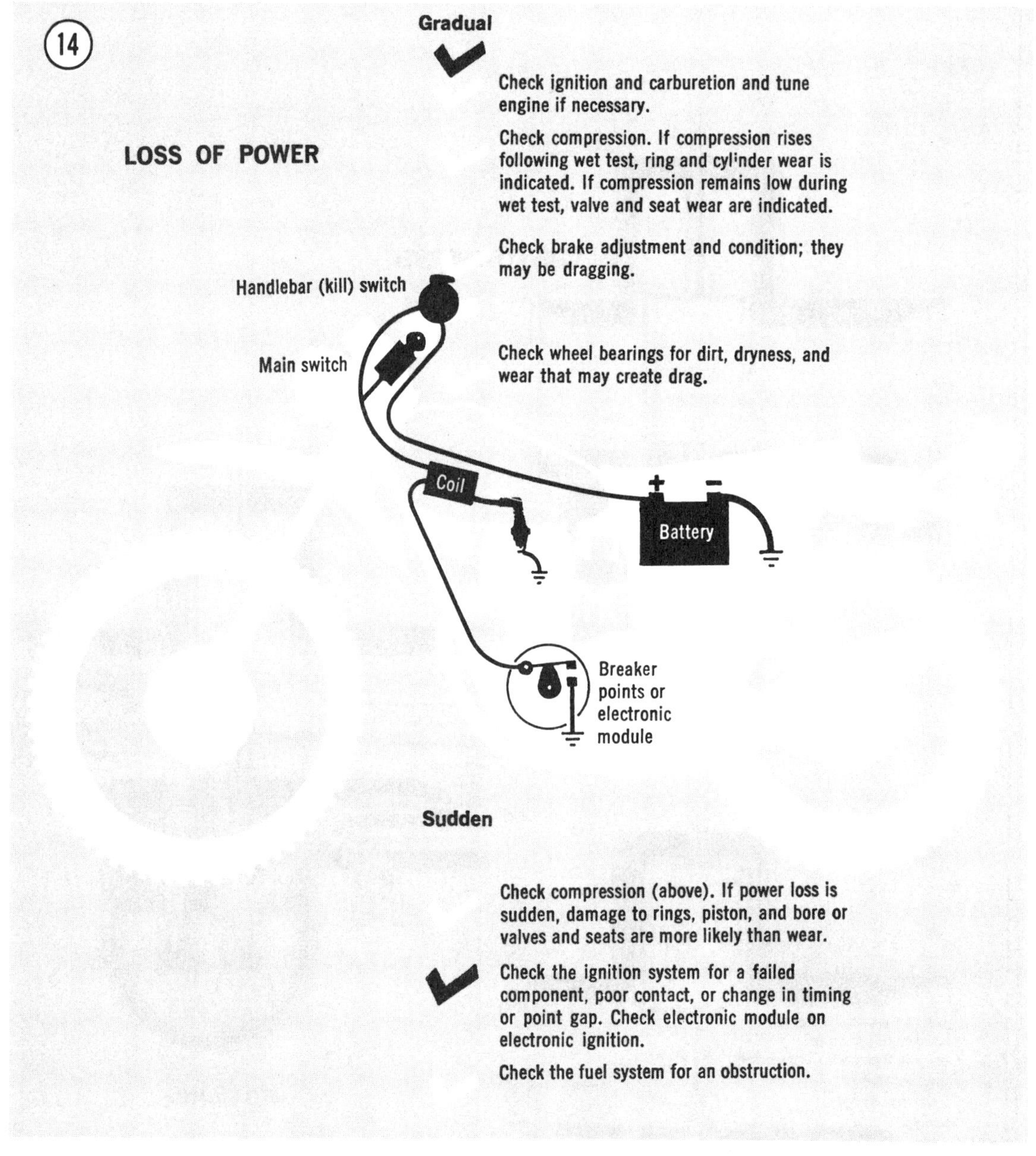

carburetion. Poor performance at idle is described earlier. Misfiring at low speed (just above idle) can be caused by a dirty low-speed circuit or jet (**Figure 13**). Poor midrange performance is attributable to a worn or incorrectly adjusted needle and needle jet. Misfiring at high speed (if not ignition related) is usually caused by a too-large main jet which causes the engine to run rich. Any of these carburetor-related conditions can be corrected by first cleaning the carburetor and then adjusting it as described in the tune-up and maintenance chapter.

14
Gradual
LOSS OF POWER
Check ignition and carburetion and tune engine if necessary.
Check compression. If compression rises following wet test, ring and cylinder wear is indicated. If compression remains low during wet test, valve and seat wear are indicated.
Check brake adjustment and condition; they may be dragging.
Handlebar (kill) switch
Main switch
Check wheel bearings for dirt, dryness, and wear that may create drag.
Coil
+
−
Battery
Breaker points or electronic module
Sudden
Check compression (above). If power loss is sudden, damage to rings, piston, and bore or valves and seats are more likely than wear.
Check the ignition system for a failed component, poor contact, or change in timing or point gap. Check electronic module on electronic ignition.
Check the fuel system for an obstruction.

Loss of Power

First determine how the power loss developed (**Figure 14**). Did it decline over a long period of time or did it drop abruptly? A gradual loss is normal, caused by deterioration of the engine's state of tune and the normal wear of the cylinder and piston rings and the valves and seats. In such case, check the condition of the

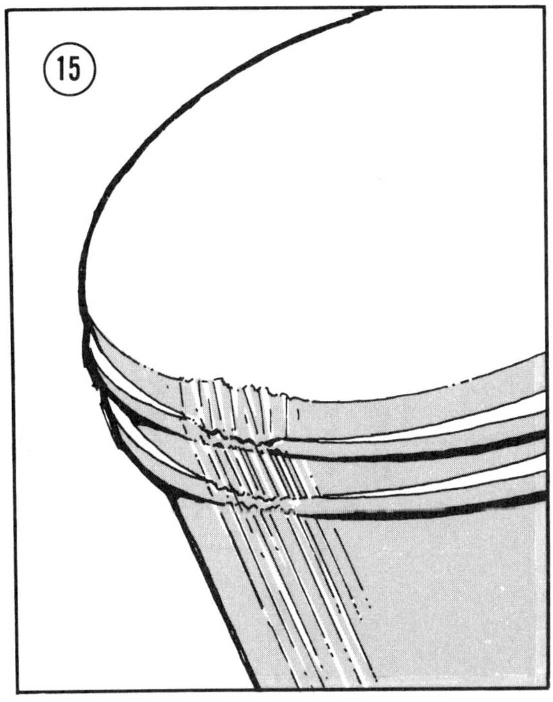

ignition and carburetion and measure the compression as described earlier.

A sudden power loss may be caused by a failed ignition component, obstruction in the fuel system, damaged valve or seat, or a broken piston ring or damaged piston (**Figure 15**).

If the engine is in good shape and tune, check the brake adjustment. If the brakes are dragging, they will consume considerable power. Also check the wheel bearings. If they are dry, extremely dirty, or badly worn they can create considerable drag.

Engine Runs Hot

A modern motorcycle engine, in good mechanical condition, correctly tuned, and operated as it was intended, will rarely experience overheating problems. However, out-of-spec conditions can create severe overheating that may result in serious engine damage. Refer to **Figure 16**.

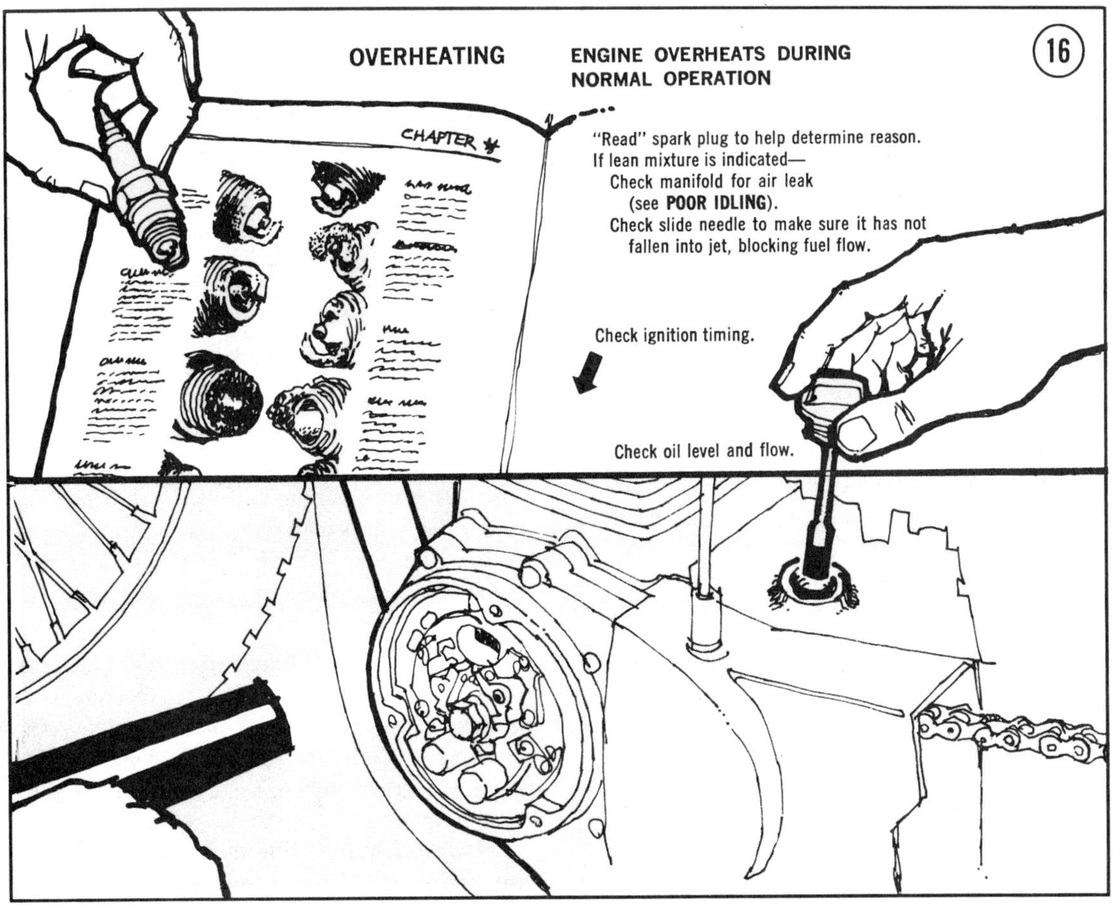

2

16

OVERHEATING

ENGINE OVERHEATS DURING NORMAL OPERATION

CHAPTER 4

"Read" spark plug to help determine reason.
If lean mixture is indicated—
Check manifold for air leak (see **POOR IDLING**).
Check slide needle to make sure it has not fallen into jet, blocking fuel flow.

Check ignition timing.

Check oil level and flow.

Overheating is difficult to detect unless it is extreme, in which case it will usually be apparent as excessive heat radiating from the engine, accompanied by the smell of hot oil and sharp, snapping noises when the engine is first shut off and begins to cool.

Unless the motorcycle is operated under sustained high load or is allowed to idle for long periods of time, overheating is usually the result of an internal problem. Most often it's caused by a too-lean fuel mixture.

Remove the spark plug and compare it to **Figure 3**. If a too-lean condition is indicated, check for leaks in the intake manifold (see *Poor Idling*). The carburetor jetting may be incorrect but this is unlikely if the overheating problem has just developed (unless, of course, the engine was jetted for high altitude and is now being run near sea level). Check the slide needle in the carburetor to make sure it hasn't come loose and is restricting the flow of gas through the main jet and needle jet (**Figure 17**).

Check the ignition timing; extremes of either advance or retard can cause overheating.

Piston Seizure and Damage

Piston seizure is a common result of overheating (see above) because an aluminum piston expands at a greater rate than a steel cylinder. Seizure can also be caused by piston-to-cylinder clearance that is too small; ring end gap that is too small; insufficient oil; spark plug heat range too hot; and broken piston ring or ring land.

A major piston seizure can cause severe engine damage. A minor seizure — which usually subsides after the engine has cooled a few minutes — rarely does more than scuff the piston skirt the first time it occurs. Fortunately, this condition can be corrected by dressing the piston with crocus cloth, refitting the piston and rings to the bore with recommended clearances, and checking the timing to ensure overheating does not occur. Regard that first seizure as a warning and correct the problem before continuing to run the engine.

CLUTCH AND TRANSMISSION

1. *Clutch slips*—Make sure lever free play is sufficient to allow the clutch to fully engage

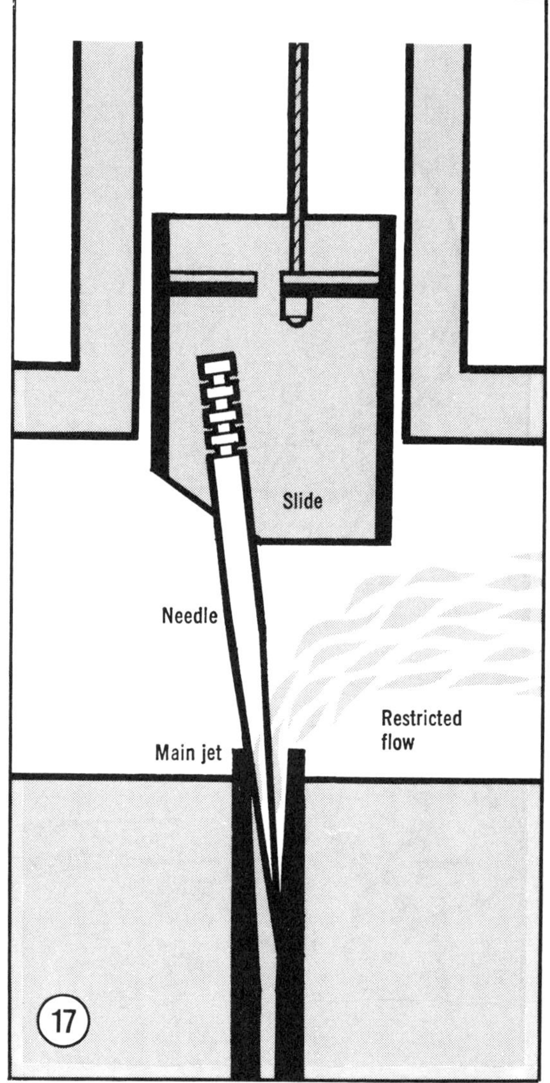

(**Figure 18**). Check the contact surfaces for wear and glazing. Transmission oil additives also can cause slippage in wet clutches. If slip occurs only under extreme load, check the condition of the springs or diaphragm and make sure the clutch bolts are snug and uniformly tightened.

2. *Clutch drags*—Make sure lever free play isn't so great that it fails to disengage the clutch. Check for warped plates or disc. If the transmission oil (in wet clutch systems) is extremely dirty or heavy, it may inhibit the clutch from releasing.

3. ***Transmission shifts hard***—Extremely dirty oil can cause the transmission to shift hard.

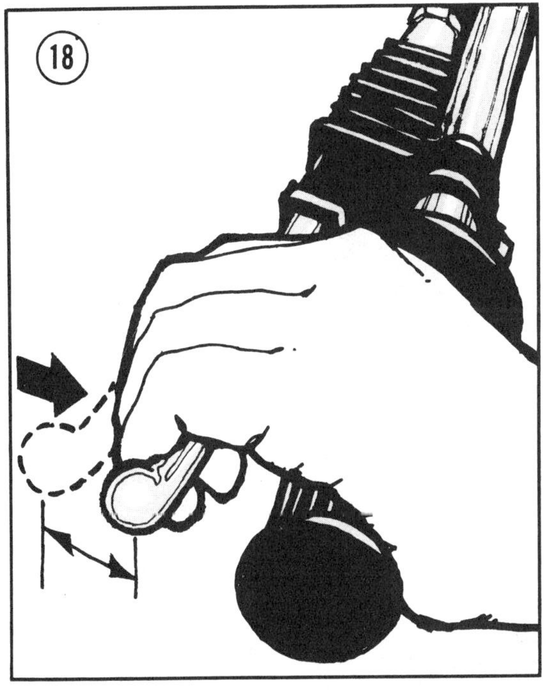

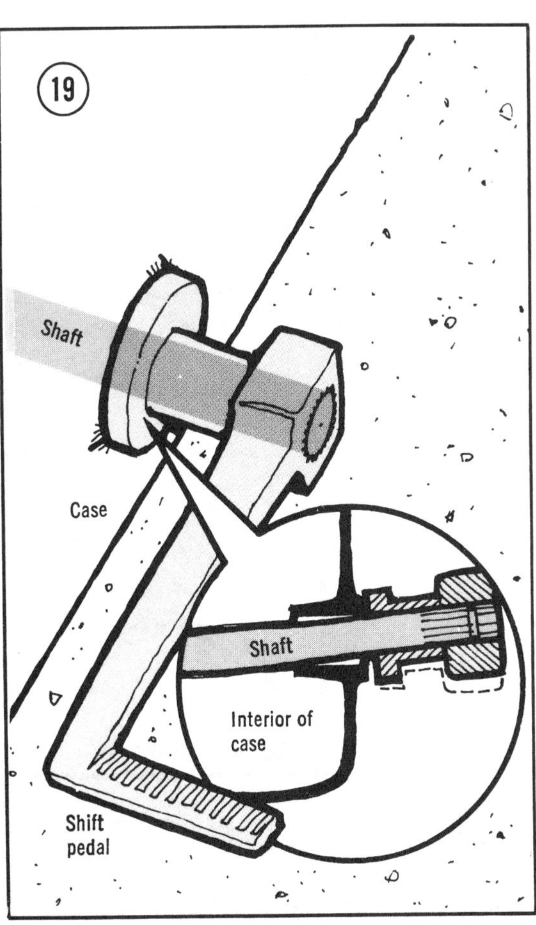

Check the selector shaft for bending (**Figure 19**). Inspect the shifter and gearsets for wear and damage.

4. ***Transmission slips out of gear***—This can be caused by worn engagement dogs or a worn or damaged shifter (**Figure 20**). The overshift travel on the selector may be misadjusted.

5. ***Transmission is noisy***—Noises usually indicate the absence of lubrication or wear and damage to gears, bearings, or shims. It's a good idea to disassemble the transmission and carefully inspect it when noise first occurs.

DRIVE TRAIN

Drive train problems (outlined in **Figure 21**) arise from normal wear and incorrect maintenance.

CHASSIS

Chassis problems are outlined in **Figure 22**.

1. ***Motorcycle pulls to one side***—Check for loose suspension components, axles, steering

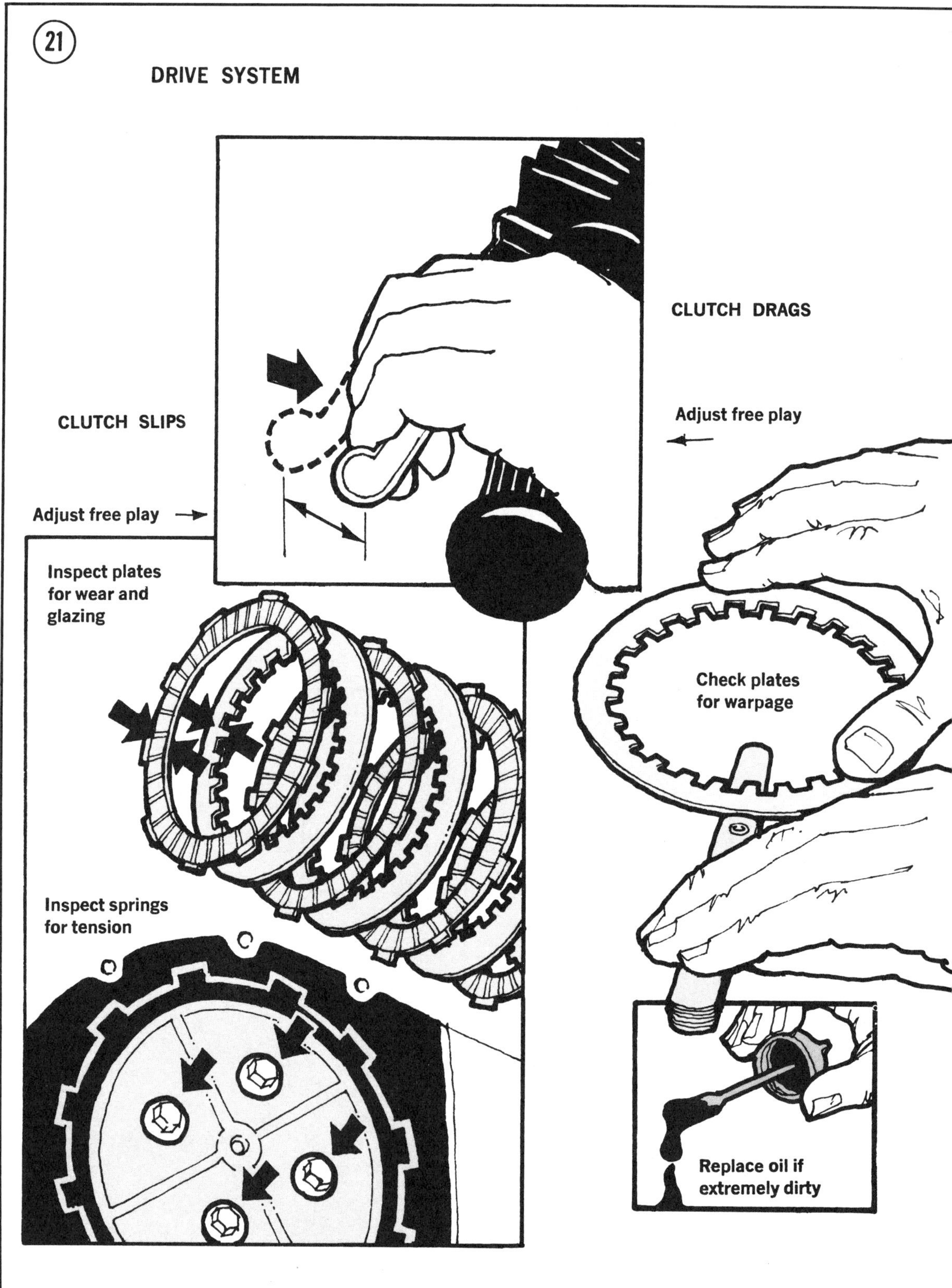
21
DRIVE SYSTEM
CLUTCH DRAGS
Adjust free play
CLUTCH SLIPS
Adjust free play
Inspect plates for wear and glazing
Check plates for warpage
Inspect springs for tension
Replace oil if extremely dirty

2

TRANSMISSION SHIFTS HARD

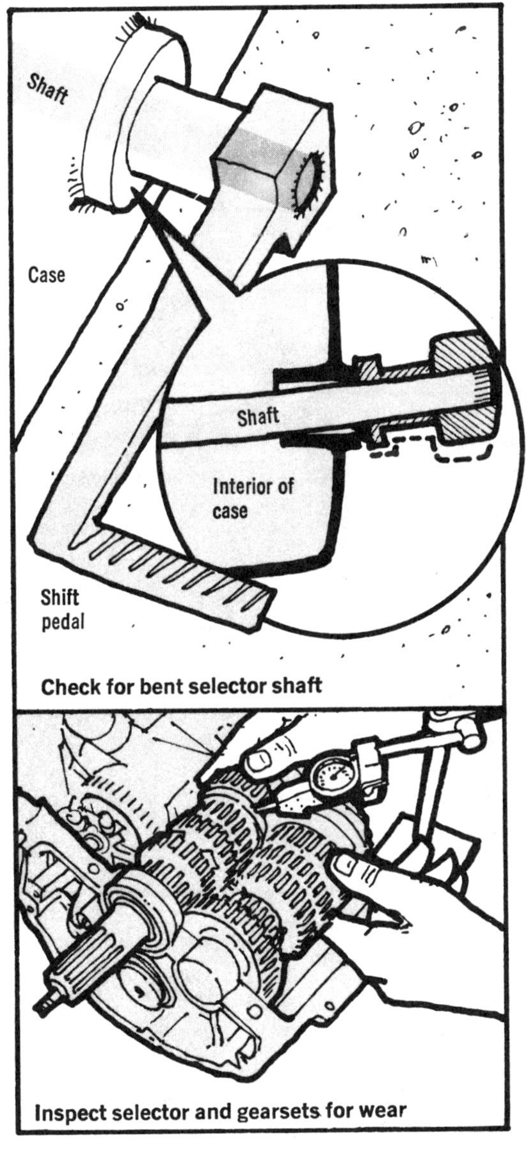

Check for bent selector shaft

Inspect selector and gearsets for wear

TRANSMISSION SLIPS OUT OF GEAR

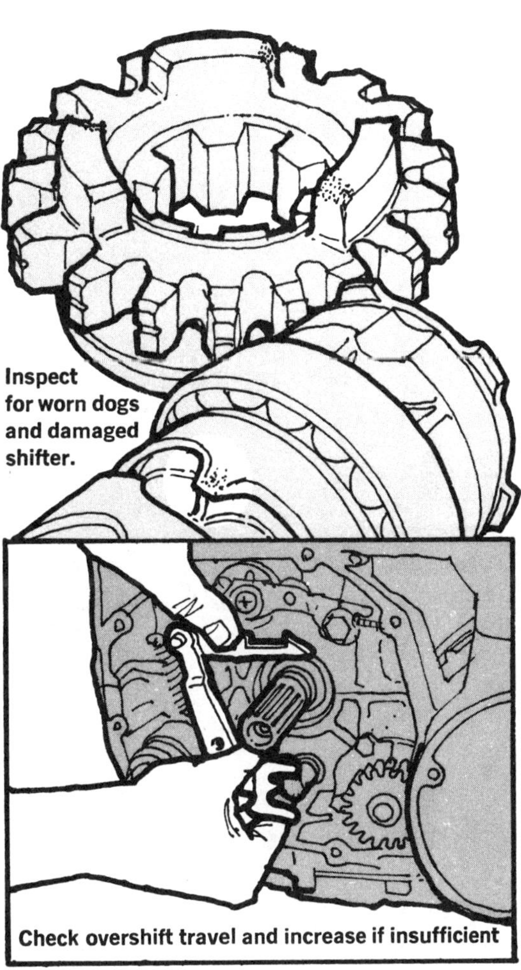

Check overshift travel and increase if insufficient

TRANSMISSION IS NOISY

Check oil level

Disassemble and inspect (see Transmission chapter)

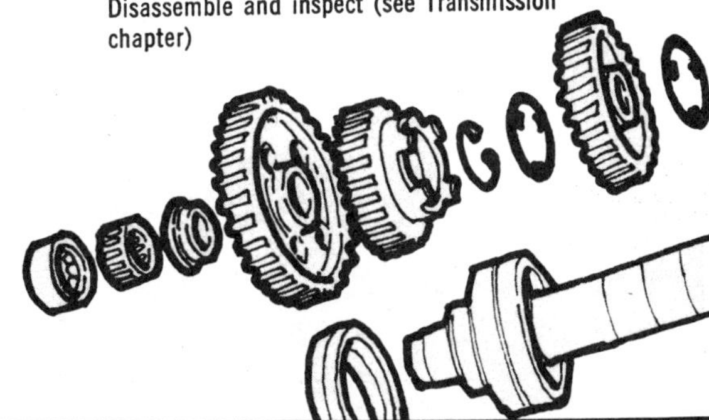

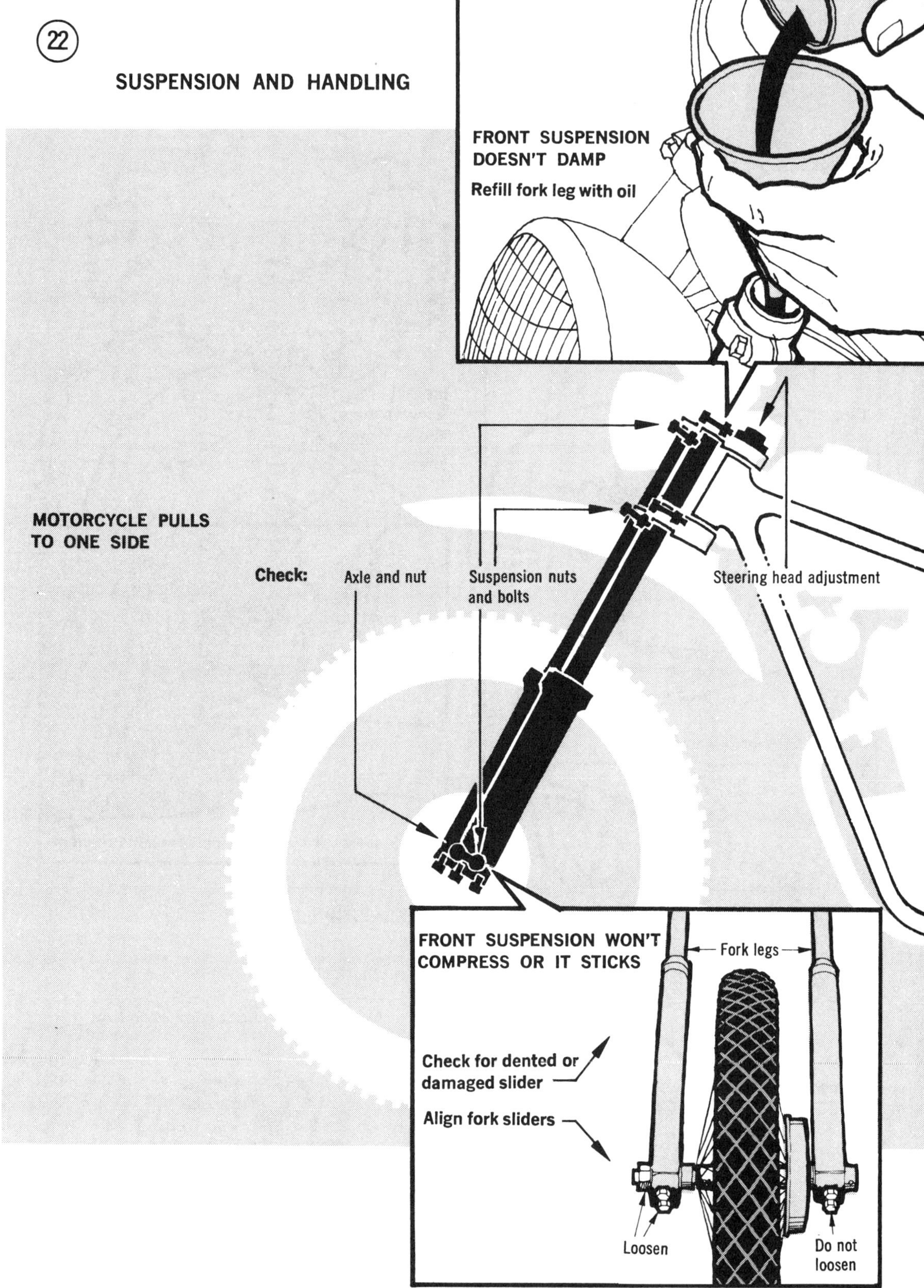
22
SUSPENSION AND HANDLING
FRONT SUSPENSION DOESN'T DAMP
Refill fork leg with oil
MOTORCYCLE PULLS TO ONE SIDE
Check:
Axle and nut
Suspension nuts and bolts
Steering head adjustment
FRONT SUSPENSION WON'T COMPRESS OR IT STICKS
Fork legs
Check for dented or damaged slider
Align fork sliders
Loosen
Do not loosen

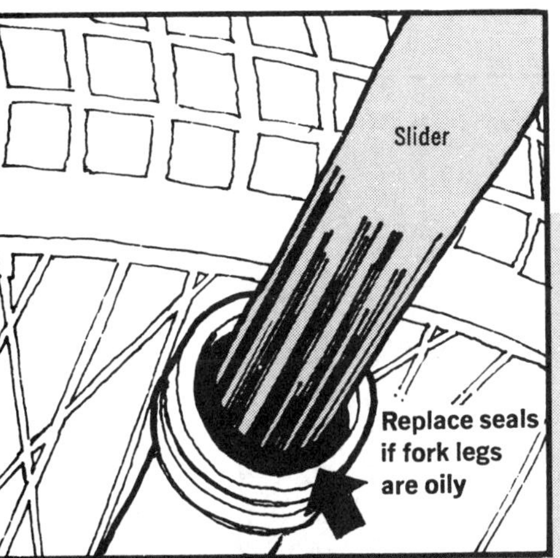

SUSPENSION AND HANDLING CONTINUED

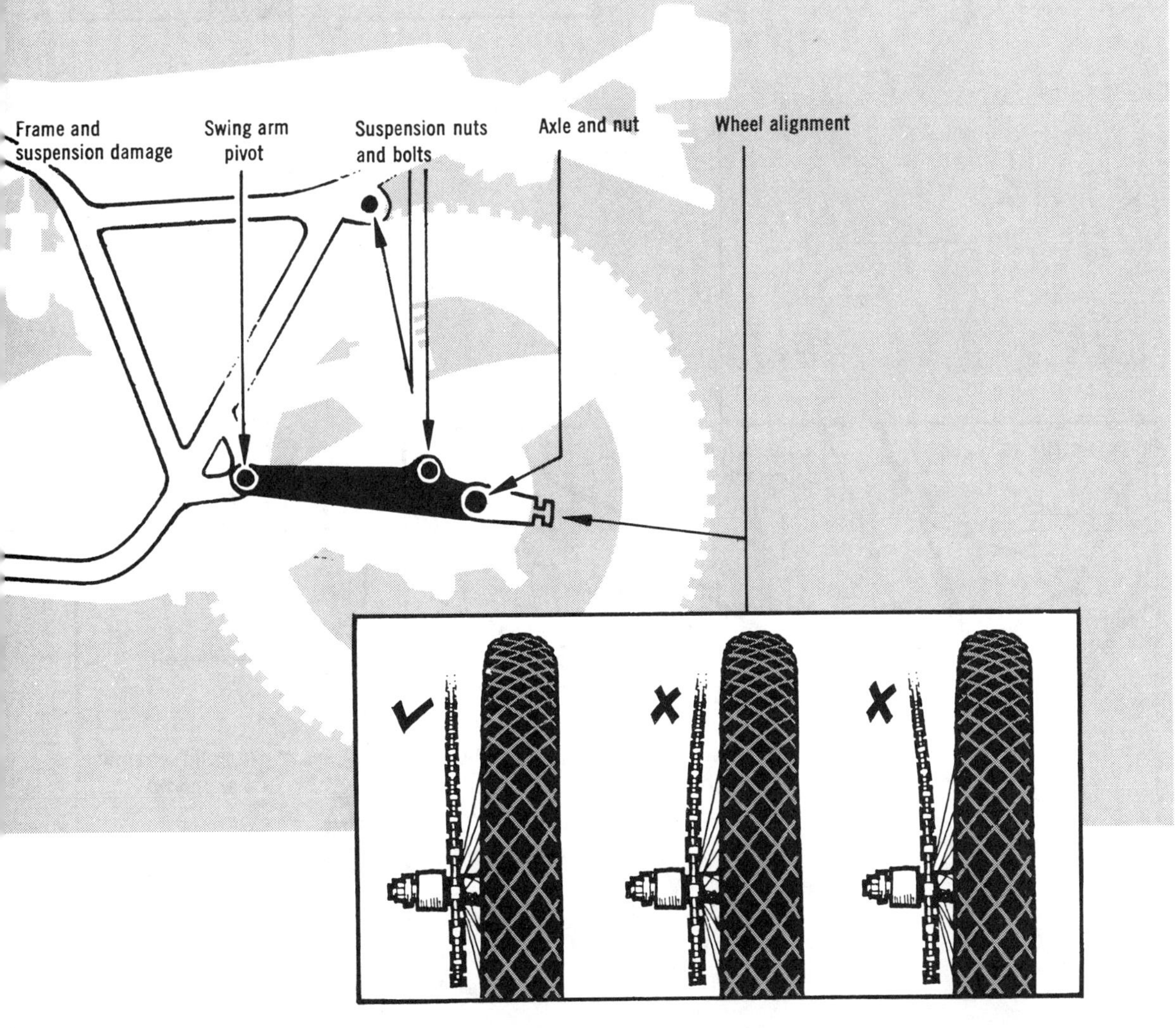

2

SUSPENSION AND HANDLING CONTINUED

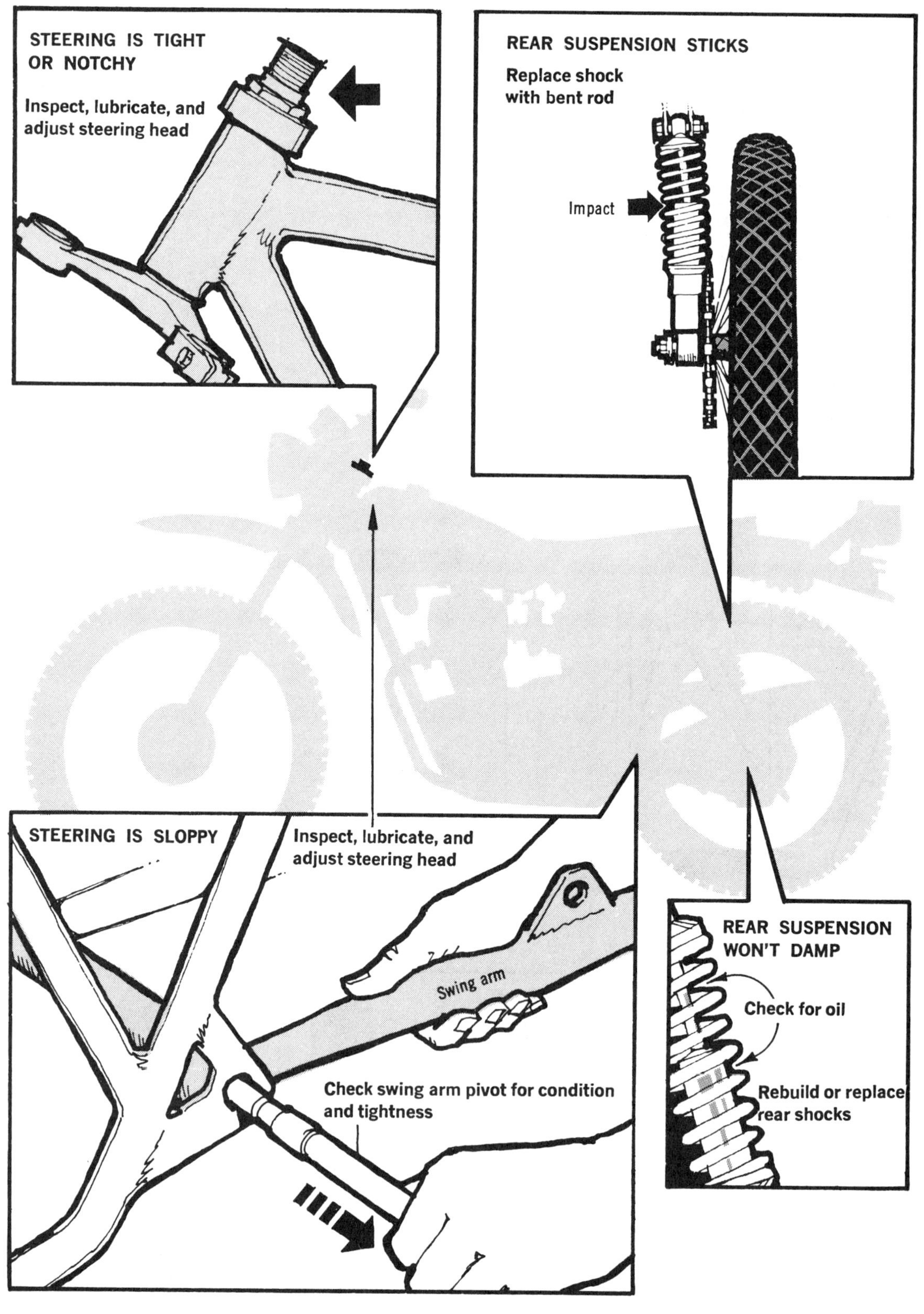
STEERING IS TIGHT OR NOTCHY
Inspect, lubricate, and adjust steering head
REAR SUSPENSION STICKS
Replace shock with bent rod
Impact
STEERING IS SLOPPY
Inspect, lubricate, and adjust steering head
Swing arm
Check swing arm pivot for condition and tightness
REAR SUSPENSION WON'T DAMP
Check for oil
Rebuild or replace rear shocks

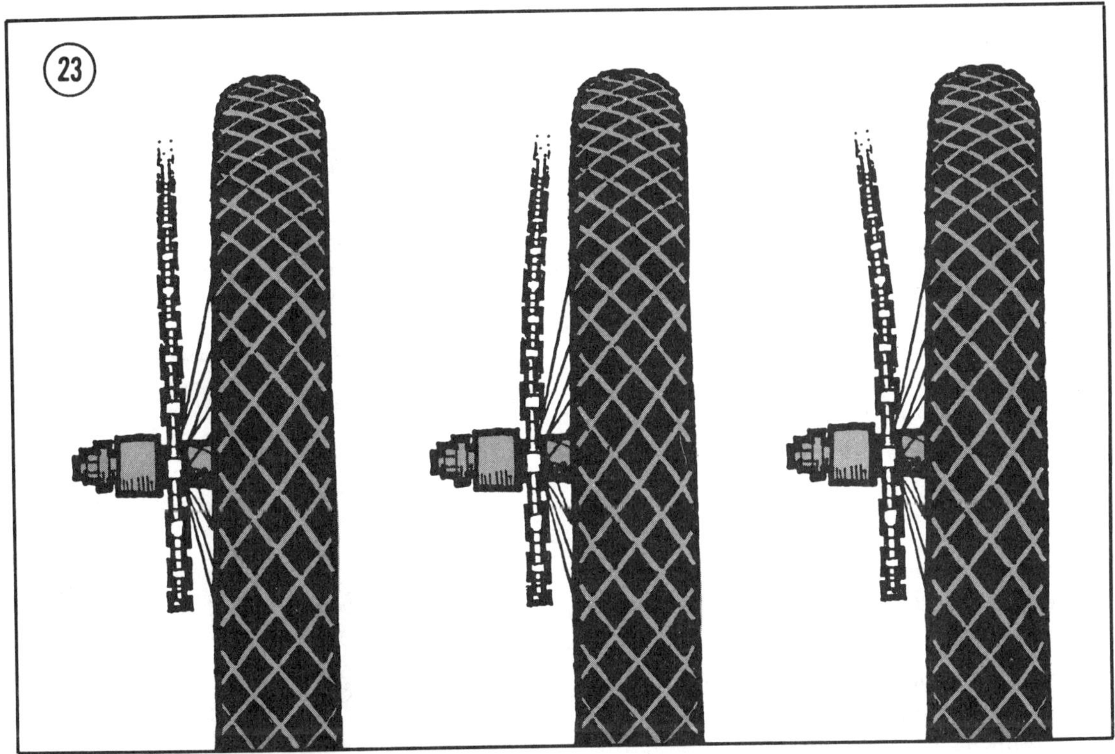

head, swing arm pivot. Check wheel alignment (**Figure 23**). Check for damage to the frame and suspension components.

2. ***Front suspension doesn't damp***—This is most often caused by a lack of damping oil in the fork legs. If the upper fork tubes are exceptionally oily, it's likely that the seals are worn out and should be replaced.

3. ***Front suspension sticks or won't fully compress***—Misalignment of the forks when the wheel is installed can cause this. Loosen the axle nut and the pinch bolt on the nut end of the axle (**Figure 24**). Lock the front wheel with the brake and compress the front suspension several times to align the fork legs. Then, tighten the pinch bolt and then the axle nut.

The trouble may also be caused by a bent or dented fork slider (**Figure 25**). The distortion required to lock up a fork tube is so slight that it is often impossible to visually detect. If this type of damage is suspected, remove the fork leg and remove the spring from it. Attempt to operate the fork leg. If it still binds, replace the slider; it's not practical to repair it.

4. ***Rear suspension does not damp***—This is usually caused by damping oil leaking past

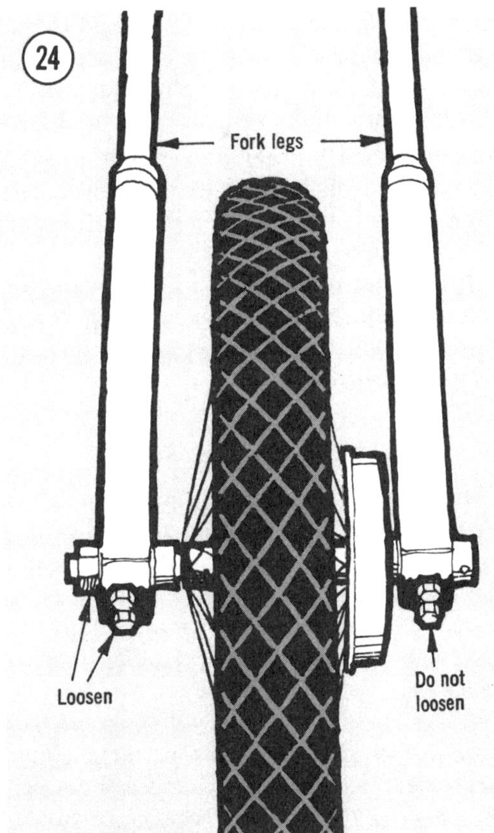

worn seals. Rebuildable shocks should be refitted with complete service kits and fresh oil. Non-rebuildable units should be replaced.

5. ***Rear suspension sticks***—This is commonly caused by a bent shock absorber piston rod (**Figure 26**). Replace the shock; the rod can't be satisfactorily straightened.

6. ***Steering is tight or "notchy"***—Steering head bearings may be dry, dirty, or worn. Adjustment of the steering head bearing pre-load may be too tight.

7. ***Steering is sloppy***—Steering head adjustment may be too loose. Also check the swing arm pivot; looseness or extreme wear at this point translate to the steering.

BRAKES

Brake problems arise from wear, lack of maintenance, and from sustained or repeated exposure to dirt and water.

1. ***Brakes are ineffective***—Ineffective brakes are most likely caused by incorrect adjustment. If adjustment will not correct the problem, remove the wheels and check for worn or glazed linings. If the linings are worn beyond the service limit, replace them. If they are simply glazed, rough them up with light sandpaper.

In hydraulic brake systems, low fluid levels can cause a loss of braking effectiveness, as can worn brake cylinder pistons and bores. Also check the pads to see if they are worn beyond the service limit.

2. ***Brakes lock or drag***—This may be caused by incorrect adjustment. Check also for foreign matter embedded in the lining and for dirty and dry wheel bearings.

ELECTRICAL SYSTEM

Many electrical system problems can be easily solved by ensuring that the affected connections are clean, dry, and tight. In battery equipped motorcycles, a neglected battery is the source of a great number of difficulties that could be prevented by simple, regular service to the battery.

A multimeter, like the volt/ohm/milliammeter described in Chapter One, is invaluable for efficient electrical system troubleshooting.

See **Figures 27 and 28** for schematics showing

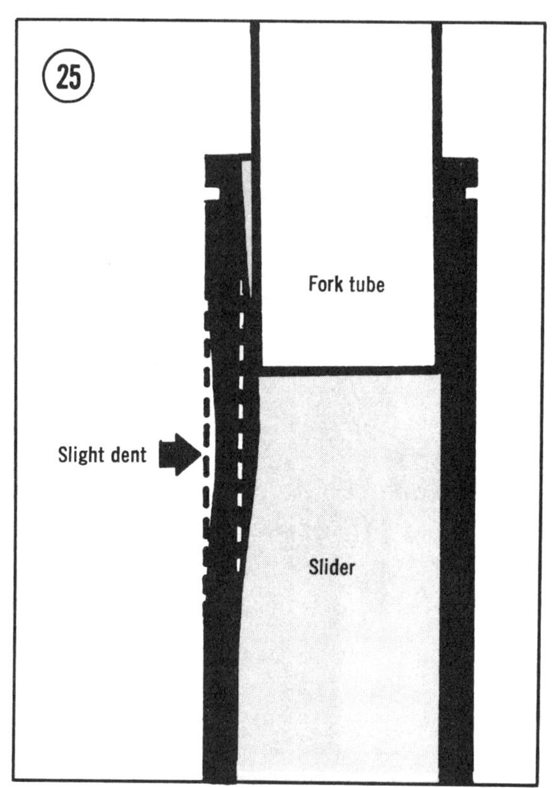

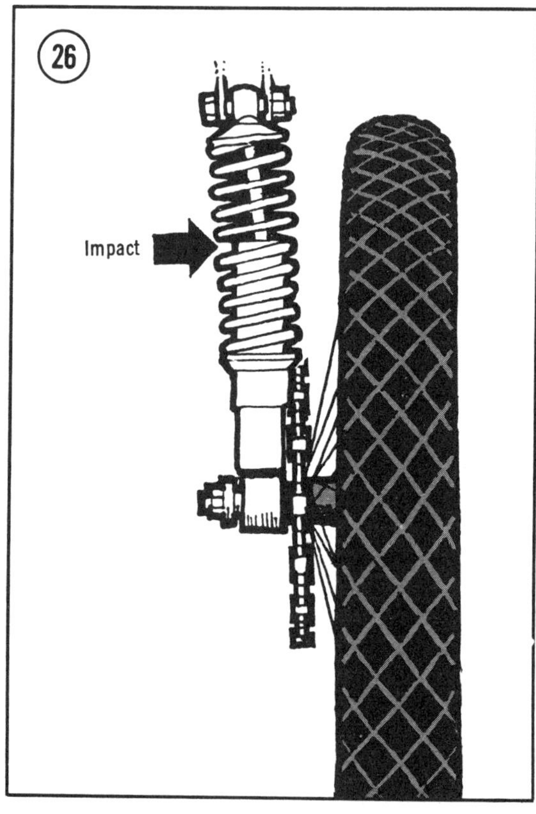

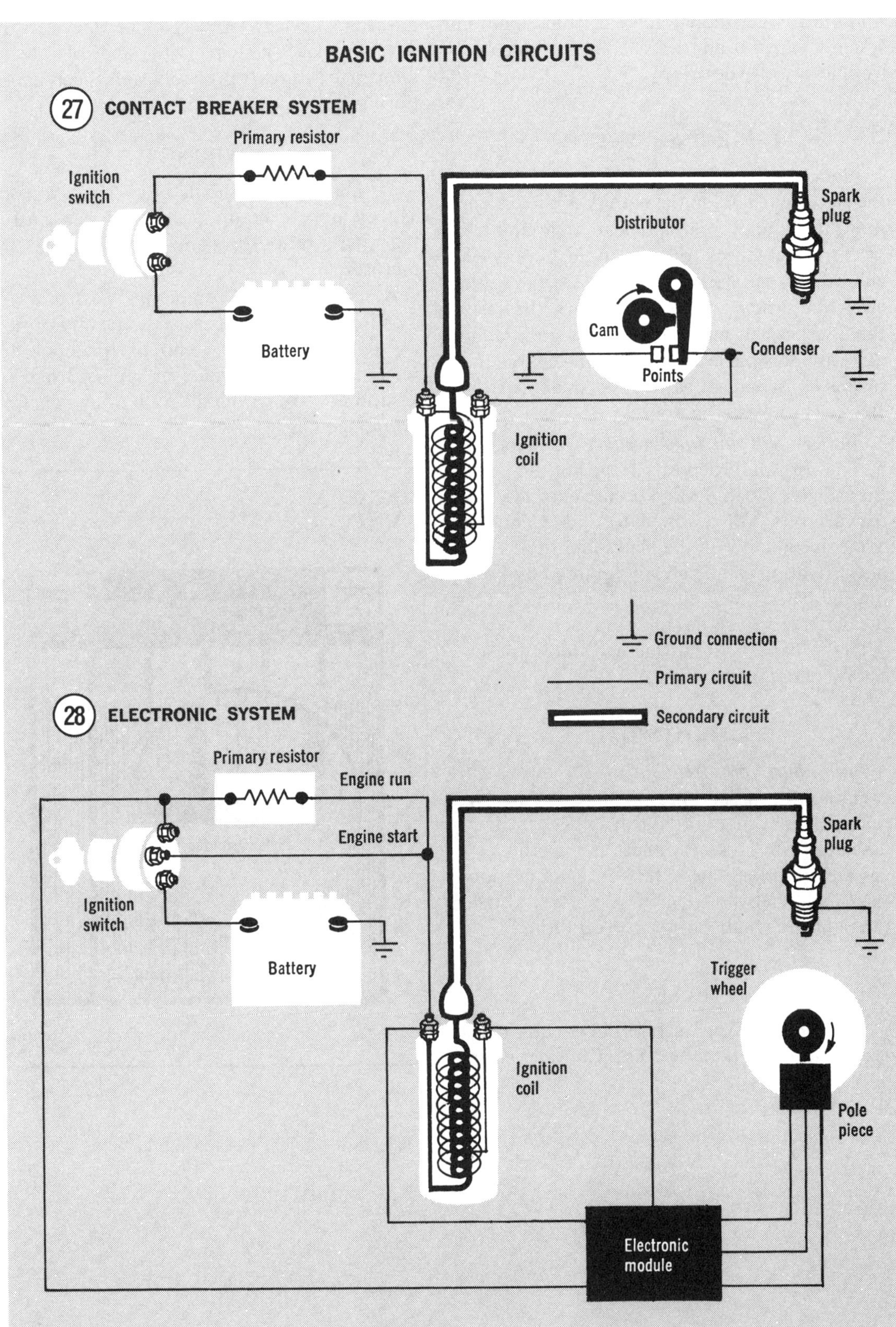
BASIC IGNITION CIRCUITS
27 CONTACT BREAKER SYSTEM
Primary resistor
Ignition switch
Battery
Distributor
Spark plug
Cam
Points
Condenser
Ignition coil
Ground connection
Primary circuit
Secondary circuit
28 ELECTRONIC SYSTEM
Primary resistor
Engine run
Engine start
Ignition switch
Battery
Spark plug
Trigger wheel
Ignition coil
Pole piece
Electronic module

simplified conventional and electronic ignition systems. Typical and most common electrical troubles are also described.

CHARGING SYSTEM

1. ***Battery will not accept a charge***—Make sure the electrolyte level in the battery is correct and that the terminal connections are tight and free of corrosion. Check for fuses in the battery circuit. If the battery is satisfactory, refer to the electrical system chapter for alternator tests. Finally, keep in mind that even a good alternator is not capable of restoring the charge to a severely discharged battery; it must first be charged by an external source.

2. ***Battery will not hold a charge***—Check the battery for sulfate deposits in the bottom of the case (**Figure 29**). Sulfation occurs naturally and the deposits will accumulate and eventually come in contact with the plates and short them out. Sulfation can be greatly retarded by keeping the battery well charged at all times. Test the battery to assess its condition.

If the battery is satisfactory, look for excessive draw, such as a short.

LIGHTING

Bulbs burn out frequently—All bulbs will eventually burn out, but if the bulb in one particular light burns out frequently check the light assembly for looseness that may permit excessive vibration; check for loose connections that could cause current surges; check also to make sure the bulb is of the correct rating.

FUSES

Fuse blows—When a fuse blows, don't just replace it; try to find the cause. Consider a fuse a warning device as well as a safety device. And never replace a fuse with one of greater amperage rating. It probably won't melt before the insulation on the wiring does.

WIRING

Wiring problems should be corrected as soon as they arise — before a short can cause a fire that may seriously damage or destroy the motorcycle.

A circuit tester of some type is essential for locating shorts and opens. Use the appropriate wiring diagram at the end of the book for reference. If a wire must be replaced make a notation on the wiring diagram of any changes in color coding.

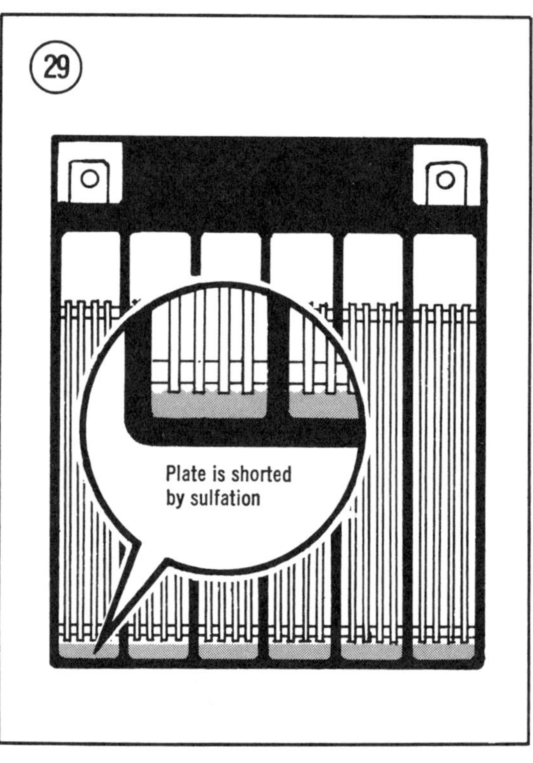
29
Plate is shorted
by sulfation

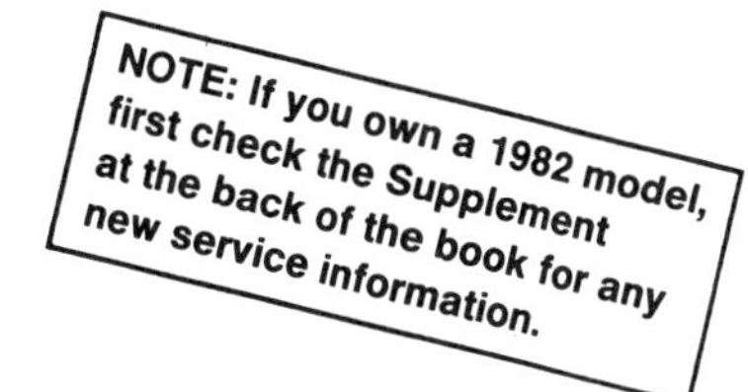
NOTE: If you own a 1982 model, first check the Supplement at the back of the book for any new service information.

CHAPTER THREE

LUBRICATION, MAINTENANCE AND TUNE-UP

A motorcycle, even in normal use, is subjected to tremendous heat, stress and vibration. When neglected, any bike becomes unreliable and actually dangerous to ride. To keep the bike properly maintained, look into the tune-up tools and parts and check out the different lubricants, motor oil, fork oil, locking compounds and greases (**Figure 1**). Also check engine degreasers, like Gunk or Bel-Ray Degreaser, for cleaning your engine prior to working on it.

The more you get involved in your Honda the more you will want to work on it. Start out by doing simple tune-up, lubrication and maintenance. Tackle more involved jobs as you become more acquainted with the bike.

The Honda CB650 is one of the most reliable bikes available but to gain the utmost in safety, performance and useful life from it, it is necessary to make periodic inspections and adjustments. It frequently happens that minor problems are found during such inspections that are simple and inexpensive to correct at the time, but which could lead to major problems if not corrected.

This chapter explains lubrication, maintenance and tune-up procedures required for the Honda CB650. **Table 1** is a suggested factory maintenance schedule (**Tables 1-7** are located at the end of this chapter).

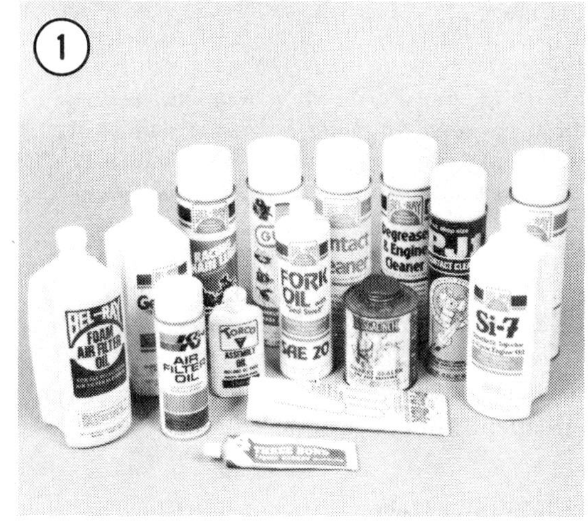

ROUTINE CHECKS

The following simple checks should be performed at each stop at a service station for gas.

Engine Oil Level

Refer to *Checking Engine Oil Level* under *Periodic Lubrication* in this chapter.

General Inspection

1. Quickly inspect the engine for signs of oil or fuel leakage.

2. Check the tires for embedded stones. Pry them out with your ignition key.
3. Make sure all lights work.

NOTE
At least check the brake light. It can burn out anytime. Motorists cannot stop as quickly as you and need all the warning you can give.

Tire Pressure

Tire pressure must be checked with the tires cold. Correct tire pressure depends a lot on the load you are carrying. See **Table 2**.

Battery

Remove the left-hand side cover and, on models since 1980, remove the owner's manual container and check the battery electrolyte level. The level must be between the upper and lower level marks on the case (**Figure 2**).

NOTE
***Figure 2** is shown with the battery removed for clarity. On models since 1980 the electrolyte level can be checked by looking through the maze of wires under the left-hand side cover.*

For complete details see *Battery Removal/Installation and Electrolyte Level Check* in this chapter.

Due to evaporation, check the level more frequently in hot weather.

Lights and Horn

With the engine running, check the following.
1. Pull the front brake lever on and check that the brake light comes on.
2. Push the rear brake pedal down and check that the brake light comes on soon after you have begun depressing the pedal.
3. Move the headlight dimmer switch up and down between the HI and LO positions and check to see that both headlight elements are working.
4. Turn the turn signal switch to the left and right positions and check that all 4 turn signals are working.

(2)

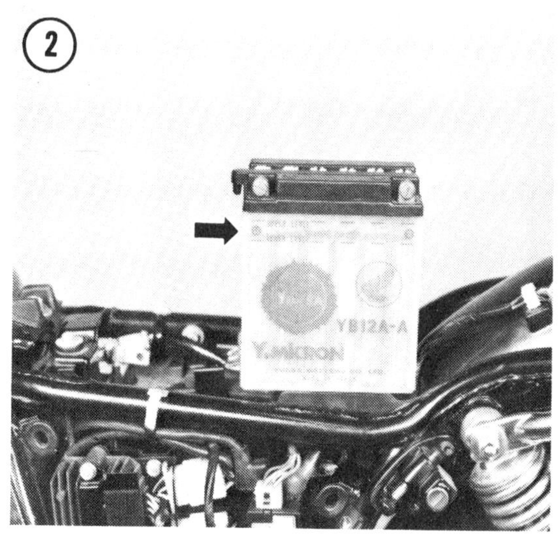

5. Push the horn button and make sure that the horn blows loudly.
6. If during these tests, the rear brake pedal traveled too far before the brake light came on, adjust the rear brake light switch as described under *Rear Brake Light Switch Adjustment* in Chapter Seven. Or if the horn or any of the lights failed to operate properly, refer to the electrical chapter, Chapter Seven.

PRE-CHECKS

The following checks should be performed prior to the first ride of the day.
1. Inspect all fuel lines and fittings for wetness.
2. Make sure the fuel tank is full of fresh gasoline.
3. Make sure the engine oil level is correct.
4. Check the operation of the clutch and adjust if necessary.
5. Check the throttle and the brake lever. Make sure they operate properly with no binding.
6. Inspect the condition of the front and rear suspension; make sure it has a good solid feel with no looseness.
7. Check the condition of the drive chain for wear and correct tension.
8. Check tire pressure. Refer to **Table 2**.
9. Check the exhaust system for damage.
10. Check the tightness of all fasteners, especially engine mounting hardware.

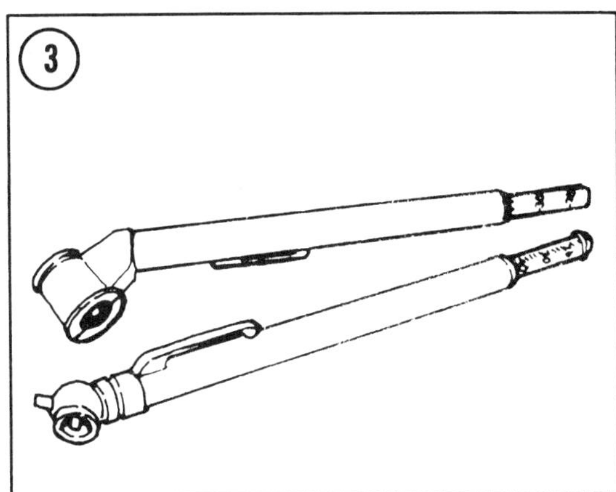

3

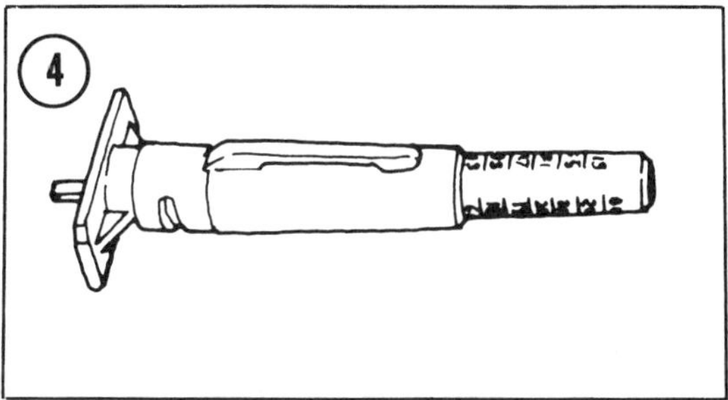

4

SERVICE INTERVALS

The services and intervals shown in **Table 1** are recommended by the factory. Strict adherence to these recommendations will insure long service from your Honda CB650. However, if the bike is run in an area of high humidity the lubrication services must be done more frequently to prevent possible rust damage.

For convenience when maintaining your motorcycle, most of the services shown in the table are described in this chapter. However, some procedures which require more than minor disassembly or adjustment are covered elsewhere in the appropriate chapter.

TIRES AND WHEELS

Tire Pressure

Tire pressure should be checked when the tires are cold and adjusted to maintain the smoothness of the tire, good traction and handling and to get the maximum life out of the tire. A simple, accurate gauge (**Figure 3**) can be purchased for a few dollars and should be carried in your motorcycle tool kit. The appropriate tire pressures are shown in **Table 2**.

Tire Inspection

The tires take a lot of punishment so inspect them periodically for excessive wear, cuts, abrasions, etc. If you find a nail or other object in the tire, mark its location with a light crayon prior to removing it. This will help locate the hole for repair. Refer to Chapter Eight for tire changing and repair information.

Check local traffic regulations concerning minimum tread depth. Measure the tread depth at the center of the tire tread using a tread depth gauge (**Figure 4**) or small ruler. Honda recommends tire replacement when the front tire tread depth is 1/16 in. (1.5 mm) or less and rear tread depth is 3/32 in. (2.0 mm) or less, or when tread wear indicators appear across the tire indicating the minimum tread depth. Replace the tire(s) at this point.

Wheel Spoke Tension

Tap each spoke with a wrench. The higher the pitch of sound it makes, the tighter the spoke. The lower the sound frequency, the looser the spoke. A "ping" is good, a "klunk" says the spoke is too loose.

If one or more spokes are loose, tighten them as described under *Wheels* in Chapter Eight.

Rim Inspection

Frequently inspect the condition of the wheel rims. If a rim has been damaged it might have been enough to knock it out of alignment. Improper wheel alignment can cause severe vibration and result in an unsafe riding condition.

CRANKCASE BREATHER HOSE (U.S. MODELS ONLY)

Remove the right-hand side cover, seat and fuel tank. Inspect the condition of the breather hose for cracks and deterioration and make sure that both hose clamps are tight (**Figure 5**).

BATTERY

Battery Removal/Installation and Electrolyte Level Check

The battery is the heart of the electrical system. It should be checked and serviced as indicated in **Table 1**. The majority of electrical system troubles can be attributed to neglect of this vital component.

The electrolyte level may be checked with the battery installed by removing the left-hand side panel. The electrolyte level should be maintained between the 2 marks on the battery case (**Figure 6**). If the electrolyte level is low, it's a good idea to remove the battery from the bike so it can be thoroughly serviced and checked.

1. Remove the left-hand side cover and seat.
2. Disconnect the battery negative (-) and positive (+) leads from the battery.
3. On 1979 models, remove the battery holder plate.
4. On models since 1980, unhook the rubber retaining strap (A, **Figure 7**) and disconnect the battery vent tube (B, **Figure 7**) from the battery and leave it routed through the bike's frame.
5. On 1979 models slide the battery and tray out of the frame.
6. On models since 1980, pull the battery up and out of its tray. Wipe off any of the highly corrosive residue that may have dripped from the battery during removal.

CAUTION
Be careful not to spill battery electrolyte on painted or polished surfaces. The liquid is highly corrosive and will damage the finish. If it is spilled, wash it off immediately with soapy water and thoroughly rinse with clean water.

7. Remove the caps from the battery cells and add distilled water to correct the fluid level. Never add electrolyte (acid) to correct the level.
8. After the fluid level has been corrected and the battery allowed to stand a few minutes,

5

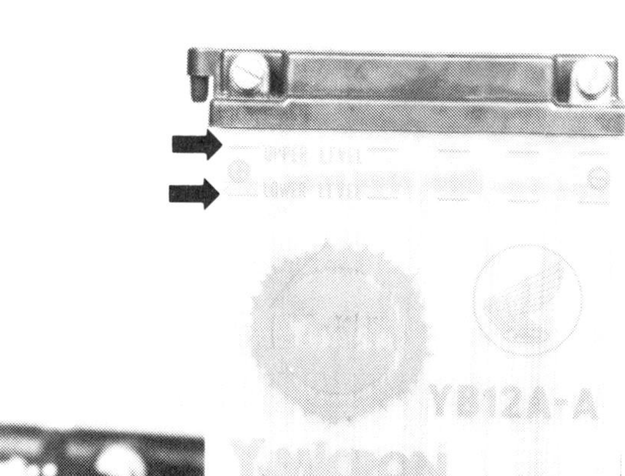

6

7

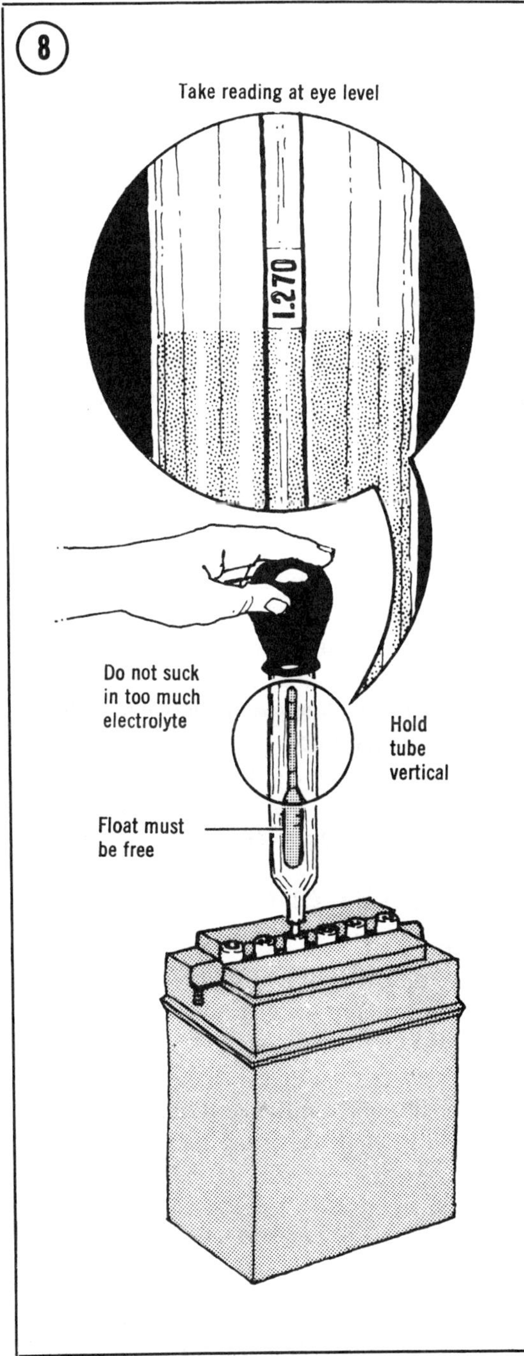
8
Take reading at eye level
1.270
Do not suck in too much electrolyte
Hold tube vertical
Float must be free

check the specific gravity of the electrolyte in each cell with a hydrometer (**Figure 8**). Follow the manufacturer's instructions for reading the hydrometer.

9. After the battery has been refilled, recharged or replaced, install it by reversing these removal steps.

CAUTION
If the breather tube was moved during battery removal be sure to route the breather tube so that any resudue from it will not drain onto any part of the bike's frame. The tube must be free of bends or twists as any restriction may pressurize the battery and damage it.

3

Testing

Hydrometer testing is the best way to check battery condition. Use a hydrometer with numbered graduations from 1.100 to 1.300 rather than one with color-coded bands. To use the hydrometer, squeeze the rubber ball, insert the tip into the cell and release the pressure on the ball. Draw enough electrolyte to float the weighted float inside the hydrometer. Note the number in line with the surface of the electrolyte; this is the specific gravity for this cell. Squeeze the rubber ball again and return the electrolyte to the cell from which it came.

The specific gravity of the electrolyte in each battery cell is an excellent indication of that cell's condition. A fully charged cell will read 1.260-1.280, while a cell in good condition reads from 1.230-1.250 and anything below 1.140 is discharged.

Specific gravity varies with temperature. For each 10° the electrolyte temperature exceeds 80° F (27° C), add 0.004 to readings indicated on the hydrometer. Subtract 0.004 for each 10° below 80° F (27° C).

If the cells test in the poor range, the battery requires recharging. The hydrometer is useful for checking the progress of the charging operation. **Table 3** shows approximate state of charge.

Charging

WARNING
During the charging process, highly explosive hydrogen gas is released from the battery. The battery should be charged only in a well-ventilated area and away from any open flames (including pilot lights on home gas appliances). Do not allow any smoking in the area. Never check the charge of the battery by arcing across the terminals; the resulting spark can ignite the hydrogen gas.

CAUTION
Always remove the battery from the bike before connecting the battery charger. Never recharge a battery in the bike's frame due to the corrosive mist that is emitted during the charging process. If this mist settles on the bike's frame it will corrode the surface.

1. Connect the positive (+) charger lead to the positive (+) battery terminal (or lead) and the negative (-) charger lead to the negative (-) battery terminal (or lead).
2. Remove all vent caps from the battery, set the charger at 12 volts and switch the charger on. If the output of the charger is variable, it is best to select a low setting—1-1/2 to 2 amps.

CAUTION
The electrolyte level must be maintained at the upper level during the charging cycle; check and refill as necessary.

3. After the battery has been charged for about 8 hours, turn the charger off, disconnect the leads and check the specific gravity. It should be within the limits specified in **Table 3**. If it is, and remains stable for 1 hour, the battery is considered charged.
4. Clean the battery terminals, surrounding case and tray and reinstall them in the bike, reversing the removal steps. Coat the battery terminals with Vaseline or silicone spray to retard corrosion and decomposition of the terminals.

CAUTION
Route the breather tube so that it does not drain onto any part of the bike's frame. The tube must be free of bends or twists as any restriction may pressurize the battery and damage it.

New Battery Installation

When replacing the old battery with a new one, be sure to charge it completely (specific gravity 1.260-1.280) before installing it in the bike. Failure to do so, or using the battery with a low electrolyte level, will permanently damage the new battery.

PERIODIC LUBRICATION

Refer to **Figure 9** for major lubrication points.

Oil

Oil is graded according to its viscosity, which is an indication of how thick it is. The Society of Automotive Engineers (SAE) system distinguishes oil viscosity by numbers called "weights." Thick (heavy) oils have higher viscosity numbers than thin (light) oils. For example, a 5 weight (SAE 5) oil is a light oil while a 90 weight (SAE 90) oil is relatively heavy. The viscosity of the oil has nothing to do with its lubricating properties.

Grease

A good quality grease (preferably water proof) should be used (**Figure 10**). Water does not wash grease off parts as easily as it washes off oil. In addition, grease maintains its lubricating qualities better than oil on long and strenuous rides. In a pinch, though, the wrong lubricant is better than none at all. Correct the situation as soon as possible.

Checking Engine Oil Level

Engine oil level is checked with the dipstick/oil filler cap, located on the rear right-hand side of the engine behind the clutch mechanism cover (**Figure 11**).

1. Place the bike on the centerstand. Start the engine and let it warm up approximately 2-3 minutes.

2. Shut off the engine and let the oil settle.

3. Unscrew the dipstick/oil filler cap and wipe it clean. Reinsert it onto the threads in the hole; do not screw it in. Remove it and check the oil level. The bike must be level for a correct reading.

4. The level should be between the 2 lines and not above the upper one (**Figure 12**). If necessary, add the recommended type oil to correct the level. Install the dipstick/oil filler cap and tighten it securely.

9

1 2 3 4 5 6 7 8

9 10 11 12 13

LUBRICATION POINTS

1. Front forks
2. Speedometer and tachometer cables
3. Steering head bearings
4. Clutch, throttle and choke cables
5. Throttle grip, clutch and brake pivots
6. Rear swing arm
7. Rear foot pegs
8. Rear wheel bearings
9. Front wheel bearings
10. Speedometer drive gear
11. Front foot pegs
12. Side and center stand pivots
13. Drive chain

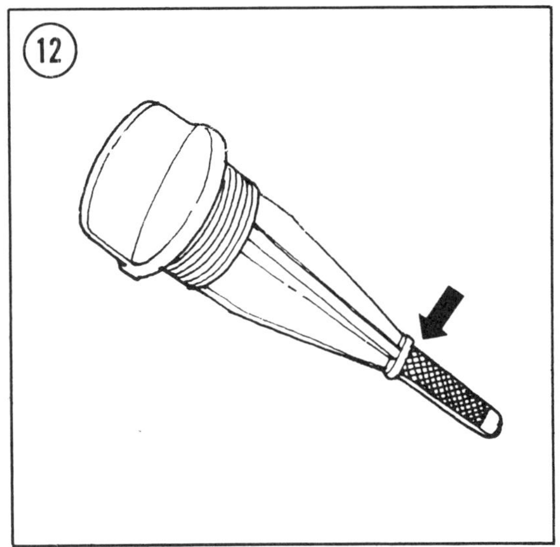
12

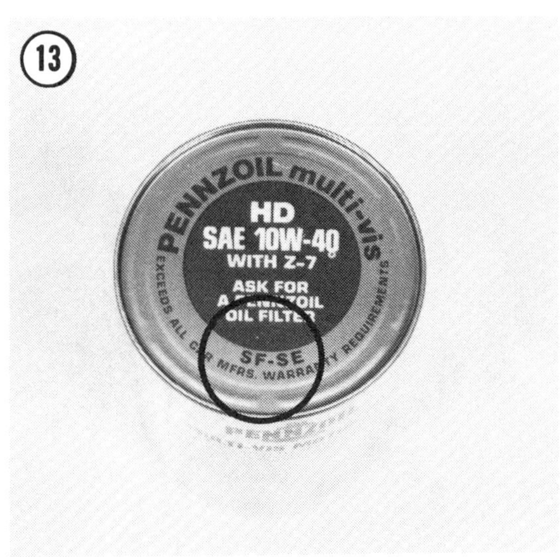

13

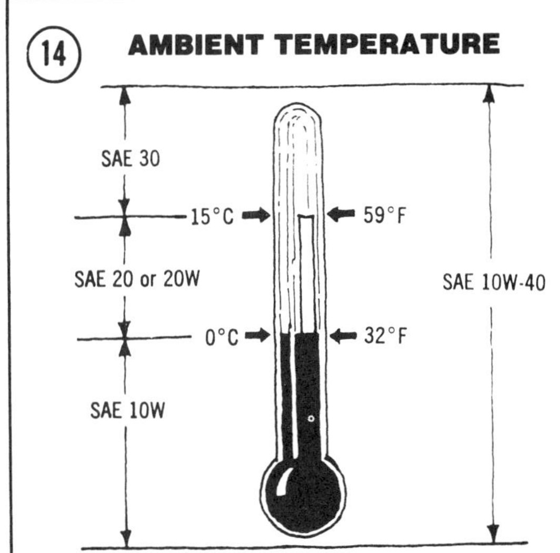

14

15

Changing Engine Oil and Filter

The factory-recommended oil and filter change interval is every 4,000 miles (6,400 km). This assumes that the motorcycle is operated in moderate climates. In extreme climates, oil should be changed every 30 days. The time interval is more important than the mileage interval because acids formed by gasoline and water vapor from combustion will contaminate the oil even if the motorcycle is not run for several months. If the motorcycle is operated under dusty conditions, the oil will get dirty more quickly and should be changed more frequently than recommended.

Use only a high quality detergent oil with an API classification of SE or SF. The classification is stamped or printed on top of the can (**Figure 13**). Try to use the same brand of oil at each change. Use of oil additives is not recommended as it may cause clutch slippage. Refer to **Figure 14** for correct oil weight to use under anticiapted ambient temperatures (not engine oil temperature).

To change the engine oil and filter you will need the following (**Figure 15**):

a. Drain pan
b. Funnel
c. Can opener or pour spout
d. 17 mm wrench (drain plug) and 12 mm wrench (filter bolt)
e. 4 quarts of oil
f. Oil filter element

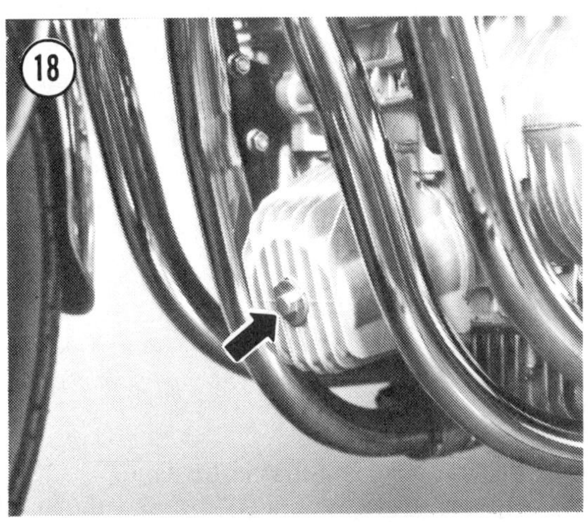

There are a number of ways to discard the old oil safely. The easiest way is to pour it from the drain pan into a gallon plastic bleach or milk bottle. Tighten the cap and place it in your household trash.

NOTE
Never dispose of motor oil in the trash, on the ground, or down a storm drain. May service stations accept used motor oil and waste haulers provide curbside used motor oil collection. Do not combine other fluids with motor oil to be recycled. To locate a recycler, contact the American Petroleum Institute (API) at ***www. recycleoil.org***.

1. Place the bike on the centerstand.

2. Start the engine and let it reach operating temperature.

3. Shut it off and place a drain pan under the engine.

4. Remove the drain plug (**Figure 16**). Remove the dipstick/oil filler cap (**Figure 17**); this will speed up the flow of oil.

5. Let it drain for at least 15-20 minutes. During this time, push the starter button a couple of times to help drain any remaining oil.

CAUTION
Do not let the engine start and run without oil in the crankcase.

6. Inspect the condition of the sealing washer on the drain plug. Replace it if its condition is in doubt.

7. Install the drain plug and tighten to 18-25 ft.-lb. (25-35 N•m).

NOTE
Before removing the oil filter cover, thoroughly clean off all road dirt and oil around it.

8. Move the drain pan under the oil filter and unscrew the bolt (**Figure 18**) securing the filter cover to the crankcase.

9. Remove the filter cover and filter. Discard the old filter and clean out the cover and the bolt with solvent. Make sure all holes in the hollow bolt are open to allow good oil flow. Dry all parts thoroughly.

CAUTION
Use only a 12 mm socket or box wrench ***(do not use an adjustable or open end wrench)*** *on this bolt. The head will round off very easily if the wrong type of wrench is used. There is an aftermarket bolt with a larger head (17 mm) which is available at some Honda dealers or motorcycle supply stores.*

10. Inspect the O-ring on the filter cover (**Figure 19**). Check for signs of deterioration and hardening. Replace if necessary.

NOTE
Prior to installing the filter cover, clean off the mating surface of the crankcase—do not allow any road dirt to enter into the oil system.

11. Insert the bolt into the filter cover and install the spring and washer. Insert the filter onto the bolt and install the spacer (**Figure 20**).
12. Install the filter assembly onto the crankcase making sure the locating tab on the filter cover is to the *top* and is indexed into the groove on the crankcase. Tighten the bolt to 20-24 ft.-lb. (27-33 N•m).
13. Insert a funnel into the oil fill hole and fill the engine with the correct weight and quantity oil.

NOTE
The capacity is approximately 3.2 U.S. qt. (3.0 liters) for oil and filter change.

14. Screw in the dipstick/oil filler cap securely.
15. Start the engine; the oil warning light should go off within 5 seconds. If it stays on, shut off the engine immediately and locate the problem. Do not run the engine with the light on.
16. Let the engine run at moderate speed and check for leaks.
17. Turn the engine off and check for correct oil level; adjust as necessary.

Front Fork Oil Change

There is no factory recommended fork oil change interval but it's a good practice to change the oil every 6,000 miles (10,000 km) or when it becomes contaminated.

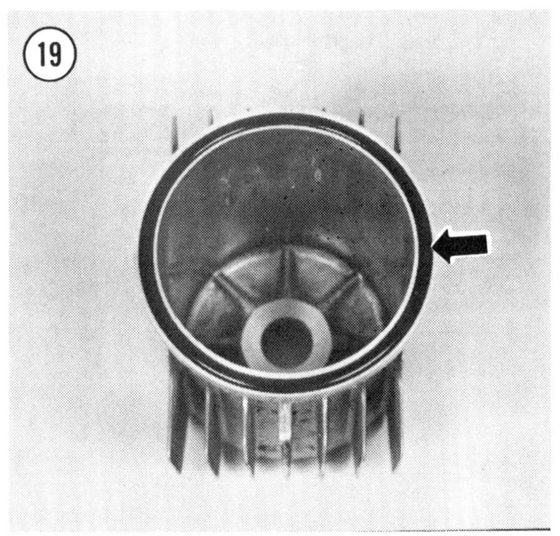

19

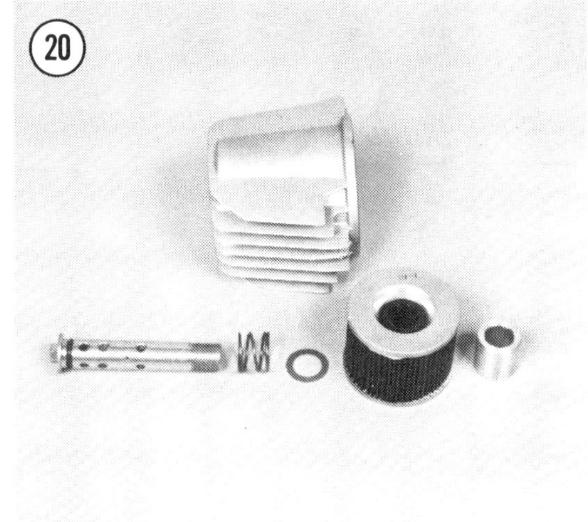

20

Models since 1981 are equipped with air assist front forks. Service is basically the same as for the conventional type fork. Where differences occur in this procedure they are identified.

1. On models since 1981, remove the dust cap (**Figure 21**) and *bleed off all air pressure* by depressing the valve stem (**Figure 22**).

NOTE
Release air pressure gradually. If it is released too fast, oil will spurt out with the air. Protect your eyes and clothing accordingly.

2. Place the bike on the centerstand.
3. On 1979-1980 models, remove the black

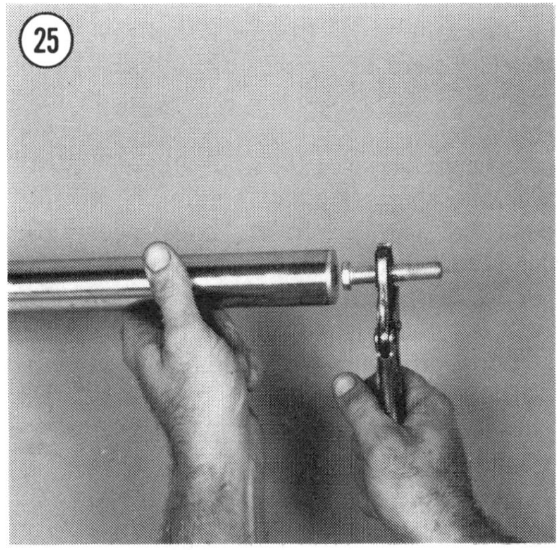

protective cap (**Figure 23**) and unscrew the top cap bolt (**Figure 24**) with a 17 mm Allen wrench. Unscrew the fork cap slowly as it is under spring pressure from the fork spring.

NOTE

*For a substitute tool, attach a pair of Vise Grips to a bolt with a head that measures 17 mm across the flats (**Figure 25**). This figure is shown with the fork assembly removed for clarity. It is not necessary to remove the fork tube for this procedure.*

4. On models since 1981, disconnect the air hose fitting from the right-hand fork cap

26

27

(**Figure 26**) and then from the fitting on the left-hand fork cap (**Figure 27**). Leave the air hose in place under the fuse holder; it is not necessary to remove it unless it is to be replaced.

5. On models since 1981, unscrew the top fork cap/air valve assembly (**Figure 28**). Unscrew the fork cap slowly as it is under spring pressure from the fork spring.

6. Place a drain pan under the drain screw (**Figure 29** or **Figure 30**) and remove the drain screw. Allow the oil to drain for at least 5 minutes. *Never reuse the oil.*

CAUTION

Do not allow the fork oil to come in contact with any of the brake components.

7. Inspect the condition of the gasket on the drain screw; replace it if necessary. Install the drain screw.

8. Repeat for the other fork.

9. Refill each fork leg with the specified quantity of Dexron ATF (automatic transmission fluid) or fork oil. Refer to **Table 4** for specified quantity.

NOTE

*In order to measure the correct amount of fluid, use a plastic baby bottle. These have measurements in fluid ounces (oz.) and cubic centimeters (cc) on the side (**Figure 31**).*

28

29

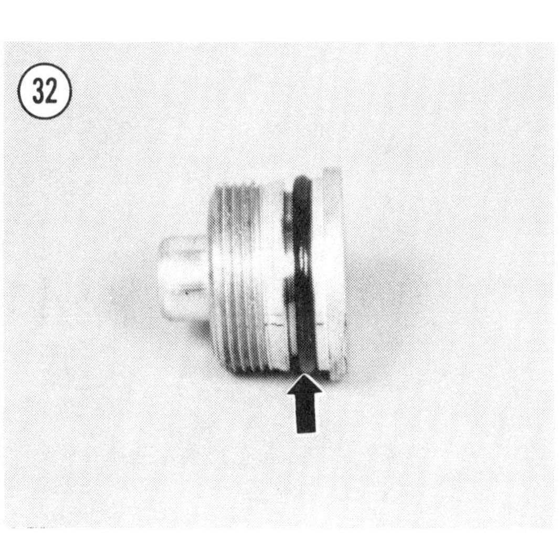

10. After filling each fork tube, slowly pump the fork tubes several times to expel air from the upper and lower fork chambers and to distribute the oil.

11. On 1979-1980 models, inspect the condition of the O-ring seal (**Figure 32**) on the fork cap bolt; replace if necessary. Install the fork top cap while pushing down on the spring. Start the fork cap bolt slowly; don't cross thread it. Tighten fork cap bolt to 22-29 ft.-lb. (30-40 N•m).

12. On models since 1981, inspect the condition of the O-ring seal on the top fork cap/air valve assembly; replace if necessary. Install the top fork cap/air valve assembly on each fork tube and tighten to 11-22 ft.-lb. (15-30 N•m). After the assemblies are tightened they must be aligned to their original position to correctly accept the air hose. If necessary, loosen the upper and lower fork bridge bolts (**Figure 33**) and rotate the fork tube until alignment is correct. Retighten the upper fork bridge bolt to 7-9 ft.-lb. (9-13 N•m) and the lower to 22-29 ft.-lb. (30-40 N•m).

13. On models since 1981, apply a light coat of grease to new O-ring seals and install them onto the air hose fittings (**Figure 34**). Install the air hose fitting first to the left-hand side fork cap and tighten to 3-5 ft.-lb. (4-7 N•m). Install the air hose to the right-hand side fork cap and tighten the fitting to 11-15 ft.-lb. (15-20 N•m).

NOTE

Hold onto the air hose connector (attached to the top fork cap/air valve assembly) with a wrench while tightening the air hose fitting.

14. On models since 1981, inflate the forks to 10-16 psi (0.7-1.1 kg/cm^2). Do not use compressed air; only use a small hand-operated air pump like the S & W Mini-Pump (**Figure 35**) or equivalent.

WARNING

Never use any type of compressed gas as an explosion may be lethal. Never heat the fork assembly with a torch or place it near an open flame or extreme heat as this will also result in an explosion.

15. Road test the bike and check for leaks.

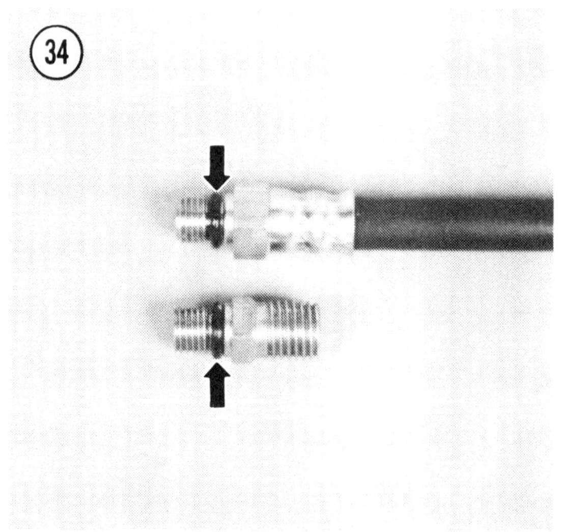

34

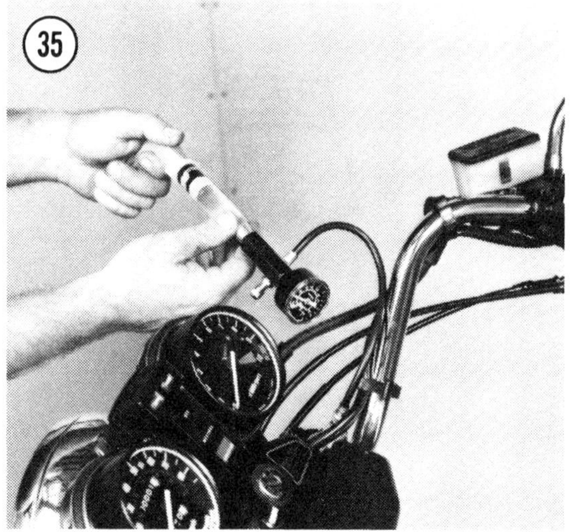

35

Drive Chain Lubrication

Oil the drive chain every 300 miles (500 km) or sooner if it becomes dry. A properly maintained chain will provide maximum service life and reliability.

1. Place the bike on the centerstand.
2. Oil the bottom run of the chain with a commercial chain lubricant (**Figure 36**) or SAE 80 or 90 weight gear oil. Concentrate on getting the lubricant down between the side plates of the chain links.

CAUTION

The drive chain is an O-ring type. Do not use engine oil as a lubricant as it will damage the O-rings. Use a chain lubricant specifically formulated for use with this type of chain or the specified gear oil.

3. Rotate the wheel to bring the unoiled portion of the chain within reach. Continue until all of the chain is lubricated.

36

Control Cables

Every 4,000 miles (6,400 km) the control cables should be lubricated. They should be also inspected at this time for fraying and the cable sheath should be checked for chafing. The cables are relatively inexpensive and should be replaced when found to be faulty.

The control cables can be lubricated either

37

38

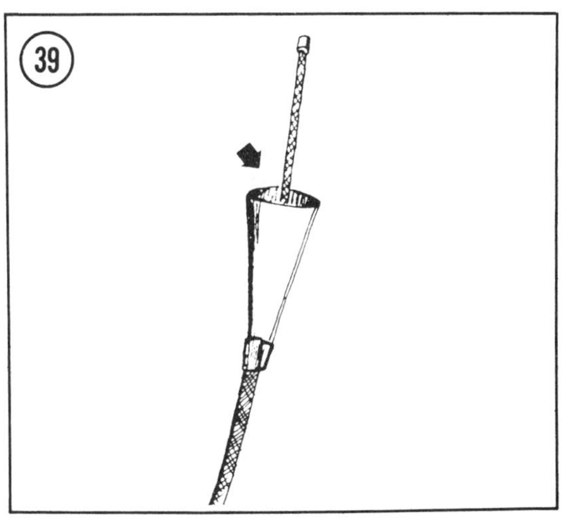
39

with oil or with any of the popular cable lubricants and a cable lubricator. The first method requires more time and the complete lubrication of the entire cable is less certain.

Examine the exposed end of the inner cable. If it is dirty or the cable feels gritty when moved up and down in its housing, spray it with a lubricant/solvent such as LPS-25 or WD-40. Let this solvent drain out, then proceed with the following steps.

Oil Method

1. Disconnect the cables from the clutch lever (**Figure 37**) and the throttle grip assembly (**Figure 38**).

NOTE

On the throttle cable it is necessary to remove the screws that clamp the housing together to gain access to the cable ends.

2. Make a cone of stiff paper and tape it to the end of the cable sheath (**Figure 39**).
3. Hold the cable upright and pour a small amount of light oil (SAE 10W/30) into the cone. Work the cable in and out of the sheath for several minutes to help the oil work its way down to the end of the cable.

NOTE

To avoid a mess, place a shop cloth at the end of the cable to catch the oil as it runs out.

4. Remove the cone, reconnect the cable and adjust the cable(s) as described in this chapter.

Lubricator Method

1. Disconnect the cables from the clutch lever (**Figure 37**) and the front brake lever (**Figure 38**).
2. Attach a lubricator following the manufacturer's instructions.
3. Insert the nozzle of the lubricant can in the lubricator, press the button on the can and hold it down until the lubricant begins to flow out of the other end of the cable.

NOTE

Place a shop cloth at the end of the cable(s) to catch all excess lubricant that will flow out.

3

4. Remove the lubricator, reconnect the cable(s) and adjust the cable(s) as described in this chapter.

Rear Swing Arm Bushing Lubrication

Lubricate the rear swing arm bushings every 4,000 miles (6,400 km) using the grease fitting (**Figure 40**) located on the bottom of the swing arm pivot bolt area. Use a good grade multipurpose grease and apply with a small hand-held grease gun (**Figure 41**).

1. Wipe the fitting clean of all road dirt and grease residue. Force the grease into the fitting until the grease runs out of both ends of the swing arm.
2. Clean off excess grease.
3. If the grease will not run out of the ends of the swing arm, unscrew the grease fitting from the swing arm. Clean it out with solvent; make sure the ball check valve is free. Reinstall the fitting or replace with a new one.
4. Apply the grease gun again. If grease still does not run out of both ends of the swing arm, remove the swing arm as described under *Rear Swing Arm Removal/Installation* in Chapter Nine. Disassemble the swing arm and thoroughly clean and regrease.

Rear Brake Cam Lubrication

Lubricate the rear brake cam every 12,000 miles (19,200 km), every 2 years or whenever the rear wheel is removed.

1. Remove the rear wheel as described under *Rear Wheel Removal/Installation* in Chapter Nine.
2. Remove the brake panel assembly from the rear wheel.
3. Remove the cotter pins, washers and plate securing the brake shoes to the backing plate.
4. Remove the brake shoes from the backing plate by pulling upon the center of each shoe as shown in **Figure 42**.

NOTE

Place a clean shop rag on the linings to protect them from oil and grease during removal.

5. Remove the return springs and separate the brake shoes.

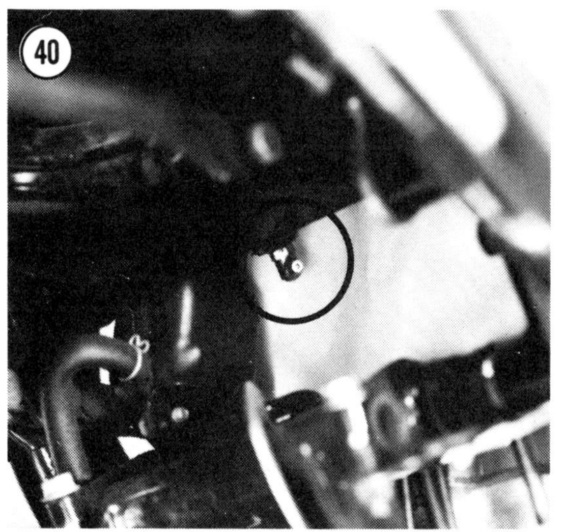
40

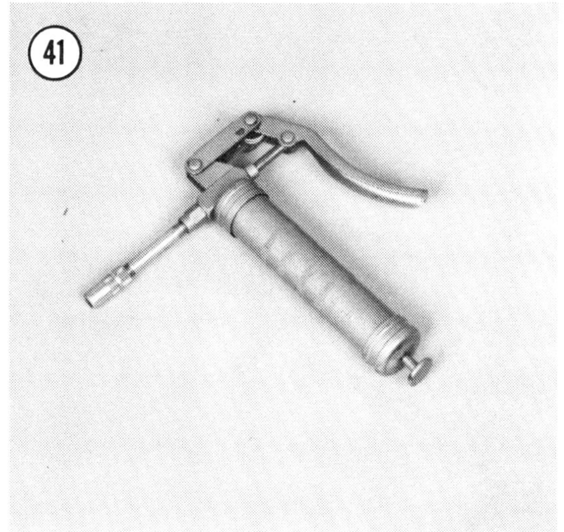
41

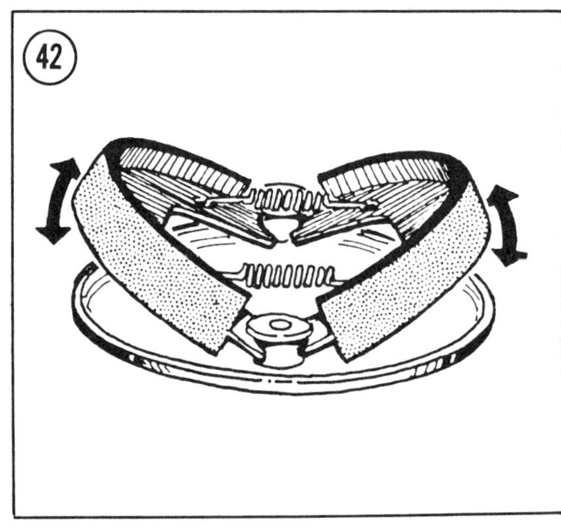
42

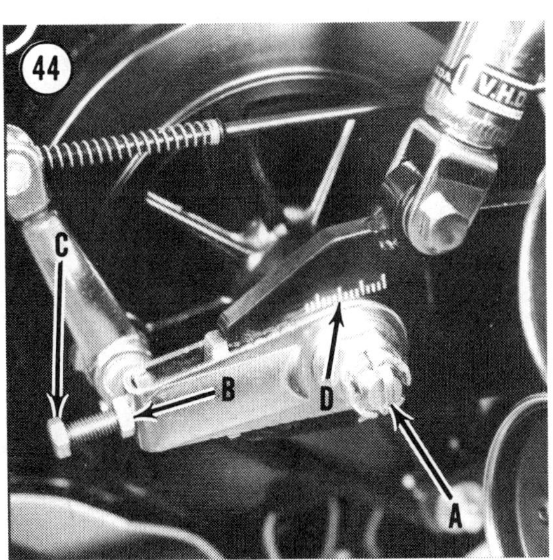

6. Wipe away old grease from the camshaft and pivot pins on the backing plate. Also clean the pivot hole and camshaft contact area of each shoe. Be careful not to get any grease on the linings.
7. Sparingly apply a high-temperature grease to all pivot and rubbing surfaces of the backing plate, brake shoes and spring ends.
8. Reassemble the brake assembly and install new cotter pins and bend the ends over completely.
9. Reinstall the brake panel assembly into the rear wheel and reinstall the rear wheel.
10. Adjust the drive chain and rear brake as described in this chapter.

Speedometer and Tachometer Cable Lubrication

Lubricate both cables every year or whenever needle operation is erratic. The procedure is the same for both instruments.

1. Unscrew the retaining collar and remove the cable from the instrument (**Figure 43**).
2. Pull the cable from the cable sheath.
3. If the grease on the cable is contaminated, thoroughly clean off all old grease.
4. Thoroughly coat the cable with a good grade multipurpose grease and reinstall into the sheath.
5. Make sure the cable is correctly seated into the drive unit.

3

PERIODIC MAINTENANCE

Drive Chain Adjustment

The drive chain should be checked and adjusted every 300 miles (500 km).

1. Place the bike on the sidestand.
2. Shift the transmission into NEUTRAL.
3. Remove the cotter pin and loosen the axle nut (A, **Figure 44**).
4. Loosen the axle adjuster locknut (B, **Figure 44**) and turn the adjuster bolts (C, **Figure 44**) in or out as required, in equal amounts. Be sure that the marks (D, **Figure 44**) on both adjusters align with the same marks on each side of the swing arm. The correct amount of chain free play pushed up midway between the sprockets, should be 5/8 to 1 in. (15-25 mm). See **Figure 45**.
5. Rotate the rear wheel to move the chain to another position and recheck the adjustment; chains rarely wear or stretch evenly and, as a result, the free play will not remain constant over the entire chain. If the chain cannot be adjusted within these limits, it is excessively worn and stretched and should be replaced. Replace the drive chain when the red zone (**Figure 46**) on the label aligns with the rear of the swing arm or when free play exceeds 1-5/8 in. (40 mm). Always replace both sprockets when replacing the drive chain; never install a new chain over worn sprockets. Replacement chain is as follows:

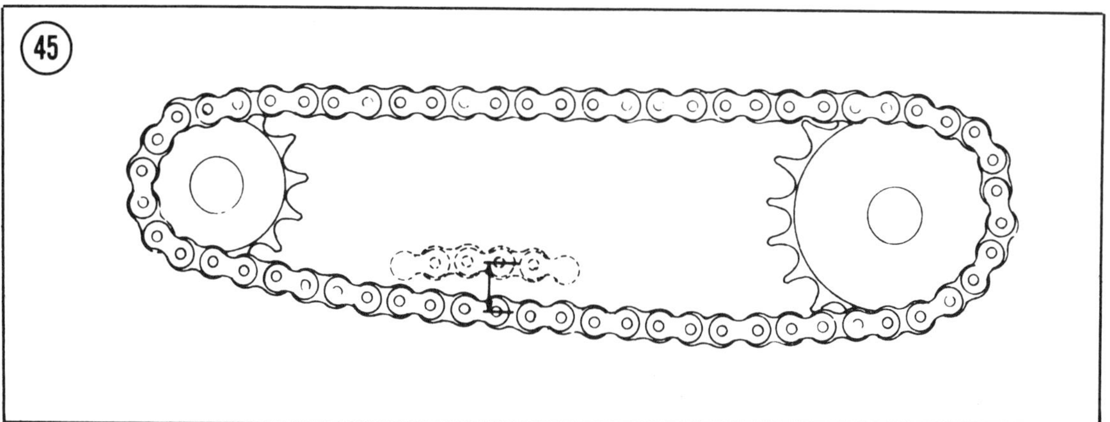

a. 1979 models—DID 50 HDK by 102 links
b. 1980 models—DID 50 V by 104 links
c. Models since 1981—DID 50 V or RK 50 MO by 104 links

WARNING
Excess free play can result in chain breakage which could cause a serious accident.

6. Sight along the top of the drive chain from the rear sprocket to see that it is correctly aligned. It should leave the top of the rear sprocket in a straight line (A, **Figure 47**). If it is cocked to one side or the other (B and C, **Figure 47**) the wheel is incorrectly aligned and must be corrected. Refer to Step 4.
7. Tighten the rear axle nut to 58-72 ft.-lb. (80-100 N•m). Install a new cotter pin and bend the ends over completely.

NOTE
Always install a new cotter pin; never reuse an old one.

8. After the drive chain has been adjusted, the rear brake pedal free play must be adjusted as described under *Rear Brake Pedal Adjustment* in this chapter.

Disc Brake

The hydraulic brake fluid in the disc brake master cylinder should be checked every month or 4,000 miles (6,400 km), whichever comes first. The brake pads should also be checked for wear at the same time. Bleeding the system, servicing brake components and

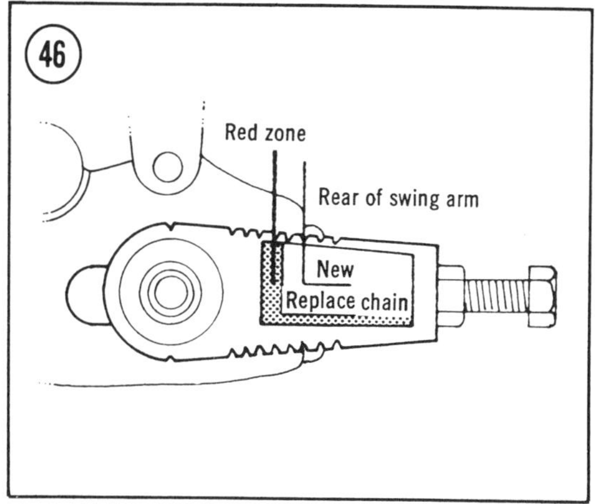

replacing the brake pads are covered in Chapter Ten.

Disc Brake Fluid Level

The fluid level in the reservoir should be up to the upper line (**Figure 48**). If necessary, correct the level by adding fresh brake fluid. Clean any dirt from the area around the cover prior to removing the cover. Remove the cover, gasket and diaphragm.

WARNING
Use brake fluid clearly marked DOT 3 only and specified for disc brakes. Others may vaporize and cause brake failure.

CAUTION
Be careful when handling brake fluid. Do not spill it on painted or plated surfaces as it will destroy the surface. Wash the area immediately with soapy water and thoroughly rinse it off.

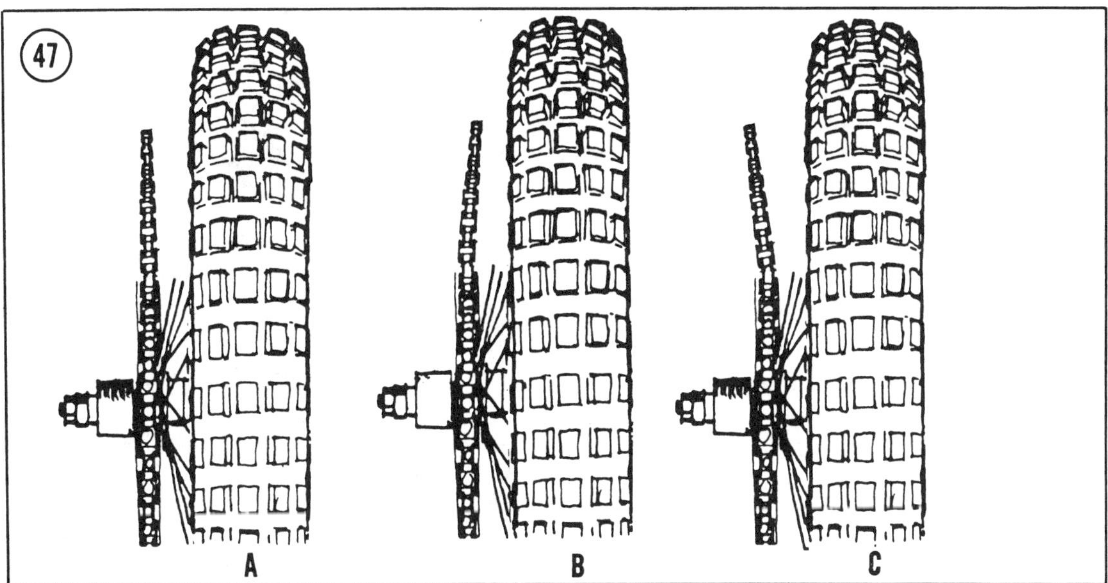

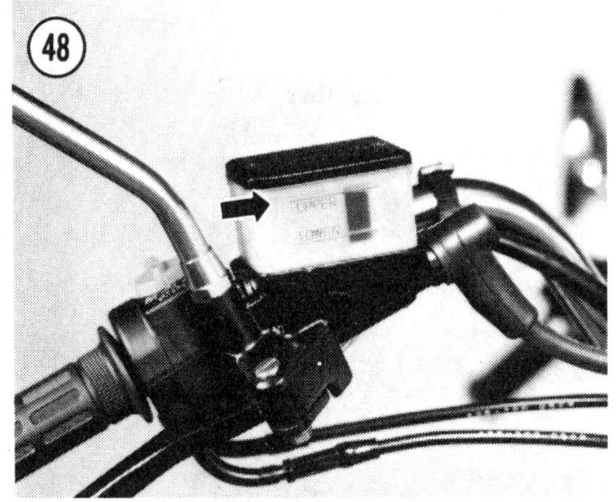

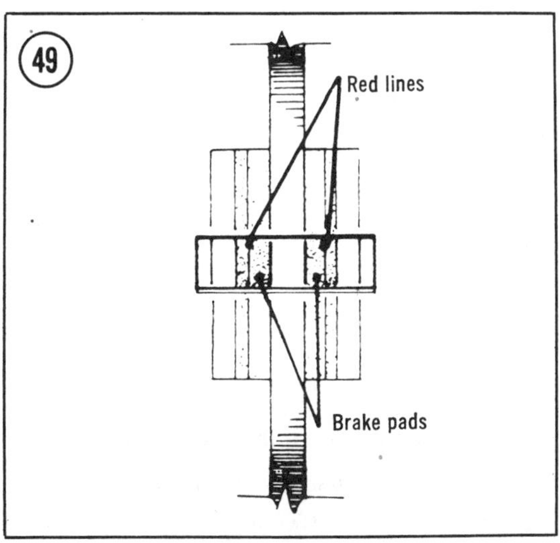

Reinstall the diaphragm, gasket and cover. Tighten the screws securely.

Disc Brake Lines

Check brake lines between the master cylinder and the brake caliper. If there is any leakage, tighten the connections and bleed the brakes as described under *Bleeding the System* in Chapter Ten. If this does not stop the leak or if a brake line is obviously damaged, cracked or chafed, replace the brake line and bleed the system.

Disc Brake Pad Wear

Inspect the brake pads for excessive or uneven wear, scoring and oil or grease on the friction surface. If the pads are worn to the red line (**Figure 49**), they must be replaced.

NOTE
Always replace both pads at the same time.

If any of these conditions exist, replace the pads as described under *Brake Pad Replacement* in Chapter Ten.

Disc Brake Fluid Change

Every time the reservoir cap is removed a small amount of dirt and moisture enters the brake fluid. The same thing happens if a leak occurs or any part of the hydraulic system is loosened or disconnected. Dirt can clog the system and cause unnecessary wear. Water in the brake fluid vaporizes at high temperature, impairing the hydraulic action and reducing the brake's stopping ability.

To maintain peak performance, change the brake fluid every 12,000 miles (19,000 km) or every 2 years, whichever comes first.

1. Remove the dust cap from the bleeder valve on the caliper assembly (**Figure 50**). Connect a small clear hose to the valve and place the free end into a container (**Figure 51**).

NOTE
On models with 2 disc brakes, start with the caliper assembly on the right-hand side first.

2. Open the bleeder valve with a wrench about 1/2 turn.

NOTE
To prevent the over travel of the piston in the master cylinder, place a 3/4 in. (20 mm) spacer between the brake lever and the throttle grip.

3. Squeeze the brake lever several times to force out as much brake fluid as possible. Close the bleeder valve.

WARNING
Do not reuse the brake fluid which has been drained from the brake system. Contaminated fluid can cause brake failure.

4. Fill the master cylinder reservoir with fresh brake fluid and install the cap.
5. For models with 2 disc brakes, repeat Step 3 for the left-hand caliper assembly.
6. Refill the master cylinder, install the cap and bleed the system as described under *Bleeding the System* in Chapter Ten.

WARNING
Use brake fluid clearly marked DOT 3 only. Others may vaporize and cause brake failure.

Rear Drum Brake Lining Inspection

Every 4,000 miles (6,400 km) inspect the rear brake lining wear indicator. Apply the rear brake fully; if the wear indicator on the brake arm aligns with the reference mark on the brake panel (**Figure 52**) the brake shoes must be replaced. Refer to *Rear Drum Brake* in Chapter Ten.

Rear Brake Pedal Height Adjustment

The rear brake pedal should be adjusted every 4,000 miles (6,400 km).

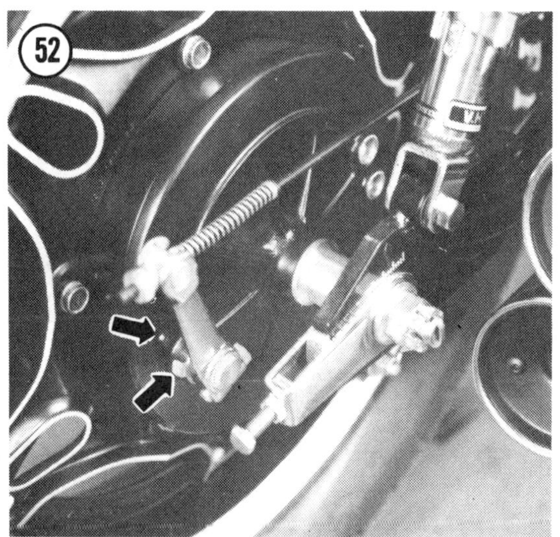

1. Place the bike on the centerstand.
2. Check that the brake pedal is in the at-rest position.
3. The correct height position below the top of the footpeg (**Figure 53**) is 3/4 in. (20 mm).

NOTE

*The adjuster and locknut are located adjacent to the rear brake pedal pivot shaft, behind the frame member (**Figure 54**).*

4. To change height position, loosen the locknut and turn the adjuster. Looking at the adjuster head, turn it *clockwise* to lower the pedal and *counterclockwise* to raise the pedal.
5. Tighten the locknut and adjust the pedal free play as described in the following procedure.

Rear Brake Pedal Adjustment

Adjust the brake pedal to the correct height as described earlier. Turn the adjustment nut on the end of the brake rod (**Figure 55**) until the pedal has 3/4 to 1-1/4 in. (20-30 mm) free play. Free play is the distance the pedal travels from the at-rest position to the applied position when the pedal is lightly depressed by hand.

Rotate the rear wheel and check for brake drag. Also operate the pedal several times to make sure it returns to the at-rest position immediately after release.

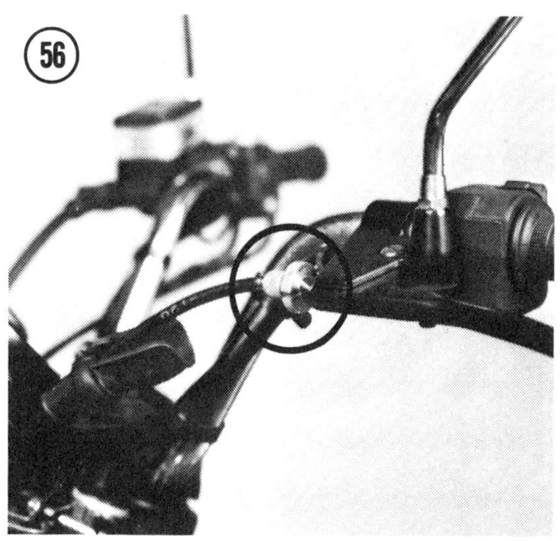

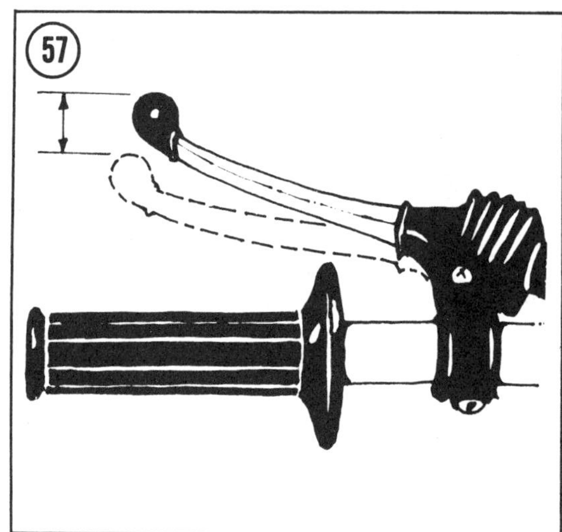

Clutch Adjustment

The clutch free play adjustment should be checked and adjusted every 4,000 miles (6,400 km).

There are 2 different clutch adjustment areas, the clutch cable and the mechanism adjustment in the engine. The cable adjustment takes up slack caused by cable stretching. The mechanism adustment takes up slack due to clutch component wear. Both areas have to be adjusted correctly for correct clutch operation.

If the proper amount of free play cannot be achieved by using these adjustment procedures, the cable has stretched to the point that it needs to be replaced. Refer to *Clutch Cable Replacement* in Chapter Five.

Cable Adjustment

1. At the cluch hand lever, loosen the locknut on the hand lever and screw in the adjuster barrel (**Figure 56**) until 3/8 to 3/4 in. (10 to 20 mm) of free play is obtained at the tip of the lever (**Figure 57**).

NOTE

If the proper amount of free play cannot be achieved at the hand lever, additional adjustment can be made at the clutch cable length adjuster.

2. At the hand lever, loosen the locknut and turn the adjuster barrel all the way in toward the hand lever. Tighten the locknut.

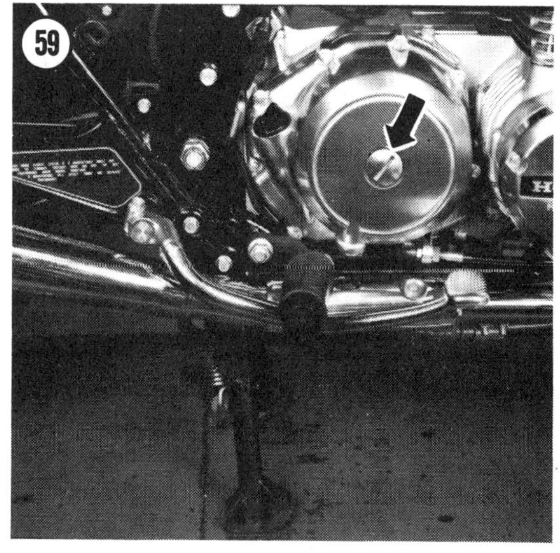

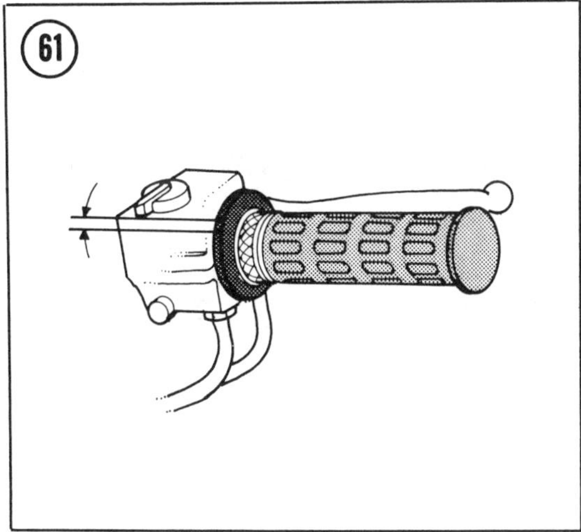

3. At the cable length adjuster (below the clutch housing) loosen the locknut and turn the adjuster barrel (**Figure 58**) until the correct amount of lever free play is obtained. Tighten the locknut.
4. If necessary, repeat Step 1 for fine adjustment.

Mechanism Adjustment

1. Remove the cap (**Figure 59**) from the clutch housing.
2. At the mechanism, loosen the locknut (A, **Figure 60**) and turn the adjuster screw (B, **Figure 60**) clockwise until *slight* resistance is felt, then *stop.*
3. From this point, back out the adjuster screw counterclockwise 3/4 of a turn and tighten the locknut. Reinstall the cap.

NOTE
Make sure the adjuster screw does not move when the locknut is tightened.

4. At the cable length adjuster (below the clutch housing) loosen the locknut and turn the adjuster barrel (**Figure 58**) until the correct amount of lever free play is obtained. Tighten the locknut.
5. If necessary, repeat Step 1 for fine adjustment.

NOTE
When making adjustments at the hand lever, do not expose the threads on the adjuster barrel by more than 5/16 in. (8 mm).

6. After adjustment is completed, check that the locknuts are tight on both the hand lever and cable length adjuster.
7. Test ride the bike and make sure the clutch is operating correctly.

Throttle Adjustment and Operation

The throttle grip should have 1/8-1/4 in. (2-6 mm) rotational free play (**Figure 61**). If adjustment is necessary, loosen the locknut and turn the adjuster (**Figure 62**) at the throttle grip in or out to achieve proper free play rotation. Tighten the locknut.

Check the throttle cables from the grip to the carburetor. Make sure they are not kinked or chafed. Replace as necessary.

Make sure the throttle grip rotates freely from a fully closed to fully open position. Check with the handlebar at center, at full right and at full left. If necessary, remove the throttle grip and apply a lithium base grease to it.

Camshaft Chain Tensioner Adjustment

In time the camshaft chain and guide will wear and develop slack. This will cause engine noise and if neglected too long will cause engine damage. The chain tension should adjusted every 4,000 miles (6,400 km).

1. Place the bike on the centerstand.
2. Turn the ignition switch to the OFF position and shift the transmission into NEUTRAL.
3. Remove all 4 spark plugs. This will make it easier to turn the engine over with a wrench.
4. Remove the ignition cover (**Figure 63**).
5. Loosen the camshaft chain tensioner locknut (**Figure 64**).

NOTE
The camshaft chain tensioner will automatically adjust itself when the locknut is loosened and the engine rotated.

6. Place a 15/16 in. wrench on the outer hex spacer (**Figure 65**) of the ignition unit. Slowly rotate the crankshaft *clockwise* when looking at the ignition unit while tightening the camshaft chain tensioner locknut (**Figure 64**). Rotate the crankshaft at least 4-5 times while tightening the locknut.
7. Reinstall the ignition cover and spark plugs.

Air Cleaner

The air cleaner element should be removed and cleaned every 4,000 miles (6,400 km) and replaced every 8,000 miles (12,800 km).

The air cleaner removes dust and abrasive particles from the air before the air enters the carburetors and engine. Without the air cleaner, very fine particles could enter into the engine and cause rapid wear of the piston rings, cylinder and bearings and might clog small passages in the carburetors. Never run the bike without the air cleaner element installed.

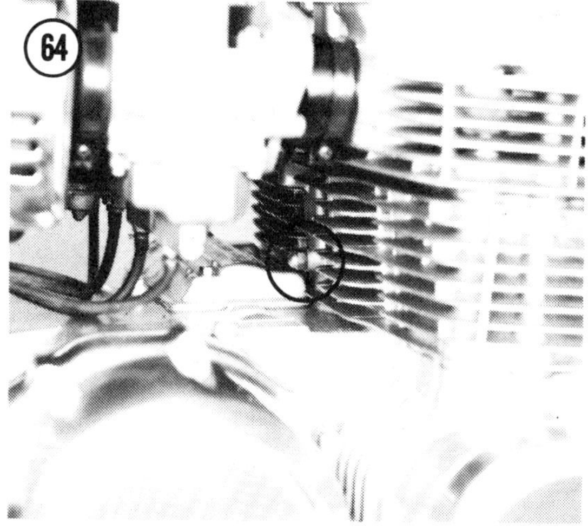

Proper air cleaner servicing can do more to ensure long service from your engine than any other single item.

Servicing

1. On 1979 models, remove the left-hand side cover.
2. On models since 1980, remove the right-hand side cover.
3. Remove the screws securing the air cleaner cover (**Figure 66**) and remove the cover.
4. Pull the element out of the air box (**Figure 67**).
5. Gently tap the element to loosen the dust. Apply compressed air from the *outside* of the element to remove all loosened dirt and dust from inside the element.
6. Inspect the element; if it is torn or broken in any area it should be replaced. Do not run with a damaged element as it may allow dirt to enter the engine.
7. Wipe out the interior of the air box with a shop rag and cleaning solvent. Remove any foreign matter that may have passed through a broken element.
8. Apply a light coat of wheel bearing grease to the sealing edges (**Figure 68**) of the element to provide a good airtight seal between the element and the air box. Install the element into the air box. Make sure it seats properly against the air box.

CAUTION

An improperly installed air cleaner element will allow dirt and grit to enter the carburetor and engine, causing expensive engine damage.

9. Install the air cleaner cover and tighten the screws securely. On 1979 models, be sure to install the cover with the "UP" arrow facing up.
10. Install the side cover.

Fuel Shutoff Valve and Filter Removal/Installation

The integral fuel filter in the fuel shutoff valve removes particles in the fuel which might otherwise enter the carburetors. This could cause the float needle(s) to stay in the open position or clog one of the jets.

1. Turn the fuel shutoff valve to the OFF position (**Figure 69**) and remove the fuel line from the valve.

NOTE

The fuel tank can either be removed or left in place; drain all fuel from it in either case.

2. Install a longer piece of clean fuel line to the valve and place the loose end into a clean, sealable metal container. If the fuel is kept clean, it can be reused.
3. Turn the fuel shutoff valve to the RES position and open the fuel filler cap. This will speed up the flow of fuel. Drain the tank completely.
4. Unscrew the locknut (**Figure 70**) securing the fuel shutoff valve to the fuel tank and remove the valve.
5. After removing the valve, insert a corner of a clean shop rag into the opening in the tank to stop the dribbling of fuel onto the engine and frame.
6. Remove the fuel filter from the shutoff valve. Clean it with a medium soft toothbrush and blow out with compressed air. Replace if it is defective.
7. Install by reversing these removal steps. Do not forget to install the gasket between the valve and the tank. Check for fuel leakage after installation is completed.

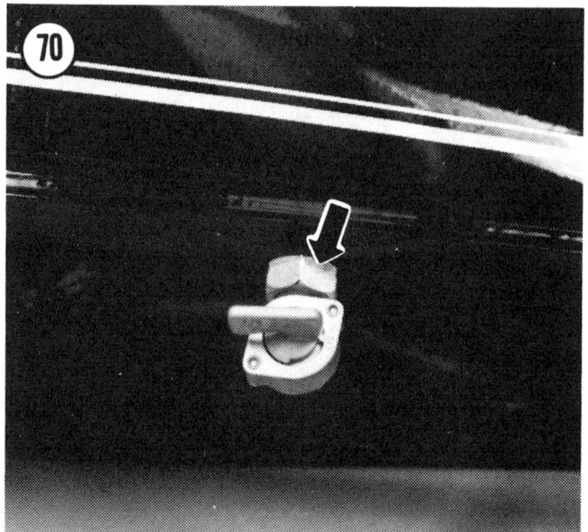

Fuel Line Inspection

Inspect the condition of the fuel line from the fuel tank to the carburetor (**Figure 71**). If it is cracked or starting to deteriorate it must be replaced. Make sure the small hose clamps are in place and holding securely.

WARNING

A damaged or deteriorated fuel line presents a very dangerous fire hazard to both the rider and the bike if fuel should spill onto a hot engine or exhaust pipe.

Wheel Bearings

There is no factory-recommended mileage interval for cleaning and repacking the wheel bearings. They should be serviced whenever they are removed from the wheel hub or

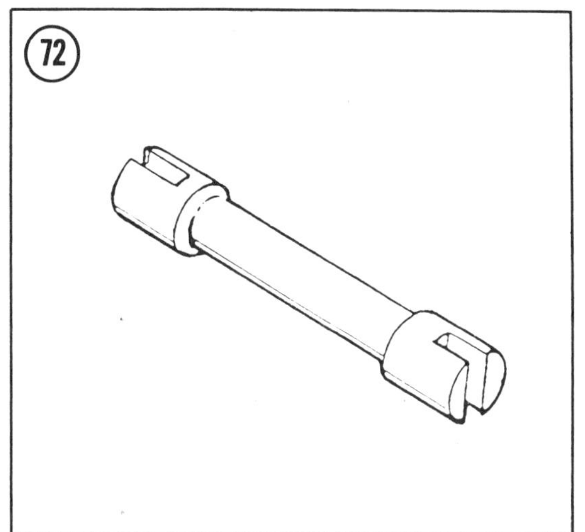

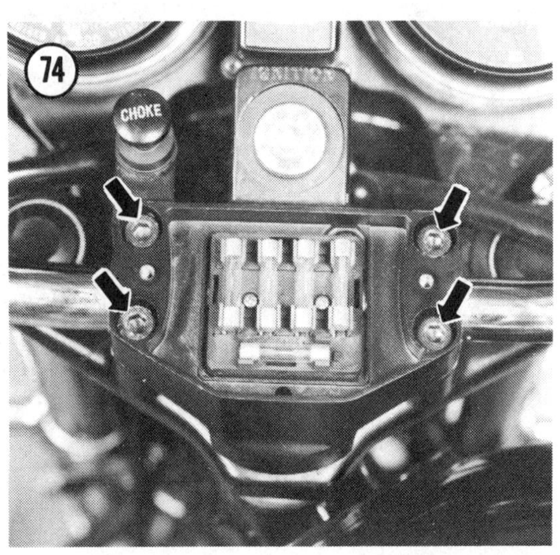

whenever there is the likelihood of water contamination. The correct service procedures are covered in Chapters Eight and Nine.

Steering Head Adjustment Check

The steering head is fitted with loose ball bearings. It should be checked every 8,000 miles (12,800 km).

Place the bike up on wood block(s) or a milk crate so that the front wheel is off the ground.

Hold onto the front fork tubes and gently rock the fork assembly back and forth. If you can feel looseness refer to *Steering Head Adjustment* in Chapter Eight.

Wheel Hubs, Rims and Spokes (Wire Wheels Only)

Check wheel hubs and rims for bends and other signs of damage. Check both wheels for broken or bent spokes. Replace damaged or broken spokes as described under *Wheels* in Chapter Eight. Pluck each spoke with your finger like a guitar string or tap each one lightly with a small hammer. All spokes should emit the same sound. A spoke that is too tight will have a higher pitch than the others; one that is too loose will have a lower pitch. If only one or two spokes are slightly out of adjustment, adjust them with a spoke wrench made for this purpose (**Figure 72**). If more are affected, the wheel should be removed and trued. Refer to *Spoke Adjustment* in Chapter Eight.

Front Suspension Check

1. Apply the front brake and pump the forks up and down as vigorously as possible. Check for smooth operation and check for any oil leaks.
2. Make sure the upper and lower fork bridge bolts (**Figure 73**) are tight.
3. Remove the fuse panel cover and check the tightness of the Allen bolts (**Figure 74**) securing the handlebar.
4. On 1979-1980 models, check that the 4 nuts (2 on each side) securing the front axle holders are tight (**Figure 75**).
5. On models since 1981, make sure the front axle and axle pinch bolt are tight (**Figure 76**).

CAUTION
If any of the previously mentioned bolts and nuts are loose, refer to Chapter Eight for correct procedures and torque specifications.

Rear Suspension Check

1. Place the bike on the centerstand.
2. Push hard on the rear wheel (sideways) to check for side play in the rear swing arm bushings.
3. Check the tightness of the upper and lower shock absorber mounting bolts and nuts (**Figure 77**).
4. Make sure the rear axle nut is tight and the cotter pin is in place (**Figure 78**).
5. Check the tightness of the rear brake torque arm bolts (**Figure 79**). Make sure the cotter pin is in place.

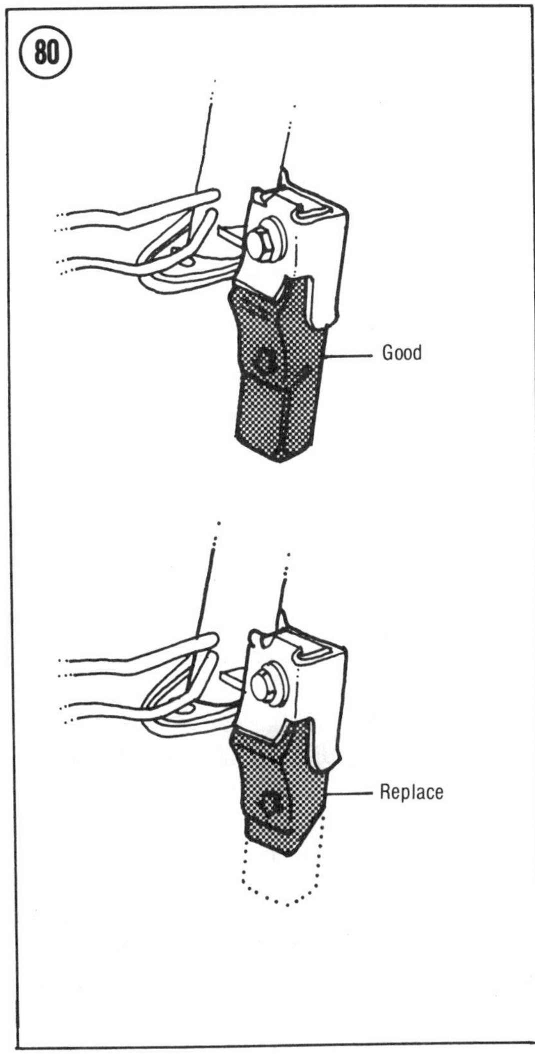

CAUTION
If any of the previously mentioned bolts and nuts are loose, refer to Chapter Nine for correct procedures and torque specifications.

Nuts, Bolts and Other Fasteners

Constant vibration can loosen many of the fasteners on the motorcycle. Check the tightness of all fasteners, especially those on:

a. Engine mounting hardware
b. Engine crankcase covers
c. Handlebar and front forks
d. Gearshift lever
e. Kickstarter lever
f. Brake pedal and lever
g. Exhaust system

Sidestand Rubber

The rubber tip on the side stand kicks the sidestand up if you should forget. If it wears down to the molded line (**Figure 80**) it will no longer be effective and must be replaced. Remove the bolt and replace the rubber tip with a new one.

Crankcase Breather (U.S. Only)

Every 4,000 miles (6,400 km); or sooner if a considerable amount of riding is done at full throttle or in the rain, remove the drain plug (**Figure 81**) and drain out all residue. Install the cap; make sure the clamp is tight.

Refer to Chapter Six for more complete details on the breather system.

ENGINE TUNE-UP

A complete tune-up should be performed every 4,000 miles (6,400 km) of normal riding. More frequent tune-ups may be required if the bike is ridden primarily in stop-and-go traffic.

The number of definitions of the term "tune-up" is probably equal to the number of people defining it. For the purposes of this book, a tune-up is general adjustment and maintenance to ensure peak engine performance.

Table 5 summarizes tune-up specifications.

The spark plugs should be routinely replaced at every other tune-up or if the electrodes show signs of erosion. Have new parts on hand before you begin.

Because different systems in an engine interact, the procedures should be done in the following order.

a. Clean or replace the air cleaner element
b. Adjust camshaft chain tension
c. Adjust valve clearances
d. Run a compression test
e. Check or replace spark plugs
f. Check and adjust the ignition timing
g. Adjust the carburetor idle speed and accelerator pump
h. Ignition timing light

To perform a tune-up on your Honda, you will need the following tools and equipment:

a. 18 mm spark plug wrench
b. Socket wrench and assorted sockets
c. Flat feeler gauge
d. Special tool for adjusting the valve clearance (Honda Valve Adjusting Wrench, part No. 07908-3230000)
e. Spark plug wire feeler gauge and gapper tool
f. Compression gauge
g. Tune-up tachometer
h. Ignition timing light
i. Carburetor synchronizing tool (1979-1980 models, Honda part No. 07908-42201000; models since 1981, Honda part No. 07908-4600200)
j. Manometer (carburetor synchronizing tool) to measure intake manifold vacuum

Air Cleaner Element

The air cleaner element should be cleaned or replaced prior to doing other tune-up procedures. Refer to *Air Cleaner Removal/Installation* in this chapter.

Camshaft Chain Adjustment

Adjust the camshaft chain as described under *Camshaft Chain Tensioner Adjustment* in this chapter.

Valve Clearance Adjustment

Valve clearance adjustment must be made with the engine cool, at room temperature (below 95° F/35° C). The correct valve clearance for all models is 0.002 in. (0.05 mm) for the *intake valves* and 0.003 in. (0.08 mm) for the *exhaust valves.*

The cylinders are numbered 1-4 starting with the No. 1 cylinder on the left-hand side and working across from left to right with the No. 2, 3 and 4. The left-hand side refers to a rider sitting on the seat facing forward. The exhaust valves are at the front of the engine and the intake valves are at the rear of the engine.

1. Remove the seat and both side panels.
2. Turn the fuel shutoff valve to the OFF position and remove the fuel line to the carburetors.
3. Remove the bolt (**Figure 82**) securing the rear of the fuel tank. Lift up and pull the tank to the rear and remove it. Remove the rubber mounting damper and keep it with the fuel tank to avoid misplacing it.
4. Remove the crankcase breather tube (A, **Figure 83**) from the breather cover.
5. Remove the breather cover (B, **Figure 83**) and both valve adjustment covers (C, **Figure 83**).
6. Remove the ignition cover (**Figure 84**).
7. Remove the spark plugs—this will make it easier to rotate the engine.
8. Rotate the crankshaft *clockwise*; use a 15/16 in. wrench on the outer hex spacer (**Figure 85**) of the ignition advance unit. Turn it until the ignition timing mark "1.4 T" aligns with the fixed index mark (**Figure 86**). The No. 1 cylinder must be at top dead center (TDC) on the compression stroke.

NOTE

A cylinder at TDC of its compression stroke will have free play in both of its rocker arms, indicating that both the intake and exhaust valves are closed.

9. With the engine and camshaft in this position measure the valve clearance of the valves marked with an "X" in **Figure 87**.
10. Check the clearance of both the intake and exhaust valves of the No. 1 cylinder (left-hand side) by inserting a flat feeler gauge between the rocker arm pad and the camshaft lobe (A, **Figure 88**). When the clearance is correct, there will be a slight resistance on the feeler gauge when it is inserted and withdrawn.

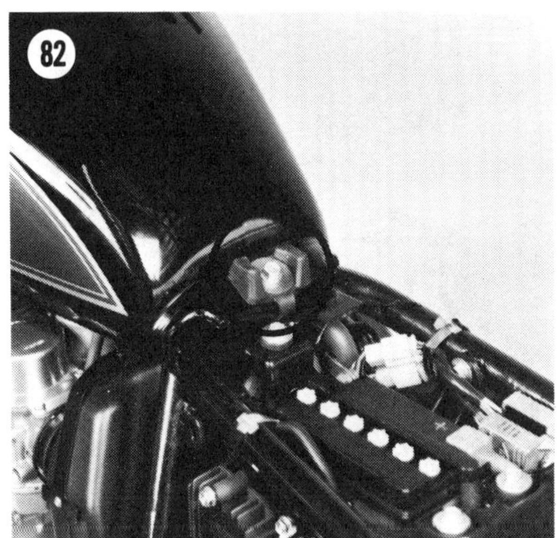
82

85

83

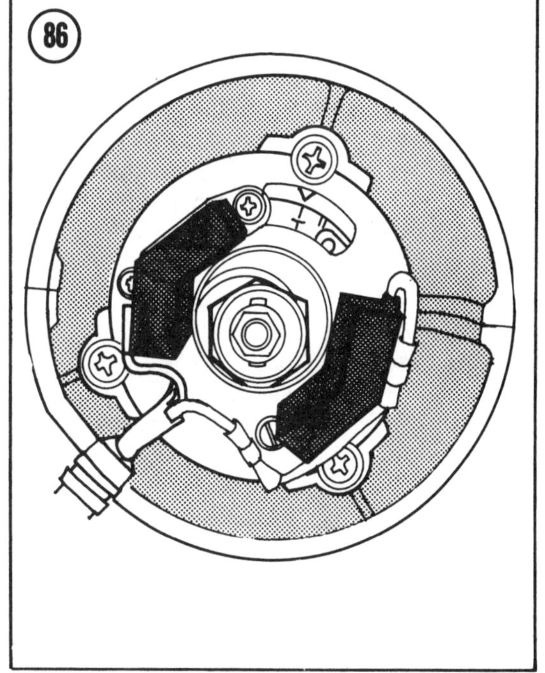
86

84

87

Cylinder No.	1	2	3	4
Intake	X	O	X	O
Exhaust	X	X	O	O

X = Adjust with No. 1 piston at TDC compression
O = Adjust with No. 4 piston at TDC compression

NOTE
*The following steps require the use of a special tool—Honda Valve Adjusting Wrench, part No. 07908-323000 (**Figure 89**), which retails for approximately $10.*

11. To correct the clearance, use the valve adjusting wrench (B, **Figure 88**) and back off the locknut. Screw the adjuster in or out so there is a slight resistance felt on the feeler gauge. Hold the adjuster to prevent it from turning further and tighten the locknut to 9-12 ft.-lb. (12-16 N•m). Then recheck the clearance to make sure the adjuster did not slip when the locknut was tightened. Readjust if necessary.
12. With the engine and camshaft in this position repeat Steps 10 and 11 for the correct valves of the No. 2 and 3 cylinder. Refer to **Figure 87**.
13. Rotate the crankshaft one full turn (360°) *clockwise*; use a 15/16 in. wrench on the outer hex spacer (**Figure 85**) of the ignition advance unit. Turn it until the ignition timing mark "1.4 T" aligns with the fixed index mark (**Figure 86**). Now the No. 4 cylinder must be at top dead center (TDC) on the compression stroke.

NOTE
A cylinder at TDC of its compression stroke will have free play in both of its rocker arms, indicating that both the intake and exhaust valves are closed.

14. With the engine and camshaft in this position measure the valve clearance of the valves marked with an "O" in **Figure 87**.
15. Repeat Steps 10 and 11 for both valves of the No. 4 cylinder and for the correct valves of the No. 2 and 3 cylinder. Refer to **Figure 87**.
16. Inspect the condition of the rubber gaskets on the breather and valve adjusting covers. Replace if they are starting to deteriorate or harden; replace as a set even if only one is bad. Install all 3 covers.
17. Attach the crankcase breather hose to the breather cover. Make sure the hose clamp is tight.
18. Install the ignition cover, fuel tank, side covers and seat.

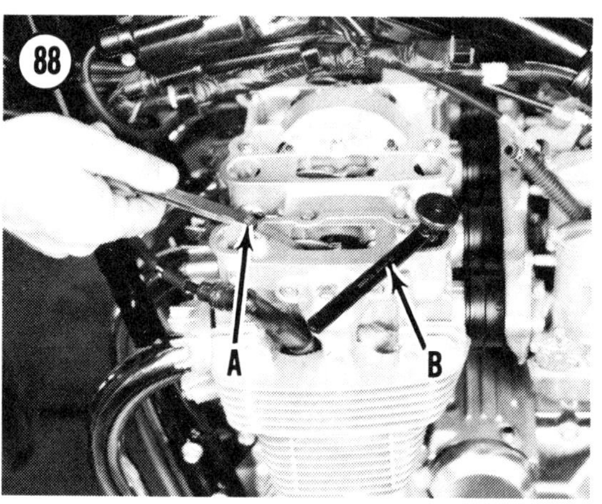

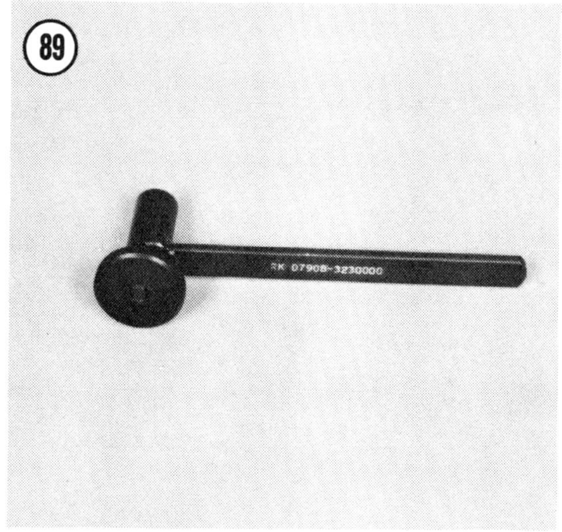

Compression Test

Every 8,000 miles (12,800 km) check compression pressure. Record the results and compare them at the next 8,000 mile (12,800 km) check. A running record will show trends in deterioration so that corrective action can be taken before complete failure occurs to a given set of parts.

The results, when properly interpreted, can indicate general cylinder, piston ring and valve condition.

1. Warm the engine and let it reach normal operating temperature. Make sure that both the throttle and choke valves are completely open.
2. Disconnect the spark plug wires and remove all 4 spark plugs.

3. Connect a compression gauge to one cylinder following manufacturer's instructions (**Figure 90**).
4. Press the starter button and turn the engine over until there is no further rise in pressure. Maximum pressure is usually reached within 4-7 seconds.

CAUTION

Do not turn the engine over more than absolutely necessary. When spark plug leads are disconnected the electronic ignition will produce the highest voltage possible and the coil may overheat and be damaged.

5. Remove the compression gauge and record the reading.

When interpreting the results, actual readings are not as important as the difference among the cylinders. Readings should be about 170 +/-28 psi (12 +/-2.0 kg/cm^2).

If the compression readings do not differ among cylinders by more than 10 psi, the piston rings and valves are in good condition.

If the reading is higher than normal, there may be a buildup of carbon deposits in the combustion chamber or on the piston crown.

If a low reading (10% or more) is obtained on one or more cylinders, it indicates valve or piston ring trouble. To determine which is faulty, pour about one teaspoon of engine oil through the spark plug hole onto the top of the piston.

NOTE

In order to do this on the 2 center cylinders it is necessary to remove the fuel tank and use a small funnel to avoid spilling oil all over the cylinder head.

Turn the engine over once to clear the oil, then take another compression reading. If the compression returns to normal, the valves are good but the piston rings are defective on that cylinder. If compression does not increase, the valves require servicing. A valve could be hanging open but not burned or a piece of carbon could be on a valve seat.

Correct Spark Plug Heat Range

Spark plugs are available in various heat ranges, hotter or colder than the plugs originally installed at the factory.

Select plugs of the heat range designed for the loads and conditions under which the bike will be run. Use of incorrect heat ranges can cause a seized piston, scored cylinder wall or damaged piston crown.

In general, use a hot plug for low speeds and low temperatures. Use a cold plug for high speeds, high engine loads and high temperatures. The plug should operate hot enough to burn off unwanted deposits, but not so hot that it is damaged or causes preignition. A spark plug of the correct heat range will show a light tan color on the portion of the insulator within the cylinder after the plug has been in service.

The reach (length) of a plug is also important. A longer than normal plug could interfere with the piston, causing permanent and severe damage; refer to **Figure 91**.

The standard heat range spark plugs are listed in **Table 6**.

Spark Plug Removal/Cleaning

1. Grasp the spark plug lead (**Figure 92**) as near the plug as possible and pull it off the plug. If it is stuck to the plug, twist it slightly to break it loose.
2. Blow away any dirt that has accumulated in the spark plug well.

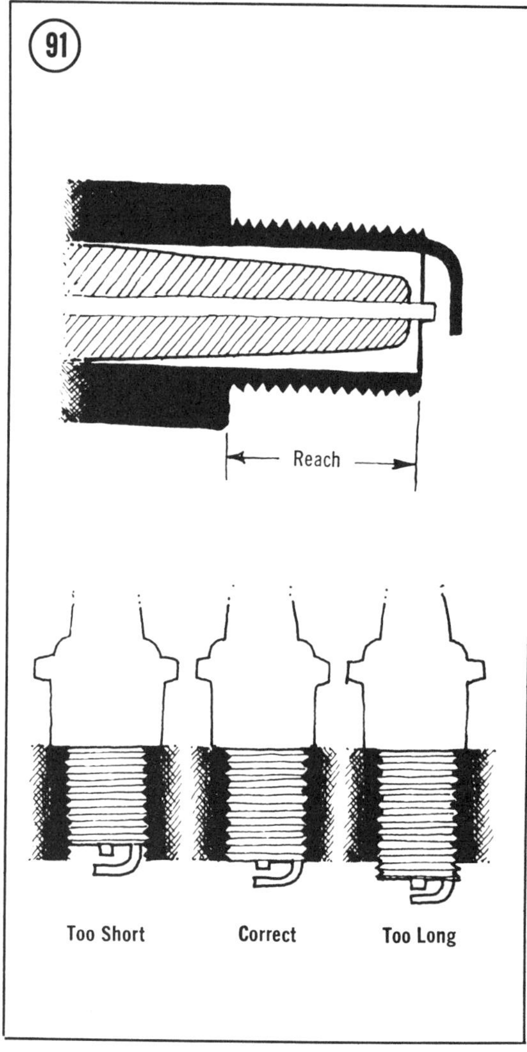

CAUTION
The dirt could fall into the cylinder when the plug is removed, causing serious engine damage.

3. Remove the spark plugs with an 18 mm spark plug wrench. Be sure to use a spark plug wrench with a rubber retainer in it. The center spark plugs are difficult to remove after they have been loosened without this type of wrench.

NOTE
If the plug is difficult to remove, apply penetrating oil, like WD-40 or Liquid Wrench ***(Figure 93)****, around the base of the plug and let it soak in about 10-20 minutes.*

4. Inspect the plug carefully. Look for a broken center porcelain, excessively eroded electrodes and excessive carbon or oil fouling. Replace such plugs. If deposits are light, the plug may be cleaned in solvent with a wire brush or cleaned in a special spark plug sandblast cleaner. Regap the plug as explained in the following section.

Gapping and Installing the Plug

A spark plug should be carefully gapped to ensure a reliable, consistant spark. You must use a special spark plug gapping tool and a wire feeler gauge.

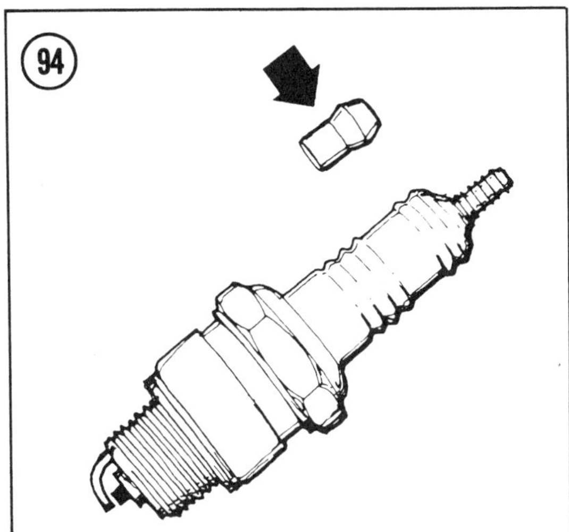

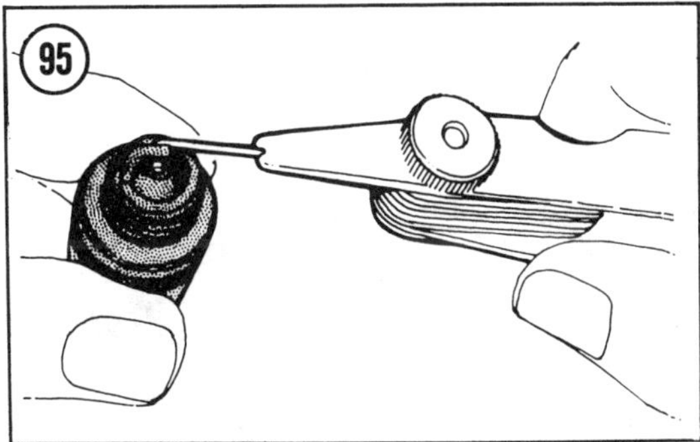

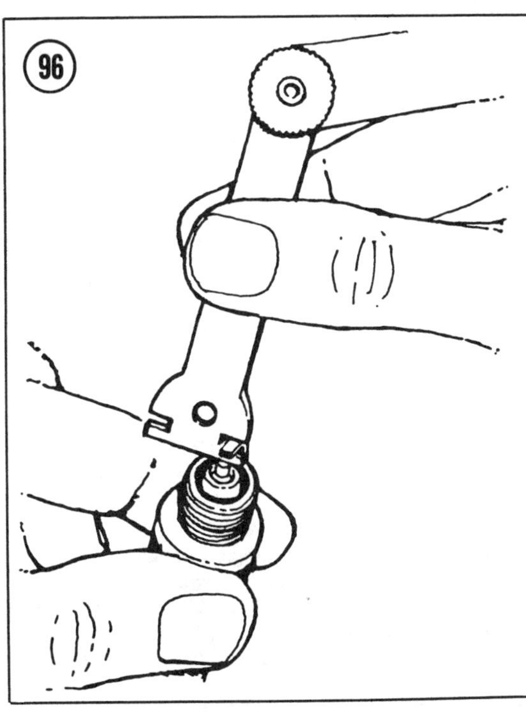

1. Remove the new plugs from their boxes. *Do not* screw on the small piece that is loose in each box (**Figure 94**); they are not used.

2. Insert a wire feeler gauge between the center and the side electrode of each plug (**Figure 95**). The correct gap is listed in **Table 6**. If the gap is correct, you will feel a slight drag as you pull the wire through. If there is no drag, or the gauge won't pass through, bend the side electrode with a gapping tool (**Figure 96**) to set the proper gap.

3. Put a small drop of oil on the threads of each spark plug.

4. Due to the strange angle and cramped quarters for your hand on the center 2 cylinders, insert the plugs into the spark plug wrench (with a rubber retainer in it) and screw the spark plug in until it seats. On the outer 2 cylinders it is not necessary to use the spark plug wrench. Screw the spark plug in by hand until it seats. Very little effort is required. If force is necessary, you have the plug cross-threaded; unscrew it and try again.

5. Use a spark plug wrench and tighten each plug an additional 1/4 to 1/2 turn after the gasket has made contact with the head. If you are installing an old, regapped plug and reusing the old gasket, only tighten an additional 1/4 turn.

NOTE
Do not overtighten. This will only squash the gasket and destroy its sealing ability.

6. Install the spark plug leads; make sure they are on tight.

Reading Spark Plugs

Much information about engine and spark plug performance can be determined by careful examination of the spark plug. This information is more valid after performing the following steps.

1. Ride the bike a short distance at full throttle in any gear.

2. Turn the kill switch to the OFF position before closing the throttle and simultaneously pull in clutch or shift to NEUTRAL; coast and brake to a stop.

97

SPARK PLUG CONDITION

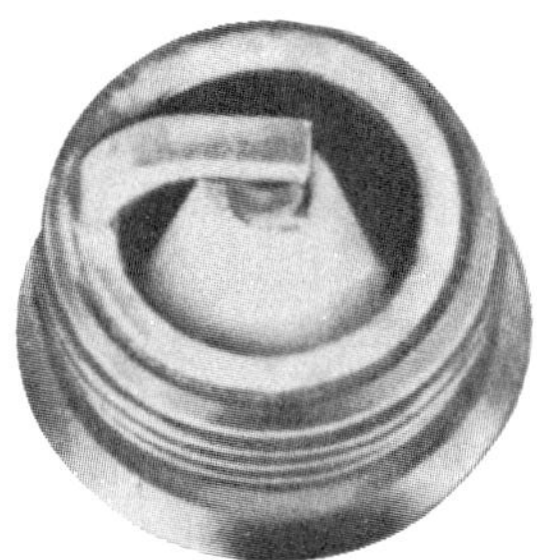

NORMAL
- Identified by light tan or gray deposits on the firing tip.
- Can be cleaned.

GAP BRIDGED
- Identified by deposit buildup closing gap between electrodes.
- Caused by oil or carbon fouling. If deposits are not excessive, the plug can be cleaned.

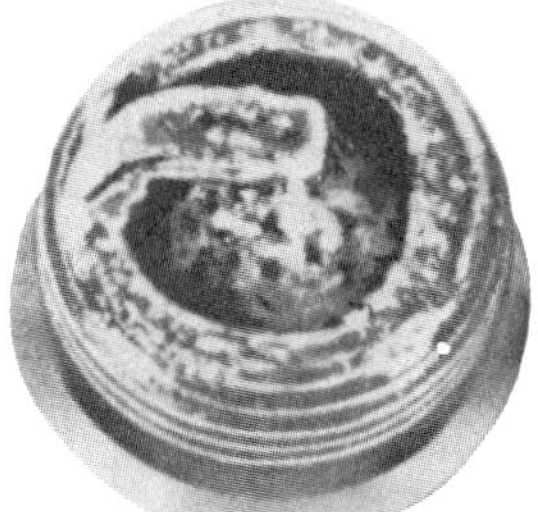

OIL FOULED
- Identified by wet black deposits on the insulator shell bore and electrodes.
- Caused by excessive oil entering combustion chamber through worn rings and pistons, excessive clearance between valve guides and stems, or worn or loose bearings. Can be cleaned. If engine is not repaired, use a hotter plug.

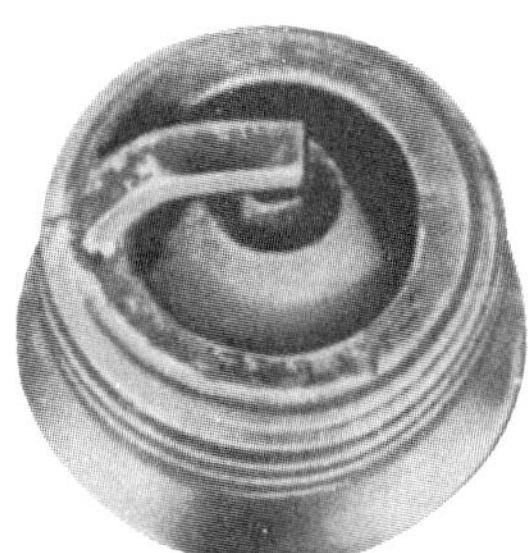

CARBON FOULED
- Identified by black, dry fluffy carbon deposits on insulator tips, exposed shell surfaces and electrodes.
- Caused by too cold a plug, weak ignition, dirty air cleaner, too rich a fuel mixture or excessive idling. Can be cleaned.

LEAD FOULED
- Identified by dark gray, black, yellow or tan deposits or a fused glazed coating on the insulator tip.
- Caused by highly leaded gasoline. Can be cleaned.

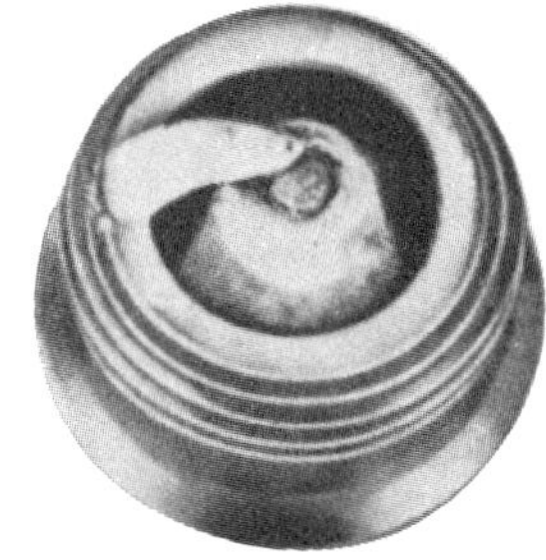

WORN
- Identified by severly eroded or worn electrodes.
- Caused by normal wear. Should be replaced.

FUSED SPOT DEPOSIT
- Identified by melted or spotty deposits resembling bubbles or blisters.
- Caused by sudden acceleration. Can be cleaned.

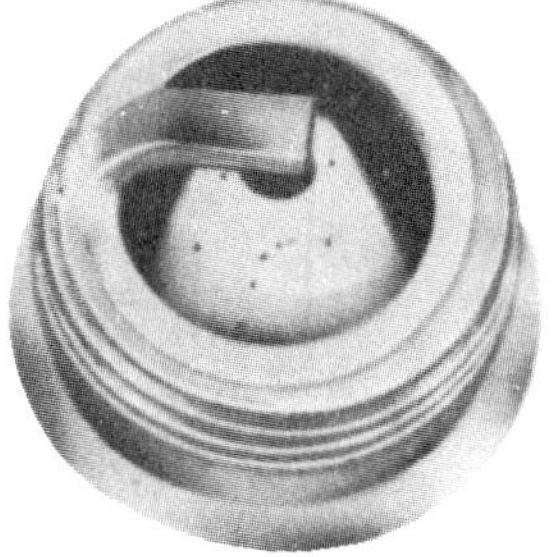

OVERHEATING
- Identified by a white or light gray insulator with small black or gray brown spots and with bluish-burnt appearance of electrodes.
- Caused by engine overheating, wrong type of fuel, loose spark plugs, too hot a plug or incorrect igntion timing. Replace the plug.

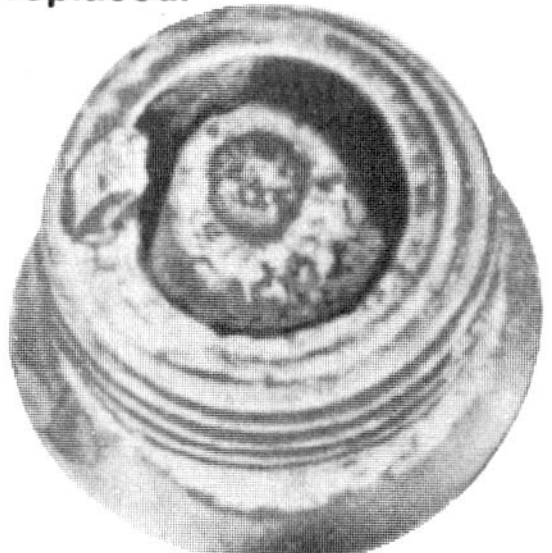

PREIGNITION
- Identified by melted electrodes and possibly blistered insulator. Metallic deposits on insulator indicate engine damage.
- Caused by wrong type of fuel, incorrect igntion timing or advance, too hot a plug, burned valves or engine overheating. Replace the plug.

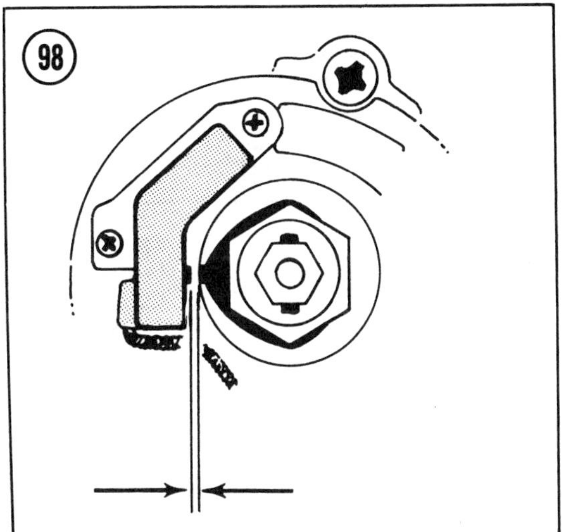

3. Remove the spark plugs and examine them. Compare them to **Figure 97**.

If the insulator is white or burned, the plug is too hot and should be replaced with a colder one.

A too-cold plug will have sooty or oily deposits ranging in color from dark brown to black. Replace with hotter plugs and check for too-rich carburetion or evidence of oil blow-by at the piston rings.

If the plug has a light tan or gray colored deposit and no abnormal gap wear or electrode erosion is evident, the plug and the engine are running properly.

If the plug exhibits a black insulator tip, a damp and oily film over the firing end and a carbon layer over the entire nose it is oil fouled. An oil fouled plug can be cleaned, but it is better to replace it.

Ignition Timing

The Honda CB650 is equipped with a capacitor discharge ignition system (CDI). This system uses no breaker points, but timing does have to be checked as the base plate may move and alter timing.

Incorrect ignition timing can cause a drastic loss of engine performance and efficiency. It may also cause overheating.

There are 2 methods to check ignition timing—static (engine not running) and dynamic (engine running). It is only necessary to check and adjust the timing on the No. 1 cylinder. Once it is adjusted correctly, the other 3 cylinders will automatically be correct. The dynamic timing procedure is the best way to insure correct timing but if a timing light is not available the static method will be satisfactory.

Before starting on this procedure, check all electrical connections related to the ignition system. Make sure all connections are tight and free from corrosion and that all ground connections are clean and tight.

NOTE

*On CB650 Custom models only, if you have experienced a general lack of performance and some surging problems check the air gap of both pulser generators. Insert a non-magnetic flat feeler gauge between the pulser generator and the projection on the rotor (**Figure 98**). The clearance should be between 0.012-0.016 in. (0.3-0.4 mm). If the clearance is incorrect, loosen either or both screws and carefully move the pulser generator to achieve the correct clearance. Perform this adjustment on both pulser generators.*

Dynamic Timing

1. Start the engine and let it reach normal operating temperature. Turn the engine off.
2. Remove the ignition cover.
3. Connect a portable tachometer (**Figure 99**) following the manufacturer's instructions. The bike's tachometer is not accurate enough in the low rpm range for this adjustment.
4. Connect a timing light (**Figure 100**) to the No. 1 cylinder (left-hand side) following the manufacturer's instructions. **Figure 101** shows typical connections if you have no instructions.

CAUTION

*The exhaust system is **hot**; protect yourself accordingly!*

5. Restart the engine and let it idle at 1,050 +/- 100 rpm.
6. Adjust the idle speed if necessary as described under *Carburetor Idle Speed Adjustment* in this chapter.

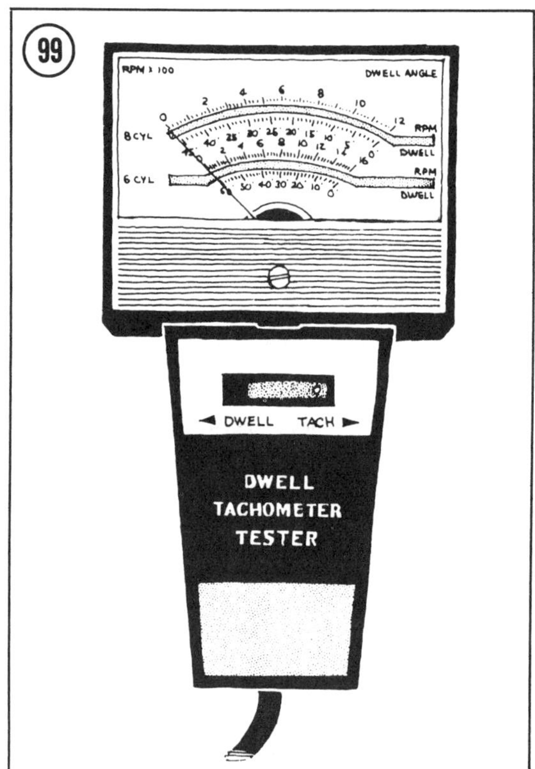

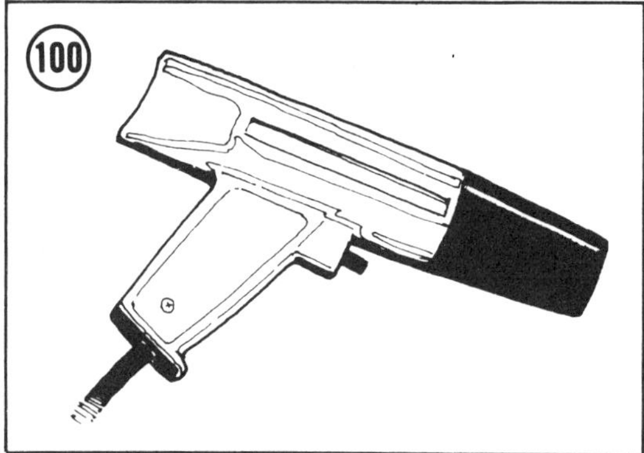

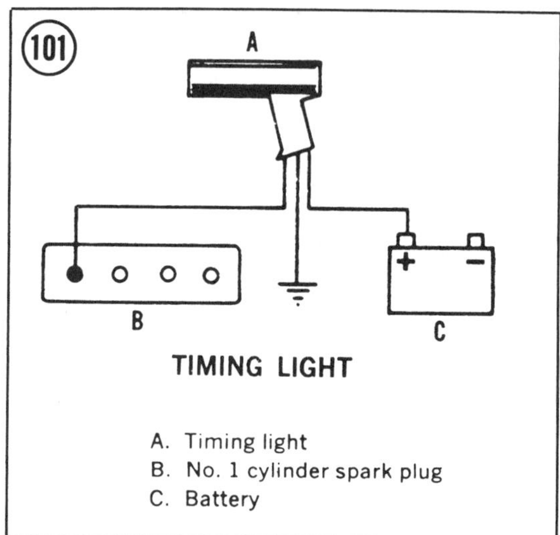

A. Timing light
B. No. 1 cylinder spark plug
C. Battery

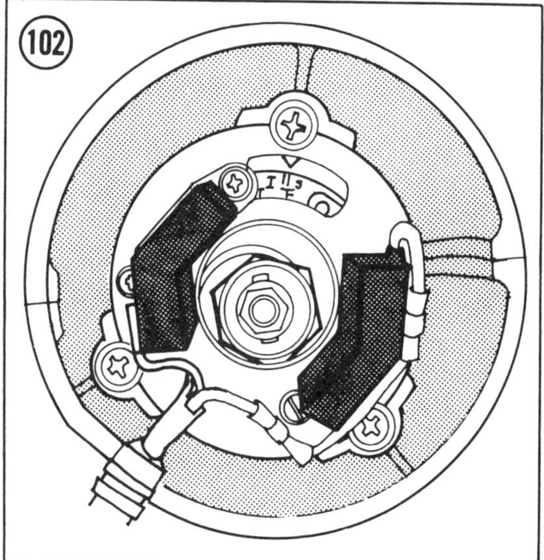

7. Shine the timing light at the timing window and pull the trigger. The timing is correct if the "1.4 F-1" mark aligns with the fixed index mark (**Figure 102**).

8. If timing is incorrect, stop the engine and loosen the screws securing the base plate (**Figure 103**). Rotate the base plate in either direction to achieve correct alignment. Tighten the screws, restart the engine and recheck the timing. Repeat this step until timing is correct. Be sure to tighten the screws securely.

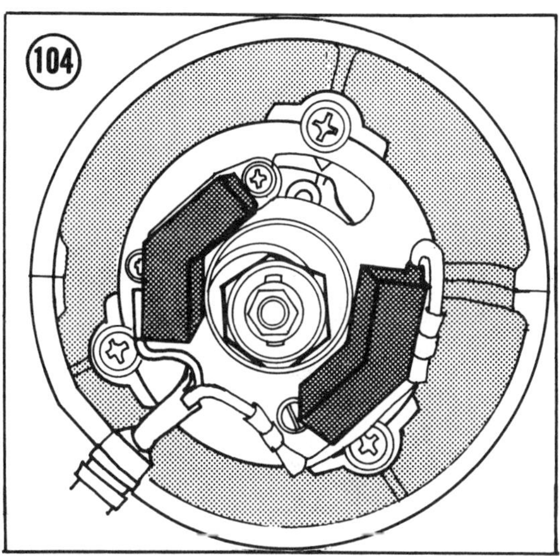

NOTE
Rotating the base plate clockwise will retard the ignition and rotating it counterclockwise will advance it.

9. Also check the ignition advance alignment. Disconnect the timing light from the No. 1 cylinder and reinstall it on the No. 4 cylinder (right-hand side). Restart the engine and increase engine speed to 2,725 rpm or higher and check that the advance marks align with the fixed index mark (**Figure 104**). If the idle speed is correct but the full advance is incorrect, refer to *Ignition Advance Mechanism Inspection* in Chapter Seven.
10. Disconnect the timing light and portable tachometer.
11. Install the ignition cover.

Static Timing

1. Place the bike on the centerstand.
2. Remove the ignition cover.
3. Rotate the crankshaft *counterclockwise*; use a 15/16 in. wrench on the outer hex spacer (**Figure 85**) of the ignition advance unit. Turn it until the ignition timing mark "1.4 S-F" aligns with the fixed index mark (**Figure 105**).

NOTE
Either the No. 1 or 4 cylinder must be at top dead center (TDC) on the compression stroke.

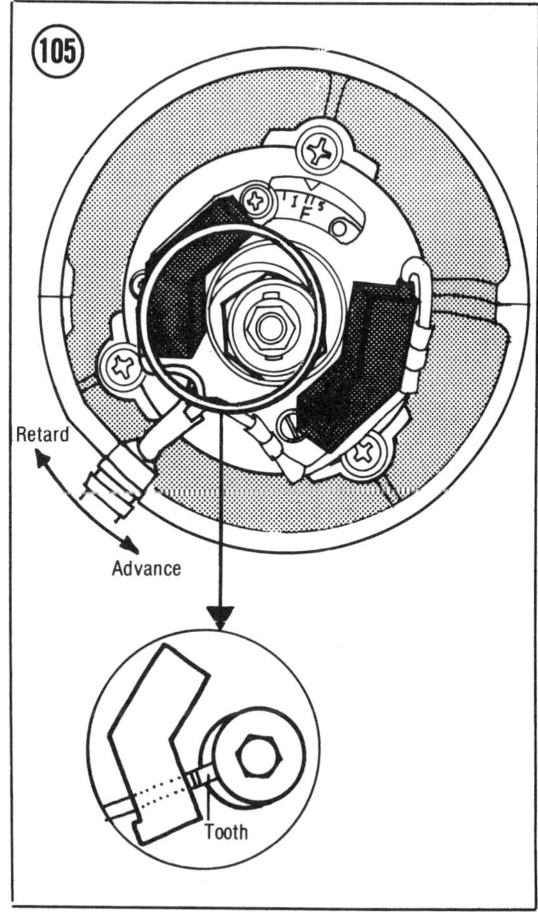

4. Timing is correct if the narrow projection on the left-hand pulser generator (No. 1 and 4 cylinder) aligns with the projection on the rotor (**Figure 105**).
5. If this alignment is incorrect, loosen the screws (**Figure 103**). Rotate the base plate in either direction until alignment is correct as shown in **Figure 106**. Tighten the screws and install the ignition cover.

NOTE
Rotating the base plate clockwise will retard the ignition and rotating it counterclockwise will advance it.

Carburetor Idle Mixture

The idle mixture (pilot screw) is preset at the factory and *is not to be reset.* This pertains to all 4 carburetors on all models (mechanical and constant velocity type). Do not adjust the pilot screws unless the carburetors have been overhauled. If so, refer to *Pilot Screw Adjustment* in Chapter Six.

3

Carburetor Fast Idle Speed Adjustment

Refer to *Fast Idle Adjustment* in Chapter Six.

Accelerator Pump Adjustment

Refer to *Accelerator Pump Adjustment* in Chapter Six.

Carburetor Synchronization

When the carburetors are properly synchronized the engine will warm up faster, and response, performance and mileage will improve.

Prior to synchronizing the carburetors, the air cleaner must be clean and the ignition timing and valve clearance must be properly adjusted.

This procedure covers both types of carburetors (mechanical and constant velocity). The only major difference between the 2 types is the location of the adjusting screws on the carburetor. Where differences occur they are noted.

This procedure requires the use of special tools. For both types of carburetors you will need a mercury manometer (carb-sync tool). This is a tool that measures the intake manifold vacuum of all 4 cylinders simultaneously. A carb-sync tool (**Figure 107**) can be purchased from a Honda dealer, motorcycle supply store or mail order firm.

NOTE
When purchasing this tool check that it is equipped with restrictors. These restrictors keep the mercury from being drawn into the engine when engine rpm is increased during the adjustment procedure. If the mercury is drawn into the engine the tool will have to be replaced.

In addition you will need an adjusting tool that is available from a Honda dealer. For 1979-1980 models, it is the Carburetor Throttle Wrench (part No. 07908-4220100) and for models since 1981 it is the Carburetor Adjusting Wrench (part No. 07908-4600200). These tools retail for about $15 and $20 respectively.

1. Place the bike on the centerstand and warm up the engine just until it will idle reliably. Do not allow it to reach full operating temperature as this may lead to overheating during the test procedure. Shut off the engine.

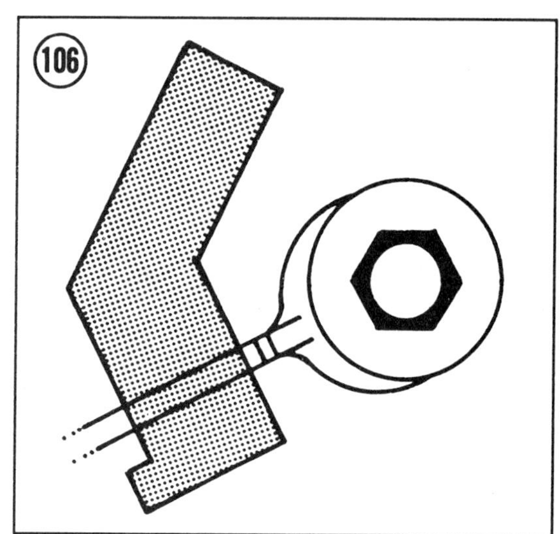

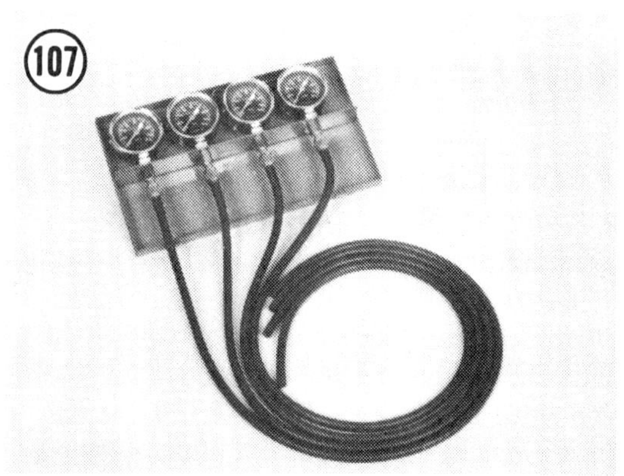

2. Remove both side covers and the seat.

3. Turn the fuel shutoff valve to the OFF position and remove the fuel line to the carburetors (A, **Figure 108**).

4. Remove the bolt (B, **Figure 108**) securing the rear of the fuel tank. Lift up and pull the tank to the rear and remove it. Remove the rubber mounting damper and keep it with the tank to avoid misplacing it.

5. Remove the vacuum plugs from the 4 carburetors. Refer to A, **Figure 109** for 1979-1980 models or **Figure 110** for models since 1981.

6. Connect the vacuum lines from the carb-sync tool to the carburetors following the manufacturer's instructions. Be sure to route the vacuum lines to the correct cylinder. Most

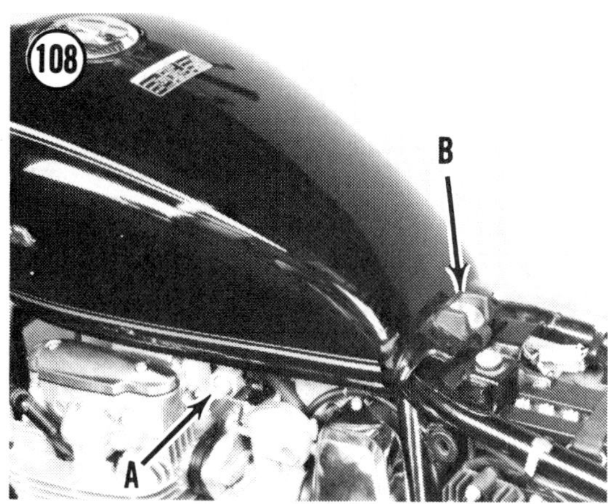

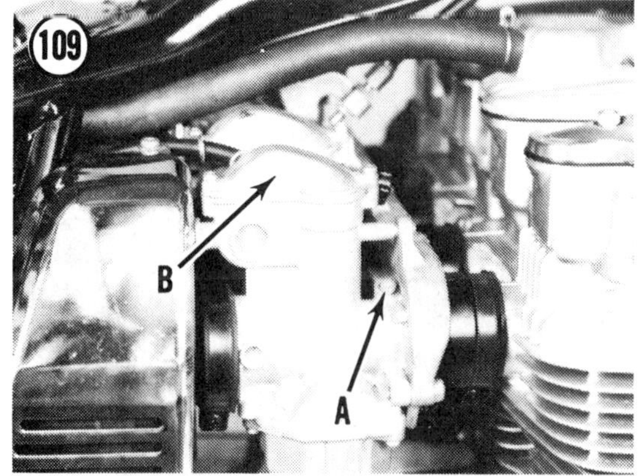

carb-sync tools have the cylinder number indicated on them adjacent to each tube containing the mercury.

7. On 1979-1980 models, remove the carburetor top covers (B, **Figure 109**) from the No. 1, 3 and 4 carburetors.

NOTE

The No. 2 carburetor has no synchronization screw; the other 3 carburetors are to be synchronized to it. The carburetors are numbered in the same sequence as the cylinders with the No. 1 on the left-hand side and continuing with the No. 2, 3 and 4 from left to right.

8. If you have a portable cooling fan, turn it on and place it in front of the engine to help prevent the engine from overheating.

9. Start the engine and let it idle at 1,050 +/-100 rpm. There should be enough fuel in the carburetor float bowls to run the bike for this procedure.

WARNING

***Do not** rig up a temporary fuel supply as this presents a real fire danger.*

10. If you start to run out of fuel during the test, shut off the engine. By this time the engine is probably too warm and should be allowed to cool off a little. After the engine has cooled, reinstall the fuel tank and refill the carburetor float bowls; remove the fuel tank and proceed with the test.

NOTE

On models since 1981, it is necessary to restart the engine as engine vacuum is required to open the fuel shutoff valve to refill the carburetors. Shut off the engine after refilling is completed and remove the fuel tank.

11. If the difference in gauge readings is 2.4 in. Hg (60 mm Hg) or less among all 4 cylinders the carburetors are considered synchronized. If not, proceed as follows.

12. Using the special tool described in the introduction to the procedure, loosen the locknut and turn the adjusting screw on the No. 1 carburetor. Refer to **Figure 111** for 1979-1980 models or **Figure 112** for models since 1981. Turn the adjusting screw until the reading is the same as that on the No. 2 carburetor. Tighten the locknut. Open the throttle a little and close it back down after each adjustment.

CAUTION

If your carb-sync tool is not equipped with restrictors, open and close the throttle very gently to avoid sucking mercury into the engine. If this happens, it will not harm the engine but will render the carb-sync tool useless.

NOTE

***Figure 111** and **Figure 112** are shown with the carburetor assembly removed for clarity. Do not remove the assembly for this procedure.*

13. Repeat Step No. 12 for the No. 3 and 4 carburetors. Repeat this step until all carburetors have the same gauge reading as the No. 2 carburetor.

NOTE

To gain the utmost performance and efficiency from the engine adjust the carburetors so that the gauge readings are as close to each other as possible.

14. After all carburetors are adjusted properly make sure all locknuts are tight.
15. Shut off the engine and remove the vacuum lines. Install the plugs into the vacuum ports in the carburetors. Make sure they are tight to prevent a vacuum leak.
16. On 1979-1980 models, install the carburetor top covers.
17. Install the fuel tank, seat and side covers.
18. Restart the engine and readjust the idle speed if necessary; refer to *Idle Speed Adjustment* in this chapter.

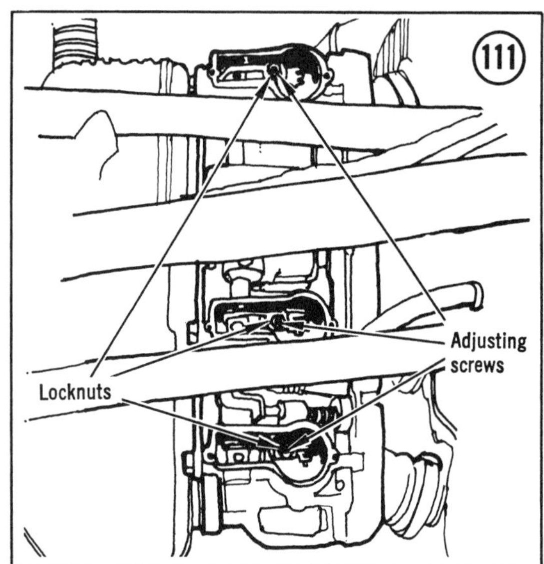

Idle Speed Adjustment

Before making this adjustment, the air cleaner must be clean, the carburetors must be synchronized and the engine must have adequate compression; see *Compression Test* in this chapter. Otherwise, this procedure cannot be done properly.

1. Connect a portable tachometer following the manufacturer's instructions.

NOTE

The bike's tachometer is not accurate enough in the low rpm range for this adjustment.

2. Start the engine and let it reach normal operating temperature.
3. Set the idle speed by turning the idle speed stop screw. Refer to **Figure 113** for 1979-1980 models or **Figure 114** for models since 1981.

NOTE

***Figure 114** is shown with the carburetor assembly partially removed for clarity. Do not remove the carburetor assembly for this adjustment.*

4. The correct idle speed is 1,050 +/- 100 rpm.
5. Open and close the throttle a couple of times; check for variation in idle speed. Readjust if necessary.

WARNING

With the engine idling, move the handlebar from side to side. If idle speed increases during this movement, the throttle cable needs adjusting or may be incorrectly routed through the frame. Correct this problem immediately. Do not ride the bike in this unsafe condition.

6. Turn the engine off and disconnect the portable tachometer.

STORAGE

Several months of inactivity can cause serious problems and a general deterioration of the bike's condition. This is especially true in areas of weather extremes. During the winter months it is advisable to specially prepare the bike for lay-up.

Selecting a Storage Area

Most cyclists store their bikes in their home garages. If you do not have a home garage, facilities suitable for long-term motorcycle storage are readily available for rent or lease in most areas. In selecting a building, consider the following points.

1. The storage area must be dry, free from dampness and excessive humidity. Heating is not necessary, but the building should be well-insulated to minimize extreme temperature variations.
2. Buildings with large window areas should be avoided or such windows should be masked if direct sunlight can fall on the bike. This is also a good security measure.
3. Buildings in industrial areas, where factories are liable to emit corrosive fumes, are not desirable nor are facilities near bodies of salt water.
4. The area should be selected to minimize the possibility of loss from fire, theft or vandalism. The area should be fully insured, perhaps with a package covering fire, theft, vandalism, weather and liability. The advice of your insurance agent should be solicited in these matters. The building should be fireproof and items such as the security of doors and windows, alarm facility and proximity of police should be considered.

Preparing Bike for Storage

Careful preparation will minimize deterioration and make it easier to restore the bike to service later. Use the following procedure.

1. Wash the bike completely. Make certain to remove all dirt in all the hard to reach parts like the cooling fins on the head and cylinder. Completely dry all parts of the bike to remove all moisture. Wax all painted and polished surfaces, including any chromed areas.
2. Run the bike for about 20-30 minutes to warm up the oil in the engine. Drain the oil, regardless of the time since the last oil change. Replace the oil filter and fill the engine with the normal quantity and type of oil.
3. Remove the battery and coat the cable terminals with petroleum jelly. If there is

evidence of acid spillage in the battery box, neutralize with a baking soda solution, wash clean and repaint the damaged area. Store the battery in a warm area and recharge it every 2 weeks.

4. Drain all gasoline from the fuel tank, the interconnecting hose and the carburetors. Leave the fuel shutoff valve in the RES position. As an alternative, a fuel preservative may be added to the fuel. This preservative is available from many motorcycle shops and marine equipment suppliers.

5. Lubricate the drive chain and control cables; refer to specific procedures in this chapter.

6. Remove the spark plugs and add about one teaspoon of SAE 10W/30 motor oil into each cylinder. Turn the engine over a few revolutions by hand to distribute the oil and then install the spark plugs.

NOTE
Since the CB650 has no kickstarter, place the transmission in gear and spin the rear wheel by hand.

7. Tape or tie a plastic bag over the end of the muffler to prevent the entry of moisture.

8. Check the tire pressure, inflate to the correct pressure and move the bike to the storage area. Place it securely on a milk crate or wood blocks with both wheels off the ground.

9. Cover the bike with a tarp, blanket or heavy plastic drop cloth. Place this cover over the bike mainly as a dust cover—do not wrap it tightly; especially if it is plastic, as it may trap moisture. Leave room for air to circulate around the bike.

Inspection During Storage

Try to inspect the bike weekly while in storage. Any deterioration should be corrected as soon as possible. For example, if corrosion of bright metal parts is observed, cover them with a light coat of grease or silicone spray after a thorough polishing.

Turn the engine over a couple of times—don't start it; shift it into gear and spin the rear wheel. Pump the front forks to keep the seals lubricated.

Restoring Bike to Service

A bike that has been properly prepared and stored in a suitable area requires only light maintenance to restore it to service. It is advisable, however, to perform a tune-up.

1. Before removing the bike from the storage area, reinflate the tires to the correct pressures. Air loss during storage may have nearly flattened the tires and moving the bike can cause damage to tires, tubes and rims.

WARNING
During the next step, place a metal container under the carburetor to catch all fuel or it will create a real fire danger if allowed to drain onto the bike and the floor. Dispose of the fuel properly.

2. When the bike is brought to the work area, drain the fuel tank if fuel preservative was used. Turn the fuel shutoff valve to the OFF position and refill the fuel tank with fresh gasoline and install the battery (fully charged).

3. Turn the fuel shutoff valve to the RES position and check for leaks in the fuel system.

WARNING
For the next step, place a metal container under the drain tubes (1979-1980 models) or outlets on the float bowls (models since 1981) to catch the expelled fuel—this presents a real fire danger if allowed to drain on the floor. Dispose of fuel properly.

4. Open the drain screws (**Figure 115**) and allow several cups of fuel to pass through the

MAJOR CONTROLS AND COMPONENTS

1. Tail/brake light and rear reflex reflector (red)
2. Shock absorber adjustment
3. Clutch lever
4. Headlight, turn signal switches
5. Fuel fill cap
6. Fuse panel
7. Speedometer, tachometer and indicator lights
8. Front turn signal (amber)
9. Rear turn signal (red)
10. Rear brake adjustment nut
11. Drive chain adjusters
12. Rear foot pegs
13. Oil dipstick/filler cap
14. Clutch
15. Rear brake pedal
16. Ignition timing cover
17. Horn

MAJOR CONTROLS AND COMPONENTS

18. Headlight
19. Start button, engine stop switch
20. Throttle grip
21. Clutch lever
22. Main fusible link
23. Seat
24. Oil filter
25. Fuel shutoff valve
26. Alternator
27. Shift lever
28. Side stand
29. Starter motor
30. Centerstand

118

119

fuel system. Turn the fuel shutoff valve to the OFF position and close the drain screws.

5. Remove the spark plug and squirt a small amount of fuel into the cylinder to help remove the oil coating.

6. Install a fresh set of spark plugs and start up the engine.

7. Perform the standard tune-up as described earlier in this chapter.

8. Check the operation of the engine kill switch and all other safety items (lights, horn, etc.). Oxidation of the switch contacts during storage may make them inoperative.

9. Clean and test ride the motorcycle.

WARNING

If any type of preservative (Armor All or equivalent) has been applied to the tire treads, be sure the tires are well "scrubbed-in" prior to any fast riding or cornering on a hard surface. If not, they will slip right out from under you.

GENERAL SPECIFICATIONS

General information and specifications are listed in **Table 7**. Refer to **Figure 116** and **Figure 117** for the location of all major controls.

SERIAL NUMBERS

You must know the model serial numbers and VIN number for registration purposes and sometimes when ordering replacement parts.

The frame serial number is stamped on the right-hand side of the steering head (**Figure 118**). The vehicle identification number (VIN) is on the left-hand side of the steering head (**Figure 119**). The engine serial number is located on the top, right-hand side of the upper crankcase (**Figure 120**). Carburetor identification numbers are located on the right-hand side of each carburetor body as shown in **Figure 121**.

PARTS REPLACEMENT

Honda makes frequent changes during a model year; some minor and some relatively major. When you order parts from a dealer or other parts distributor, always order by engine or chassis number. Write the numbers down and carry them with you. Compare new parts to old parts before purchasing them. If they are not alike, have the parts manager explain the difference to you. This is especially true with electrical components as few dealers or parts houses will allow you to return them for an exchange or a refund.

3

Tables are on the following pages.

TABLE 1 MAINTENANCE SCHEDULE*

Every 300 miles (500 km)—or when it is dry, lubricate and adjust the drive chain	
Every 600 miles (1,000 km) or 6 months	Check engine oil level Check battery specific gravity and electrolyte level Lubricate rear brake pedal and shift lever Lubricate side and center stand pivot point(s) Inspect front steering for looseness Check wheel bearings for smooth operation Check wheel spoke condition (wire wheels only) Check wheel runout—both wire type and Comstar wheels Check and adjust clutch lever free play
Every 4,000 miles (6,400 km)	Change engine oil and replace oil filter Clean air cleaner element Complete engine tune-up Check and adjust valve clearance Adjust the cam chain tension Check and adjust ignition timing Check and adjust the carburetors Check and synchronize the carburetors Inspect spark plugs, regap if necessary Check and adjust clutch free play Check and adjust throttle operation and free play Adjust rear brake pedal height and free play Clean fuel shutoff valve and filter Inspect hydraulic brake fluid level Inspect brake pads and shoes for wear Inspect crankcase breather hose for cracks or loose hose clamps—drain out all residue

(continued)

TABLE 1 MAINTENANCE SCHEDULE* (continued)

Every 4,000 miles (6,400 km)	Inspect fuel line for chafed, cracked or swollen ends Check engine mounting bolts for tightness Inspect and repack rear swing arm bushings Check all suspension components Lubricate control cables
Every 6,000 miles (10,000 km)	Change front fork oil Lubricate speedometer housing Inspect wheel bearings
Every 8,000 miles (12,800 km)	Dismantle and clean the carburetors Replace the spark plugs Replace the air filter element Run a compression test Inspect and repack the steering head bearings Lubricate the speedometer and tachometer drive cables
Every 12,000 miles (19,000 km) or every 2 years	Lubricate rear brake camshaft Replace the hydraulic brake fluid
Every 4 years	Replace all hydraulic brake hoses

*This Honda Factory maintenance schedule should be considered as a guide to general maintenance and lubrication intervals. Harder than normal use and exposure to mud, water, sand, high humidity, etc. will naturally dictate more frequent attention to most maintenance items.

TABLE 2 TIRE INFLATION PRESSURE

Load	Air Pressure
Up to 200 lb. (90 kg)	
Front—all models	28 psi (2.0 kg/cm^2)
Rear	
Standard models	28 psi (2.0 kg/cm^2)
Custom models	28 psi (2.0 kg/cm^2)
Maximum load limit *	
Front—all models	28 psi (2.0 kg/cm^2)
Rear	
Standard models	36 psi (2.5 kg/cm^2)
Custom models	32 psi (2.25 kg/cm^2)

*Maximum load limit includes total weight of motorcycle with accessories, rider(s) and luggage.

Table 3 STATE OF CHARGE

Specific Gravity	State of Charge	Specific Gravity	State of Charge
1.110-1.130	Discharged	1.200-1.220	One-half charged
1.140-1.160	Almost discharged	1.230-1.250	Three-quarters charged
1.170-1.190	One-quarter charged	1.260-1.280	Fully charged

3

TABLE 4 FRONT FORK OIL CAPACITY*

Year	Drain	Rebuild
1979	5.0 oz. (150 cc)	5.7 oz. (170 cc)
1980		
Standard	5.3 oz. (155 cc)	5.9 oz. (175 cc)
Custom	6.5 oz. (190 cc)	7.1 oz. (209 cc)
Since 1981		
Standard	6.4 oz. (190 cc)	7.1 oz. (210 cc)
Custom	7.6 oz. (225 cc)	8.3 oz. (245 cc)

*Capacity for each fork leg.

TABLE 5 TUNE-UP SPECIFICATIONS

Valve clearance	
Intake	0.002 in. (0.05 mm)
Exhaust	0.003 in. (0.08 mm)
Compression pressure	
(at sea level)	170 +/- 28 psi (12.0 +/- 2.0 kg/cm^2)
Spark plug type	
Standard heat range	ND X24ES-U or NGK D8ES-U
Canadian	ND X24ESR-U or NGK DR8ES-L
Cold weather*	ND X22ES-U or NGK D7EA
Canadian	ND X22ESR-U or NGK DR7ES
Extended high speed riding	ND X27ES-U or NGK D9EA
Canadian	ND X27ESR-U or NGK DR8ES
Spark plug gap	0.024-0.028 in. (0.6-0.7 mm)
Ignition timing	"1.4 F-1" at 1,050 +/- 100 rpm Advance timing mark "II" at 2,725 rpm
Idle speed	1,050 +/- 100 rpm

*Cold weather climate—below 41° F (5° C)

TABLE 6 SPARK PLUG HEAT RANGE

Standard heat range	ND X24ES-U or NGK D8ES-U
Canadian	ND X24ESR-U or NGK DR8ES-L
Cold weather*	ND X22ES-U or NGK D7EA
Canadian	ND X22ESR-U or NGK DR7ES
Extended high speed riding	ND X27ES-U or NGK D9EA
Canadian	ND X27ESR-U or NGK DR8ES
Spark plug gap	0.24-0.28 in. (0.6-0.7 mm)
Torque specification	9-12 ft.-lb. (12-16 N.)

*Cold weather climate—below 41° F (5° C)

TABLE 7 GENERAL SPECIFICATIONS

Engine type	Air-cooled, 4-stroke, SOHC, transverse mounted inline 4
Bore and stroke	2.354 X 2.197 in. (59.8 X 55.8 mm)
Displacement	38.2 cu.in. (627 cc)
Compression ratio	9.0 to 1
Carburetion	4 Keihin carburetors with accelerator pump on No. 2 carburetor only
1979-1980	PD50A or PD50B Mechanical type
Since 1981	VB 44A Constant velocity type
Ignition	Capacitor discharge ignition (CDI)
Lubrication	Wet-sump, filter, oil pump
Clutch	Wet, multi-plate (7)
Transmission	5-speed, constant mesh
Transmission ratios	
1st	2.500
2nd	1.722
3rd	1.333
4th	1.074
5th	0.885
Final reduction ratio	2.500 (16/40)
Drive chain	
1979	DID 50DK or RK 50NK by 102 links
1980	DID 50HDK or RK 50NK by 104 links
Since 1981	DID 50V or RK 50MO by 104 links
Starting system	Electric starter only
Battery	12 Volt, 12 amp/hour
Alternator	Three phase, A.C., 0.26 kw/5000 rpm
Firing order	1-2-4-3
Wheelbase	
1979	56.3 in. (1,430 mm)
1980, 1981 Standard	57.1 in. (1,450 mm)
1980 Custom	58.3 in. (1,480 mm)
Since 1981 Custom	57.9 in. (1,470 mm)
Steering head angle	
1979	27° 30'
1980, 1981 Standard	26° 50'
1980 Custom	29° 20'
Since 1981 Custom	30° 10'

(continued)

TABLE 7 GENERAL SPECIFICATIONS (continued)

Trail	
1979	4 in. (105 mm)
1980,1981 Standard	4 in. (105 mm)
1980 Custom	4.8 in. (121 mm)
Since 1981 Custom	5.2 in. (131 mm)
Front suspension	Telescopic forks
1979-1981 Standard, 1980 Custom	5.6 in. (142 mm)
Since 1981 Custom	6.3 in. (160 mm)
Rear suspension	Swing arm, adjustable shock absorbers
1979	3.0 in. (77 mm)
1980,1981 Standard, 1980 Custom	3.6 in. (91 mm)
1981 Custom	4.0 in. (102 mm)
Front tire	
1979-1981 Standard	3.50 H19 4PR
1980, 1981 Custom	3.50 S19 4PR
Rear tire	
1979-1981 Standard	4.50 H17 4PR
1980, 1981 Custom	130/90-16 X 67S
Ground clearance	
1979	6.3 in. (160 mm)
1980,1981 Standard	6.1 in. (155 mm)
1980 Custom	5.7 in. (145 mm)
1981 Custom	5.5 in. (140 mm)
Overall height	
1979	46.3 in. (1,175 mm)
1980,1981 Standard	45.5 in. (1,155 mm)
1980 Custom	45.5 in. (1,155 mm)
1981 Custom	45.7 in. (1,160 mm)
Overall width (handlebar)	
1979	33.5 in. (850 mm)
Since 1980 Standard	34.1 in. (865 mm)
Since 1980 Custom	34.3 in. (870 mm)
Overall length	
1979	85.4 in. (2,170 mm)
Since 1980 Standard	85.8 in. (2,180 mm)
Since 1980 Custom	87.2 in. (2,215 mm)
Weight	
1979	431.2 lb. (196 kg)
Since 1980 Standard	437 lb. (199 kg)
1980 Custom	442 lb. (201 kg)
Since 1981 Custom	450 lb. (204 kg)
Fuel capacity	
1979	4.8 U.S.gal. (18 liters, 3.9 Imp.gal.)
Since 1980	3.5 U.S.gal. (13.5 liters, 3.0 Imp.gal.)

(continued)

TABLE 7 GENERAL SPECIFICATIONS (continued)

Oil capacity		
Oil and filter change		3.2 U.S.qt. (3.0 liters, 2.6 Imp.qt.)
At overhaul		3.7 U.S.qt. (3.5 liters, 3.0 Imp.qt.)
Front fork oil	Drain	Rebuild capacity*
1979	5.0 oz. (150 cc)	5.7 oz. (170 cc)
1980		
Standard	5.3 oz. (155 cc)	5.9 oz. (175 cc)
Custom	6.5 oz. (190 cc)	7.1 oz. (209 cc)
Since 1981		
Standard	6.4 oz. (190 cc)	7.1 oz. (210 cc)
Custom	7.6 oz. (225 cc)	8.3 oz. (245 cc)

*Capacity for each fork leg

CHAPTER FOUR

ENGINE

The CB650 engine is an air-cooled, 4-stroke, 4-cylinder engine with a single overhead camshaft. The crankshaft is supported by 5 main bearings and power is delivered to the primary shaft via a Hy-Vo chain within the crankcase. The camshaft is chain driven from the timing sprocket on the crankshaft and operates rocker arms that are individually adjustable.

Engine lubrication is by wet sump with the oil pump located on the left-hand side of the engine under the rear crankcase cover. The oil pump delivers oil under pressure throughout the engine and is gear driven off of the primary shaft.

The starter motor is located in the upper crankcase half on the left-hand side just behind the cylinder block.

This chapter contains information for removal, inspection, service and reassembly of the engine. **Tables 1-4** at the end of the chapter provide complete specifications for the engine. Although the clutch and transmission are located within the engine they are covered in Chapter Five to simplify this material.

Prior to removing the engine or any major assembly, clean the entire engine and frame with a good grade commercial degreaser like Gunk or Bel-Ray Degreaser (**Figure 1**). It is easier to work on a clean engine and you will do a better job.

Make certain that you have all the necessary tools available, especially any special tool(s), and purchase replacement parts prior to disassembly. Also make sure you have a clean place to work.

It is a good idea to identify and mark parts as they are removed to help during assembly and installation. Clean all parts thoroughly upon removal, then place them in trays or boxes

(2)

4-STROKE OPERATING PRINCIPLES

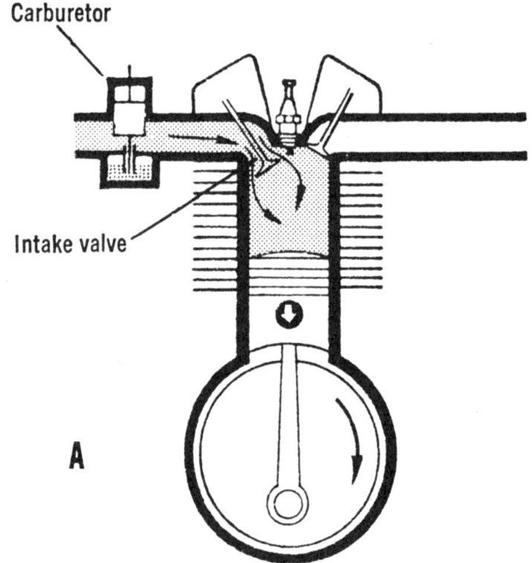

As the piston travels downward, the exhaust valve is closed and the intake valve opens, allowing the new fuel/air mixture from the **carburetor** to be drawn into the cylinder. When the piston reaches the bottom of its travel (BDC), the **intake valve** closes and remains closed for the next revolution-and-a-half of the crankshaft.

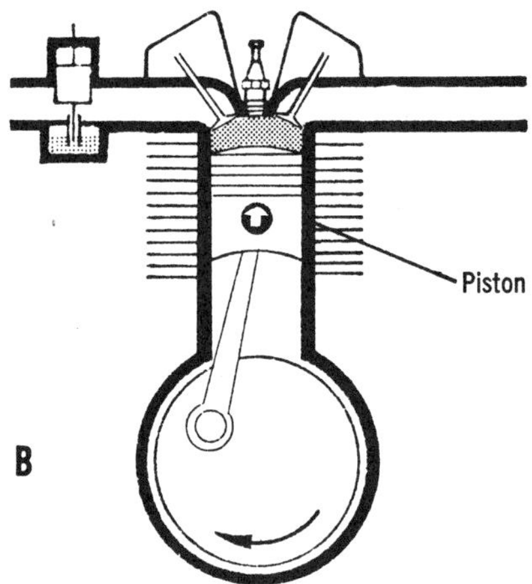

While the crankshaft continues to rotate, the **piston** moves upward, compressing the fuel/air mixture.

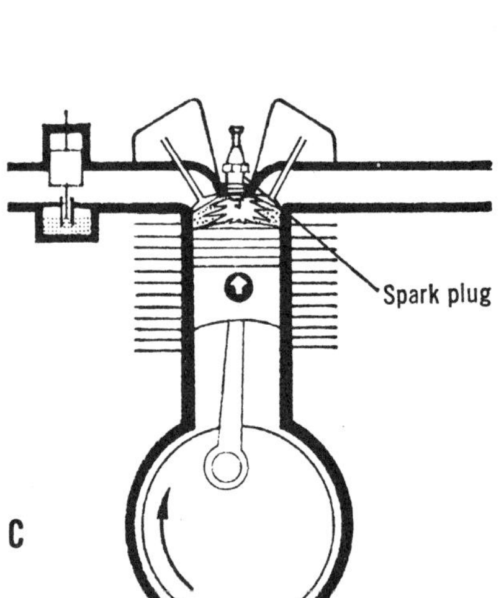

As the piston almost reaches the top of its travel, the **spark plug** fires, igniting the compressed fuel/air mixture. The piston continues to top dead center (TDC) and is pushed downward by the expanding gases.

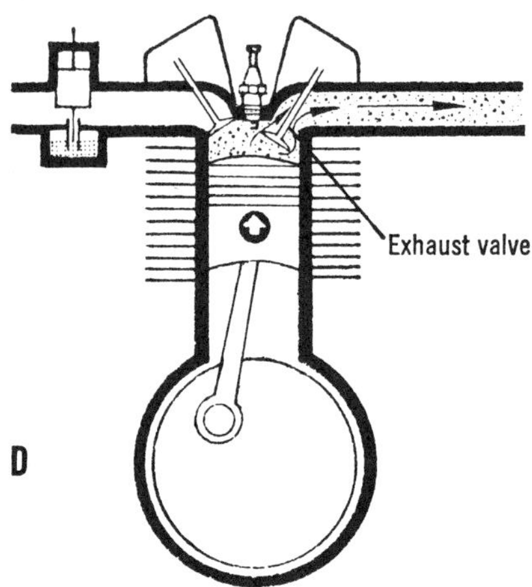

When the piston almost reaches BDC, the **exhaust valve** opens and remains open until the piston is near TDC. The upward travel of the piston causes the exhaust gases to be pushed out of the cylinder. After the piston has reached TDC, the exhaust valve closes and the cycle starts all over again.

with their associated mounting hardware. Do not rely on memory alone as it may be days or weeks before you complete the job.

Throughout the text there is frequent mention of the right-hand and left-hand side of the engine. This refers to the engine as it sits in the bike's frame, not as it sits on your workbench. The right- and left-hand refers to a rider sitting on the seat facing forward.

ENGINE PRINCIPLES

Figure 2 explains how the engine works. This will be helpful when troubleshooting or repairing the engine.

ENGINE COOLING

Cooling is provided by air passing over the cooling fins on the engine cylinder head and cylinder. It is very important to keep these fins free from buildup of dirt, oil, grease and other foreign matter. Brush out the fins with a whisk broom or small stiff paint brush.

CAUTION

Remember, these fins are thin in order to dissipate heat and may be damaged if struck too hard.

SERVICING ENGINE IN FRAME

The following components can be serviced while the engine is mounted in the frame (the bike's frame is a great holding fixture for breaking loose stubborn bolts and nuts):

a. Camshaft and cylinder head
b. Cylinder block
c. Pistons
d. Carburetor assembly
e. Alternator
f. Clutch
g. External shift mechanism

ENGINE

Removal/Installation

1. Drain the engine oil as described under *Changing Oil and Filter* in Chapter Three.

NOTE

Do not reinstall the oil filter housing as it must be off in order for the engine to clear the frame.

2. Place the bike on the centerstand and remove the seat and side covers.
3. Disconnect the battery negative lead.
4. Turn the fuel shutoff valve to the OFF position (**Figure 3**) and remove the fuel line to the carburetor.
5. Remove the bolt securing the rear of the fuel tank (**Figure 4**), pull the tank up and to the rear and remove it. Remove the rubber mounting damper and keep it with the fuel tank to avoid misplacing it.
6. Disconnect the spark plug leads (**Figure 5**) and tie them up out of the way.

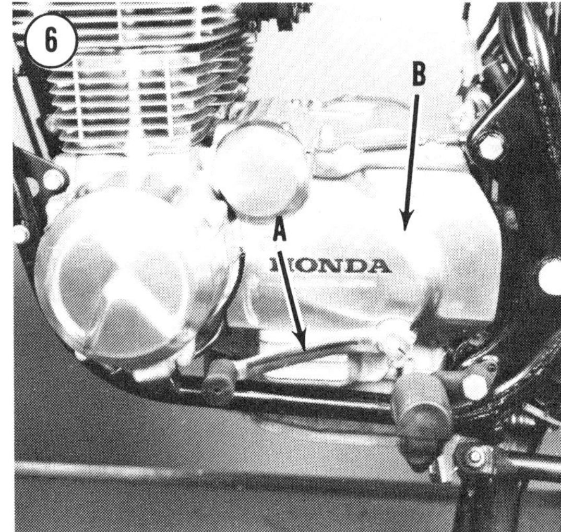

7. Remove the exhaust system as described under *Exhaust System Removal/Installation* in Chapter Six.
8. Remove the carburetor assembly as described under *Carburetor Removal/ Installation* in Chapter Six.
9. Remove the gearshift lever (A, **Figure 6**) and left-hand crankcase cover (B, **Figure 6**).
10. Remove the cotter pin and rear axle nut (A, **Figure 7**).
11. Loosen the drive chain adjuster locknuts and loosen the adjusters (B, **Figure 7**).
12. Remove the 2 bolts (A, **Figure 8**) securing the drive sprocket holding plate (B, **Figure 8**). Rotate the plate to clear the shaft splines and remove the plate. Slide off the drive sprocket and drive chain.
13. Disconnect the rear brake switch return spring.
14. Remove the rear brake pedal (**Figure 9**).
15. Loosen the bolt securing the tachometer drive cable (**Figure 10**) and remove it from the cylinder head cover.
16. Remove the alternator as described under *Alternator Removal/Installation* in this chapter.
17. Remove the clutch assembly as described under *Clutch Removal/Installation* in Chapter Five.

NOTE

If you are only removing the engine assembly and do not intend to disassemble it, do not perform Steps 18 and 19; proceed to Step 20.

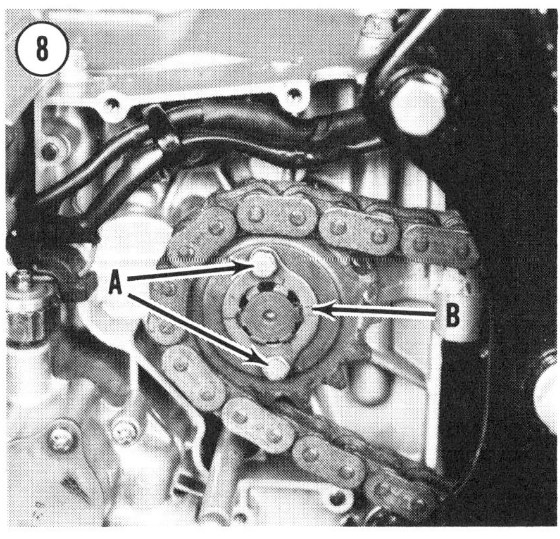

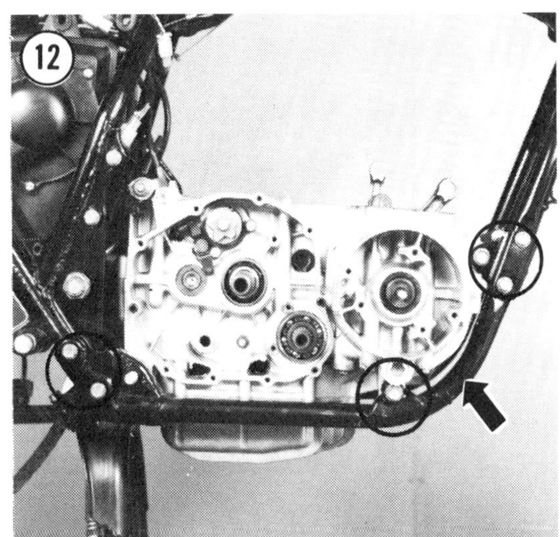

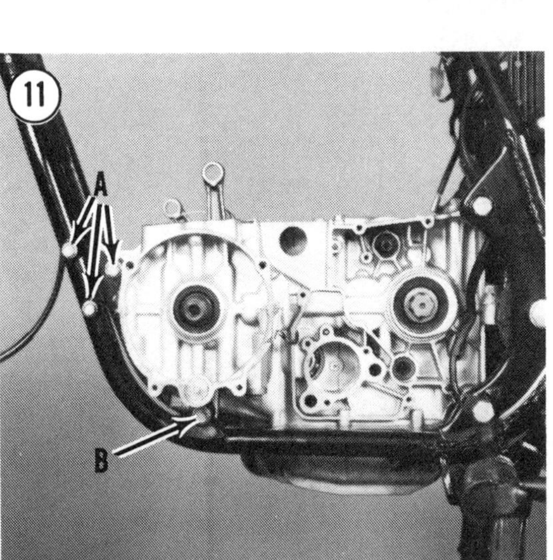

18. Remove the cylinder head cover, camshaft, cylinder head and cylinder block as described under *Cylinder Block Removal/Installation* in this chapter.

19. Remove the pistons as described under *Piston Removal* in this chapter.

NOTE

The CB650 has a removable frame section on the right-hand side to aid in the removal of the engine.

20. Remove the left-hand side front engine hanger bracket bolts and nuts (A, **Figure 11**) and lower mounting bolt and nut (B, **Figure 11**).

21. On the right-hand side, remove all mounting bolts and nuts (**Figure 12**) and remove the removable frame section.

22. Place a suitable size hydraulic jack, with a piece of wood to protect the oil pan, under the engine. Apply a *small amount* of jack pressure up on the engine.

23. Remove the lower rear through bolt from the left-hand side.

CAUTION

The following steps require the aid of a helper to safely remove the crankcase assembly from the frame.

24. Remove the upper rear through bolt from the left-hand side. Don't lose the frame spacer (**Figure 13**). The engine ground strap is attached to the right-hand end of this bolt.

4

25. Pull the engine up and slightly forward. Remove the engine from the right-hand side. Take it to a work bench for further disassembly.
26. Install by reversing these removal steps, noting the following.

NOTE

Due to the weight of the complete engine assembly, it is suggested that all components removed be left off until the crankcase assembly is reinstalled in the bike's frame. If you choose to install a complete engine assembly, it requires a minimum of 2 people. It must be installed from the right-hand side of the frame.

27. Be sure to install the engine ground strap on the upper rear through bolt (**Figure 14**).
28. Install the right-hand removable frame section and install the short bolt into the lower rear hole (**Figure 15**).
29. Tighten the bolts and nuts to the following torque specifications. Refer to **Figure 16**. The letter designation on the figure relates to the text letters in the following list:
   a. 8 mm flange bolts and nut: 19-23 ft.-lb. (26-32 N•m)
   b. 10 mm flange bolt and nut: 22-29 ft.-lb. (30-40 N•m)
   c. 12 mm flange bolt and nut: 58-72 ft.-lb. (80-100 N•m)
30. Fill the engine with the recommended type and quantity oil; refer to Chapter Three.
31. Adjust the clutch, drive chain and rear brake pedal as described in Chapter Three.
32. Start the engine and check for leaks.

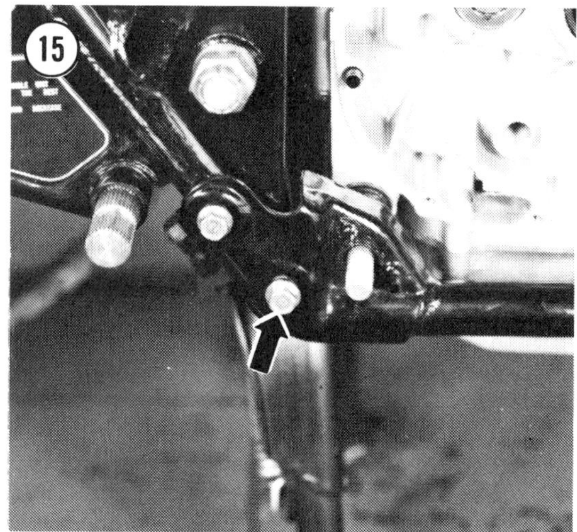

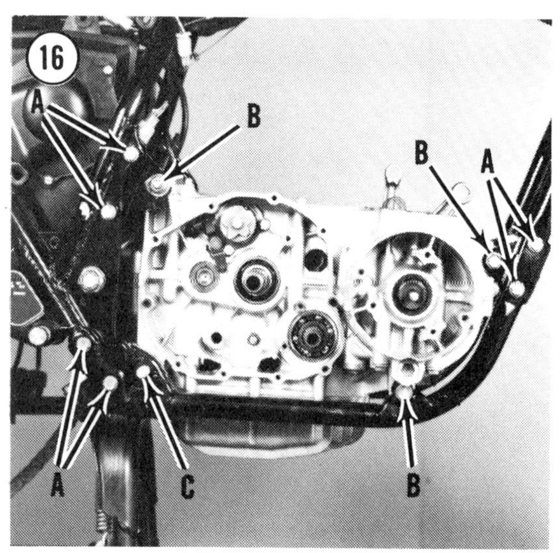

CYLINDER HEAD COVER

Removal

CAUTION
To prevent any warpage and damage, remove the cylinder head cover only when the engine is at room temperature.

1. Remove the seat, side covers and the fuel tank.
2. Disconnect the battery negative lead.
3. Disconnect the spark plug wires and tie them up out of the way.
4. Remove the spark plugs with an 18 mm spark plug wrench.

NOTE
Use a spark plug wrench with a rubber insert that holds onto the spark plug. This is necessary on the 2 inside cylinders as the spark plugs are installed at a severe angle and are difficult to remove without this type of tool.

5. Disconnect the engine breather hose from the cover (A, **Figure 17**).
6. Disconnect the tachometer drive cable.
7. Remove the bolts and Allen bolts securing the center breather cover (B, **Figure 17**) and both valve adjustment covers (C, **Figure 17**). Remove all 3 covers.
8. Loosen the cylinder head cover bolts evenly in 2-3 stages in a crisscross pattern. Remove the cylinder head cover (**Figure 18**) by lifting it up and slightly forward to clear the cam sprocket; withdraw the cover from either side.

4

Disassembly/Inspection/Assembly

Refer to **Figure 19** for this procedure.

It is recommended that one rocker arm assembly be disassembled, inspected and then assembled to avoid the intermixing of parts. This is especially true on a well run-in bike as the different sets of parts have taken a set and wear pattern unique to themselves.

1. Remove the bolt securing the tachometer driven gear unit (**Figure 20**) and remove it.
2. Remove the rocker arm shaft threaded cotter pin nut and washer (**Figure 21**).
3. Carefully tap out the threaded cotter pin.
4. Remove the rocker arm shaft cap bolt (**Figure 22**).
5. Screw in a 6 mm bolt (**Figure 23**) and withdraw the rocker arm shaft.
6. Remove the rocker arm and spring.
7. Wash all parts in cleaning solvent and thoroughly dry.
8. Inspect the condition of the rocker arm pad where it rides on the cam lobe and where the adjuster rides on the valve stem. If the pad is scratched or unevenly worn, inspect the condition of the cam lobe for scoring, chipping or flat spots. Replace the rocker arm if defective.

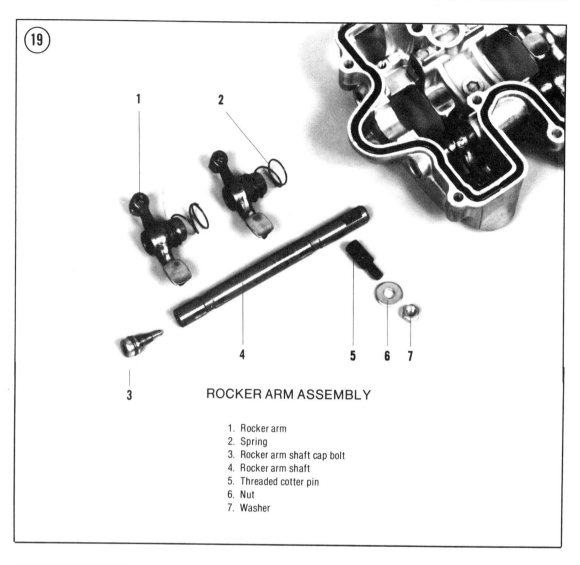

19

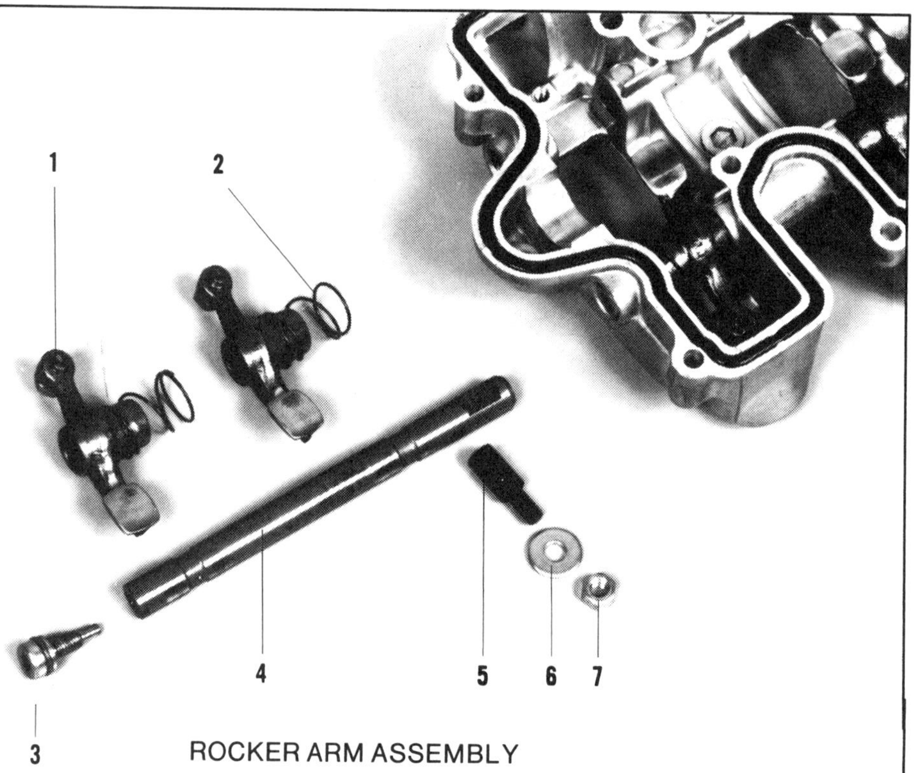

1 2

3 4 5 6 7

ROCKER ARM ASSEMBLY

1. Rocker arm
2. Spring
3. Rocker arm shaft cap bolt
4. Rocker arm shaft
5. Threaded cotter pin
6. Nut
7. Washer

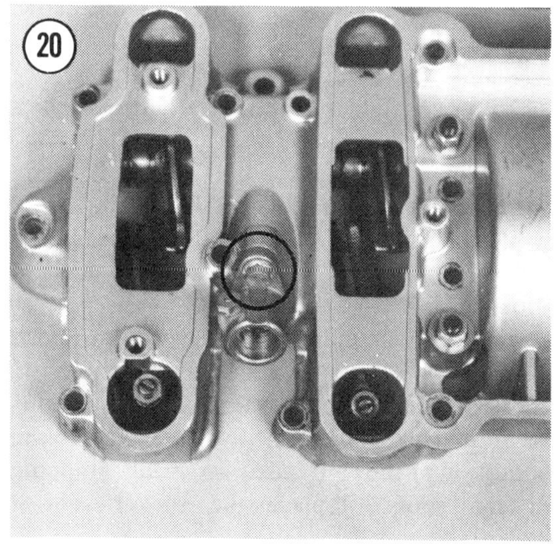

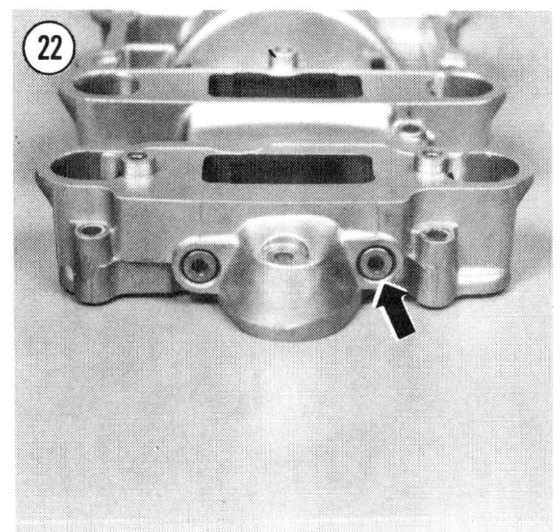

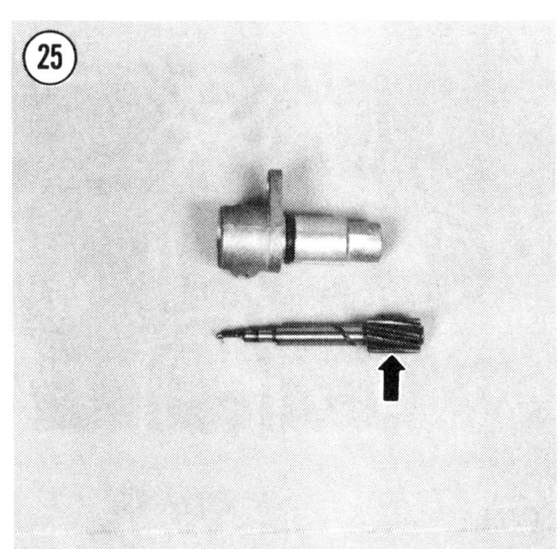

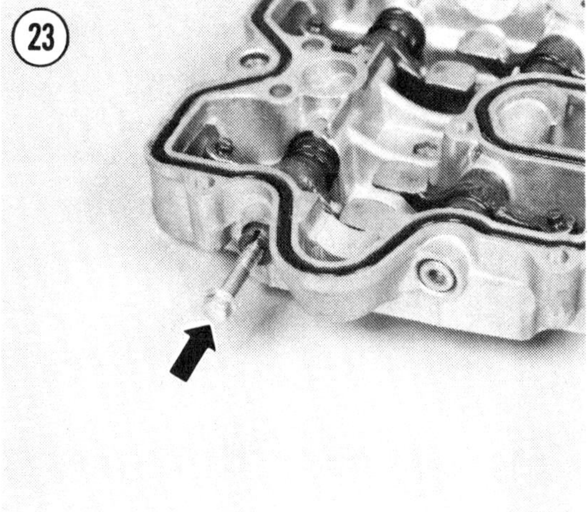

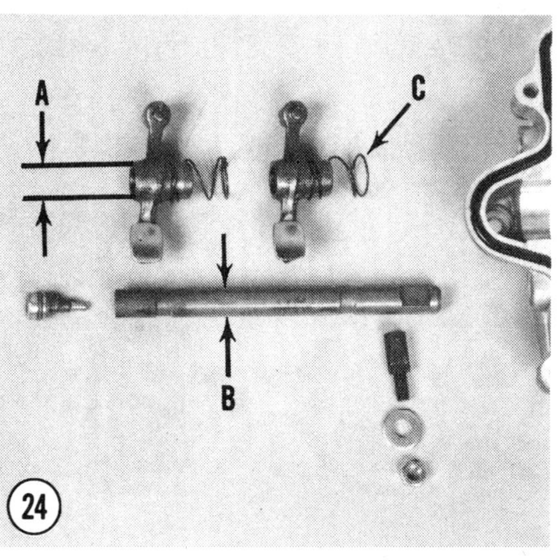

4

9. Measure the inside diameter of the rocker arm bore (A, **Figure 24**) with an inside micrometer and check against dimensions in **Table 1**. Replace if worn to the service limit or greater.

10. Inspect the rocker arm shaft for signs of wear or scoring. Measure the outside diameter (B, **Figure 24**) with a micrometer and check against dimensions in **Table 1**. Replace if worn to the service limit or less.

11. Check the condition of the spring (C, **Figure 24**) for breakage or distortion; replace if necessary.

12. Inspect the condition of the cam bearing surfaces for excessive wear. If worn excessively, the cylinder head cover must be replaced.

13. Inspect the condition of the tachometer driven gear and housing (**Figure 25**). If the gear teeth are damaged, replace the assembly. Make sure the O-ring seal is in good condition; replace if necessary.

14. Coat the rocker arm shaft and rocker arm bore with assembly oil.

15. Install the rocker arm shaft with the threaded hole facing out. Partially insert the rocker arm shaft into the cover while assembling the rocker arms and springs (**Figure 26**).

16. The slot in the end of the rocker arm (**Figure 27**) must be vertical. This is necessary so that the threaded cotter pin can align with the locking relief in the rocker arm shaft.

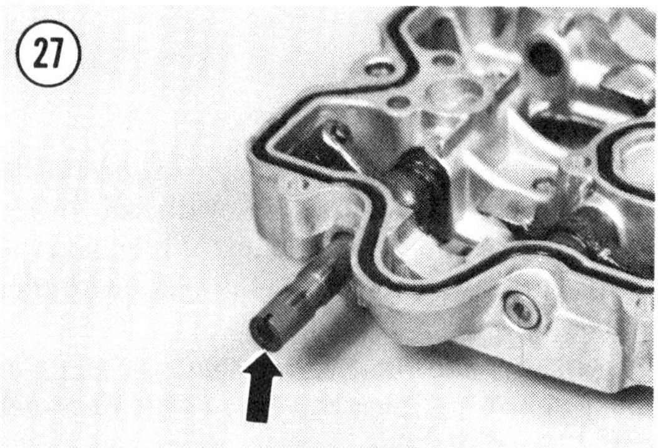

17. Make sure the locking relief in the rocker arm shaft is aligned with the hole in the cylinder head to allow the threaded cotter pin to be inserted. Use the slot in the end of rocker arm shaft to rotate for proper alignment.
18. Install the threaded cotter pin (**Figure 28**) with the flat side facing the locking relief on the rocker arm shaft.
19. Install the washer and nut on the threaded cotter pin and tighten to 7-10 ft.-lb. (10-14 N•m).
20. Install the rocker arm shaft cap bolt and O-ring seal (**Figure 29**). Tighten the cap bolt to 6-9 ft.-lb. (8-12 N•m).

NOTE

To prevent an oil leak don't forget to install the O-ring seal on the cap bolt.

21. Repeat Step 2-19 for the other 3 rocker arm assemblies.
22. Inspect the condition of the rubber seal (**Figure 30**) on the bottom of the cylinder head cover and on the breather and valve adjuster covers (**Figure 31**). Replace as necessary.

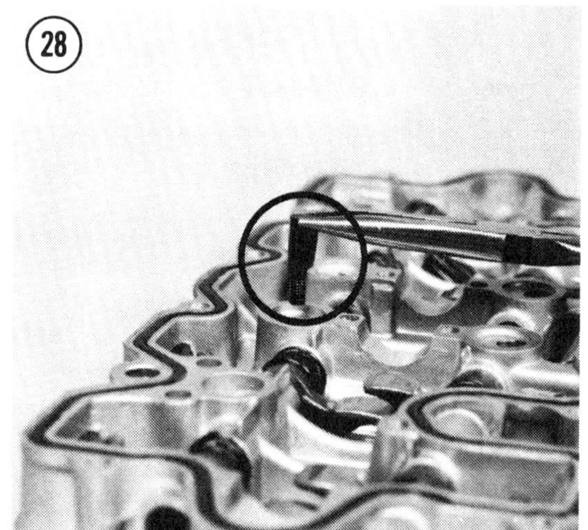

Installation

CAUTION

Do not install the tachometer driven gear unit until the cylinder head cover is installed. If the unit is installed, the drive gear may not mesh properly with the drive gear on the cam. This may damage the drive gear when the cylinder head cover is installed and tightened.

1. Loosen all valve adjusters fully. This is to relieve strain on the rocker arms and cylinder head cover during installation.
2. Make sure the rubber seal is in place. Install the cylinder head cover onto the cylinder head.

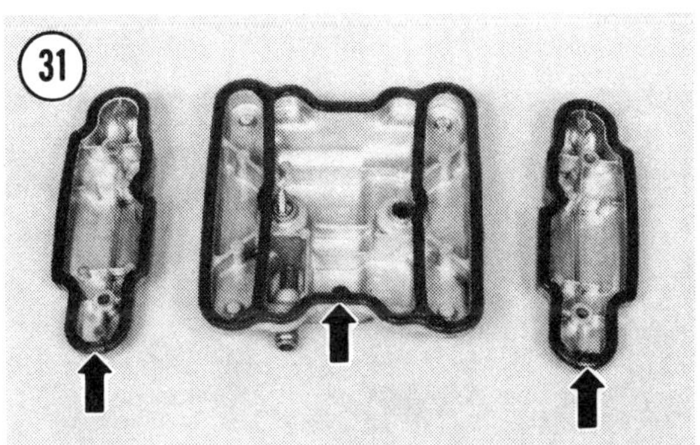

3. Install the sealing washers under the bolts as indicated by squares drawn around the circled bolts in **Figure 32**. Install all bolts and tighten in 5-6 stages in the sequence indicated in **Figure 32**. Tighten the bolts to 6-9 ft.-lb. (8-12 N•m).
4. Adjust the valve clearance as described under *Valve Clearance Adjustment* in Chapter Three.
5. Install the breather cover and valve adjustment covers. Be sure to attach the breather hose to the breather cover.
6. Install the spark plugs.

NOTE

Use an 18 mm spark plug wrench with a rubber insert that holds onto the spark plug. This is necessary on the 2 inside cylinders as the spark plugs are installed at a severe angle and are difficult to install without this type of tool.

7. Install the tachometer driven gear unit and attach the tachometer drive cable.
8. Attach the battery negative lead.
9. Install the fuel tank, side covers and seat.

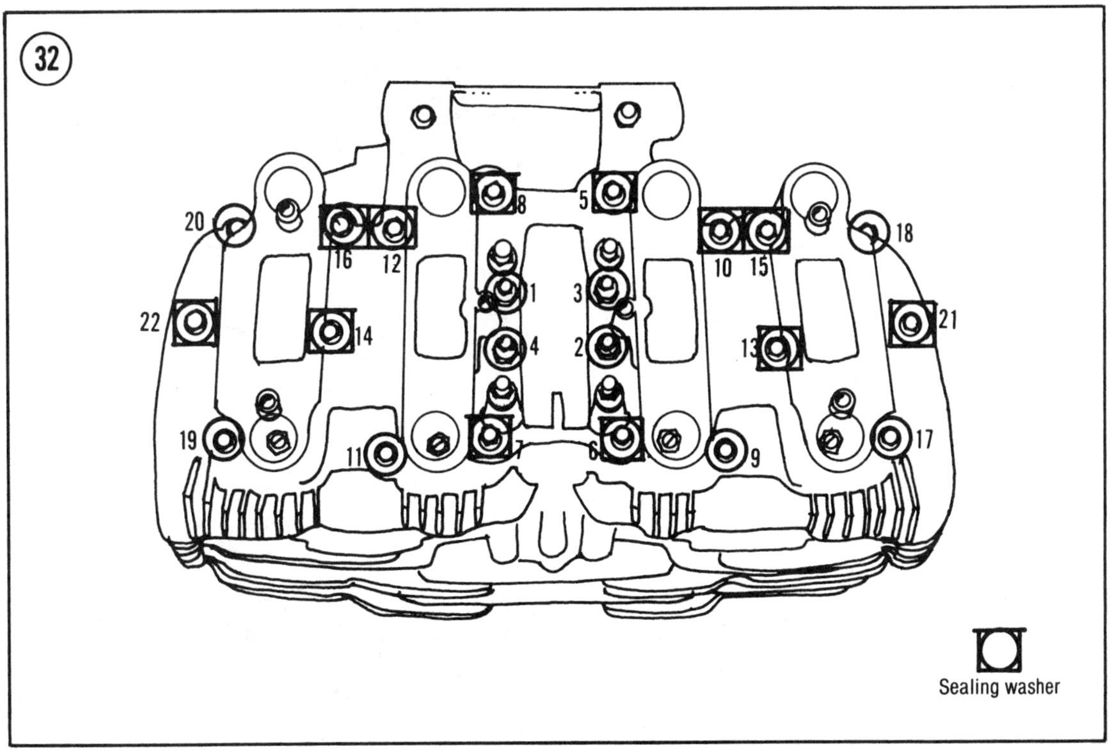

32

20 16 12 8 5 10 15 18
22 14 1 3 13 21
4 2
19 11 7 6 9 17

Sealing washer

CYLINDER HEAD

Removal/Installation

CAUTION
To prevent any warpage and damage, remove the cylinder head only when the engine is at room temperature.

1. Place the bike on the centerstand.
2. Remove the seat, side covers and fuel tank.
3. Disconnect the battery negative lead.
4. Remove the cylinder head cover (A, **Figure 33**) as described under *Cylinder Head Cover Removal* in this chapter.
5. Remove the carburetor assembly as described under *Carburetor Removal/ Installation* in Chapter Six.
6. Remove the exhaust system as described under *Exhaust System Removal/Installation* in Chapter Six.
7. Remove the rubber seals (**Figure 34**) on both sides of the cam drive sprocket. The cylinder head bolts are beneath these rubber seals.
8. Remove the cam as described under *Camshaft Removal/Installation* in this chapter.
9. Remove the cam chain tensioner set bolt (B, **Figure 33**).
10. To prevent warpage of the cylinder head, remove the 2 outer 6 mm bolts first. Refer to **Figure 35** and **Figure 36**. Then loosen the 12 internal 8 mm bolts (**Figure 37**) in 2-3 stages in the sequence shown in **Figure 38**. Remove all cylinder bolts.

NOTE
*The 2 center front bolts are difficult to completely withdraw due to the ignition coils and wiring harness directly above them. Pull them partially up and wrap with masking tape **(Figure 39)** to hold them in place in the head. Use the same setup when installing the cylinder head.*

11. Loosen the head by tapping around the perimeter with a rubber or plastic mallet. If necessary, *gently* pry the head loose with a broad-tipped screwdriver.

CAUTION
Remember, the cooling fins are fragile and may be damaged if tapped or pried on too hard. Never use a metal hammer.

NOTE
Sometimes it is possible to loosen the cylinder head with engine compression. Reinstall the spark plugs. Rotate the engine with the outer hex spacer on the ignition advance unit with a 15/16 in. socket or box wrench. As the pistons reach TDC on their compression stroke, the head may pop loose.

12. Untie the wire securing the cam chain and retie it to the cylinder head.

37

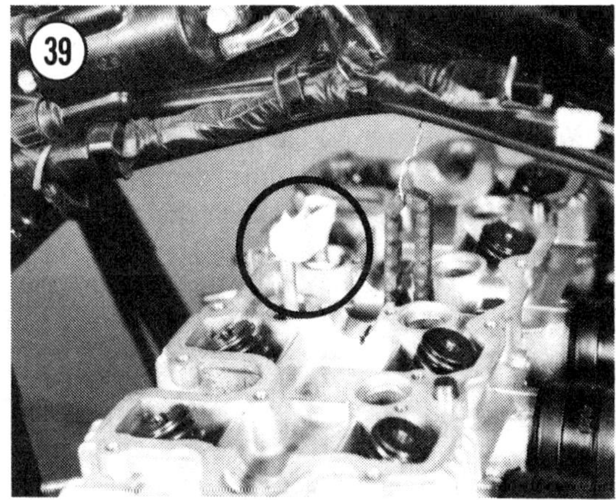
39

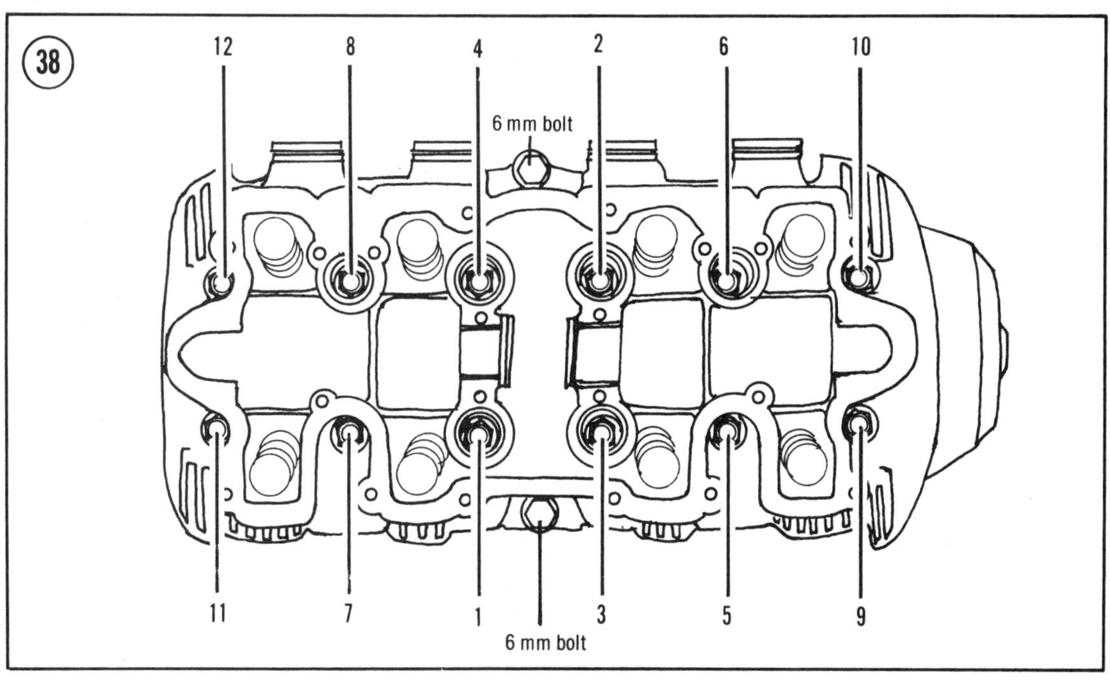

38

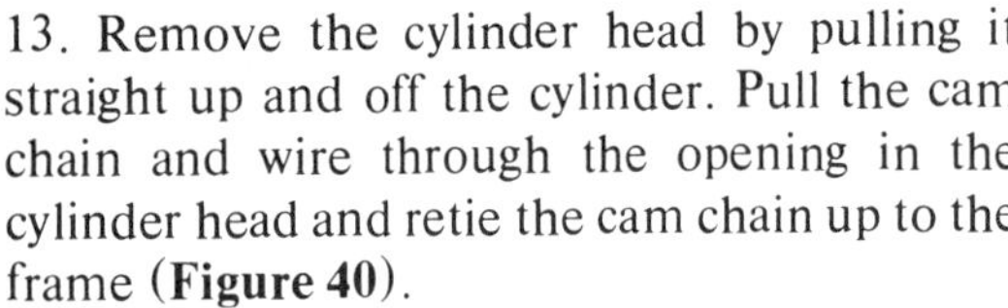
13. Remove the cylinder head by pulling it straight up and off the cylinder. Pull the cam chain and wire through the opening in the cylinder head and retie the cam chain up to the frame (**Figure 40**).

14. Remove the cylinder head gasket and discard it.

NOTE
Don't lose the 2 locating dowels. Discard the 2 small O-rings.

15. Place a clean shop cloth into the cam chain opening in the cylinder block to prevent the entry of foreign matter.

16. Install by reversing these removal steps; note the following.

17. Clean the mating surfaces of the head and cylinder block of any gasket material.

18. Install both locating dowels (**Figure 41**).

19. Install a new head gasket (A, **Figure 42**) and install new O-ring seals (B, **Figure 42**).

20. Loosen the cam chain tensioner locknut (A, **Figure 43**) and pull the tensioner (B, **Figure 43**) *up* as far as it will go. Tighten the locknut. This allows the maximum amount of cam chain slack for ease of cam installation.

NOTE
The 2 rear center bolts are longer than all other inner 8 mm bolts.

21. Install the cylinder head and secure it with the bolts. Tighten the inner 12 bolts in the torque pattern shown in **Figure 38**. Tighten in

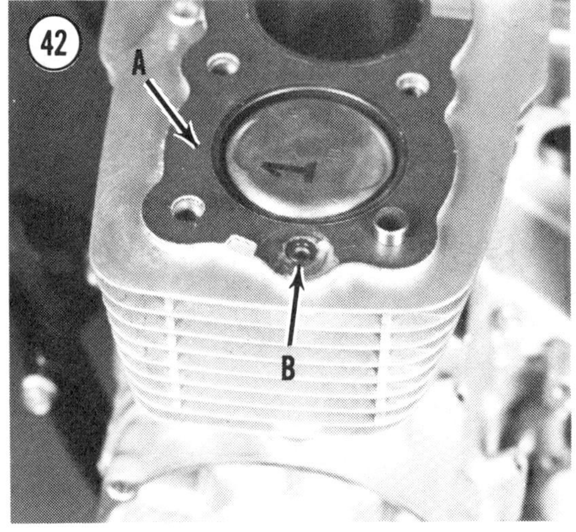

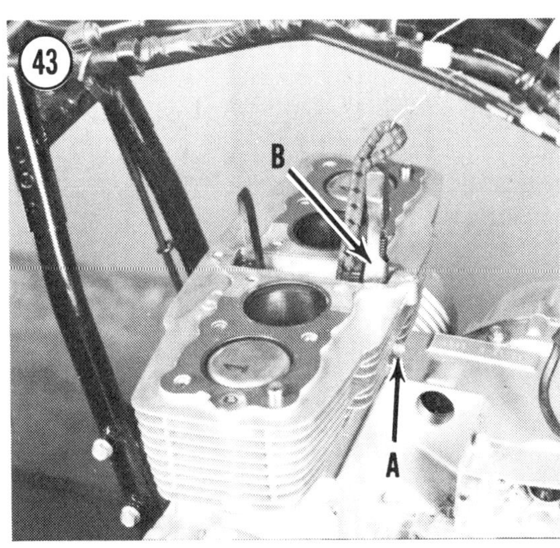

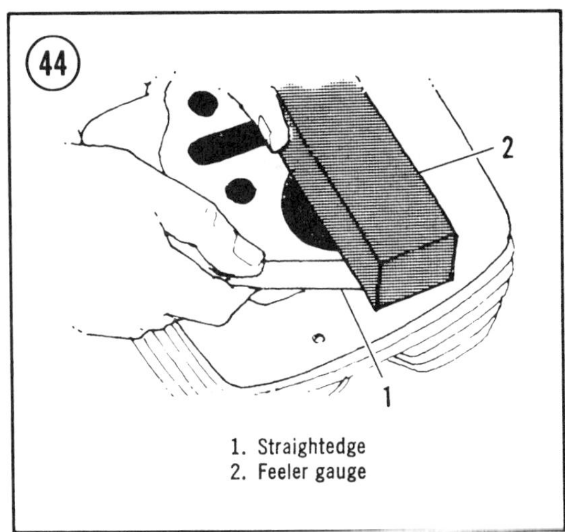

1. Straightedge
2. Feeler gauge

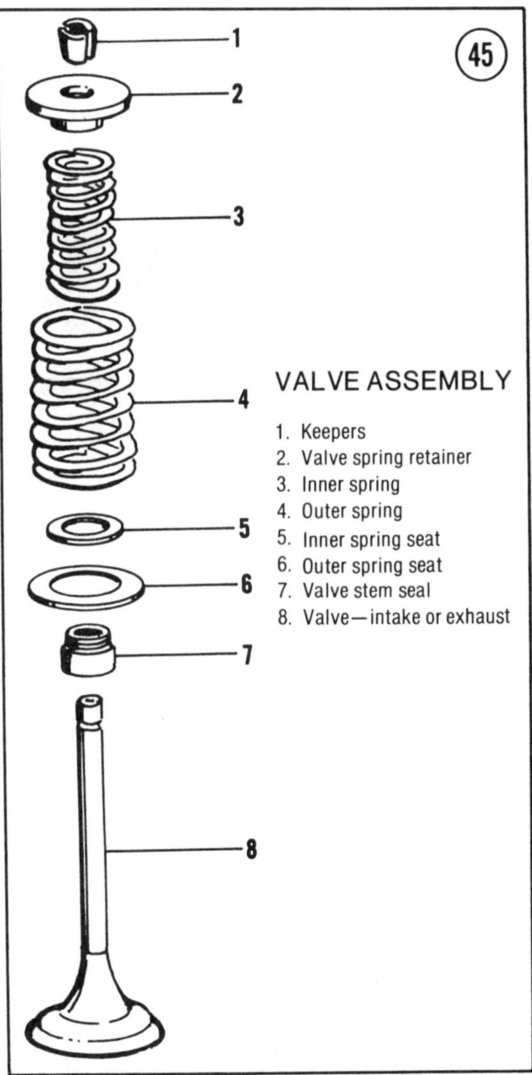

VALVE ASSEMBLY

1. Keepers
2. Valve spring retainer
3. Inner spring
4. Outer spring
5. Inner spring seat
6. Outer spring seat
7. Valve stem seal
8. Valve—intake or exhaust

2-3 stages to a final torque of 17-22 ft.-lb. (24-30 N•m).

22. Install the 2 outer 6 mm bolts and tighten to 7-10 ft.-lb. (10-14 N•m).

23. Don't forget to install the rubber seals.

Inspection

1. Remove all traces of gasket material from the cylinder head mating surfaces.
2. *Without removing the valves*, remove all carbon deposits from the combustion chambers and valve ports with a wire brush. A blunt screwdriver or chisel may be used if care is taken not to damage the head, valves and spark plug threads.
3. After the carbon is removed from the combustion chambers and the valve intake and exhaust ports, clean the entire head in cleaning solvent. Blow dry with compressed air.
4. Clean away all carbon from the piston crowns. Do not remove the carbon ridge at the top of each cylinder bore.
5. Check for cracks in the combustion chamber and exhaust ports. A cracked head must be replaced.
6. After the head has been thoroughly cleaned, place a straightedge across the cylinder head/cylinder block gasket surface (**Figure 44**) at several points. Measure the warp by inserting a feeler gauge between the straightedge and the cylinder head at each location. There should be no warpage; if a small amount is present, it can be resurfaced by a dealer or qualified machine shop.
7. Check the cylinder head cover mating surface using the procedure in Step 6. There should not be warpage.
8. Check the condition of the valves and valve guides as described under *Valve and Valve Components* in this chapter.

VALVE AND VALVE COMPONENTS

Removal

Refer to **Figure 45** for this procedure.

1. Remove the cylinder head as described under *Cylinder Head Removal/Installation* in this chapter.
2. Compress the valve springs with a valve compressor tool (**Figure 46**). Remove the

4

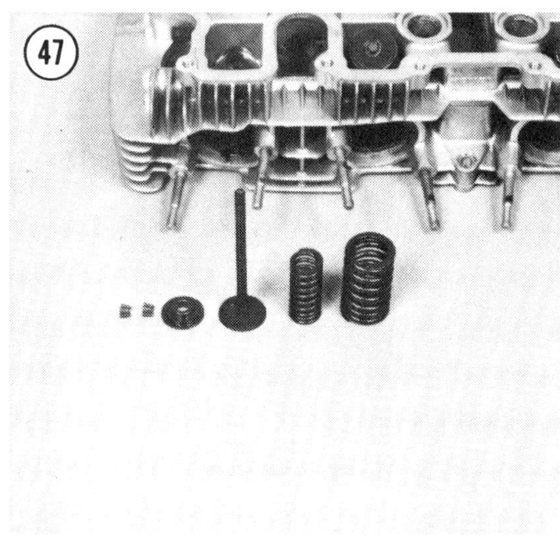

valve keepers and release the compression. Remove the valve compressor tool.

CAUTION
To avoid loss of spring tension, do not compress the springs any more than necessary to remove the keepers.

3. Remove the valve spring retainer and valve springs (**Figure 47**).

NOTE
*The inner and outer valve seats and valve stem seal **(Figure 48)** will stay in the cylinder head.*

4. Prior to removing the valve, remove any burrs from the valve stem (**Figure 49**). Otherwise, the valve guide will be damaged.
5. Mark all parts as they are disassembled so that they will be installed in their same locations.

Inspection

1. Clean valves with a wire brush and solvent.
2. Inspect the contact surface of each valve for burning (**Figure 50**). Minor roughness and pitting can be removed by lapping the valves as described under *Valve Lapping* in this chapter. Excessive unevenness of the contact surface is an indication that the valve is not serviceable. The valve contact surface can be ground on a valve grinding machine, but it best to replace a burned or damaged valve with a new valve.

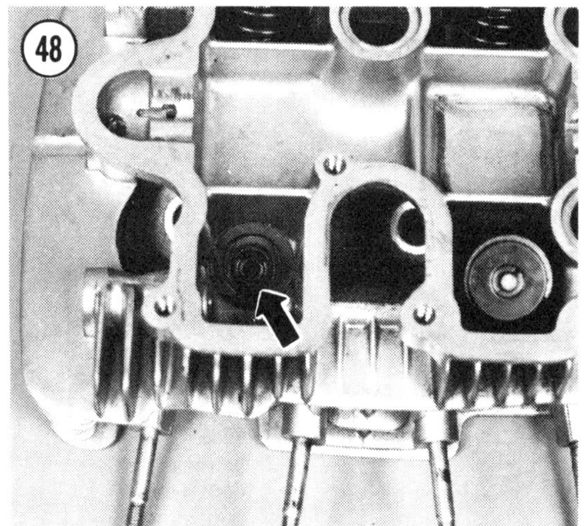

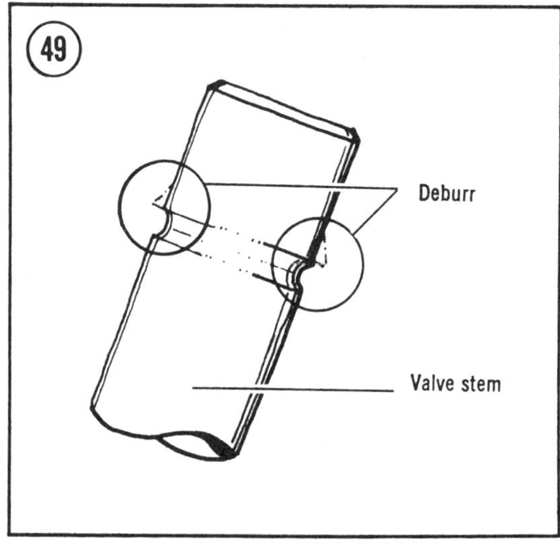

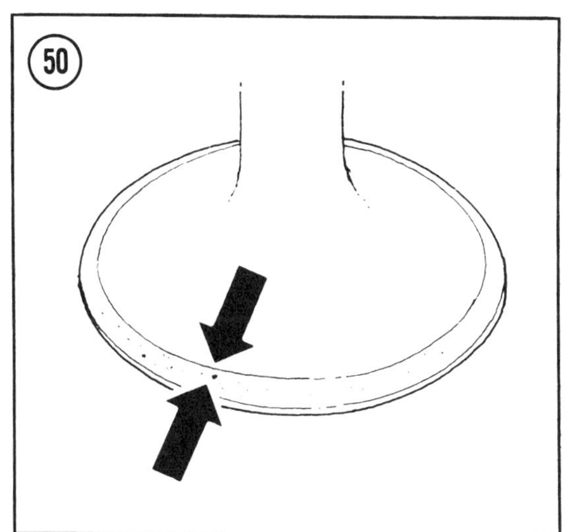

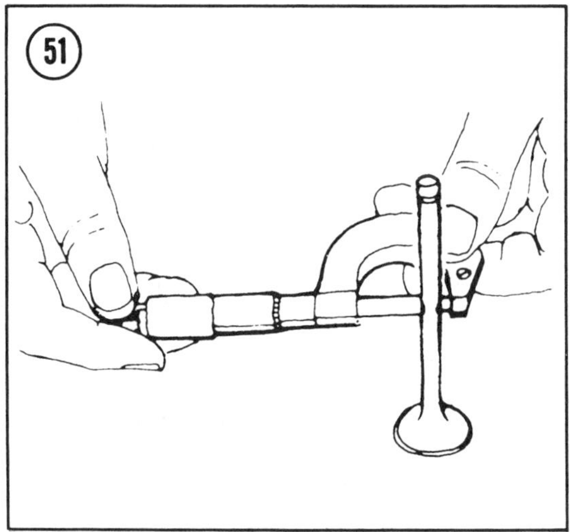

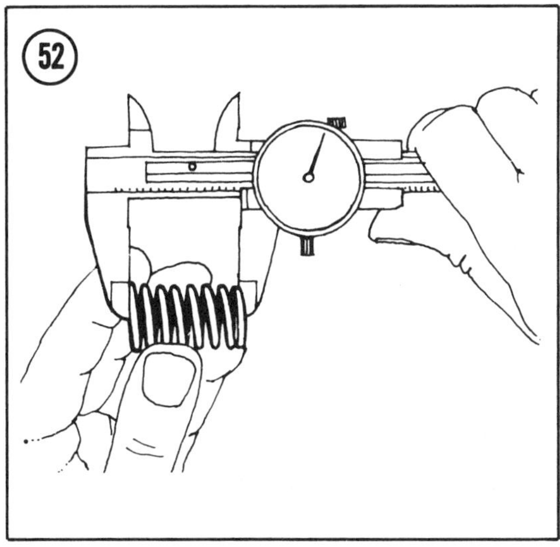

3. Measure the valve stem for wear (**Figure 51**). Compare with specifications given in **Table 1**.
4. Remove all carbon and varnish from the valve guide with a stiff spiral wire brush.

5. Insert each valve in its guide. Hold the valve with the head just slightly off the valve seat and rock it sideways. If it rocks more than slightly, the guide is probably worn and should be replaced. As a final check, take the head to a dealer and have the valve guides measured.

6. Measure the valve spring free length with a vernier caliper (**Figure 52**). All should be within the length specified in **Table 1** with no signs of bends or distortion. Replace defective springs in pairs (inner and outer).

7. Check the valve spring retainer and valve keepers. If they are in good condition they may be reused; replace as necessary.
8. Inspect the valve seats. If worn or burned, they must be reconditioned. This should be performed by a dealer or qualified machine shop. Seats and valves in near-perfect condition can be reconditioned by lapping. Refer to *Valve Lapping* in this chapter.

Installation

1. Coat the valve stems with molybdenum disulfide grease (**Figure 53**). To avoid damage to the valve stem seal, turn the valve slowly while inserting the valve into the cylinder head.

4

2. Install the valve springs with the narrow pitch end (end with the coils closest together) facing the head. Refer to **Figure 54**.
3. Install the valve spring retainer.
4. Compress the valve springs with a compressor tool (**Figure 46**) and install the valve keepers.

CAUTION
To avoid loss of spring tension, do not compress the springs any more than necessary to install the keepers.

5. After all springs have been installed, gently tap the end of the valve stems with a soft aluminum or brass drift and hammer (**Figure 55**). This will ensure that the keepers are properly seated.

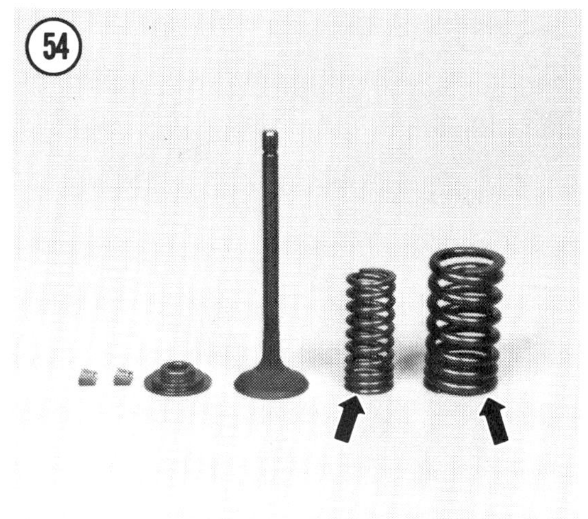

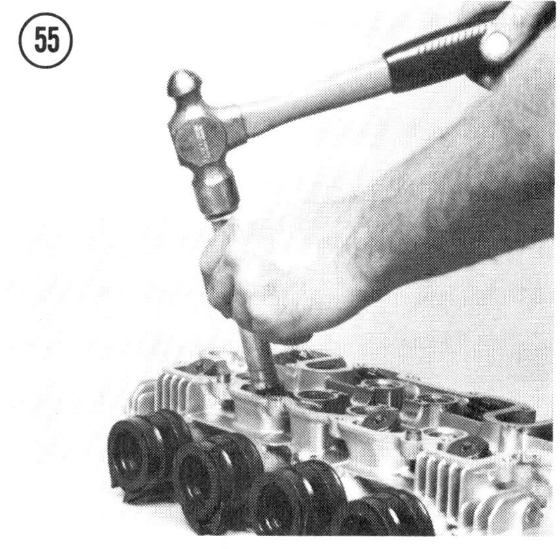

Valve Guide Replacement

When valve guides are worn so that there is excessive stem-to-guide clearance or valve tipping, the guides must be replaced. Replace all, even if only one is worn. This job should only be done by a dealer as special tools are required.

Valve Seat Reconditioning

This job is best left to a dealer or qualified machine shop. They have special equipment and knowledge for this exacting job. You can still save considerable money by removing the cylinder head and taking the head to the shop for repairs.

Valve Lapping

Valve lapping is a simple operation which can restore the valve seal without machining, providing the amount of wear or distortion is not too severe.

1. Coat the valve seating area in the cylinder head with a lapping compound such as Carborundum or Clover Brand.
2. Insert the valve into the cylinder head.
3. Wet the suction cup of the lapping stick (**Figure 56**) and stick it onto the head of the valve. Lap the valve to the seat by rotating the lapping stick in both directions. Every 5-10 seconds, rotate the valve 180° in the valve seat; continue lapping until the contact surfaces of the valve and the valve seat are a

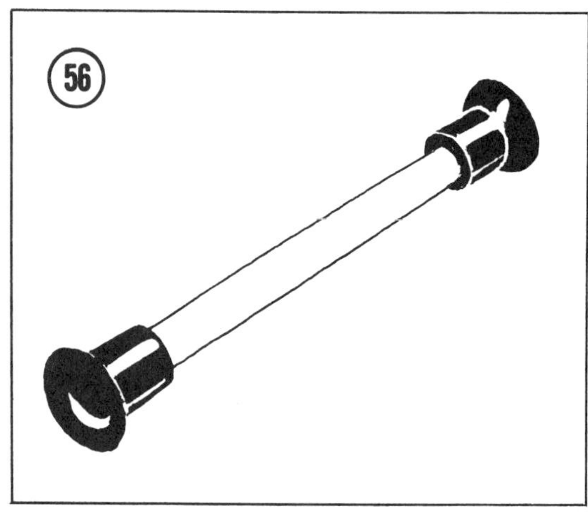

uniform grey. Stop as soon as they are; avoid removing too much material.

4. Thoroughly clean the valves and cylinder head in solvent to remove all traces of the grinding compound. Any compound left on the valves or cylinder head will cause damage.

5. After the lapping has been completed and the valve assemblies have been reinstalled into the head, the valve seat sealing ability should be tested. Check the seal of each valve seat by pouring solvent into both the intake and exhaust ports. The solvent should not flow past the valve seat and the valve head. Perform on all 4 sets of valves. If fluid does pass by any of the seats, disassemble that valve assembly and repeat the lapping procedure until there is no leakage.

CAMSHAFT

The cam is driven by a chain off of the timing sprocket on the crankshaft. The cam can be removed with the engine in the frame.

1. Place the bike on the centerstand.
2. Remove the seat, side covers and fuel tank.
3. Disconnect the battery negative lead.
4. Remove the cylinder head cover as described under *Cylinder Head Cover Removal* in this chapter.
5. Remove the screws securing the alternator cover (**Figure 57**) and remove the cover and the gasket.
6. Using a 15/16 in. socket or box wrench on the outer hex spacer, rotate the engine *clockwise* until one of the camshaft sprocket bolts is exposed. Remove the exposed bolt. Be careful not to drop the bolt down the cam chain cavity.
7. Again rotate the crankshaft *clockwise* until the other bolt is exposed (**Figure 58**). Remove that bolt; again be careful not to drop it into the cam chain cavity.
8. Pull the cam chain and cam sprocket off of the shoulder on the cam. Pull up and slide the cam chain off the cam sprocket.
9. Tie a piece of wire to the cam chain and tie it to the frame (**Figure 59**). This will prevent the chain from falling into the crankcase.
10. Hold onto the cam sprocket and withdraw the cam from the cam chain and sprocket. Pull it out from the right-hand side.
11. Remove the cam sprocket.

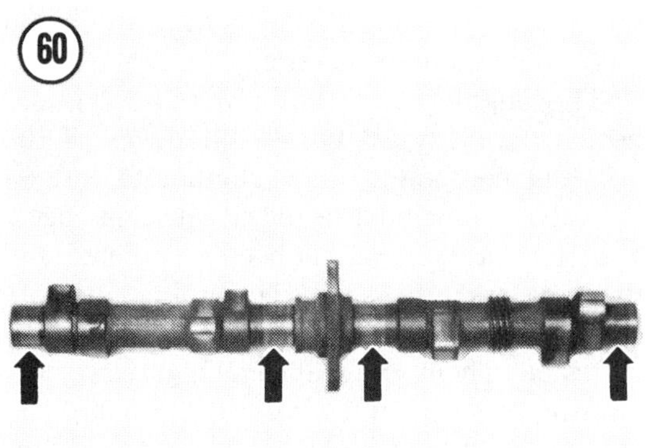

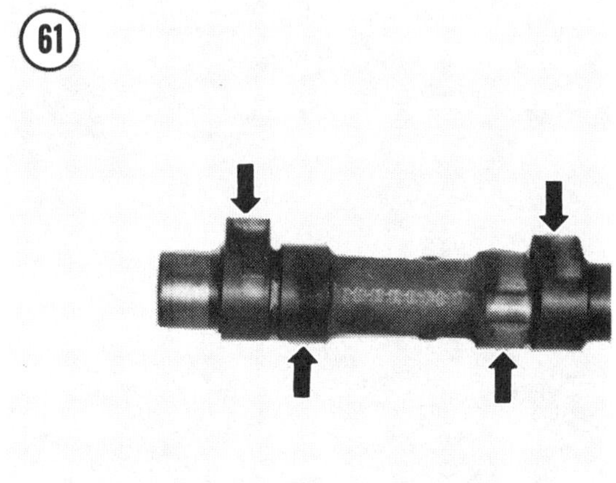

CAUTION

If the crankshaft must be rotated when the camshaft is removed, pull up on the cam chain and keep it taut while rotating the crankshaft. Make certain that the chain is positioned onto the crankshaft timing sprocket. If this is not done, the chain may become kinked and may damage both the chain and the timing sprocket on the crankshaft.

Inspection

1. Check the cam bearing journals for wear and scoring (**Figure 60**).

2. Check the cam lobes for wear (**Figure 61**). The lobes should show no signs of scoring and the edges should be square. Slight damage may be removed with a silicone carbide oilstone. Use No. 100-120 grit stone initially, then polish with a No. 280-320 grit stone.

3. Even though the cam lobe surface appears to be satisfactory, with no visible signs of wear, the cam lobes must be measured with a micrometer as shown in **Figure 62**.

4. Check the cam bearing surfaces in the cylinder head (**Figure 63**) and cylinder head cover (**Figure 64**). They should not be scored or excessively worn. Replace either part if wear is evident.

5. Inspect the condition of the cam sprocket for wear; replace if necessary.

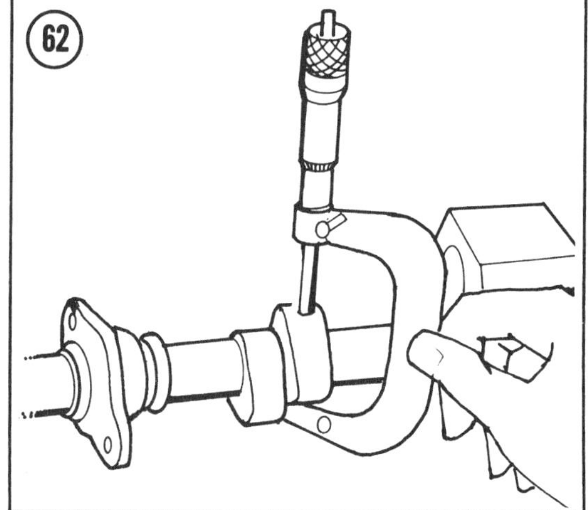

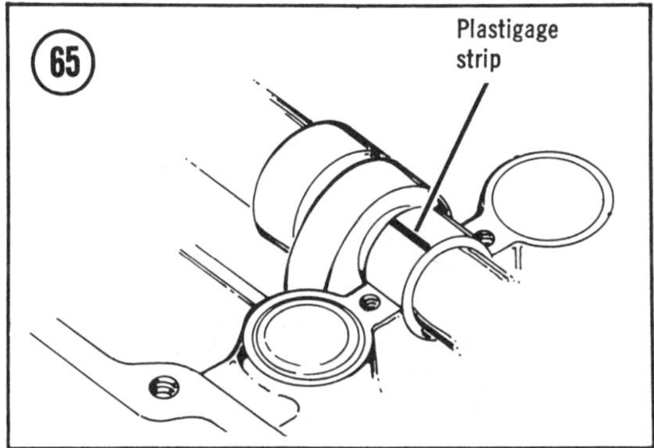

Camshaft Bearing Clearance

This procedure requires the use of a Plastigage set.

1. Wipe all oil residue from each cam bearing journal and bearing surface on the cylinder head and cylinder head cover.
2. Insert the cam through the cam chain. It is not necessary to install the cam sprocket. Lay the cam chain on top of the cam in the same area where the sprocket would be. Make sure it will not interfere with the cylinder head cover when it is installed.
3. Place a strip of Plastigage material on top of each cam bearing journal, lengthwise with the cam as shown in **Figure 65**.
4. Carefully install the cylinder head cover and install all of the bolts holding the cover in place. Tighten the bolts to 6-9 ft.-lb. (8-12 N•m) in the torque sequence shown in **Figure 66**.

NOTE
Do not rotate the camshaft with the Plastigage material in place.

5. Remove the bolts securing the cylinder head cover in the same torque sequence as they were tightened.

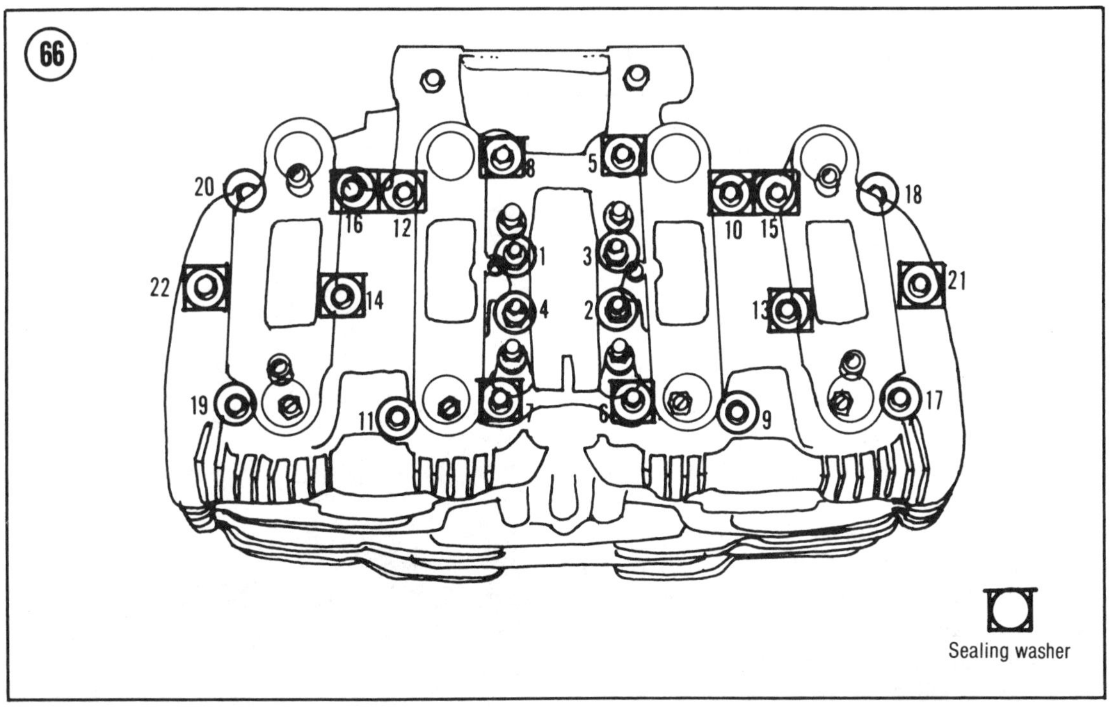

6. Carefully lift up and remove the cylinder head cover.
7. Measure the width of the flattened Plastigage according to manufacturer's instructions (**Figure 67**).
8. If the clearance exceeds the wear limit in **Table 1**, measure the cam bearing journals with a micrometer and compare with dimensions given in **Table 1**. Replace the cam if it is worn, but if the cam is within specifications, the cylinder head and cylinder head cover must be replaced.

CAUTION
Remove all particles of Plastigage material from all bearing journals on all parts. This material must not be left in the engine as it can plug up a small oil control orifice and cause severe engine damage.

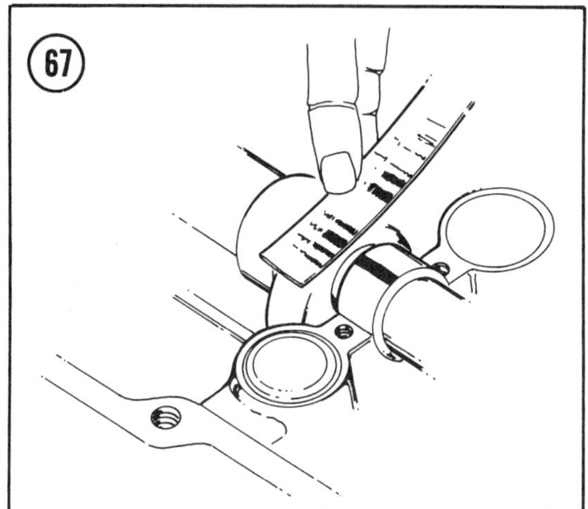

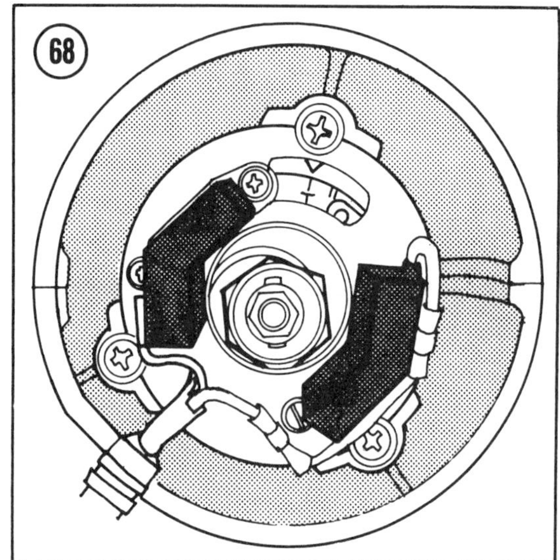

Installation

1. Lubricate all cam lobes and bearing journals with assembly oil. Also coat the bearing surfaces in the cylinder head and cylinder head cover with assembly oil.

CAUTION
When rotating the crankshaft, keep the cam chain taut and engaged with the timing sprocket on the crankshaft.

2. Rotate the crankshaft *clockwise* until the "1.4 T" timing mark aligns with the stationary pointer (**Figure 68**). Use a 15/16 in. socket or box wrench on the outer hex head spacer (**Figure 69**) of the ignition advance unit.
3. Install the cam with the index mark on the end toward the right-hand side of the engine. Position the cam sprocket with alignment punch marks toward the left-hand side.
4. Insert the cam from the right-hand side through the cam chain and chain sprocket.
5. On the right-hand side of the engine, align the index mark in the end of the cam with the *front* top surface of the cylinder head (**Figure 70**).
6. As viewed from the left-hand side, position the chain sprocket with the 2 punch marks level with the top surface of the cylinder head. Place the cam chain up and onto the cam sprocket. Pull the chain and chain sprocket up onto the shoulder on the cam. The cam and

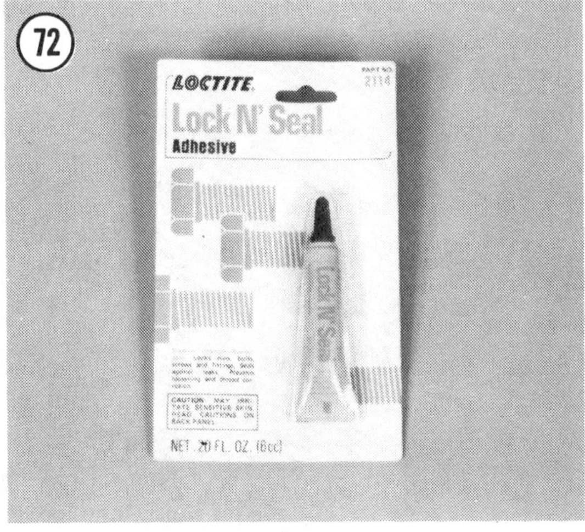

sprocket bolt holes should align at this time (**Figure 71**). If alignment is not correct, reposition the cam chain on the sprocket so alignment is correct.

CAUTION
Very expensive damage could result from improper cam and chain alignment. Recheck your work several times to be sure alignment is correct.

7. When alignment is correct install the bolt—only finger-tight at this time.

8. Rotate the crankshaft *clockwise* until the other bolt hole is accessible. Apply Loctite 242 (**Figure 72**) to the bolt threads and install the bolt. Tighten to 16-19 ft.-lb. (22-26 N·m).

NOTE
*Use a 15/16 in. socket or box wrench on the outer hex head spacer (**Figure 69**) of the ignition advance unit.*

9. Again rotate the crankshaft *clockwise* until the first bolt is accessible. Remove the bolt and apply Loctite 242 (**Figure 72**) to the bolt threads and reinstall the bolt. Tighten to 16-19 ft.-lb. (22-26 N·m).

10. Make one final check to make sure alignment is correct. The "1.4 T" timing mark must be aligned with the stationary pointer (**Figure 68**) and the index mark on the right-hand end of the cam must be aligned with the *front* top surface of the cylinder head (**Figure 70**). Also the cam sprocket alignment punch marks on the left-hand side must align with the top surface of the cylinder head (**Figure 71**).

11. Fill all oil pockets with fresh engine oil (**Figure 73**) so the cam lobes will be covered for the initial engine start up.

12. Install the cylinder head cover as described under *Cylinder Head Cover Installation* in this chapter.

13. Adjust the valves and cam chain tension as described in Chapter Three.

CAMSHAFT CHAIN

Replacement

In order to replace the cam chain the engine must be removed from the frame and the crankcase split.

Inspection

Refer to *Camshaft and Primary Chain Inspection* in this chapter.

Camshaft Chain Tensioner Adjustment

After the cam chain has been replaced, adjust the chain as described under *Camshaft Chain Tensioner Adjustment* in Chapter Three.

Camshaft Chain Sprocket

Inspect the condition of the cam chain sprocket. Replace it if it shows signs of wear or has any teeth missing.

CYLINDER BLOCK

Removal

1. Remove the cylinder head as described under *Cylinder Head Removal/Installation* in this chapter.
2. Remove the front cam chain guide (A, **Figure 74**) and untie the wire securing the cam chain to the frame (B, **Figure 74**). Tie the wire to the cylinder block.
3. Loosen the cylinder block by tapping around the perimeter with a rubber or plastic mallet. If necessary, *gently* pry the cylinder block loose with a broad-tipped screwdriver.
4. Pull the cylinder block straight up and then tip it slightly to the rear (**Figure 75**) so that the cam chain tensioner assembly will clear the opening in the crankcase. Work the cam chain wire through the opening in the cylinder block and retie the wire to the frame or crankcase so the chain will not fall into the crankcase.
5. Remove the cylinder base gasket and discard it. Remove the 2 oil control dowel pins and O-rings.
6. Install a piston holding fixture under 2 of the pistons (**Figure 76**) to protect the piston skirt from damage. This fixture may be purchased or may be a homemade unit of wood. See **Figure 77**.

73

74

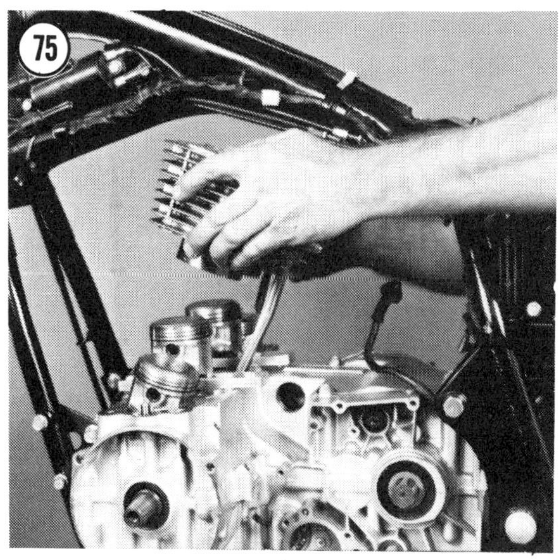
75

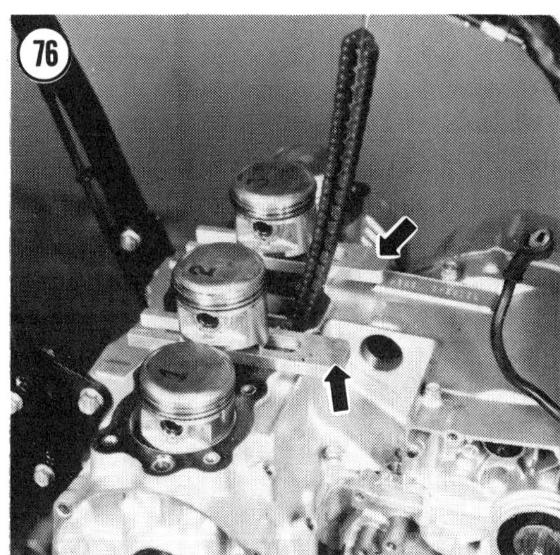

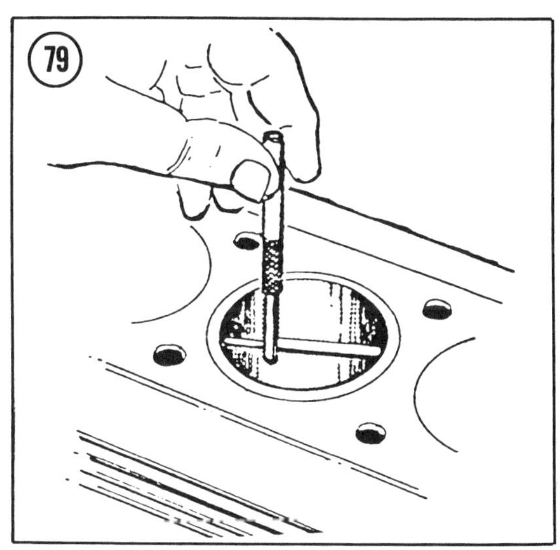

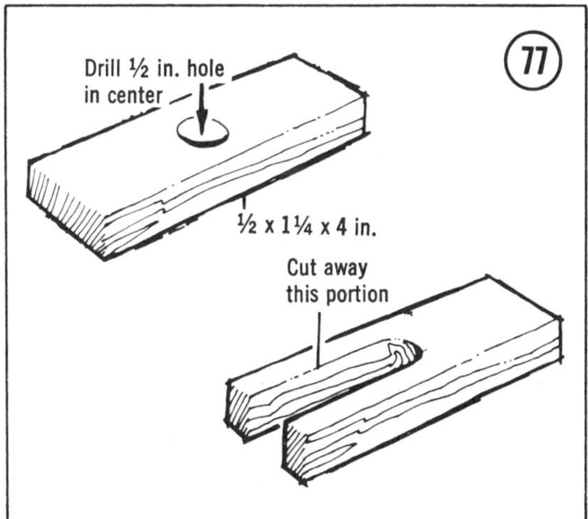

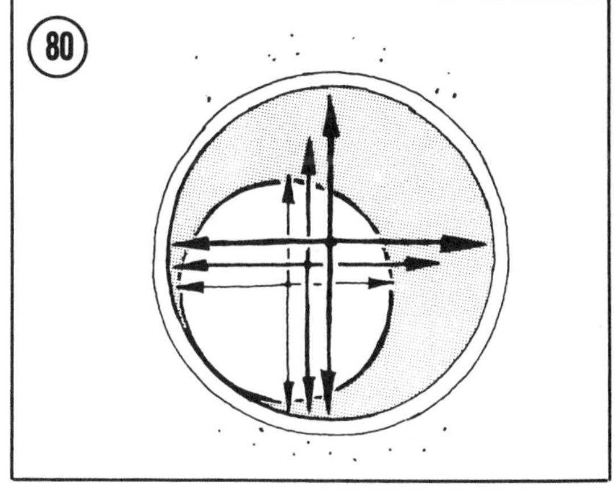

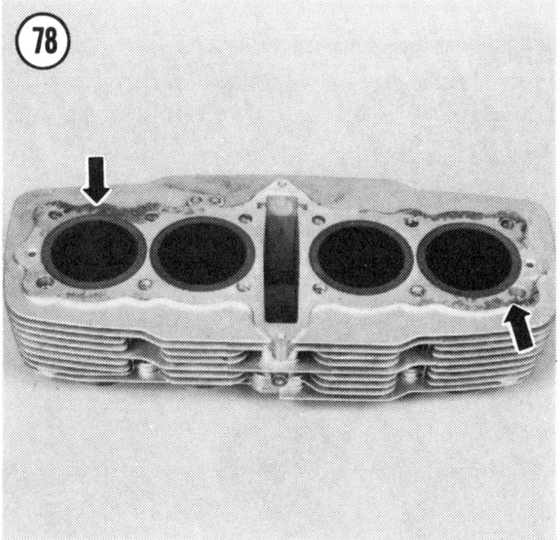

7. Remove the cam chain tensioner assembly locknut and remove the chain tensioner assembly.

Inspection

The following procedure requires the use of highly specialized and expensive measuring instruments. If such equipment is not readily available, have the measurements performed by a dealer or qualified machine shop.

1. Soak with solvent any old cylinder head gasket material (**Figure 78**) on the cylinder block. Use a broad-tipped *dull* chisel and gently scrape off all gasket residue. Do not gouge the sealing surface as oil and air leaks will result.
2. Measure the cylinder bore with a cylinder gauge (**Figure 79**) or inside micrometer at the points shown in **Figure 80**.

3. Measure in 2 axes—in line with the piston pin and at 90° to the pin. If the taper or out-of-round is 0.002 in. (0.05 mm) or greater, the cylinders must be rebored to the next oversize and new pistons installed.

NOTE

The new pistons should be obtained before the cylinder block is rebored so that the pistons can be measured; slight manufacturing tolerances must be taken into account to determine the actual size and working clearance. Piston-to-cylinder wear limit is 0.004 in. (0.10 mm).

4. Check the cylinder walls for scratches; if evident, the cylinders should be rebored.

NOTE

The maximum wear limit on a cylinder is 2.358 in. (59.90 mm). If any cylinder is worn to this limit, the cylinder block must be replaced. Never rebore a cylinder if the finished rebore diameter will be this dimension or greater.

5. Inspect the condition of the large O-ring seal at the base of each cylinder (**Figure 81**). Replace all 4 if any are deteriorated or damaged.
6. Inspect the slipper portion of the cam chain tensioner assembly (A, **Figure 82**) for damage or excessive wear. Also check the spring tension (**Figure 83**) for weakness. Replace as necessary.
7. Inspect the condition of the front cam chain guide (B, **Figure 82**) for excessive wear. Replace as necessary.

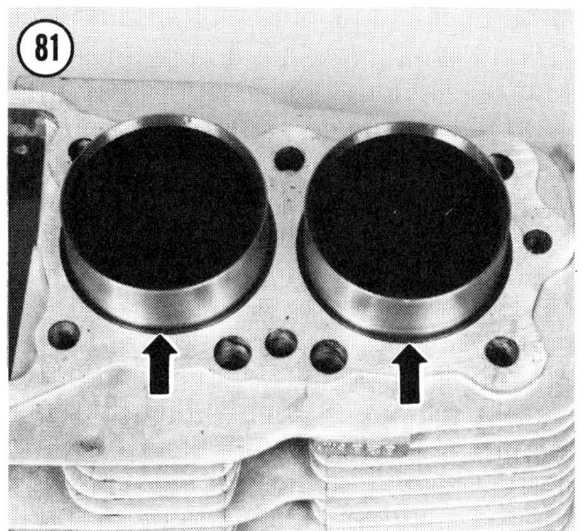

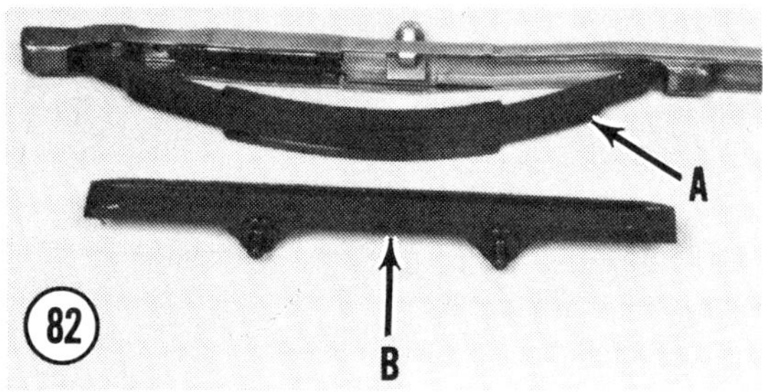

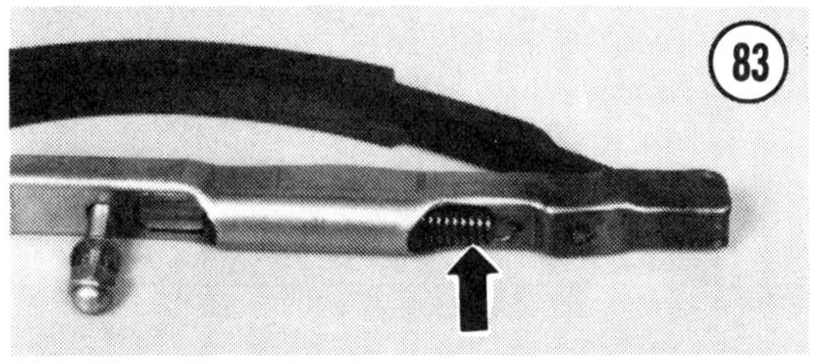

Installation

1. Check that the top surface of the crankcase and the bottom surface of the cylinder block are clean prior to installing a new base gasket.
2. Install a new cylinder block base gasket (A, **Figure 84**).
3. Install the 2 oil control dowel pins and 2 new O-ring seals (B, **Figure 84**).
4. Install a piston holding fixture under the 2 pistons protruding out of the crankcase (**Figure 76**).
5. Install the cam chain tensioner assembly and tighten the locknut only finger-tight at this time.

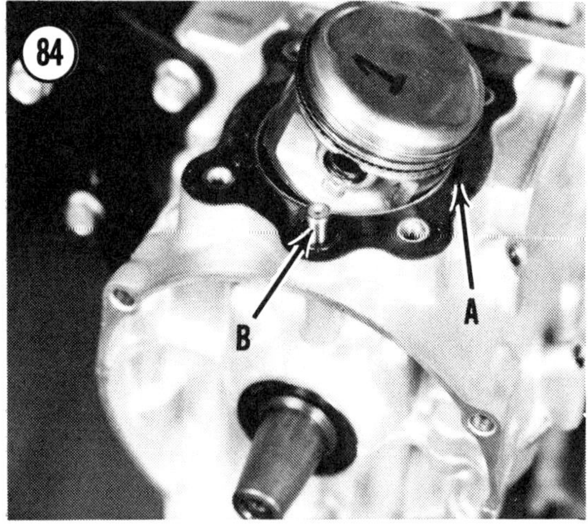

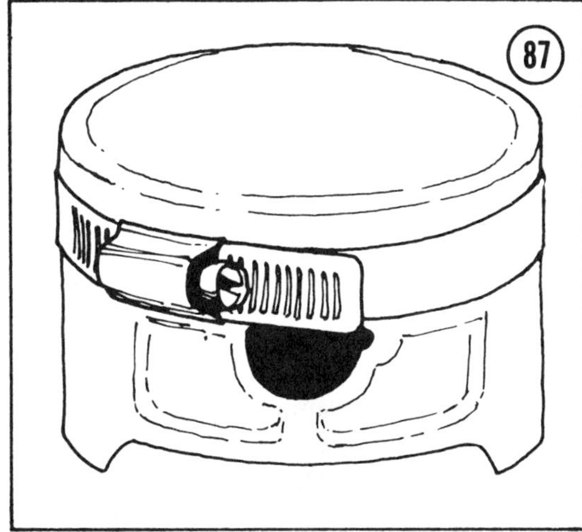

6. Make sure the end gaps of the piston rings are *not* lined up with each other—they must be staggered. Lightly oil the piston rings and the inside of the cylinder bores with assembly oil.
7. Untie the cam chain wire and tie it to the cylinder block.
8. Start the cylinder block in an almost laid back position and guide the cam chain tensioner assembly into the cam chain slot in the crankcase (**Figure 85**).
9. Continue to rotate the cylinder block forward and down until it aligns with the pistons (**Figure 86**).
10. Carefully feed the cam chain and wire up through the opening in the cylinder block and tie it to the frame.
11. Start the cylinder block down over the 2 protruding pistons. Compress each piston ring as it enters the cylinder either with your fingers or by using aircraft type hose clamps (**Figure 87**) of appropriate size.
12. Slide the cylinder block down until it bottoms on the piston holding fixtures (**Figure 88**).
13. Remove the piston holding fixtures and slide the cylinder block down into place on the crankcase.

NOTE
*Make sure the lower end of the cam chain tensioner seats correctly into the groove in the upper crankcase (**Figure 89**).*

14. Install the cylinder head as described under *Cylinder Head Removal/Installation* in this chapter.

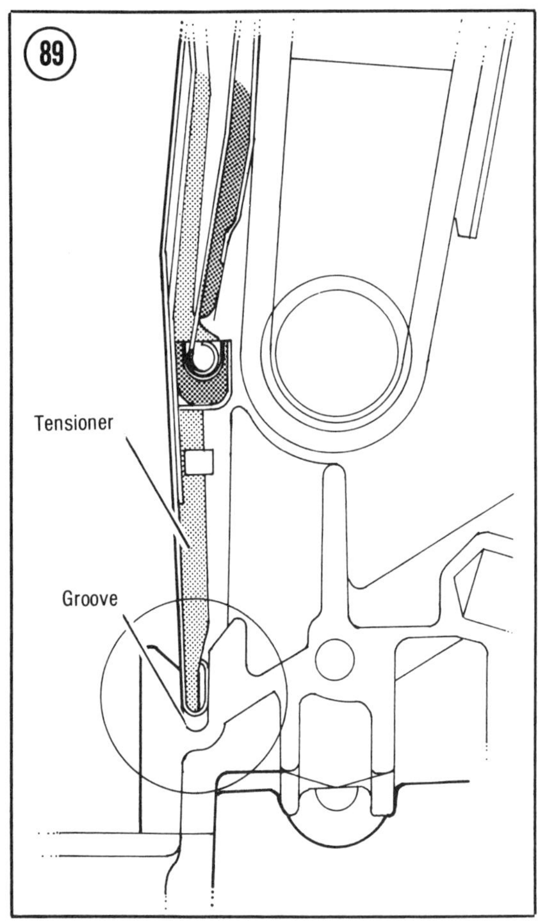

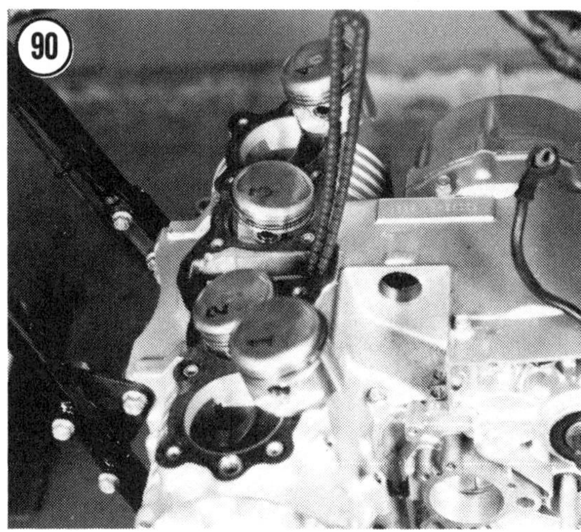

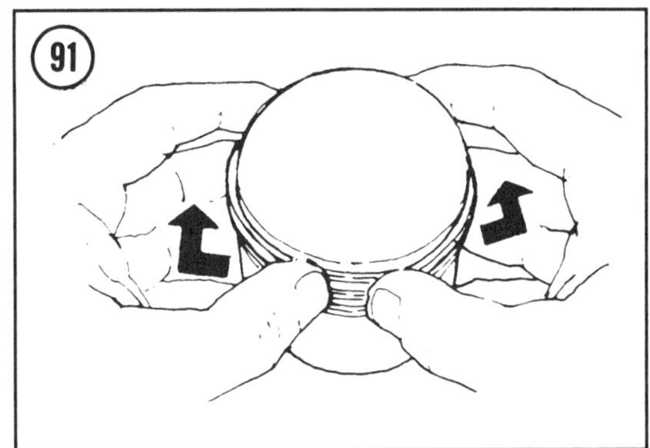

15. Adjust the valves, cam chain tensioner and ignition timing as described in *Tune-up* in Chapter Three.
16. Follow the *Break-in Procedure* in this chapter if the cylinder block was rebored or honed or a new pistons or piston rings were installed.

PISTON, PISTON PIN AND PISTON RINGS

The pistons used in the CB650 are made of an aluminum alloy. The piston pin is a precision fit and is held in place by a clip at each end.

The pistons can be removed with the engine in the frame.

Piston Removal

1. Remove the cylinder head and cylinder block as described under *Cylinder Block Removal* in this chapter.
2. Mark the top of each piston with the correct cylinder number "1," "2," "3" and "4" as shown in **Figure 90**. The No. 1 cylinder is on the left-hand side of the bike; No. 2, 3, and 4 continue from left to right across the engine.

WARNING

The edges of all piston rings are very sharp. Be careful when handling them to avoid cut fingers.

3. Remove the top ring with a ring expander tool or by spreading the ends with your thumbs just enough to slide the ring up over the piston (**Figure 91**). Repeat for the remaining rings.
4. Before removing the piston, hold the rod tightly and rock the piston as shown in **Figure 92**. Any rocking motion (do not confuse with the normal sliding motion) indicates wear on the piston pin, rod bearing or piston pin bore (more likely a combination of all three).

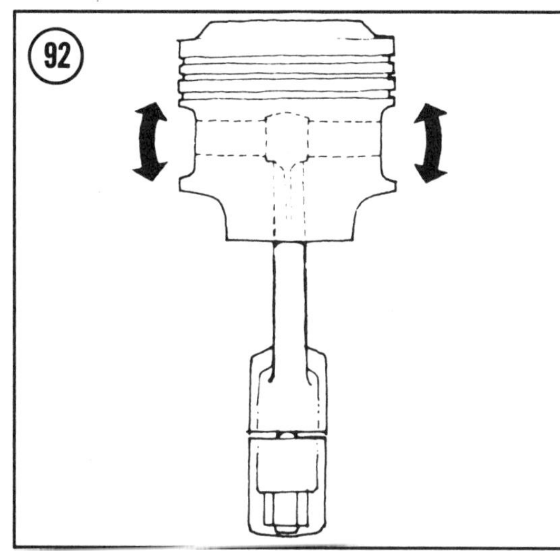

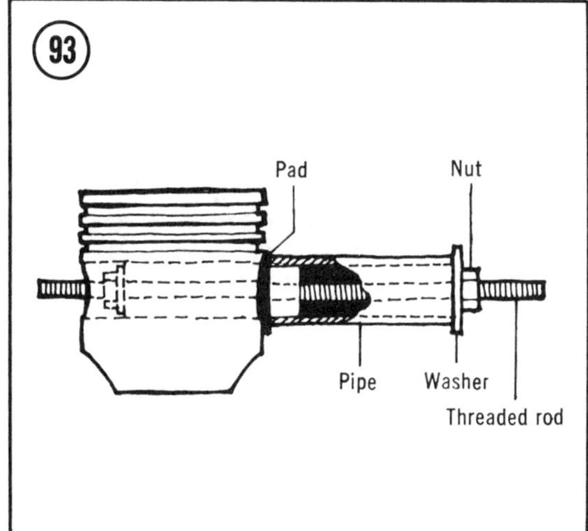

NOTE
Wrap a clean shop cloth under the piston so that the piston pin clip will not fall into the crankcase.

5. Remove the clips from each side of the piston pin bore with a small screwdriver or scribe. Hold your thumb over one edge of the clip when removing it to prevent it from springing out.
6. Use a proper size wooden dowel or socket extension and push out the piston pin. Mark the piston pin with the same number as the piston so they will be reassembled in the same set.

CAUTION
Be careful when removing the pin to avoid damaging the connecting rod. If it is necessary to gently tap the pin to remove it, be sure that the piston is properly supported so that lateral shock is not transmitted to the lower connecting rod bearing.

7. If the piston pin is difficult to remove, heat the piston and pin with a butane torch. The pin will probably push right out. Heat the piston to only about 140° F (60° C), i.e., until it is too warm to touch, but not excessively hot. If the pin is still difficult to push out, use a homemade tool as shown in **Figure 93**.
8. Lift the piston off the connecting rod.
9. If the piston is going to be left off for some time, place a piece of foam insulation tube over the end of the rod to protect it.

Inspection

1. Carefully clean the carbon from the piston crown with a chemical remover or with a soft scraper (**Figure 94**). Do not remove or damage the carbon ridge around the circumference of the piston above the top ring. If the pistons, rings, and cylinders are found to be dimensionally correct and can be reused, removal of the carbon ring from the top of the pistons or the carbon ridge from the top of each cylinder will promote excessive oil consumption.

CAUTION
Do not wire brush the piston skirts.

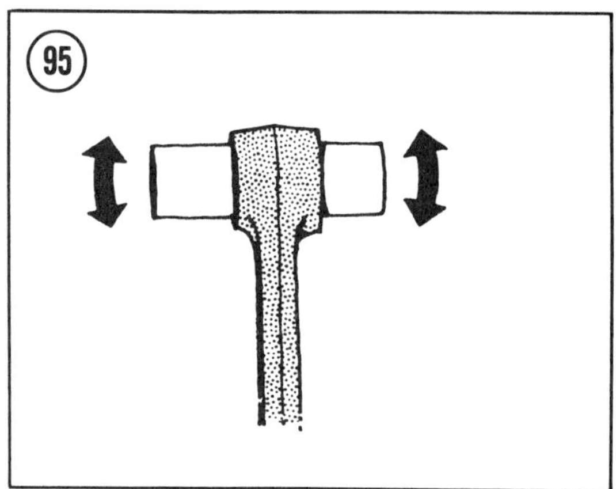

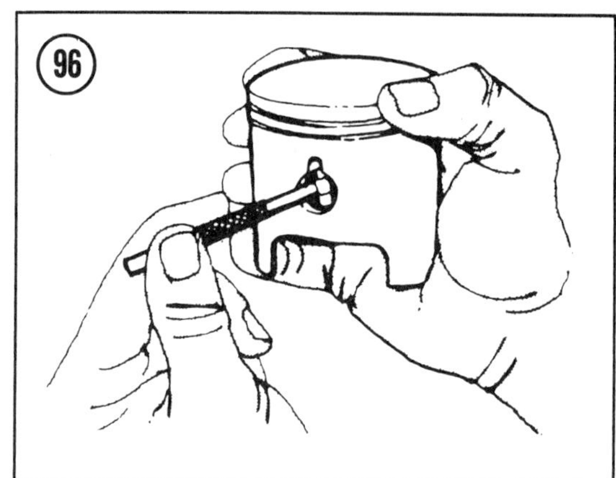

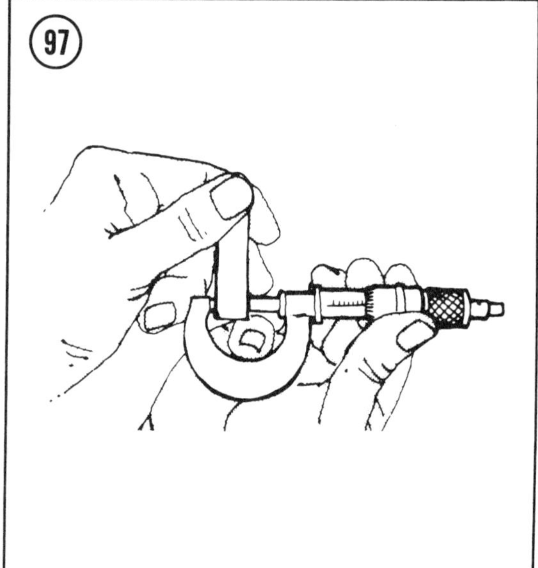

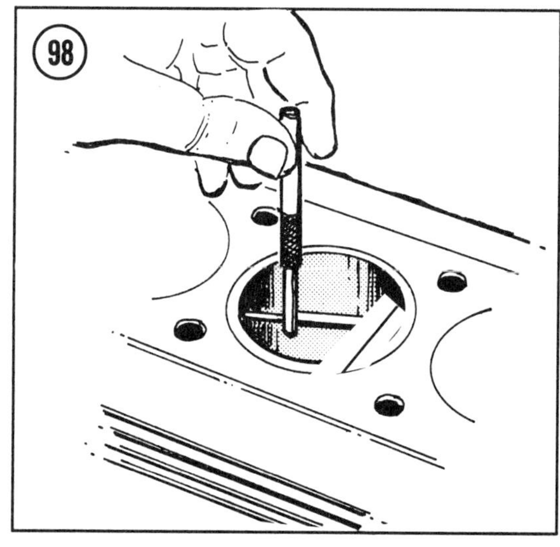

2. Examine each ring groove for burrs, dented edges and wide wear. Pay particular attention to the top compression ring groove as it usually wears more than the others.
3. Measure piston-to-cylinder clearance as described under *Piston Clearance* in this chapter.
4. If damage or wear indicates piston replacement, select a new piston as described under *Piston Clearance* in this chapter.
5. Oil the piston pin and install it in the connecting rod. Slowly rotate the piston pin and check for radial and axial play (**Figure 95**). If any play exists, the piston pin should be replaced, providing the rod bore is in good condition. Measure the inside diameter of the piston pin bore with a snap gauge (**Figure 96**) and measure the outside diameter of the piston pin with a micrometer (**Figure 97**). Compare with dimensions given in **Table 1**. Replace the piston and piston pin as a set if either or both are worn.
6. Check the piston skirt for galling and abrasion which may have been caused by piston seizure. If light galling is present, smooth the affected area with No. 400 emery paper and oil or a fine oilstone. However, if galling is severe or if the piston is deeply scored, replace it.

Piston Clearance

1. Make sure the piston and cylinder walls are clean and dry.
2. Measure the inside diameter of the cylinder bore at a point 1/2 in. (13 mm) from the upper edge with a bore gauge (**Figure 98**).

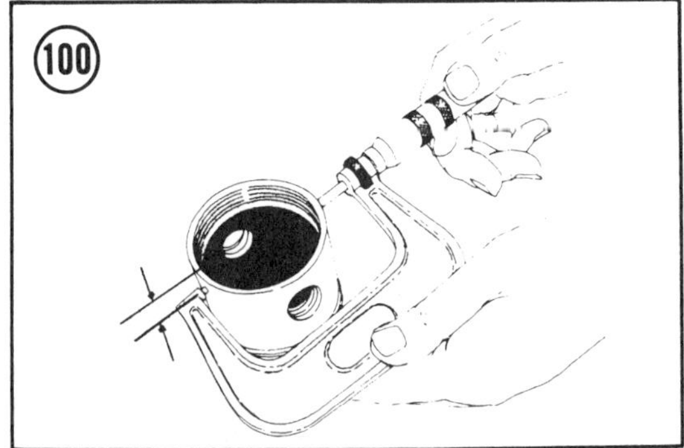

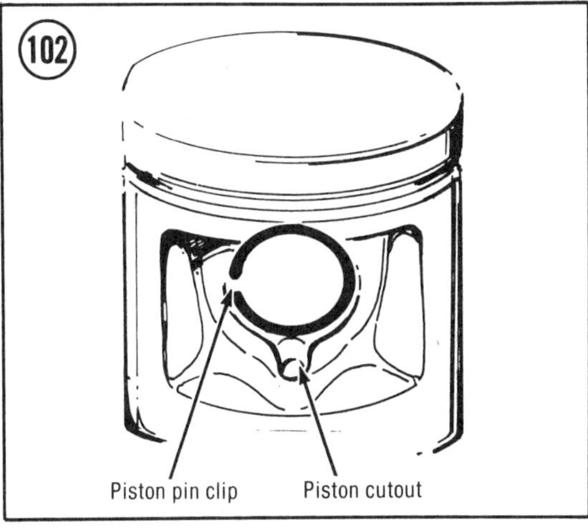

3. Measure the outside diameter of the piston across the skirt (**Figure 99**) at right angles to the piston pin. Measure at a distance 0.40 in. (10 mm) up from the bottom of the piston skirt (**Figure 100**).
4. Piston clearance is the difference between the maximum piston diameter and the minimum cylinder diameter. Subtract the dimension of the piston from the cylinder dimension. If the clearance exceeds the dimension of 0.004 in. (0.10 mm) the cylinder should be rebored to the next oversize and a new piston installed.
5. To establish a final overbore dimension with a new piston, add the piston skirt measurement to the specified clearance. This will determine the dimension for the cylinder overbore size. Remember, do not exceed the cylinder maximum service limit inside diameter of 2.358 in. (59.90 mm).

4

Piston Installation

1. Apply molybdenum disulfide grease to the inside surface of the connecting rod.
2. Oil the piston pin with assembly oil and install it in the piston until its end extends slightly beyond the inside of the boss.
3. Place the piston over the connecting rod with the IN on the piston crown toward the rear (**Figure 101**). Be sure to install the correct piston (No. 1, 2, 3 and 4) onto the same rod from which it was removed.
4. Line up the piston pin with the holes in the piston and connecting rod and push the pin into the piston until it is even with the piston pin clip grooves.

CAUTION

If it is necessary to tap the piston pin into the connecting rod, do so gently with a block of wood or a soft-faced hammer. Make sure you support the piston to prevent the lateral shock from being transmitted to connecting rod bearing.

NOTE

*In the next step, install the clips with the gap away from the cutout in the piston (**Figure 102**).*

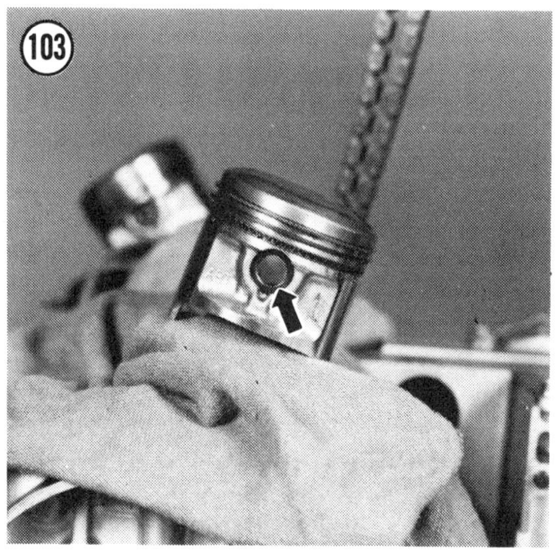

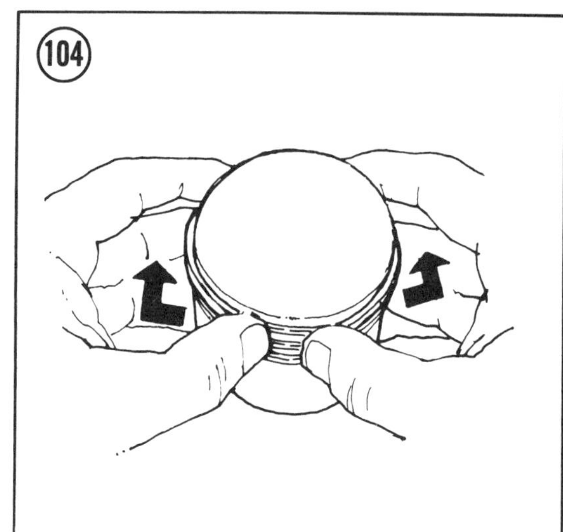

5. Install new piston pin clips in the ends of the pin boss (**Figure 103**). Make sure they are seated in the grooves.
6. Check the installation by rocking the piston back and forth around the pin axis and from side to side along the axis. It should rotate freely back and forth but not from side to side.
7. Install the piston rings as described under *Piston Ring Replacement* in this chapter.
8. Install the cylinder block and cylinder head as described under *Cylinder Block Installation* in this chapter.

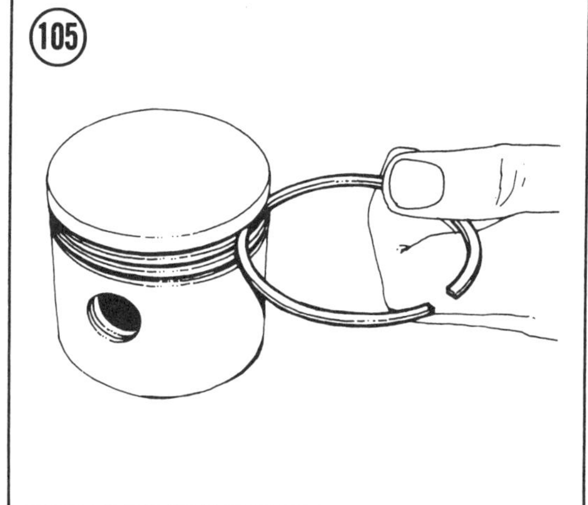

Piston Ring Replacement

WARNING
The edges of all piston rings are very sharp. Be careful when handling them to avoid cut fingers.

1. Remove the top ring by spreading the ends with your thumbs just enough to slide the ring up over the piston (**Figure 104**). Repeat for the remaining rings.
2. Carefully remove all carbon buildup from the ring grooves. Inspect the grooves carefully for burrs, nicks or broken and cracked lands. Recondition or replace the piston if necessary.
3. Roll each ring around its piston groove as shown in **Figure 105** to check for binding. Minor binding may be cleaned up with a fine cut file.
4. Measure the side clearance of each ring in its groove with a flat feeler gauge (**Figure 106**)

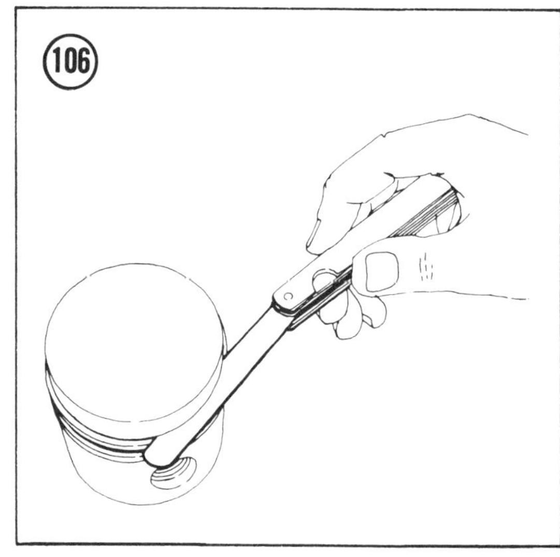

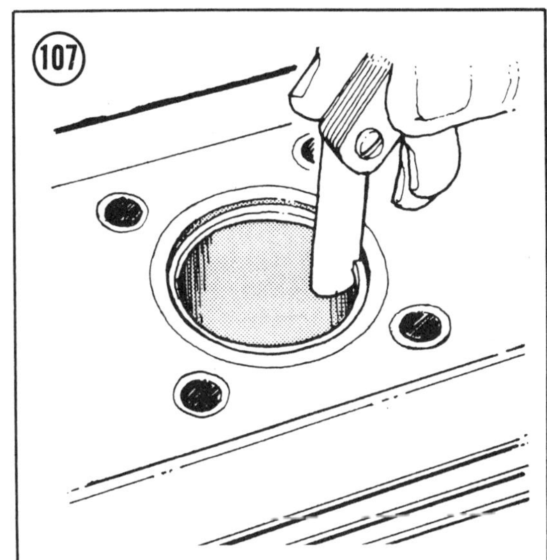

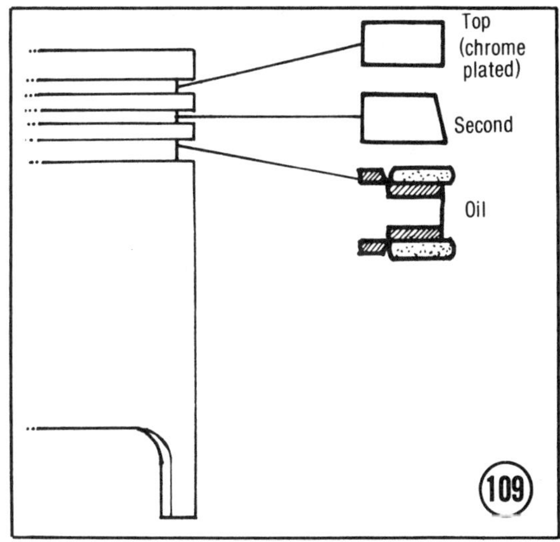

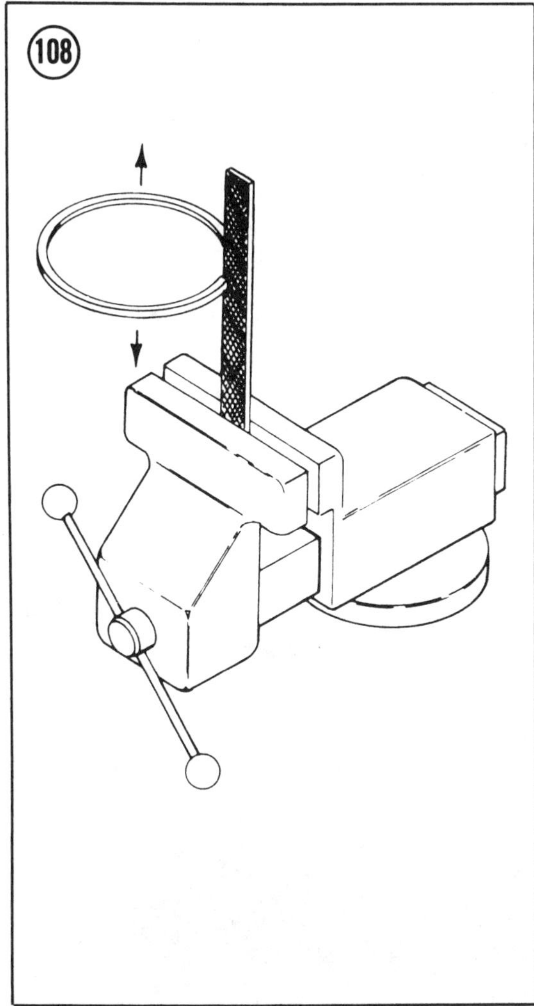

and compare to dimensions given in **Table 1**. If the clearance is greater than specified, the rings must be replaced. If the clearance is still excessive with the new rings, the piston must also be replaced.

5. Measure each ring for wear as shown in **Figure 107**. Place each ring, one at a time, into the cylinder and push it in about 3/4 in. (20 mm) with the crown of the piston to ensure that the ring is square in the cylinder bore. Measure the gap with a flat feeler gauge and compare to dimensions in **Table 1**. If the gap is greater than specified, the rings should be replaced. When installing new rings, measure their end gap in the same manner as for old ones. If the gap is less than specified, carefully file the ends with a fine cut file (**Figure 108**) until the gap is correct.

6. Install the piston rings in the order shown in **Figure 109**.

NOTE

Install all rings with their markings facing up.

7. Install the piston rings—first the bottom one, then the top—by carefully spreading the ends of the ring with your thumbs and slipping the ring over the top of the piston. Remember that the marks on the piston rings are toward the top of the piston.

8. Make sure the rings are seated completely in their grooves all the way around the piston and that the ends are distributed around the

piston as shown in **Figure 110**. The important thing is that the ring gaps are not aligned with each other when installed.

9. If new rings were installed, measure the side clearance of each ring in its groove with a flat feeler gauge (**Figure 106**) and compare to dimensions given in **Table 1**.

10. Follow the *Break-in Procedure* in this chapter if a new piston or piston rings have been installed or the cylinder block was rebored or honed.

IGNITION ADVANCE AND PULSER GENERATOR

Removal/Installation

1. Remove the seat and left-hand side cover.
2. Disconnect the battery negative lead.
3. Disconnect the pulser generator electrical connector containing 4 wires (2 yellow and 2 blue). Refer to **Figure 111**.

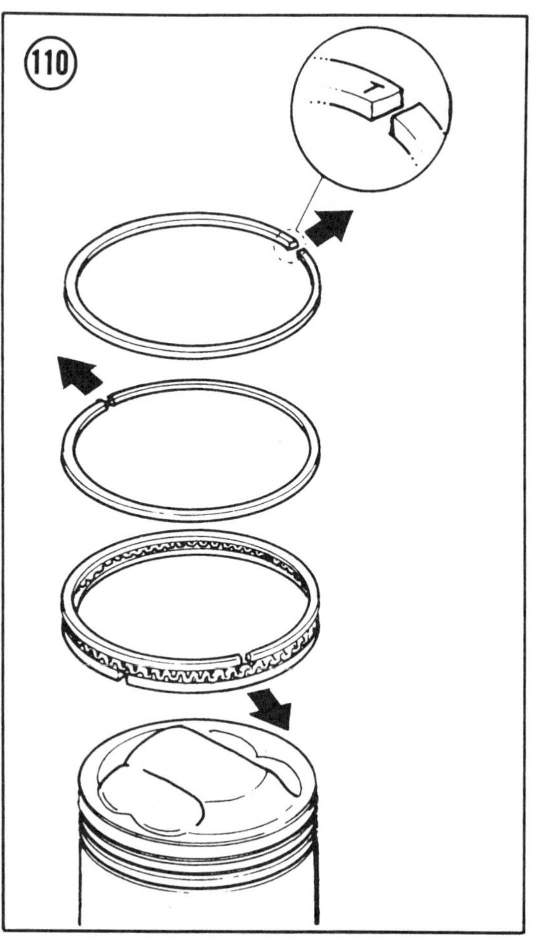

4. Remove the screws securing the ignition cover (**Figure 112**) and remove it.
5. Prior to removing the pulser generator assembly, make a mark on the base plate that lines up with the centerline of one of the attachment screws. This will assure correct ignition timing when the assembly is installed (providing it was correct prior to removal).
6. Remove the screws (A, **Figure 113**) securing the pulser generator assembly.
7. Carefully pull the electrical harness out along with the rubber grommet (B, **Figure 113**) from the crankcase.
8. Remove the pulser generator assembly.
9. Hold onto the outer hex spacer with a 15/16 in. box wrench and remove the inner bolt (**Figure 114**).

CAUTION

To avoid internal damage to the ignition advance unit, be sure to securely hold the hex spacer while removing the inner bolt.

10. Slide the ignition advance unit (**Figure 115**) off the thin shaft on the crankshaft.

NOTE

*If the ignition advance components have been separated assemble by aligning the raised tooth on the rotor with the "O" mark on the backing plate (**Figure 116**).*

11. When installing the ignition advance unit, index the pin on the backside of the advance unit into the slot in the end of the crankshaft (**Figure 117**).

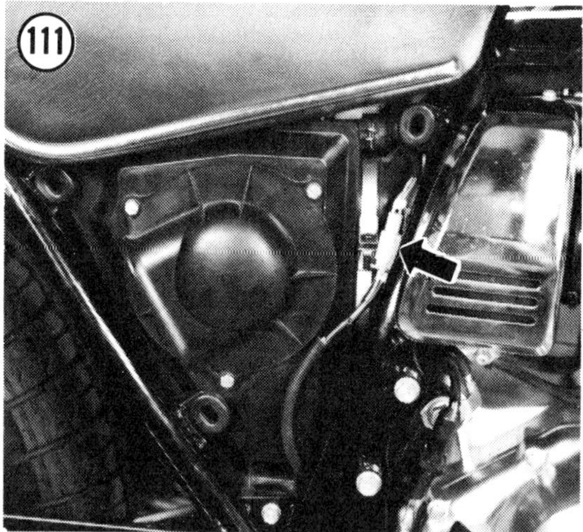

112
HONDA
MADE IN JAPAN

115

113
B
A
A
A

116

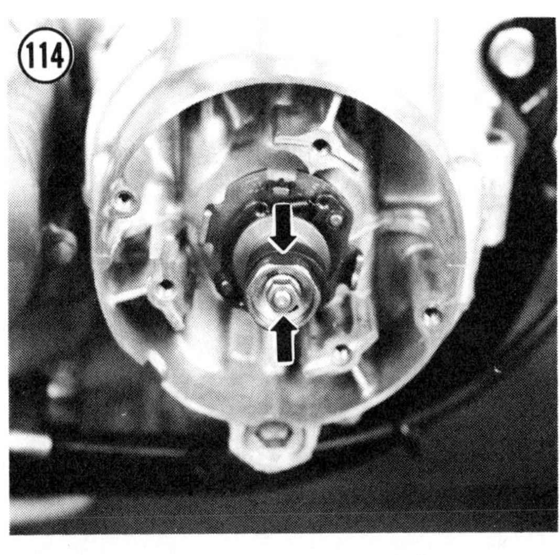
114

117

12. Hold the ignition advance unit in place. Align the notches in the hex spacer with the tangs on the advance unit and install the hex spacer (**Figure 118**).
13. Hold the hex spacer and install the inner bolt. Tighten the inner bolt to 6-7 ft.-lb. (8-12 N•m).

CAUTION
To avoid internal damage to the ignition advance unit, be sure to securely hold the hex spacer while installing the inner bolt.

14. Install the ignition pulser generator assembly aligning the mark made in Step 5 for preliminary ignition timing. Tighten the screw securely.
15. Route the electrical harness the same way it was. Make sure the rubber grommet is in place (B, **Figure 113**). Be sure to keep the harness away from the exhaust system.
16. Install the ignition cover.
17. Connect the pulser generator electrical connector containing 4 wires (2 yellow and 2 blue). Refer to **Figure 111**.
18. Connect the battery negative lead.
19. Install the seat and left-hand side cover.
20. Adjust the ignition timing as described under *Ignition Timing* in Chapter Three.

Testing/Inspection

For inspection of the ignition advance unit and test procedures for the ignition pulser, refer to *Ignition Advance Inspection* and *Ignition Pulser Testing* in Chapter Seven.

OIL PUMP

The oil pump is located on the left-hand side of the engine under the rear crankcase cover and can be removed with the engine in the frame.

Removal/Installation

1. Place the bike on the centerstand.
2. Drain the engine oil as described under *Changing Engine Oil and Filter* in Chapter Three.
3. Remove the exhaust system on the left-hand side. Refer to *Exhaust System Removal/Installation* in Chapter Six.

4. Remove the shift lever and the left-hand rear crankcase cover.
5. Disconnect the electrical wire from the oil pressure switch on top of the oil pump (**Figure 119**).
6. Remove the bolts (**Figure 120**) securing the oil pump to the crankcase and remove it.
7. Install the oil pump by reversing these removal steps, note the following.
8. Make sure the O-ring seals and collars are in place (**Figure 121**).
9. If the oil pump switch was removed, apply a liquid sealant to the threads prior to installation.
10. Refill the engine with the recommended type and quantity oil; refer to *Changing Engine Oil and Filter* in Chapter Three.

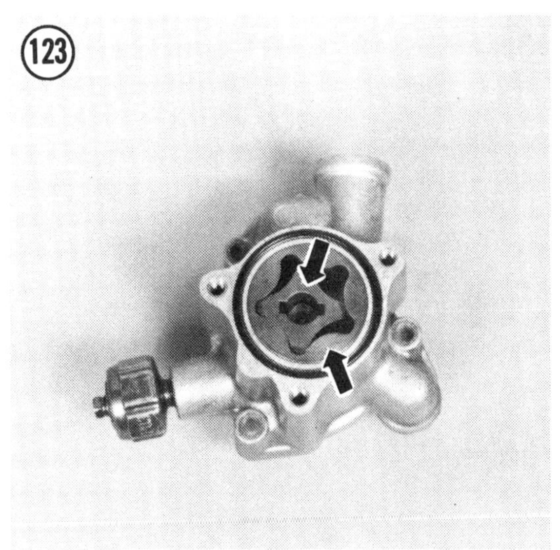

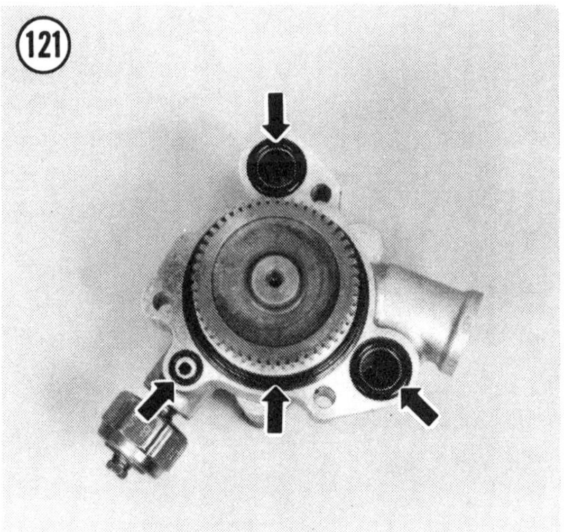

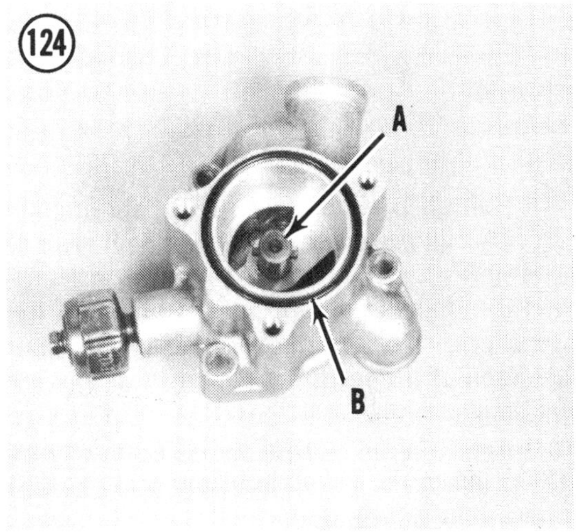

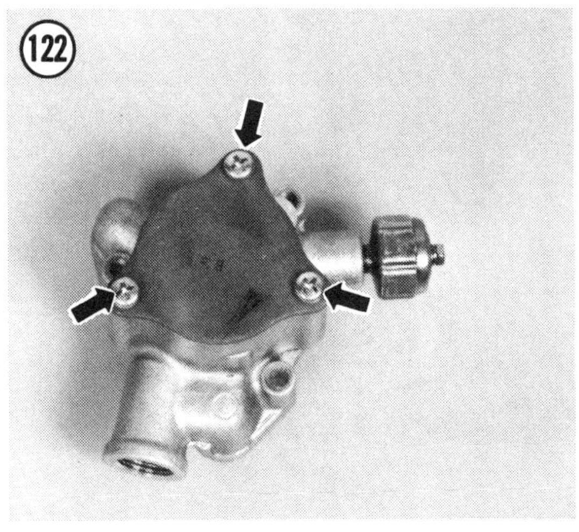

Disassembly/Inspection/Assembly

1. Inspect the outer body for cracks.
2. Remove the Phillips head screws (**Figure 122**) securing the pump cover to the body and remove the cover.
3. Remove the outer small O-rings and dowels (**Figure 121**).
4. Remove the inner and outer rotor (**Figure 123**). Inspect both parts for scratches and abrasions. Replace both parts if evidence of this is found.
5. Remove the dowel pin and push out the drive gear and shaft assembly (A, **Figure 124**).
6. Remove the large O-ring (B, **Figure 124**) from the oil pump body.

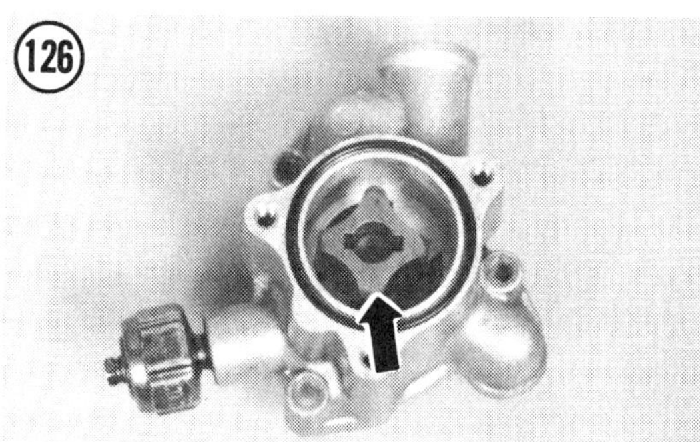

7. Clean all parts in solvent and thoroughly dry. Coat all parts with fresh engine oil prior to assembly.

8. Inspect the condition of the teeth on the drive gear. Replace the drive gear and shaft assembly if the teeth are damaged or any are missing.

9. Inspect the oil control orifice hole (**Figure 125**) next to the switch housing. Make sure it is clean and not clogged with dirt or oil sludge.

10. Install the large O-ring (B, **Figure 124**).

11. Install the drive gear and shaft and install the dowel pin (A, **Figure 124**). Center the dowel pin in the shaft.

12. Install the inner rotor (**Figure 126**) and outer rotor (A, **Figure 127**) into the oil pump body. Install both parts with the punch marks facing *up*. It is not necessary to align the 2 marks upon installation. Make sure the slot in the inner rotor aligns with the dowel pin.

13. Measure the clearance between the inner rotor tip and the outer rotor as shown in **Figure 128**. If the clearance is 0.006 in. (0.15 mm) or greater, replace the worn part.

14. Measure the clearance between the outer rotor and the oil pump body with a flat feeler gauge (**Figure 129**). If the clearance is 0.014

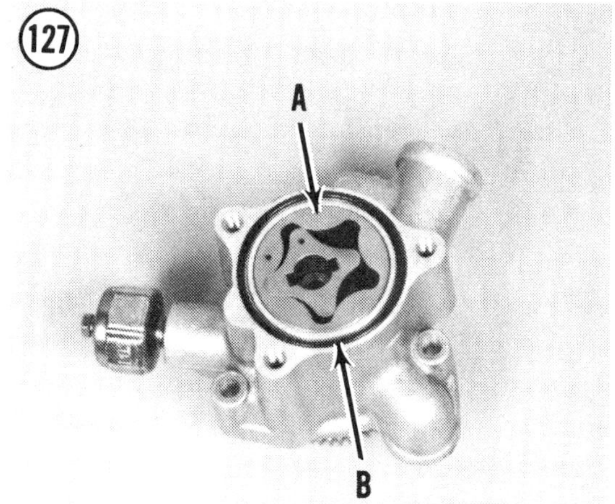

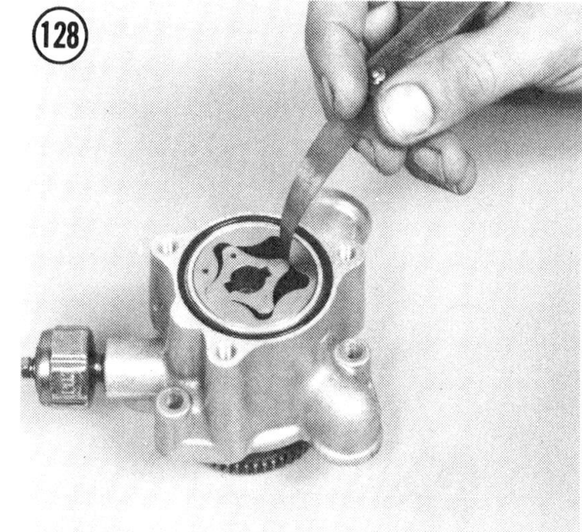

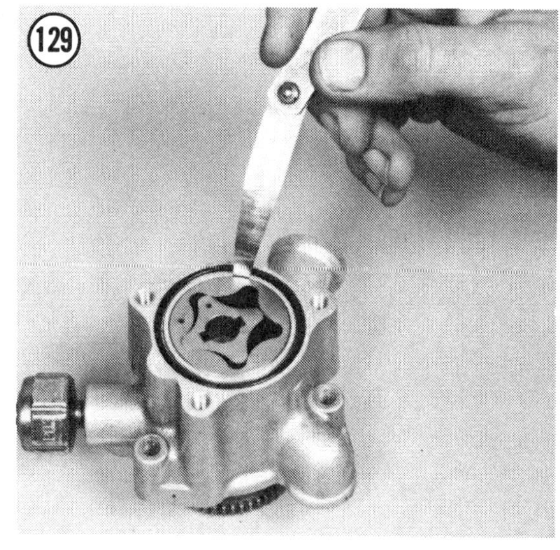

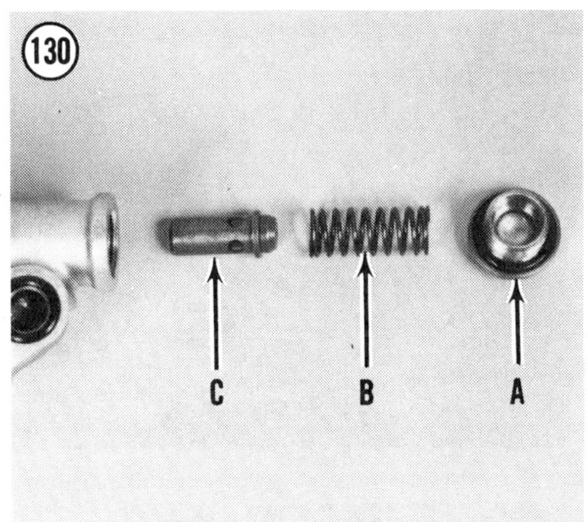

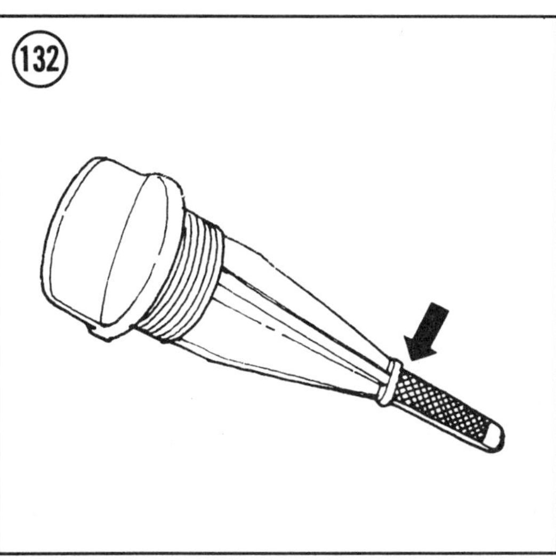

in. (0.35 mm) or greater, replace the worn part.

15. Inspect the rotor end clearance. Place a straightedge across the oil pump body and both rotors. Insert a flat feeler gauge between the rotors and the straightedge. If the clearance is 0.004 in. (0.1 mm) or greater replace either both rotors or the oil pump assembly.

16. Install the large O-ring (B, **Figure 127**) and install the cover and screws. Tighten the screws securely.

17. Install the outer small O-rings and dowels (**Figure 121**).

Oil Pump Pressure Relief Valve Disassembly/Assembly

1. Remove the sealing bolt and O-ring seal (A, **Figure 130**).
2. Remove the spring (B, **Figure 130**) and pressure relief valve (C, **Figure 130**).
3. Clean all parts in solvent and thoroughly dry. Make sure the holes in the relief valve are clear of any oil sludge buildup.
4. Inspect all components for wear or damage. If the spring is broken or the relief valve damaged replace all parts.
5. Make sure the O-ring seal is pliable and not deteriorating. Replace as necessary.
6. Coat all parts with assembly oil. Install the pressure relief valve with the long end in first. Insert the spring and install the sealing bolt with the O-ring seal. Tighten the bolt securely.

Oil Pump Pressure Test

If the oil pump output is doubtful, the following test can be performed.

1. Warm the engine up to normal operating temperature (176° F/80° C). Approximately 10-15 minutes of stop-and-go riding is usually sufficent to reach this temperature.
2. Turn the engine off.
3. Place the bike on the centerstand and make sure the bike is level.
4. Check to make sure the engine oil level is correct. Unscrew the oil fill cap/dipstick (**Figure 131**). Wipe it clean and set it on the case threads; do not screw it in. Remove and check the level. It must be between the 2 lines but not above the upper one (**Figure 132**).

Correct oil level if necessary, otherwise, the test reading will be incorrect.

WARNING

The exhaust system is ***hot****; protect yourself accordingly.*

5. Remove the gearshift lever and left-hand rear crankcase cover (**Figure 133**).
6. Disconnect the electrical wire from the oil pressure switch (A, **Figure 134**).
7. Unscrew the oil pressure switch from the oil pump (B, **Figure 134**).
8. Screw a portable oil pressure gauge into the oil pressure switch hole in the oil pump. Make sure the gauge attachment is screwed in tight or *hot oil* will spurt out, maybe on your left leg. Protect yourself accordingly.

NOTE

An oil pressure gauge can be purchased from a motorcycle or automotive supply house or from a dealer. The Honda part numbers are No. 07506-3000000 (Oil Pressure Gauge) and No. 07510-4220100 (Oil Pressure Gauge Attachment).

9. Start the engine and let it idle at 3,000 rpm. The standard pressure is 54-60 psi (3.8-4.2 kg/cm^2) at 3,000 rpm and at 176° F (80° C). Stop the engine.
10. If the oil pressure is less than specified, again check for correct oil level. If oil level is correct, remove the oil pan and check that the oil strainer screen is not partially clogged; refer to *Oil Strainer Removal/Installation* in this chapter.
11. If oil level is correct and the oil strainer screen is clean the oil pump must be rebuilt or replaced.
12. Disconnect the portable oil pump gauge and gauge attachment.
13. Apply a liquid sealant to the threads of the oil pressure switch and install it into the oil pump housing securely. Tighten the switch to 7-15 ft.-lb. (10-20 N•m). Attach the electrical wire to the top of the switch. This connection must be free of oil to make good electrical contact.
14. Start the engine and check that the oil pressure warning light goes out. If the light stays on, stop the engine immediately and determine the cause. Also make sure there is no oil leak around the pressure switch threads; tighten if necessary.

OIL STRAINER

Removal/Installation

The components can be removed with the engine in the frame. This procedure is shown with the engine removed for clarity.

1. Drain the engine oil as described under *Changing Engine Oil and Filter* in Chapter Three.
2. Remove the bolts securing the oil pan (**Figure 135**) and remove the oil pan.
3. Pull the oil strainer (A, **Figure 136**) from the lower crankcase.
4. Clean the strainer in solvent and thoroughly dry with compressed air.

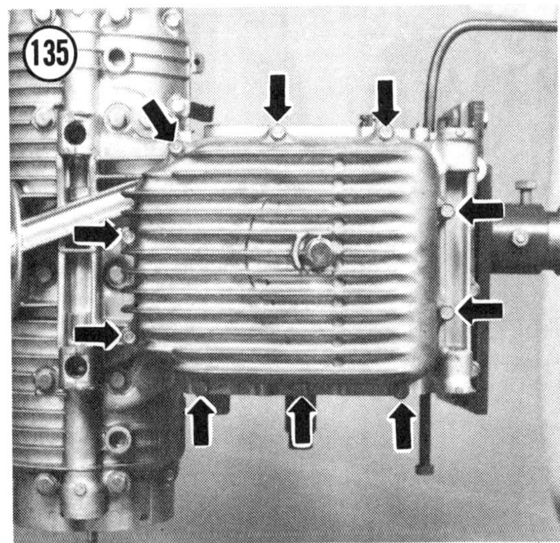

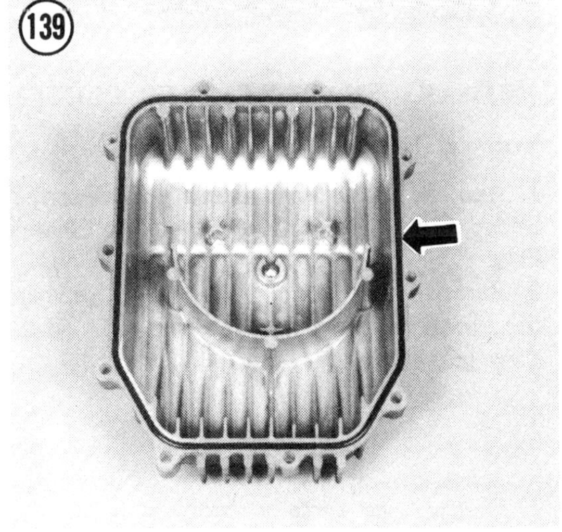

5. Inspect the condition of the screen (**Figure 137**). If the screen has any holes the strainer must be replaced.

6. Inspect the condition of the O-rings (**Figure 138**). Replace them if they show signs of deterioration or will not securely hold the strainer in position in the crankcase.

7. Install the strainer onto the crankcase making sure the strainer notch goes onto the web in the crankcase (B, **Figure 136**).

8. Check the condition of the oil pan rubber gasket (**Figure 139**); replace if necessary. Install the oil pan and tighten the bolts securely.

9. Fill the crankcase with the recommended type and quantity engine oil; refer to Chapter Three.

10. Start the engine and check for oil leaks.

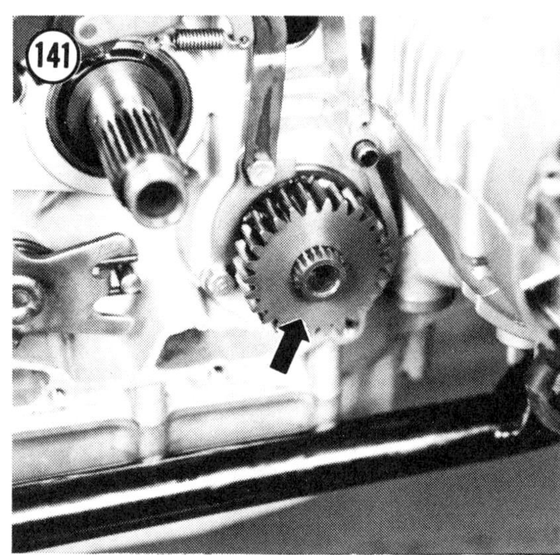

PRIMARY SHAFT/STARTER CLUTCH

Removal/Installation

1. Remove the clutch assembly as described under *Clutch Removal/Installation* in Chapter Five.
2. Remove the circlip (**Figure 140**) securing the primary shaft drive gear and slide off the drive gear (**Figure 141**).

NOTE
*It is not necessary to remove the outer circlip, inner circlip or thrust washer (A, **Figure 142**).*

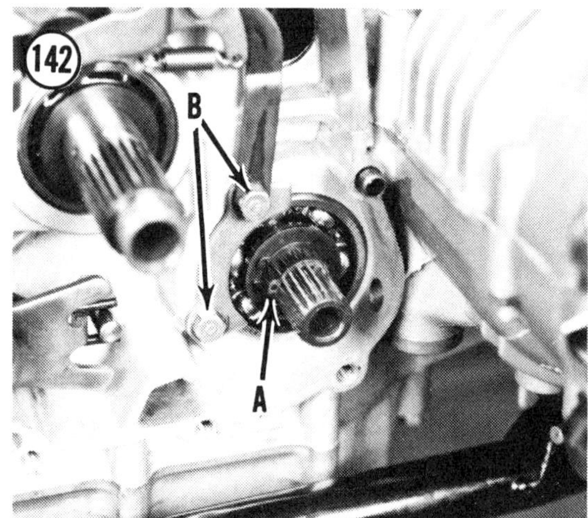

3. Remove the bolts (B, **Figure 142**) securing the bearing retainer and remove the bearing retainer.
4. Remove the engine from the frame as described under *Engine Removal/Installation* in this chapter.
5. Separate the crankcase as described under *Crankcase Disassembly* in this chapter.
6. This step requires the use of special tools. Onto the left-hand end of the primary shaft (**Figure 143**) attach the slide hammer shaft (Honda part No. 07936-3740100) and slide hammer weight (Honda part No. 07945-3000500). Withdraw the shaft from the left-hand side.
7. Lift up the damper/starter clutch assembly and primary drive chain (**Figure 144**).

146

8. Disengage the damper/starter clutch assembly from the primary drive chain and remove the damper assembly.
9. Install by engaging the damper/starter clutch assembly with the primary drive chain.
10. Pivot it down and insert the shaft from the left-hand side (**Figure 145**).
11. With a broad-tipped screwdriver press down on the lower run of the primary drive chain (**Figure 146**). This will relieve spring tension on the primary drive chain tensioner assembly.
12. Complete installation by tapping on the end of the primary drive shaft with a plastic or soft-faced hammer (**Figure 147**). Tap it in until it completely seats.
13. Install the bearing retainer, primary shaft drive gear and circlip (**Figures 142-149**).

Disassembly/Inspection/Assembly

Refer to **Figure 148** for this procedure.

Primary Shaft Damper Assembly

1. Slide off the spacer and needle bearing.
2. Slide off the primary shaft damper/starter clutch assembly (A, **Figure 149**) and the starter gear (B, **Figure 149**).
3. Inspect the condition of the internal splines (A, **Figure 150**) and the wide teeth on the sprocket (B, **Figure 150**). Replace as necessary.

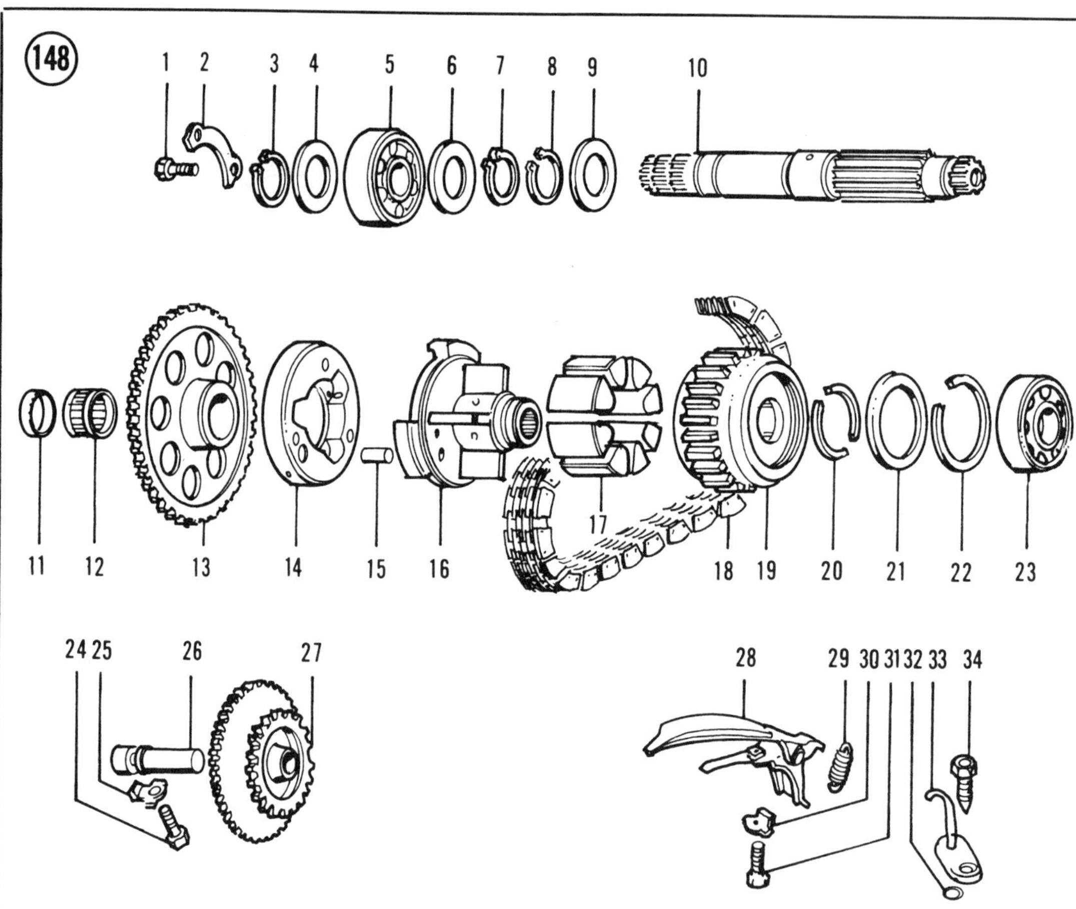

PRIMARY SHAFT/STARTER CLUTCH ASSEMBLY

1. Bolt
2. Bearing stopper plate
3. Circlip
4. Thrust washer
5. Bearing
6. Thrust washer
7. Circlip
8. Circlip
9. Thrust washer
10. Primary shaft
11. Spacer
12. Needle bearing
13. Starter drive gear
14. Starter clutch
15. Roller
16. Hub
17. Rubber dampers
18. Hy-Vo drive chain
19. Primary drive sprocket
20. Cotters
21. Collar
22. Circlip (52 mm)
23. Bearing
24. Bolt
25. Locking tab
26. Starter idle gear shaft
27. Starter idle gear
28. Tensioner assembly
29. Spring
30. Locking tab
31. Bolt
32. O-ring
33. Oil nozzle
34. Bolt

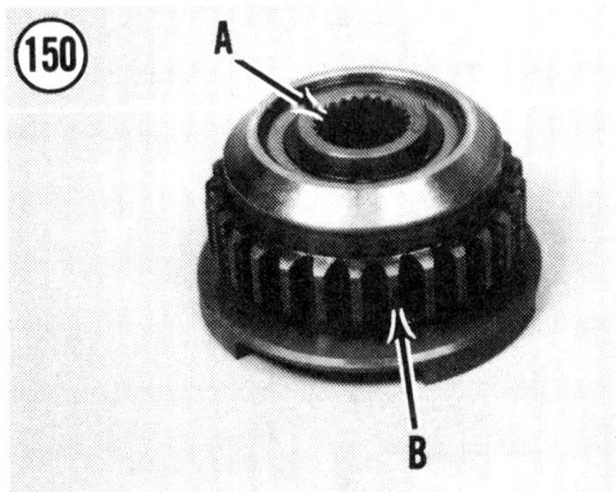

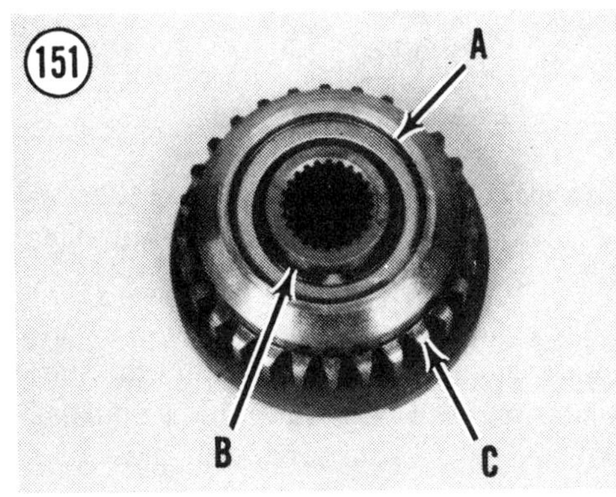

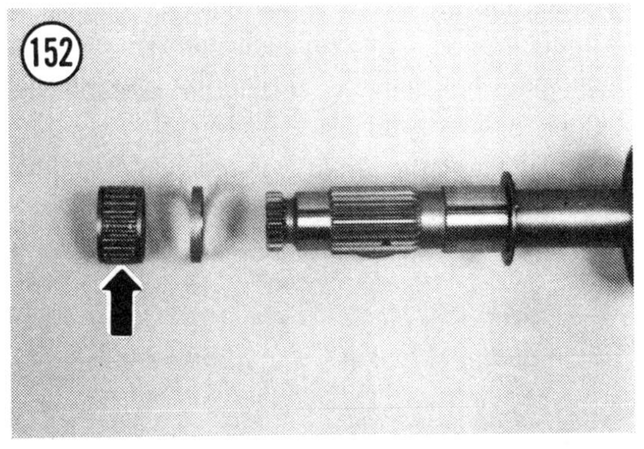

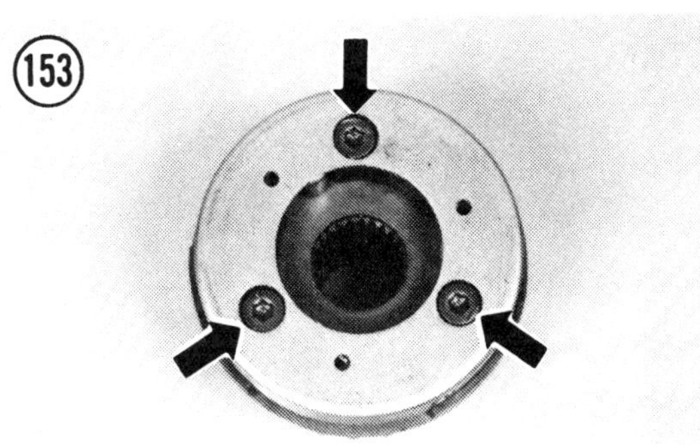

4. Remove the 52 mm inside circlip (A, **Figure 151**).

NOTE

This is not an easy task even with a good pair of circlip pliers. If you are unable to remove the circlip, take the assembly to a Honda dealer and have them remove it.

5. Remove the collar and cotters (B, **Figure 151**).
6. Slide off the primary drive sprocket (C, **Figure 151**).
7. Inspect the condition of the rubber dampers. Replace as a set if any are worn or starting to deteriorate.
8. Inspect the webs in the hub and drive sprocket for cracks. If any are found replace as necessary.
9. Assemble by reversing these removal steps. Make sure the large circlip is properly seated after installation.
10. Inspect the condition of the needle bearing (**Figure 152**). It must rotate freely with no signs of binding.

Starter Clutch Assembly

1. Slide off the spacer and needle bearing.
2. Slide off the primary shaft damper/starter clutch assembly (A, **Figure 149**) and the starter gear (B, **Figure 149**).
3. With the starter drive gear facing up, slightly rotate the gear *clockwise* while lifting up and remove the gear from the starter clutch assembly.
4. Remove the Torx bolts (**Figure 153**) securing the starter clutch to the damper assembly and remove the starter clutch assembly.

4

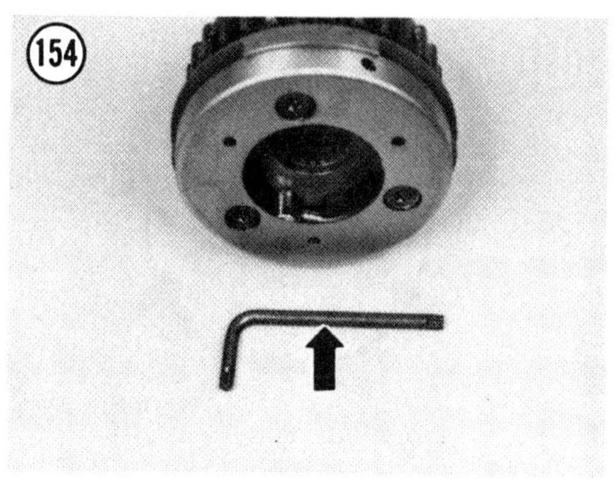

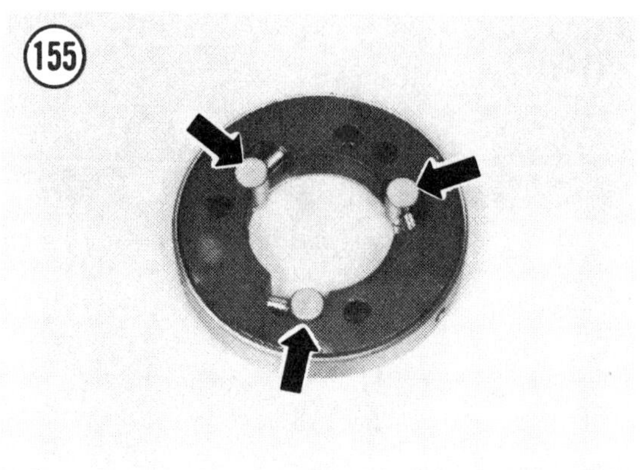

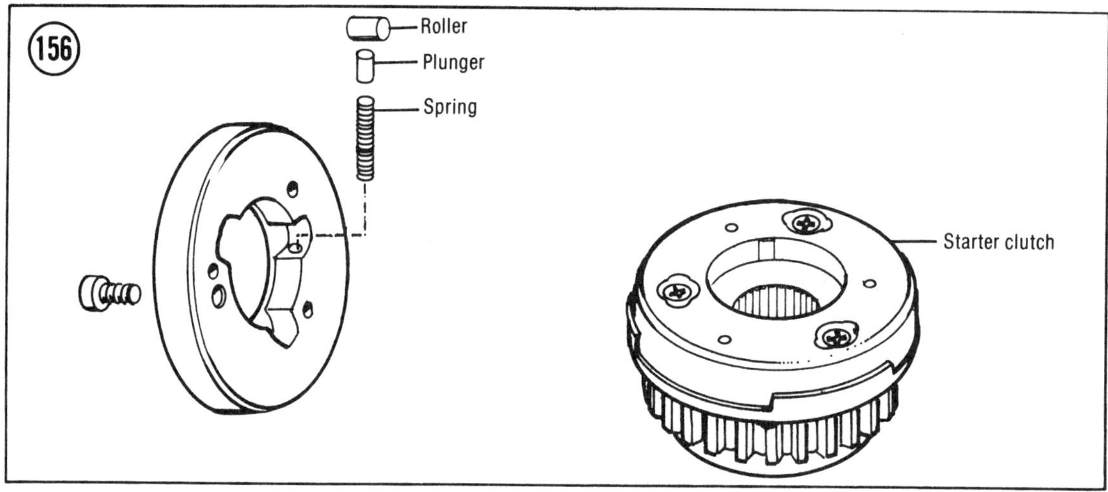

NOTE

*A special tool is required to remove the Torx bolts. Its size is T-27 and it is available in the Allen wrench configuration as shown in **Figure 154** or in a configuration similar to a screwdriver. These tools are manufactured by Proto and Apex and are available from most large hardware, automotive and motorcycle supply stores. Honda also has a removal tool—Torx driver bit (Honda part No. 07703-0010200) and the driver attachment (Honda part No. 07947-6710100).*

5. Inspect the condition of the rollers (**Figure 155**) in the starter clutch for uneven or excessive wear. Replace as a set if any are bad. Install the rollers, plungers and springs (**Figure 156**).

6. Inspect the condition of the teeth (A, **Figure 157**) on the starter drive gear. Check for chipped or missing teeth; replace if necessary.

7. Measure the outside diameter of the starter drive gear shoulder that rides within the starter clutch housing (B, **Figure 157**). If the dimension is 1.650 in. (41.93 mm) or less it must be replaced.

8. Reinstall the starter clutch onto the damper assembly. Apply Loctite 242 to the threads of the Torx bolts prior to installation. Install the Torx bolts and tighten to 9-12 ft.-lb. (12-16 N·m).

9. Install the startter drive gear into the starter clutch assembly.

NOTE

*With the starter drive gear facing up, slightly rotate the gear **counterclockwise** while installing it into the starter clutch assembly.*

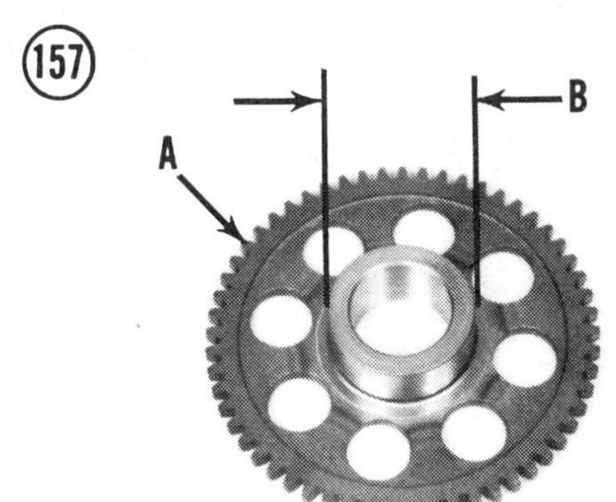

PRIMARY SHAFT TENSIONER

Removal/Inspection/Installation

1. Remove the engine from the frame as described under *Engine Removal/Installation* in this chapter.
2. Separate the crankcase as described under *Crankcase Disassembly* in this chapter.
3. Remove the primary shaft assembly as described under *Primary Shaft/Starter Clutch Removal/Installation* in this chapter.
4. Remove the crankshaft assembly as described under *Crankshaft Removal/Installation* in this chapter.
5. Inspect the condition of the Teflon coating on the contact surface of the tensioner slipper (**Figure 158**). If the surface is damaged or worn the tensioner assembly should be replaced.
6. Inspect the condition of the spring. If it is weak or distorted it must be replaced.
7. Straighten the tabs on the lockwasher and remove the bolt (**Figure 159**) securing the tensioner in place and remove the tensioner assembly.
8. Remove the bolt (**Figure 160**) securing the oil control nozzle and remove the nozzle.
9. Clean out the nozzle in solvent and blow out with compressed air. A lot of oil passes through this nozzle to lubricate the primary drive chain; make sure it is not clogged. If its condition is doubtful, replace it.
10. Install by reversing these removal steps; note the following.
11. Tighten the primary chain oil control nozzle to 6-9 ft.-lb. (8-12 N•m) and the bolt securing the primary chain tensioner to 7-10 ft.-lb. (10-14 N•m).

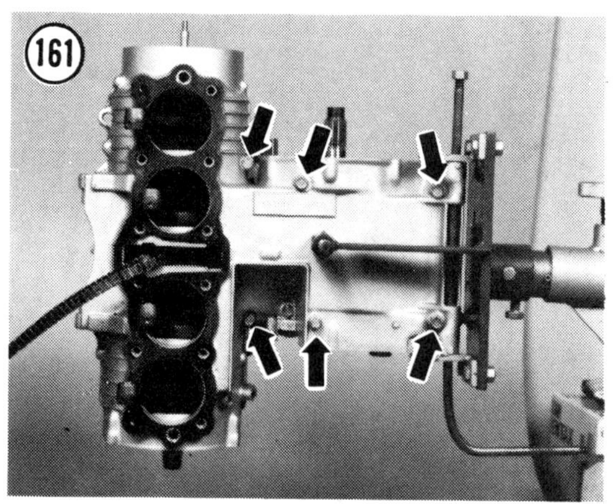

CRANKCASE

Service to the lower end requires that the crankcase be removed from the bike's frame.

Disassembly

1. Remove all exterior assemblies (cylinder head, cylinder block, pistons, oil pump, clutch, alternator, external shift mechanism) from the crankcase as described in this chapter and Chapter Five. Remove the engine from the frame as described under *Engine Removal/Installation* in this chapter.
2. Loosen the upper crankcase bolts (**Figure 161**) in 2-3 stages in a crisscross pattern to avoid warpage. Remove all bolts.
3. Turn the engine upside down and place it on wood blocks to protect the ends of the exposed connecting rods. Remove the bolts securing the oil pan (**Figure 162**) and remove the pan.
4. Remove the oil strainer (**Figure 163**).
5. Loosen the lower crankcase bolts (**Figure 164**) in 2-3 stages in a crisscross pattern to avoid warpage. Leave the 10 crankshaft bearing bolts for last; remove all bolts.

NOTE

Don't forget the one bolt ***(Figure 165)*** *within the oil pan recess area.*

6. Tap around the perimeter of the crankcase with a plastic mallet or soft-faced hammer—do not use a metal hammer as it will cause damage.
7. Pull the lower case half off of the upper case half. Don't lose the 2 locating dowels.

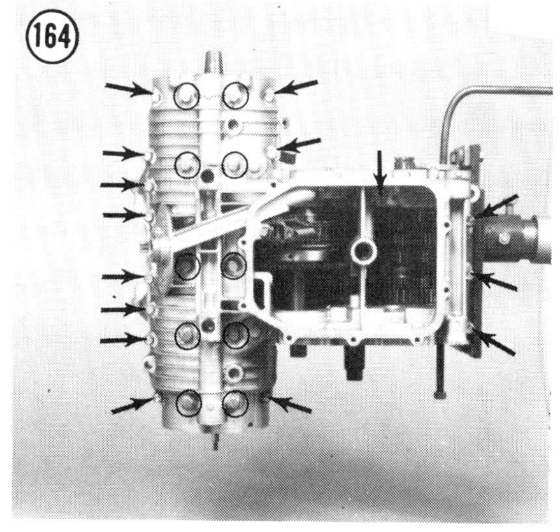

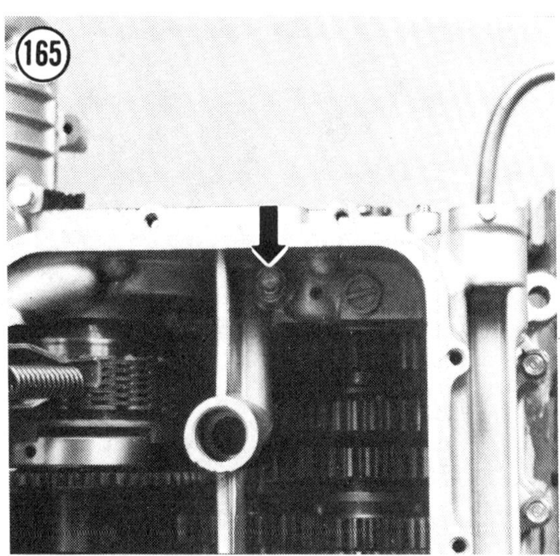

CAUTION

Honda's thin-walled crankcase castings are just that—thin. To avoid damage to the cases do not hammer on the projected walls that surround the clutch or alternator areas. These areas are easily damaged if stressed beyond what they are designed for.

CAUTION

If it is necessary to pry the crankcase apart, do it very carefully so that you do not mar the gasket surfaces. If you do, the cases will leak oil and must be replaced. They cannot be repaired.

8. Remove the transmission assemblies.
9. Remove the primary shaft assembly as described under *Primary Shaft/Starter Clutch Removal/Installation* in this chapter.
10. Lift out the crankshaft, cam drive chain and primary drive chain.
11. Remove the primary drive chain tensioner and oil nozzle as described under *Primary Shaft Tensioner Removal/Inspection/Installation* in this chapter.
12. Remove the shift drum and shift forks as described under *Gearshift Drum and Shift Fork Removal/Installation* in Chapter Five.
13. Staighten the locking tabs on the lockwasher and loosen the set bolt (**Figure 166**) securing the starter idle gear shaft in place. Push the shaft out and remove the idle gear.

14. Remove the crankshaft bearing inserts from the upper and lower crankcase halves. Mark the backside of the inserts with numbers "1," "2," "3" or "4" and "U" (upper) or "L" (lower). Start from the left-hand side with No. 1 and work across from left to right.

NOTE

The left-hand side refers to the engine as it sits in the bike frame—not as it sits on your workbench.

Inspection

1. Thoroughly clean the inside and outside of both crankcase halves with cleaning solvent. Dry with compressed air. Make sure there is no solvent residue left in the cases as it will contaminate the new engine oil.
2. Make sure all oil passages are clean (**Figure 167**). After a thorough cleaning, blow all passages clean with compressed air.
3. Check the crankcase for possible damage such as cracks, fractures or other damage. Especially check the front portion of the lower crankcase half as this area gets hit with "road trash" from the highway. The interior of both case halves must be free of gouges, burrs or any other damage that could cause an oil leak.

Assembly

1. Install the main bearing inserts in both the upper and lower crankcase halves. If reusing

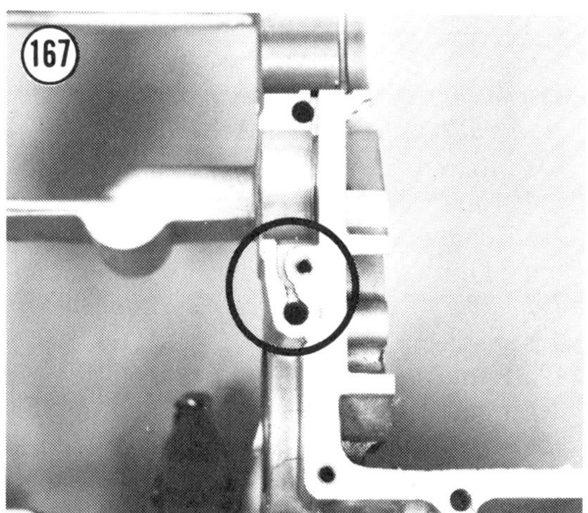

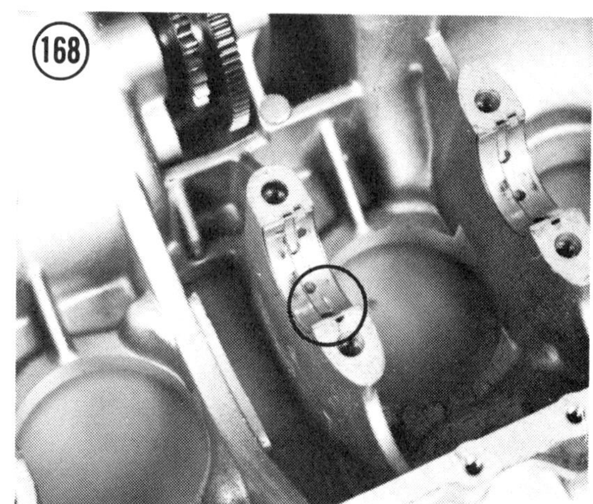

old bearing inserts, make sure they are installed in the same location. Refer to marks made in *Disassembly*, Step 13. Make sure they are locked in place (**Figure 168**).

2. Install the starter idle gear and shaft. Tighten the set bolt and bend up the locking tabs against the flats of the set bolt.
3. Install the shift drum and shift forks as described under *Gearshift Drum and Shift Fork Removal/Installation* in Chapter Five.
4. Install the primary drive chain tensioner and oil nozzle as described under *Primary Shaft Tensioner Removal/Inspection/Installation* in this chapter.
5. Apply molybdenum disulfide grease to all main bearing inserts and install the crankshaft, cam drive chain and primary drive chain into the lower crankcase half (**Figure 169**).

NOTE

*Make sure the oil seals **(Figure 170)** at both ends of the crankshaft are positioned in the crankcase groove correctly.*

6. Install the primary shaft assembly as described under *Primary Shaft/Starter Clutch Removal/Installation* in this chapter.
7. Set the upper crankcase upside down on wooden blocks. The blocks should be high enough to allow the cam drive chain and connecting rod ends to pass through the openings in the upper crankcase.
8. Install the locating dowels (**Figure 171**) into the upper crankcase half.
9. Make sure case half sealing surfaces are perfectly clean and dry.

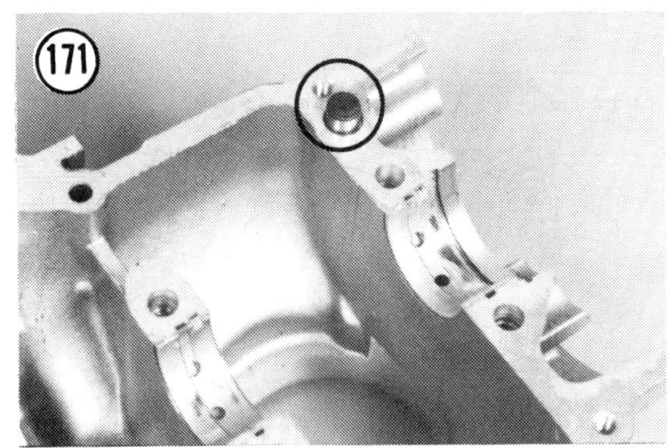

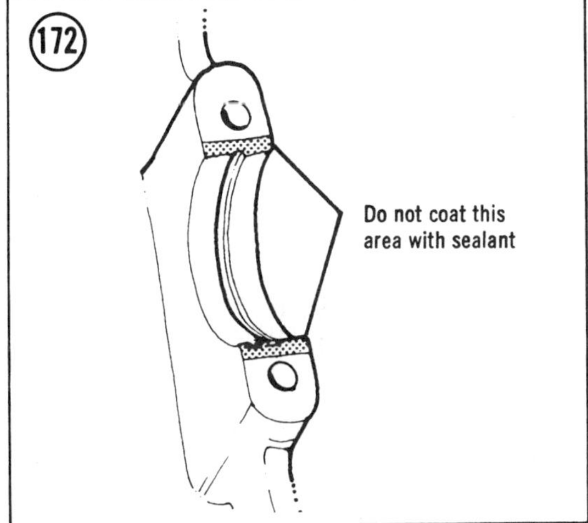

10. Apply a light coat of gasket sealer to the sealing surfaces of both case halves. Cover only flat surfaces, not curved bearing surfaces. Make the coating as thin as possible or the case can shift and hammer out the bearings. Do not apply sealant close to the edge of the bearing inserts (**Figure 172**) as it will restrict oil flow.

NOTE
*Use Gasgacinch Gasket Sealer, 4 Three Bond (**Figure 173**) or equivalent. When selecting an equivalent, avoid thick or hard setting materials.*

11. Into the upper crankcase half, install the transmission assemblies (**Figure 174**) as described under *Transmission Removal/Installation* in Chapter Five.

NOTE
The following step requires the aid of a helper—do not attempt this procedure by yourself.

12. Securely hold onto the crankshaft ends to hold the crankshaft into the lower crankcase. Carefully turn this assembly upside down and locate it onto the upper crankcase. Have the helper guide the connecting rods and cam drive chain through the openings in the upper crankcase half. Make sure the starter gears mesh properly.
13. After the lower crankcase is properly located, tap it into place with your hands until it completely seats. Then tap around the perimeter of the case half with a rubber or soft-faced hammer until it is completely seated.

CAUTION
Do not force the case halves together. Do not install any crankcase bolts until the crankcase sealing surfaces around the entire perimeter have seated completely.

14. Prior to installing the bolts, slowly spin the transmission shafts and shift the transmission through all 5 gears. Make sure there is no binding.
15. Apply engine oil to the threads of the 6 mm crankcase bolts and molybdenum disulfide grease to the threads and to the under side of the heads of the ten 8 mm bolts.

4

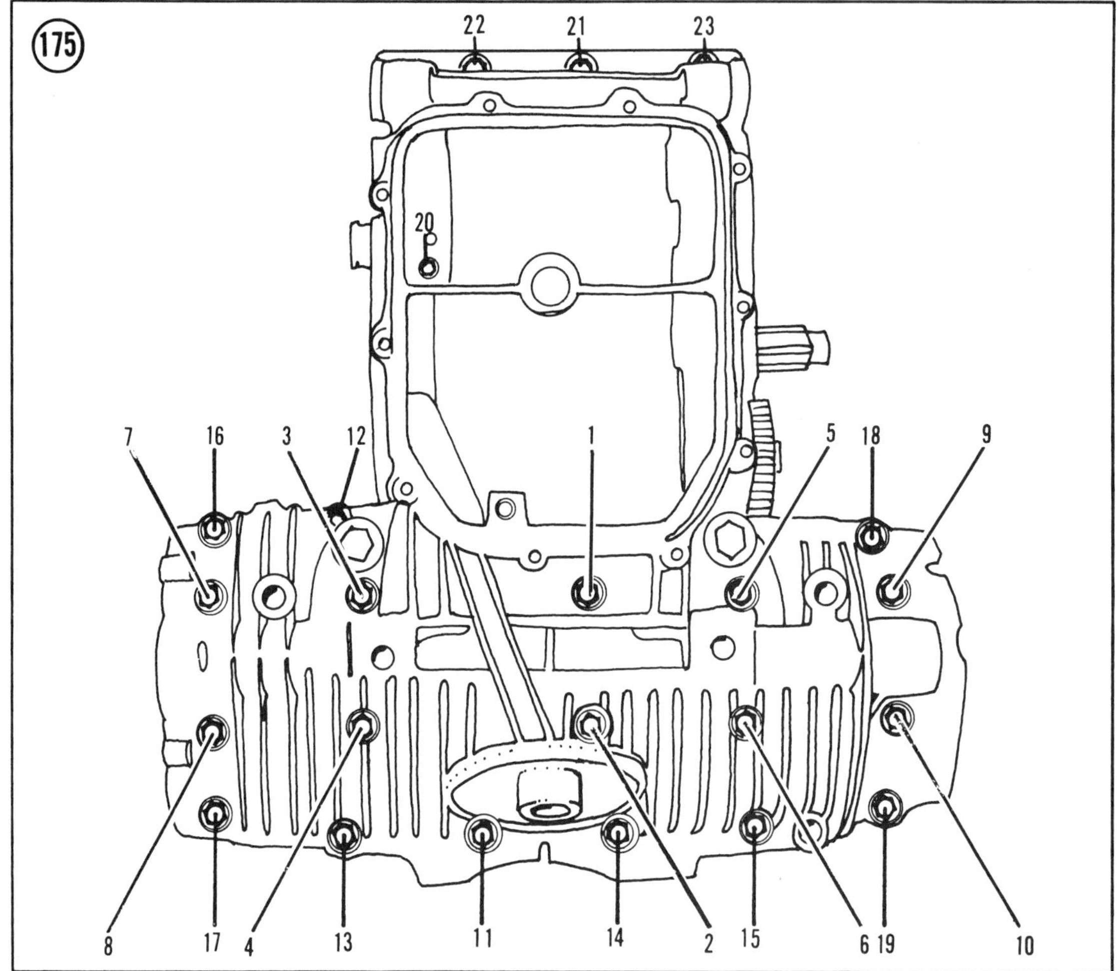

16. Install the lower crankcase bolts only finger-tight at this time.

17. Tighten all bolts in 2-3 steps in the torque sequence shown in **Figure 175**. Tighten the 8 mm bolts to 16-19 ft.-lb. (22-26 N•m) and the 6 mm bolts to 7-10 ft.-lb. (10-14 N•m).

18. Turn the crankcase assembly over and install the upper crankcase bolts. Tighten in 2-3 steps in a criss cross pattern to a final torque of 7-10 ft.-lb. (10-14 N•m).

19. Install all engine assemblies that were removed.

20. Install the engine as described under *Engine Removal/Installation* in this chapter.

21. Fill the crankcase with the recommended type and quantity engine oil. Refer to Chapter Three.

CRANKSHAFT AND CONNECTING RODS

Crankshaft Removal/Installation

1. Split the crankcases as described under *Crankcase Disassembly* in this chapter.
2. Remove the crankshaft assembly.

NOTE

Prior to disassembly, mark the rods and caps. Number them "1," "2," "3" and "4" starting from the left-hand side. The left-hand side refers to the engine sitting in the bike frame—not as it sits on your workbench.

3. Remove the connecting rods from the crankshaft. Mark the back of each bearing insert with its cylinder number and "U" (upper) or "L" (lower).

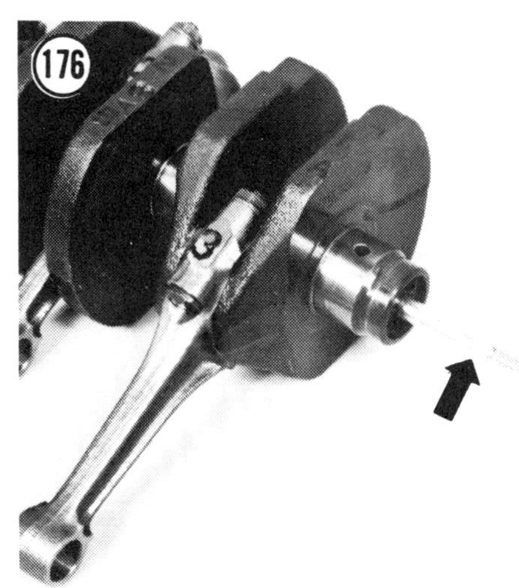

4. Install by reversing these removal steps, noting the following.
5. Install the bearing inserts into each connecting rod and cap. Make sure they are locked into place correctly.

NOTE
If the old bearing inserts are reused, be sure they are installed into their original positions; refer to Step 3.

6. Apply molybdenum disulfide grease to the bearing inserts, crankpins and connecting rod bolt threads. Install the connecting rods and rod caps. Tighten the rod cap nuts evenly in 2-3 steps to 17-20 ft.-lb. (24-28 N•m).
7. After all rod caps have been installed, rotate the crankshaft several times and check that the bearings are not too tight. Make sure there is no binding.

Crankshaft Inspection

1. Clean crankshaft thoroughly with solvent. Clean oil holes with rifle cleaning brushes; flush thoroughly with new solvent and dry with compressed air. Lightly oil all bearing journal surfaces immediately to prevent rust.
2. Carefully inspect each journal for scratches, ridges, scoring, nicks, etc. Very small nicks and scratches may be removed with crocus cloth. More serious damage must be removed by grinding—a job for a machine shop or dealer.
3. If the surface on all journals is satisfactory, take the crakshaft to a Honda dealer or machine shop. They can check for out-of-roundness, taper and wear on the bearing journals. They can also check crankshaft run-out which has a service limit of 0.002 in. (0.05 mm).
4. Inspect the condition of the threaded rod in the right-hand end of the crankshaft (**Figure 176**). If it is bent or damaged replace with a new one.
5. Inspect the condition of the sprocket teeth for the cam and primary drive chains. If damaged the crankshaft must be replaced.

Crankshaft Main Bearing and Journal Inspection

1. Check the inside and outside surfaces of the bearing inserts for wear, bluish tint (burned), flaking abrasion and scoring. If the bearings are good, they may be reused. If any insert is questionable, replace the entire set.
2. Measure the main bearing oil clearance. Clean the bearing surfaces of the crankshaft and the main bearing inserts.
3. Set the upper crankcase upside down on the workbench on wood blocks.
4. Install the existing main bearing inserts into the upper crankcase.
5. Install the crankshaft into the upper crankcase.
6. Place a strip of Plastigage material over each main bearing journal parallel to the crankshaft.

NOTE
Do not rotate the crankshaft while the Plastigage strips are in place.

7. Install the existing bearing inserts into the lower crankcase.
8. Carefully turn the lower crankcase over and install it onto the upper crankcase.
9. Apply oil to the threads of the 8 mm lower crankcase bolts. Tighten them in 2-3 steps in the torque sequence shown in **Figure 177**. Tighten to a final torque of 16-19 ft.-lb. (22-26 N•m).
10. Remove the 8 mm bolts in the reverse order of installation.

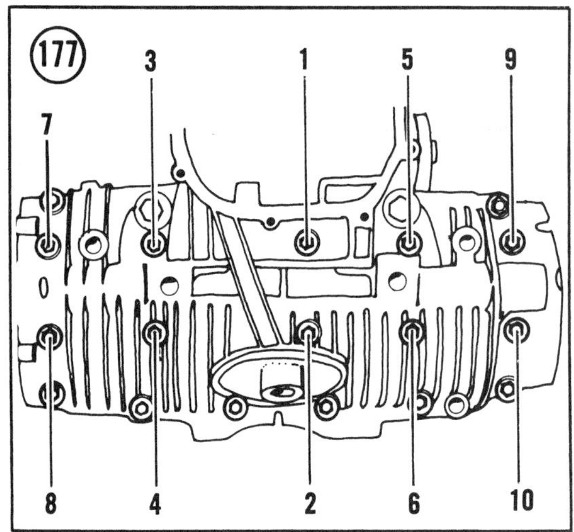

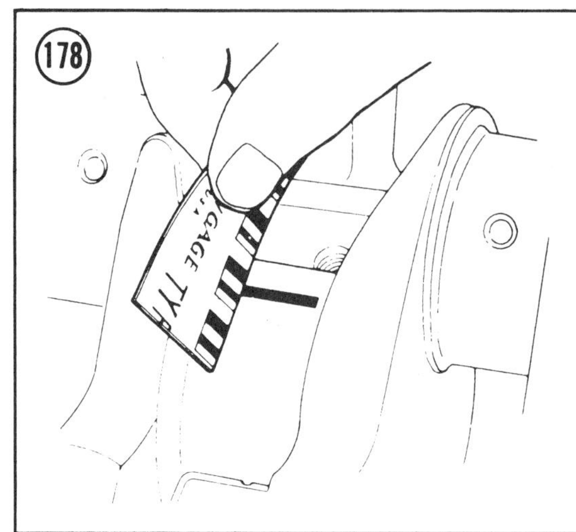

11. Carefully remove the lower crankcase and measure the width of the flattened Plastigage material following manufacturer's instructions. Measure both ends of the Plastigage strip (**Figure 178**). A difference of 0.001 in. (0.025 mm), or more, indicates a tapered journal. Confirm with a micrometer. New bearing oil clearance should be 0.0008-0.0019 in. (0.020-0.048 mm) with a service limit of 0.003 in. (0.08 mm). Remove the Plastigage strips from all bearing journals.

12. If the bearing clearance is greater than specified, use the following steps for new bearing selection.

13. The crankshaft main journals are marked with either number "1" or "2" (A, **Figure 179**). The upper rear portion of the upper crankcase is marked with a series of letters "A," "B" or "C" (**Figure 180**).

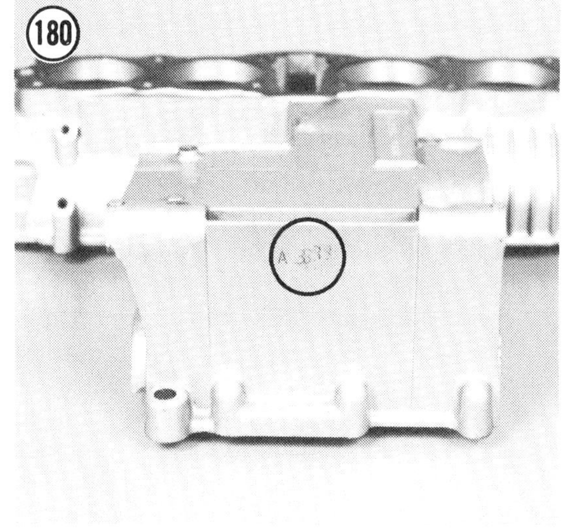

NOTE

The letter on the left-hand end relates to the bearing insert in the left-hand side and so on working across from left to right. Remember the left-hand side relates to the engine as it sits in the bike frame, not as it sits on your workbench.

14. Select new bearings by cross-referencing the main journal number (A, **Figure 179**) in the horizontal column of **Table 2** to the crankcase bearing letter (**Figure 180**) in the vertical column. Where the 2 columns intersect, the new bearing color is indicated. Always replace as a set of 10 at the same time.

15. After new bearings have been installed, recheck clearance by repeating this procedure.

Connecting Rod Removal/Installation

1. Split the crankcases as described under *Crankcase Disassembly* in this chapter.
2. Remove the crankshaft assembly.

NOTE

Prior to disassembly, mark the rods and caps. Number them "1," "2," "3" and "4" starting from the left-hand side. The left-hand side refers to the engine sitting in the bike frame—not as it sits on your workbench.

3. Remove the connecting rods from the crankshaft. Mark the back of each bearing insert with the cylinder number and "U" (upper) or "L" (lower).
4. Install by reversing these removal steps, note the following.
5. Install the bearing inserts into each connecting rod and cap. Make sure they are locked into place correctly.

NOTE

If the old bearing inserts are reused, be sure they are installed into their original positions; refer to Step 3.

6. Apply molybdenum disulfide grease to the bearing inserts, crankpins and connecting rod bolt threads. Install the connecting rods and rod caps. Tighten the cap nuts evenly in 2-3 steps to 17-20 ft.-lb. (24-28 N•m).
7. After all rod caps have been installed, rotate the crankshaft several times and check that the bearings are not too tight. Make sure there is no binding.

Connecting Rod Inspection

NOTE

Prior to disassembly, mark the rods and caps. Number them "1," "2," "3" and "4" starting from the left-hand side. The left-hand side refers to the engine sitting in the bike frame—not as it sits on your workbench.

1. Remove the connecting rods from the crankshaft if not already removed.
2. Clean the connecting rods and inserts in solvent and dry with compressed air.
3. Carefully inspect each rod journal on the crankshaft for scratches, ridges, scoring, nicks, etc. Very small nicks and scratches may be removed with crocus cloth. More serious damage must be removed by grinding—a job for a machine shop or dealer.
4. If the surface on all journals is satisfactory, take the crankshaft to a dealer or machine shop. They can check for out-of-roundness, taper and wear on the rod bearing journals.

4

Connecting Rod Bearing and Journal Inspection

1. Check the inside and outside surfaces of the bearing inserts for wear, bluish tint (burned), flaking abrasion and scoring. If the bearings are good, they may be reused. If any insert is questionable, replace the entire set.
2. Clean the rod bearing surfaces of the crankshaft and the rod bearing inserts and measure the rod bearing oil clearance.
3. Place a strip of Plastigage material over each rod bearing journal parallel to the crankshaft.

NOTE

Do not rotate the crankshaft while the Plastigage strips are in place.

4. Install the rod cap and tighten the nuts to 17-20 ft.-lb. (24-28 N•m).
5. Remove the rod cap and measure the width of the flattened Plastigage material following manufacturer's instructions. Measure both ends of the Plastigage strip. A difference of 0.001 in. (0.025 mm), or more, indicates a tapered journal. Confirm with a micrometer. New bearing oil clearance should be 0.0007-0.0019 in. (0.018-0.047 mm) and the service limit is 0.003 in. (0.08 mm). Remove the Plastigage strip.
6. If the rod bearing clearance is greater than specified, use the following steps for new bearing selection.
7. The crankshaft rod journals are marked with either letter "A" or "B" (B, **Figure 179**) on the counterbalance weights. The

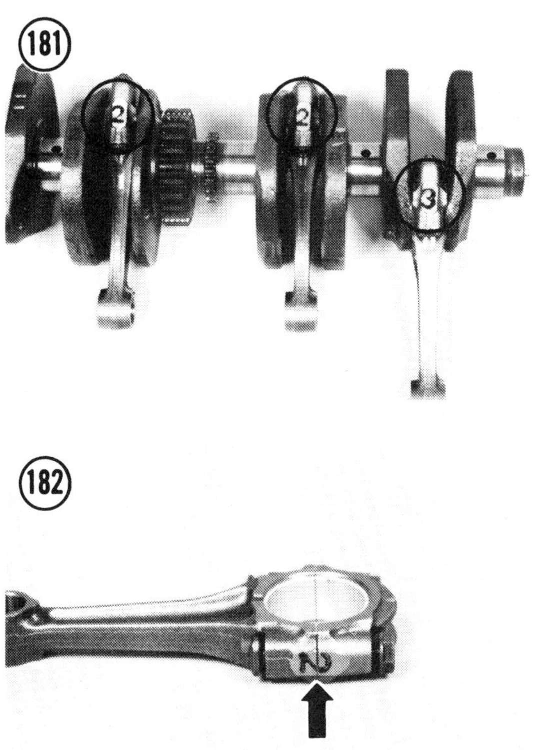

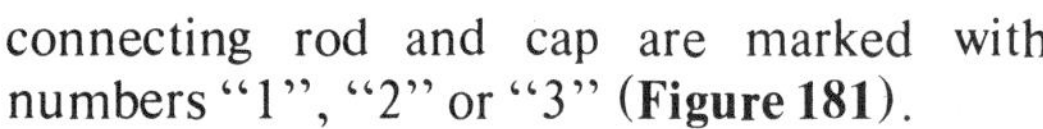

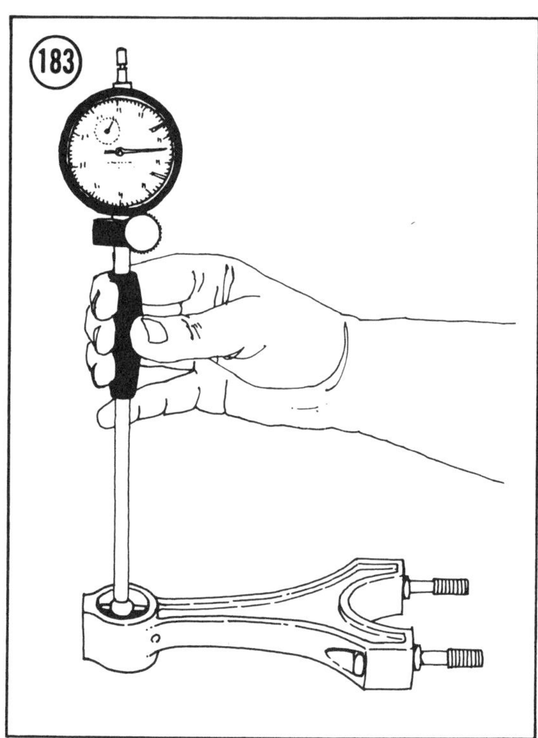

connecting rod and cap are marked with numbers "1", "2" or "3" (**Figure 181**).

8. Select new bearings by cross-referencing the rod journal letter (B, **Figure 179**) in the horizontal column of **Table 3** to the rod bearing number (**Figure 182**) in the vertical column. Where the 2 columns intersect, the new bearing color is indicated.

9. After new bearings have been installed, recheck clearance by repeating this procedure.

10. Repeat Steps 3-8 for the other 3 cylinders.

11. Measure the inside diameter of the small end of the connecting rods with an inside dial gauge (**Figure 183**). Check dimension given in **Table 1** at the end of the chapter; replace the rod as necessary.

12. Install the bearing inserts into each connecting rod and cap. Make sure they are locked into place correctly.

NOTE

If the old bearing inserts are reused, be sure they are installed into their original positions; refer to ***Connecting Rod Removal/Installation****; Step 3.*

13. Apply molybdenum disulfide grease to the bearing inserts, crankpins and connecting rod bolt threads. Install the connecting rods and rod caps. Tighten the cap nuts evenly in 2-3 steps to 17-20 ft.-lb. (24-28 N•m).

14. After all rod caps have been installed, rotate the crankshaft several times and check that the bearings are not too tight. Make sure there is no binding.

CAMSHAFT AND PRIMARY CHAIN INSPECTION

Inspection

1. Split the crankcase and remove the crankshaft. Refer to *Crankcase Disassembly* in this chapter.

2. Inspect the condition of the links on both the cam and primary chains (**Figure 184**).

3. Place the cam chain onto the sprocket on the crankshaft and the cam drive sprocket. Attach a scale (a portable fish scale will do) and apply 29 lb. (13 kg) of tension on the components. Measure the distance between the 2 sprockets as shown in **Figure 185**. Replace the chain if the length exceeds the service wear limit of 7.34 in. (186.4 mm).

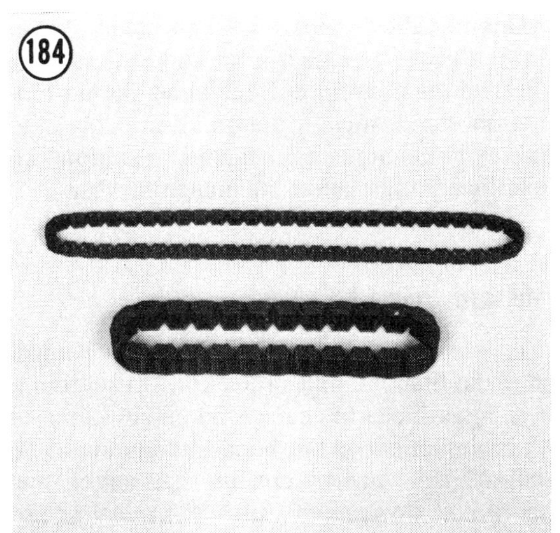

4. Place the primary chain onto the sprocket on the crankshaft and the primary drive sprocket. Attach a scale (a portable fish scale will do) and apply 71 lbs. (32 kg) of tension on the components. Measure the distance between the 2 sprockets as shown in **Figure 186**. Replace the chain if the length exceeds the service wear limit of 4.55 in. (115.5 mm).

BREAK-IN PROCEDURE

If the rings were replaced, new pistons installed, the cylinders rebored or honed or major lower end work performed, the engine should be broken in just as though it were new. The performance and service life of the engine depends greatly on a careful and sensible break-in.

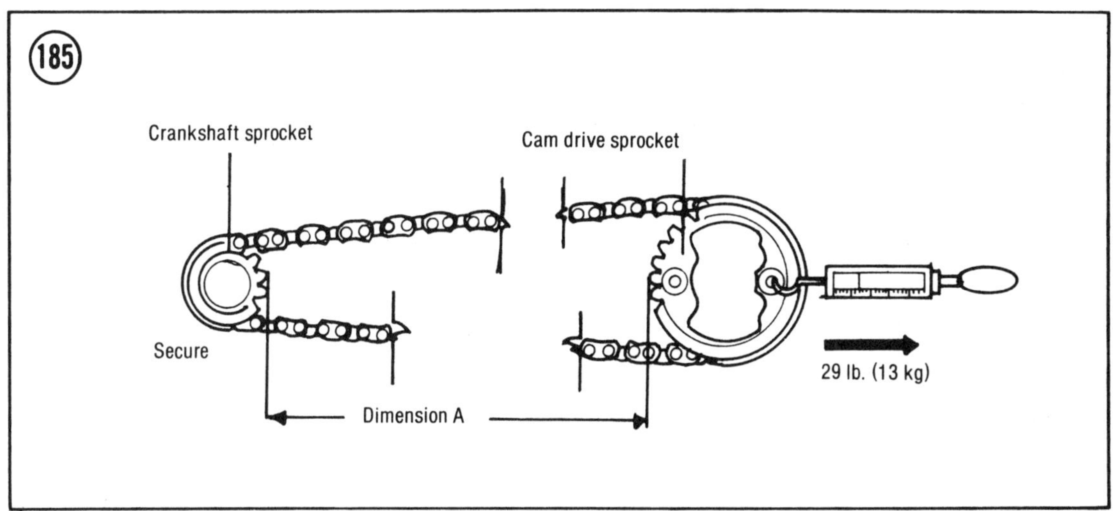

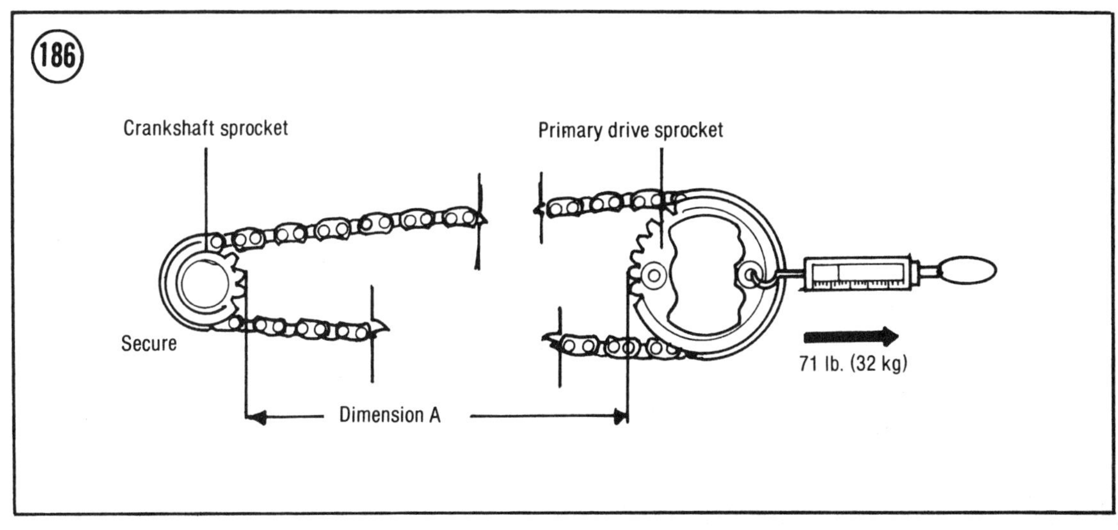

For the first 100 miles (805 km), no more than one-third throttle should be used and speed should be varied as much as possible within the one-third throttle limit. Prolonged steady running at one speed, no matter how moderate, is to be avoided as well as hard acceleration.

Following the *500 Mile (805 km) Service* described in this chapter more throttle should not be used until the motorcycle has covered at least 1,000 miles (1,601 km) and then it should be limited to short bursts of speed until 1,500 miles (2,414 km) have been logged.

The mono-grade oils recommended for break-in and normal use provide a better bedding pattern for rings and cylinders than do multi-grade oils. As a result, piston ring and cylinder bore life are greatly increased. During this period, oil consumption will be higher than normal. It is therefore important to frequently check and correct oil level. At no time, during the break-in or later, should the oil level be allowed to drop below the bottom line on the dipstick; if the oil level is low, the oil will become overheated resulting in insufficient lubrication and increased wear.

500 Mile (805 km) Service

It is essential that oil and filter be changed after the first 500 miles (805 km). In addition, it is a good idea to change the oil and filter at the completion of the break-in (about 1,500 miles/2,414 km) to ensure that all of the particles produced during break-in are removed from the lubrication system. The small added expense may be considered a smart investment that will pay off in increased engine life.

TABLE 1 ENGINE SPECIFICATIONS

Item	Specifications	Wear Limit
General		
Type	4-Stroke, air-cooled, SOHC	
Number of cylinders	4	
Bore and stroke	2.354 X 2.197 in. (59.8 X 55.8 mm)	
Displacement	38.2 cu. in. (627 cc)	
Compression ratio	9.0 to 1	
Compression pressure	170 +/- 28 psi (12.0 +/- 2.0 kg/cm^2)	
Lubrication	Wet sump	
Engine weight	156.6 lb. (71 kg)	
Cylinders		
Bore	2.3543-2.3547 in. (59.800-59.810 mm)	2.358 in.(59.90 mm)
Out of round	—	0.002 in. (0.05 mm)
Piston/cylinder clearance	—	0.004 in. (0.10 mm)
Pistons		
Diameter	2.353-2.354 in. (59.77-59.79 mm)	2.348 in.(59.65 mm)
Clearance in bore	—	0.004 in. (0.10 mm)
Piston pin bore	0.5906-0.5909 in. (15.002-15.008 mm)	0.594 in. (15.08 mm)
Piston pin outer diameter	0.5903-0.5906 in. (14.994-15.000 mm)	0.590 in. (14.98 mm)
Piston Rings		
Number per piston		
Compression	2	
Oil control	1	
Ring end gap		
Top and second	0.004-0.012 in. (0.10-0.30 mm)	0.028 in. (0.7 mm)
Oil (side rail)	0.012-0.035 in. (0.3-0.9 mm)	0.043 in. (1.1 mm)
Ring side clearance		
Top and second	0.0006-0.0018 in. (0.015-0.045 mm)	0.006 in. (0.15 mm)
Connecting Rod		
Small end inner diameter	0.5912-0.5919 in (15.016-15.034 mm)	0.593 in. (15.07 mm)
Crankshaft		
Runout	—	0.002 in. (0.05 mm)
Main bearing oil clearance	0.0008-0.0019 in. (0.020-0.048 mm)	0.003 in. (0.08 mm)

(continued)

TABLE 1 ENGINE SPECIFICATIONS (continued)

Item	Specifications	Wear Limit
Connecting rod oil clearance	0.0007-0.0019 in. (0.018-0.047 mm)	0.003 in. (0.08 mm)
Connecting rod big end side clearance	0.005-0.011 in. (0.12-0.27 mm)	0.014 in. (0.35 mm)
Camshaft		
Valve Timing		
Intake valve		
Opens	5° (BTDC) at 1 mm lift 58° (BTDC) at 0 lift	
Closes	35° (ABDC) at 1 mm lift 127° (ABDC) at 0 lift	
Exhaust valve		
Opens	40° (BBDC) at 1 mm lift 121° (BBDC) at 0 lift	
Closes	5° (ATDC) at 1 mm lift 65° (ATDC) at 0 lift	
Cam lobe height		
Intake	1.4026-1.4089 in. (35.627-35.787 mm)	1.40 in. (35.6 mm)
Exhaust	1.3903-1.3966 in. (35.314-35.474 mm)	1.39 in. (35.3 mm)
Runout	—	0.004 in. (0.1 mm)
Oil clearance	0.0063-0.0080 in. **(0.160-0.202 mm)**	0.008 in. (0.21 mm) 0.004 in. (0.1 mm)
End clearance	0.0013-0.0020 in. **(0.035-0.050 mm)**	
Camshaft chain length	7.279-7.280 in. (184.87-184.90 mm)	7.34 in. (186.4 mm)
Valves		
Valve stem outer diameter		
Intake	0.2156-0.2161 in. (5.475-5.490 mm)	0.215 in. (5.47 mm)
Exhaust	0.2148-0.2154 in. (5.455-5.470 mm)	0.214 in. (5.54 mm)
Valve guide inner diameter		
Intake and exhaust	0.2165-0.2171 in. (5.500-5.515 mm)	0.219 in. (5.55 mm)
Stem to guide clearance		
Intake	0.0004-0.0016 in. (0.010-0.040 mm)	0.003 in. (0.08 mm)
Exhaust	0.0012-0.0020 in. (0.030-0.050 mm)	0.004 in. (0.10 mm)
Valve seat width		
Intake and exhaust	0.05 in. (1.2 mm)	0.06 in. (1.5 mm)
Valve length		
Intake	3.55 in. (90.2 mm)	3.53 in. (89.7 mm)
Exhaust	3.49 in. (88.7 mm)	3.47 in. (88.0 mm)
Valve Springs		
Free length		
Inner	1.54 in. (39.2 mm)	1.49 in. (37.9 mm)
Outer	1.77 in. (44.8 mm)	1.70 in. (43.3 mm)
Rocker Arm Assembly		
Rocker arm bore I.D.	0.4724-0.4731 in. (12.000-12.018 mm)	0.474 in. (12.05 mm)
Rocker arm shaft O.D.	0.4714-0.4718 in. (11.973-11.984 mm)	0.0470 in. (11.94 mm)

(continued)

TABLE 1 ENGINE SPECIFICATIONS (continued)

Item	Specifications	Wear Limit
Cylinder Head Warpage	4.494-4.504 in.	0.010 in.(0.25 mm)
Primary chain length	(114.15-114.40 mm)	4.55 in. (115.5 mm)
Oil Pump		
Inner to outer rotor tip clearance	—	0.006 in. (0.15 mm)
Outer rotor to body clearance	—	0.014 in. (0.35 mm)
End clearance to body	—	0.004 in. (0.1 mm)

TABLE 2 MAIN JOURNAL BEARING SELECTION

	Main journal OD size code number and dimension	
	Number 1 1.2988-1.2992 in. (32.990-33.000 mm)	Number 2 1.2944-1.2988 in. (32.880-32.990 mm)
Crankcase ID code letter and dimension		
Letter A 1.4173-1.4176 in (36.000-36.008 mm)	Yellow (D)	Green (C)
Letter B 1.4176-1.4179 in. (36.008-36.016 mm)	Green (C)	Brown (B)
Letter C 1.4179-1.4183 in. (36.016-36.024 mm)	Brown (B)	Black (A)

TABLE 3 CONNECTING ROD BEARING SELECTION

	Crankpin journal OD size code letter and dimension	
	Letter A 1.3777-1.3782 in. (34.996-35.006 mm)	Letter B 1.3774-1.3777 in. (34.986-34.996 mm)
Connecting rod ID code number and dimension		
Number 1 1.4960-1.4963 in. (38.000-38.007 mm)	Yellow (D)	Green (C)
Number 2 1.4963-1.4966 in. (38.007-38.014 mm)	Green (C)	Brown (B)
Number 3 1.4966-1.4969 in. (38.014-38.021 mm)	Brown (B)	Black (A)

Table 4 ENGINE TORQUE SPECIFICATIONS

Item	Foot-pounds (ft.-lb.)	Newton meters (N•m)
Engine mounting bolts		
8 mm flange bolt	19-23	26-32
10 mm flange bolt	22-29	30-40
12 mm flange bolt	58-72	80-100
Cylinder head cover, breather cover and tachometer driven gear housing	6-9	8-12
Valve adjusting locknut	9-12	12-16
Rocker arm cotter pin	7-10	10-14
Rocker arm shaf cap bolt	6-9	8-12
Cylinder head bolt (*)		
6 mm	7-10	10-14
8 mm	17-22	24-30
Spark plug	9-12	12-16
Camshaft sprocket bolts (**)	16-19	22-26
Cam chain tensioner bolt	7-10	10-14
Crankcase bolts (*)		
6 mm	7-10	10-14
8 mm	16-19	22-26
Connecting rod cap nuts	17-20	24-28
Alternator bolt	36-43	50-60
Starter clutch assembly bolts (**)	9-12	12-16
Oil pressure switch (***)	7-15	10-20
Primary chain tensioner base bolt	7-10	10-14
Primary chain oil nozzle bolt	6-9	8-12

(*) Apply molybdenum disulfide grease to the threads prior to installation.

(**) Apply Loctite 242 to the threads prior to installation.

(***) Apply liquid sealant to threads prior to installation.

CHAPTER FIVE

CLUTCH AND TRANSMISSION

5

CLUTCH

The clutch used on the Honda CB650 is a wet multiplate type immersed in the oil supply it shares with the transmission and engine. The clutch center is splined to the transmission main shaft and the clutch outer housing can rotate freely on the main shaft. The clutch outer housing is geared to the primary shaft.

The clutch release mechanism is mounted within the clutch cover. The mechanism consists of a lifter shaft, operated by the clutch cable, and an adjusting arm. Pulling the clutch lever and cable pivots the lifter shaft which in turn raises the adjusting arm. The arm pushes in on the lifter guide and the lifter plate disengages the clutch mechanism.

The clutch can be removed while the engine is in the frame.

Refer to **Table 1** for all clutch specifications. **Tables 1-3** are located at the end of this chapter.

Figure 1 shows the clutch assembly and **Figure 2** shows the release mechanism.

Removal/Disassembly

1. Drain the engine oil as described under *Changing Engine Oil and Filter* in Chapter Three.

2. Place the bike on the centerstand or place a milk crate or wood block(s) under the engine or frame to support the bike securely.

3. Slacken the clutch cable at the hand lever (**Figure 3**) and remove the clutch cable.

4. At the clutch mechanism, loosen the locknut (A, **Figure 4**) and remove the clutch cable from the lifter shaft lever.

5. Remove the rear brake lever (B, **Figure 4**).

NOTE
Steps 6 through 12 are shown with the engine partially disassembled. It is not necessary to do so for clutch removal and disassembly.

6. Remove the screws securing the clutch cover (**Figure 5**) and remove the cover and gasket. Remove and save the 2 locating dowels.

7. Remove the lifter guide, bearing and bearing retainer (**Figure 6**).

8. Using a crisscross pattern remove the clutch bolts (**Figure 7**) securing the clutch lifter plate and remove the lifter plate.

9. Remove the clutch springs (**Figure 8**).

(1)

CLUTCH ASSEMBLY

1. Circlip
2. Primary drive gear
3. Washer
4. Clutch outer housing
5. Pressure plate
6. Guide spacer
7. Friction disc "A" (7)
8. Clutch plate (7)
9. Friction disc "B" (1)
10. Disc pressure springs
11. Clutch center
12. Clutch spring (4)
13. Lockwasher
14. Lock nut
15. Clutch lifter plate
16. Clutch bolt (4)
17. Bearing retainer
18. Bearing
19. Lifter guide

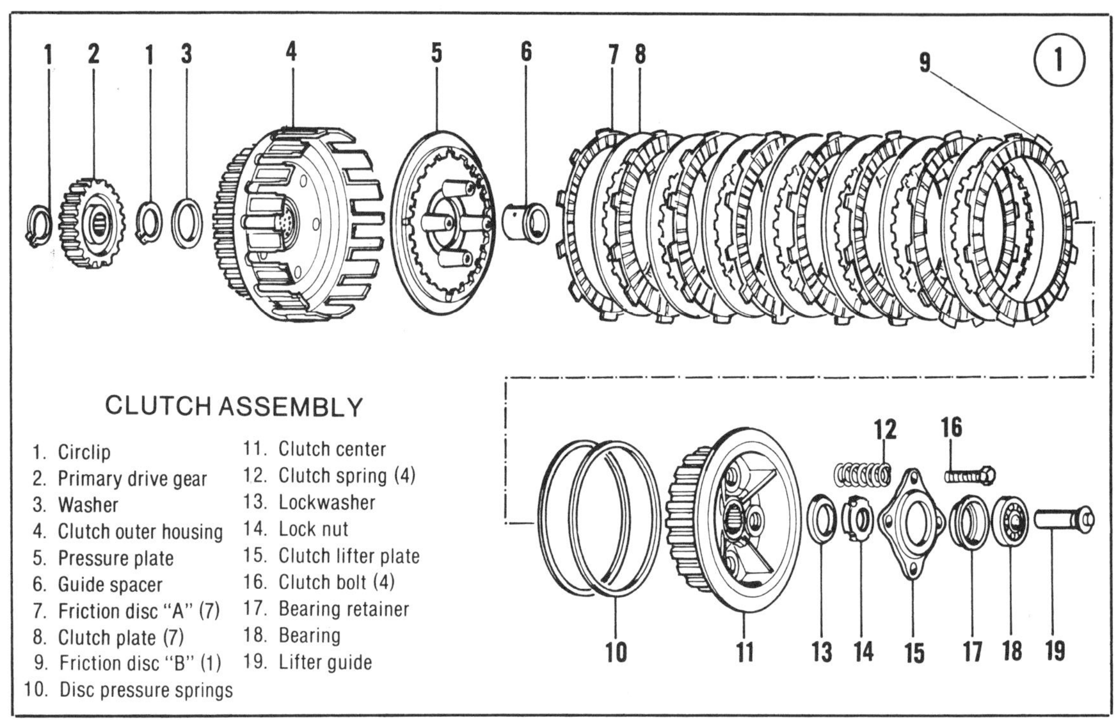

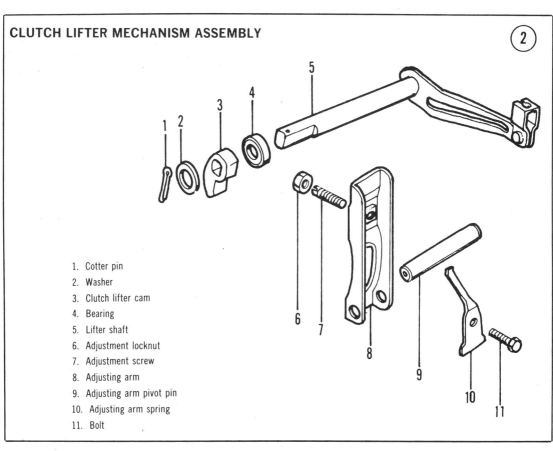

CLUTCH LIFTER MECHANISM ASSEMBLY

(2)

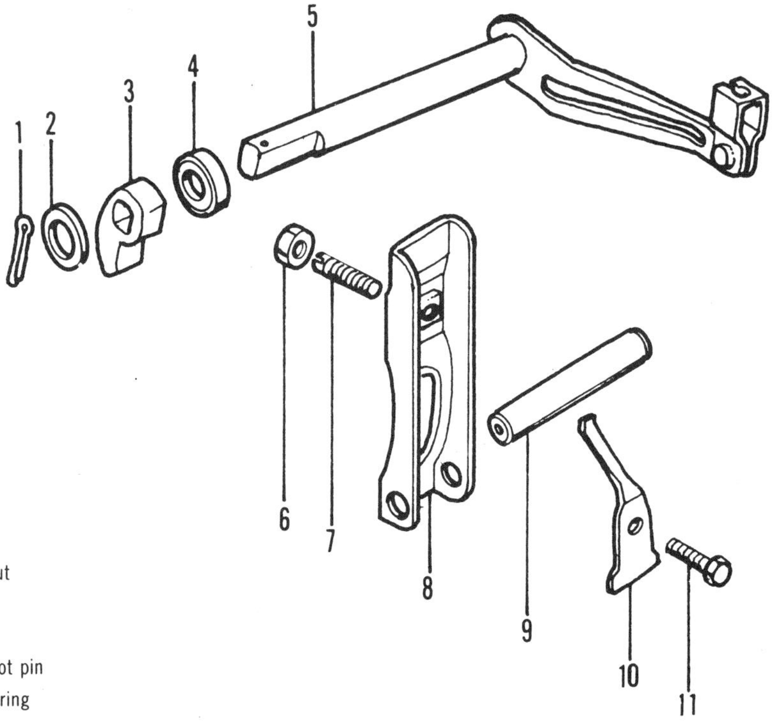

1. Cotter pin
2. Washer
3. Clutch lifter cam
4. Bearing
5. Lifter shaft
6. Adjustment locknut
7. Adjustment screw
8. Adjusting arm
9. Adjusting arm pivot pin
10. Adjusting arm spring
11. Bolt

3

6

4
A
B
HONDA
MADE IN JAPAN

7

5

8

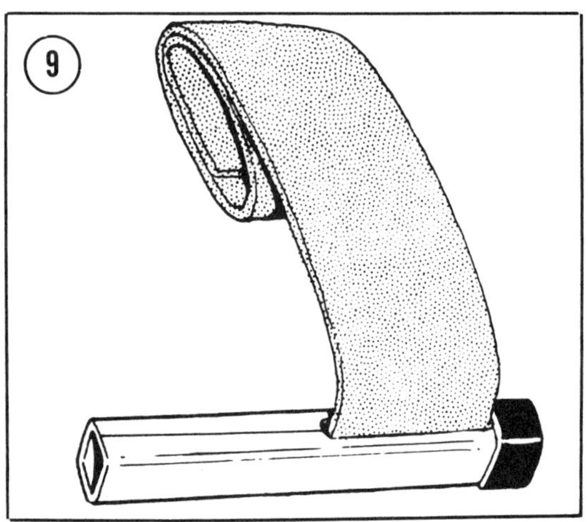

10. Remove the clutch nut and lockwasher. To keep the clutch boss from turning hold it with a strap wrench (**Figure 9**).

NOTE
Clutch nut removal requires a special tool available from a Honda dealer (Locknut Wrench Socket part No. 07716-0020202). Refer to ***Figure 10****.*

11. Remove the clutch center, plates, discs and pressure plate.
12. Remove the clutch outer housing and guide spacer (**Figure 11**).
13. Remove the inner thrust washer.

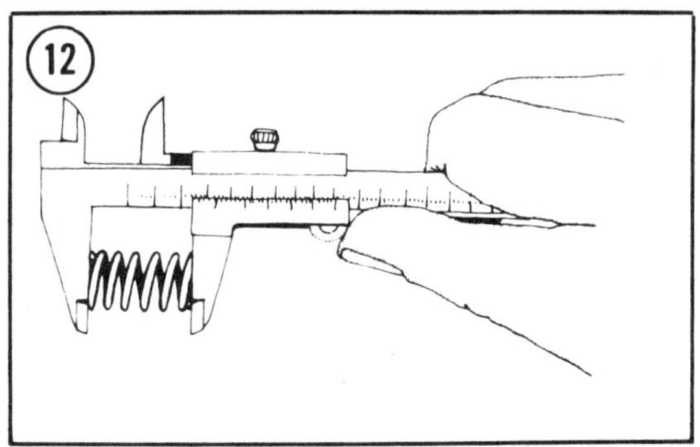

Inspection

1. Clean all parts in a petroleum based solvent such as kerosene and thoroughly dry with compressed air.

2. Measure the free length of each clutch spring as shown in **Figure 12**. If any of the springs are worn to 1.39 in. (35.4 mm) or less, replace all springs as a set.

3. Measure the thickness of each friction disc at several places around the disc as shown in **Figure 13**. Replace any disc "A" that is worn to 0.13 in. (3.2 mm) or less. Replace disc "B" if it is worn to 0.009 in. (2.4 mm) or less. For optimum performance, replace all discs as a set even if only a few need replacement.

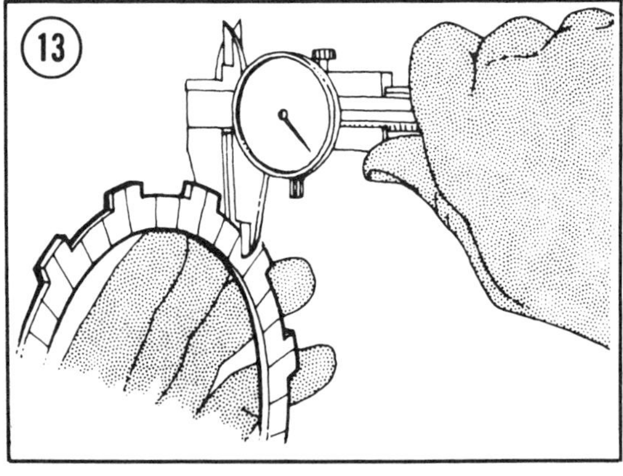

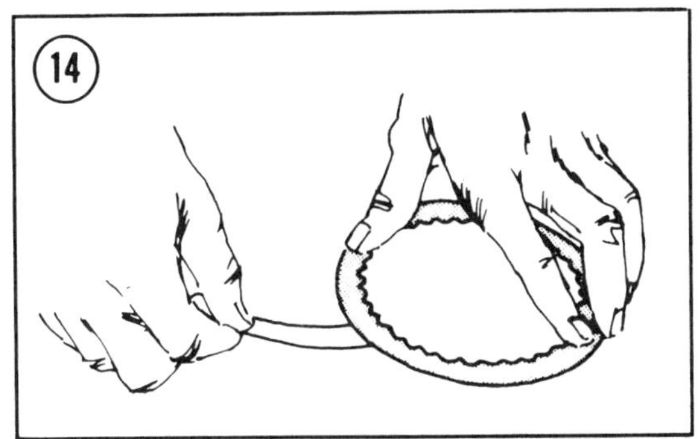
14

18

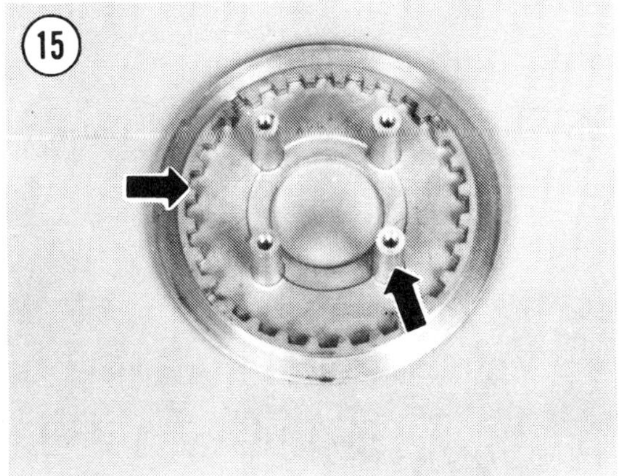
15

19

16

17

4. Check the clutch plates for warpage on a surface plate such as a piece of plate glass (**Figure 14**). Replace any that are warped 0.012 in. (0.30 mm) or more. For optimum performance, replace all plates as a set even if only a few need replacement.

5. Inspect the condition of the grooves and studs in the pressure plate (**Figure 15**). If either show signs of wear or galling the plate should be replaced.

6. Inspect the condition of the inner splines (**Figure 16**) and outer grooves (**Figure 17**) in the clutch center; if damaged, the clutch center should be replaced.

7. Inspect the condition of the teeth on the outer housing (**Figure 18**). Remove any small nicks on the gear teeth with an oilstone. If damage is severe the clutch housing should be replaced. Also check the condition of the teeth on the driven gear (**Figure 19**); it may also require replacing.

8. Inspect the condition of the slots in the clutch outer housing (**Figure 20**) for cracks, nicks or galling where it comes in contact with the friction disc tabs. If any severe damage is evident, the clutch housing must be replaced.
9. Measure the inside diameter of the clutch outer housing (A, **Figure 21**) and the outside diameter of the guide spacer (B, **Figure 21**) with vernier calipers. Replace the clutch outer housing if worn to 1.183 in. (30.05 mm) or more. Replace the guide spacer if worn to 1.179 in. (29.94 mm) or less.
10. Inspect the condition of the lifter guide bearing. Make sure it rotates smoothly with no signs of wear or damage. Replace as necessary.
11. Check the lifter guide bearing retainer for signs of wear or cracks. This part has a lot of stress placed on it during normal clutch operation. Replace the retainer if there is the slightest crack on either the inner or outer edge.
12. Check the movement of the clutch adjuster arm and lifter shaft in the clutch cover (**Figure 22**). They must operate smoothly or be replaced.

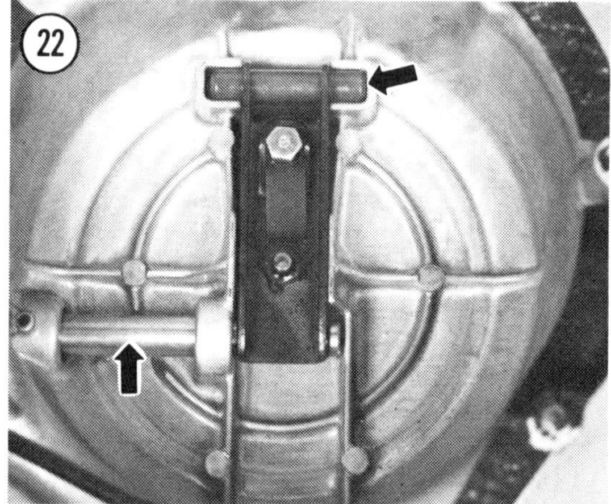

Assembly/Installation

1. Install the disc pressure spring onto the clutch center with the convex or cupped side facing out (**Figure 23**).

NOTE

If either or both friction discs and clutch plates have been replaced with new ones, apply new engine oil to all surfaces to avoid having the clutch lock up when used for the first time.

2. Install a friction disc "A" (**Figure 24**), a

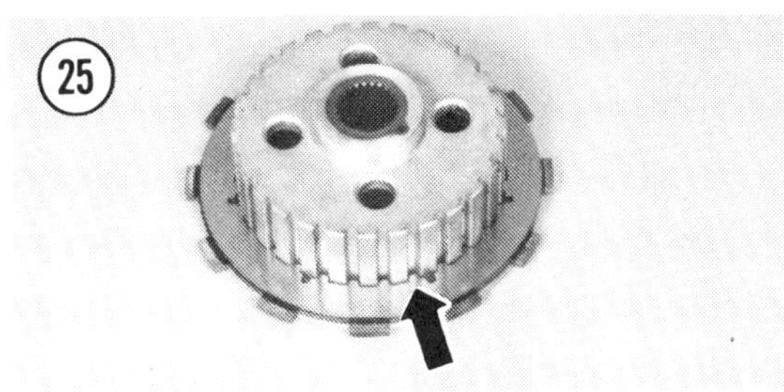

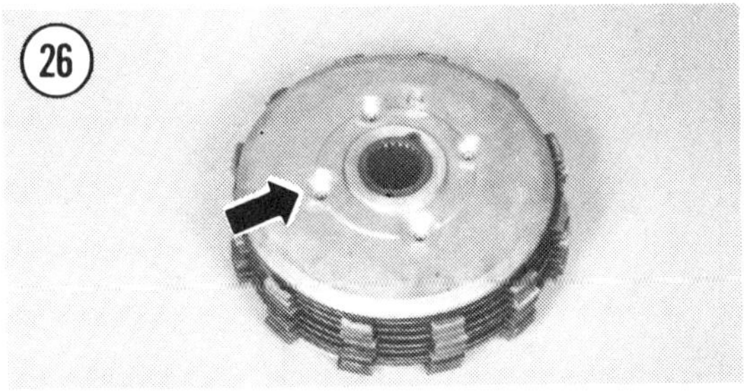

clutch plate (**Figure 25**) and another friction disc until all are installed. Install friction disc "B" last (this disc is the only one that has thicker tabs than those on friction discs "A").

3. Install the pressure plate (**Figure 26**).
4. Turn the assembly over and install one clutch spring and one bolt with washer to hold the assembly together. This will aid in installation.

NOTE

Do not tighten the bolt as some play is needed for final alignment of friction plate tabs when installing it into the clutch outer housing.

5. Install the inner thrust washer (**Figure 27**) onto the transmission main shaft.
6. Install the clutch outer housing (A, **Figure 28**) and the guide spacer (B, **Figure 28**).
7. Slide on the clutch parts (clutch center, friction discs, clutch plates and pressure plate) assembled in Steps 1 through 4 (**Figure 29**). Push the assembly on slowly, carefully aligning the tabs of the friction discs into the slots in the clutch outer housing.

NOTE

Friction disc "B," installed last in Step 2, has the wider tabs and will only fit into the outermost section of the clutch outer housing. This is a check for correct location of disc "B" onto the clutch center.

5

30

31

32

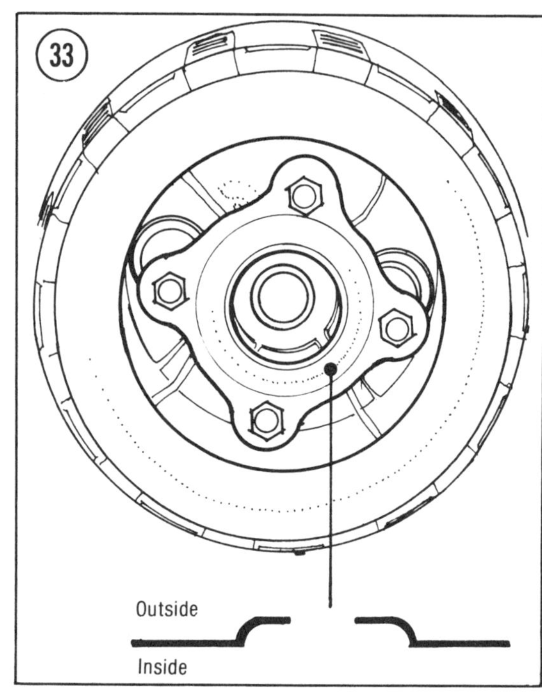
33
Outside
Inside

34

35

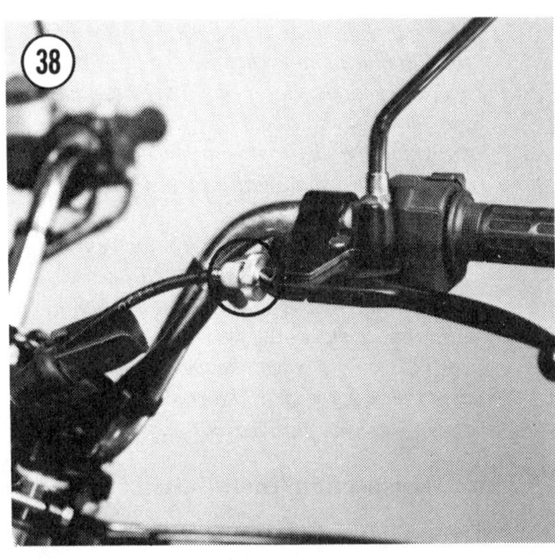

8. Install the lockwasher with the dished side facing toward the outside. The word "OUTSIDE" stamped on it must face outward (**Figure 30**).

9. Install the locknut (**Figure 31**) and tighten to 34-38 ft.-lb. (47-53 N•m). Use the same tool setup as used for removal (**Figure 10**).

10. Remove the one clutch bolt and washer. Install all of the clutch springs (**Figure 32**).

11. Install the clutch lifter plate with the convex or dished side facing outward (**Figure 33**).

12. Install the clutch bolts and tighten them securely in a crisscross pattern in 2 or 3 stages.

13. Install the lifter guide bearing retainer, bearing and lifter guide (**Figure 34**).

14. Install the 2 locating dowels (**Figure 35**) and gasket.

15. Install the clutch cover and the rear brake pedal.

16. Install the clutch cable to the lower adjuster (**Figure 36**) and to the hand lever.

17. Refill the engine with the recommended type and quantity oil; refer to *Changing Engine Oil and Filter* in Chapter Three.

18. Adjust the clutch as described under *Clutch Adjustment* in Chapter Three.

CLUTCH CABLE

Replacement

In time the clutch cable will stretch to the point that it will have to be replaced.

1. Turn the fuel shutoff valve to the OFF position and remove the fuel line to the carburetor.

2. Remove the seat and fuel tank.

3. Pull back the rubber protective boot (**Figure 37**) covering the cable adjuster.

4. At the clutch lever loosen the locknut and turn the adjuster barrel (**Figure 38**) all the way toward the cable sheath. Slip the cable end out of the hand lever.

5

5. At the lower adjuster, loosen the locknut (**Figure 39**) and remove the cable from the bracket and lifter shaft lever.

NOTE
The piece of string attached in the next step will be used to pull the new clutch cable back through the frame so it will be routed in the exact same position.

6. Tie a piece of heavy string or cord (approximately 6-8 ft./1.8-2.4 m long) to the clutch mechanism end of the cable. Wrap this end with masking or duct tape. Do not use an excessive amount of tape as it must be pulled through the frame loops during removal. Tie the other end of the string to the foot peg.
7. At the handlebar end of the cable, carefully pull the cable (and attached string) out through the frame loops (**Figure 40**) and from behind the headlight housing. Make sure the attached string follows the same path of the cable through the frame and behind the headlight.

NOTE
Step 7 is shown with the right-hand exhaust system removed for clarity. It is not necessary to remove it for this procedure.

8. Remove the tape and untie the string from the old cable.
9. Lubricate the new cable as described under *Control Cables* in Chapter Three.
10. Tie the string to the clutch mechanism end of the new clutch cable and wrap it with tape.
11. Carefully pull the string back through the frame routing the new cable through the same path as the old cable.
12. Remove the tape and untie the string from the cable and the footpeg. Attach the new cable to the clutch lever and the clutch mechanism.
13. Adjust the clutch cable as described under *Clutch Lever Free Play Adjustment* in Chapter Three.

EXTERNAL SHIFT MECHANISM

The external shift mechanism is located on the same side of the crankcase as the clutch assembly and can be removed with the engine

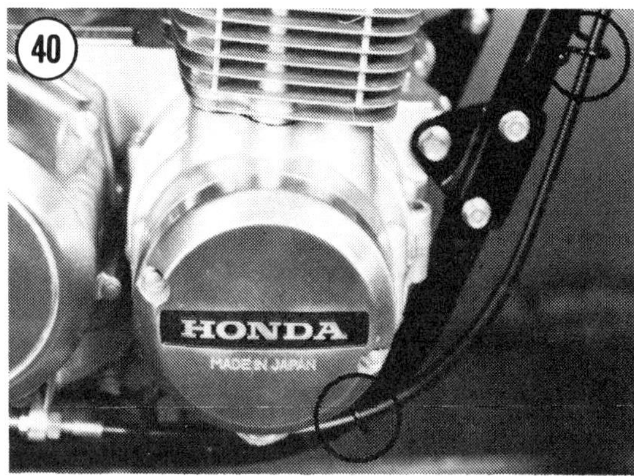

in the frame. To remove the shift drum and shift forks it is necessary to remove the engine and split the crankcase. This procedure is covered under *Shift Drum and Shift Forks* in this chapter.

NOTE
The gearshift lever is subject to a lot of abuse. If the motorcycle has been in a hard spill, the gearshift lever may have been hit and the shift shaft bent. It is very hard to straighten the shaft without subjecting the crankcase to abnormal stress where the shaft enters the case.

If the shaft is bent enough to prevent it from being withdrawn from the crankcase, there is little recourse but to cut the shaft off with a hacksaw very close to the crankcase. It is much cheaper in the long run to replace the shaft than risk damaging a very expensive crankcase.

Removal/Inspection/Installation

Refer to **Figure 41** for this procedure.

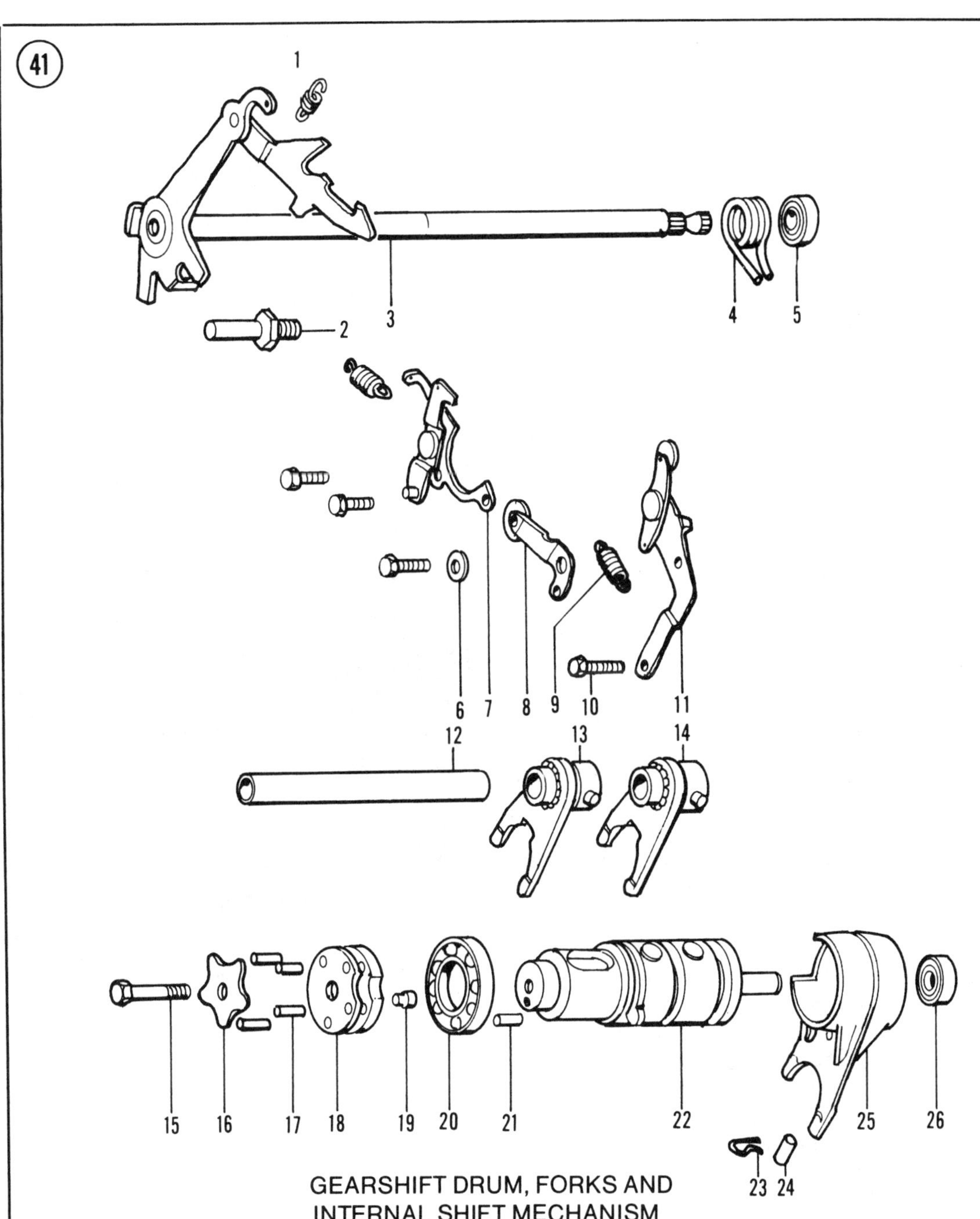

GEARSHIFT DRUM, FORKS AND INTERNAL SHIFT MECHANISM

1. Shift arm return spring
2. Stopper plate bolt
3. Gearshift lever assembly
4. Return spring
5. Oil seal
6. Washer
7. Shift drum retainer
8. Shift drum stopper arm
9. Return spring
10. Bolt
11. Neutral stopper
12. Shift fork shaft
13. Shift fork (right-hand side)
14. Shift fork (left-hand side)
15. Bolt
16. Shift drum cam plate
17. Pin (4)
18. Shift drum center
19. Pin
20. Bearing
21. Locator pin
22. Shift drum
23. Clip
24. Shift fork set pin
25. Large shift fork (center)
26. Oil seal

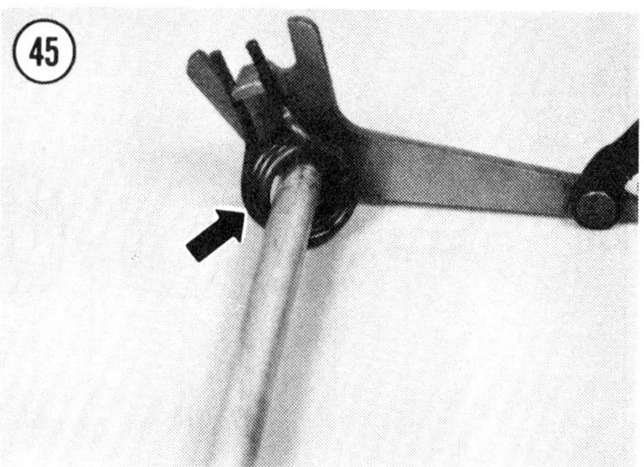

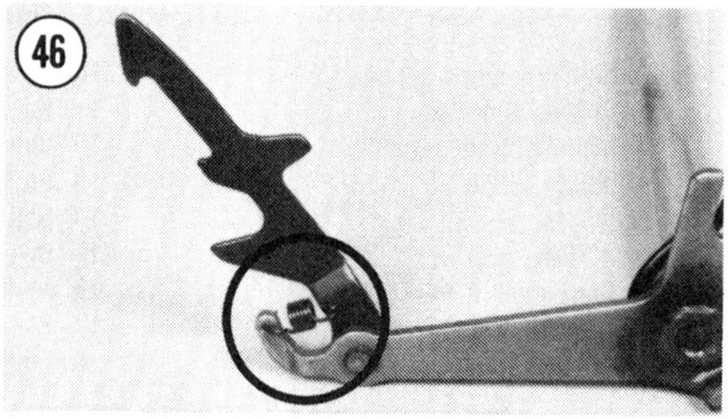

1. Remove the clutch assembly as described under *Clutch Removal/Installation* in this chapter.
2. Remove the gearshift lever.
3. Remove the bolt (**Figure 42**) securing the lower end of the shift drum stopper.
4. Remove the upper bolt (**Figure 43**) and remove the neutral stopper arm and drum stopper arm assembly.
5. Disengage the shift arm from the shift drum (**Figure 44**) and withdraw the gearshift lever assembly. See the *NOTE* in the introduction to this procedure regarding a bent shaft if the assembly is difficult to remove.
6. Inspect the condition of the return spring on the shift lever assembly (**Figure 45**). If broken or weak it must be replaced.
7. Inspect the shift arm assembly spring (**Figure 46**). If broken or weak remove and replace the spring.
8. Inspect the gearshift lever assembly shaft (**Figure 47**) for bending, wear or other damage; replace if necessary.
9. Inspect the condition of the rollers and spring on the neutral stopper arm and drum stopper arm assembly (**Figure 48**).
10. Install the gearshift lever assembly. Make sure the return spring is correctly positioned onto the stopper plate bolt (**Figure 49**).
11. Install the neutral stopper arm and drum stopper arm assembly. Make sure it is engaged properly in the shift drum (**Figure 50**).
12. Install the clutch assembly as described in this chapter.

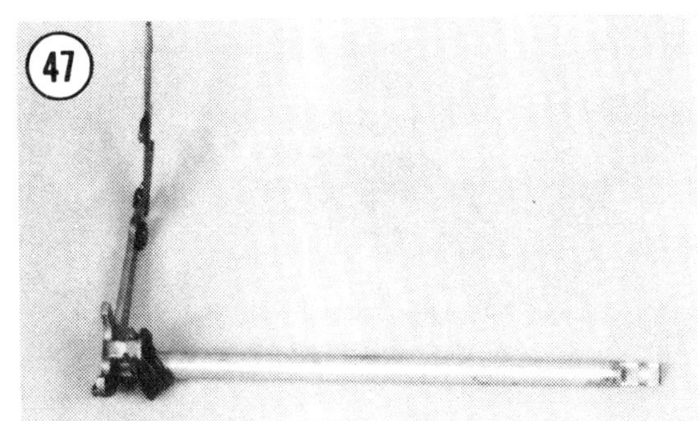

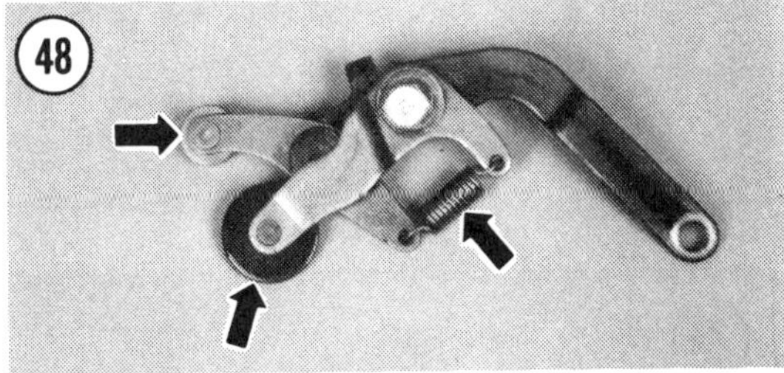

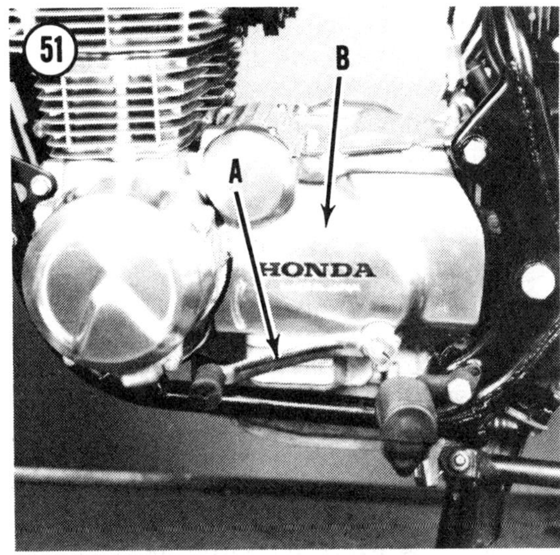

DRIVE SPROCKET

Removal/Installation

1. Place the bike on the centerstand or place a milk crate or wood block(s) under the engine or frame to support the bike securely.

2. Remove the gear shift lever (A, **Figure 51**) and left-hand rear crankcase cover (B, **Figure 51**).

3. Remove the rear axle nut cotter pin and loosen the axle nut (A, **Figure 52**).

4. Loosen the drive chain adjusters (B, **Figure 52**) and push the rear wheel forward to allow slack in the drive chain.

5. Remove the bolts (A, **Figure 53**) securing the drive sprocket and drive sprocket holding plate (B, **Figure 53**).
6. Rotate the drive sprocket holding plate slightly and slide it off the shaft.
7. Slide off the drive sprocket and drive chain.

WARNING
The drive chain is manufactured as a continuous closed loop with no master link. ***Do not cut*** *it with a chain cutter as it will result in future chain failure and possible loss of control under riding conditions.*

8. Install by reversing these removal steps, noting the following.
9. Align the punch marks on the shift lever with the shaft when installing the shift lever.
10. Adjust the drive chain as described under *Drive Chain Adjustment* in Chapter Three.

Inspection

Inspect the condition of the teeth on the drive sprocket. If the teeth are visibly worn (**Figure 54**), replace the sprocket with a new one.

If the sprocket requires replacement, the drive chain is probably worn also. Refer to *Drive Chain Adjustment* in Chapter Three.

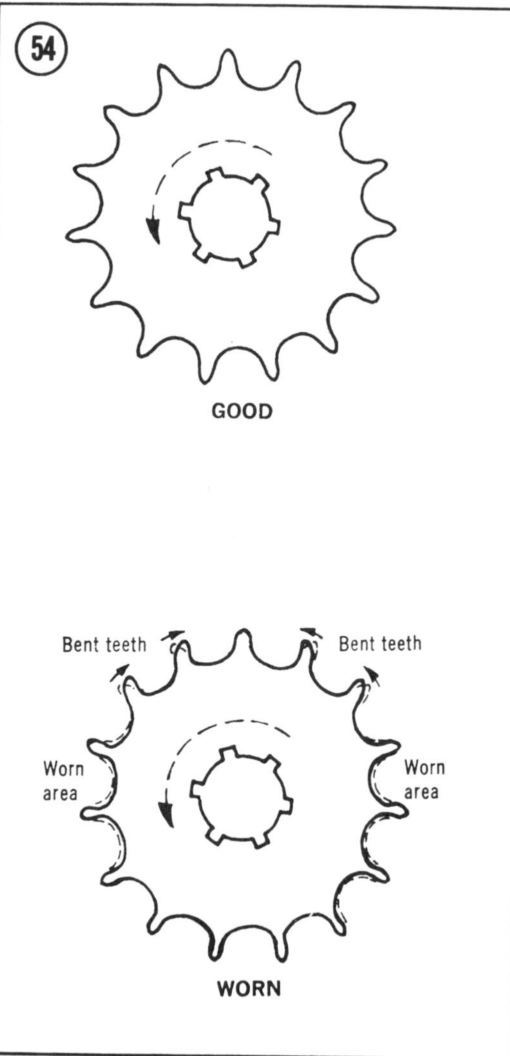

TRANSMISSION

To gain access to the transmission and internal shift mechanism it is necessary to remove the engine and split the crankcase. Once the crankcase has been split removal of the transmission is a simple task of pulling the assemblies up and out of the crankcase. Installation is more complicated and is covered more completely than the removal sequence.

Pay particular attention to the location of spacers, washers and bearings during disassembly. If disassembling a used, well run-in engine for the first time by yourself, pay particular attention to any additional shims that may have been added by a previous owner. These may have been added to take up the tolerance of worn components and must be reinstalled in the same position since the shims have developed a wear pattern. If new parts are going to be installed these shims may

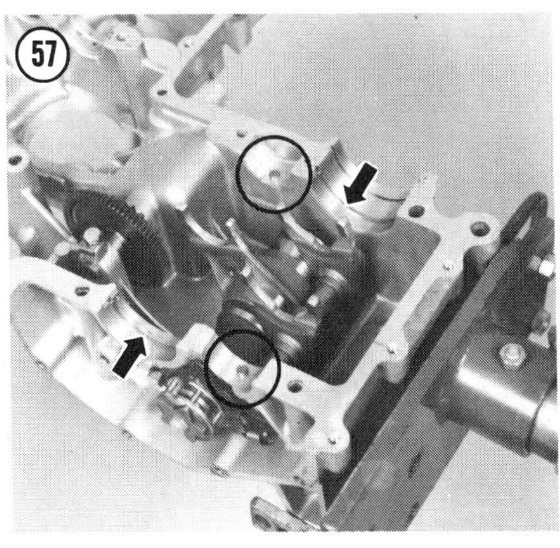

be eliminated. This is something you will have to determine upon reassembly.

Removal/Installation

1. Disassemble the crankcase as described under *Crankcase Disassembly* in Chapter Four.
2. Remove the main shaft assembly (A, **Figure 55**).
3. Remove the countershaft assembly (B, **Figure 55**).
4. Install by reversing these removal steps, noting the following.

NOTE

Prior to installing any components, coat all bearing surfaces with assembly oil ***(Figure 56)****.*

5. In the upper crankcase make sure that both locating dowels and both bearing set rings are correctly positioned (**Figure 57**).
6. Position the shift forks as shown in **Figure 58**.
7. Install the countershaft assembly (A, **Figure 59**). Make sure the locating dowel is

indexed into the hole in the bearing outer race. When properly installed the alignment lines on the bearing outer race will line up with the split line on the crankcase (**Figure 60**).

NOTE

*To prevent an oil leak, make sure that the countershaft oil seal (B, **Figure 59**) is completely seated in the groove in the crankcase.*

8. Install the main shaft assembly (**Figure 61**). Make sure the locating dowel is indexed into the hole in the bearing outer race. When properly installed the alignment lines on the bearing outer race will line up with the split line on the crankcase (**Figure 62**).
9. Make sure that the shift forks are properly engaged into their respective grooves in both transmission assemblies. Spin the transmission shafts and shift through the gears using the shift drum. Make sure you can shift into all gears. This is the time to find that something may be installed incorrectly—not after the crankcase is completely assembled.
10. Assemble the crankcase as described under *Crankcase Assembly* in Chapter Four.

60

61

62

Main Shaft Disassembly/ Inspection/Assembly

Refer to **Figure 63** for this procedure.

NOTE

*A helpful "tool" that should be used for transmission disassembly is a large egg flat (the type that restaurants get their eggs in). As you remove a part from the shaft set it in one of the depressions in the same position from which it was removed (**Figure 64**). This is an easy way to remember the correct relationship of all parts.*

1. Place the assembled shaft into a large can or plastic bucket and thoroughly clean with solvent and a stiff brush. Dry with compressed air or let it sit on rags to drip dry.
2. Remove the bearing outer race and the bearing.
3. Remove the thrust washer and slide off the 5th gear, 5th gear bushing and shim.

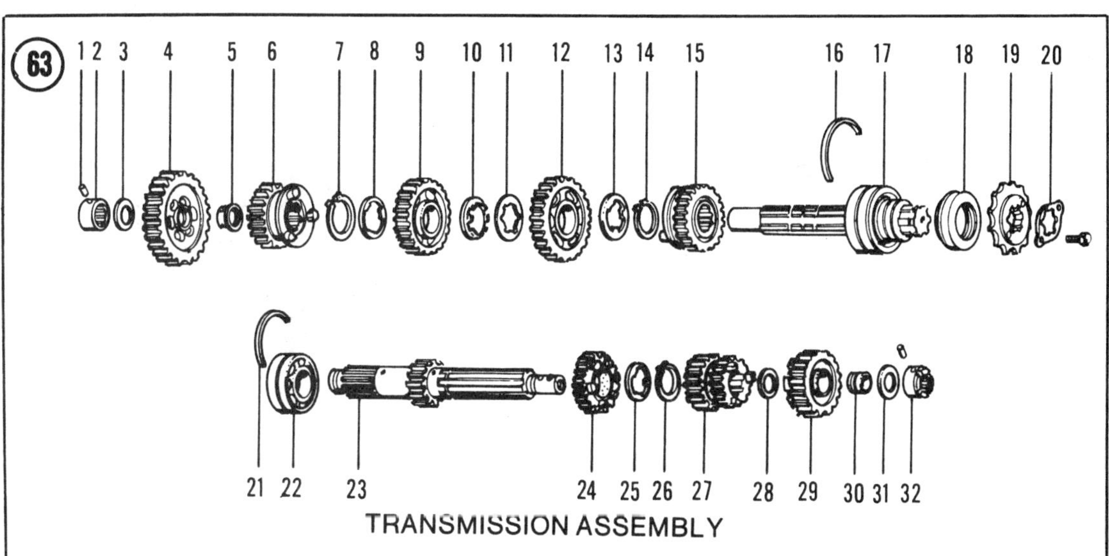

1. Locating dowel
2. Bearing and outer race
3. Thrust washer
4. Countershaft 1st gear
5. Countershaft 2nd gear bushing
6. Countershaft 4th gear
7. Circlip
8. Splined washer
9. Countershaft 3rd gear
10. Splined lockwasher
11. Splined washer
12. Countershaft 2nd gear
13. Splined washer
14. Circlip
15. Countershaft 5th gear
16. Set ring
17. Countershaft/bearing
18. Oil seal
19. Drive sprocket
20. Drive sprocket holding plate
21. Set ring
22. Bearing
23. Main shaft (including 1st gear)
24. Main shaft 4th gear
25. Splined washer
26. Circlip
27. Mainshaft 2nd/3rd combination gear
28. Shim
29. Main shaft 5th gear
30. Main shaft 5th bushing
31. Thrust washer
32. Bearing and outer race

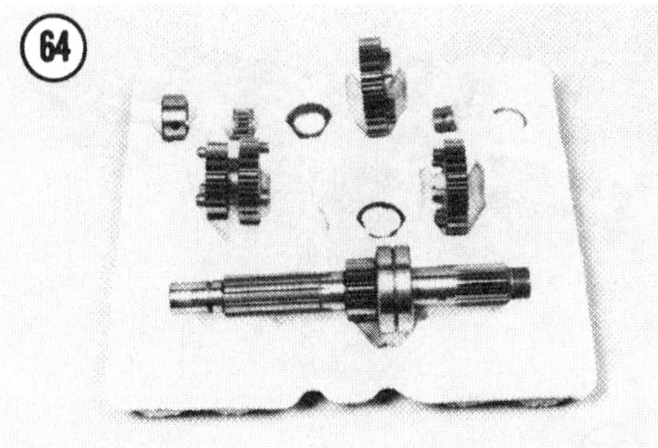

4. Slide off the 2nd/3rd combination gear.
5. Remove the circlip and splined washer and slide off the 4th gear.
6. If necessary, remove the ball bearing from the shaft.
7. Check each gear for excessive wear, burrs, pitting or chipped or missing teeth. Make sure the lugs (**Figure 65**) on the gears are in good condition.

NOTE

Defective gears should be replaced. It is a good idea to replace the mating gear on the countershaft even though it may not show as much wear or damage.

NOTE

The 1st gear is part of the shaft, therefore, if the gear is defective the shaft must be replaced.

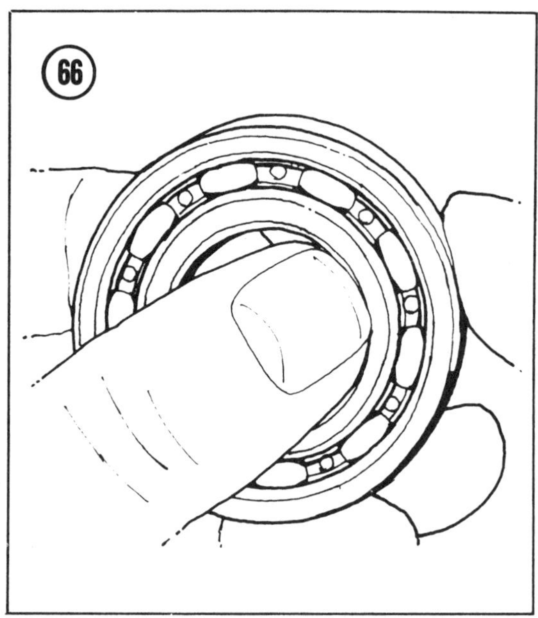

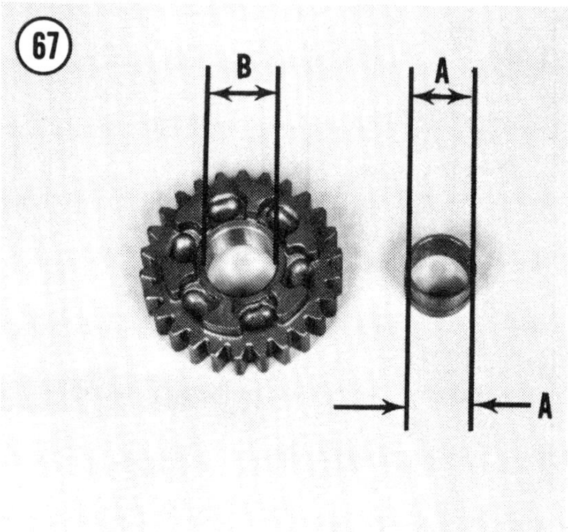

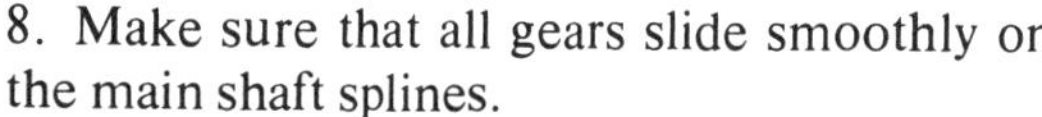

8. Make sure that all gears slide smoothly on the main shaft splines.
9. Check the condition of the bearing. Make sure it rotates smoothly (**Figure 66**) with no signs of wear or damage. Replace if necessary.
10. Measure the inside and outside diameter of the 5th gear bushing (A, **Figure 67**) and the inside diameter of the 5th gear (B, **Figure 67**). Compare with dimensions given in **Table 2**.
11. Measure the inside diameter of the 4th gear and compare with dimensions given in **Table 2**.
12. Measure the outside diameter of the transmission shaft at the locations of the 4th gear (A, **Figure 68**) and the 5th gear bushing (B, **Figure 68**). Compare with dimensions given in **Table 2**.

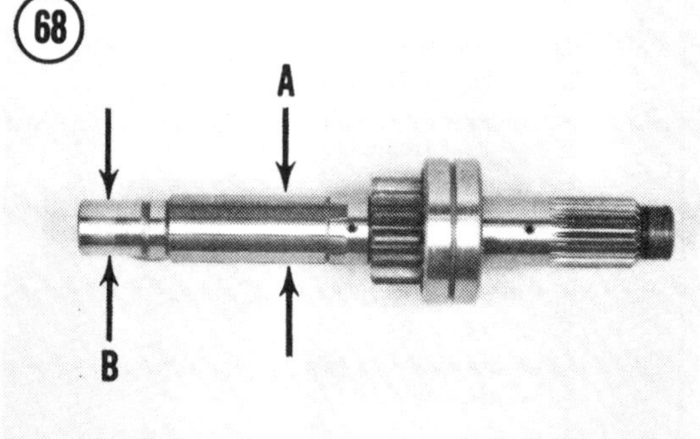

NOTE

It is a good idea to replace the circlip every other time the transmission is disassembled to ensure proper gear alignment.

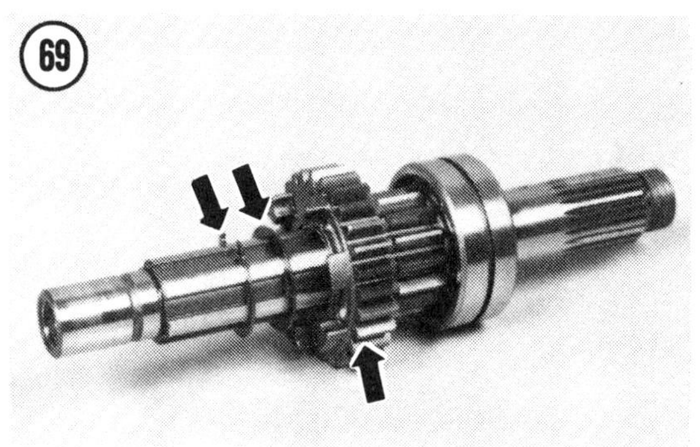

13. Slide on the 4th gear and install the splined washer and circlip (**Figure 69**).
14. Slide on the 2nd/3rd combination gear (**Figure 70**). Install the gears with the larger diameter gear (3rd gear) on first.

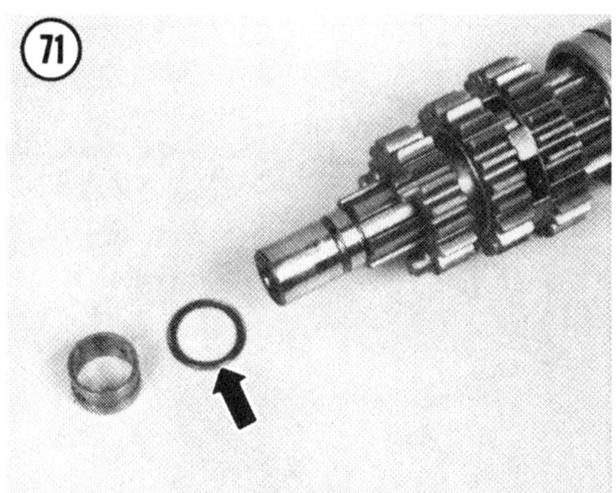
(71)

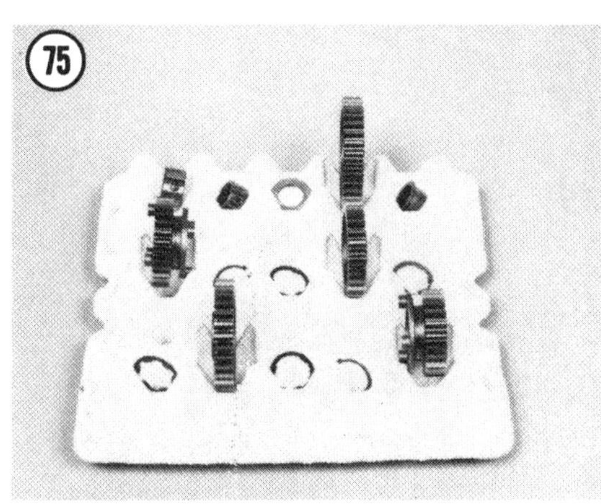
(75)

(72)

(73)

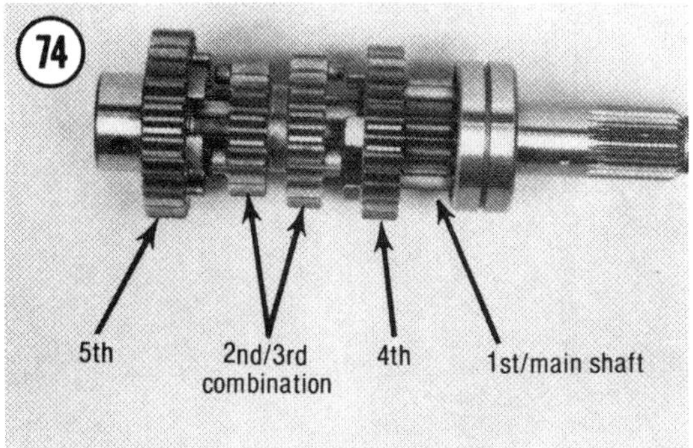

(74)

15. Install the shim (**Figure 71**) and the 5th gear bushing (**Figure 72**).
16. Install the 5th gear (**Figure 73**).
17. Install the thrust washer, bearing and bearing outer race.
18. After assembly is complete refer to **Figure 74** for the correct placement of all gears. Make sure the circlip is seated correctly in the main shaft groove.
19. Make sure each gear engages properly with the adjoining gears where applicable.

Countershaft Disassembly/ Inspection/Assembly

Refer to **Figure 63** for this procedure.

NOTE

*Use the same large egg flat (used on the main shaft disassembly) during the countershaft disassembly (**Figure 75**). This is an easy way to remember the correct relationship of all parts.*

1. Place the assembled shaft into a large can or plastic bucket and thoroughly clean with solvent and a stiff brush. Dry with compressed air or let it sit on rags to drip dry.
2. Slide off the bearing outer race, bearing and thrust washer.
3. Slide off the 1st gear and 1st gear bushing.
4. Slide off 4th gear.
5. Remove the circlip and splined washer and slide off the 3rd gear.

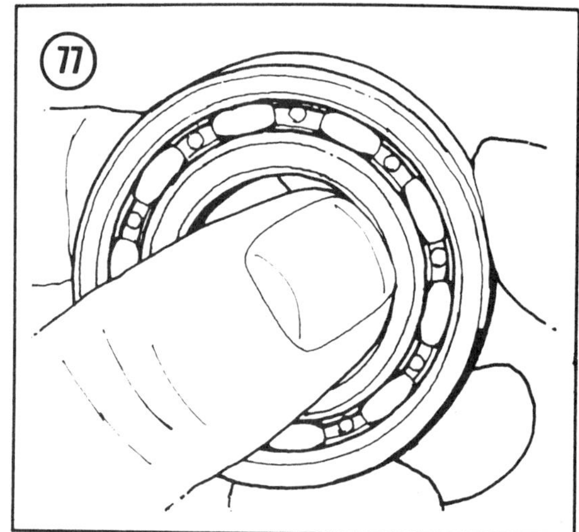

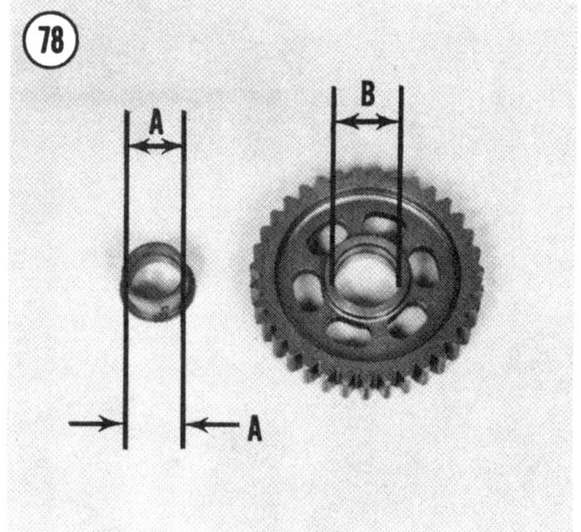

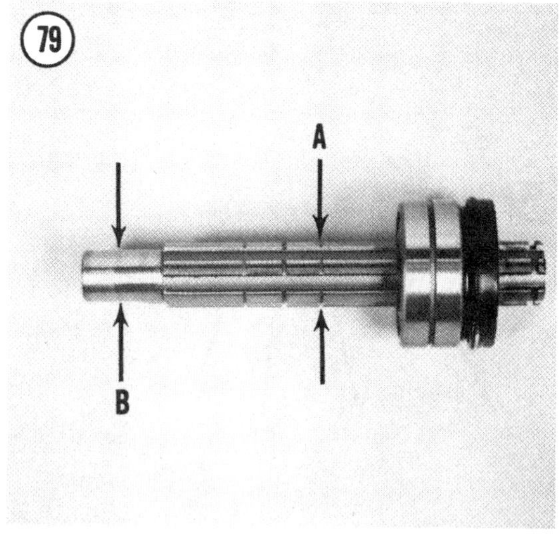

6. Remove the splined lockwasher, then rotate the splined washer in either direction so its tangs will clear the transmission spline grooves and slide it off the shaft.
7. Slide off the 2nd gear.
8. Remove the splined washer, circlip and the 5th gear.
9. Check each gear for excessive wear, burrs, pitting or chipped or missing teeth. Make sure the lugs (**Figure 76**) on the gears are in good condition.

NOTE
Defective gears should be replaced. It is a good idea to replace the mating gear on the main shaft even though it may not show as much wear or damage.

10. Make sure that all gears slide smoothly on the countershaft splines.
11. Check the condition of the bearing. Make sure it rotates smoothly (**Figure** 77) with no signs of wear or damage. Replace if necessary.
12. Measure the inside and outside diameter of the 1st gear bushing (A, **Figure 78**) and the inside diameter of the 1st gear (B, **Figure 78**). Compare with dimensions given in **Table 2**. Replace as necessary.
13. Measure the inside diameter of the 2nd and the 3rd gear and compare with dimensions given in **Table 2**. Replace as necessary.
14. Measure the outside diameter of the transmission shaft at the locations of the 2nd and 3rd gear (A, **Figure 79**) and the 5th gear bushing (B, **Figure 79**). Compare with

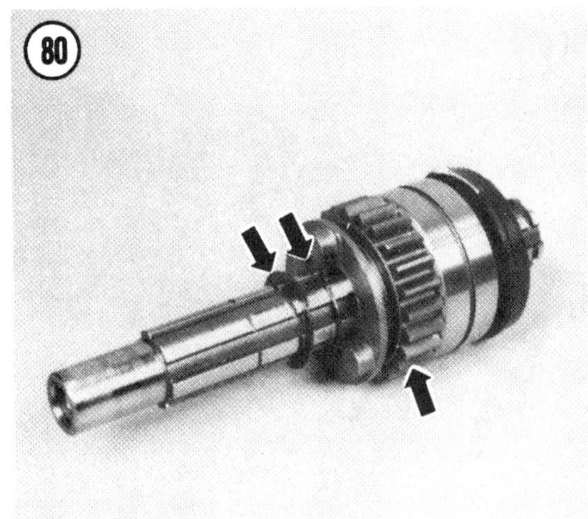
80

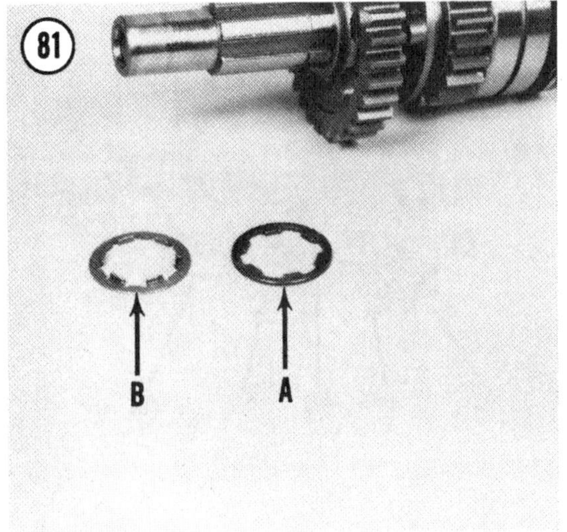

81

82

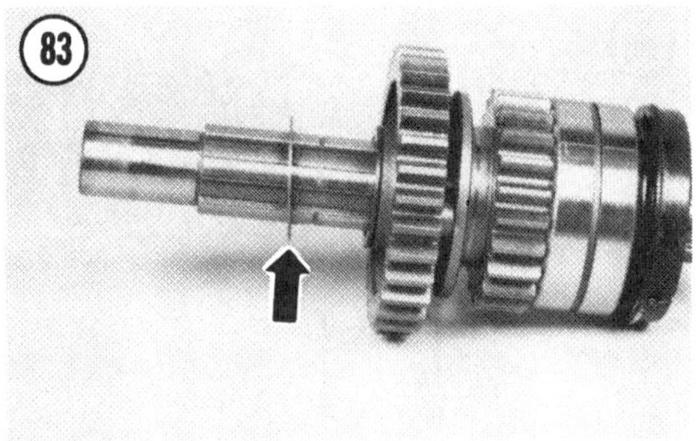
83

84

dimensions given in **Table 2**. Replace as necessary.

NOTE
It is a good idea to replace all circlips every other time the transmission is disassembled to ensure proper gear alignment.

15. Slide on the 5th gear and install the circlip and splined washer (**Figure 80**).
16. Slide on the 2nd gear and install the splined washer (A, **Figure 81**) and splined lockwasher (B, **Figure 81**).

NOTE
*Slide on the splined washer **(Figure 82)** and rotate it in either direction so its tangs are engaged into the groove in the raised splines of the transmission shaft. Slide on the splined lockwasher **(Figure 83)** so that its tangs go into the open areas of the splined washer and lock the washer in place.*

17. Slide on the 3rd gear and install the splined washer and circlip (**Figure 84**).

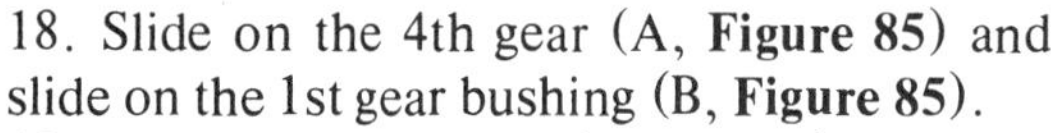

18. Slide on the 4th gear (A, **Figure 85**) and slide on the 1st gear bushing (B, **Figure 85**).
19. Install the 1st gear (**Figure 86**) with the machined side on first.
20. Slide on the thrust washer, bearing and bearing outer race (**Figure 87**).
21. After assembly is complete refer to **Figure 88** for the correct placement of all gears. Make sure all circlips are seated correctly in the countershaft grooves.

NOTE

*After both transmission shafts have been assembled, mesh the 2 assemblies together in the correct position (**Figure 89**). Check that all gears meet correctly. This is your last check prior to installing the assemblies into the crankcase; make sure both shaft assemblies are correctly assembled.*

GEARSHIFT DRUM AND SHIFT FORKS

Refer to **Figure 90** for this procedure.

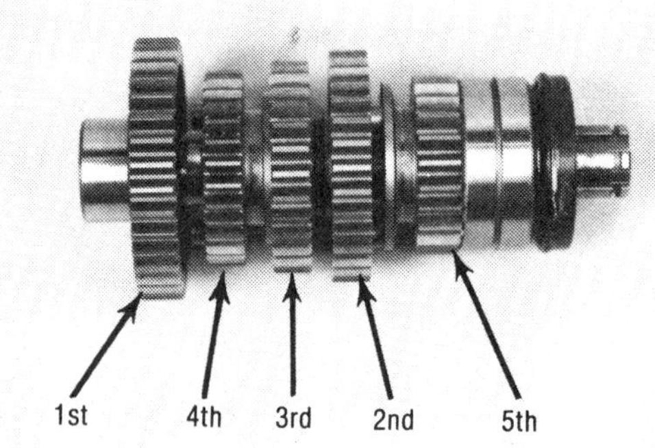

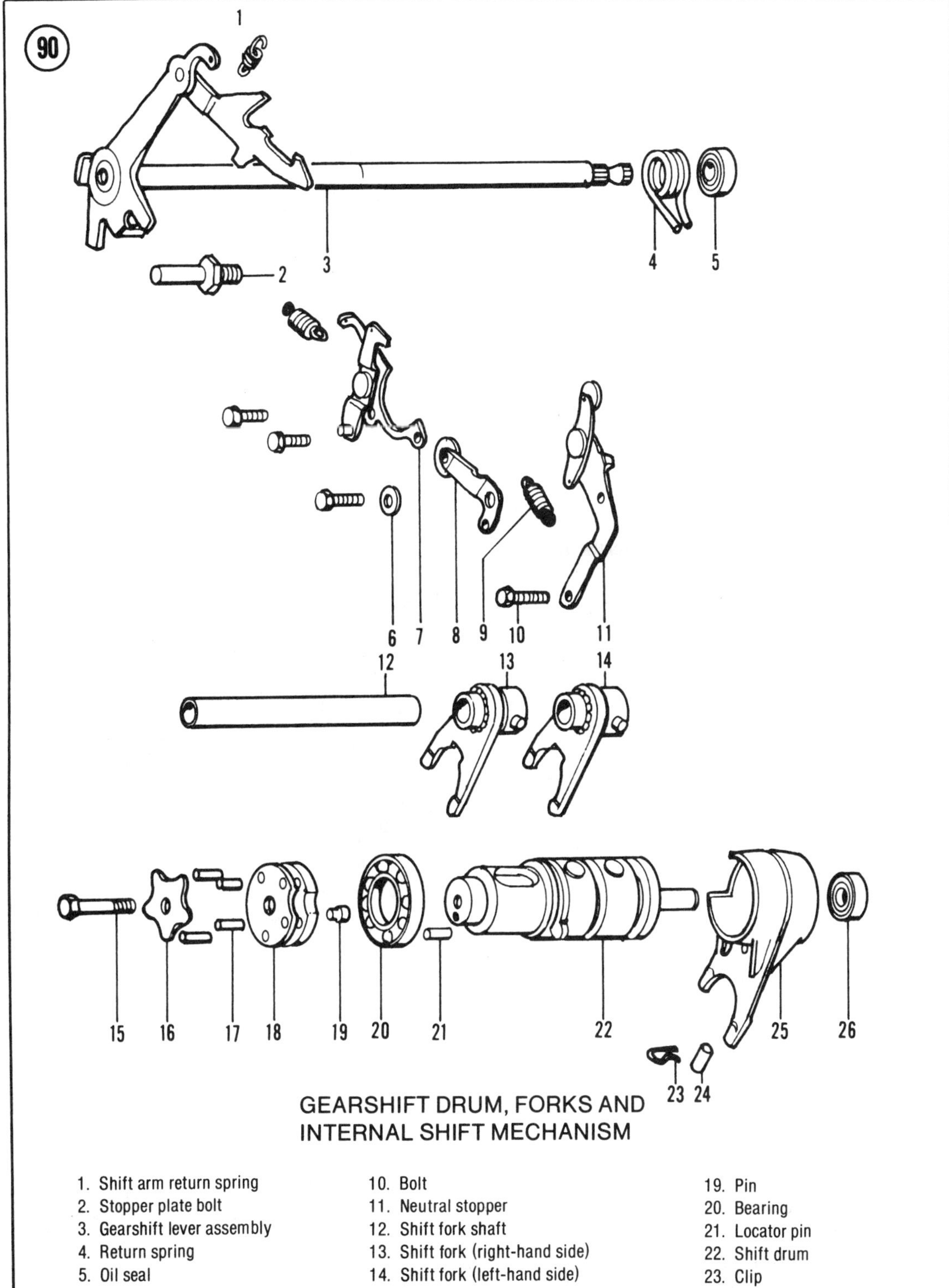

GEARSHIFT DRUM, FORKS AND INTERNAL SHIFT MECHANISM

1. Shift arm return spring
2. Stopper plate bolt
3. Gearshift lever assembly
4. Return spring
5. Oil seal
6. Washer
7. Shift drum retainer
8. Shift drum stopper arm
9. Return spring
10. Bolt
11. Neutral stopper
12. Shift fork shaft
13. Shift fork (right-hand side)
14. Shift fork (left-hand side)
15. Bolt
16. Shift drum cam plate
17. Pin (4)
18. Shift drum center
19. Pin
20. Bearing
21. Locator pin
22. Shift drum
23. Clip
24. Shift fork set pin
25. Large shift fork (center)
26. Oil seal

91

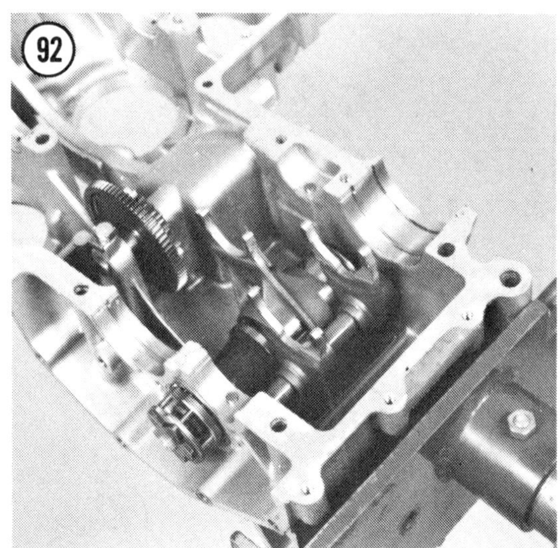
92

Removal

1. Separate the crankcase as described under *Crankcase Disassembly* in Chapter Four.

2. Remove the transmission assemblies as described under *Transmission Removal/Installation* in this chapter.

3. Remove the neutral switch from the left-hand end of the shift drum.

4. Remove the bolts (**Figure 91**) securing the shift drum bearing stopper plate and remove the stopper plate.

5. Withdraw the shift fork shaft and both shift forks (**Figure 92**).

6. Remove the clip (**Figure 93**) securing the shift fork set pin.

7. Remove the shift fork set pin.

8. Withdraw the shift drum from the right-hand side. Hold onto the large shift fork while removing the shift drum. Remove the large shift fork.

93

Inspection

Refer to **Table 3** for shift fork and shift shaft specifications.

1. Inspect each shift fork for signs of wear or cracking. Check for bending and make sure each fork slides smoothly on its shaft (**Figure 94**) or shift drum. Replace any worn or damaged forks.

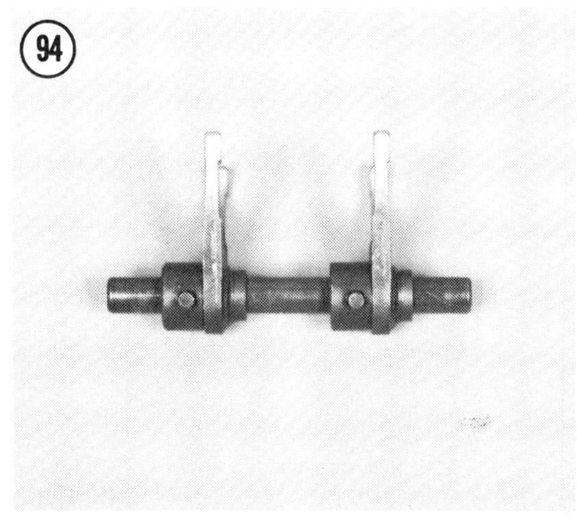
94

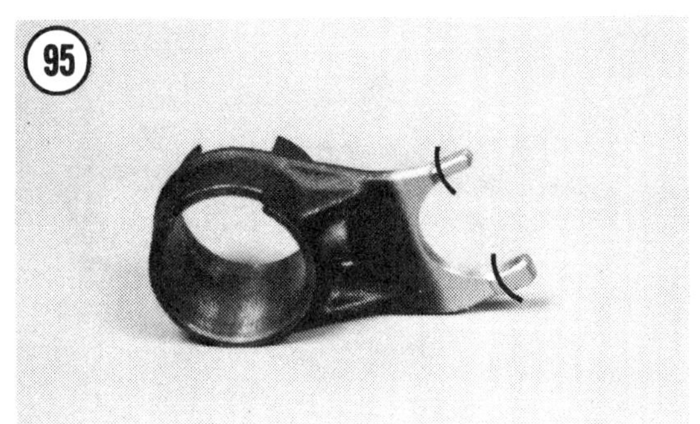

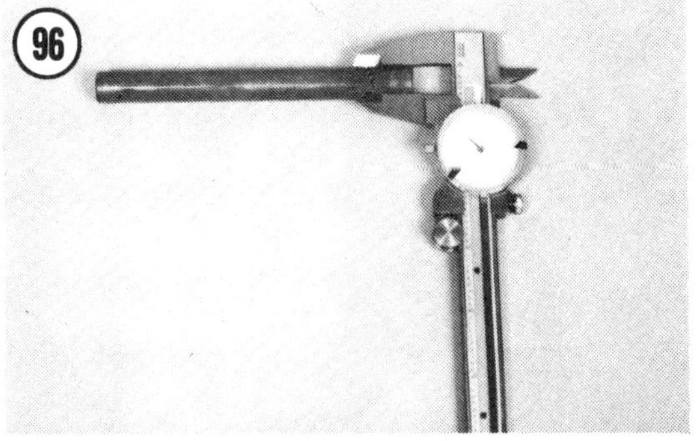

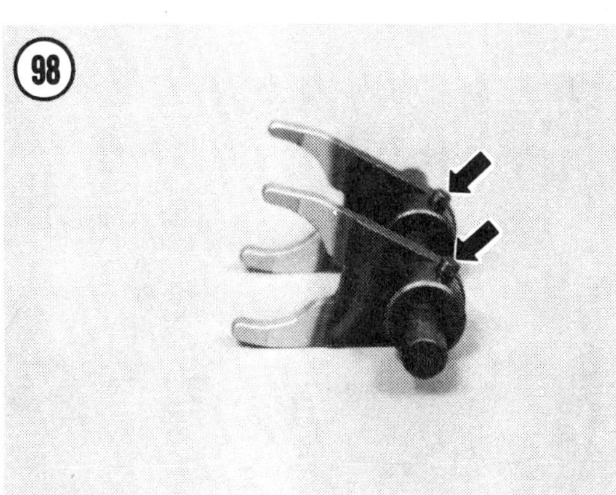

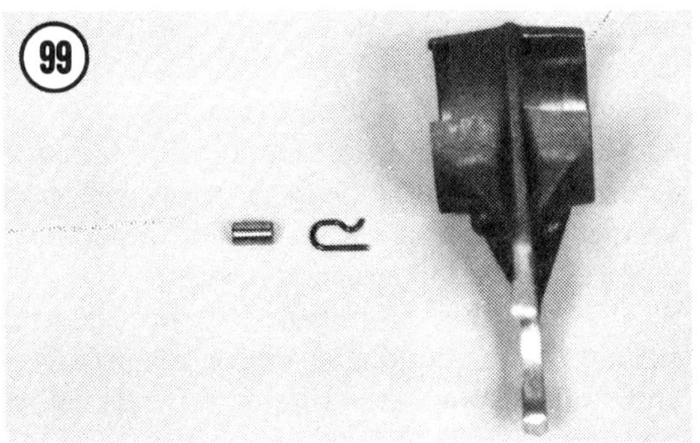

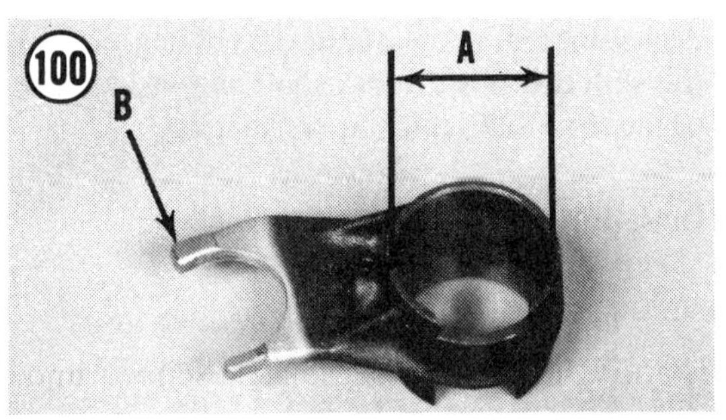

NOTE

Check for any arc-shaped wear or burned marks on the shift forks (**Figure 95**)*. This indicates that the shift fork has come in contact with the gear. The fork fingers are excessively worn and the fork must be replaced.*

2. Roll the shift fork shaft on a flat surface such as a piece of plate glass and check for any bends. If the shaft is bent, replace it.
3. Measure the outside diameter of the shift fork shaft with a micrometer or vernier caliper (**Figure 96**). Replace if worn beyond the specifications in **Table 3**.
4. Check the grooves in the shift drum (**Figure 97**) for wear or roughness. If any of the groove profiles have excessive wear or damage, replace the shift drum.
5. Check the cam pin followers (**Figure 98**) in each shift fork for wear or burrs. Replace the shift fork if they are damaged.
6. On the large shift fork, inspect the condition of the fork set pin and clip (**Figure 99**). All parts must fit snugly and be free of burrs. Replace as necessary.
7. Measure the inside diameter of the large shift fork (A, **Figure 100**) and the thickness of the gearshift fingers (B, **Figure 100**) with a

micrometer or vernier caliper. Compare with dimensions given in **Table 3**. Replace if either dimension is worn to the service limit.

8. Measure the outside diameter of the shift drum (**Figure 101**) with a micrometer or vernier caliper and compare with dimensions given in **Table 3**. Replace as necessary.

9. Inspect the condition of the bearing surfaces in the crankcase where the shift fork and shift drum ride. Check for scoring or scratches.

10. If shift fork assemblies have been disassembled, apply a light coat of engine oil to the shift drum, shift fork shaft and inside bores of the shift forks prior to installation.

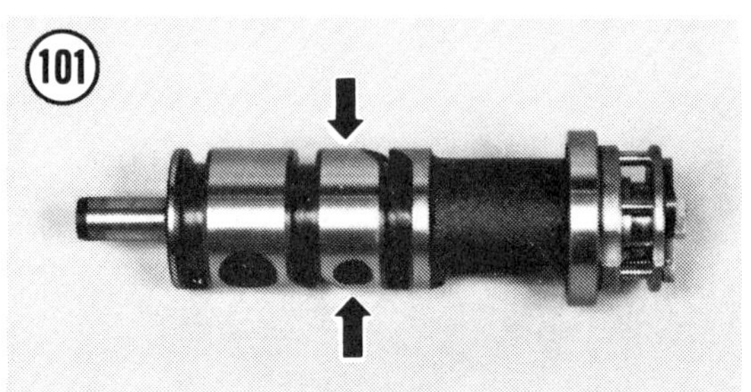

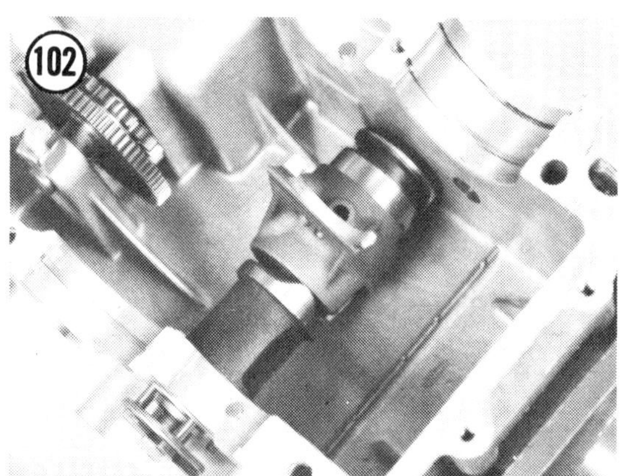

Installation

NOTE
In the following procedure, remember that the right- and left-hand side of the engine refers to the engine installed in the bike's frame—not as it sits on your workbench.

1. Coat all bearing surfaces with assembly oil.
2. Partially slide in the shift drum. Position the large shift fork and slide the shift drum all the way in until it seats completely in the crankcase.
3. Position the large shift fork so the set pin hole is located on the middle shift drum groove (**Figure 102**).
4. Install the shift drum set pin (**Figure 103**) and install the retaining clip (**Figure 104**).

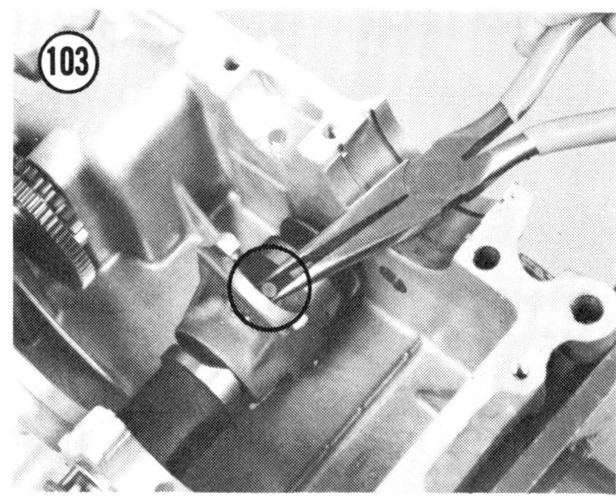

NOTE
In the next step, position the shift forks with the guide pin facing toward the left-hand side of the engine.

5. Partially insert the shift fork shaft and position one shift fork onto it (**Figure 105**). Slide it in further and install the other shift fork (**Figure 92**).

NOTE
Make sure the guide pins are properly meshed into the shift drum.

6. Install the shift drum bearing stopper plate and install the bolts (**Figure 91**). Tighten the bolts securely.

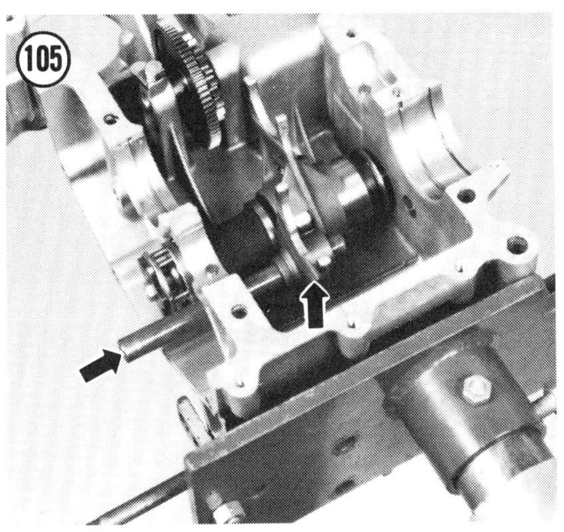

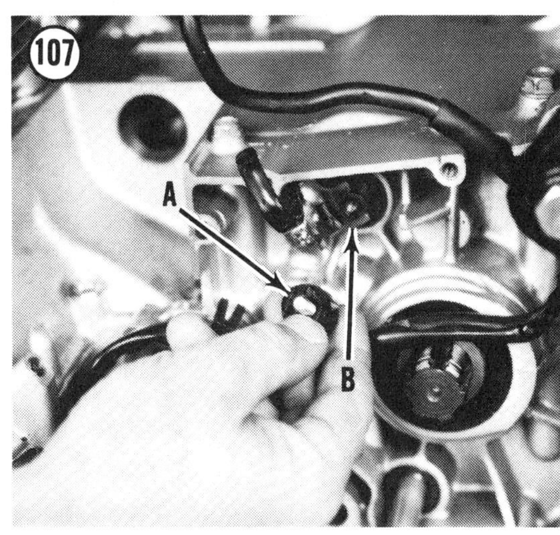

7. Install the neutral switch on the left-hand end of the shift drum (**Figure 106**). Align the tab on the switch (A, **Figure 107**) with the slot on the end of the shift drum (B, **Figure 107**).

NOTE

***Figure 106** and **Figure 107** are shown with the engine assembled and installed in the frame. The switch can be either installed now or installed later as shown in these figures.*

8. Install the transmission components and assemble the crankcase halves as described under *Transmission Removal/Installation* in this chapter.

TABLE 1 CLUTCH SPECIFICATIONS

Item	Standard	Wear Limit
Friction disc thickness		
Disc A	0.135-0.141 in. (3.42-3.58 mm)	0.13 in. (3.2 mm)
Disc B	0.103-0.109 in. (2.62-2.78 mm)	0.09 in. (2.4 mm)
Clutch plate warpage	—	0.012 in. (0.3 mm)
Clutch springs free length	1.45 in. (36.8 mm)	1.39 in. (35.4 mm)
Clutch outer housing ID	1.1808-1.1813 in. (29.990-30.005 mm)	1.183 in. (30.05 mm)
Clutch outer housing guide OD	1.1795-1.1803 in. (29.959-29.980 mm)	1.179 in. (29.94 mm)

TABLE 2 TRANSMISSION SPECIFICATIONS

Item	Specifications	Wear Limit
Gear backlash		
1st, 2nd, 3rd	0.0017-0.0052 in. (0.044-0.133 mm)	0.008 in. (0.20 mm)
4th, 5th	0.0018-0.0055 in. (0.046-0.140 mm)	0.008 in. (0.20 mm)
Gear ID/Main shaft		
4th gear	0.9850-0.9859 in. (25.020-25.041 mm)	0.987 in. (25.06 mm)
5th gear	0.9055-0.9068 in. 23.000-23.033 mm)	0.908 in. (23.06 mm)
Gear I.D./Countershaft		
1st	0.9449-0.9462 in. (24.000-24.033 mm)	0.947 in. (24.06 mm)
2nd, 3rd	0.9850-0.9859 in. (25.020-25.041 mm)	0.987 in. (25.07 mm)
Gear Bushing		
Main shaft/ 5th gear OD	0.9849-0.9052 in. (22.984-22.993 mm)	0.904 in. (22.96 mm)
5th gear ID	0.8665-0.7886 in. (20.010-20.030 mm)	0.790 in. (20.07 mm)
Countershaft/		
1st gear OD	0.9443-0.9556 in. (23.984-23.993 mm)	0.943 in. (23.95 mm)
1st gear ID	0.8665-0.7886 in. (20.010-20.030 mm)	0.790 in. (20.07 mm)
Main shaft OD		
at 4th gear	0.9826-0.9835 in. (24.959-24.980 mm)	0.981 in. (24.93 mm)
at 5th gear	0.7869-0.7874 in. (19.987-20.000 mm)	0.785 in. (19.93 mm)
Countershaft OD		
at 1st gear	0.7869-0.7874 in. (19.987-20.000 mm)	0.785 in. (19.93 mm)
at 2nd and 3rd	0.7869-0.7874 in. (19.987-20.000 mm)	0.785 in. (19.93 mm)
Gear to shaft or gear to bushing clearance/ all gears—both shafts	—	0.0040 in. (0.10 mm)
End clearance		
Main shaft 5th gear	0.012-0.020 in. (0.3-0.5 mm)	—
Countershaft 1st gear	0.004-0.012 in. (0.1-0.3 mm)	—

TABLE 3 SHIFT FORK AND SHAFT SPECIFICATIONS

Item	Specifications	Wear Limit
Shift fork ID		
Center	1.4961-1.4970 in. (38.000-38.025 mm)	1.499 in. (38.075 mm)
Left and right	0.5118-0.5125 in. (13.000-13.018 mm)	0.513 in. (13.04 mm)
Shift fork finger thickness—all	0.2333-0.236 in. (5.93-6.00 mm)	0.22 in. (5.6 mm)
Shift fork shaft OD	0.5104-0.5112 in. (12.966-12.984 mm)	0.508 in. (12.90 mm)
Shift fork drum OD	1.4941-1.4951 in. (37.950-37.975 mm)	1.492 in. (37.90 mm)

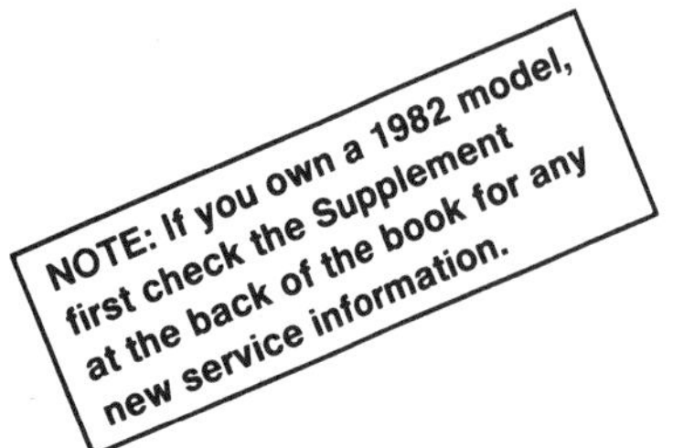

NOTE: If you own a 1982 model,
first check the Supplement
at the back of the book for any
new service information.

CHAPTER SIX

FUEL AND EXHAUST SYSTEMS

The fuel system consists of the fuel tank, the shutoff valve, 4 Keihin carburetors and the air cleaner assembly. The carburetors used on the 1979-1980 models have mechanically operated throttle valves (slides) while models since 1981 use the constant velocity (CV) type.

The exhaust system consists of 4 exhaust pipes and 2 mufflers on the standard model while the Custom model uses 4 exhaust pipes and 4 short mufflers.

This chapter includes service procedures for all parts of the fuel system and exhaust system. **Table 1** is at the end of the chapter.

AIR CLEANER

The air cleaner must be cleaned frequently. Refer to Chapter Three for specific procedures and service intervals.

CARBURETOR OPERATION

An understanding of the function of each of the carburetor components and their relation to one another is a valuable aid for pinpointing a source of carburetor trouble.

The carburetor's purpose is to supply and atomize fuel and to mix it in correct proportions with the air that is drawn in through the air intake. At the primary throttle opening—at idle—a small amount of fuel is siphoned through the pilot jet by the incoming air. As the throttle is opened further, the air stream begins to siphon fuel through the main jet and needle jet. The tapered needle increases the effective flow capacity of the needle jet as it is lifted, in that it occupies decreasingly less of the area of the jet. In addition, the amount of cutaway in the leading edge of the throttle valve (or vacuum cylinder) aids in controlling the fuel/air mixture during partial throttle openings.

At full throttle, the carburetor venturi is fully opened and the needle is lifted far enough to permit the main jet to flow at full capacity.

Both types of carburetors are equipped with an accelerator pump. This supplies an additional amount of fuel to the carburetors during acceleration. There is only one accelerator pump with a distribution tube leading to all 4 carburetors.

CARBURETOR SERVICE

Major carburetor service (removal and cleaning) should be performed at 10,000 mile (16,093 km) intervals or when poor engine performance, hesitation and little or no response to mixture adjustment is observed. Alterations in jet size, throttle slide or cylinder

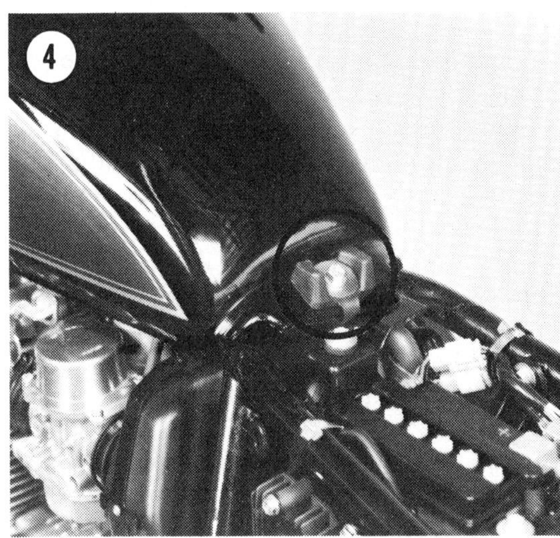

cutaway, etc., should be attempted only if you're experienced in this type of "tuning" work; a bad guess could result in costly engine damage or, at least, poor performance. If after servicing the carburetors and making the adjustments described in this chapter, the motorcycle does not perform correctly (and assuming that other factors affecting performance are correct, such as ignition timing and condition, valve adjustment, etc.), the motorcycle should be checked by a dealer or a qualified performance tuning specialist.

Carburetor specifications are covered in **Table 1** at the end of this chapter.

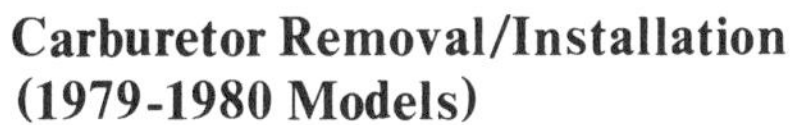

Carburetor Removal/Installation (1979-1980 Models)

1. Place a milk crate or wood block(s) under the engine or frame to support it securely.
2. Turn the fuel shutoff valve to the OFF position and remove the fuel line to the carburetor (**Figure 1**).
3. Remove the seat and side covers (**Figure 2**).
4. Disconnect the battery negative and positive leads (**Figure 3**) and remove the battery.
5. Remove the bolt (**Figure 4**) securing the rear of the fuel tank. Lift up and pull the tank to the rear and remove it. Remove the rubber mounting damper and keep it with the fuel tank to avoid misplacing it.

6. Place a suitable container under the carburetor drain tubes located next to the rear swing arm pivot area. Open the drain screw (**Figure 5**) on each carburetor and drain the gasoline from the float bowls. Tighten the drain screws after draining is complete. Dispose of this gasoline properly; *do not reuse it* as it is dirty after flowing out through the drain tubes.
7. Remove the chrome trim plates on each side of the air box. Loosen the clamping screw (**Figure 6**) on the band securing the air cleaner assembly to the air box.
8. Pull the air cleaner assembly and air box as far back as possible to gain as much working room as possible.
9. At the throttle grip, loosen the locknut and adjuster on the throttle cables and turn the adjusting barrel (**Figure 7**) all the way in.
10. Disconnect the engine breather tube (**Figure 8**) from the engine and air box and remove it.
11. Loosen the front and back clamping screws on all 4 carburetors (**Figure 9**).
12. Slide the clamps away from the carburetors.
13. Pull the carburetor assembly to the rear to clear the carburetor throats from the rubber intake ports on the cylinder head.
14. Pull the drain tubes free from the frame area; leave them attached to the carburetors.
15. Pull the carburetor assembly out toward the right-hand side.

NOTE
This is not an easy task and it is a lot easier with the aid of a helper. One or more of the rubber intake tubes on the air box may come off during disassembly; just push it back into place after the carburetor assembly is removed.

16. Loosen the cable locknuts (**Figure 10**) and disconnect the choke cable (**Figure 11**) and the throttle cables (**Figure 12**). Watch your fingers as the throttle assembly return spring is very strong; protect yourself accordingly. Tie the loose ends of the cables up to the frame.
17. Take the carburetor assembly to your workbench for disassembly and cleaning.

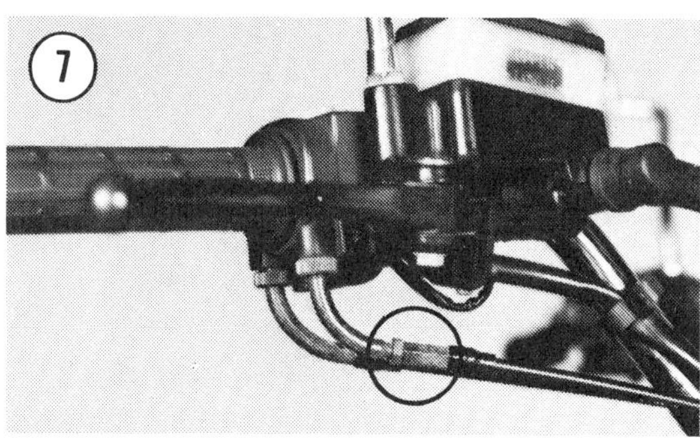

18. Install by reversing these removal steps, noting the following.
19. Prior to installing the carburetor assembly, move each carburetor clamp on the air box toward the rear. This will allow the tube to flex the maximum amount for ease of installation. Also pull the air box as far back as possible and hold it in place with a Bungee cord (**Figure 13**).
20. Be sure the throttle and choke cables are in the correct position in the frame and that they are not twisted or kinked and do not have any sharp bends.
21. Install the throttle cables (**Figure 12**) and choke cable (**Figure 11**). Tighten the cable locknuts. Remove the Bungee cord.

8

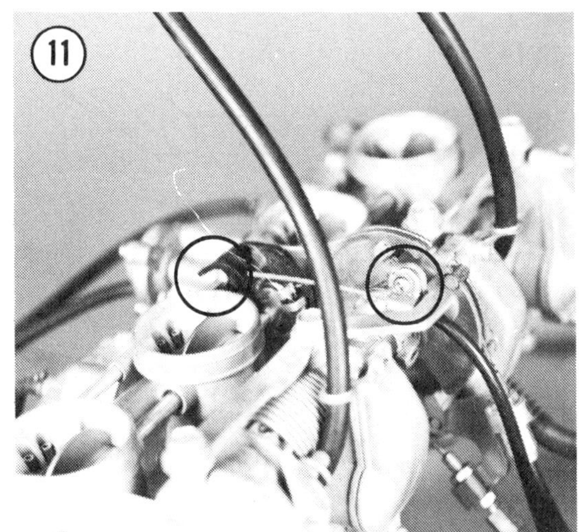
11

9

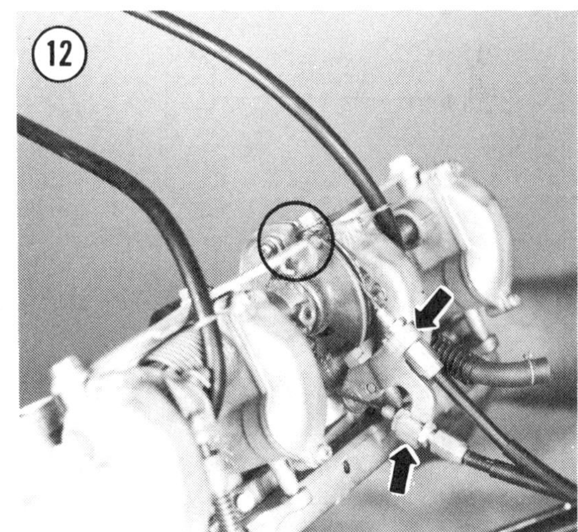
12

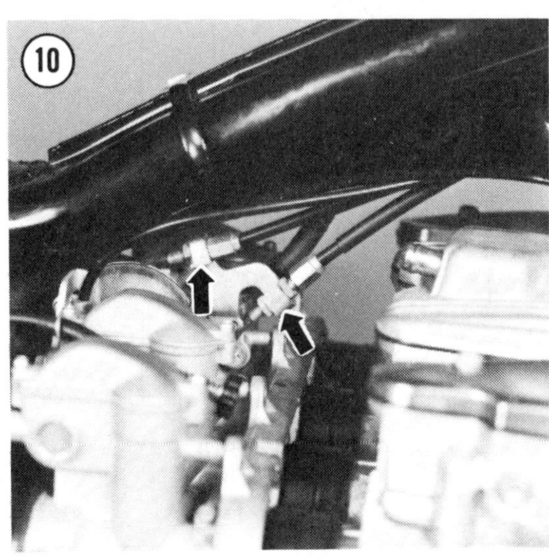
10

13

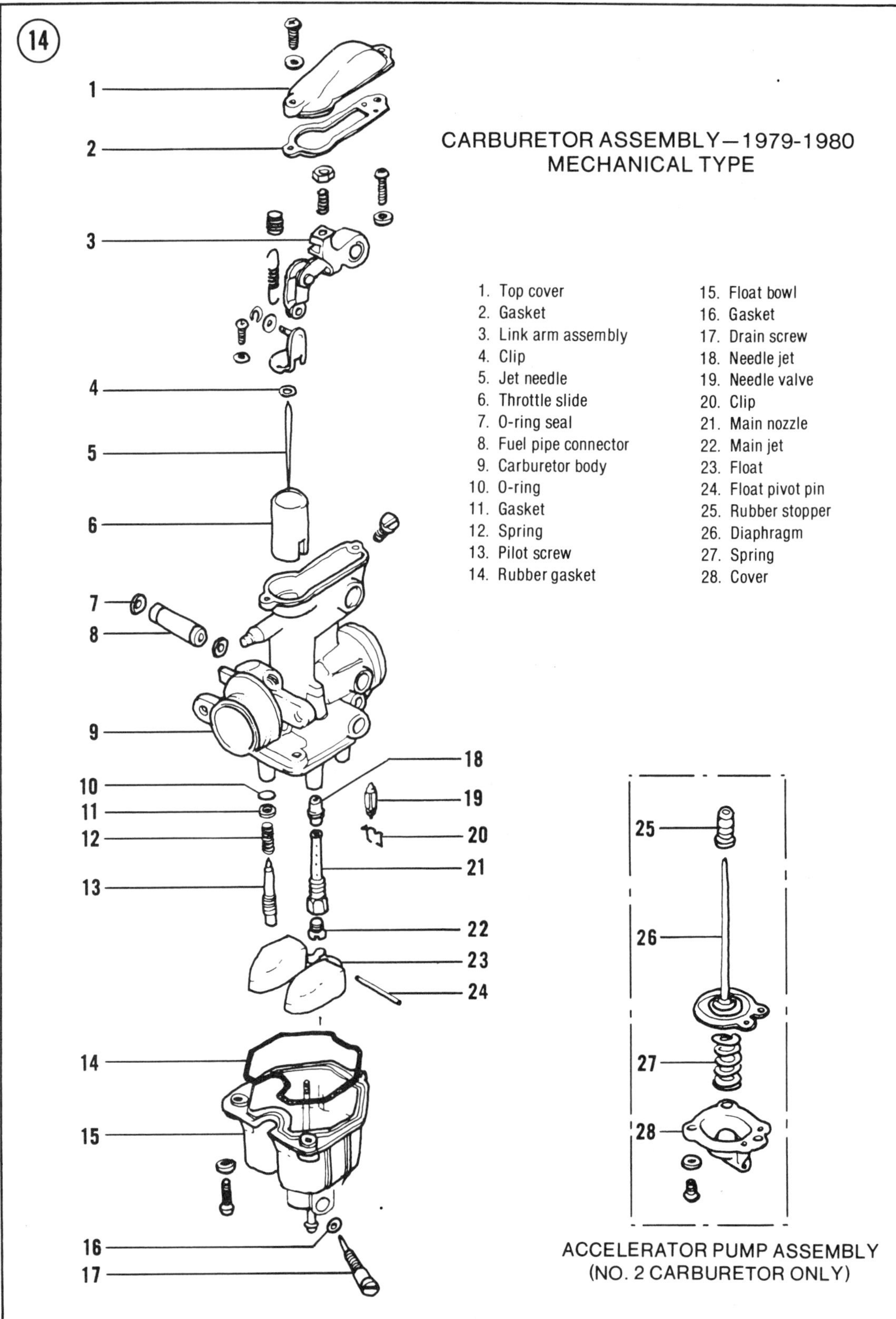
14
CARBURETOR ASSEMBLY—1979-1980
MECHANICAL TYPE
1. Top cover
2. Gasket
3. Link arm assembly
4. Clip
5. Jet needle
6. Throttle slide
7. O-ring seal
8. Fuel pipe connector
9. Carburetor body
10. O-ring
11. Gasket
12. Spring
13. Pilot screw
14. Rubber gasket
15. Float bowl
16. Gasket
17. Drain screw
18. Needle jet
19. Needle valve
20. Clip
21. Main nozzle
22. Main jet
23. Float
24. Float pivot pin
25. Rubber stopper
26. Diaphragm
27. Spring
28. Cover
ACCELERATOR PUMP ASSEMBLY
(NO. 2 CARBURETOR ONLY)

15

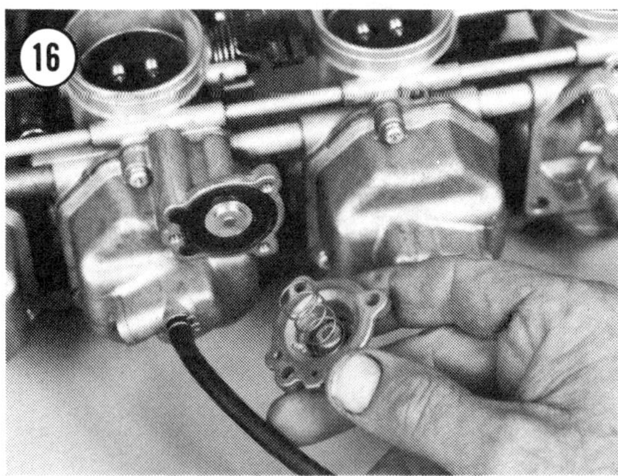
16

17

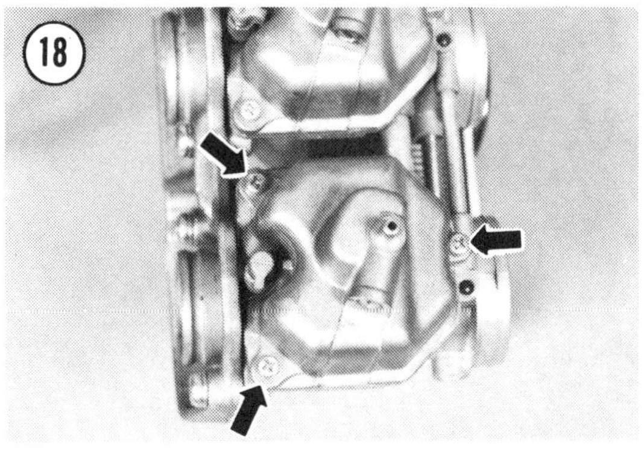
18

Disassembly/Cleaning/Inspection/ Assembly (1979-1980 Models)

Refer to **Figure 14** for this procedure.

It is recommended that only one carburetor be disassembled and cleaned at one time. This will prevent the intermix of parts.

NOTE

All 4 carburetors look the same, but slight differences exist among all of them. Take note of this prior to disassembly.

All components that require cleaning can be removed from the carburetor body without removing the carburetors from the mounting plates. If separation is necessary it is covered under *Carburetor Separation/Assembly—1979-1980 Models* in this chapter.

The carburetors are not separated in this procedure to help simplify this material.

NOTE

The carburetors are numbered in the same sequence as the engine cylinders. The No. 1 carburetor is on the left-hand side and No. 2, 3 and 4 continue from left to right. Remember that the left-hand side refers to the carburetor assembly as it sits in the bike's frame, not as it sits on your workbench.

1. On the No. 2 carburetor only, disassemble the accelerator pump assembly. Remove the 3 screws (**Figure 15**) securing the accelerator pump cover. Remove the cover and spring (**Figure 16**). Withdraw the diaphragm assembly from the carburetor body (**Figure 17**). Don't lose the small external O-ring gasket on the end of the diaphragm rod.
2. On the No. 2 carburetor only, disassemble the air cutoff valve. Remove the 2 screws securing the air cutoff valve cover and remove it. Remove the spring and diaphragm. Remove the small O-ring seal.
3. Remove the drain tube from the carburetor that is going to be disassembled.
4. Remove the screws securing the float bowl (**Figure 18**) and remove the float bowl.

6

5. Carefully push out the float pivot pin (**Figure 19**).
6. Lift the float and needle valve (**Figure 20**) out of the main body.
7. Remove the main jet (**Figure 21**).
8. Remove the main jet holder (**Figure 22**).

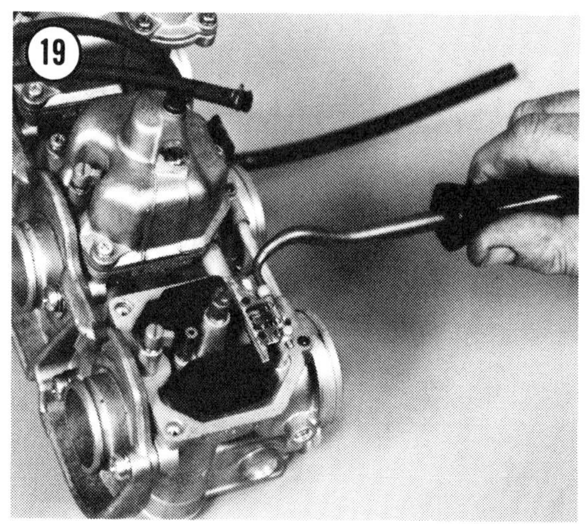

NOTE
Prior to removing the pilot screw, record the number of turns necessary until the screw lightly seats. Record the number of turns for all 4 carburetors as they must be reinstalled into the same exact setting.

9. Unscrew the pilot screw (A, **Figure 23**), spring, plain washer and O-ring (**Figure 24**).
10. The slow jet (B, **Figure 23**) is not removable as it is pressed into place.
11. Remove the float bowl gasket (**Figure 25**).
12. If the throttle valve (slide) is suspected of hanging up, remove the screws (**Figure 26**) securing the top cover and remove the top cover.

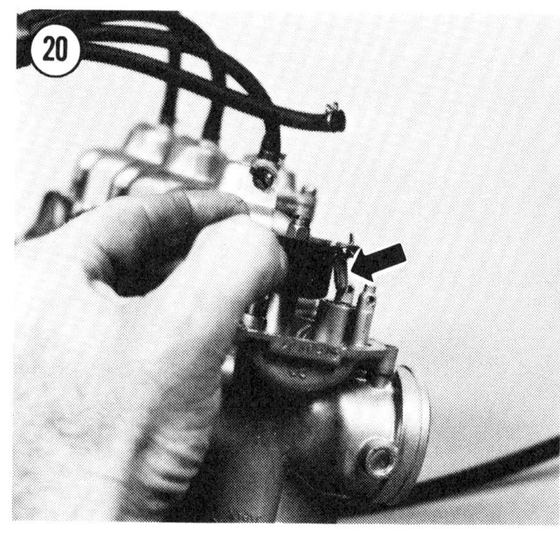

NOTE
Further disassembly is neither necessary nor recommended. If throttle or choke shafts or butterflies are damaged, take the carburetor body to a dealer for replacement.

13. Clean all parts, except rubber or plastic parts, in a good grade of carburetor cleaner. This solution is available at most automotive or motorcycle supply stores in a small, resealable tank with a dip basket for just a few dollars (**Figure 27**). If it is tightly sealed when not in use, the solution will last for several cleanings. Follow the manufacturer's instructions for correct soak time (usually about 1/2 hour).
14. Remove all parts from the cleaner and blow dry with compressed air. Blow out the jets with compressed air. *Do not* use a piece of wire to clean them as minor gouges in the jet can alter flow rate and upset the fuel/air mixture.
15. Be sure to clean out the overflow tube.

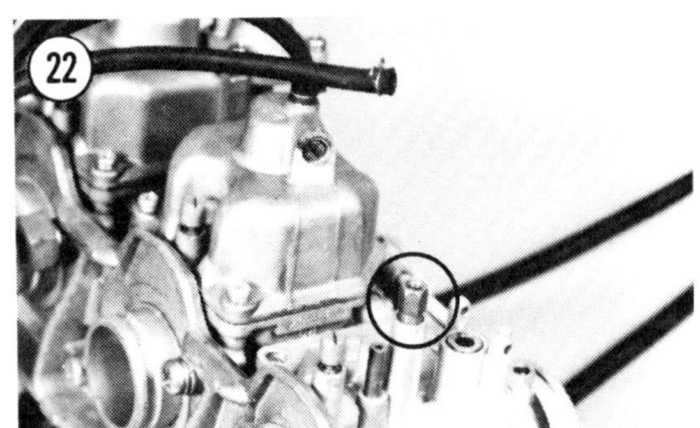

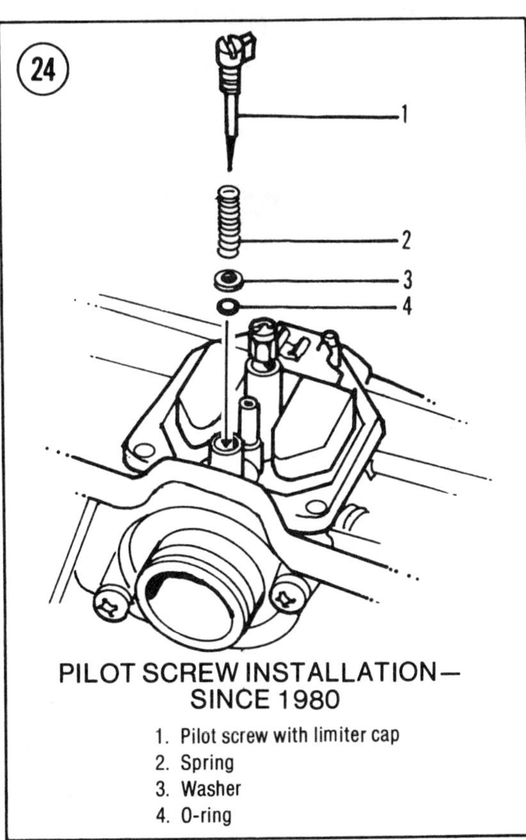

PILOT SCREW INSTALLATION—
SINCE 1980

1. Pilot screw with limiter cap
2. Spring
3. Washer
4. O-ring

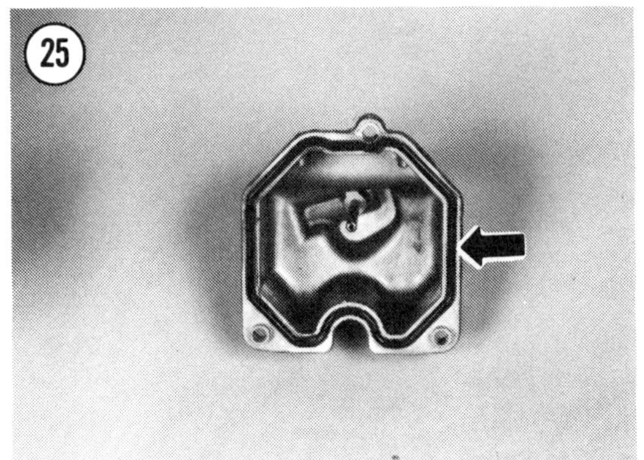

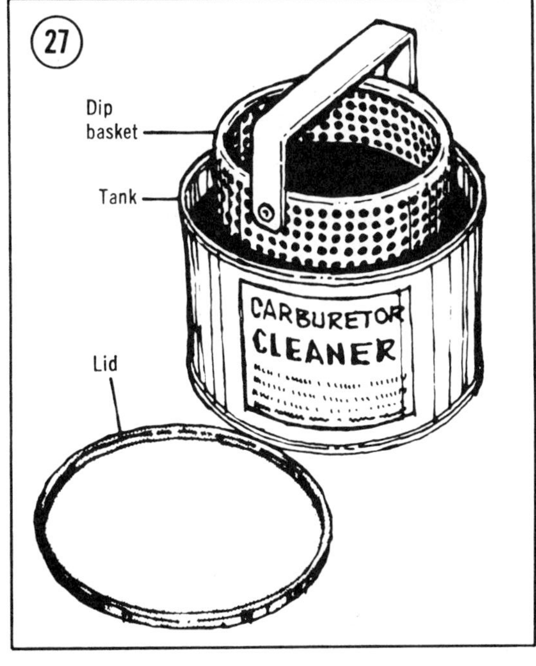

16. If the throttle valve (slide) area in the carburetor body is dirty (**Figure 28**), spray some carburetor cleaner into it while working the throttle linkage back and forth. Carefully blow out the area with compressed air.
17. Inspect the condition of the end of the float valve needle and seat (**Figure 29**) for wear or damage; replace either or both parts if necessary.
18. Repeat Steps 1-17 for the other 3 carburetors; note that Step 1 and Step 2 are performed only on specific carburetors, as designated.
19. Inspect the condition of all O-ring seals. O-ring seals tend to become hardened after prolonged use and heat and therefore lose their ability to seal properly. Replace as necessary.
20. Screw the pilot screw into the exact same position (same number of turns) as recorded in Step 9.

NOTE

*On 1980 models, if a new pilot screw was installed, turn it 2-1/8 turns out from the **lightly** seated position and position the limiter to the right of the stop on the float bowl (**Figure 30**).*

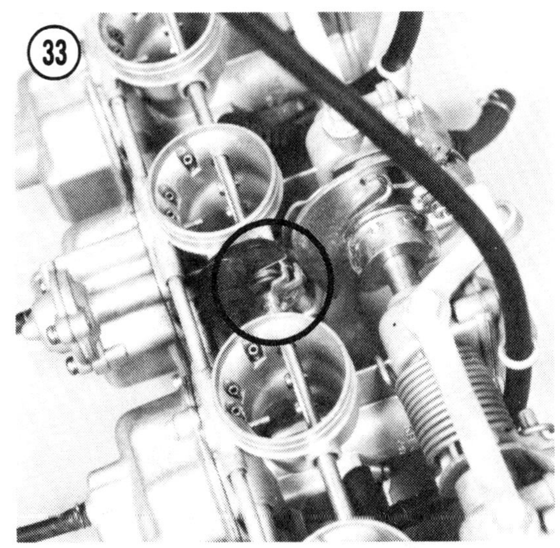

33

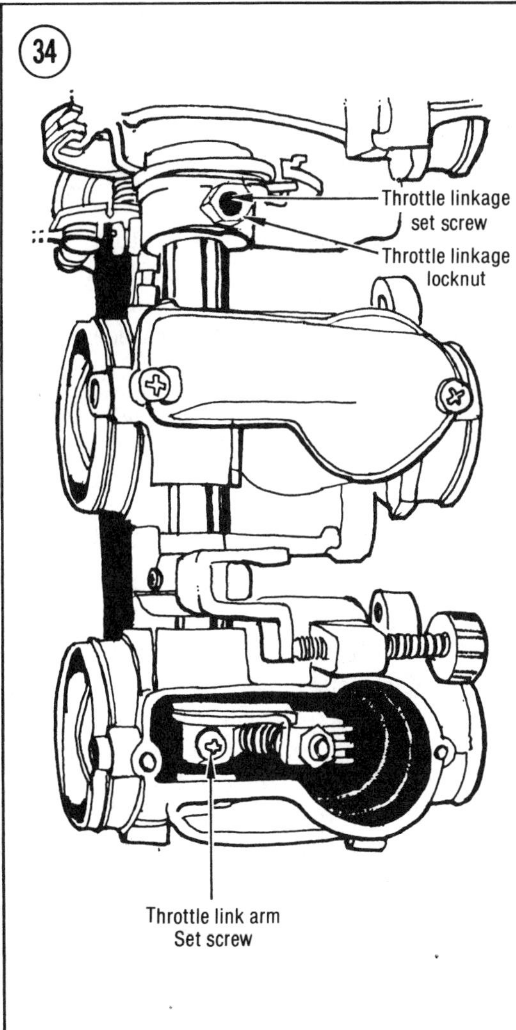

34

21. Inspect the condition of the accelerator pump diaphragm for cracks and hardening; ensure that the rod is not bent.

22. When installing the diaphragm on the accelerator pump make sure the 2 tabs on the diaphragm align with the notches in the float bowl (**Figure 31**). Install the small O-ring gasket (**Figure 32**) onto the outer end of the diaphragm rod and push it all the way down to the carburetor body.

23. On the No. 1 carburetor, install the diaphragm on the air cutoff valve with the flat surface in toward the carburetor body. Make sure to install the small O-ring seal.

24. Check the float height and adjust if necessary. Refer to *Float Adjustment* in this chapter.

25. After assembly and installation are completed, adjust the carburetors as described under *Pilot Screw Adjustment—1979 Models* or *Pilot Screw Adjustment—1980 Models (And New Limiter Cap Installation—U.S. Only)* in this chapter and *Carburetor Synchronization* in Chapter Three.

6

Carburetor Separation/Assembly (1979-1980 Models)

1. Remove the carburetor assembly as described under *Carburetor Removal/Installation—1979-1980 Models* in this chapter.

2. Unhook the choke relief spring from the choke shaft arm on the No. 2 and No. 3 carburetors (**Figure 33**).

NOTE

The carburetors are numbered in the same sequence as the engine cylinders. The No. 1 carburetor is located on the left-hand side and No. 2, 3 and 4 continue from left to right. Remember that the right-hand side relates to the carburetor assembly as it sits in the bike's frame, not as it sits on your workbench.

3. Remove the screws securing the carburetor's top covers and remove all 4 top covers.

4. Remove the throttle link arms' set screws (**Figure 34**).

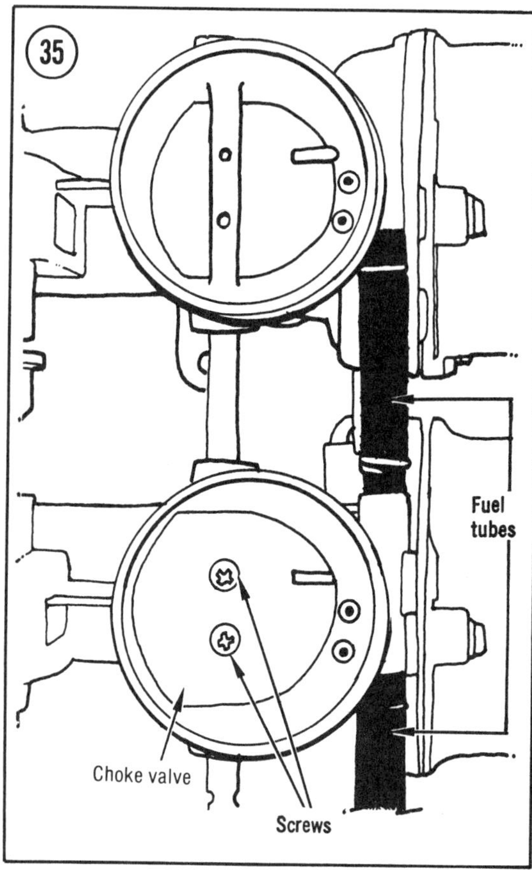

5. Hold the carburetor assembly with the choke side facing downward and file off the staked ends of the choke valve holding screws. Don't allow the metal filings to enter into the carburetor body. Remove the screws and all 4 choke valves (**Figure 35**). Discard these screws as they will be replaced with small bolts and lockwashers upon assembly.
6. Remove the bolts securing the rear brackets (**Figure 36**) and remove both brackets.
7. Remove the screws securing the front bracket (**Figure 37**) and remove the bracket.
8. While holding the carburetor assembly in the horizontal position and in one plane, carefully remove the No. 1 and No. 4 carburetor.

CAUTION
Avoid damage to the fuel and air joint pipes and the choke linkage that join the subassemblies.

9. Loosen the throttle linkage set screw locknut and screw (**Figure 34**).

10. Disengage the throttle return spring from the rib on the No. 3 carburetor.
11. Hold the remaining carburetors in the horizontal position and in one plane and carefully separate the No. 2 and No. 3 carburetors, throttle shaft and throttle linkage.

CAUTION
Avoid damage to the fuel and air joint pipes and the choke linkage that joins the 2 carburetors.

12. With the exception of the throttle valve (slide) assembly further disassembly is not recommended and should be entrusted to a dealer or carburetor specialist.
13. Assemble the subassemblies by performing the following steps.
14. If disassembled, install the throttle valve (slide) to the link arm so that the cutaway is facing the choke valve (**Figure 38**).
15. Install the throttle valve assemblies into the carburetor bodies. The assembly without the adjust screw (**Figure 39**) is fitted to the No. 2 carburetor body.
16. Insert the throttle shaft into the No. 3 carburetor through the throttle spring.
17. Apply a light coat of oil to *new O-rings* on the fuel joint pipes.

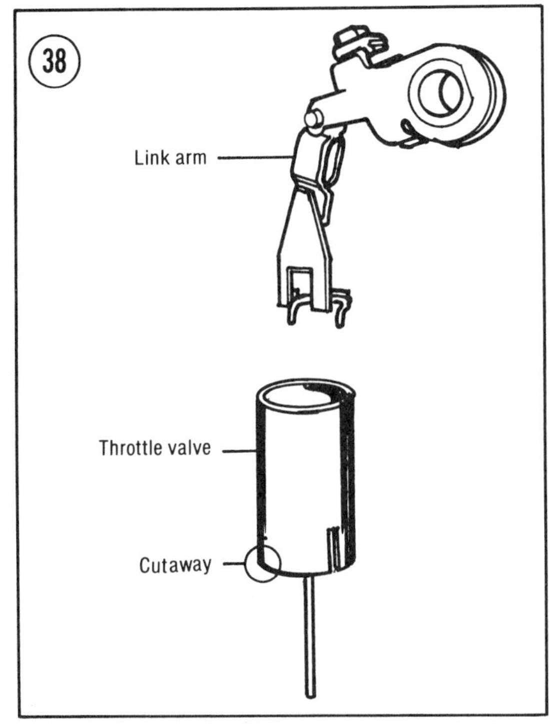

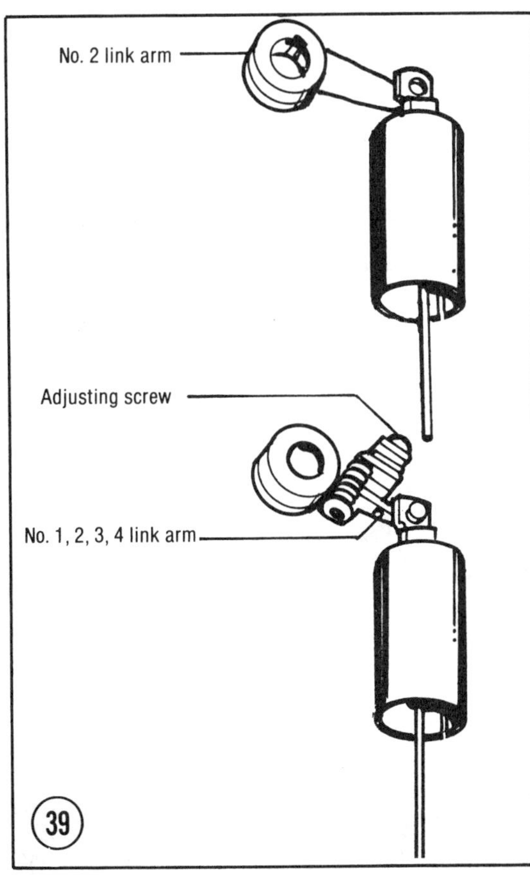

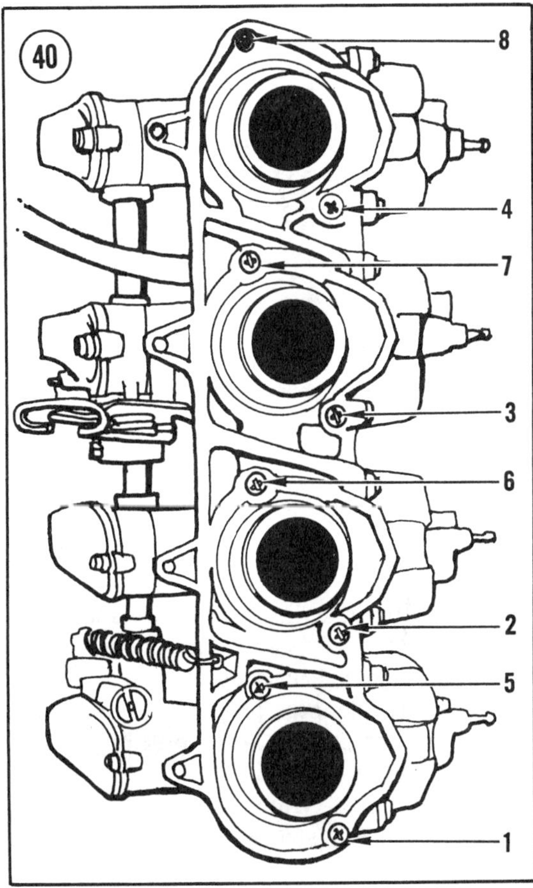

18. Insert a new choke shaft into the No. 2 and No. 3 carburetors.
19. Install the throttle linkage and nylon washer onto the throttle shaft. The nylon washer goes next to the No. 2 carburetor.
20. Holding the carburetors horizontal and in one plane, carefully press the No. 2 and No. 3 carburetors together.
21. Align the hole in the throttle shaft with the throttle linkage set screw and tighten the set screw and locknut. Attach the small coil return spring.
22. Holding the carburetors horizontal and in one plane, carefully press the No. 1 and No. 4 carburetors into place onto the subassembly.
23. Lay the carburetor assembly on a flat surface.
24. Install the front bracket and tighten the screws finger-tight. Tighten the screws in 2 or 3 steps in the sequence shown in **Figure 40**. While tightening the screws continue to check that the choke shaft operates smoothly. If it

does not, check carburetor alignment and adjust as necessary.

25. Install rear brackets and tighten the bolts securely.

26. Align the holes in the throttle shaft with each throttle valve (slide) arm set screw hole. Install and tighten each set screw.

27. Use needlenose pliers and hook the throttle return spring ends onto the throttle shaft arm (**Figure 41**) and onto the boss on the No. 3 carburetor. Watch your fingers as the spring is very strong; protect yourself accordingly.

28. After the spring is installed check the throttle operation. Open the linkage slightly by pressing on the throttle linkage (A, **Figure 42**) and then releasing it. It should return to the closed position smoothly with no hesitation or drag. If throttle operation is not correct, check for proper alignment of the throttle shaft and also make sure the throttle valves (slides) are not binding within the carburetor body. Make sure that the linkage is not bent. Replace the linkage or realign the carburetors.

29. Install all 4 choke valves, lockwashers and small bolts (**Figure 43**). Tighten the bolts finger-tight at this time.

30. Hook the choke relief spring to the choke shaft arm of the No. 2 and No. 3 carburetors.

31. Close the choke valves with the choke linkage (B, **Figure 42**) and release it. Make sure it operates smoothly and returns completely with no hesitation or drag. If it does not, the carburetors are not properly aligned or the linkage is bent. Replace the linkage or realign the carburetors.

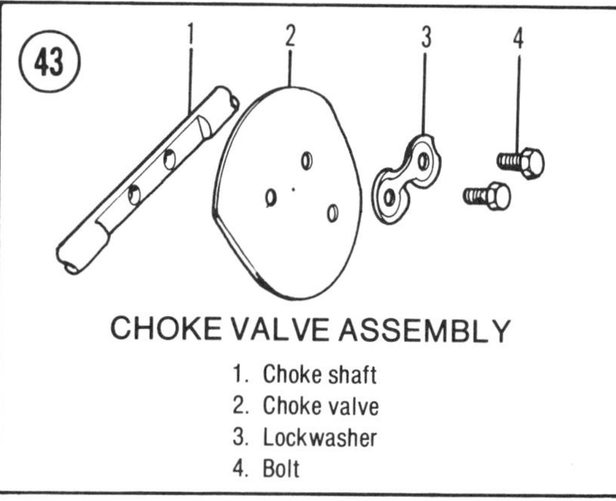

CHOKE VALVE ASSEMBLY

1. Choke shaft
2. Choke valve
3. Lockwasher
4. Bolt

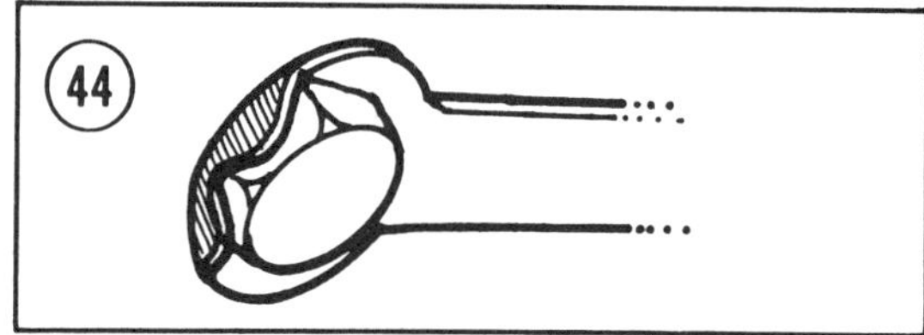

32. Tighten the choke valve bolts to 0.4-0.9 ft.-lb. (0.06-0.12 N•m) and fold the tabs of the lockwasher up against the flats of the bolts (**Figure 44**).
33. Again check the choke for smooth operation.

6

Carburetor Removal/Installation (Models Since 1981)

1. Place a milk crate or wood block(s) under the engine or frame to support it securely.
2. Turn the fuel shutoff valve to the OFF position and remove the fuel line to the carburetor (**Figure 45**).
3. Remove the seat and side covers.
4. Disconnect the battery negative and positive leads (**Figure 46**) and remove the battery.
5. Remove the bolt (**Figure 47**) securing the rear of the fuel tank. Lift up and pull the tank to the rear and remove it. Remove the rubber mounting damper and keep it with the fuel tank to avoid misplacing it.
6. Place a suitable container under the carburetor drain outlet on the bottom of float bowl. Open the drain screw (**Figure 48**) on the carburetor and drain the gasoline from the float bowl. Tighten the drain screw after draining is complete. Repeat for all carburetors.
7. Loosen the clamping screw on the band securing the air cleaner assembly to the air box. Remove the chrome trim plates on each side of the air box.
8. Pull the air cleaner assembly and air box as far back as possible to gain as much working room as possible.
9. At the throttle, loosen the locknut and adjuster on the throttle cables and turn the adjusting barrel all the way in (**Figure 49**).

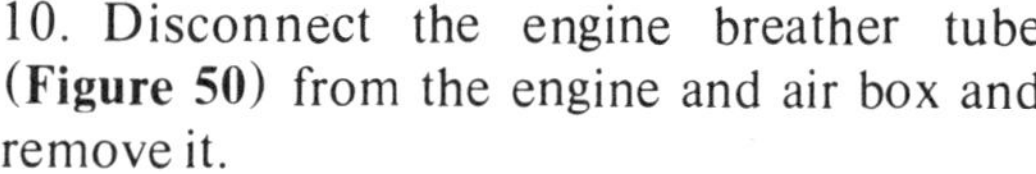

10. Disconnect the engine breather tube (**Figure 50**) from the engine and air box and remove it.
11. Loosen the front and back clamping screws on all 4 carburetors (**Figure 51**).
12. At the rear, slide the clamps away from the carburetors.
13. Pull the carburetor assembly to the rear to clear the carburetor throats from the rubber intake ports on the cylinder block.
14. Pull the vent tube (**Figure 52**) free from the frame area; leave it attached to the carburetors.
15. Loosen the throttle cable locknuts (**Figure 53**).
16. Pull the carburetor assembly out toward the left-hand side (**Figure 54**).
17. Disconnect the choke cable (**Figure 55**) and the throttle cables (**Figure 56**).
18. Take the carburetor assembly to your workbench for disassembly and cleaning.
19. Install by reversing these removal steps, noting the following.
20. Prior to installing the carburetor assembly, move each carburetor clamp on the air box toward the rear. This will allow the tube to flex the maximum amount for ease of installation.
21. Be sure the throttle and choke cables are in the same position in the frame and that they are not twisted or kinked and do not have any sharp bends.
22. Install the throttle cables (**Figure 56**) and choke cable (**Figure 55**). Tighten the cable locknuts.

23. Be sure to pull or push the carburetor assembly all the way forward until it completely seats in the intake tubes.

Disassembly/Cleaning/Inspection/ Assembly (Models Since 1981)

Refer to **Figure 57** for this procedure.

It is recommended that only one carburetor be disassembled and cleaned at one time. This will prevent the intermixing of parts.

NOTE

All 4 carburetors look the same, but slight differences exist among all of them. Take note of this prior to disassembly.

All components that require cleaning can be removed from the carburetor body without removing the carburetors from the mounting plates. If separation is necessary it is covered under *Carburetor Separation/Assembly—Models Since 1981* in this chapter.

The carburetors are not separated in this procedure to help simplify this material.

NOTE

The carburetors are numbered in the same sequence as the engine cylinders. The No. 1 carburetor is on the left-hand side and No. 2, 3 and 4 continue from left to right. Remember that the left-hand side refers to the carburetor assembly as it sits in the bike's frame not as it sits on your workbench.

1. On the No. 2 carburetor only, disassemble the accelerator pump assembly. Remove the 3 screws (**Figure 58**) securing the accelerator pump cover. Remove the cover and spring (**Figure 59**). Withdraw the diaphragm assembly from the carburetor body. Don't lose the small external O-ring on the end of the diaphragm rod.
2. On the No. 1 carburetor only, disassemble the air cutoff valve. Remove the 2 screws securing the air cutoff valve cover and remove it. Remove the spring and diaphragm. Remove the small O-ring seal.

NOTE

The air cutoff valve was installed on some early 1981 models only.

6

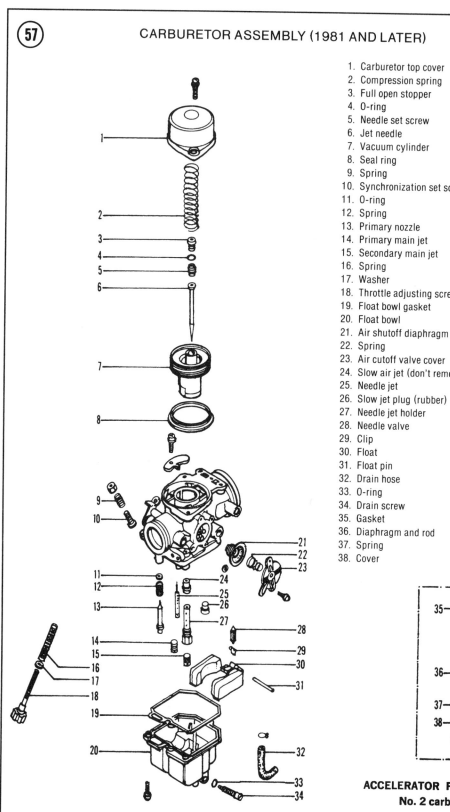

(57) CARBURETOR ASSEMBLY (1981 AND LATER)

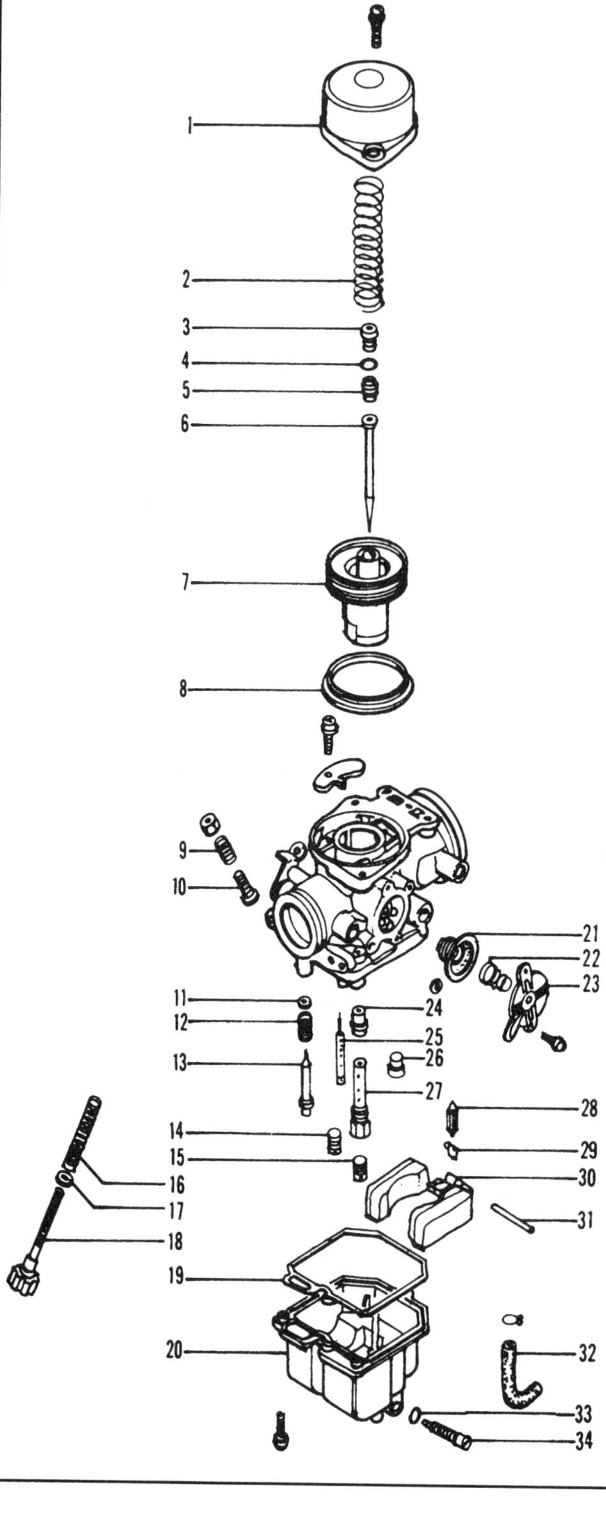

1. Carburetor top cover
2. Compression spring
3. Full open stopper
4. O-ring
5. Needle set screw
6. Jet needle
7. Vacuum cylinder
8. Seal ring
9. Spring
10. Synchronization set screw
11. O-ring
12. Spring
13. Primary nozzle
14. Primary main jet
15. Secondary main jet
16. Spring
17. Washer
18. Throttle adjusting screw
19. Float bowl gasket
20. Float bowl
21. Air shutoff diaphragm
22. Spring
23. Air cutoff valve cover
24. Slow air jet (don't remove)
25. Needle jet
26. Slow jet plug (rubber)
27. Needle jet holder
28. Needle valve
29. Clip
30. Float
31. Float pin
32. Drain hose
33. O-ring
34. Drain screw
35. Gasket
36. Diaphragm and rod
37. Spring
38. Cover

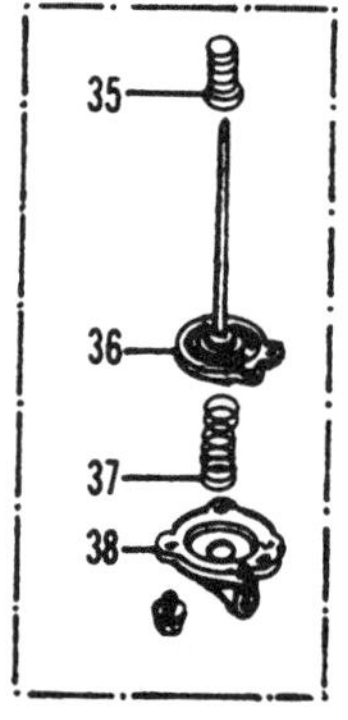

ACCELERATOR PUMP ASSEMBLY
No. 2 carburetor only

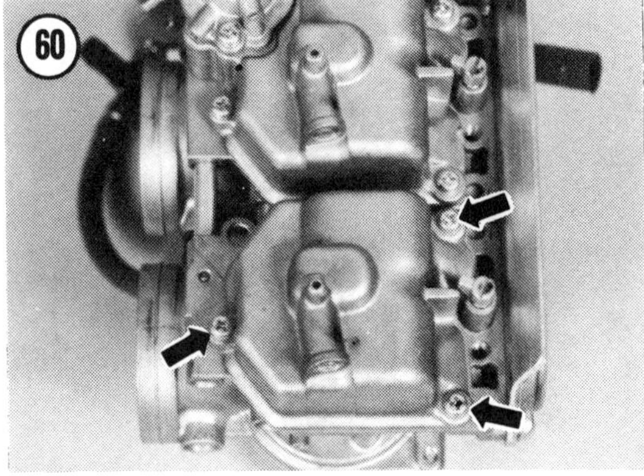

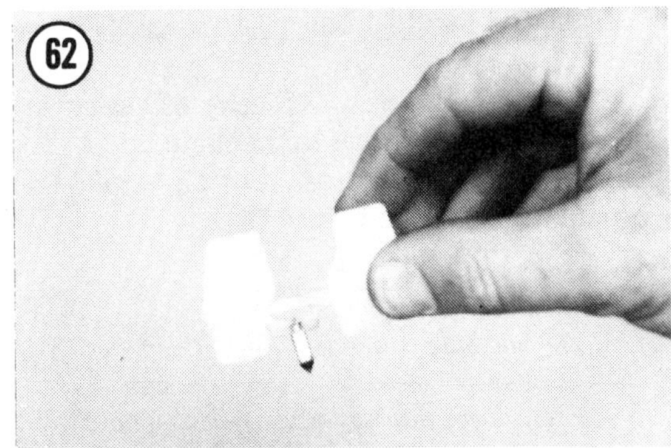

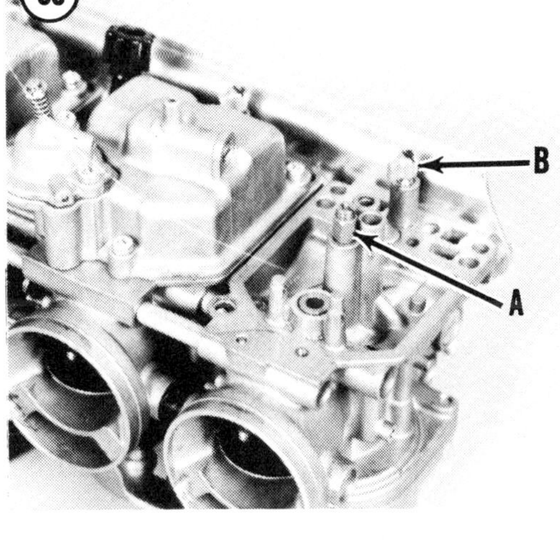

3. Remove the screws securing the float bowl (**Figure 60**) and remove the float bowl.
4. Carefully push out the float pivot pin (**Figure 61**).
5. Lift the float and needle valve (**Figure 62**) out of the main body.
6. Remove the main jet and main jet holder (A, **Figure 63**).
7. Tilt the carburetor and remove the needle jet.

NOTE

*Prior to removing the pilot screw, record the number of turns necessary until the screw **lightly** seats. Record the number of turns for all 4 carburetors as they must be reinstalled into the exact same setting.*

8. Unscrew the pilot screw (B, **Figure 63**), spring, plain washer and O-ring (**Figure 24**).
9. The slow jet is not removable as it is pressed into place.

10. Remove the float bowl O-ring seal (**Figure 64**).
11. Remove the screws (**Figure 65**) securing the carburetor top cover to the main body.
12. Remove the top cover and the compression spring (**Figure 66**).

NOTE
*The outboard carburetors (No. 1 and No. 4) have polished top covers. Be sure to install them this way when reassembling. This is for **appearance only** and has no effect on performance or operation of the carburetors.*

13. Remove the vacuum cylinder assembly (**Figure 67**).
14. Remove the seal ring (**Figure 68**) and air screw cover assembly (**Figure 69**).
15. Disassemble the vacuum cylinder assembly (**Figure 70**).

NOTE
Further disassembly is neither necessary nor recommended. If throttle or choke shafts or butterflies are damaged, take the carburetor body to a dealer for replacement.

16. Clean all parts, except rubber or plastic parts, in a good grade of carburetor cleaner. This solution is available at most automotive or motorcycle supply stores in a small, resealable tank with a dip basket for just a few dollars (**Figure 71**). If it is tightly sealed when not in use, the solution will last for several cleanings. Follow the manufacturer's instructions for correct soak time (usually about 1/2 hour).
17. Remove all parts from the cleaner and blow dry with compressed air. Blow out the jets with compressed air. *Do not* use a piece of wire to clean them as minor gouges in the jet can alter flow rate and upset the fuel/air mixture.
18. Make sure the air jets are clean (**Figure 72**).
19. Inspect the end of the float valve needle and seat (**Figure 73**) for wear or damage; replace either or both parts if necessary.
20. Repeat Steps 1-19 for the other 3 carburetors; note that Step 1 and Step 2 are

64

65

66

67

68

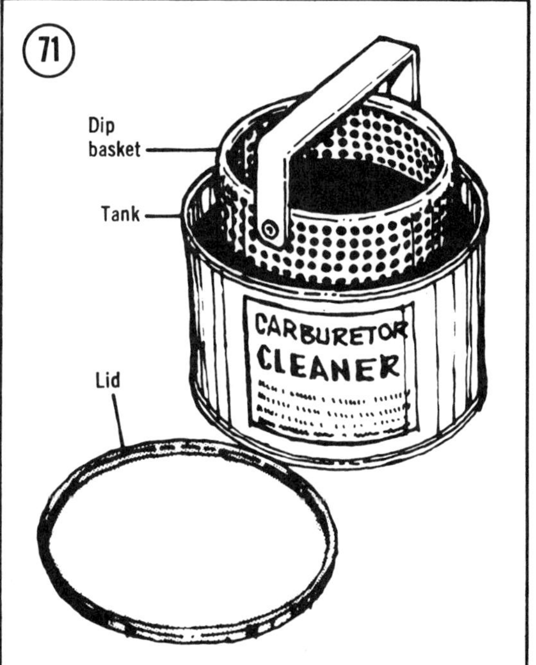
71
Dip basket
Tank
Lid
CARBURETOR
CLEANER

69

72

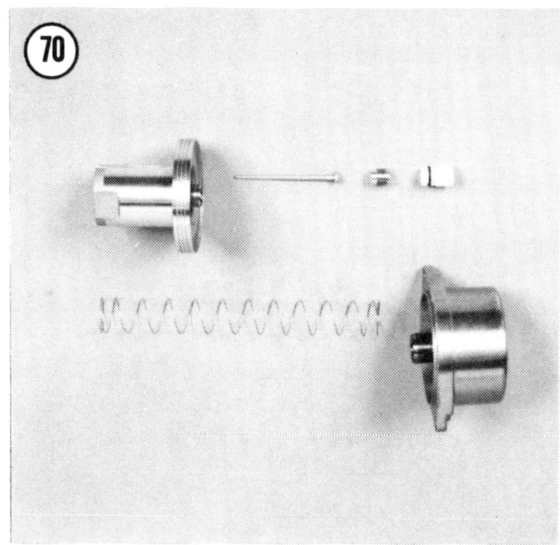
70

73

performed only on specific carburetors, as designated.

21. Inspect the condition of all O-ring seals. O-ring seals tend to become hardened after prolonged use and heat and therefore lose their ability to seal properly. Replace as necessary.

22. Screw the pilot screw into the exact same position (same number of turns) as recorded in Step 8.

NOTE

*If a new pilot screw was installed, turn it 2-1/4 turns out from the **lightly** seated position and position the limiter to the right of the stop on the float bowl (**Figure 74**).*

23. Inspect the condition of the accelerator pump diaphragm for cracks and hardening; ensure that the rod is not bent.

24. When installing the diaphragm on the accelerator pump make sure the 2 tabs on the diaphragm align with the notches in the float bowl (**Figure 75**). Install the small O-ring seal onto the outer end of the diaphragm rod and push it all the way down to the carburetor body.

25. Assemble the vacuum cylinder. Insert the jet needle into the vacuum cylinder (**Figure 76**) and screw in the needle set screw (**Figure 77**). Push in the full open stopper (**Figure 78**).

NOTE

Make sure the O-ring seal is installed on the full open stopper before installation.

26. Install the gasket, air jet cover and screw (**Figure 79**).

27. Install the seal ring (**Figure 68**) with the flat side on first.

28. Install the vacuum cylinder, compression spring and top cover.

29. Install the needle jet (**Figure 80**) with the chamfered side facing up toward the jet needle holder. Install the jet needle holder (**Figure 81**).

30. Install the main jet (**Figure 82**).

31. Install the float and needle valve and install the float pin (**Figure 83**).

32. Check the float height and adjust if necessary. Refer to *Float Adjustment* in this chapter.

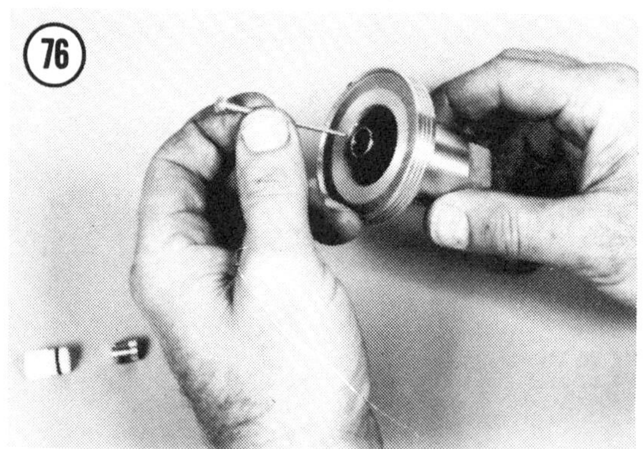

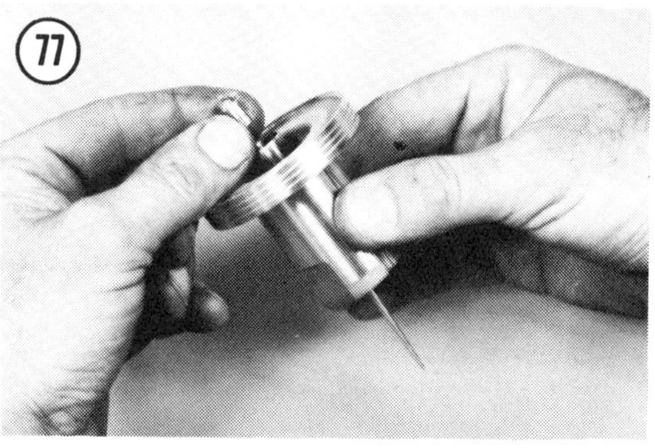

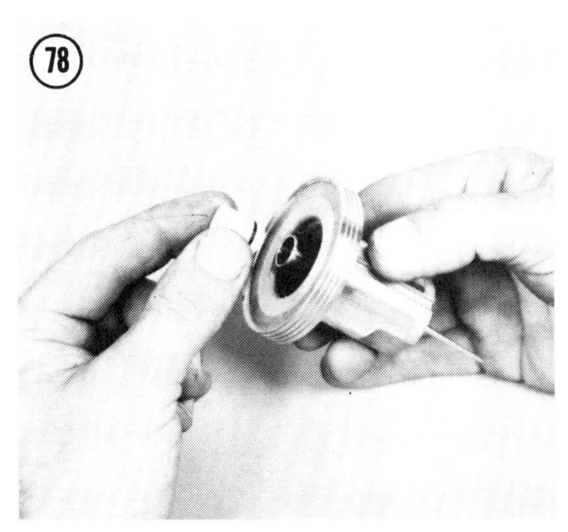
78

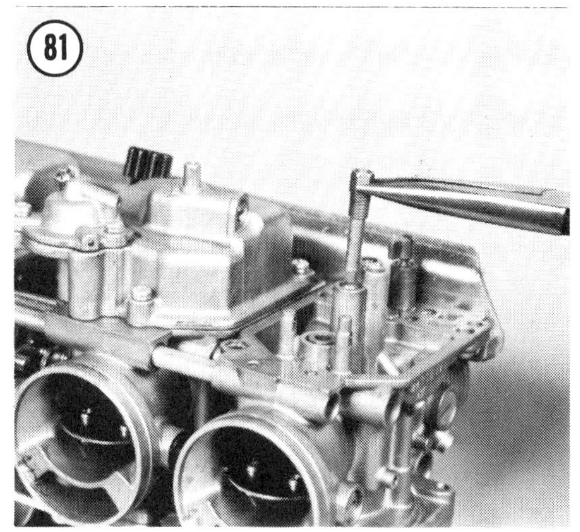
81

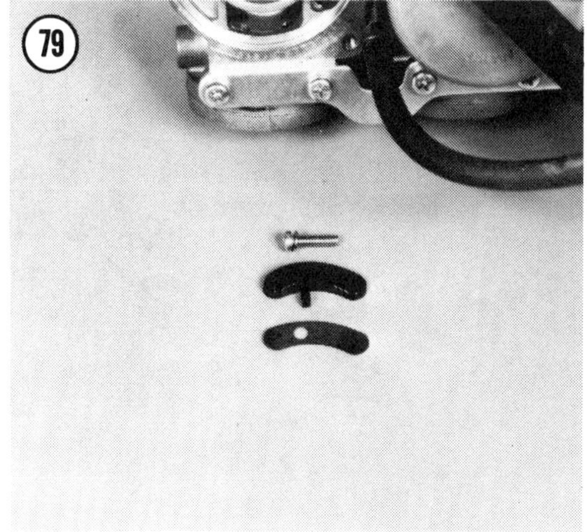
79

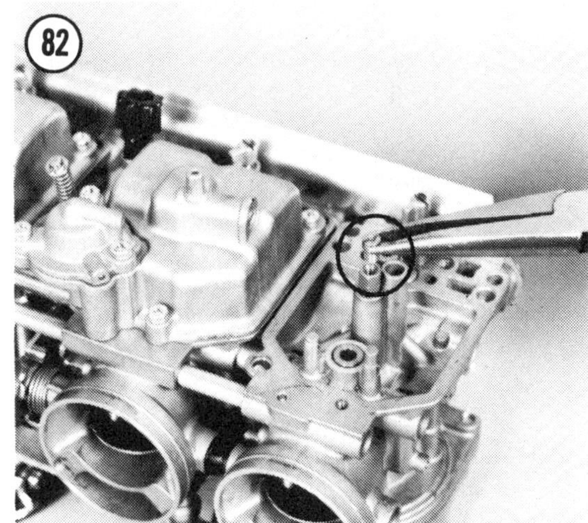
82

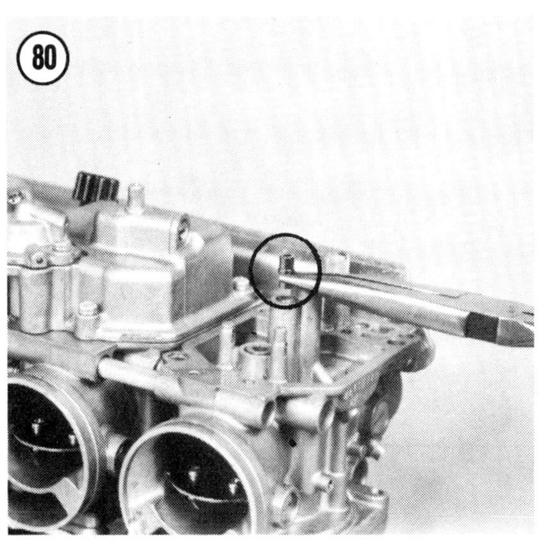
80

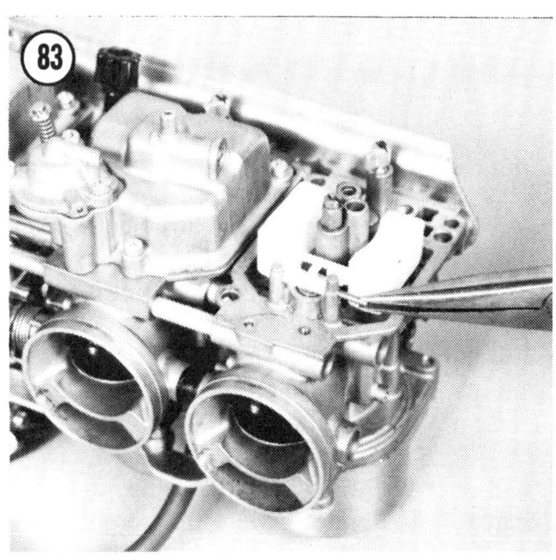
83

33. Install the float bowl.
34. On the No. 1 carburetor (on models so equipped), install the diaphragm on the air cutoff valve with the flat surface in toward the carburetor body. Make sure to install the small O-ring seal.
35. After assembly and installation are completed, adjust the carburetors as described under *Pilot Screw Adjustment—Models Since 1981 (And New Limiter Cap Installation—U.S. Only)* in this chapter and *Carburetor Synchronization* in Chapter Three.

Carburetor Separation/Assembly (Models Since 1981)

1. Remove the carburetor assembly as described under *Carburetor Removal/Installation—Models Since 1981* in this chapter.

NOTE

The carburetors are numbered in the same sequence as the engine cylinders. The No. 1 carburetor is located on the left-hand side and No. 2, 3 and 4 continue from left to right. Remember that the right-hand side relates to the the carburetor assembly as it sits in the bike's frame, not as it sits on your workbench.

2. Unhook the choke relief spring from the choke shaft arm on the No. 2 and No. 3 carburetors (**Figure 84**).

NOTE

Turn the adjuster screw in until it seats. Record the number of turns so it can be adjusted to the same position. Record all 4 different carburetor settings.

3. Loosen the synchronizing adjuster screw locknut (**Figure 85**); loosen the adjuster screw until it is under no tension. Perform this on all carburetors except the No. 2 carburetor, which has no adjuster screw.
4. Remove the screws securing the front bracket (**Figure 86**) and remove the bracket.
5. Remove the fuel line diaphragm (A, **Figure 87**).
6. Remove the screws securing the rear bracket (B, **Figure 87**) and remove the bracket.

84

85

86

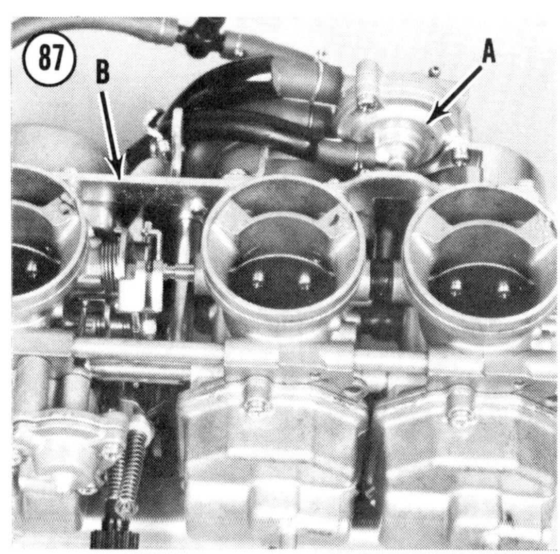

7. While holding the carburetor assembly in the horizontal position and one plane, carefully separate the No. 1 and 2 carburetors from the No. 3 and 4 carburetors.

CAUTION
Avoid damage to the fuel and air joint pipes and the choke linkage that joins the subassemblies.

8. Further disassembly is not recommended and should be entrusted to a dealer or carburetor specialist.
9. Assemble the subassembies by performing the following steps.
10. Apply a light coat of oil to *new O-rings* on the fuel joint pipes.

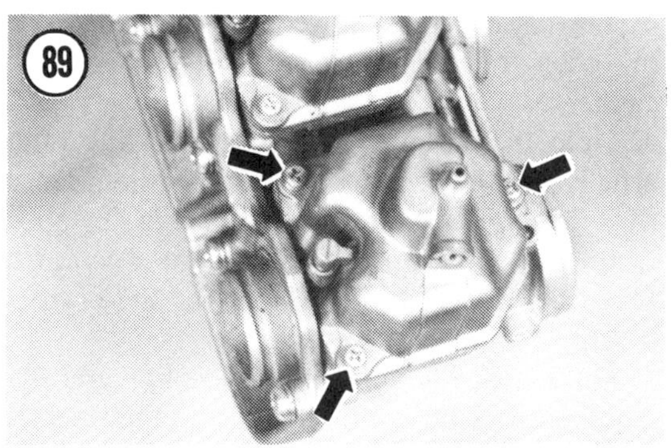

11. Assemble the 2 subassemblies and install the front bracket and screws—leave the screws loose at this time. Set the carburetor assembly on a flat surface with the float bowls facing up. Press the 2 subassemblies together and tighten the screws in 2 or 3 steps to a final torque of 2-3 ft.-lb. (2.8-4.2 N•m). Use the torque pattern shown in **Figure 88**. While tightening the screws continue to check that the choke shaft operates smoothly. If it does not, check carburetor alignment and adjust as necessary.
12. Install the rear bracket using the same sequence used in Step 11. Do not place screws where the fuel line diaphragm is going to be attached.
13. Install the fuel line diaphragm.
14. Turn the synchronizing adjuster screws back to their original positions as noted in Step 3. Tighten the locknuts.
15. Hook the choke relief spring to the choke shaft arm of the No. 2 and No. 3 carburetors.
16. Close the choke valves with the choke linkage and release it. Make sure it operates smoothly and returns completely with no hesitation or drag. If it does not, the carburetors are not properly aligned or the linkage is bent. Replace the linkage or realign the carburetors.

CARBURETOR ADJUSTMENTS

Float Adjustment—All Models

The carburetor assembly has to be removed and partially disassembled for this adjustment.
1. Remove the carburetor as described under *Carburetor Removal/Installation* (for your specific model) in this chapter.
2. Remove the screws (**Figure 89**) securing the float bowls to the main bodies and remove

6

them. It is necessary to remove all float bowls in order to gain clearance for a float bowl gauge.

3. Hold the carburetor assembly so the float arm is just touching the float needle. Use a float level gauge and measure the distance from the carburetor body to the float arm (**Figure 90**). Refer to **Table 1** for the correct height.

4. On 1979-1980 models, adjust by carefully bending the tang on the float arm (**Figure 91**). On models since 1981 the float assembly is plastic and cannot be adjusted; it must be replaced if the float is not within specifications.

CAUTION
The floats on all 4 carburetors must be adjusted to exactly the same height to maintain the same fuel/air mixture to all 4 cylinders.

5. If the float level is set too high, the result will be a rich fuel/air mixture. If it is set too low the mixture will be too lean.

6. Reassemble and install the carburetor.

Needle Jet Adjustment—All Models

The needle jet is *non-adjustable* on all CB650 models.

Accelerator Pump Adjustment (No. 2 Carburetor Only)—All Models

1. Remove the carburetor assembly as described under *Carburetor Removal/Installation* (for your specific model) in this chapter.

NOTE
For the following step the throttle valve must be in the closed position.

2. Measure the distance between the accelerator pump rod and the adjusting arm. Refer to **Figure 92** for 1979-1980 models or **Figure 93** for models since 1981. Refer to **Table 1** for correct clearance.

3. If adjustment is necessary, carefully bend the adjusting arm and repeat Step 2 until correct clearance is obtained.

Choke Adjustment—All Models

1. Remove the side covers, seat and fuel tank.

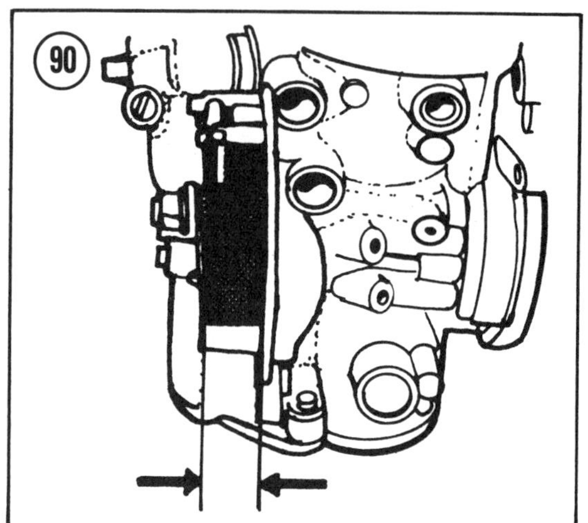

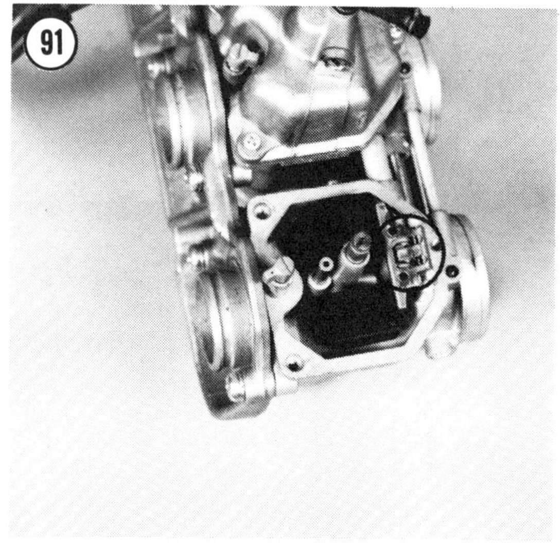

93

94

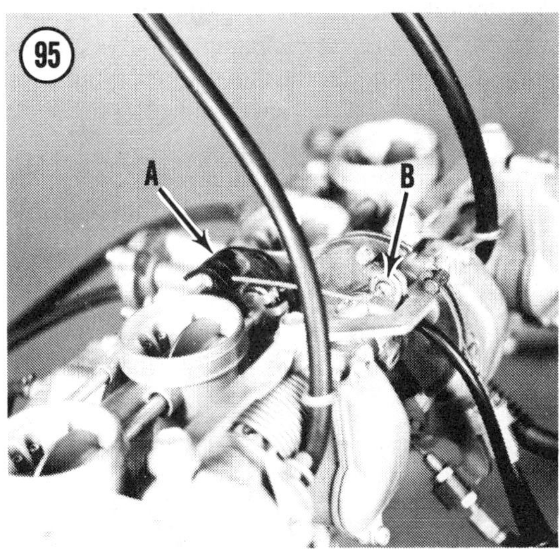

95

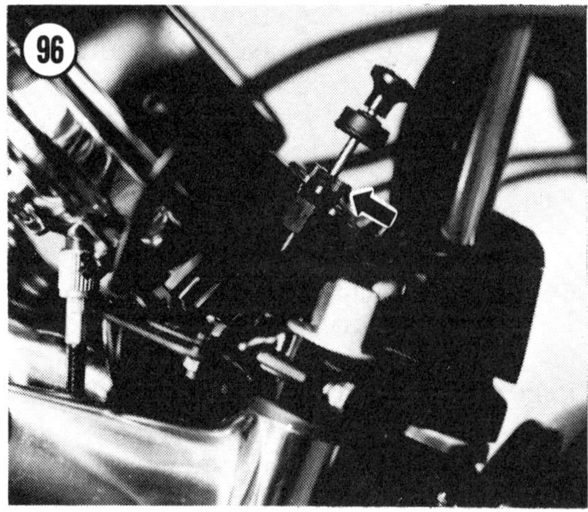
96

2. Operate the choke knob and check for smooth operation of the cable and choke mechanism.

3. Pull the knob all the way *up* to the closed position (**Figure 94**).

4. At the carburetor assembly, pull up on the choke lever (A, **Figure 95**) to make sure it is at the end of its travel thus closing the choke valves. If you can move the choke lever an additional amount it must be adjusted.

NOTE

Figure 95 *is shown with the carburetor assembly removed from the engine for clarity.*

5. To adjust, loosen the cable clamping screw (B, **Figure 95**) and move the cable sheath *up* until the choke lever is fully closed. Hold the choke lever in this position and tighten the cable clamping screw securely.

6. Push the choke knob all the way *down* to the fully open position.

7. At the carburetor assembly, check that the choke lever (A, **Figure 95**) is fully open by checking for free play between the cable and the choke lever. The cable should move slightly as there should be no tension on it.

8. If proper adjustment cannot be achieved using this procedure the cable has stretched and must be replaced. Refer to *Choke Cable Replacement* in this chapter.

9. The choke knob should remain in whatever position it is placed from fully closed to fully open. If it does not, pull up on the rubber cover and turn the adjuster (**Figure 96**). Look

down onto the knob and turn it either clockwise to increase resistance or counterclockwise to decrease resistance.

10. Reinstall the fuel tank, seat and side covers.

Fast Idle Adjustment—1979-1980 Models

The engine must be *cold* to perform this inspection and adjustment procedure.

1. Connect a portable tachometer following the manufacturer's instructions. The bike's tachometer is not accurate enough at this rpm range.
2. Pull the choke knob all the way *up* to the closed position.
3. Start the engine and *immediately* check the fast idle speed. The idle speed should be 2,000 +/-700 rpm.
4. Turn the engine off.
5. If the engine speed is not within specifications, remove the side covers, seat and fuel tank.
6. Turn the fast idle adjust screw (**Figure 97**) until it touches the cam surface.
7. Push the choke knob all the way *in* and then turn the fast idle adjust screw *in* an additional 2-1/2 turns.
8. Install the fuel tank, repeat Step 2 and Step 3 and if fast idle speed is not within specifications, turn the engine off, remove the fuel tank and slightly readjust the fast idle adjust screw until the engine rpm is correct.
9. Install the side covers and seat (and the fuel tank if it was not reinstalled).

Fast Idle Adjustment—Models Since 1981

The engine must be *cold* to perform this inspection and adjustment procedure.

1. Connect a portable tachometer following the manufacturer's instructions. The bike's tachometer is not accurate enough at this rpm range.
2. Pull the knob all the way *up* to the closed position.
3. Start the engine and *immediately* check the fast idle speed. The idle speed should be between 1,000-2,700 rpm.
4. Turn the engine off.
5. If the engine speed is not within specifications, remove the carburetor assembly as described under *Carburetor Removal/Installation—Models Since 1981* in this chapter.

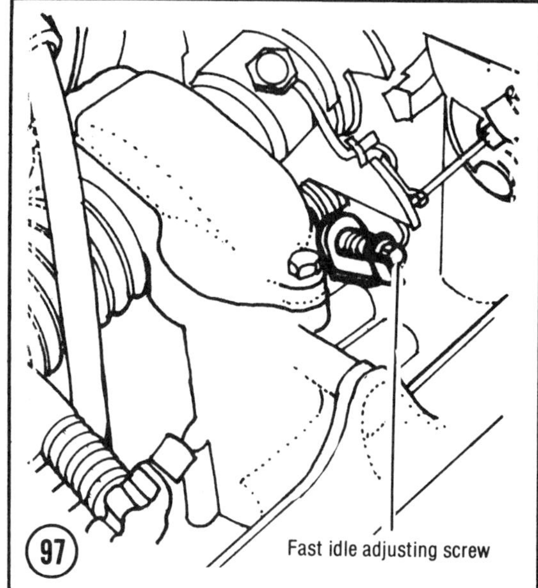

6. Close the throttle valve and open the choke valve. Measure the clearance between the throttle link and the fast idle adjusting arm pin (**Figure 98**). The specified clearance is 0.03-0.04 in. (0.7-1.0 mm).
7. If the clearance is incorrect, adjust by opening or closing the fork end of the fast idle adjusting arm.
8. Install the carburetor assembly and repeat Step 2 and Step 3.

Pilot Screw Adjustment—1979 Models

NOTE

The pilot screw is pre-set at the factory and adjustment is not necessary unless the carburetor has been overhauled or someone has misadjusted it.

The air cleaner must be cleaned before starting this procedure or the results will be inaccurate.

1. For the preliminary adjustment, carefully turn the pilot screw on each carburetor in until it *lightly seats* and then back it out 1-5/8 turns.
2. Start the engine and let it reach normal operating temperature. Stop-and-go riding for approximately 10 minutes is sufficient.
3. Connect a portable tachometer following the manufacturer's instructions. The bike's tachometer is not accurate enough at a low rpm.
4. Start the engine and turn the idle adjust screw (**Figure 99**) in or out to achieve the idle speed of 1,050 +/-100 rpm.
5. Turn each pilot screw *out* 1/2 turn from the initial setting of Step 1. If engine speed *does not* increase by 50 rpm or more, proceed to Step 8.
6. Turn the pilot screw on the No. 1 carburetor 1/2 turn *out.* Repeat for the No. 2, 3 and 4 carburetors. When the engine speed does not change by 50 rpm or more, discontinue the 1/2 turn out increments at the No. 4 carburetor.

NOTE
All 4 carburetor pilot screws should now be turned out the exact same number of turns.

7. Turn the idle adjust screw in or out again to achieve the desired idle speed of 1,050 +/-100 rpm.
8. Turn the pilot screw on the No. 1 carburetor *in* until engine speed drops by 50 rpm.
9. Turn the pilot screw on the No. 1 carburetor *out* 7/8 of a turn from the position in Step 8.
10. Turn the idle adjust screw in or out again to achieve the desired idle speed of 1,050 +/-100 rpm.
11. Perform Steps 8, 9 and 10 on the No. 2, 3 and 4 carburetors.

WARNING
With the engine idling, move the handlebar from side to side. If idle speed increases during this movement, the throttle cables need adjustment or they may be incorrectly routed through the frame. Correct this problem immediately. Do not ride the bike in this unsafe condition.

12. Turn the engine off and disconnect the portable tachometer.
13. After this adjustment is completed, test ride the bike. Throttle response from idle should be rapid and without any hesitation.

Pilot Screw Adjustment—1980 Models (And New Limiter Cap Installation—U.S. Only)

To comply with U. S. emission control standards, a limiter cap is attached to each pilot screw. This is to prevent the owner from readjusting the factory setting. The limiter cap will allow a maximum of 7/8 of a turn of the pilot screw to a leaner mixture only. *The pilot screw is preset at the factory and should not be reset unless the carburetor has been overhauled.*

CAUTION
Do not try to remove the limiter cap from the pilot screw as it is bonded in place and will break off and damage the pilot screw if removal is attempted.

NOTE
Perform Steps 1, 2 and 3 only if new pilot screws have been installed or the carburetors have been overhauled. ***Do not install*** *the new limiter caps onto the pilot screws until this procedure is completed.*

1. Remove the carburetor assembly as described under *Carburetor Removal/ Installation—Models Since 1981* in this chapter.
2. Remove the screws securing the float bowls and remove the float bowls.
3. For the preliminary adjustment, carefully turn the pilot screw on each carburetor in until it *lightly seats* and then back it out 2-1/8 turns. Remember, do not install the limiter caps at this time.
4. Install the float bowls and install the carburetor assembly.
5. Proceed with Steps 2-13 of *Pilot Screw Adjustment—1979 Models* in this chapter.
6. Perform this step only if new limiter caps are to be installed. Apply Loctite No. 601, or equivalent, to the limiter cap and install it on the pilot screw. Position the limiter cap against the stop on the float bowl (**Figure 100**) so that the pilot screw can *only turn clockwise*, not counterclockwise.

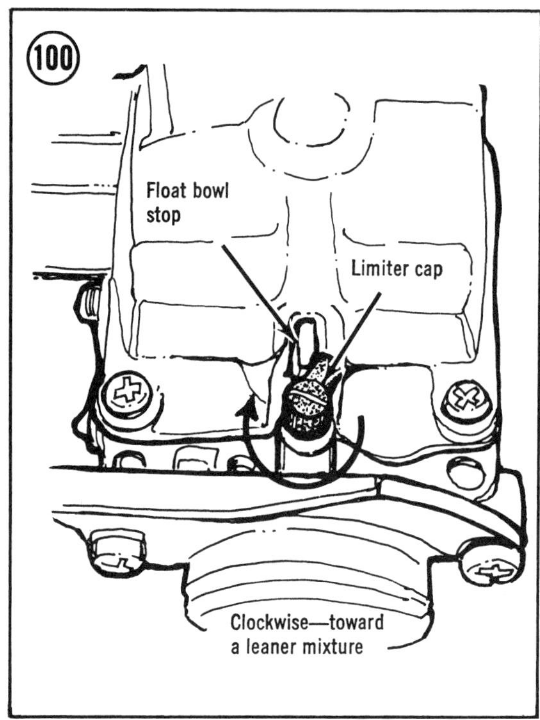

Pilot Screw Adjustment—Models Since 1981 (And New Limiter Cap Installation—U.S. Only)

To comply with U. S. emission control standards, a limiter cap is attached to each pilot screw. This is to prevent the owner from readjusting the factory setting. The limiter cap will allow a maximum of 7/8 of a turn of the pilot screw to a leaner mixture only. *The pilot screw is preset at the factory and should not be reset unless the carburetor has been overhauled.*

CAUTION
Do not try to remove the limiter cap from the pilot screw as it is bonded in place and will break off and damage the pilot screw if removal is attempted.

NOTE
Perform Steps 1, 2 and 3 only if new pilot screws have been installed or the carburetors have been overhauled. ***Do not install*** *the new limiter caps onto the pilot screws until this procedure is completed.*

1. Remove the carburetor assembly as described under *Carburetor Removal/ Installation—Models Since 1981* in this chapter.
2. Remove the screws securing the float bowls and remove the float bowls.
3. For the preliminary adjustment, carefully turn the pilot screw on each carburetor in until it *lightly seats* and then back it out 2-1/4 turns. Remember, do not install the limiter caps at this time.
4. Install the float bowls and install the carburetor assembly.
5. Start the engine and let it reach normal operating temperature. Stop-and-go riding for approximately 10 minutes is sufficient.
6. Connect a portable tachometer following the manufacturer's instructions. The bike's tachometer is not accurate enough at a low rpm.
7. Start the engine and turn the idle adjust screw (**Figure 101**) in or out to achieve the idle speed of 1,050 +/-100 rpm.

NOTE
Figure 101 *is shown with the carburetor assembly partially removed for clarity. Do not remove it for this procedure.*

8. Turn each pilot screw *out* 1/2 turn from the initial setting of Step 3.

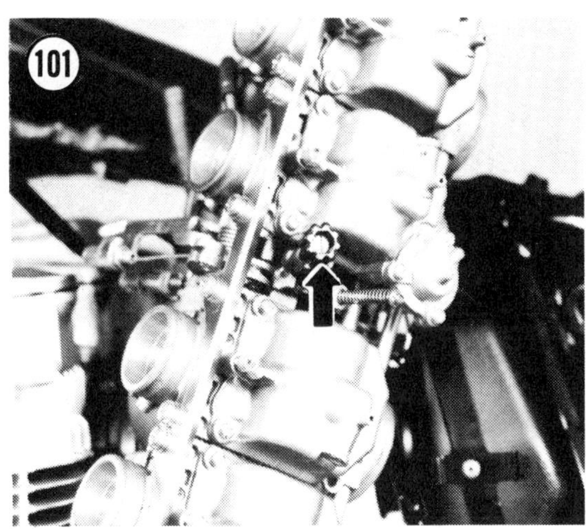

9. If the engine speed increases by 50 rpm or more, continue to turn each pilot screw *out* by 1/2 turns until it drops by 50 rpm or more.
10. Turn the idle adjust screw in or out again to achieve the desired idle speed of 1,050 +/-100 rpm.
11. Turn the pilot screw on the No. 1 carburetor *in* until engine speed drops by 50 rpm.
12. Turn the pilot screw on the No. 1 carburetor *out* one full turn from the position in Step 11.
13. Turn the idle adjust screw in or out again to achieve the desired idle speed of 1,050 +/-100 rpm.
14. Perform Steps 11, 12 and 13 on the No. 2, 3 and 4 carburetors.
15. Perform this step only if new limiter caps are to be installed. Apply Loctite No. 601, or equivalent, to the limiter cap and install it on the pilot screw. Position the limiter cap against the stop on the float bowl (**Figure 100**) so that the pilot screw can only turn clockwise, *not counterclockwise.*

WARNING

With the engine idling, move the handlebar from side to side. If idle speed increases during this movement, the throttle cables need adjustment or they may be incorrectly routed through the frame. Correct this problem immediately. Do not ride the bike in this unsafe condition.

16. Turn the engine off and disconnect the portable tachometer.
17. After this adjustment is completed, test ride the bike. Throttle response from idle should be rapid and without any hesitation.

Rejetting The Carburetors

Do not try to solve a poor running engine problem by rejetting the carburetors if all of the following conditions hold true.
1. The engine has held a good tune in the past with the standard jetting.
2. The engine has not been modified.
3. The motorcycle is being operated in the same geographical region under the same general climatic conditions as in the past.
4. The motorcycle was and is being ridden at average highway speeds.

If those conditions all hold true, the chances are that the problem is due to a malfunction in the carburetor or in another component that needs to be adjusted or repaired. Changing carburetion jet size probably won't solve the problem. Rejetting the carburetors may be necessary if any of the following conditions hold true.
1. A non-standard type of air filter element is being used.
2. A non-standard exhaust system is installed on the motorcycle.
3. Any of the top end components in the engine (pistons, cam, valves, compression ratio, etc.) have been modified.
4. The motorcycle is in use at considerably higher or lower altitudes or in a considerably hotter or colder climate than in the past.
5. The motorcycle is being operated at considerably higher speeds than before and changing to colder spark plugs does not solve the problem.
6. Someone has previously changed the carburetor jetting.
7. The motorcycle has never held a satisfactory engine tune.

If it is necessary to rejet the carburetors check with a dealer or motorcycle performance tuner for recommendations as to the size of jets to install for your specific situation.

If you do change the jets do so only one size at a time. After rejetting, test ride the bike and perform a spark plug test; refer to *Reading Spark Plugs* in Chapter Three.

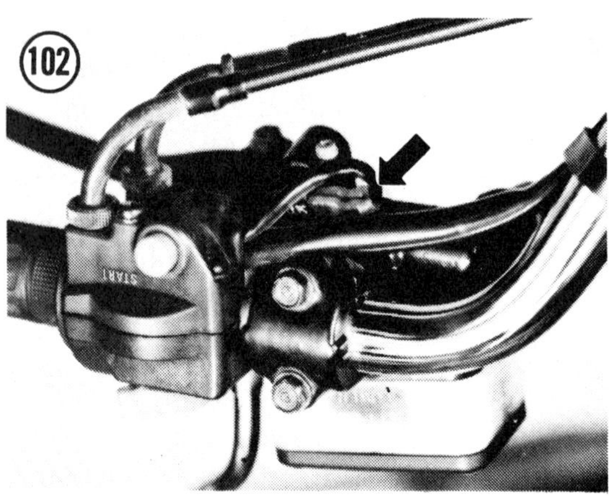

Throttle Cable Replacement

1. Remove the seat and fuel tank.
2. Disconnect the front brake light switch electrical connectors (**Figure 102**).
3. Remove the screws (**Figure 103**) securing the upper and lower right-hand switch/throttle housing together.
4. Remove the housing from the handlebar and disengage the throttle cables from the throttle grip.
5. Remove the carburetor assembly as described under *Carburetor Removal/ Installation* (for your specific year) in this chapter.

NOTE

It may not look like it, but it is practically impossible to remove the throttle cables from the carburetors with the carburetor assembly in place. There is not enough room for 2 hands within the area.

6. Loosen the throttle cable locknuts and remove both cables from the carburetor assembly. Refer to **Figure 104** for 1979-1980 models or **Figure 105** for models since 1981.

NOTE

The piece of string attached in the next step will be used to pull the new throttle cables back through the frame so they will be routed in the exact same position.

7. Tie a piece of heavy string or cord (approximately 6-8 ft./1.8-2.4 m long) to the carburetor end of the throttle cables. Wrap this end with masking or duct tape. Do not use an excessive amount of tape as it will be pulled

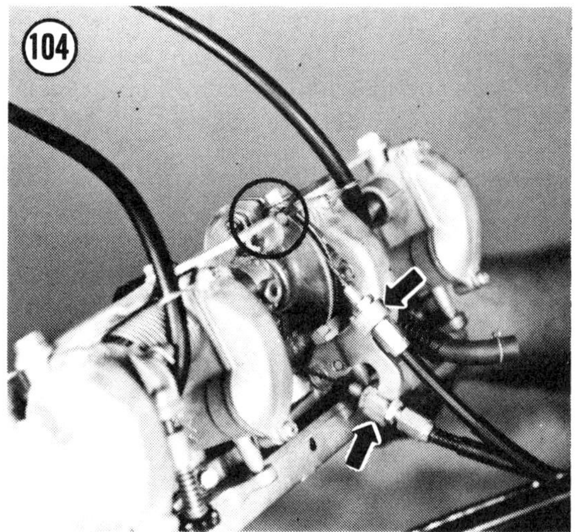

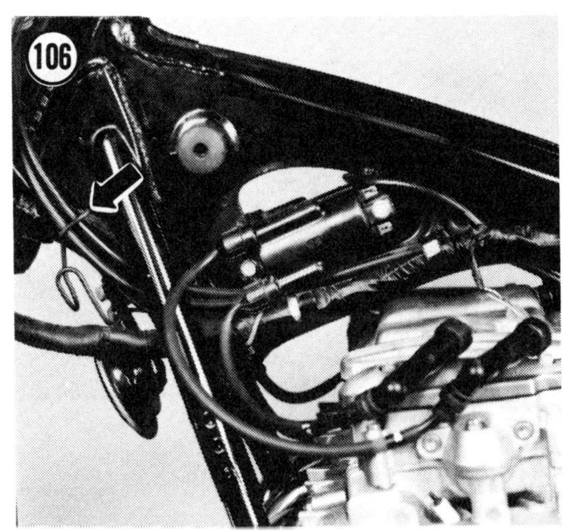

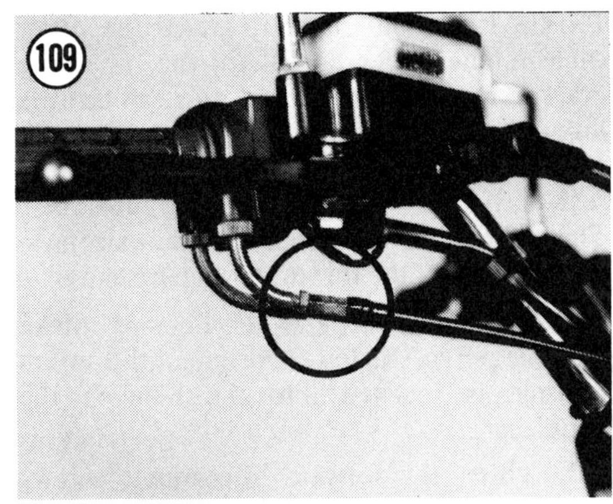

through the frame loop during removal. Tie the other end of the string to the frame or air box.

8. At the throttle grip end of the cables, carefully pull the cables (and attached string) out through the frame loop, past the electrical harness (**Figure 106**) and from behind the headlight housing. Make sure the attached string follows the same path of the cables through the frame and behind the headlight.

9. Remove the tape and untie the string from the old cables.

10. Lubricate the new cables as described under *Control Cables* in Chapter Three.

11. Tie the string to the new throttle cables and wrap it with tape.

12. Carefully pull the string back through the frame routing the new cables through the same path as the old cables.

13. Remove the tape and untie the string from the cables and the frame.

CAUTION

*The throttle cables are the push/pull type and must be installed as described and shown in Steps 14 and 15. **Do not intermix the 2 cables**.*

14. On 1979-1980 models, attach the throttle cable with the adjustment nuts to the lower portion of the mounting bracket and into the rear slot in the throttle linkage wheel (**Figure 107**). On models since 1981, attach the throttle cable to the front portion of the bracket (A, **Figure 108**). The other end is attached to the front receptacle (**Figure 109**) of the throttle/switch housing.

6

15. On 1979-1980 models, attach the other cable to the upper portion of the mounting bracket and into the front slot in the throttle linkage wheel (**Figure 110**). On models since 1981, attach the other end of the cable to the rear portion of the bracket (B, **Figure 108**). The other end is attached to the rear receptacle (**Figure 111**) of the throttle/switch housing.

16. Install the throttle/switch housing. Make sure the pin on the lower portion of the switch housing is indexed into the hole in the handlebar.

17. Tighten the forward attachment screws first and then the rear screws. Attach the front brake light switch connectors.

18. Operate the throttle grip and make sure the carburetor throttle linkage is operating correctly and with no binding. If operation is incorrect or there is binding carefully check that the cables are attached correctly and there are no tight bends in the cables.

19. Install the carburetor assembly, fuel tank and seat.

20. Adjust the throttle cables as described under *Throttle Operation/Adjustment* in Chapter Three.

21. Test ride the bike and make sure the throttle is operating correctly.

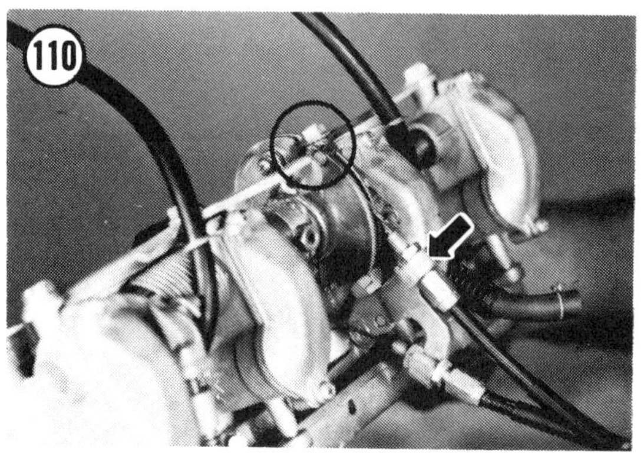
110

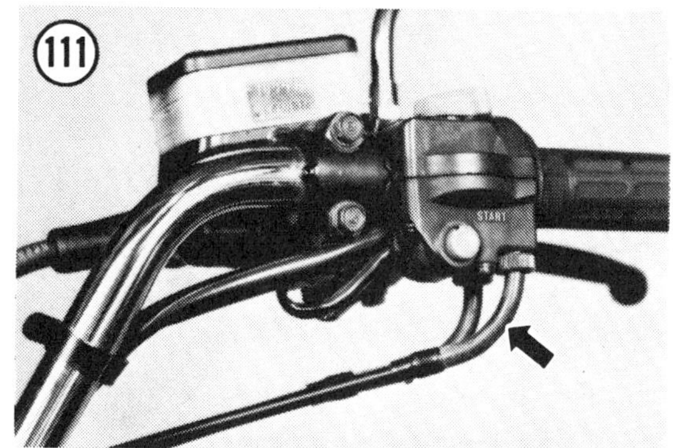

111

Choke Cable Replacement

1. Remove the seat and fuel tank.
2. Remove the carburetor assembly as described under *Carburetor Removal/ Installation* (for your specific year) in this chapter.

NOTE
It may not look like it, but it is practically impossible to remove the choke cable from the carburetors with the carburetor assembly in place. There is just not enough room for 2 hands within the area.

3. Loosen the choke cable clamp screw and remove the cable end from the choke linkage. Refer to **Figure 112** for 1979-1980 models or **Figure 113** for models since 1981.

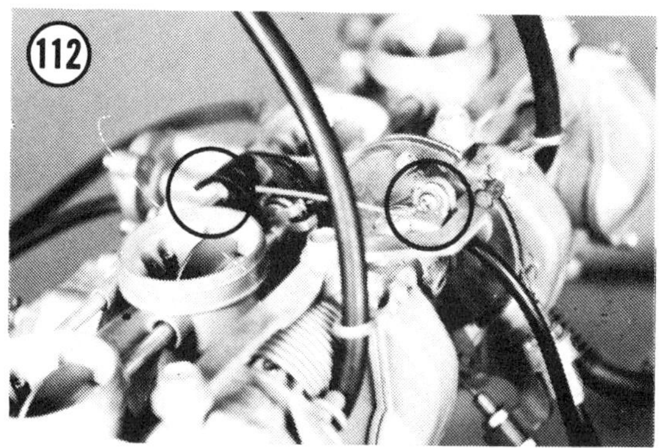
112

113

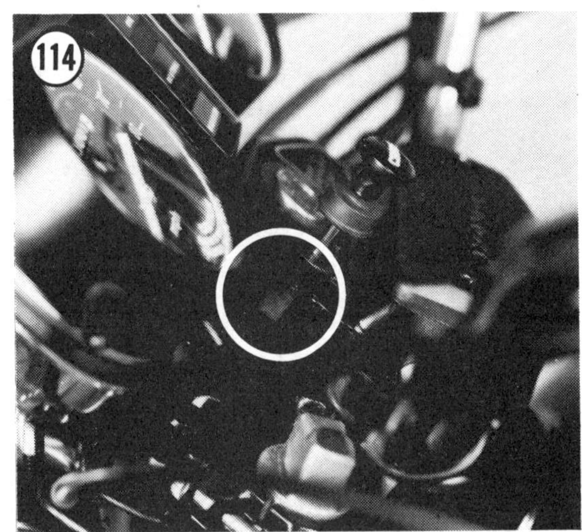

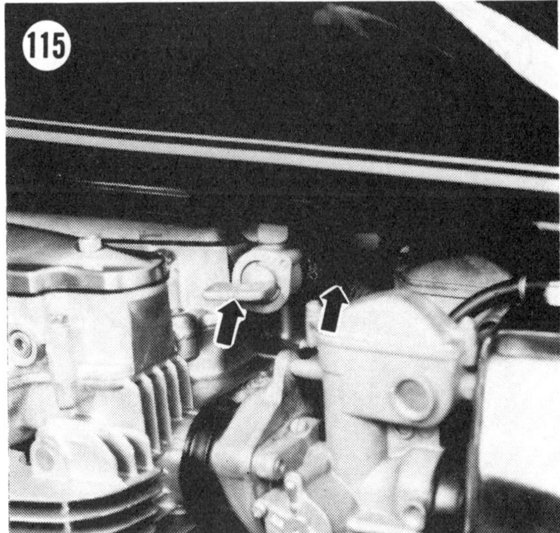

NOTE
The piece of string attached in the next step will be used to pull the new choke cable back through the frame so it will be routed in the same position as the old cable.

4. Tie a piece of heavy string or cord (approximately 6-8 ft./1.8-2.4 m long) to the carburetor end of the choke cable. Wrap this end with masking or duct tape. Do not use an excessive amount of tape as it will be pulled through the frame loop during removal. Tie the other end of the string to the frame or air box.
5. Completely unscrew the locknut (**Figure 114**) securing the choke knob assembly to the bracket.
6. At the choke knob end of the cable, carefully pull the cable (and attached string) out through the frame loop, past the electrical harness (**Figure 106**) and from behind the headlight housing. Make sure the attached string follows the same path that the cable does through the frame and behind the headlight.
7. Remove the tape and untie the string from the old cable.
8. Lubricate the new cable as described under *Control Cables* in Chapter Three.

NOTE
Make sure the locknut is positioned on the string so it will be located below the mounting bracket when the cable is installed.

9. Tie the string to the new choke cable and wrap it with tape.
10. Carefully pull the string back through the frame routing the new cable through the same path as the old cable.
11. Remove the tape and untie the string from the cable and the frame.
12. Screw the locknut onto the choke cable knob assembly and tighten securely.
13. Attach the choke cable to the carburetor choke linkage as shown in **Figure 112**.
14. Operate the choke knob and make sure the carburetor choke linkage is operating correctly and with no binding. If operation is incorrect or there is binding carefully check that the cable is attached correctly and there are no tight bends in the cable.
15. Adjust the choke cable as described under *Choke Adjustment—All Models* in this chapter.
16. Install the carburetor assembly, fuel tank and seat.

FUEL SHUTOFF VALVE

Removal/Cleaning/Installation

1. Turn the fuel shutoff valve to the OFF position and remove the flexible fuel line (**Figure 115**) to the carburetor.
2. Place the loose end into a clean, sealable metal container. This fuel can be reused if kept clean.
3. Open the valve to the RESERVE position and remove the fuel filler cap. This will allow

air to enter the tank and speed up the flow of fuel. Drain the tank completely.

4. Unscrew the locknut from the tank (**Figure 116**) and remove the valve.

NOTE

***Figure 116** is shown with the fuel tank removed for clarity. It is not necessary to remove it for this procedure.*

5. After removing the valve, insert a corner of a clean shop rag into the opening in the tank to stop the fuel from dribbling onto the engine and frame.
6. Remove the filter cup on the bottom of the valve and remove the filter and O-ring gasket.
7. Install by reversing these removal steps. Do not forget to install the washer between the valve and the tank.
8. After installation is complete, thoroughly check for fuel leaks.

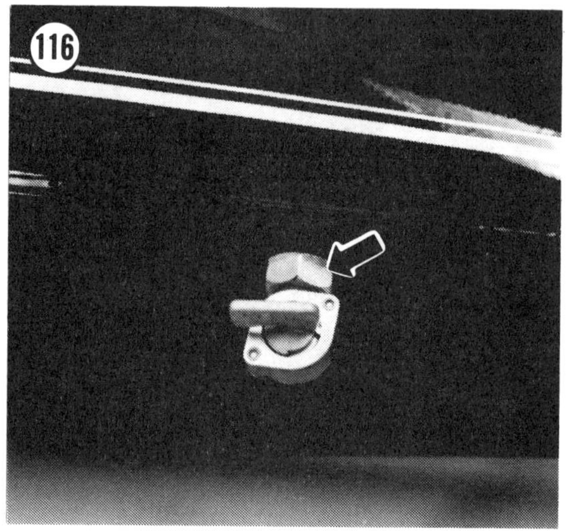

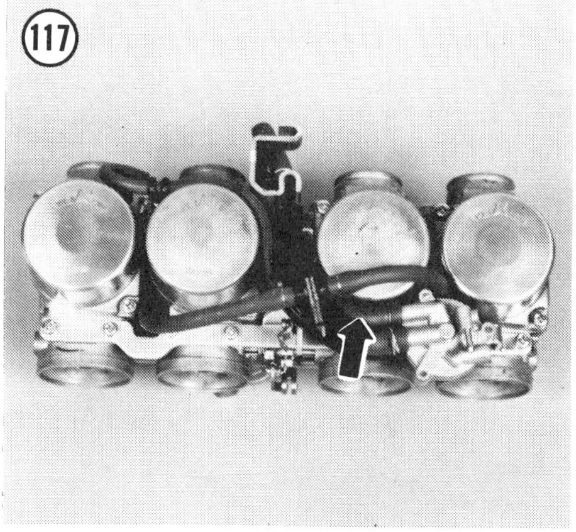

FUEL LINE DIAPHRAGM (MODELS SINCE 1981)

On models since 1981 the fuel shutoff valve can be left in the ON or RES position at all times. Vacuum from the engine opens the valve only when the engine is running and automatically closes the valve to stop the flow of fuel when the engine is shut off. The OFF position is used only when the motorcycle is stored for any length of time or when servicing the fuel system.

Removal/Testing/Installation

1. Remove the carburetors as described under *Carburetor Removal/Installation—Models Since 1981* in this chapter.
2. Remove the fuel tube to the carburetors (**Figure 117**), the vacuum line (A, **Figure 118**) and the air vent tube from the carburetor assembly (leave them attached to the fuel line diaphragm assembly).
3. Remove the screws (B, **Figure 118**) securing the fuel line diaphragm assembly to the carburetors and remove it.
4. Place the fuel tank up on a box so it is higher than the work surface of your workbench. Attach a test piece of long fuel line from the fuel shutoff valve to the fuel inlet fitting on the fuel line diaphragm.

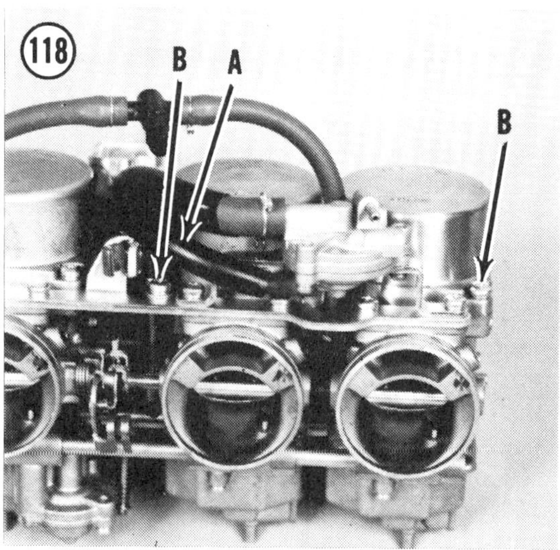

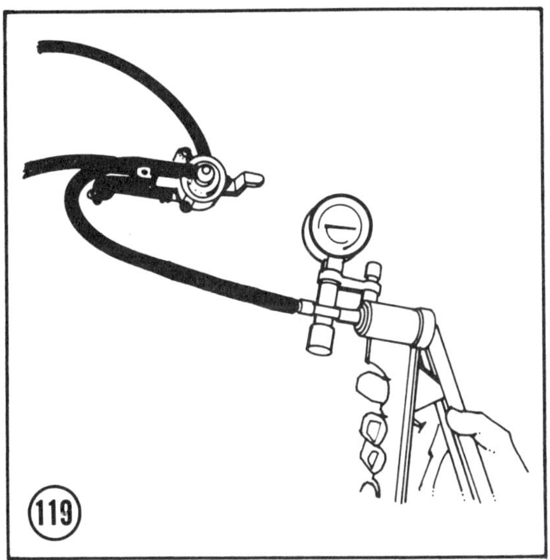

5. Connect a portable hand vacuum pump to the vacuum hose on the fuel line diaphragm (**Figure 119**).
6. Place a suitable clean metal container under the carburetor fuel hose (the one that normally leads to the carburetors).

NOTE

If this fuel is kept clean it can be reused. If it becomes contaminated during this procedure dispose of it properly. Check with local regulations for proper disposal of gasoline.

7. Turn the fuel shutoff valve to the ON or RES position. Fuel should *not* flow from the carburetor fuel hose.
8. Apply vacuum to the diaphragm with the hand pump. Fuel *should flow* out when 10-20 mm Hg (0.4-0.8 in. Hg) of vacuum is applied.
9. If fuel does not flow the diaphragm is not operating correctly and must be replaced; it cannot be serviced.
10. Disconnect the portable hand vacuum pump.
11. Turn the fuel shutoff valve to the OFF position and remove the test fuel line from the fuel tank to the diaphragm assembly.
12. Install the fuel line diaphragm to the carburetor assembly and route the fuel lines as shown in **Figure 117**.
13. Install the carburetors as described under *Carburetor Removal/Installation—Models Since 1981* in this chapter.

FUEL TANK

Removal/Installation

1. Place a milk crate or wood block(s) under the engine or frame to support it securely.
2. Turn the fuel shutoff valve to the OFF position and remove the fuel line to the carburetor.
3. Remove the seat and side panels.
4. Disconnect the battery negative lead.
5. Remove the bolt securing the rear of the fuel tank. Lift up and pull the tank to the rear and remove it. Remove the rubber mounting damper and keep it with the fuel tank to keep from misplacing it.
6. Install by reversing these removal steps.

6

Sealing (Pin-Hole Size)

A pin hole size leak can be sealed with the use of a product called Theroxite Gas Tank Sealer Stick or equivalent. Follow the manufacturer's instructions.

Sealing (Small Hole Size)

This procedure requires the use of a non-petroleum, non-flammable solvent.

If you feel unqualified to accomplish it, take the tank to a dealer and have them seal the tank for you.

WARNING

Before attempting any service on the fuel tank be sure to have a fire extinguisher rated for gasoline or chemical fires within reach. Do not smoke or allow any one to smoke or work where there are any open flames (i.e. water heater or clothes dryer gas pilot). The work area must be well-ventilated.

1. Remove the fuel tank as described under *Fuel Tank Removal/Installation* in this chapter.
2. Mark the spot on the tank where the leak is visible with a grease pencil.
3. Remove the fuel filler cap and turn the fuel shutoff valve to the RESERVE position. Use compressed air and direct the air nozzle into the fuel filler neck; blow the interior of the tank dry.
4. Turn the fuel shutoff valve to the OFF position and pour about 1 quart (1 liter) of

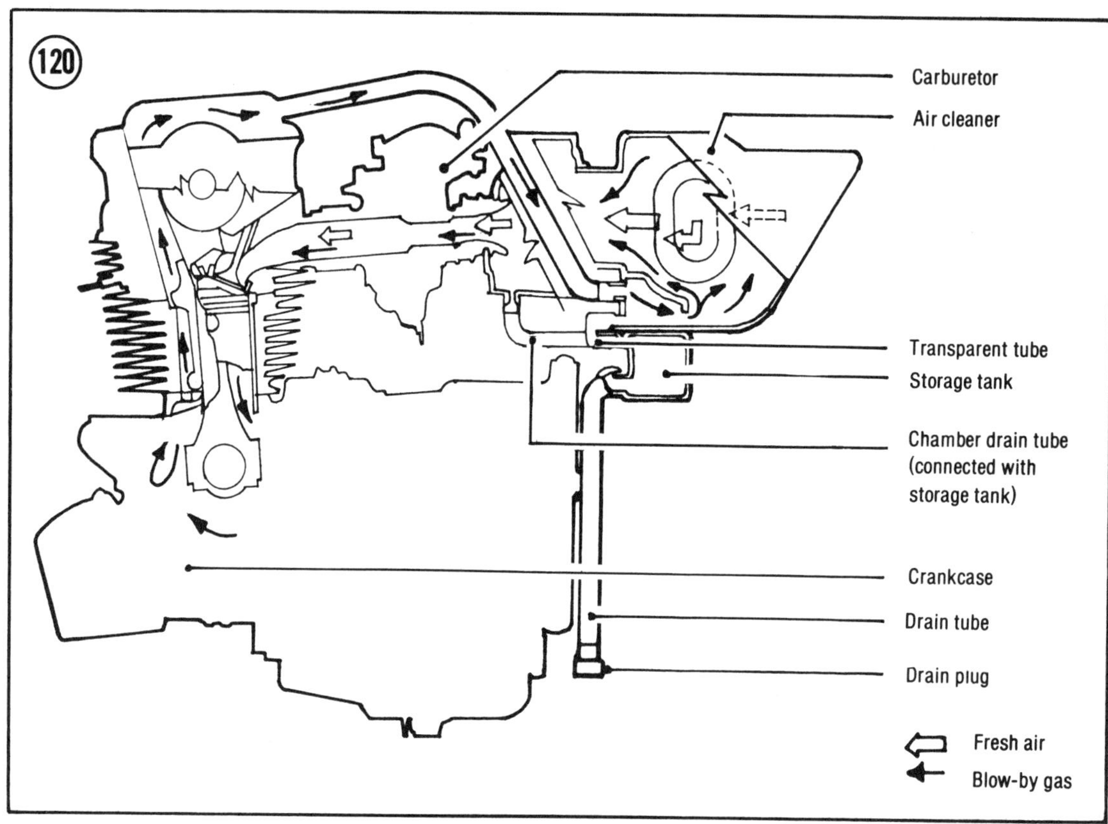

non-petroleum solvent into the tank; install the fuel filler cap and shake the tank vigorously 1 or 2 minutes. This is to remove all fuel residue.

5. Drain the non-petroleum based solution into a safe storable container. This solution may be reused. Let the tank air out overnight before using the sealant.

6. Remove the fuel shutoff valve from the tank. If necessary, plug the tank opening with a cork and/or tape it closed with duct tape. Thoroughly clean the surrounding area with ignition contact cleaner so the tape will stick securely.

7. Again blow the tank interior completely dry with compressed air.

8. The following step is best done out of doors as the fumes are very strong and flammable. Pour a sealant into the tank (a silicone rubber base sealer like Pro-Tech or Kreem Super Sealer or equivalent). These are available at most motorcycle supply stores.

CAUTION

Do not spill the sealant onto the painted surface of the tank as it will destroy the finish.

9. Position the tank so that the point of the leak is at the lowest part of the tank. This will allow the sealant to accumulate at the point of the leak.

10. Let the tank sit in this position for at least 48 hours.

11. After the sealant has dried, install the fuel shutoff valve, turn it to the OFF position and refill the tank with fuel.

12. After the tank has been filled, let it sit for at least 2 hours and recheck the leak area.

13. Install the tank on the bike.

CRANKCASE BREATHER SYSTEM (U.S. ONLY)

In order to comply with air pollution standards, the Honda CB650 is equipped with a crankcase breather system. The system shown in **Figure 120** is used to draw out blow-by gases generated in the crankcase and

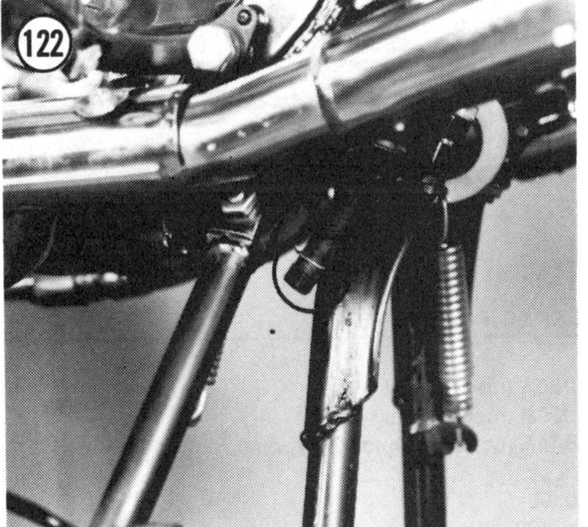

recirculate them into the fuel/air mixture and thus into the engine to be burned.

Inspection

Make sure all hose clamps are tight (**Figure 121**). Check all hoses for deterioration and replace as necessary.

Remove the plug (**Figure 122**) from the drain hose and drain out all residue. This cleaning procedure is needed more frequently if a considerable amount of riding is done at full throttle or in the rain.

NOTE

Be sure to install the drain plug and clamp.

EXHAUST SYSTEM

The exhaust system consists of 4 exhaust pipes and 2 mufflers on the standard model while the Custom model has 4 exhaust pipes and 4 short mufflers.

Removal/Installation

1. Place the bike on the centerstand or place a milk crate or wood block(s) under the frame to support it securely.
2. Remove the nuts and lockwashers (**Figure 123**) securing the exhaust pipe flanges to the cylinder head.
3. Slide the flanges down and remove the split keepers.
4. Remove the bolt and nut (**Figure 124**) securing the rear footpeg and muffler(s) to the frame.

5. Remove the exhaust system on one side by pushing the muffler(s) and exhaust pipe assembly forward to clear the exhaust port studs and remove it. Repeat for the other side.

6. Inspect the condition of the gaskets at all joints; replace as necessary.

7. Install one of the assemblies into position and install the frame bolt, footpeg and nut only finger-tight until the exhaust flange nuts and washers are installed and securely tightened. This will minimize an exhaust leak at the cylinder head.

8. Install the split keepers, exhaust flanges, washers and nuts. Tighten the nuts securely.

9. Tighten the frame bolt and nut securing the rear footpeg (**Figure 125**) securely.

10. Repeat for the other side.

11. After installation is complete, make sure there are no exhaust leaks. On models with 2 mufflers, make sure the 2 into 1 collector joint on each side (**Figure 126**) is tight.

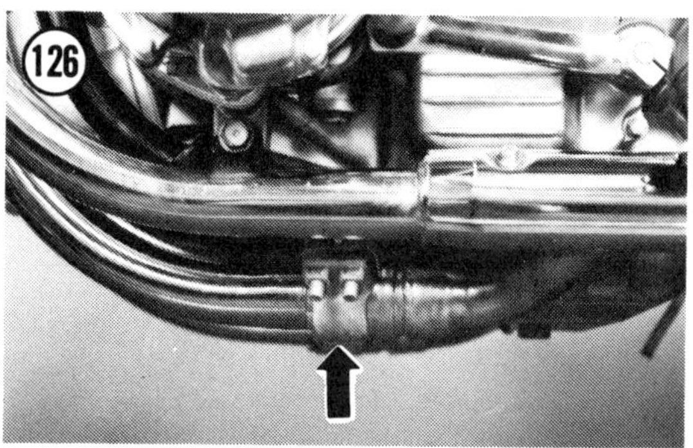

Table 1 CARBURETOR SPECIFICATIONS

Carburetor model number	
1979	PD50A (mechanical type)
1980	PD50B (mechanical type)
Since 1981	VB44A (constant velocity type)
Main jet number	
1979, 1980	No. 90
Since 1981	No. 120
Main air jet (CV type only)	
Since 1981	No. 100
Jet needle clip setting, all models	Non-adjustable
Float level	
1979-1980	0.50 in. (12.5 mm)
Since 1981	0.61 in. (15.5 mm)
Idle speed	
All models	1050 ± 100 rpm
Fast idle speed	
1979-1980	2000 ± 700 rpm
Since 1981	1000-2700 rpm
Accelerator pumprod clearance (#2 carburetor only)	0.00-0.04 mm (0.0000-0.0016 in.)

NOTE: If you own a 1982 model, first check the Supplement at the back of the book for any new service information.

CHAPTER SEVEN

ELECTRICAL SYSTEM

The electrical system consists of the following systems:

a. Charging system
b. Ignition system
c. Lighting system
d. Directional signal system
e. Horn

Tables 1-2 are at the end of the chapter.

CHARGING SYSTEM

The charging system consists of the battery, alternator and a voltage regulator/rectifier (**Figure 1**).

Alternating current generated by the alternator is rectified to direct current. The voltage regulator maintains the voltage to the battery and additional electrical load (lights, ignition, etc.) at a constant voltage regardless of variations in engine speed and load.

Charging System Output Test

Whenever a charging system trouble is suspected, make sure the battery is fully charged and in good condition before going any further. Clean and test the battery as described under *Battery Testing* in Chapter Three.

Prior to starting the test, start the bike and let it reach normal operating temperature; shut off the engine.

To test the charging system, connect a 0-15 *DC* voltmeter to the battery as shown in **Figure 2**. Connect the voltmeter positive (+) lead to the battery positive (+) terminal and the voltmeter negative (-) lead to ground.

NOTE

Do not disconnect either the positive or negative battery cables; they are to remain in the circuit as is.

Connect a 0-10 *DC* ammeter in line with the main fuse connectors (fusible link). Loosen the screws securing the fusible link (**Figure 3**) and remove the fusible link. Install an in-line fuse/fuse holder (available at most auto supply or electronic supply stores) along with the ammeter as shown in **Figure 4**. Use alligator clips on the test leads for a good electrical connection.

NOTE

During the test if the needle of the ammeter reads in the opposite direction on the scale, reverse the polarity of the test leads.

CAUTION

In order to protect the ammeter, always run the test with the in-line fuse in the circuit.

CAUTION

Do not try to test the charge system by connecting an ammeter between the positive (+) battery terminal and the starter cable. The ammeter will burn out when the electric starter is operated.

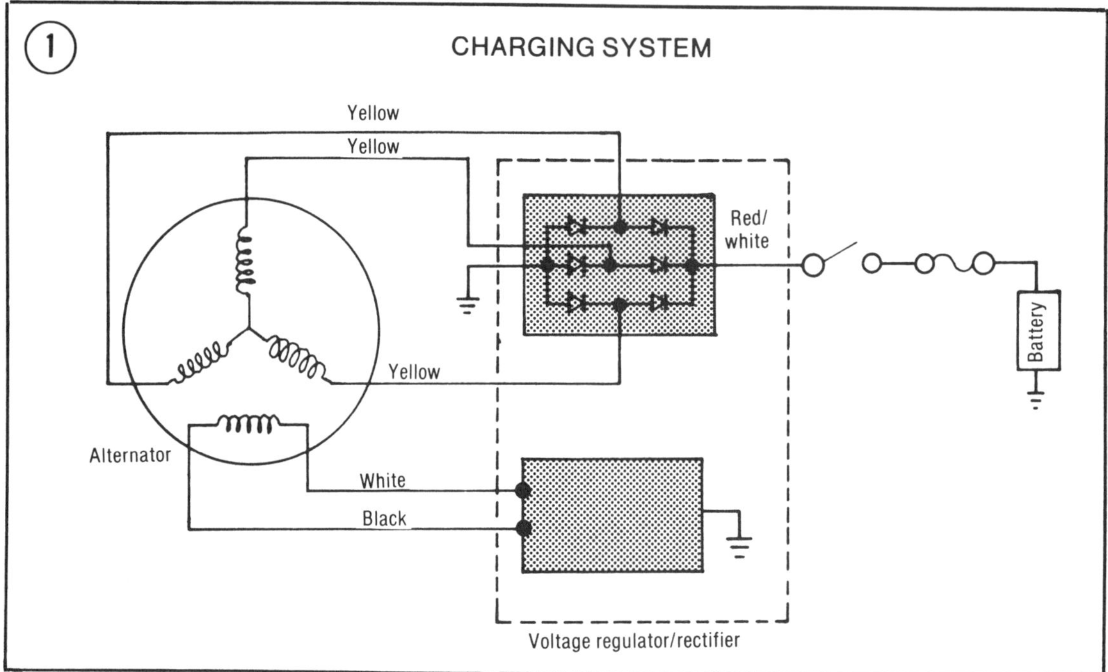

Turn the headlight to high beam. Start the engine and run at 5,000 rpm. Minimum charging current should be 0 amperes. Voltage should read 14.5 volts.

If the charging voltage is considerably lower than specified, check the alternator and voltage regulator/rectifier. Less likely is the possibility that the voltage is too high; in that case the voltage regulator is probably at fault.

Test the separate charging system components as described under the appropriate headings in this section.

BATTERY

For complete battery information, refer to *Battery* in Chapter Three.

ALTERNATOR

The alternator is a form of electrical generator in which a magnetized field called a rotor revolves within a set of stationary coils called a stator. As the rotor revolves, alternating currect is induced in the stator. The current is then rectified and used to operate the electrical accessories on the motorcycle and for charging the battery. The rotor is an electromagnet and receives its electricity through 2 brushes connected to the stator

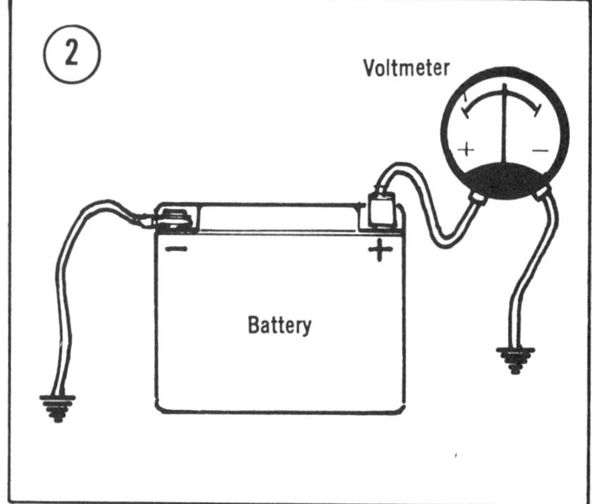

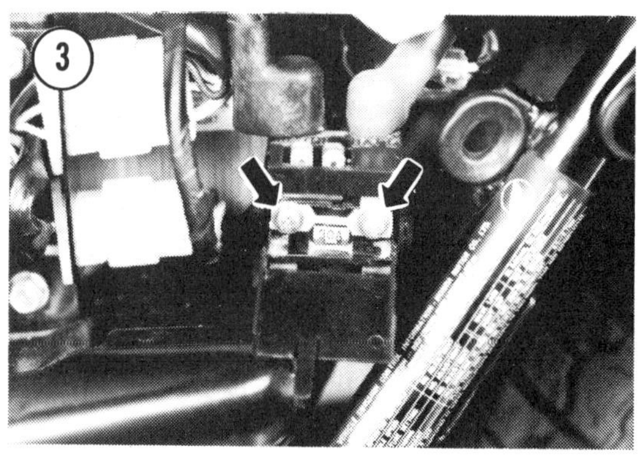

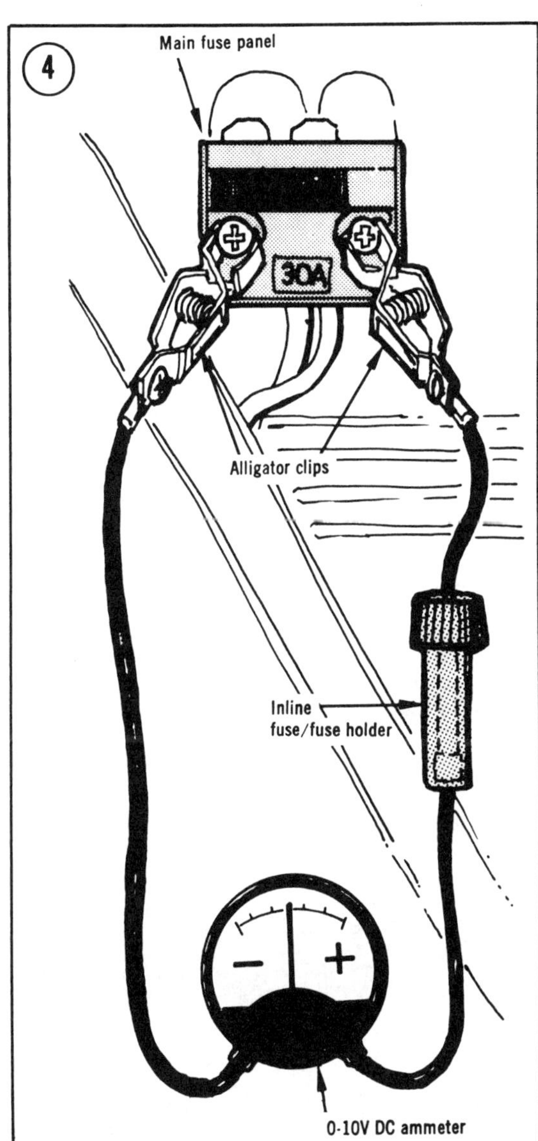

wiring harness and located within the alternator cover. Refer to **Figure 5** for alternator components.

Removal/Installation

1. Place the bike on the centerstand.

2. Remove the seat and left-hand side cover. Disconnect the battery negative lead (**Figure 6**).

3. Disconnect the alternator electrical connection. Refer to **Figure 7** for 1979 models or **Figure 8** for models since 1980.

4. Remove the shift lever (A, **Figure 9**) and left-hand crankcase cover (B, **Figure 9**).

5. Disconnect the oil pump pressure switch connector (**Figure 10**) and the neutral indicator connector (**Figure 11**).

6. Remove the electrical harness from the clips on the frame and engine.

7. Remove the bolts securing the alternator cover and remove the cover and gasket. Don't lose the 2 locating dowels in the crankcase (**Figure 12**). It is not necessary to remove them if they are secure in the case.

8. Remove the bolt (**Figure 13**) securing the alternator rotor.

NOTE

*If necessary use a strap wrench (**Figure 14**) to keep the rotor from turning while removing the nut.*

9. Screw in a flywheel puller until it stops. Use the Honda flywheel puller or equivalent.

CAUTION

Don't try to remove the rotor without a puller; any attempt to do so will ultimately lead to some form of damage to the engine and/or rotor. Many aftermarket types of pullers are available from most motorcycle dealers or mail order houses. The cost of one of these pullers is about $10 and it makes an excellent addition to any mechanic's tool box. If you can't buy or borrow one, have a dealer remove the rotor.

10. Turn the puller gradually until the rotor disengages from the crankshaft.

NOTE

If the rotor is difficult to remove, strike the puller with a hammer a few times. This will usually break it loose.

CAUTION

If normal rotor removal attempts fail, do not force the puller as the threads may be stripped out of the rotor causing expensive damage. Take it to a dealer and have them remove it.

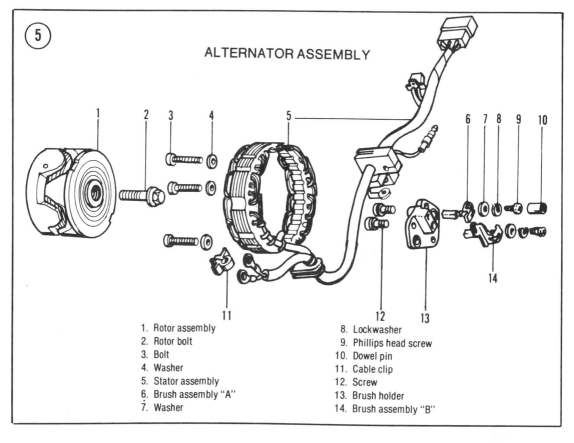

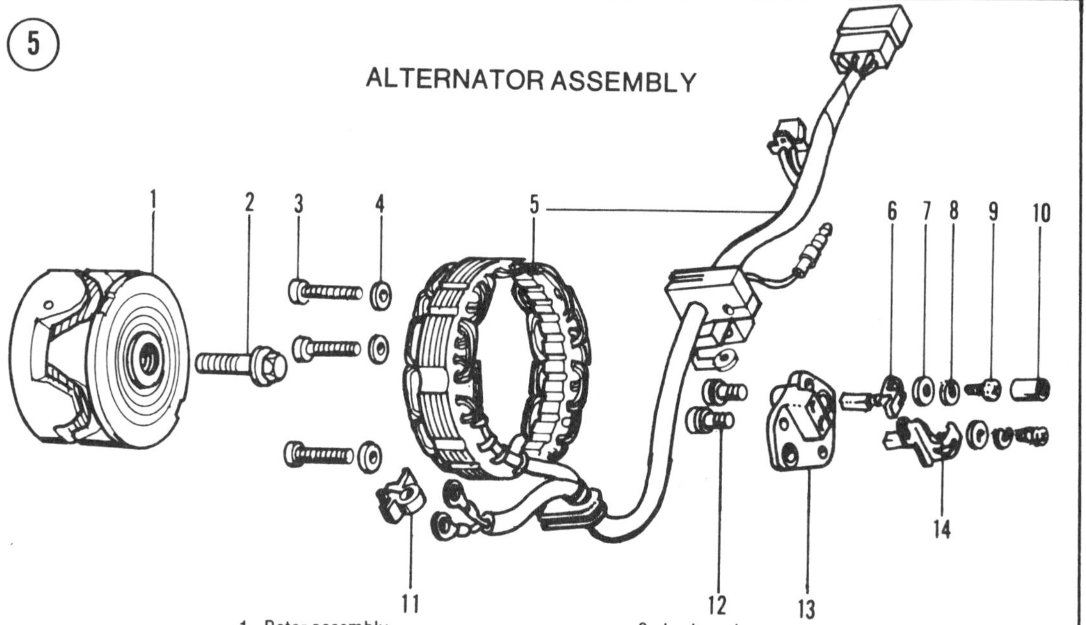

5

ALTERNATOR ASSEMBLY

1. Rotor assembly
2. Rotor bolt
3. Bolt
4. Washer
5. Stator assembly
6. Brush assembly "A"
7. Washer
8. Lockwasher
9. Phillips head screw
10. Dowel pin
11. Cable clip
12. Screw
13. Brush holder
14. Brush assembly "B"

6

8

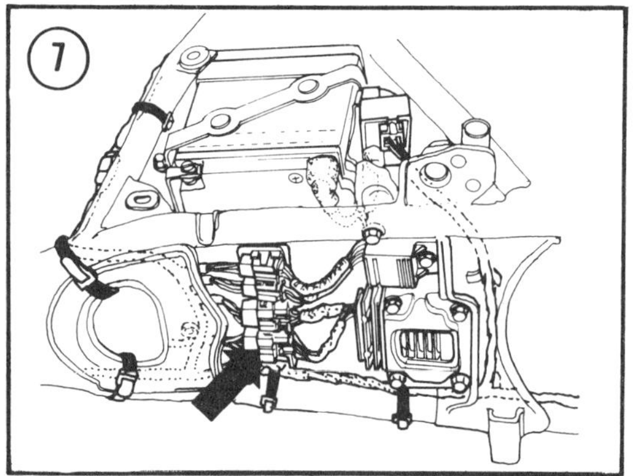
7

9

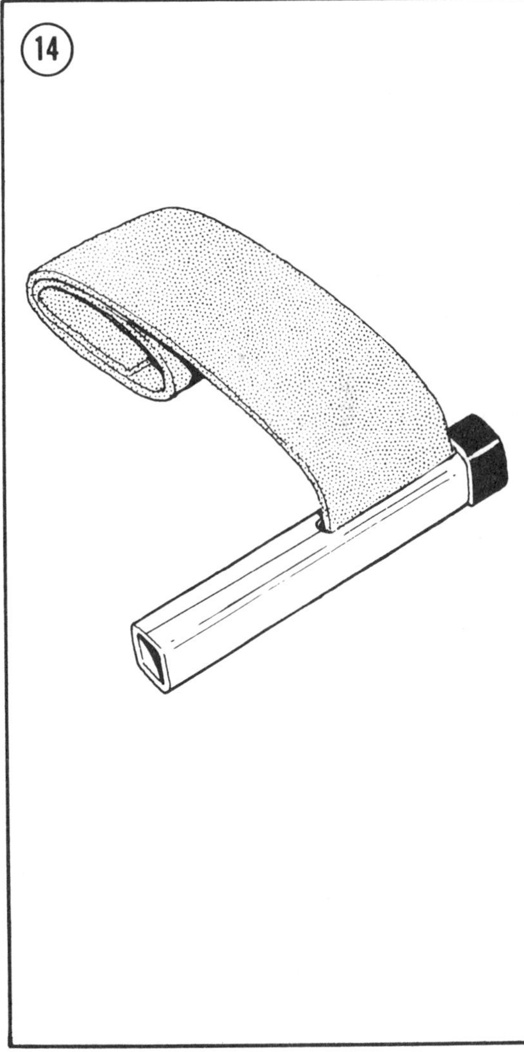

7

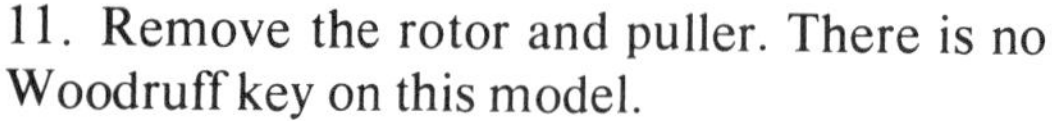

11. Remove the rotor and puller. There is no Woodruff key on this model.
12. Install by reversing these removal steps. Tighten the rotor bolt to 36-43 ft.-lb. (50-60 N•m) and route the electrical harness as shown in **Figure 15**.

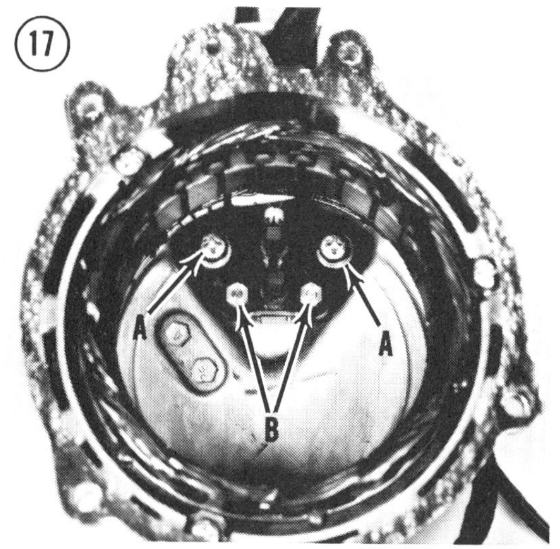

Brush Inspection and Replacement

1. Inspect the length of both brushes within the stator housing (**Figure 16**). The brushes must be replaced if worn to the scribe line on them. Always replace both brushes as a set.
2. If replacement is necessary, remove the Phillips head screws (A, **Figure 17**) securing the brush holder in place.
3. Remove the small screws and washers (B, **Figure 17**) securing each brush assembly and replace with new brushes.

Stator Testing

It is not necessary to remove the stator assembly to perform this test. The stator is removed in this procedure for clarity only.

1. Remove the left-hand side cover (**Figure 18**) and disconnect the alternator electrical connection (**Figure 19**). This connection contains 5 wires—3 yellow, 1 black and 1 white.
2. Use an ohmmeter and check continuity between each yellow terminal (**Figure 20**). The specified resistance between all yellow terminals is 0.41-0.51 ohms. Replace the stator if any yellow terminal shows no continuity to any other. This would indicate an open in the winding.

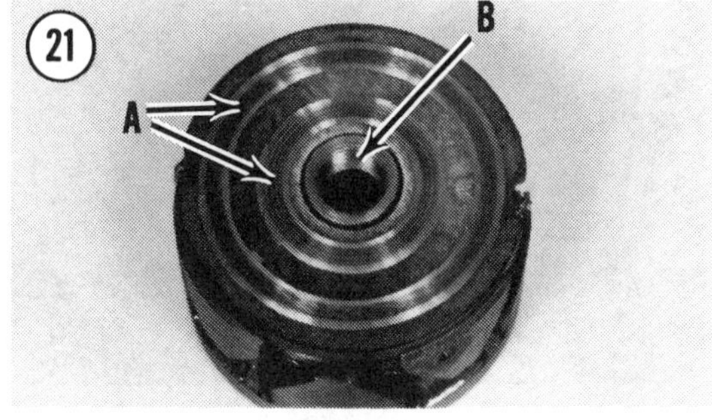

NOTE
Prior to replacing the stator with a new one, check the electrical wires to and within the terminal connector for any opens or poor connections.

3. Use an ohmmeter and check for continuity between all 5 terminals and to ground. Replace the stator if any of the terminals show continuity to ground. This would indicate a short within a winding.

Rotor Testing

1. Clean the 2 slip rings (A, **Figure 21**) with contact cleaner (**Figure 22**) and a clean shop rag to remove any carbon deposits.

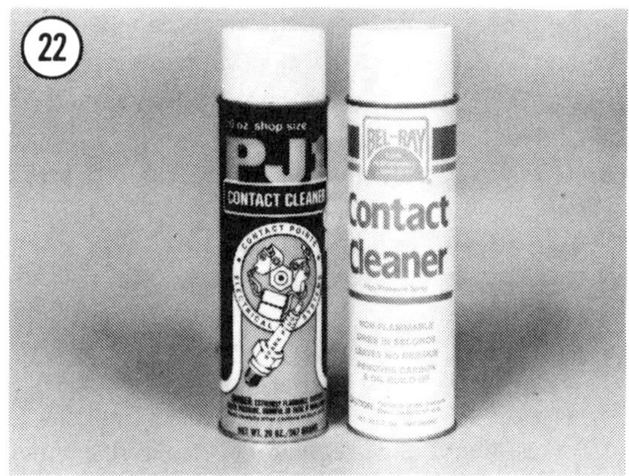

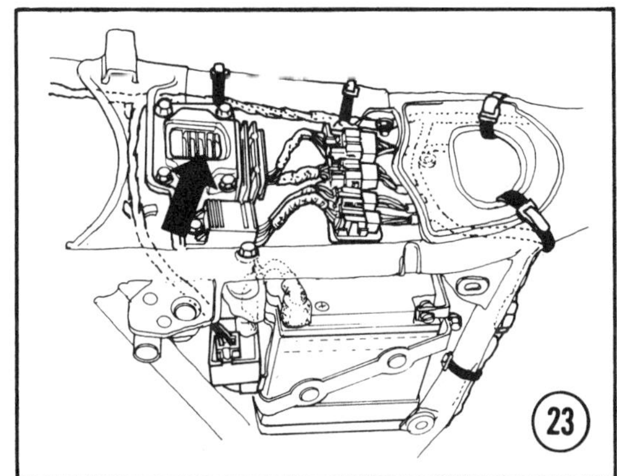

2. Use an ohmmeter and check for continuity between the 2 slip rings. There is no factory specified resistance; some resistance should be present but it should be very low (approximately 4-6 ohms). If there is very high resistance (infinity reading on the scale) this indicates there is an open and the rotor should be replaced.
3. Use an ohmmeter and check for continuity between each slip ring and the center core (B, **Figure 21**) which is the ground. The reading should be infinity for each ring. Replace the rotor if either ring shows continuity to ground which would indicate a short within a winding.

VOLTAGE REGULATOR/RECTIFIER

Removal/Installation

1. Remove the seat and both side covers.
2. Disconnect the battery negative lead.
3. On 1979 models, disconnect the electrical connections. Remove the bolts securing the voltage regulator/rectifier in place (**Figure 23**).

4. On models since 1980, disconnect the electrical connections (A, **Figure 24**). Remove the bolts (B, **Figure 24**) securing the document holder and voltage regulator/rectifier in place.
5. Remove the voltage regulator/rectifier and the 2 electrical connectors and wires.
6. Install by reversing these removal steps. Make sure all electrical connections are tight.

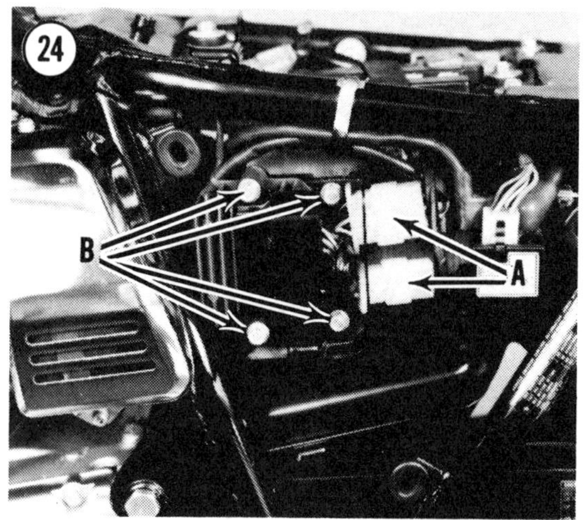

Testing – 1979-1980 Models

To test the voltage regulator/rectifier, disconnect the 2 electrical connectors from the harness. One connector terminal contains 3 wires – 1 green, 1 black and 1 red/white. The other terminal contains 5 wires – 3 yellow, 1 black and 1 white. Refer to **Figure 25**.

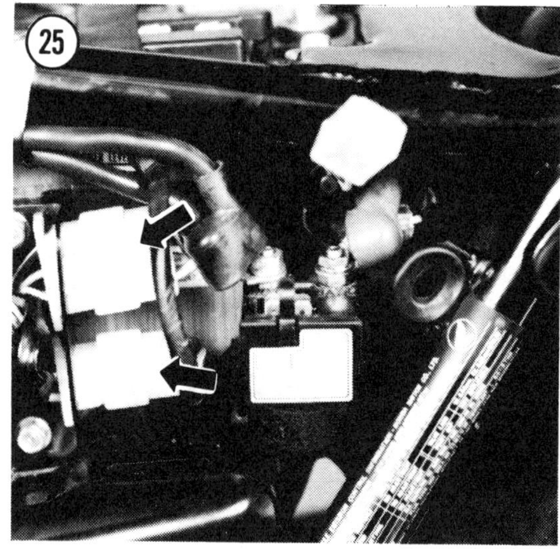

Make the following measurements using an ohmmeter and referring to **Figure 26**.

1. Connect either ohmmeter lead to the green rectifier lead. Connect the other ohmmeter lead to each of the yellow leads. These 3 measurements must be the same, either all very high resistance (2,000 ohms minimum) or very low resistance (5-40 ohms). If one or more differ, the voltage regulator/rectifier is defective and must be replaced.
2. Reverse the ohmmeter leads and repeat Step 1. This time, the readings must also be the same, but just the opposite from the measurements in Step 1. For example, if all readings in Step 1 were low, all readings in this step must be high and vice versa.
3. Connect either ohmmeter lead to the red/white voltage regulator/rectifier lead. Connect the other ohmmeter lead to each of the yellow leads. These 3 measurements must be the same–either all very high or all very low.
4. If the voltage regulator/rectifier fails to pass any of these tests the unit is defective and must be replaced.

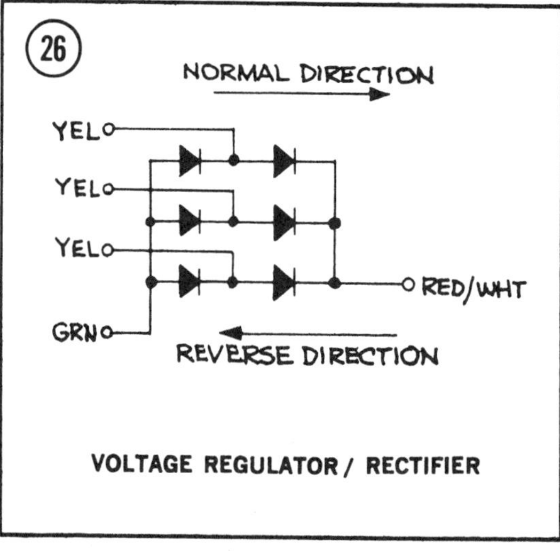

VOLTAGE REGULATOR / RECTIFIER

Testing – Models Since 1981

To test the voltage regulator/rectifier, disconnect the 2 electrical connectors from the harness. One connector terminal contains 3 wires – 1 green, 1 black and 1 red/white. The other terminal contains 5 wires – 3 yellow, 1 black and 1 white. Refer to **Figure 25**.

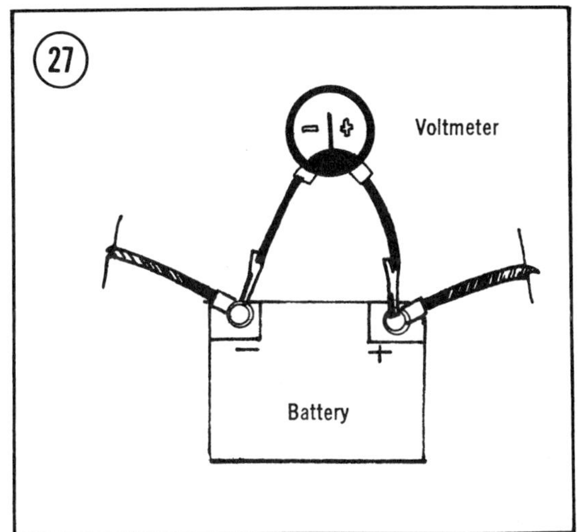

Make the following measurements using an ohmmeter with a positive ground. If a negative ground ohmmeter is used reverse the test leads in the following tests.

1. Connect the negative ohmmeter lead to the green rectifier lead. Connect the positive ohmmeter lead to each of the yellow leads. These 3 measurements must be the same (0.5-50 ohms).
2. **Reverse the ohmmeter leads and repeat Step 1. This time, the readings must all be the same, but just the opposite—they should read infinity.**
3. Connect the positive ohmmeter lead to the red/white rectifier lead. Connect the negative ohmmeter lead to each of the yellow leads and to the green lead. These 4 measurements must be the same (0.5-50 ohms).
4. Reverse the ohmmeter leads and repeat Step 3. This time, the readings must all be the same, but just the opposite—they should read infinity.
5. Connect the negative ohmmeter lead to the regulator black lead. Connect the positive ohmmeter lead to the regulator white lead and then to the green lead. The measurements should be 1-30 ohms for the white lead and 0.5-20 ohms for the green lead.
6. Connect the negative ohmmeter lead to the regulator white lead. Connect the positive ohmmeter lead to the regulator black lead and then to the green lead. The measurements should be 0.5-30 ohms for the black lead and 1-50 ohms for the green lead.
7. Connect the negative ohmmeter lead to the regulator green lead. Connect the positive ohmmeter lead to the regulator black lead and then to the white lead. The measurements should be 0.5-20 ohms for the black lead and 0.5-30 ohms for the white lead.
8. Connect the positive ohmmeter lead to the regulator black lead. Connect the neagrive ohmmeter lead to the regulator white lead and then to the green lead. The measurements should be 0.5-30 ohms for the white lead and 0.5-20 ohms for the green lead.
9. Connect the positive ohmmeter lead to the regulator white lead. Connect the negative ohmmeter lead to the regulator black lead and then to the green lead. The measurements should be 1-30 ohms for the black lead and 0.5-30 ohms for the green lead.
10. Connect the positive ohmmeter lead to the regulator green lead. Connect the negative ohmmeter lead to the regulator black lead and then to the white lead. The measurements should be 0.5-20 ohms for the black lead and 1-50 ohms for the white lead.
11. If the voltage regulator/rectifier fails to pass any of these tests the unit is defective and must be replaced.

Voltage Regulator Performance Test

Connect a voltmeter to the battery negative and positive terminals (**Figure 27**). Leave the battery cables attached. Start the engine and let it idle; increase engine speed until the voltage going to the battery reaches 14.0-15.0 volts. At this point, the voltage regulator/rectifier should prevent any further increase in voltage. If this does not happen, and the voltage increases above specifications, the voltage regulator/rectifier is faulty and must be replaced.

IGNITION SYSTEM

The ignition system consists of 2 ignition coils, a spark unit, an ignition pulser generator and 4 spark plugs. Refer to **Figure 28** for a diagram of the ignition circuit.

CAPACITOR DISCHARGE IGNITION

All CB650's are equipped with a fully transistorized ignition system. This solid state

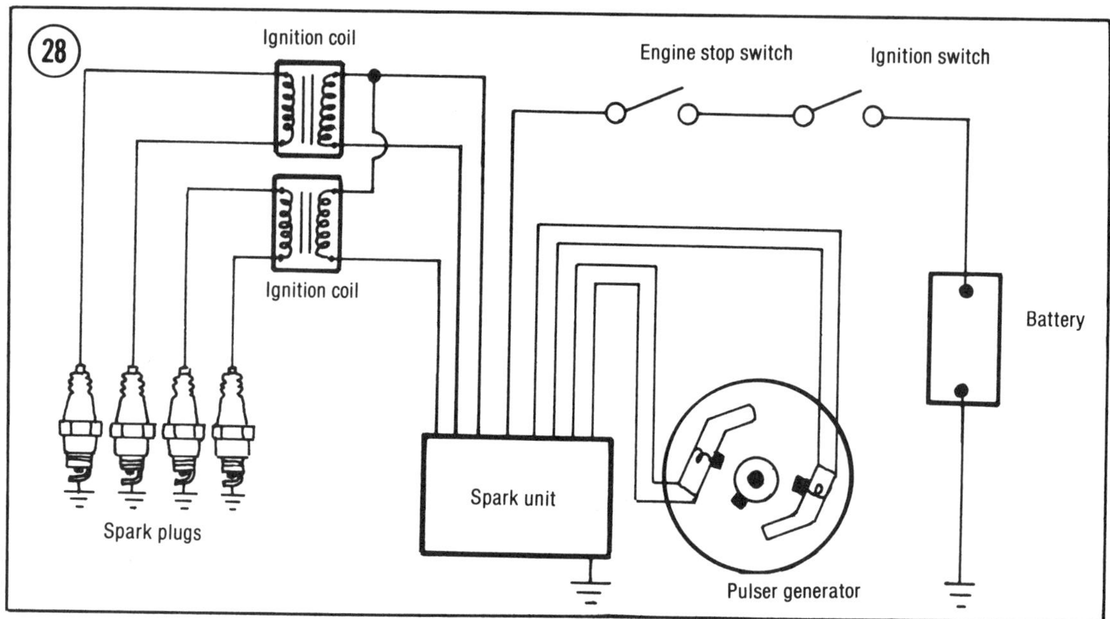

system is the capacitor discharge ignition (CDI) system that uses no breaker points. This system provides a longer life for components and delivers a more efficient spark throughout the entire speed range of the engine. Ignition timing is maintained for a longer time without periodic adjustment.

Alternating current from the alternator is rectified to direct current and is used to charge the capacitor. As the piston approaches the firing position, a pulse from the pulser generator coil is used to trigger the silicone controlled rectifier. The rectifier in turn allows the capacitor to discharge quickly into the primary circuit of the ignition coil, where the voltage is stepped up in the secondary circuit to a value sufficient to fire the spark plugs of the No. 1 and No. 4 cylinder, causing the plugs to fire. The same sequence happns to the No. 2 and No. 3 cylinders and is controlled by the rotation of the driven rotor in the ignition pulser generator.

NOTE

The spark plugs will fire at the same time (No. 1 and 4 and No. 2 and 3) but only one of the cylinders will be at TDC on the compression stroke. The other cylinder is on the exhaust stroke and the spark in that cylinder has no effect on it.

CDI Precautions

Certain measures must be taken to protect the capacitor discharge system. Damage to the semiconductors in the system may occur if the following precautions are not observed.

1. Never connect the battery backwards. If the connected battery polarity is wrong, damage will occur to the voltage regulator/rectifier, the alternator and spark unit.
2. Do not disconnect the battery when the engine is running. A voltage surge will occur which will damage the voltage regulator/rectifier and possibly burn out the lights.
3. Keep all connections between the various units clean and tight. Be sure that the wiring connections are pushed together firmly to help keep out moisture.
4. Do not substitute another type of ignition coil.
5. Each component is mounted within a rubber vibration isolator. Always be sure that the isolator is in place when installing any units of the system.

CDI Troubleshooting

Problems with the capacitor discharge system are usually the production of a weak spark or no spark at all.

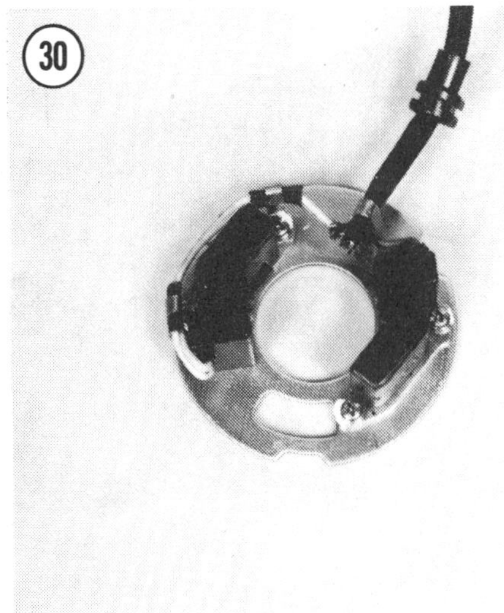

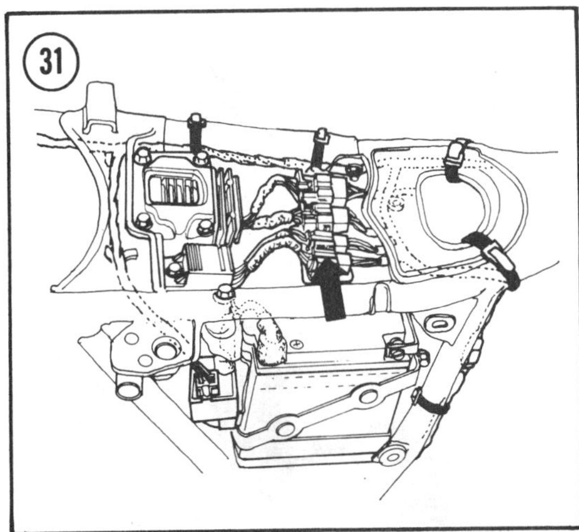

1. Check all connections to make sure they are tight and free of corrosion.
2. Check the ignition coils as described under *Ignition Coil Testing* in this chapter.
3. Check the pickup coils in the ignition pulser generator with an ohmmeter. Remove the right-hand side cover and disconnect the ignition pulser generator electrical connector (**Figure 29**). Connect the ohmmeter leads between both blue leads (No. 1 and 4 cylinders) and then between both yellow leads (No. 2 and 3 cylinders). Each coil's resistance should be 530 +/- 50 ohms at 68° F (20° C). If the pickup coils do not meet these specifications the ignition pulser generator assembly (**Figure 30**) must be replaced. It cannot be serviced; refer to *Ignition Pulser Generator Removal/Installation* in this chapter.
4. If the ignition coils and ignition pulser generator assembly check out okay, the spark unit is at fault and must be replaced.

Spark Unit Replacement

1. Remove the seat and both side covers.
2. Disconnect the battery negative lead.
3. Disconnect the electrical connector going to the spark unit. Refer to **Figure 31** for 1979 models or **Figure 32** for models since 1980.
4. Disconnect the spark unit from the frame.
5. Install by reversing these removal steps.

Spark Unit Testing

Tests may be performed on the unit but a good one may be damaged by someone unfamiliar with the test equipment. To be safe, have the test made by a dealer or substitute a known good unit for a suspected one.

7

IGNITION COIL

There are 2 ignition coils; the one on the left-hand side fires the No. 1 and 4 cylinders and the one on the right-hand side fires the No. 2 and 3 cylinders.

Removal/Installation

1. Remove the seat and right-hand side cover.
2. Disconnect the battery negative lead.
3. Remove the bolt (**Figure 33**) securing the rear of the fuel tank. Lift up and pull the tank to the rear and remove it. Remove the rubber mounting damper and keep it with the fuel tank to avoid misplacing it.
4. Disconnect the spark plug leads (**Figure 34**).
5. Disconnect the primary wire connectors (A, **Figure 35**) for both coils (black and black/white—left-hand coil; yellow and black/white—right-hand coil).
6. Remove the bolts securing the ignition coils to the frame and remove both coils.
7. Install by reversing these removal steps. Note the following.
8. Be sure to install the ground strap onto the front mounting bolt (B, **Figure 35**).
9. Make sure all electrical connections are tight and free of corrosion.
10. Route the spark plug wires to the correct cylinder (**Figure 36**).

Testing

The ignition coil is a form of transformer which develops the high voltage required to jump the spark plug gap. The only maintenance required is that of keeping the electrical connections clean and tight and occasionally checking to see that the coils are mounted securely.

If the condition of the coil(s) is doubtful, there are several checks which may be made.

First as a quick check of coil condition, disconnect the high voltage lead from the spark plug. Remove the spark plug from the cylinder head. Connect a new or known good spark plug to the high voltage lead and place the spark plug base on a good ground like the engine cylinder head (**Figure 37**). Position the spark plug so you can see the electrode.

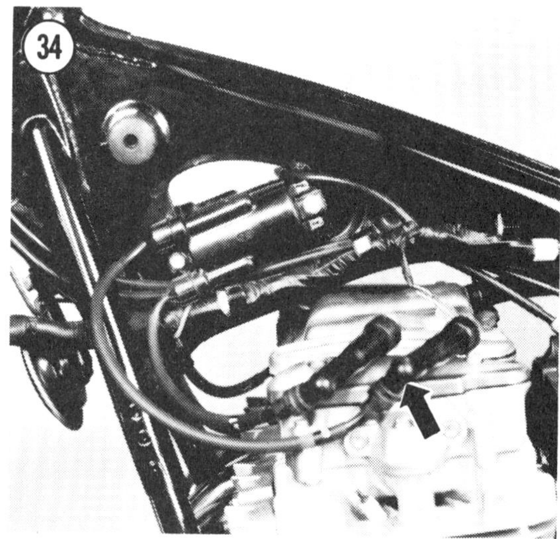

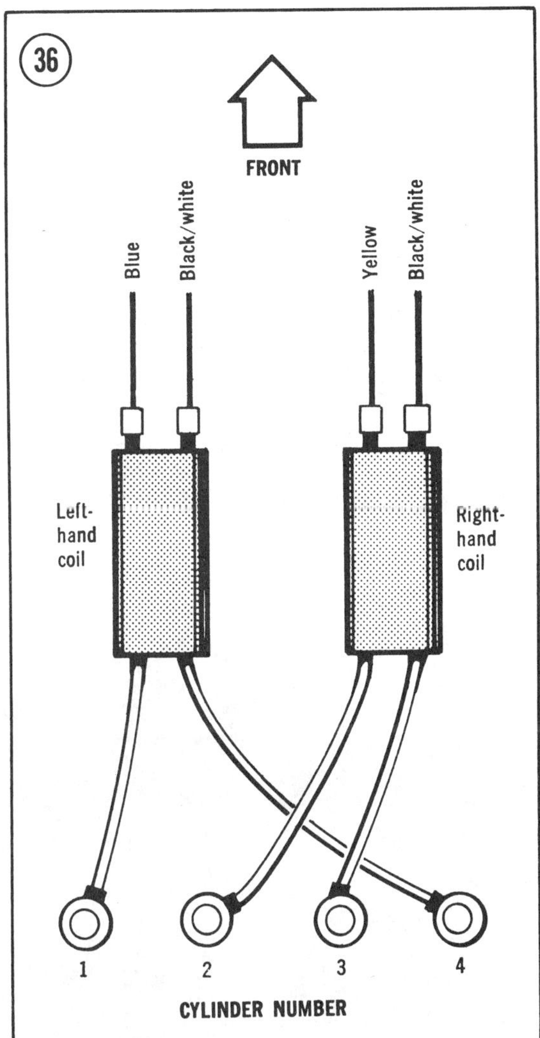

WARNING
If it is necessary to hold the high voltage lead, do so with an insulated pair of pliers. The high voltage generated could produce serious or fatal shocks.

Push the starter button to turn the engine over a couple of times. If a fat blue spark occurs the coil is in good condition; if not it must be replaced. Make sure that you are using a known good spark plug for this test. If the spark plug used is defective the test results will be incorrect.

Reinstall the spark plug in the cylinder head.

PULSER GENERATOR

Removal/Installation

1. Remove the seat and right-hand side cover.
2. Disconnect the battery negative lead.
3. Disconnect the pulser generator electrical connector containing 4 wires (2 yellow and 2 blue). Refer to **Figure 38**.
4. Remove the screws securing the ignition cover (**Figure 39**) and remove it.

5. Prior to removing the pulser generator assembly, make a mark on the base plate that lines up with the centerline of one of the attachment screws. This will assure correct ignition timing when the assembly is installed (providing it was correct prior to removal).
6. Remove the screws (A, **Figure 40**) securing the pulser generator assembly.
7. Carefully pull the electrical harness, along with the rubber grommet (B, **Figure 40**), out from the crankcase.
8. Remove the pulser generator assembly.
9. Install by reversing these removal steps; note the following.
10. When installing the assembly align the mark made in Step 5 for preliminary ignition timing.
11. Route the electrical harness the same way it was. Make sure to keep it away from the exhaust system.
12. Adjust the ignition timing as described under *Ignition Timing* in Chapter Three.

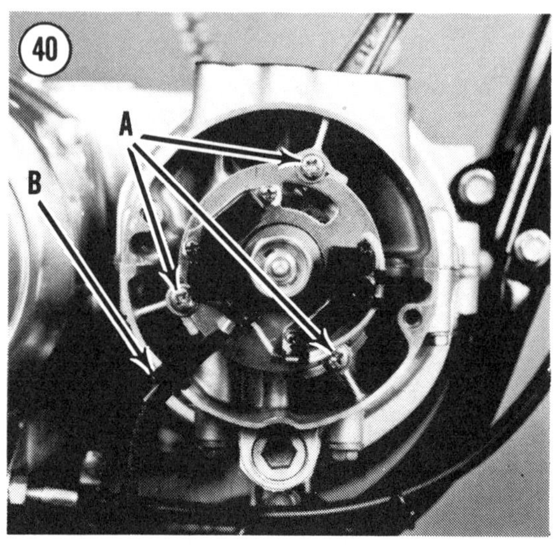

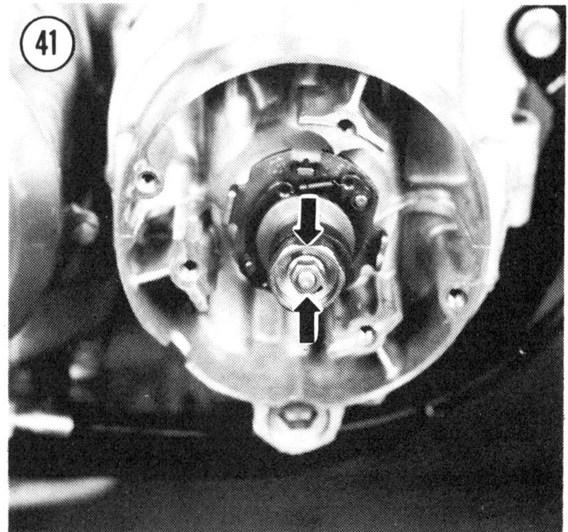

IGNITION ADVANCE MECHANISM

The ignition advance mechanism advances the ignition (fires the spark plugs sooner) as engine speed increases. If it does not advance properly and smoothly, the ignition will be incorrect at high engine rpm. It must be inspected periodically to make certain it operates freely.

Removal/Installation

1. Remove the pulser generator as described under *Pulser Generator Removal/Installation* in this chapter.
2. Hold onto the outer hex spacer with a 15/16 in. box wrench and remove the inner bolt (**Figure 41**).

CAUTION
To avoid internal damage to the ignition advance unit, be sure to securely hold the hex spacer while removing the inner bolt.

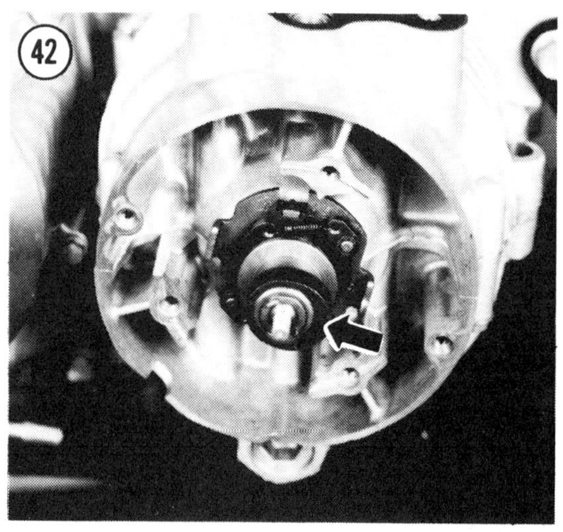

3. Remove the ignition advance unit (**Figure 42**).

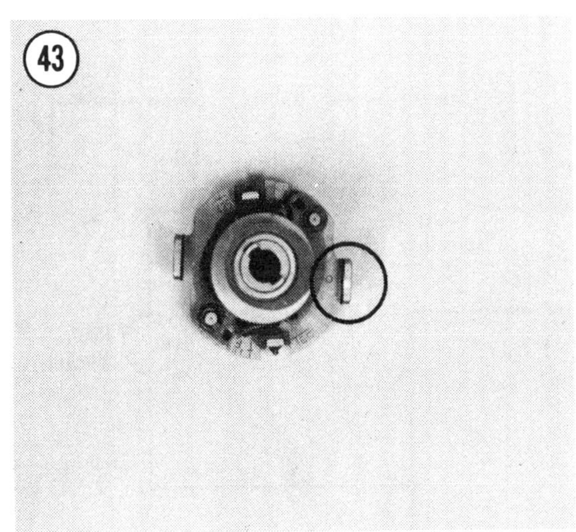

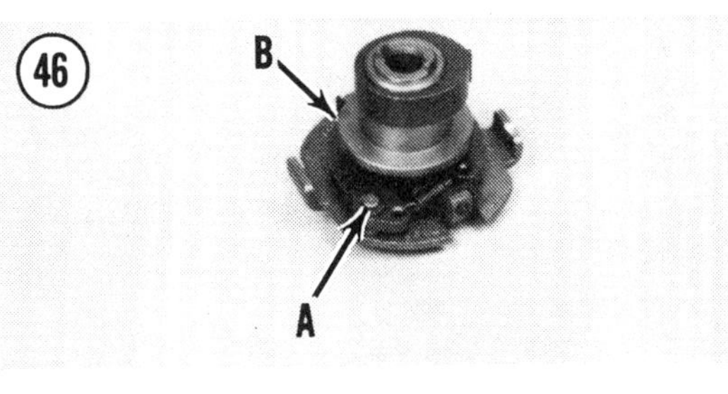

NOTE

If the ignition advance unit is separated, assemble by aligning the raised tooth on the rotor with the "O" mark on the backing plate ***(Figure 43)****.*

4. When installing the ignition advance unit, index the pin on the backside of the advance unit into the slot in the end of the crankshaft (**Figure 44**).
5. Hold the ignition advance unit in place. Align the notches in the hex spacer with the tangs on the advance unit and install the hex spacer (**Figure 45**).
6. Hold the hex spacer and install the inner bolt. Tighten the inner bolt to 6-7 ft.-lb. (8-12 N•m).

CAUTION

To avoid internal damage to the ignition advance unit, be sure to securely hold the hex spacer while installing the inner bolt.

Inspection

1. Inspect the condition of the pivot points (A, **Figure 46**) of each weight. It must pivot freely to maintain proper ignition advance. Apply lightweight grease to the pivot pins and all sliding surfaces.
2. Inspect the pivot cam (B, **Figure 46**) operation on the shaft. It must operate freely.
3. Make sure the centrifugal advance weight return springs (**Figure 47**) completely retract the weights. If not, replace the ignition advance unit.

48

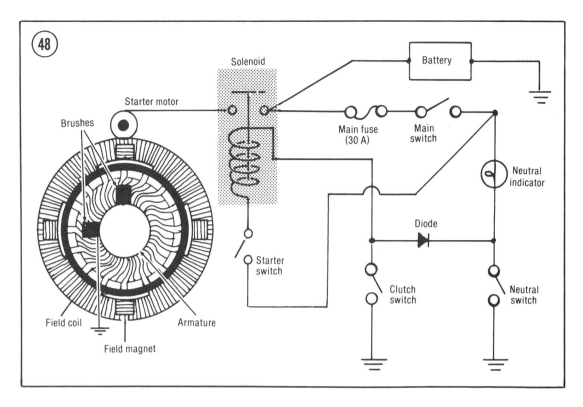

Solenoid
Battery
Starter motor
Brushes
Main fuse (30 A)
Main switch
Neutral indicator
Diode
Starter switch
Clutch switch
Neutral switch
Field coil
Armature
Field magnet

SPARK PLUG

The spark plug recommended by the factory is usually the most suitable for your motorcycle. If riding conditions are mild, it may be advisable to go to a plug one step hotter than normal. Unusually severe riding conditions may require a slightly colder plug. See Chapter Three for details.

STARTING SYSTEM

The starting system consists of the starter motor, starter gears, solenoid and the starter button.

The layout of the starting system is shown in **Figure 48.** When the starter button is pressed, it engages the starter solenoid switch that completes the circuit allowing electricity to flow from the battery to the starter motor.

CAUTION

Do not operate the starter for more than 5 seconds at a time. Let it rest approximately 10 seconds, then use it again.

The starter gears are covered in Chapter Four.

Table 1 at the end of the chapter lists possible starter problems, probable causes and most common remedies.

STARTER

Removal/Installation

1. Place the bike on the centerstand.
2. Remove the seat and side covers.
3. Disconnect the battery negative lead.
4. Remove the shift lever (A, **Figure 49**) and left-hand crankcase cover (B, **Figure 49**).
5. Remove the bolts (**Figure 50**) securing the starter cover and remove the cover.
6. Remove the bolts (**Figure 51**) securing the starter in place. Pull the starter out and disconnect the electrical wires to it (**Figure 52**).
7. Install by reversing these removal steps.

Disassembly/Inspection/Assembly

Refer to **Figure 53** for this procedure.

The overhaul of a starter motor is best left to an expert. This procedure shows how to detect a defective starter.

1. Remove the case screws and separate the case and covers.

NOTE

Write down the number of shims used on the shaft next to the commutator. Be sure to install the same number when reassembling the starter.

2. Clean all grease, dirt and carbon from the armature, case and end covers (**Figure 54**).

CAUTION

Do not immerse brushes or the wire windings in solvent as the insulation may be damaged. Wipe the windings with a cloth lightly moistened with solvent and dry thoroughly.

3. Remove the screws (**Figure 55**) securing the brushes in their holders and remove both brushes. Measure the length of each brush with a vernier caliper (**Figure 56**). If the length is 0.30 in. (7.5 mm) or less it must be replaced. Replace both brushes as a set even though only one may be worn to this dimension.
4. Inspect the condition of the commutator (**Figure 57**). The mica in a good commutator is below the surface of the copper bars. On a worn commutator the mica and copper bars may be worn to the same level. This condition must be corrected by undercutting the mica (**Figure 58**) but should be done by a specialist. Have this performed by a dealer or motorcycle or automotive electrical repair shop.
5. Inspect the commutator copper bars for discoloration. If a pair of bars are discolored grounded armature coils are indicated.
6. Use an ohmmeter and check for continuity between the commutator bars (**Figure 59**); there should be continuity between pairs of bars. Also check continuity between the commutator bars and the shaft (**Figure 60**); there should be no continuity. If the unit fails either of these tests the armature is faulty and must be replaced.
7. Use an ohmmeter and inspect the field coil by checking continuity between the starter cable terminal and the starter case; there should be no continuity. Also check continuity between the starter cable terminal and each brush wire terminal; there should be

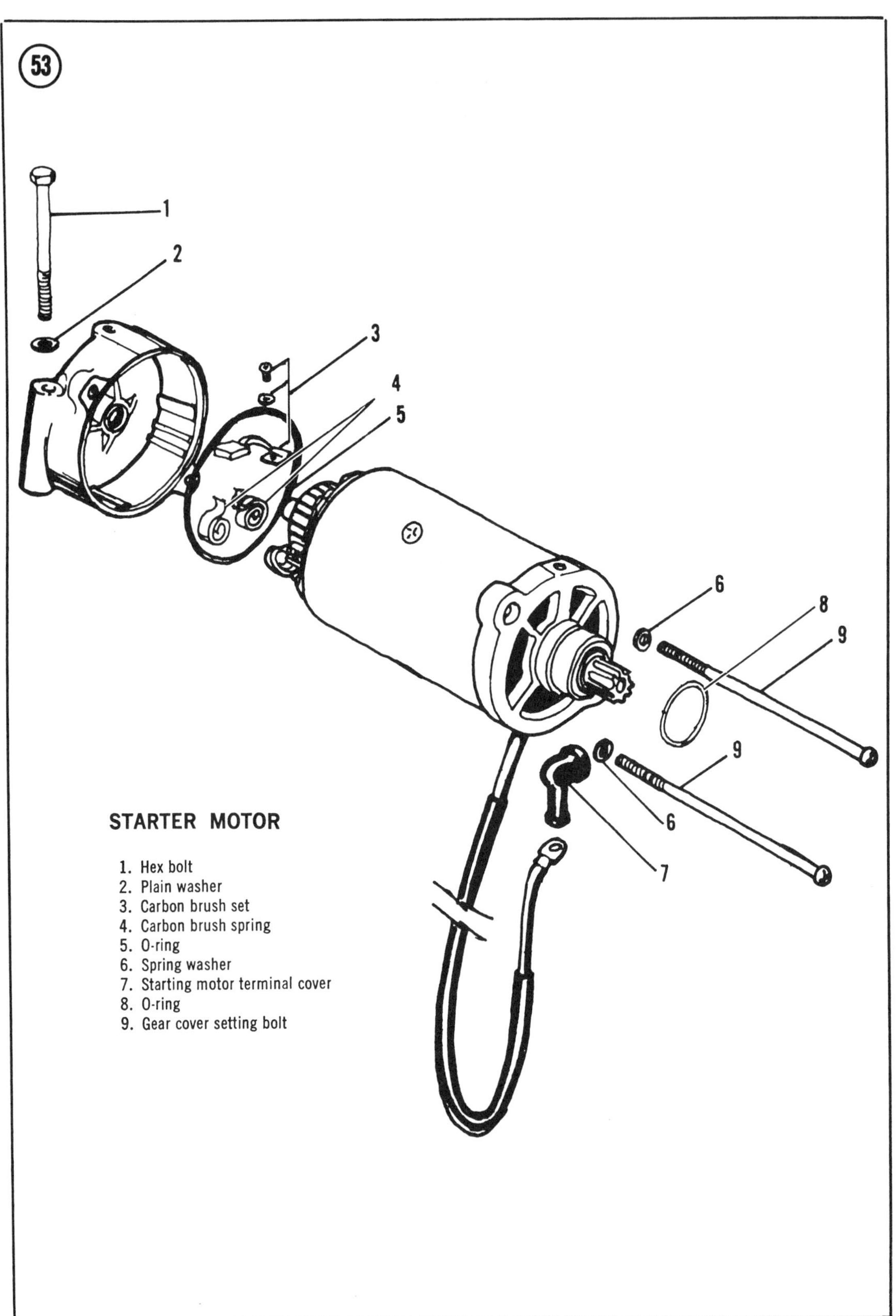
53
1
2
3
4
5
6
8
9
9
6
7
STARTER MOTOR
1. Hex bolt
2. Plain washer
3. Carbon brush set
4. Carbon brush spring
5. O-ring
6. Spring washer
7. Starting motor terminal cover
8. O-ring
9. Gear cover setting bolt

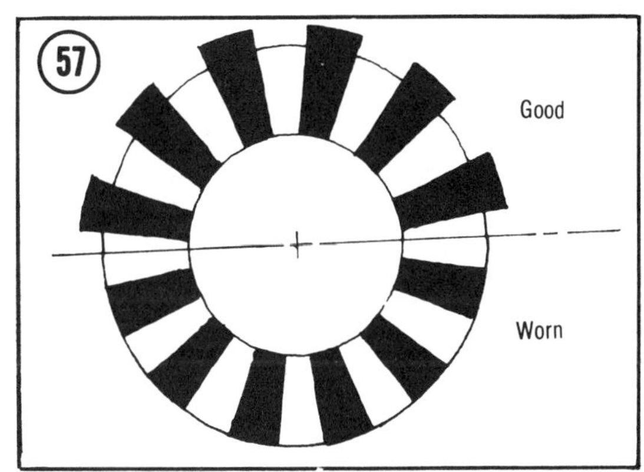

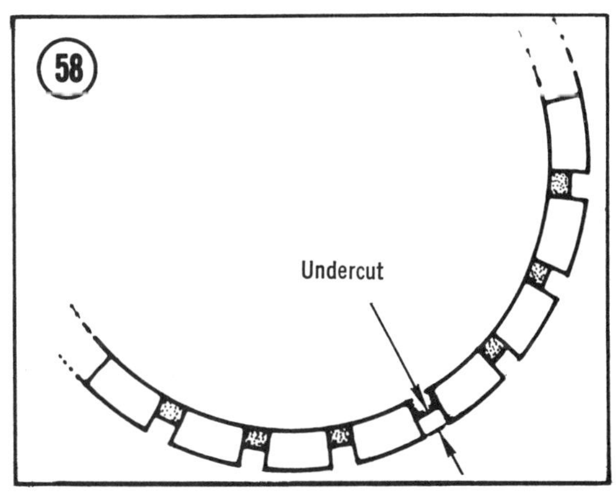

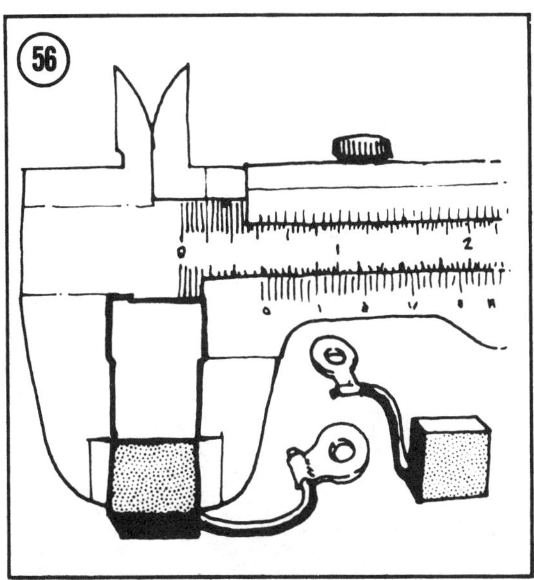

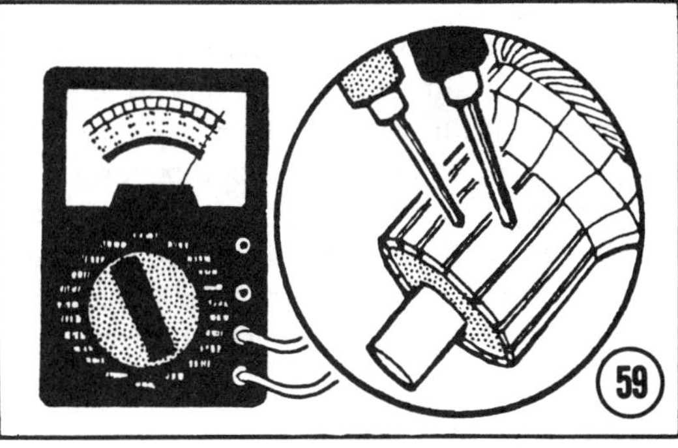

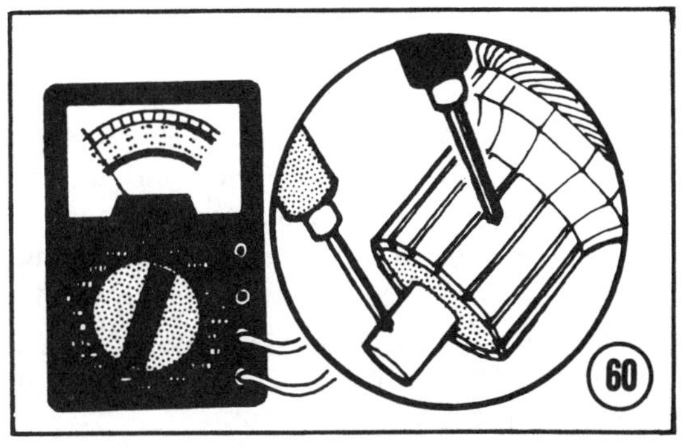

7

continuity. If the unit fails either of these tests the case/field coil assembly must be replaced.

8. Assemble the case; be sure to align the marks on both the case and end covers (**Figure 61**).

9. Inspect the condition of the gear and O-ring seal (**Figure 62**). If the gear is chipped or worn the armature must be replaced.

STARTER SOLENOID

Removal/Installation

1. On 1979 models, remove the right-hand side cover and disconnect the electrical connector to the main fuse.
2. On models since 1980, remove the left-hand side cover and disconnect the electrical connector to the main fuse (**Figure 63**).
3. On all models, slide off the rubber protective boots and disconnect the electrical wires from the top terminals (**Figure 64**).
4. Remove the solenoid from the frame along with the main fuse holder that is attached to it.
5. Replace by reversing these removal steps.

LIGHTING SYSTEM

The lighting system consists of a headlight, taillight/brakelight combination, directional signals, indicator lights and speedometer and tachometer illumination lights. **Table 2** lists replacement bulbs for these components.

Always use the correct wattage bulb as indicated in this section. The use of a larger wattage bulb will give a dim light and a smaller wattage bulb will burn out prematurely.

Headlight Replacement (U.S., Canada and U.K.)

Models since 1981 are equipped with a quartz halogen headlight and special handling is required as specified in this procedure.

Refer to **Figure 65** for this procedure.

1. Remove the screws (**Figure 66**) on each side securing the headlight assembly.
2. Pull out on the bottom of the headlight assembly and disengage it from the locating tab on top of the headlight housing.
3. Disconnect the electrical connector (**Figure 67**) from the headlight lens unit.

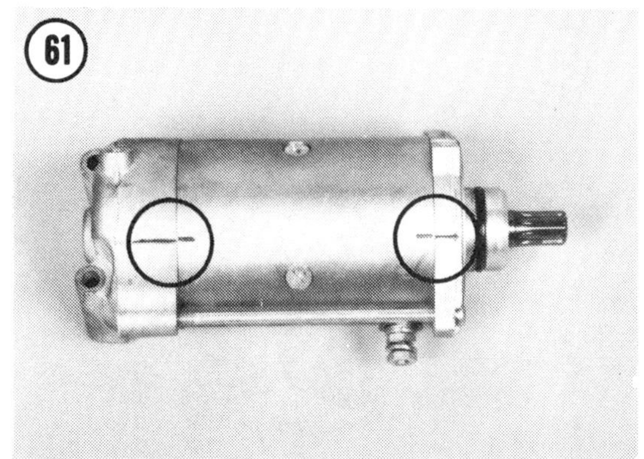
61

62

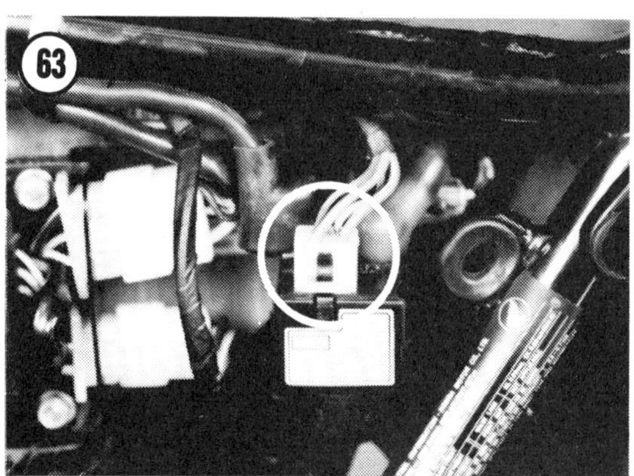
63

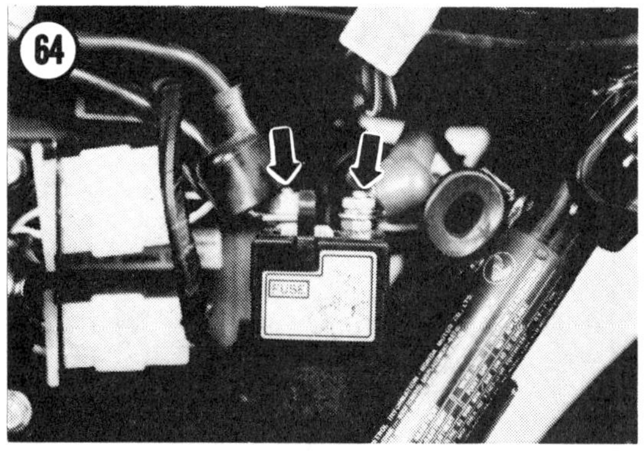

64

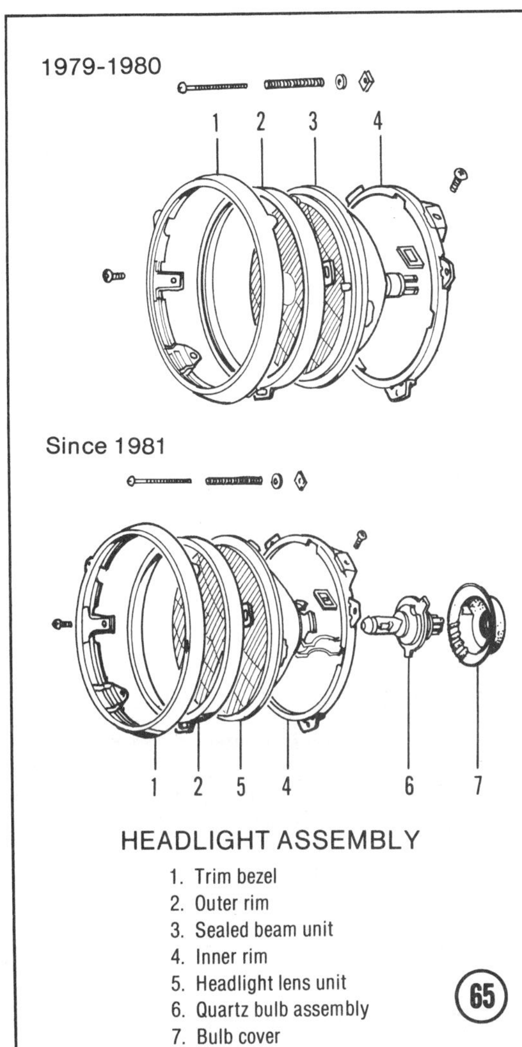

HEADLIGHT ASSEMBLY

1. Trim bezel
2. Outer rim
3. Sealed beam unit
4. Inner rim
5. Headlight lens unit
6. Quartz bulb assembly
7. Bulb cover

65

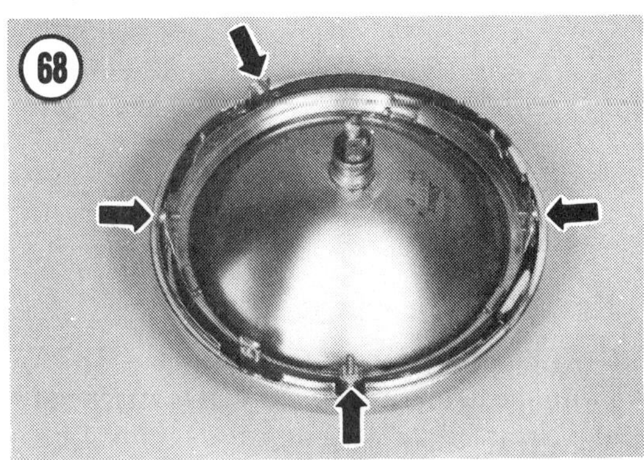

4. On 1979-1980 models, remove the retaining screws, the horizontal adjust screw and the 2 headlight retaining screws (**Figure 68**). Remove the inner rim and remove the sealed beam unit. Assemble by reversing this sequence; make sure to install the sealed beam unit with the "TOP" facing up.

5. On models since 1981, for bulb replacement remove the bulb cover, set spring and bulb assembly. Replace with a new bulb assembly—do not touch the bulb with your fingers. Assemble by reversing this sequence.

CAUTION

Carefully read all instructions shipped with the replacement bulb. Do not touch the bulb glass with your fingers because of oil on your skin. Any traces of oil on the quartz halogen bulb will drastically reduce the life of the bulb. Clean any traces of oil from the bulb with a cloth moistened in alcohol or lacquer thinner.

6. Install by reversing these removal steps.

7. Adjust the headlight as described under *Headlight Adjustment* in this chapter.

City (Pilot) Lamp Replacement (U.K.)

The U.K. models of the CB650 use the same headlight assembly as those for U.S. and Canada with the addition of the city (pilot) lamp.

Pull the city lamp out of the housing. Insert new bulb and push it back into the housing.

CAUTION
Models equipped with a quartz headlight also have a quartz city (pilot) lamp. Carefully read all instructions shipped with the replacement bulb. Do not touch the bulb glass with your fingers because of oil on your skin. Any traces of oil on the quartz halogen bulb will drastically reduce the life of the bulb. Clean any traces of oil from the bulb with a cloth moistened in alcohol or lacquer thinner.

Headlight Adjustment

Adjust the headlight horizontally and vertically according to Department of Motor Vehicle regulations in your area.

To adjust the headlight horizontally, turn the screw (A, **Figure 69**) on the right-hand side of the headlight trim bezel. Screwing in turns the light toward the right-hand side of the rider and loosening the screw will direct the light to the left-hand side of the rider.

To adjust the headlight vertically, remove the side reflex reflectors (**Figure 70**) on each side of the headlight assembly. Loosen the mounting bolt (B, **Figure 69**) on each side and position the headlight correctly. Retighten the bolts and reinstall the reflex reflectors.

Taillight/Brakelight Replacement

Remove the screws securing the lens (**Figure 71**) and remove the lens. Wash out the inside and outside of the lens with a mild detergent and wipe dry. Wipe off the reflective base surrounding the bulbs with a soft cloth.

Inspect the condition of the lens gasket (**Figure 72**) and replace if it is damaged or deteriorated.

Replace the bulb(s) and install the lens; do not overtighten the screws as the lens may crack.

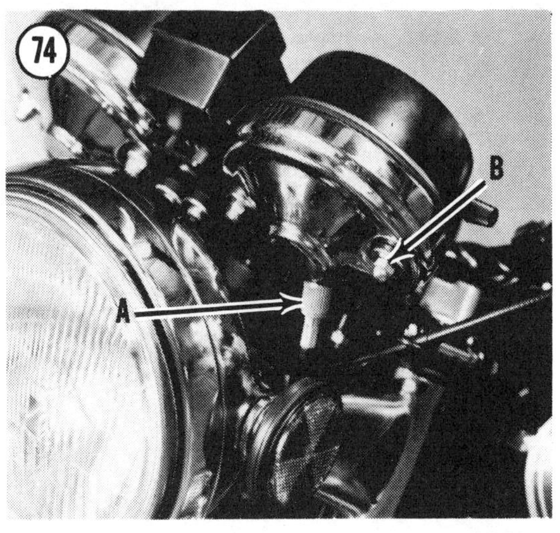

Directional Signal Light Replacement

Remove the screws securing the lens (**Figure 73**) and remove the lens. Wash out the inside and outside of the lens with a mild detergent and wipe dry.

Inspect the condition of the lens gasket and replace if it is damaged or deteriorated.

Replace the bulb and install the lens; do not overtighten the screws as the lens may crack.

Speedometer and Tachometer Illumination Light Replacement

1. Disconnect either or both speedometer and tachometer drive cables (A, **Figure 74**).
2. Unscrew the nuts, washers, and rubber dampers (B, **Figure 74**).

NOTE
In the next step do not pull up too hard on the housing as there is very little slack in the electrical wires—they are very short.

3. Carefully pull the housing up and off of the mounting bracket. Carefully pull the socket/bulb assembly out of the backside of the housing (**Figure 75**).

4. Replace the defective bulb(s). See **Figure 76**.

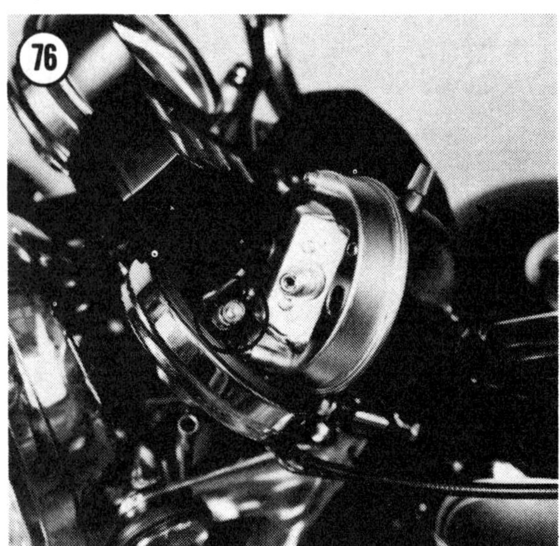

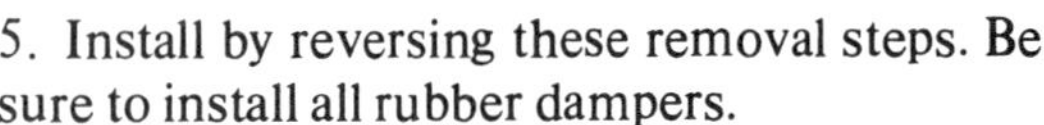

5. Install by reversing these removal steps. Be sure to install all rubber dampers.

Indicator Light Replacement

1. Remove the screws securing the indicator light panel (**Figure 77**) and remove the panel.
2. Remove the defective bulb(s) and replace with new ones.
3. Reinstall the indicator light panel.

SWITCHES

Front Brake Light Switch Replacement

Pull the electrical wires from the front brake switch (**Figure 78**). Remove the screw (A, **Figure 79**) securing the switch and carefully pull the switch assembly (B, **Figure 79**) out of the brake lever. Install a new switch and reconnect the electrical wires.

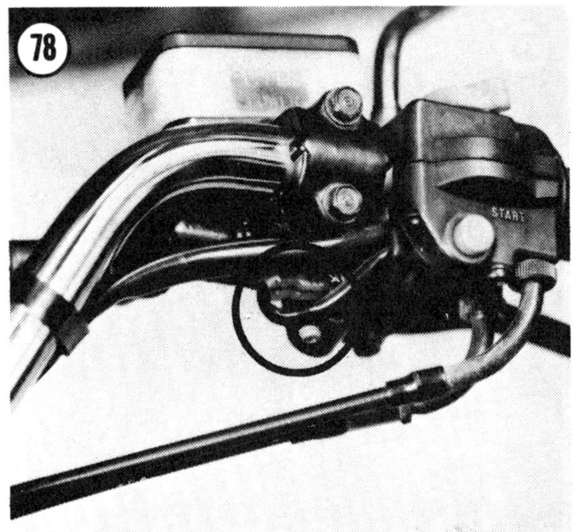

Rear Brake Light Switch Replacement

1. Remove the right-hand side cover (**Figure 80**).
2. Unhook the switch spring from the brake arm (A, **Figure 81**).
3. Unscrew the switch housing and adjust nut (B, **Figure 81**) from the frame bracket.
4. Disconnect the electrical connectors (C, **Figure 81**) from the wiring harness.
5. Replace the switch; reinstall and adjust as described under *Rear Brake Light Switch Adjustment* in this chapter.

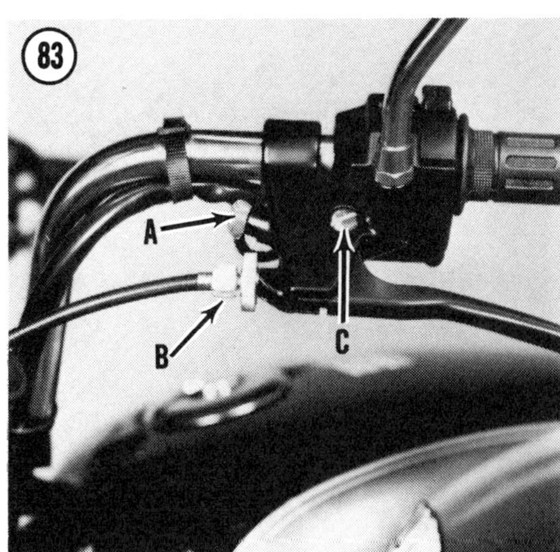

Rear Brake Light Switch Adjustment

1. Turn the ignition switch to the ON position.
2. Depress the brake pedal. The light should come on just as the brake begins to work.
3. To make the light come on earlier, hold the switch body and turn the adjusting nut *clockwise* as viewed from the top. Turn *counterclockwise* to delay the light from coming on. Refer to **Figure 82**.

NOTE

Some riders prefer the light to come on a little early. This way, they can tap the pedal without braking to warn drivers who are following too closely.

Clutch Switch Replacement

1. Disconnect the electrical wire (A, **Figure 83**).
2. Adjust the clutch cable for maximum slack and remove the cable (B, **Figure 83**) from the clutch lever.
3. Remove the bolt (C, **Figure 83**) securing the clutch lever and remove it.
4. Remove the clutch switch.
5. Install by reversing these removal steps. Position the small protrusion on the switch toward the handlebar when installing the switch.

Oil Pressure Switch Replacement

1. Remove the gearshift lever and left-hand crankcase cover.

2. Disconnect the electrical connector from the top of the switch (**Figure 84**).
3. Unscrew the switch from the oil pump.
4. Apply Loctite Lock N' Seal to the switch threads. Install the switch and tighten to 7-15 ft.-lb. (10-20 N•m).
5. Attach the electrical wire. Make sure the connection is tight and free from oil.
6. Install the left-hand crankcase cover and gearshift cover.

Neutral Indicator Switch Replacement

1. Remove the shift lever and left-hand crankcase cover.
2. Disconnect the electrical connections to the switch.
3. Remove the screws securing the neutral indicator switch (**Figure 85**) and remove it.

NOTE

Figure 85 *is shown with some engine components removed for clarity. It is not necessary to remove them for switch replacement.*

4. Install a new switch and connect the electrical wire securely.
5. Install the left-hand crankcase cover and shift lever.

ELECTRICAL COMPONENTS

Turn Signal Relay Replacement

On 1979 models, remove the seat and right-hand side cover. Remove the voltage

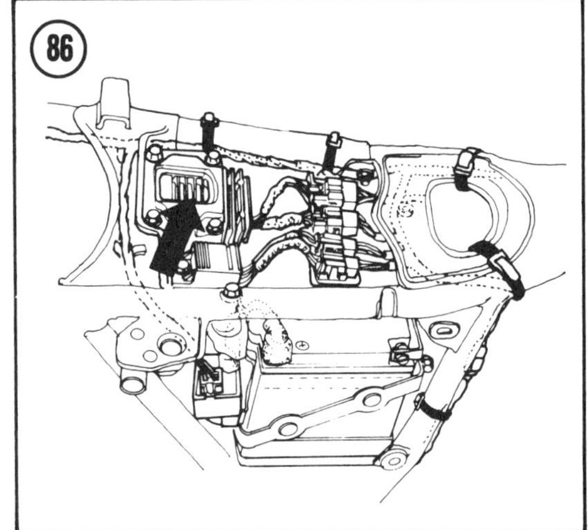

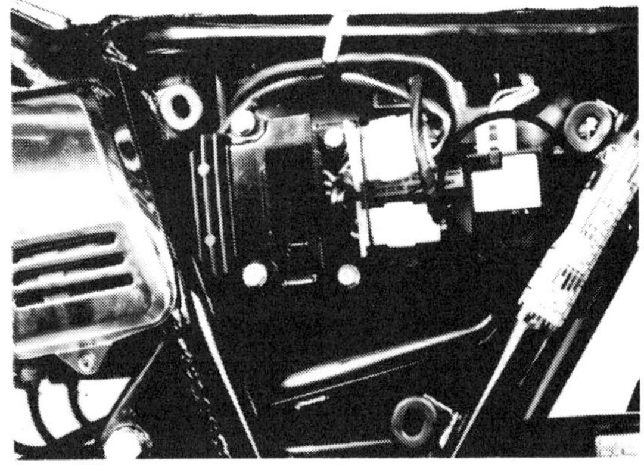

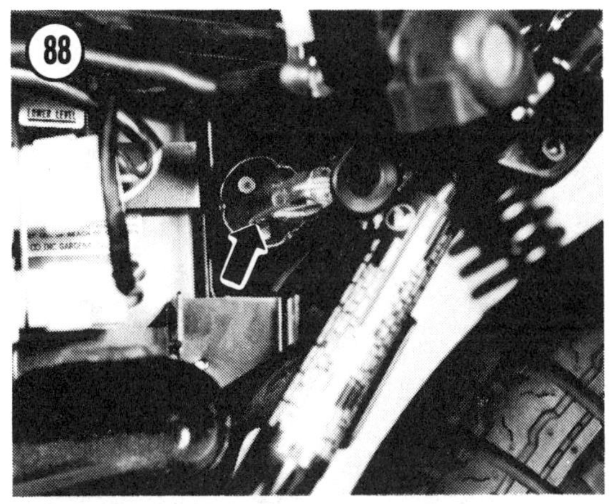

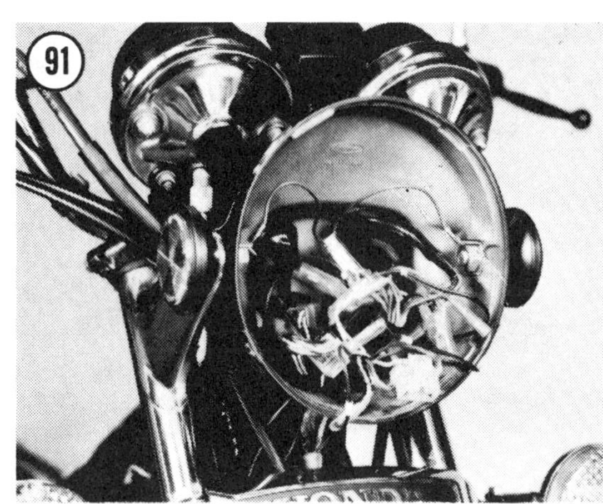

regulator/rectifier (**Figure 86**). Pull the turn signal relay out of the rubber mount and transfer the electrical wires to the new relay. Install the relay in the rubber mount. Install the regulator/rectifier, seat and side cover.

On models since 1980, remove the left-hand side cover. Pull the starter solenoid (**Figure 87**) out of its rubber mount and pivot it up and out of the way. Pull the turn signal relay (**Figure 88**) out of the rubber mount. Transfer the electrical wires to the new relay and install the relay in the rubber mount. Install the solenoid and side cover.

Horn Removal/Installation

1. Disconnect the electrical connections (**Figure 89**) on the horn.
2. Remove the screw and washer securing the horn to the frame and remove it.
3. Install by reversing these removal steps.

Horn Testing

Remove the horn as described under *Horn Removal/Installation* in this chapter. Connect a 12-volt battery to the horn. If the horn is good, it will sound. If not, replace it.

Instrument Cluster Removal/Installation

1. Disconnect the speedometer and tachometer drive cables (**Figure 90**).
2. Remove the headlight as described under *Headlight Replacement* in this chapter.
3. Within the headlight housing (**Figure 91**) trace the electrical wires from the instrument cluster. Disconnect the electrical connector containing 8 wires.

7

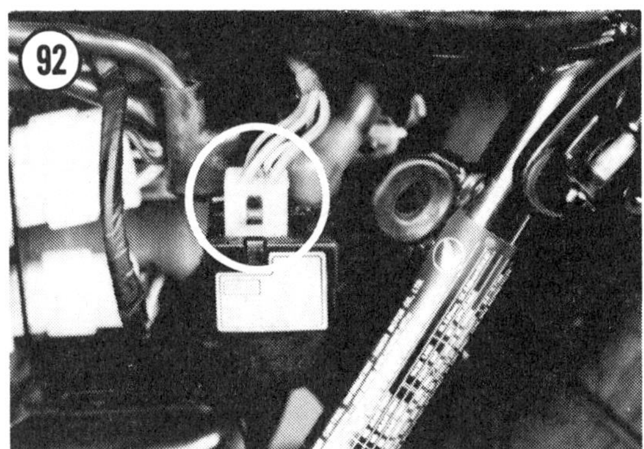

4. Unscrew the nuts securing the instrument cluster to the mounting bracket and remove it. Carefully pull the electrical wires through the rear opening in the headlight housing.
5. Install by reversing these removal steps. Make sure to install all rubber dampers.

Fuse

There are 5 fuses used on the CB650. The main fuse (fusible link) is located next to the starter solenoid and the remaining 4 are located in the fuse panel on the handlebar base.

If the main fusible link blows, disconnect the electrical connector (**Figure 92**) and open the fuse door. Remove the Phillips screws securing the fusible link and replace it (A, **Figure 93**). There is a spare link inside the panel (B, **Figure 93**). The remaining fuses are accessible by removing the cover (**Figure 94**) on the handlebar base. There is one spare fuse (**Figure 95**) here also; always carry spares.

Whenever a fuse blows, find out the reason for the failure before replacing the fuse. Usually the trouble is a short circuit in the wiring. This may be caused by worn-through insulation or a disconnected wire shorted to ground.

CAUTION

Never substitute aluminum foil or wire for a fuse. Never use a higher amperage fuse than specified. An overload could cause a fire and complete loss of the motorcycle.

WIRING DIAGRAMS

Full color wiring diagrams are located at the end of this book.

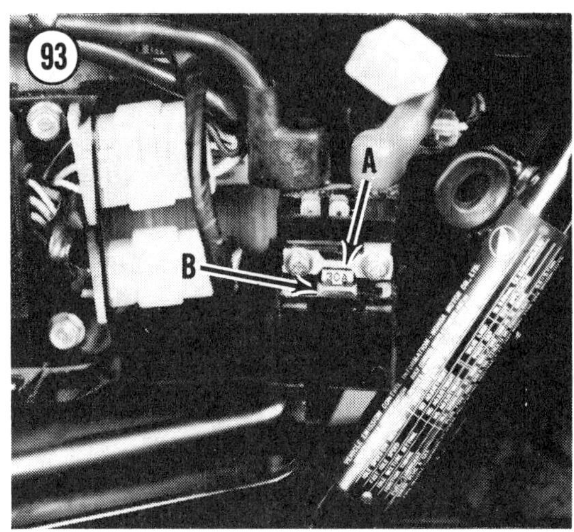

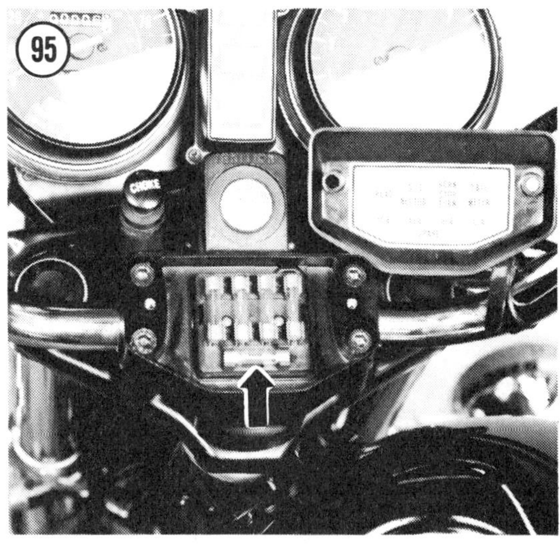

Table 1 STARTER TROUBLESHOOTING

Symptom	Probable Cause	Remedy
Starter does not work	Low battery Worn brushes Defective relay Defective switch Defective wiring or connection Internal short circuit	Recharge battery Replace brushes Repair or replace Repair or replace Repair wire or clean connection Repair or replace defective component
Starter action is weak	Low battery Pitted relay contacts Worn brushes Defective connection Short circuit in commutator	Recharge battery Clean or replace Replace brushes Clean and tighten Replace armature
Starter runs continuously	Stuck relay	Replace relay
Starter turns; does not turn engine	Defective starter clutch	Replace starter clutch

TABLE 2 REPLACEMENT BULBS

Headlight	
1979-1980	12V 65/50W (sealed beam)
1981-on	12V H4 Phillips No. 12341/99 or equivalent (quartz bulb)
Tail/brakelight	12V 8/27W—SAE No. 1157
Directionals	
Front	12V 23W—SAE No. 1034
Rear	12V 23 W—SAE No. 1073
Speedometer and tachometer illumination	12V 3.4W—SAE No. 57
Indicator lights (all)	12V 3.4W—SAE No. 57
Pilot (city)	
Used with regular headlight	12V 3W (Stanley)
Used with quarts headlight	12V 4W (Stanley)

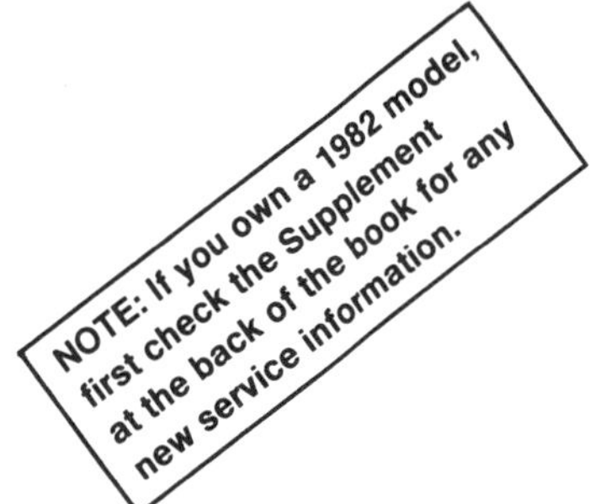

NOTE: If you own a 1982 model,
first check the Supplement
at the back of the book for any
new service information.

CHAPTER EIGHT

FRONT SUSPENSION AND STEERING

This chapter describes repair and maintenance of the front wheel, forks and steering components.

Refer to **Table 1** for torque specifications for the front suspension. **Tables 1-3** are located at the end of this chapter.

FRONT WHEEL

Single Disc Brake Models Removal

1. Place a milk crate or wood block(s) under the engine or frame to support it securely with the front wheel off the ground.
2. Unscrew the speedometer cable set screw (**Figure 1**). Pull the speedometer cable free from the hub.
3. Loosen the axle clamp nuts evenly then remove the nuts, lockwashers, washers and clamps (**Figure 2**) from each side.
4. Pull the wheel down and forward, being careful not to damage the studs on the fork end.

CAUTION

*Do not set the wheel down on the disc surface as it may get scratched or warped. Set it on 2 wood blocks (**Figure 3**).*

NOTE

Insert a piece of wood in the caliper in place of the brake disc. That way if the brake lever is inadvertently squeezed, the piston will not be forced out of the cylinder. If this does happen, the caliper may have to be disassembled to reseat the piston and the system will have to be bled. By using the wood, bleeding the brake is not necessary when installing the wheel.

Single Disc Brake Models Installation

1. Make sure the axle bearing surfaces of the fork sliders, lower clamps and axle are free from burrs and nicks.
2. Remove the piece of wood from the brake caliper.
3. Position the wheel into place, carefully inserting the brake disc between the brake pads.
4. Install the axle clamps with the "F" mark or arrow (**Figure 4**) facing forward. Install the washers, lockwashers and nuts.
5. Position the speedometer housing so the cable inlet is at the 3 o'clock position.
6. Tighten the front axle clamp nut first and then the rear nut to 13-18 ft.-lb. (18-25 N•m).

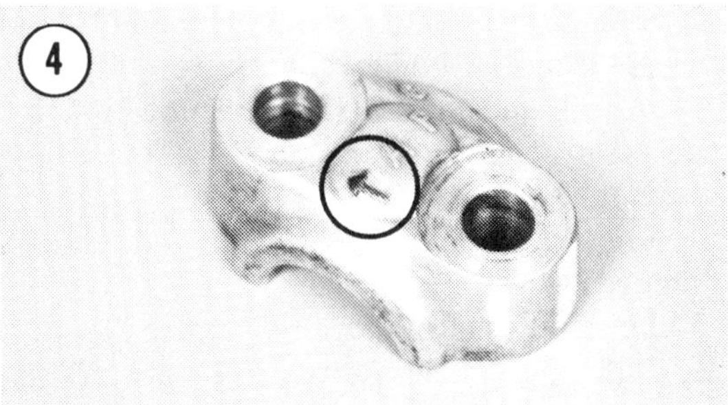

WARNING

The clamp nuts must be tightened in this manner and to this torque value. After installation is complete, there will be a slight gap at the rear, with no gap at the front. If done incorrectly, the studs could fail, resulting in loss of control of the bike when riding.

7. Slowly rotate the wheel and install the speedometer cable into the speedometer housing. Install and tighten the cable set screw.
8. After the wheel is completely installed, rotate it several times and apply the brakes a couple of times to make sure that it rotates freely and that the brake pads are against the disc correctly.

Dual Disc Brake Models
Removal

1. Place a milk crate or wood block(s) under the engine or frame to support it securely with the front wheel off the ground.
2. Expand the speedometer cable set spring (**Figure 5**). Pull the speedometer cable free from the hub.

3. On one side only, remove the bolts (**Figure 6**) securing the brake caliper assembly to the front fork and tie it up to the front fork. It is necessary to remove only one of the caliper assemblies, not both.
4. Loosen the axle pinch bolt and nut (A, **Figure 7**).
5. Unscrew the front axle (B, **Figure 7**).
6. Pull the wheel down and forward and remove it.

CAUTION
Do not set the wheel down on the disc surface as it may get scratched or warped. Set it on 2 wood blocks.

NOTE
Insert a piece of wood in both calipers in place of the brake discs. That way if the brake lever is inadvertently squeezed, the piston will not be forced out of the cylinder. If this does happen, the caliper may have to be disassembled to reseat the piston and the system will have to be bled. By using the wood, bleeding the brake is not necessary when installing the wheel.

Dual Disc Brake Models Installation

1. Make sure the axle bearing surfaces of the fork slider and axle are free from burrs and nicks.
2. Remove the pieces of wood from the brake calipers.
3. Position the wheel into place, carefully inserting the brake disc between the brake pads.
4. Position the speedometer housing so that it is perpendicular to the left-hand fork leg.
5. Insert the front axle from the right-hand side and screw it into the left-hand fork leg.
6. Tighten the front axle to 40-47 ft.-lb. (55-65 N•m).
7. Install the pinch bolt and nut and tighten it finger-tight only.
8. Install the caliper that was removed, being careful not to damage the brake pads.
9. Tighten the caliper mounting bolts to 22-29 ft.-lb. (30-40 N•m).
10. Slowly rotate the wheel and install the speedometer cable into the speedometer housing. Install the cable set spring.

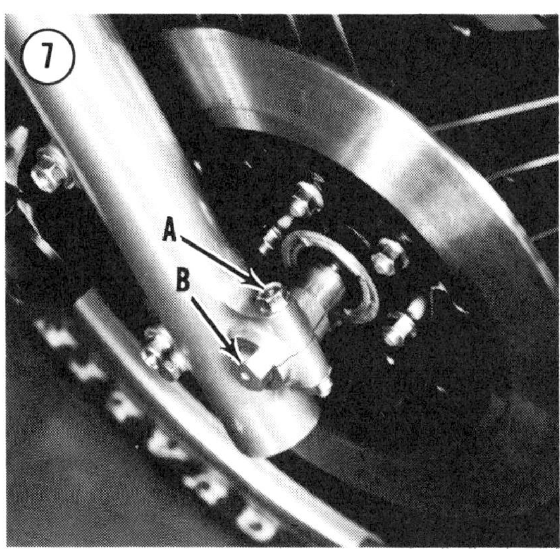

11. With a flat feeler gauge, measure the distance between the outside surface of the disc and the left-hand caliper holder. The clearance must be 0.028 in. (0.7 mm) or more. If clearance is insufficient, loosen the axle pinch bolt and pull the left-hand fork leg out until this dimension is achieved. Tighten the pinch bolt and nut to 11-18 ft.-lb. (15-25 N•m).

12. After the wheel is completely installed, rotate it several times and apply the brakes a couple of times to make sure that it rotates freely and that the brake pads are against the disc correctly.

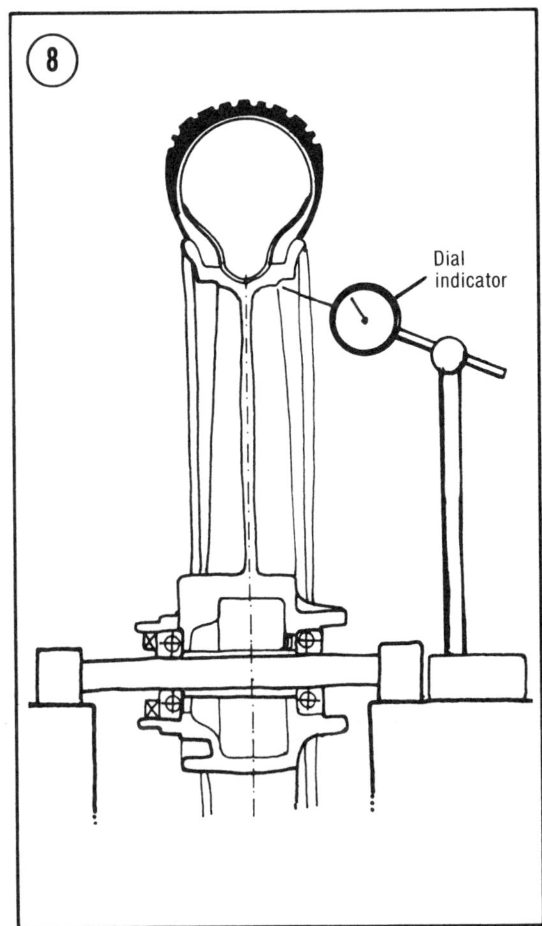

Inspection—All Models

Measure the radial and axial runout of the wheel rim with a dial indicator as shown in **Figure 8**. The standard value for both radial and axial runout is 0.02 in. (0.5 mm). The maximum permissible limit for both the wire spoke type and ComStar wheel is 0.08 in. (2 mm).

On models with wire wheels, some of this condition can be corrected by either tightening or replacing any loose or bent spokes. Refer to *Spoke Adjustment* or *Spoke Inspection and Replacement (Wire Spoke Type Wheels)* in this chapter.

On models with the ComStar wheels, if the runout exceeds this dimension the wheel will have to be replaced as it cannot be serviced. Inspect the ComStar wheel for signs of cracks, fractures, dents or bends. If it is damaged in any way, it must be replaced.

WARNING
Do not try to repair any damage to a ComStar wheel as it will result in an unsafe condition.

Check the axle runout as described under *Front Hub Inspection* in this chapter.

FRONT HUB

Refer to **Figure 9** or **Figure 10** for this procedure.

Removal of the bearing retainers can be accomplished with a small drift and hammer or with the use of special tools. These are available from a Honda dealer and are as follows:

a. Retainer wrench body (Honda part No. 07710-0010401).
b. Retainer wrench "B" (Honda part No. 07710-0010200).

8

Disassembly

1. Remove the front wheel as described under *Front Wheel Removal* in this chapter.
2. On single disc brake models, unscrew the axle nut (**Figure 11**) from the axle.
3. Withdraw the axle (**Figure 12**) and speedometer housing (**Figure 13**).
4. Turn the wheel over and remove the spacer (**Figure 14**).
5. On wire spoke wheel models, remove the bolts (**Figure 15**) securing the brake disc and remove it.
6. On single disc brake ComStar wheels, remove the bolts and nuts securing the brake disc and front cover. Remove the brake disc and cover.
7. On dual disc brake ComStar wheels, remove the bolts and nuts securing the brake discs and remove them.
8. Remove the oil seal (**Figure 16**).
9. Use a small drift and hammer or special tools (Honda part No. 07710-0010200 and 07710-0010401) and unscrew the bearing retainer from the hub.
10. Remove the grease seal and speedometer drive dog (**Figure 17**).

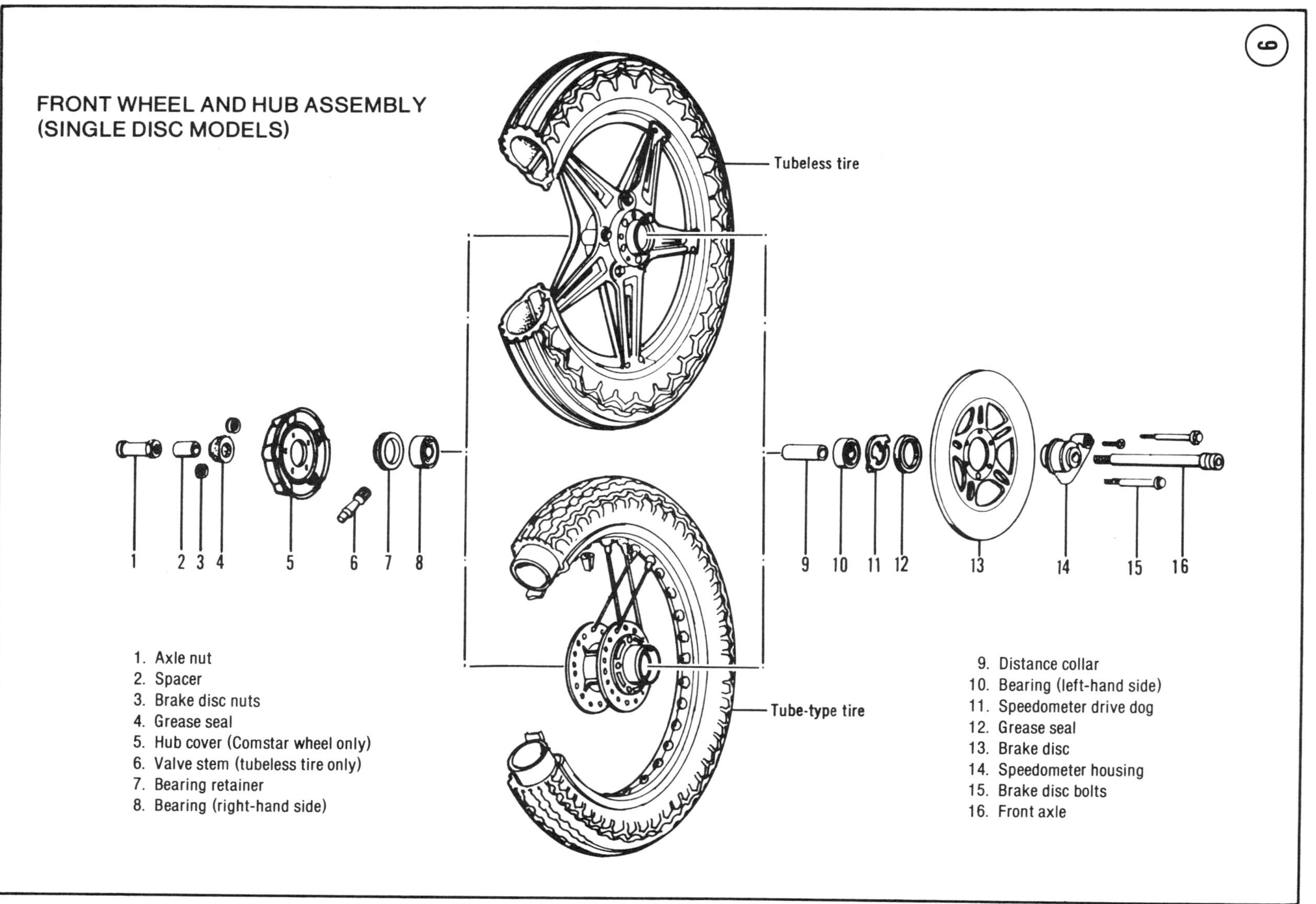
9
FRONT WHEEL AND HUB ASSEMBLY
(SINGLE DISC MODELS)
Tubeless tire
Tube-type tire
1. Axle nut
2. Spacer
3. Brake disc nuts
4. Grease seal
5. Hub cover (Comstar wheel only)
6. Valve stem (tubeless tire only)
7. Bearing retainer
8. Bearing (right-hand side)
9. Distance collar
10. Bearing (left-hand side)
11. Speedometer drive dog
12. Grease seal
13. Brake disc
14. Speedometer housing
15. Brake disc bolts
16. Front axle

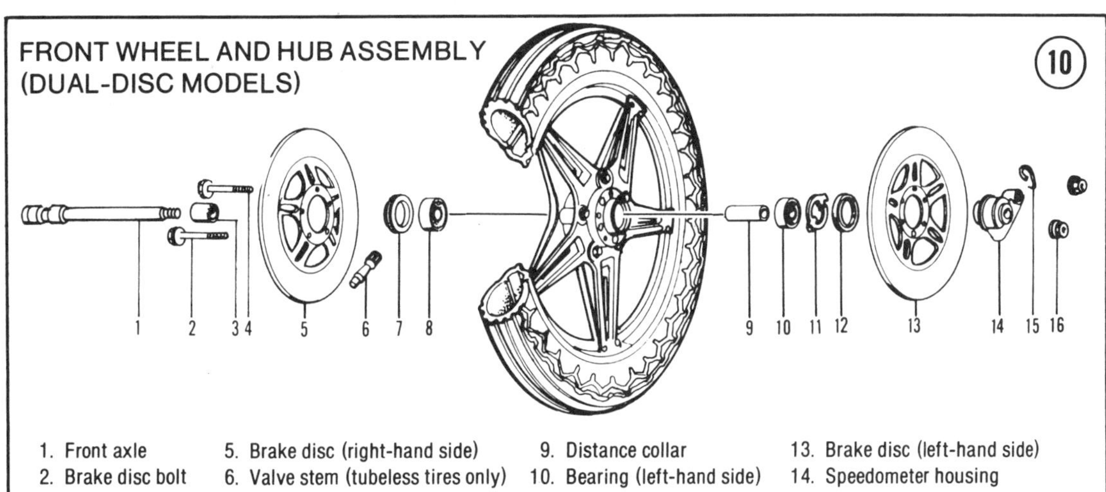

FRONT WHEEL AND HUB ASSEMBLY (DUAL-DISC MODELS)

1. Front axle
2. Brake disc bolt
3. Spacer
4. Brake disc bolt
5. Brake disc (right-hand side)
6. Valve stem (tubeless tires only)
7. Bearing retainer
8. Bearing (right-hand side)
9. Distance collar
10. Bearing (left-hand side)
11. Speedometer drive dog
12. Grease seal
13. Brake disc (left-hand side)
14. Speedometer housing
15. Speedometer cable retainer clip
16. Brake disc nut

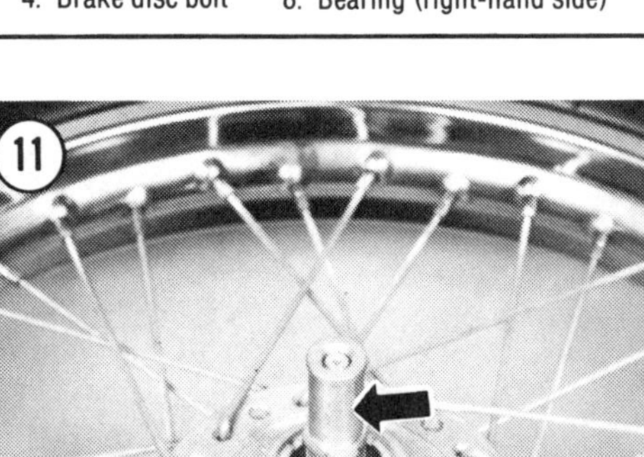

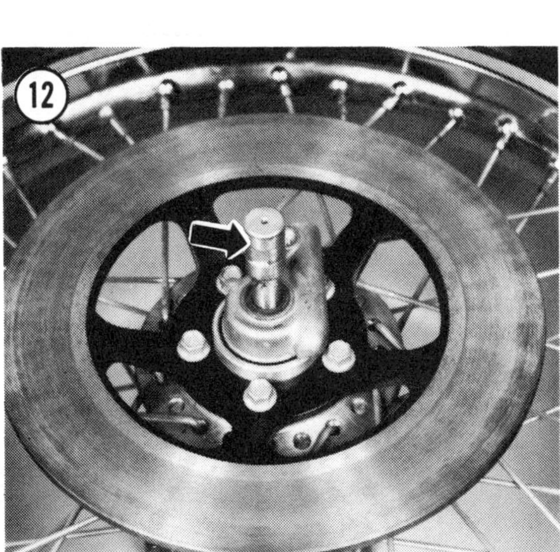

11. To remove the right- and left-hand bearings and distance collar, insert a soft aluminum or brass drift into one side of the hub. Push the distance collar over to one side and place the drift on the inner race of the lower bearing. Tap the bearing out of the hub with a hammer, working around the perimeter of the inner race.
12. Remove the distance collar and tap out the opposite bearing.

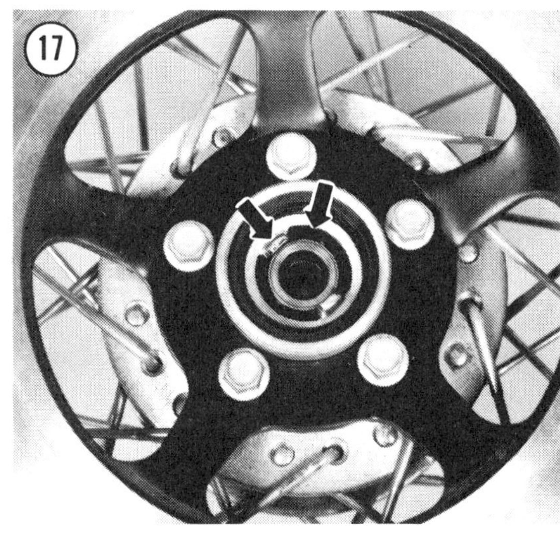

Inspection

1. Thoroughly clean out the inside of the hub with solvent and dry with compressed air or a shop cloth.
2. Do not clean sealed bearings. If non-sealed bearings are installed, thoroughly clean them in solvent and thoroughly dry with compressed air. Do not let the bearing spin while drying.
3. Turn each bearing by hand (**Figure 18**). Make sure the bearings turn smoothly.

NOTE
Some axial play is normal, but radial play should be negligible. The bearing should turn smoothly.

4. On non-sealed bearings, check the balls for evidence of wear, pitting or excessive heat (bluish tint). Replace bearings if necessary; always replace as a complete set. When replacing, be sure to take your old bearings along to ensure a perfect matchup.

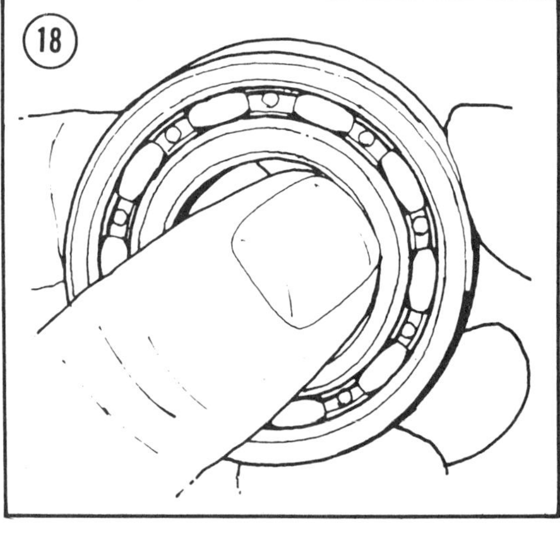

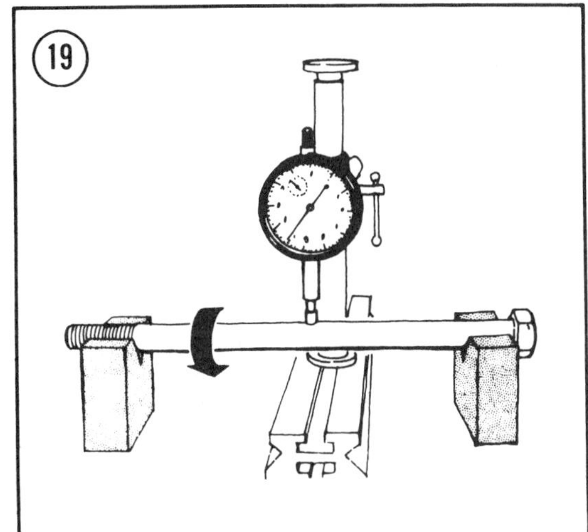

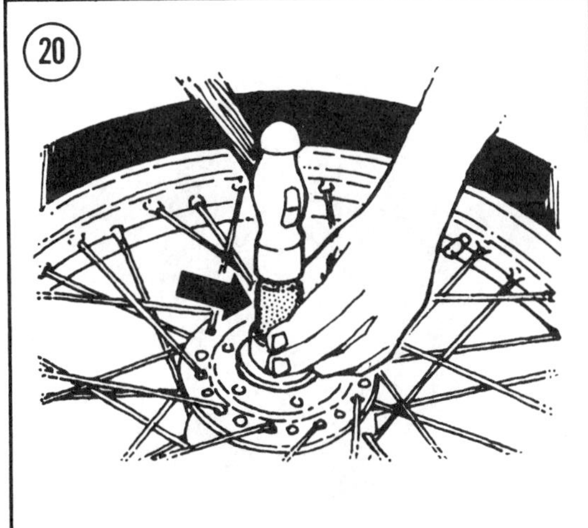

NOTE

Fully sealed bearings are available from many good bearing specialty shops. Fully sealed bearings provide better protection from dirt and moisture that may get into the hub.

5. Check the axle for wear and straightness. Use V-blocks and a dial indicator as shown in **Figure 19**. If the runout is 0.008 in. (0.2 mm) or greater, the axle should be replaced.

Assembly

1. On non-sealed bearings, pack the bearings with a good quality bearing grease. Work the grease in between the balls thoroughly. Turn the bearing by hand a couple of times to make sure the grease is distributed evenly inside the bearing.
2. Pack the wheel hub and distance collar with multipurpose grease.

CAUTION

Install the wheel bearings with the sealed side facing out. During installation, tap the bearings squarely into place and tap on the outer race only. Use a socket ***(Figure 20)*** *that matches the outer race diameter. Do not tap on the inner race or the bearing may be damaged. Be sure that the bearings are completely seated.*

3. Install the right-hand bearing and press the distance collar into place.
4. Install the left-hand bearing.
5. Inspect the condition of the threads on the bearing retainer; replace if the threads are damaged. Screw the bearing retainer into the right-hand side of the hub.
6. After the bearing retainer has been screwed in securely, lock it into place by staking it (**Figure 21**) with a center punch and hammer.
7. Lubricate the oil seal with grease and install the oil seal.
8. Pack the speedometer drive gear housing with multipurpose grease. Align the tangs of the drive dog (**Figure 22**) and install the housing.
9. Install the brake disc(s) and tighten the bolts and nuts (on models so equipped) to 20-24 ft.-lb. (27-33 N•m).

10. Install the front wheel as described under *Front Wheel Installation* in this chapter.

WHEELS

Wheels should be inspected prior to a long ride. This little time spent will help keep you out of trouble on the highway.

Wheel Balance

An unbalanced wheel is unsafe. Depending on the degree of unbalance and the speed of the bike, the rider may experience anything from a mild vibration to a violent shimmy and loss of control.

On wire spoke type wheels, the balance weights are applied to the spokes on the light side of the wheel to correct the condition.

On ComStar wheels, weights are attached to the rim. A kit of Tape-A-Weight, or equivalent, may be purchased from most motorcycle dealers or motorcycle supply stores. This kit contains test weights that can be cut to the desired weight and attached directly to the rim.

NOTE

Be sure to balance the front wheel with the brake disc(s) attached and the rear wheel with the driven flange assembly attached as they affect the balance.

Before you attempt to balance the wheel, check to be sure that the wheel bearings are in good condition and properly lubricated. The wheel must rotate freely.

1. Remove the wheel as described under *Front Wheel Removal* in this chapter or *Rear Wheel Removal* in Chapter Nine.
2. Mount the wheel on a fixture such as the one shown in **Figure 23** so it can rotate freely.
3. Give the wheel a spin and let it coast to a stop. Mark the tire at the lowest point.
4. Spin the wheel several more times. If the wheel keeps coming to rest at the same point, it is out of balance.
5. On wire spoke type wheels, attach a weight to the upper (or light) side of the wheel on the spoke (**Figure 24**). Weights come in 4 sizes: 5, 10, 15 and 20 grams. Crimp the weights onto the spoke with ordinary gas pliers.

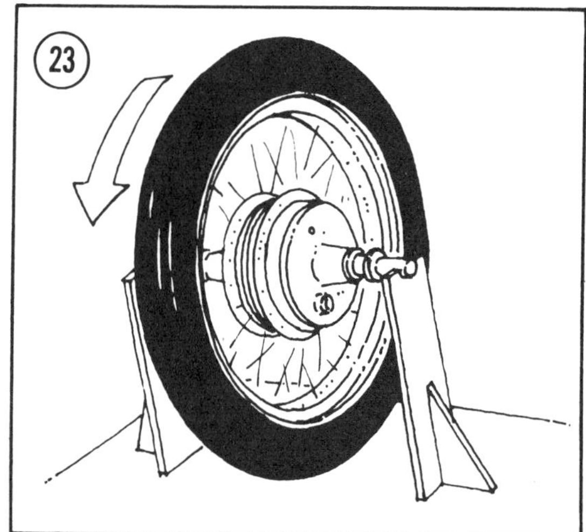

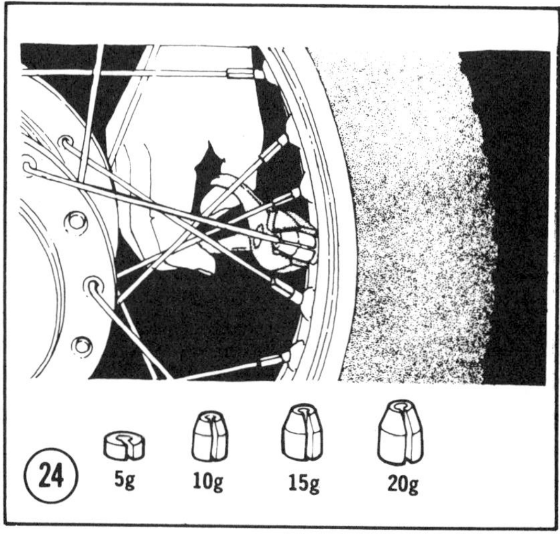

6. On ComStar wheels, tape a test weight to the upper (or light) side of the wheel.

7. On both types of wheels, experiment with different weights until the wheel comes to rest at a different position each time it is spun. When this happens, consider the wheel balanced. On wire spoke type wheels, tighten the weights so they won't be thrown off.

8. On ComStar wheels, remove the test weight and install the correct size adhesive backed or clamp-on weight (**Figure 25**).

Spoke Inspection and Replacement (Wire Spoke Type Wheels)

Spokes loosen with use and should be checked periodically. The "tuning fork" method for checking spoke tightness is simple and works well. Tap each spoke with a spoke wrench or the shank of a screwdriver and listen for a tone. A tightened spoke will emit a clear, ringing tone and a loose spoke will sound flat. All the spokes in a correctly tightened wheel will emit tones of similar pitch but not necessarily the same precise tone.

Bent or stripped spokes should be replaced as soon as they are detected, as they can destroy an expensive hub. Unscrew the nipple from the spoke and depress the nipple into the rim far enough to free the end of the spoke; take care not to push the nipple all the way in. Remove the damaged spoke from the hub and use it to match a new spoke of identical length. If necessary, trim the new spoke to match the original and dress the end of the thread with a thread die. Install the new spoke in the hub and screw on the nipple; tighten it until the spoke's tone is similar to the tone of the other spokes in the wheel. Periodically check the new spoke; it will stretch and must be retightened several times before it takes its final set.

Spoke Adjustment

If all spokes appear loose, tighten all on one side of the hub, then tighten all on the other side. One-half to one turn should be sufficient; do not overtighten.

After tightening the spokes, check rim runout to be sure you haven't pulled the rim out of shape.

One way to check rim runout is to mount a dial indicator on the front fork or swing arm, so that it bears against the rim.

If you don't have a dial indicator, improvise one as shown in **Figure 26**. Adjust the position of the bolt until it just clears the rim. Rotate the rim and note whether the clearance increases or decreases. Mark the tire with chalk or light crayon at areas that produce significantly large or small clearance. Clearance must not change by more than 0.08 in. (2 mm).

To pull the rim out, tighten spokes which terminate on the same side of the hub and loosen spokes which terminate on the opposite side of the hub (**Figure 27**). In most cases, only a slight amount of adjustment is necessary to true a rim. After adjustment, rotate the rim and make sure another area has not pulled out of true. Continue adjustment and checking until runout does not exceed 0.08 in. (2 mm).

ComStar Wheels

The ComStar wheel cannot be serviced and must be replaced if it is severely out of balance. If it is damaged in any way, it must be replaced.

WARNING

Do not try to repair any damage to a ComStar wheel as it will result in an unsafe riding condition.

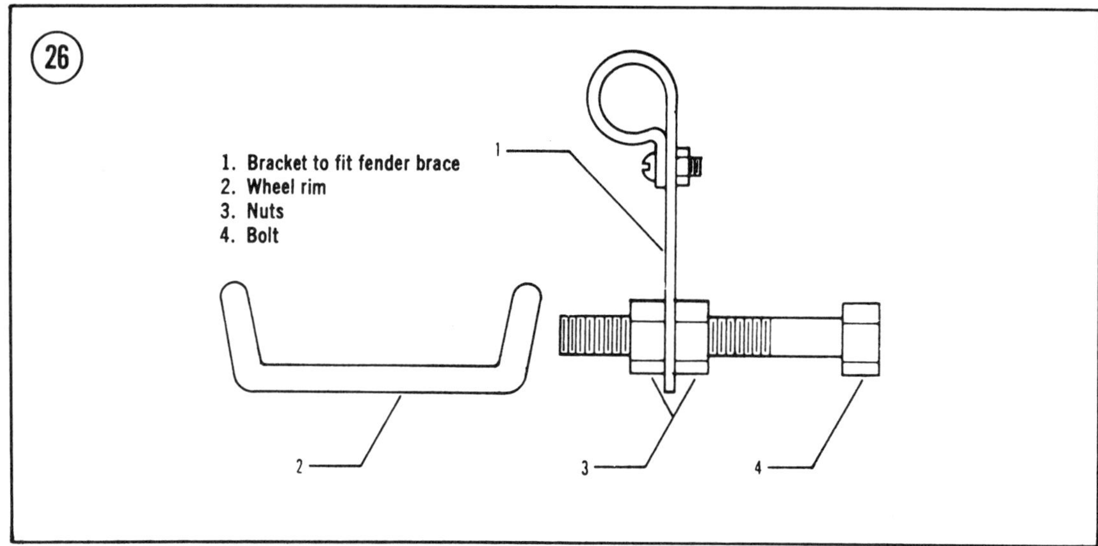

TIRE CHANGING

The rim of the ComStar wheel is aluminum and the exterior appearance can easily be damaged. Special care must be taken with tire irons when changing a tire to avoid scratches and gouges to the outer rim surface. Insert scraps of leather between the tire iron and the rim to protect the rim from damage. Honda offers rim protectors (part No. 07772-0020200) for this purpose that are very handy to use.

Some models are factory equipped with tubeless tires and Comstar wheels designed specifically for use with tubeless tires.

WARNING

*Do not install tubeless tires on wheels designed for use only with tube-type tires. Personal injury and tire failure may result from rapid deflation while riding. Wheels designed for use with tubeless tires are so marked (**Figure 28**).*

Tire removal and installation are basically the same for tube and tubeless tires; where differences occur they are noted. Tire repair is different and is covered in separate procedures.

When removing a tubeless tire, take care not to damage the tire beads, inner liner of the tire or the wheel rim flange. Use Honda tire levers (part No. 07772-0020100) or flat handled tire irons with rounded ends.

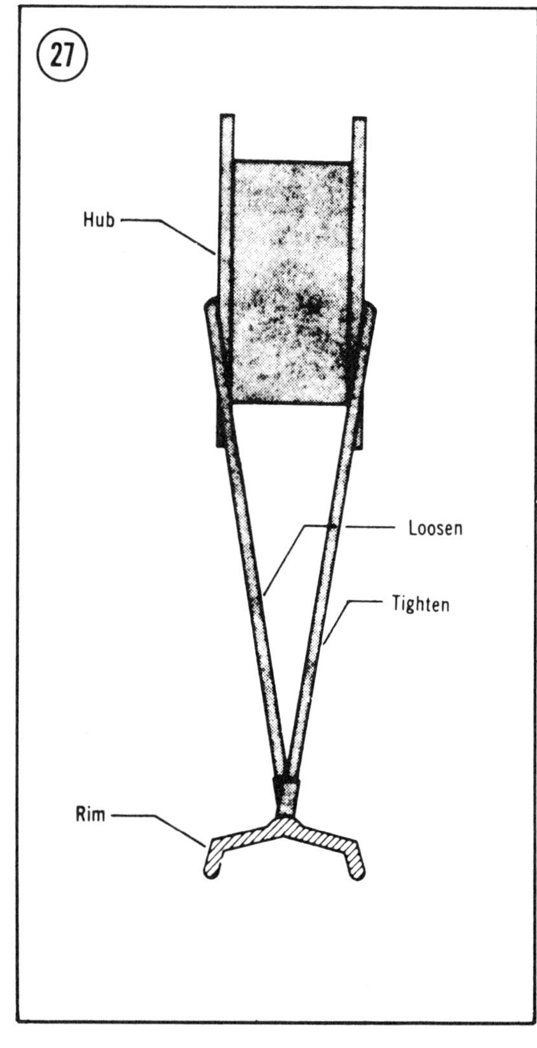

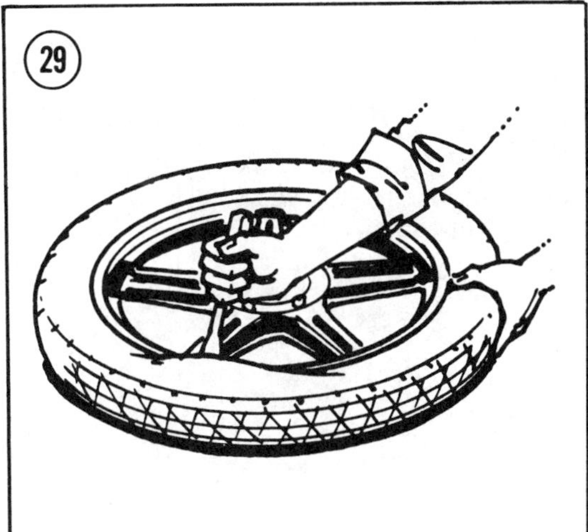

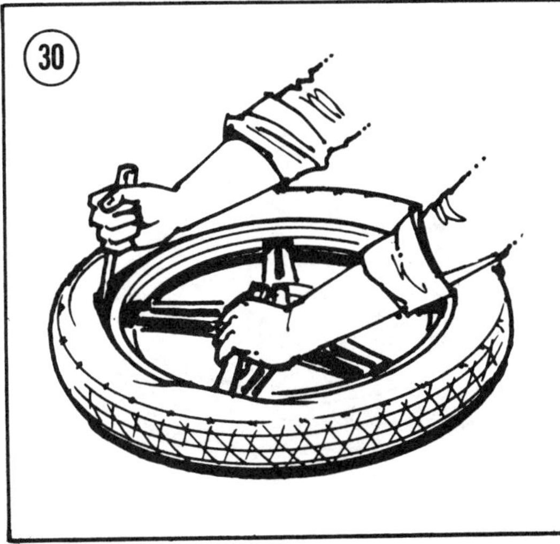

Removal

1. Remove the valve core and deflate the tire.
2. Press the entire bead on both sides of the tire into the center of the rim.
3. Lubricate the beads with soapy water.

NOTE
When performing the following steps on models with ComStar wheels, use leather scraps or Honda rim protectors to protect the rim from damage.

4. Insert the tire iron under the bead next to the valve (**Figure 29**). Force the bead on the opposite side of the tire into the center of the rim and pry the bead over the rim with the tire iron.
5. Insert a second tire iron next to the first to hold the bead over the rim (**Figure 30**). Then work around the tire with the first tire iron, prying the bead over the rim. On tube-type tires be careful not to pinch the inner tube with the tire irons.
6. Remove the valve from the hole in the rim and remove the tube from the tire (tube-type tires only).

NOTE
Step 7 is required only if it is necessary to completely remove the tire from the rim, such as for tire replacement or tubeless tire repair.

7. Stand the tire upright. Insert the tire iron between the second bead and the side of the rim that the first bead was pried over (**Figure 31**). Force the bead on the opposite side from the tire iron into the center of the rim. Pry the second bead off of the rim, working around the wheel with 2 tire irons as with the first bead.
8. On tubeless tires, Honda recommends that the tire valve stem be replaced whenever the tire is removed from the wheel.

Installation

1. Carefully check the tire for any damage, especially inside.
2. A new tire may have balancing rubbers inside. These are not patches and should not be disturbed. A colored spot near the bead indicates a lighter point on the tire. This should be placed next to the valve (**Figure 32**).

3. On wire spoke type wheels, check that the spoke ends do not protrude through the nipples into the center of the rim where they can puncture the tube. File off any protruding spoke ends. Be sure the rim rubber tape is in place with the rough side toward the rim.

4. Install the valve stem core and tighten securely.

5. On tube-type tires, inflate the tube just enough to round it out. Too much air will make installing it in the tire difficult and too little will increase the chances of pinching the tube with the tire irons. Install the tube into the tire.

6. Lubricate the tire beads and rim with soapy water.

7. On tube-type tires, pull the tube partly out of the tire at the valve. Squeeze the beads together to hold the tube and insert the valve into the hole in the rim. The lower bead should go into the center of the rim with the upper bead outside it.

8. Press the lower bead into the rim center on each side of the valve, working around the tire in both directions (**Figure 33**). Use a tire iron for the last few inches of the bead (**Figure 34**).

9. Press the upper bead into the rim opposite the valve (**Figure 35**). Pry the bead into the rim on both sides of the initial point with a tire iron, working around the rim to the valve (**Figure 36**).

10. On tube-type tires, wiggle the valve to be sure the tube is not trapped under the bead. Set the valve squarely in its hole before screwing on the valve nut to hold it against the rim.

11. Check the bead on both sides of the tire for even fit around the rim.

12. On tube-type tires, inflate the tire slowly to seat the beads in the rim. It may be necessary to bounce the tire to complete the seating. Inflate to the required pressure; refer to **Table 2**. Balance the wheel as described previously.

13. On tubeless tires, bounce the wheel several times, rotating it each time. This will force the tire beads against the rim flanges. After the tire beads are in contact with the rim evenly, inflate the tire to seat the beads.

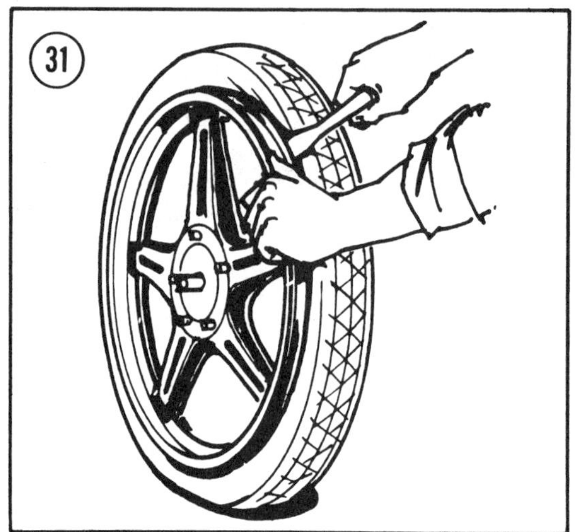
31

32

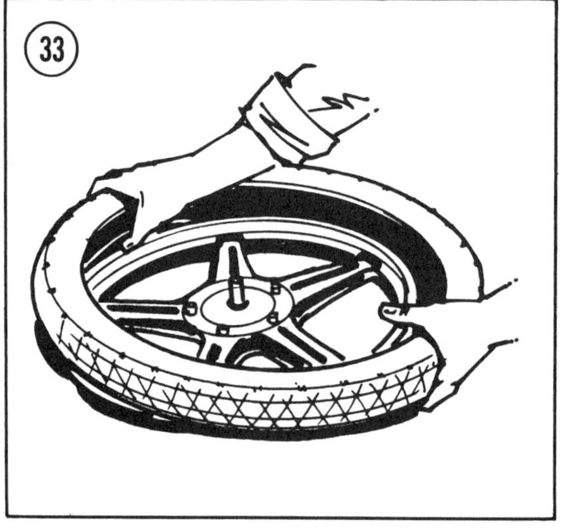
33

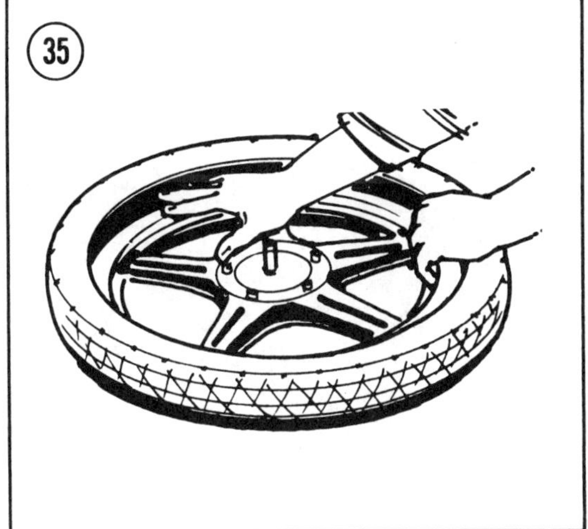

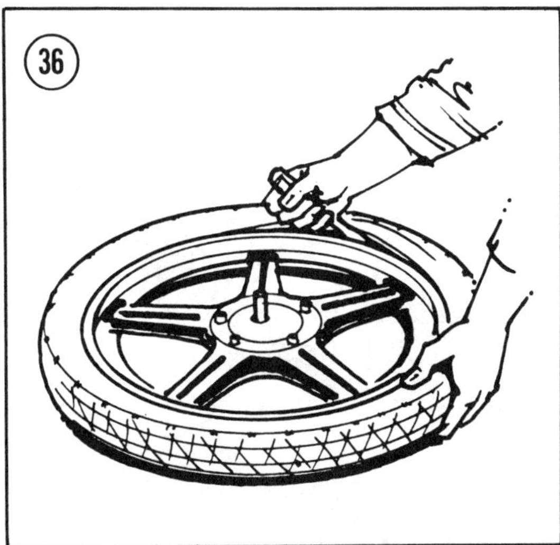

NOTE

If you are unable to get an air-tight seal this way, install an inflatable band around the circumference of the tire. Slowly inflate the band until the beads are seated against the rim flanges, then inflate the tire. If you still encounter trouble, deflate the inflation band and the tire. Apply additional lubricant to the beads and repeat the inflation procedure. Also try rolling the tire back and forth while inflating it.

14. On tubeless tires, inflate the tire to more than the recommended inflation pressure for the initial seating of the rim flanges. Once the beads are seated correctly, deflate the tire to the correct pressure. Refer to **Table 2**.

WARNING

Never exceed 56 psi (4.0 k/cm^2) inflation pressure as the tire could burst causing severe injury. Never stand directly over the tire while inflating it.

TIRE REPAIRS—TUBE-TYPE TIRES

Every rider will eventually experience trouble with a tire or tube. Repairs and replacement are fairly simple and every rider should know the techniques.

Patching a motorcycle tube is only a temporary fix. The tire flexes too much and the patch could rub right off. However, a patched tire will get you far enough to buy a new tube.

Tire Repair Kits

Tire repair kits can be purchased from motorcycle dealers and some auto supply stores. When buying, specify that the kit you want is for motorcycles.

There are 2 types of tire repair kits:

a. Hot patch

b. Cold patch

Hot patches are stronger because they actually vulcanize to the tube, becoming part of it. However, they are far too bulky to carry for roadside repairs and the strength is unnecessary for a temporary repair.

Cold patches are not vulcanized to the tube; they are simply glued to it. Though not as strong as hot patches, cold patches are still very durable. Cold patch kits are less bulky than hot and more easily applied under adverse conditions. A cold patch kit contains everything necessary and tucks easily in with your emergency tool kit.

Tube Inspection

1. Remove the inner tube as previously described.
2. Install the valve core into the valve stem (**Figure 37**) and inflate the tube slightly. Do not overinflate.
3. Immerse the tube in water a section at a time (**Figure 38**). Look carefully for bubbles indicating a hole. Mark each hole and continue checking until you are certain that all holes are discovered and marked. Also make sure that the valve core is not leaking; tighten it if necessary.

NOTE

If you do not have enough water to immerse sections of the tube, try running your hand over the tube slowly and very close to the surface. If your hand is damp, it works even better. If you suspect a hole anywhere, apply some saliva to the area to verify it ***(Figure 39)****.*

4. Apply a cold patch using the techniques described under *Cold Patch Repair* in this chapter.

5. Dust the patch area with talcum powder to prevent it from sticking to the tire.

6. Carefully check the inside of the tire casing for small rocks or sand which may have damaged the tube. If the inside of the tire is split, apply a patch to the area to prevent it from pinching and damaging the tube again.

7. Check the inside of the rim. Make sure the rim band is in place, with no spoke ends protruding which could puncture the tube.

8. Deflate the tube prior to installation in the tire.

Cold Patch Repairs

1. Remove the tube from the tire as previously described.

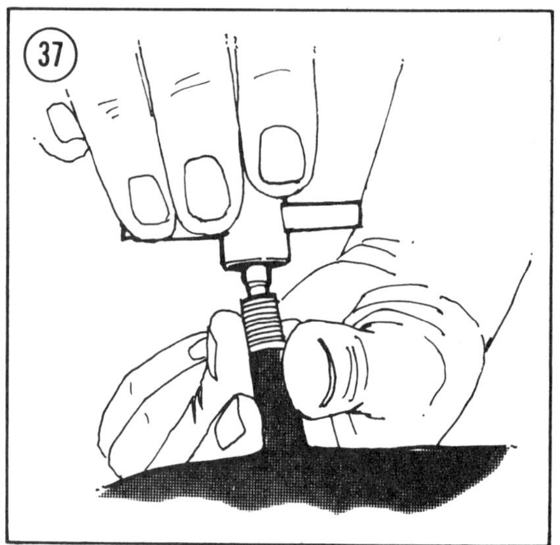

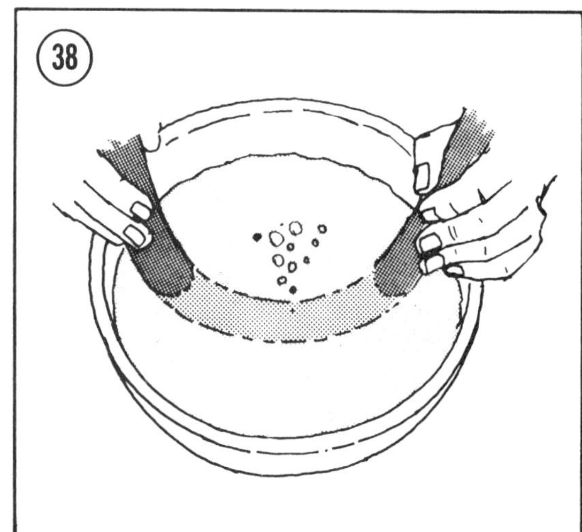

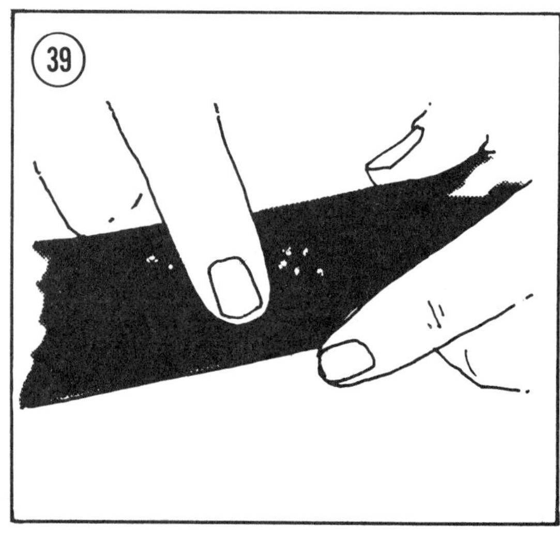

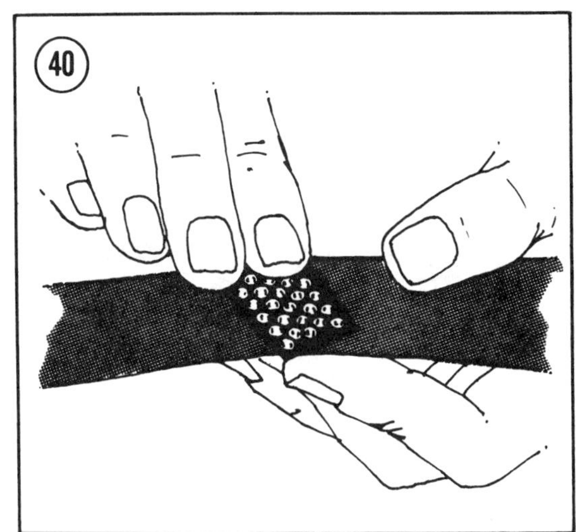

40

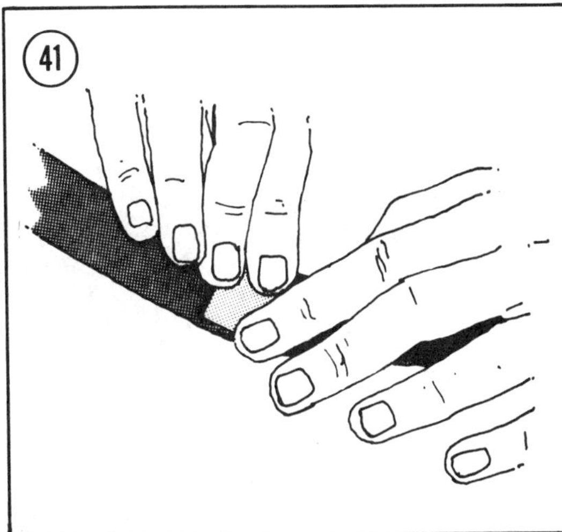

41

42

2. Roughen an area around the hole slightly larger than the patch, using a cap from the tire repair kit or a pocket knife. Do not scrape too vigorously or you may cause additional damage.
3. Apply a small quantity of special cement to the puncture and spread it evenly with your finger (**Figure 40**).
4. Allow the cement to dry until tacky—usually 30 seconds or so is sufficient.
5. Remove the backing from the patch.

CAUTION
Do not touch the newly exposed rubber with your fingers or the patch will not stick firmly.

6. Center the patch over the hole. Hold the patch firmly in place for about 30 seconds to allow the cement to set (**Figure 41**).
7. Dust the patched area with talcum powder to prevent sticking.
8. Install the tube as previously described.

TIRE REPAIRS—TUBELESS TYPE

Patching a tubeless tire on the road is very difficult. If both beads are still in place against the rim, a can of pressurized tire sealant (**Figure 42**) may inflate the tire and seal the hole. The beads must be against the wheel for this method to work.

Another solution is to carry a spare innertube that could be temporarily installed and inflated. This will enable you to get to a service station where the tire can be correctly repaired. Be sure that the tube is designed for use with a tubeless tire.

Honda (and the tire industry) recommends that the tubeless tire be patched from the inside. Therefore do not patch the tire with an external type plug. If you find an external patch on a tire, it is recommended that it be patch-reinforced from the inside.

Due to the variations of material supplied with different tubeless tire repair kits, follow the instructions and recommendations supplied with the repair kit.

Honda recommends that the valve stem be replaced each time the tire is removed from the wheel.

HANDLEBAR

Removal

1. Remove the rear view mirrors, seat and fuel tank.
2. Disconnect the battery negative lead from the battery.
3. Remove the screws (A, **Figure 43**) securing the right-hand handlebar switch assembly and remove the electrical wires from the clips on the handlebar.

CAUTION

Cover the frame with a heavy cloth or plastic tarp to protect it from accidental spilling of brake fluid. Wash any spilled brake fluid off any painted or plated surface immediately, as it will destroy the finish. Use soapy water and rinse thoroughly.

4. Remove the 2 bolts (B, **Figure 43**) securing the master cylinder and lay it over the frame. Keep the reservoir in the upright position to minimize the loss of brake fluid and to keep air from entering into the brake system. It is not necessary to remove the hydraulic brake line.
5. Remove the screws (A, **Figure 44**) securing the left-hand handlebar switch assembly and remove the electrical wires from the clips on the handlebar.
6. Slacken the clutch cable (A, **Figure 45**) and disconnect the cable from the clutch hand lever. Disconnect the clutch safety switch wires (B, **Figure 45**).
7. Loosen the clutch bracket bolt (B, **Figure 44**) and slide off the clutch lever assembly.
8. Remove the throttle assembly and carefully lay the throttle assembly and cables over the fender or back over the frame. Be careful that the cables do not get crimped or damaged.
9. Remove the screws (**Figure 46**) securing the fuse panel cover and remove it.
10. Remove the Allen bolts (**Figure 47**) securing the handlebar holder/fuse panel and move it up and out of the way.
11. Remove the handlebar.
12. To maintain a good grip on the handlebar and to prevent it from slipping down, clean the knurled section of the handlebar with a wire brush. It should be kept rough so it will be held

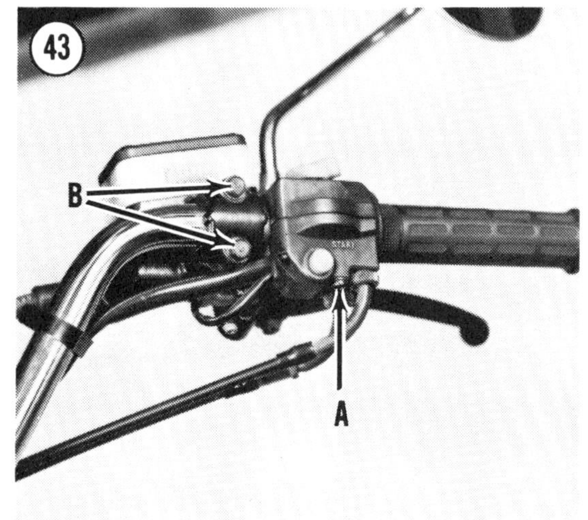

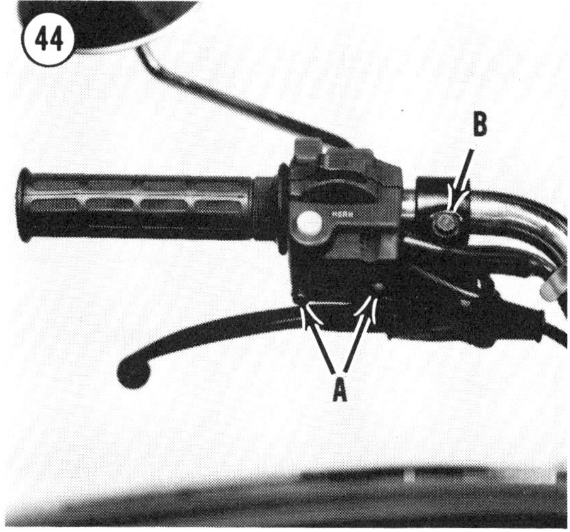

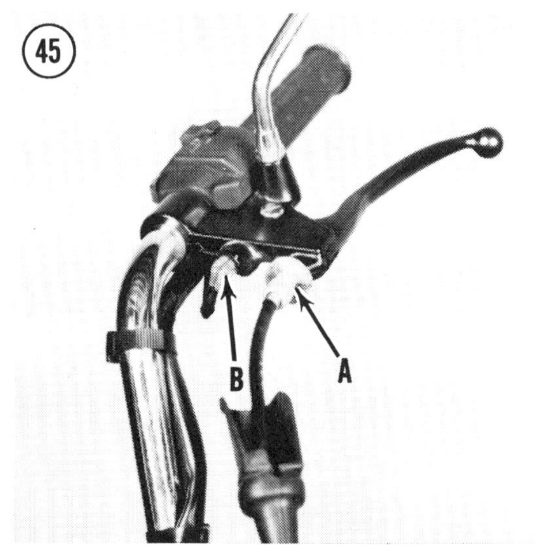

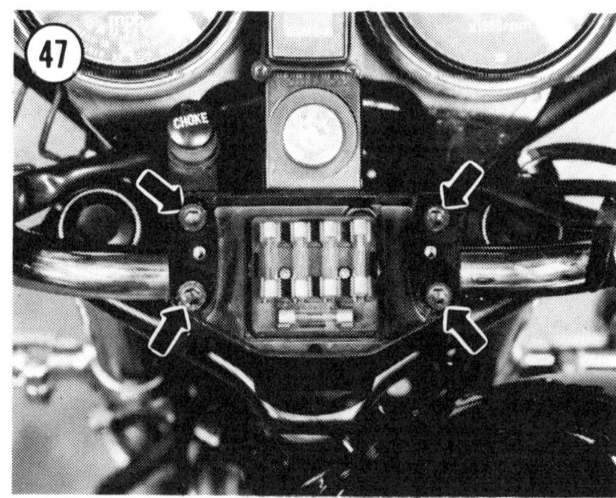

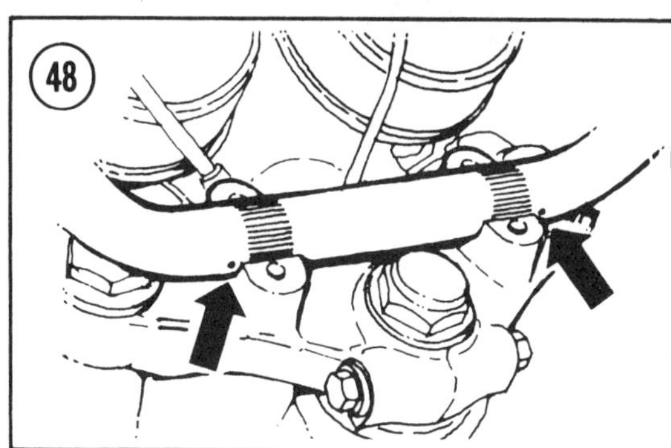

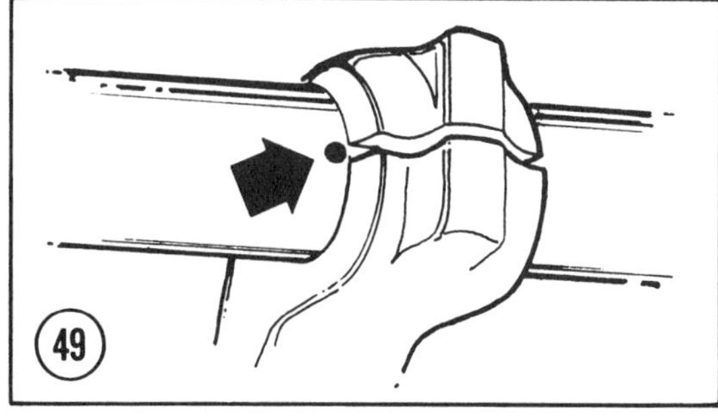

securely by the holders. The holders should also be kept clean and free of any metal that may have been gouged loose by handlebar slippage.

Installation

1. Position the handlebar on the fork bridge so the punch mark on the handlebar is aligned with the top surface of the fork bridge (**Figure 48**).
2. Install the handlebar holder/fuse panel and install the Allen bolts. Tighten the forward bolts first and then the rear bolts. Tighten all to 20-23 ft.-lb. (28-32 N•m). After installation is complete, recheck the alignment of the punch mark.
3. Install the fuse panel cover.
4. Apply a light coat of multipurpose grease to the throttle grip area on the handlebar prior to installing the throttle grip assembly.

NOTE

When installing all assemblies, align the punch mark on the handlebar with the slit on the mounting bracket (***Figure 49***).

5. Install the throttle grip assembly and right-hand switch assembly.
6. Install the master cylinder onto the handlebar. Install the clamp with the wire relief facing down and align the clamp mating surface with the punch mark on the handlebar. Tighten the upper bolt first and then the lower bolt.

WARNING

After installation is completed, make sure the brake lever does not come in contact with the throttle grip assembly when it is pulled on fully.

7. Install the clutch lever assembly and attach the clutch cable to the hand lever.
8. Install the left-hand handlebar switch assembly.
9. Connect the battery negative lead to the battery.
10. Install the fuel tank, seat and rear view mirrors.
11. Adjust the clutch and throttle operation as described under *Clutch Adjustment* and *Throttle Operation/Adjustment* in Chapter Three.

STEERING HEAD

Disassembly

Refer to **Figure 50** for this procedure.

1. Remove the front wheel as described under *Front Wheel Removal* in this chapter.
2. Remove the handlebar as described under *Handlebar Removal* in this chapter.
3. Remove the instrument cluster as described under *Instrument Cluster Removal/Installation* in Chapter Seven.
4. Remove the headlight assembly as described under *Headlight Assembly Removal/Installation* in Chapter Seven.
5. Remove the front forks as described under *Front Fork Removal/Installation* in this chapter.
6. Loosen the steering stem flange bolt.
7. Remove the upper fork bridge assembly.
8. Remove the steering head adjusting nut. Use a large drift and hammer or use the easily improvised tool shown in **Figure 51**.

NOTE

Have an assistant hold a large pan under the steering stem to catch the loose ball bearings while you carefully lower the steering stem.

9. Lower the steering stem assembly down and out of the steering head (**Figure 52**). Remove the 19 ball bearings from the lower race.
10. Remove the upper 18 ball bearings from the upper race in the steering stem.

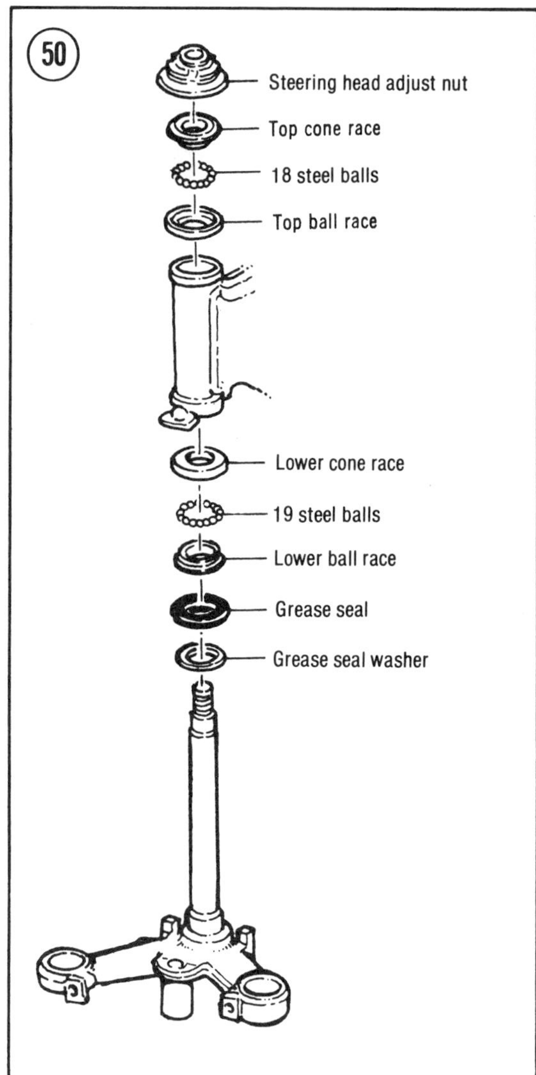

Inspection

1. Clean the bearing races in the steering head, the steering stem races and the bearings with solvent.
2. Check the welds around the steering head for cracks and fractures. If any are found, have them repaired by a competent frame shop or welding service.
3. Check the balls for pitting, scratches or discoloration indicating wear or corrosion. Replace them in sets if any are bad.
4. Check the races for pitting, galling and corrosion. If any of these conditions exist, replace the races as described under *Bearing Race Replacement* in this chapter.

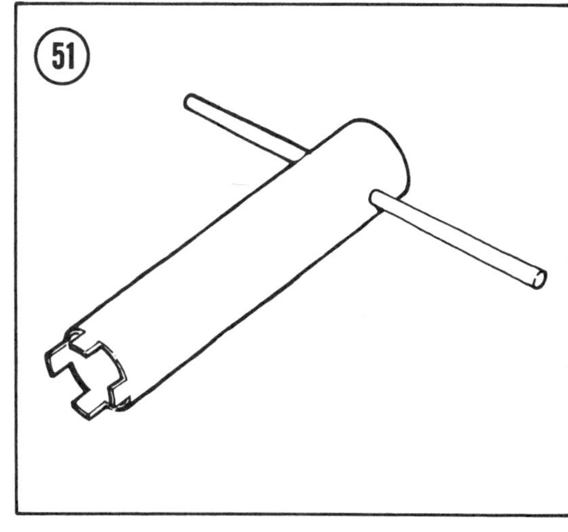

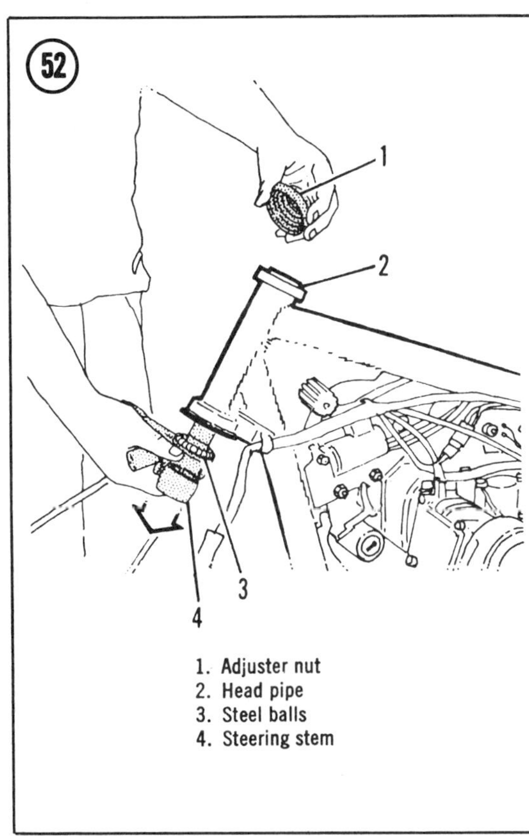

1. Adjuster nut
2. Head pipe
3. Steel balls
4. Steering stem

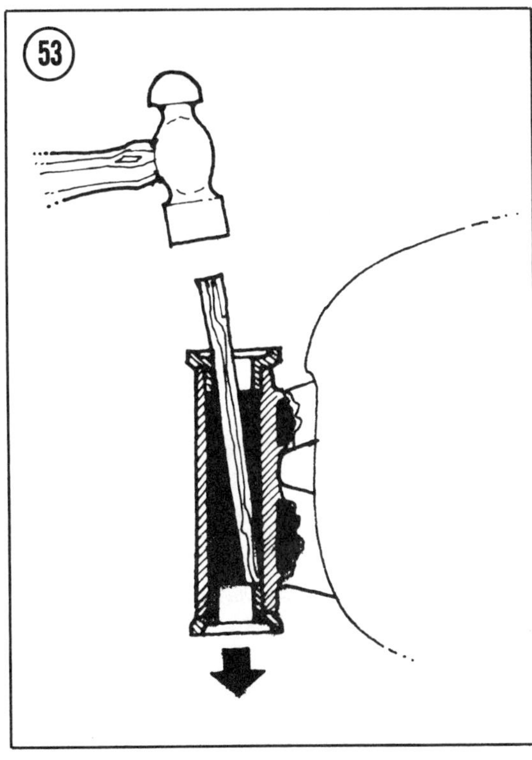

5. Check the steering stem for cracks and check its race for damage or wear. If this race or any race is damaged, the bearings should be replaced as a complete bearing set. Take the old races and bearings to your dealer to ensure accurate replacement.

Steering Head Bearing Races

The headset and steering stem bearing races are pressed into place. Because they are easily bent, do not remove them unless they are worn and require replacement.

NOTE

The upper and lower bearings and races are not the same size. The lower one is the larger of the two. Be sure that you install them at the proper ends of the head tube.

Headset bearing race removal/installation

To remove the headset race, insert a hardwood stick or soft punch into the head tube (**Figure 53**) and carefully tap the race out from the inside. After it is started, tap around the race so that neither the race nor the head tube is damaged. To install the headset race, tap it in slowly with a block of wood, a suitable size socket or piece of pipe (**Figure 54**). Make sure that the race is squarely seated in the headset race bore before tapping it into place. Tap the race in until it is flush with the steering head surface.

Steering stem bearing race and grease seal removal/installation

To remove the steering stem race, try twisting and pulling it up by hand. If it will not come off, carefully pry it up with a screwdriver; work around in a circle, prying a little at a time. Remove the race and the grease seal.

Install the new grease seal. Slide the lower race over the steering stem with the bearing surface pointing up. Tap the race down with a piece of hardwood; work around in a circle so the race will not be bent. Make sure it is seated squarely and is all the way down.

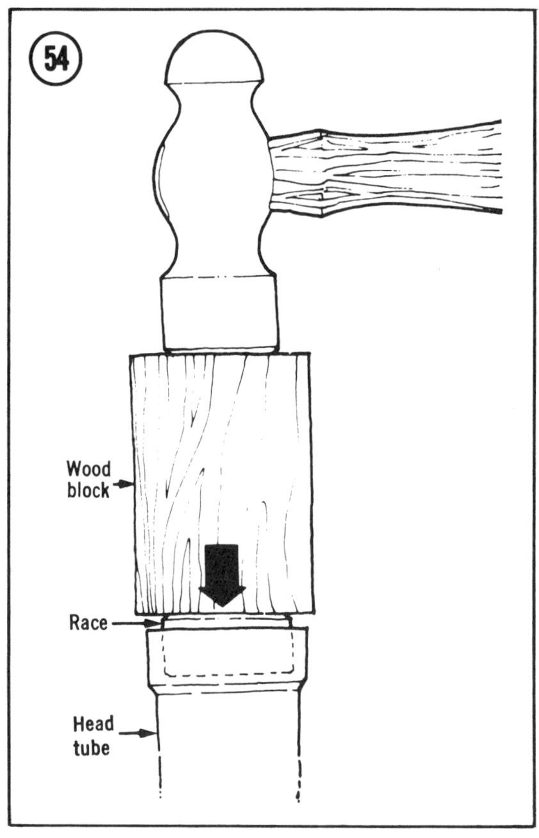

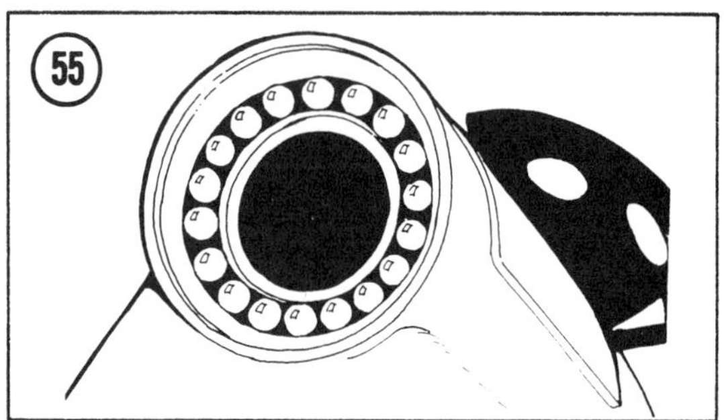

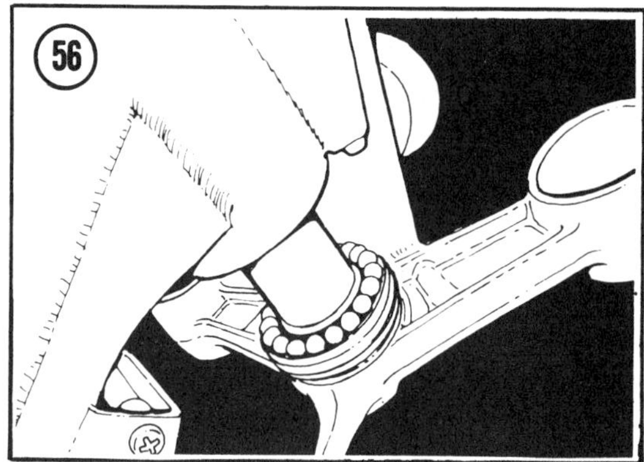

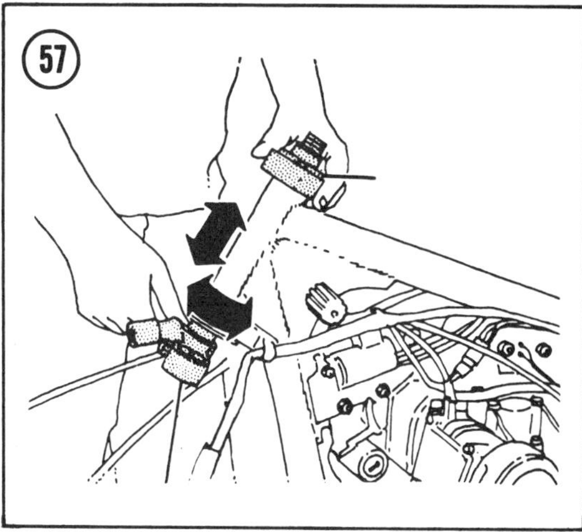

Steering Head Assembly

Refer to **Figure 50** for this procedure.

1. Make sure the steering head and stem races are properly seated.
2. Apply a coat of cold grease to the upper bearing race cone and fit 18 ball bearings around it (**Figure 55**).
3. Apply a coat of cold grease to the lower bearing race cone and fit 19 ball bearings around it (**Figure 56**).
4. Install the steering stem into the head tube and hold it firmly in place.
5. Install the upper bearing race.
6. Install the steering stem adjusting nut and tighten it until it is snug against the upper race, then back it off 1/8 turn.

NOTE

*The adjusting nut should be just tight enough to remove both horizontal and vertical play (**Figure 57**), yet loose enough so that the assembly will turn to both lock positions under its own weight after an assist.*

7. Install the upper fork bridge and steering stem flange bolt finger-tight.

NOTE

Steps 8-10 must be performed in this order to assure proper upper and lower fork bridge to fork alignment.

8. Slide the fork tubes into position and tighten the lower fork bridge bolts to the torque specifications in **Table 1**.

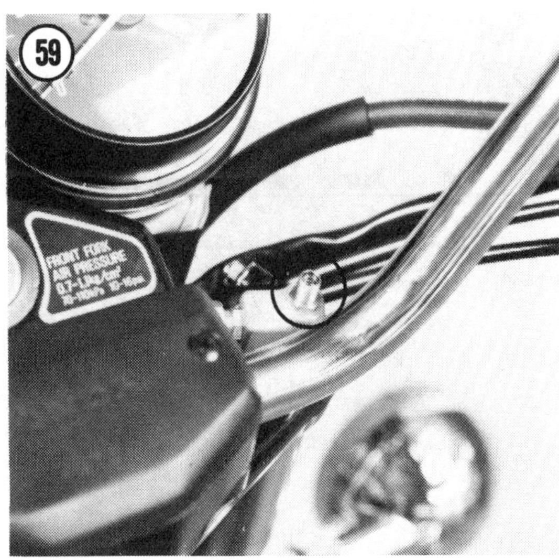

NOTE

Install the fork tubes so that the line on the fork tube aligns with the top surface of the upper fork bridge.

9. Tighten the steering stem flange bolt to the torque specifications in **Table 1**.
10. Tighten the upper fork bridge bolts to the torque specifications in **Table 1**.
11. Continue assembly by reversing Steps 1-3, *Steering Stem Disassembly.*
12. After a few hours of riding, the bearings have had a chance to seat; readjust the free play in the steering stem with the steering stem adjusting nut. Refer to Step 6.

Steering Stem Adjustment

If play develops in the steering system, it may only require adjustment. However, don't take a chance on it. Disassemble the stem and look for possible damage. Then reassemble and adjust as described in Step 6 of the *Steering Head Assembly* procedure.

FRONT FORK

The front suspension uses a spring controlled, hydraulically damped, telescopic fork. Models since 1981 have air assist and the disassembly should be entrusted to a Honda dealer. These forks require the use of special tools and a hydraulic press. Removal and installation are basically the same on all models and where differences occur they are identified.

Before suspecting major trouble, drain the front fork oil and refill with the proper type and quantity; refer to *Front Fork Oil Change* in Chapter Three. If you still have trouble, such as poor damping, a tendency to bottom or top out or leakage around the rubber seals, follow the service procedures in this section.

To simplify fork service and to prevent the mixing of parts, the legs should be removed, serviced and installed individually.

Removal/Installation—All Models

1. Remove the front wheel as described under *Front Wheel Removal/Installation* in this chapter.
2. On 1979-1980 models, remove the black protective cap (**Figure 58**) from the fork top bolt.
3. On models since 1981, remove the air valve cap and *bleed off all air pressure* by depressing the valve stem (**Figure 59**).

WARNING

Always bleed off all air pressure; failure to do so may cause personal injury when disassembling the fork assembly.

NOTE

Release the air pressure gradually. If released too fast, fork oil will spurt out with the air. Protect your eyes and clothing accordingly.

4. On models since 1981, disconnect the air hose fitting from the right-hand fork cap (**Figure 60**) and then from the fitting on the left-hand fork cap (**Figure 61**). Leave the air hose in place under the fuse holder; it is not necessary to remove it unless it is to be replaced. Unscrew the air hose connector from the right-hand fork cap (**Figure 62**).

5. Remove the bolts (**Figure 63**) securing the front fender and remove the fender.

6. Loosen the upper and lower fork bridge bolts (**Figure 64**).

7. Remove the fork tube. It may be necessary to slightly rotate the fork tube while pulling it down and out.

65

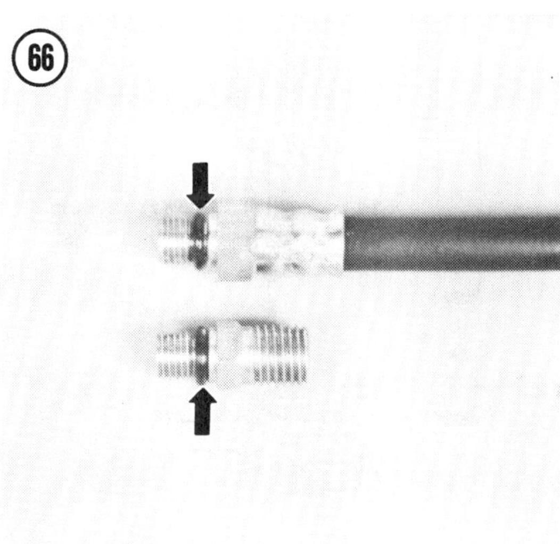
66

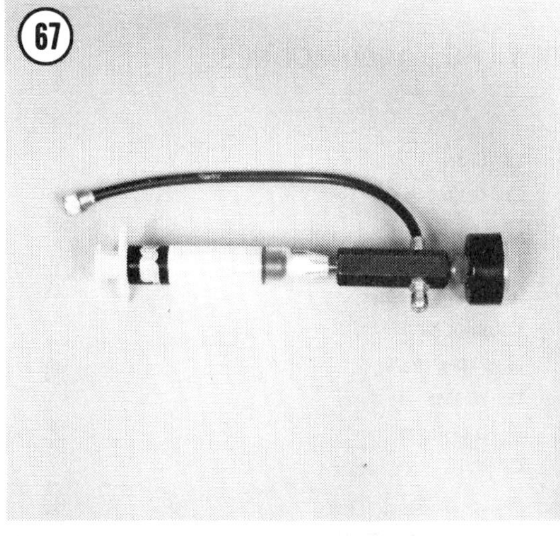
67

8. Install by reversing these removal steps, noting the following.
9. On all models, install the fork tubes so that the line on the fork tube aligns with the top surface of the upper fork bridge (**Figure 65**).
10. Tighten the bolts to the following torque specifications:
   a. Upper fork bridge bolts: 7-9 ft.-lb. (9-13 N•m)
   b. Lower fork bridge bolts: 22-29 ft.-lb. (30-40 N•m.)
   c. Caliper mounting bolts: 22-29 ft.-lb. (30-40 N•m)
11. On models since 1981, apply a light coat of grease to new O-ring seals and install them onto the air hose fittings (**Figure 66**). Install the air hose connector into the fork top cap/air valve assembly and tighten to 3-5 ft.-lb. (4-7 N•m). Install the air hose fitting first to the left-hand side fork cap and tighten to 3-5 ft.-lb. (4-7 N•m). Install the air hose to the right-hand side fork cap and tighten the fitting to 11-15 ft.-lb. (15-20 N•m).

NOTE
Hold onto the air hose connector (attached to the top fork cap/air hose assembly) with a wrench while tightening the air hose fitting.

12. On models since 1981, inflate the forks to 10-16 psi (0.7-1.1 kg/cm^2). Do not use compressed air, only use a small hand-operated air pump like the S & W Mini-Pump (**Figure 67**) or equivalent.

WARNING
Never use any type of compressed gas as an explosion may be lethal. Never heat the fork assembly with a torch or place it near an open flame or extreme heat as this will also result in an explosion.

Disassembly—1979-1980 Models

Refer to **Figure 68** during the disassembly and assembly procedures.

1. Hold the upper fork tube in a vise with soft jaws. Remove the top bolt and flat washer.

WARNING
Be careful when removing the top bolt as the spring is under pressure.

8

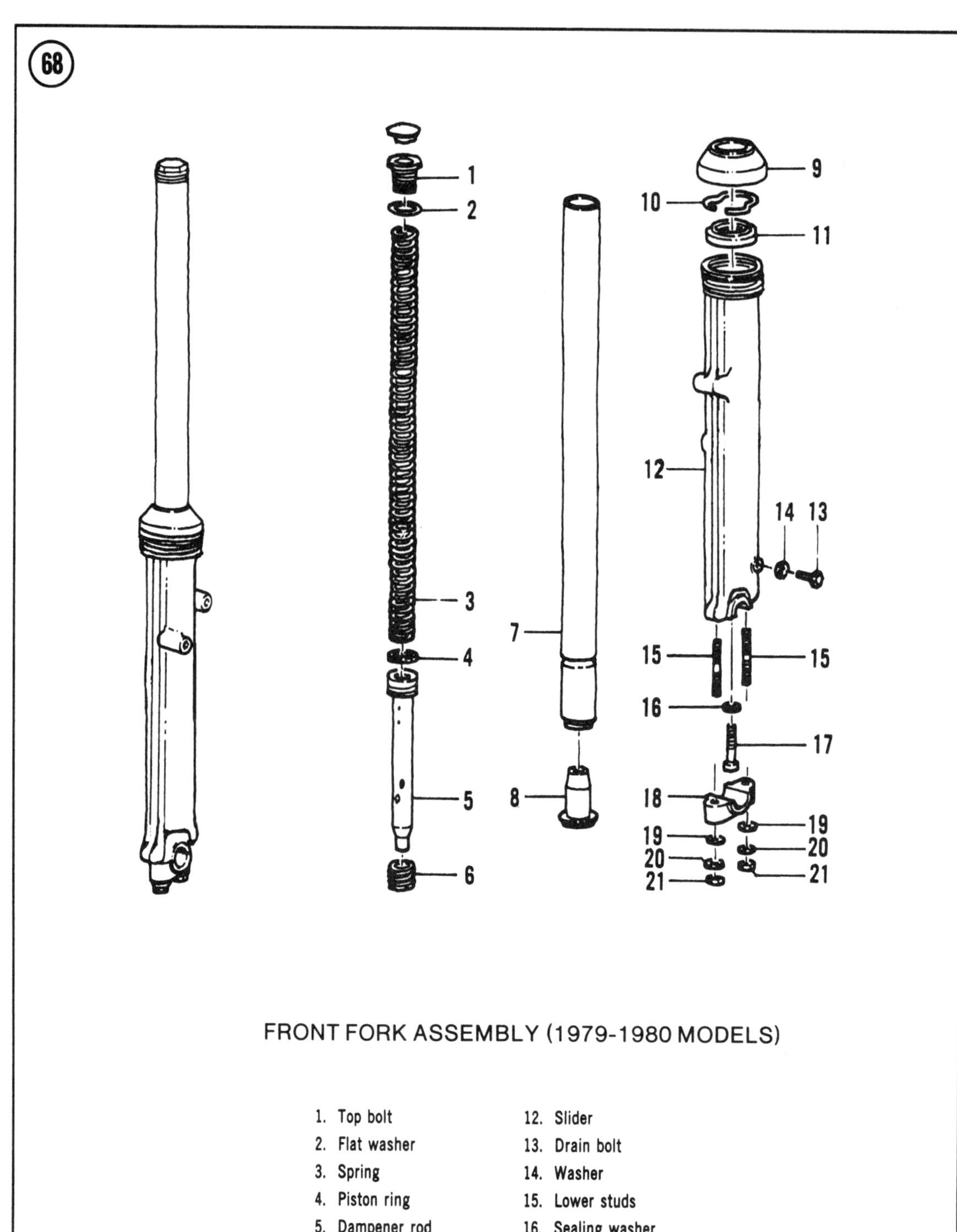

FRONT FORK ASSEMBLY (1979-1980 MODELS)

1. Top bolt
2. Flat washer
3. Spring
4. Piston ring
5. Dampener rod
6. Rebound spring
7. Upper fork tube
8. Oil lock piece
9. Dust seal
10. Snap ring
11. Oil seal
12. Slider
13. Drain bolt
14. Washer
15. Lower studs
16. Sealing washer
17. Allen bolt
18. Axle clamp
19. Washer
20. Lockwasher
21. Nut

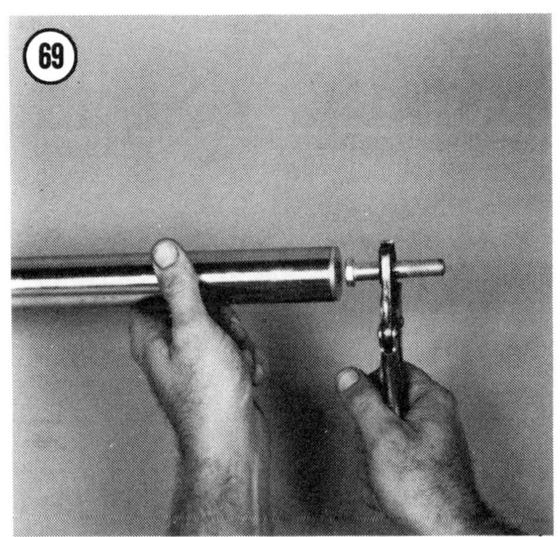

69

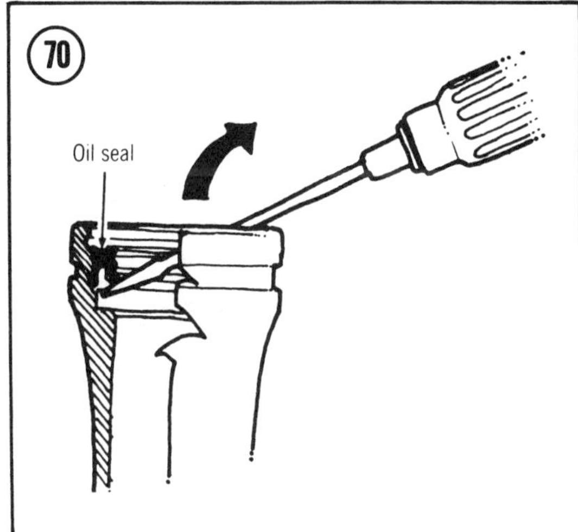

70

71

2. Remove the top bolt from the fork. Use a 17 mm Allen wrench or insert the head of a 17 mm bolt (17 mm across the flats of the head) or a 5/8 in. bolt head into the socket and turn it with Vise Grip pliers (**Figure 69**).
3. Remove the fork spring.
4. Remove the fork from the vise, pour the fork oil out and discard it. Pump the fork several times by hand to expel most of the remaining oil.
5. Clamp the slider in a vise with soft jaws.
6. Remove the Allen head screw and gasket from the bottom of the slider.

NOTE

This screw has been secured with Loctite and is often very difficult to remove because the damper rod will turn inside the slider. It sometimes can be removed with an air impact driver. If you are unable to remove it, take the fork tubes to a dealer and have them remove the screws.

7. Pull the fork tube out of the slider.
8. Remove the oil lock piece, the damper rod and rebound spring.
9. If oil has been leaking from the top of the slider, remove the dust seal, snap ring and oil seal.
10. It may be necessary to slightly heat the area on the slider around the oil seal prior to removal. Use a rag soaked in hot water; do not apply a flame directly to the fork slider.

CAUTION

*Use a dull screwdriver blade to remove the oil seal (**Figure 70**). Do not damage the outer edge or inner surface of the slider.*

11. Inspect the components as described under *Inspection—1979-1980 Models* in this chapter.

Inspection—1979-1980 Models

1. Thoroughly clean all parts in solvent and dry them. Check the fork tube for signs of wear or scratches.
2. Check the damper rod for straightness. **Figure 71** shows one method. The rod should be replaced if the runout is 0.008 in. (0.2 mm) or greater.

8

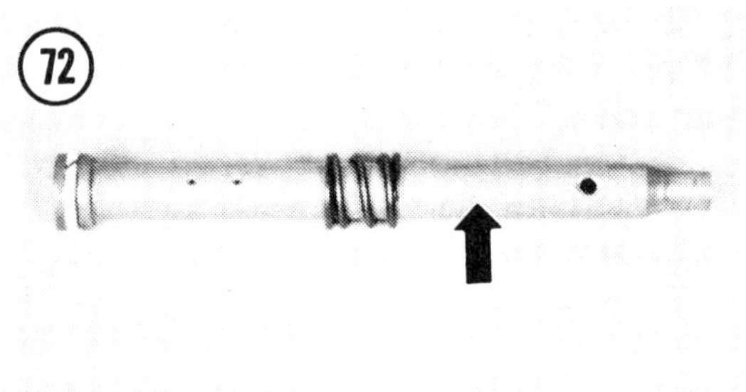

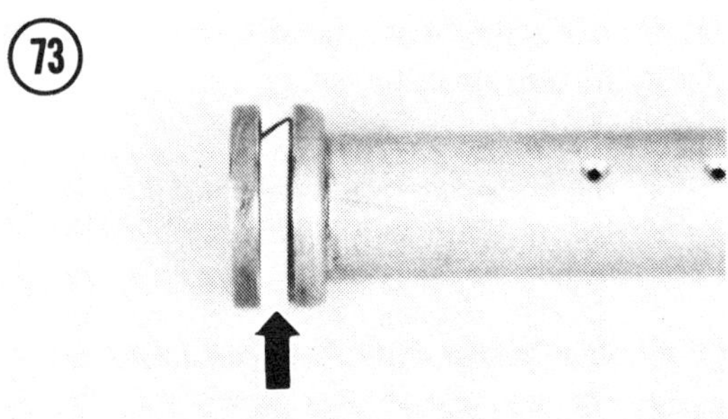

3. Carefully check the damper rod (**Figure 72**) and piston ring (**Figure 73**) for wear or damage.
4. Inspect the oil seals for scoring, nicks and loss of resiliency. Replace if their condition is questionable.
5. Check the upper fork tube for straightness. If bent or severely scratched, it should be replaced. Measure the outside diameter, where it rides in the slider, with a micrometer. If the dimension is 1.374 in. (34.90 mm) or less it should be replaced.
6. Check the lower slider for dents or exterior damage that may cause the upper fork tube to hang up during riding. Replace if necessary. Measure the inside diameter of the slider with a cylinder gauge (**Figure 74**). If the dimension is 1.384 in. (35.15 mm) or greater it must be replaced.
7. Measure the uncompressed length of the fork spring (not rebound spring) as shown in **Figure 75**. If the spring has sagged to 19.4 in. (492.7 mm) or less it must be replaced.
8. Any parts that are worn or damaged should be replaced. Simply cleaning and reinstalling unserviceable components will not improve performance of the front suspension.

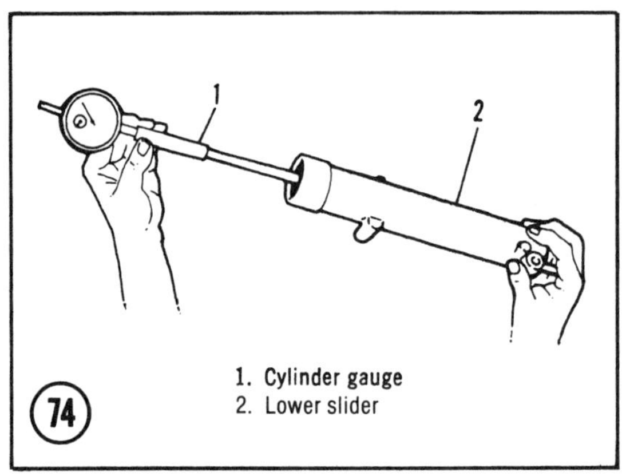

1. Cylinder gauge
2. Lower slider

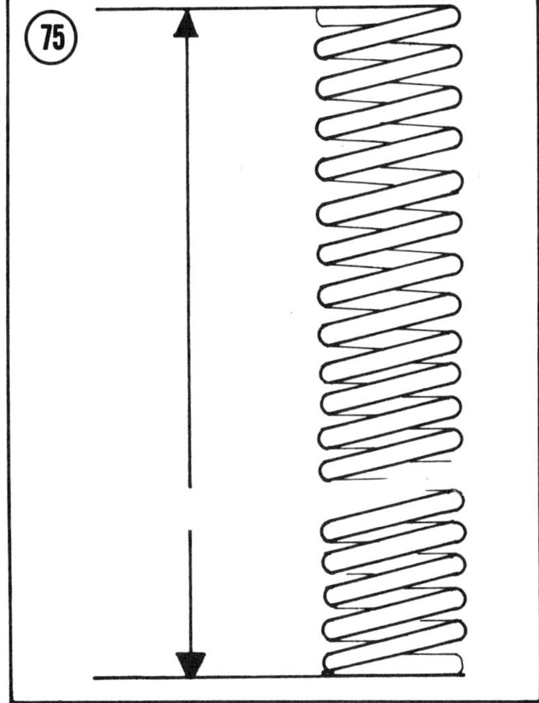

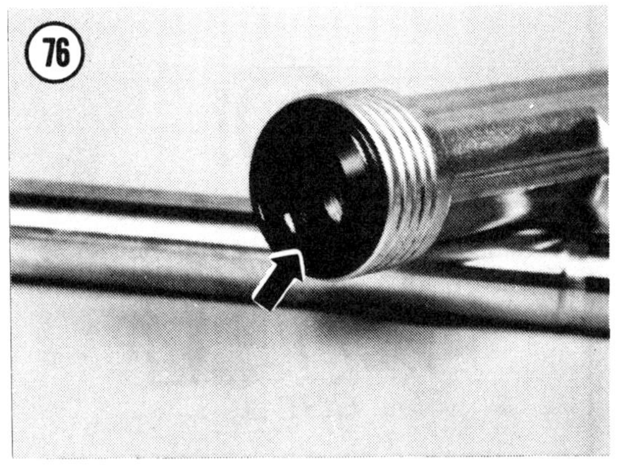

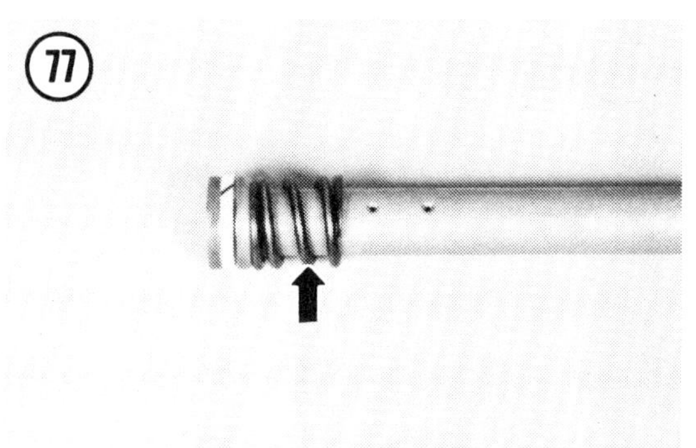

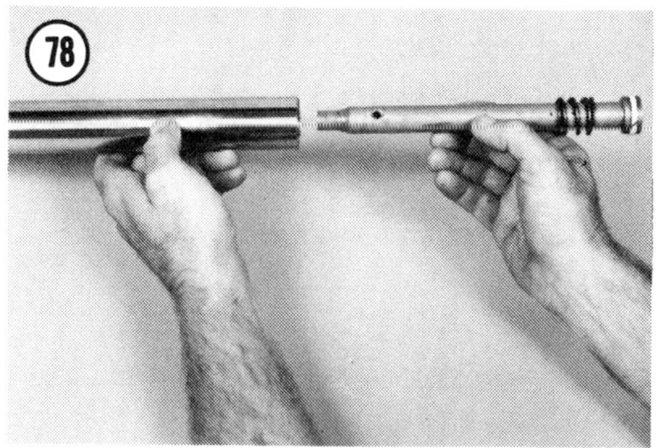

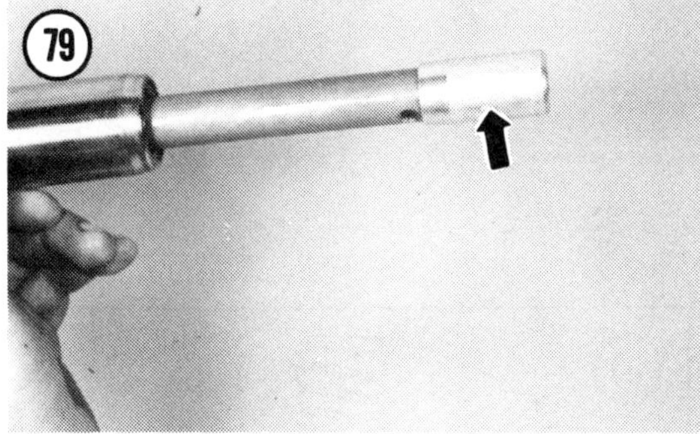

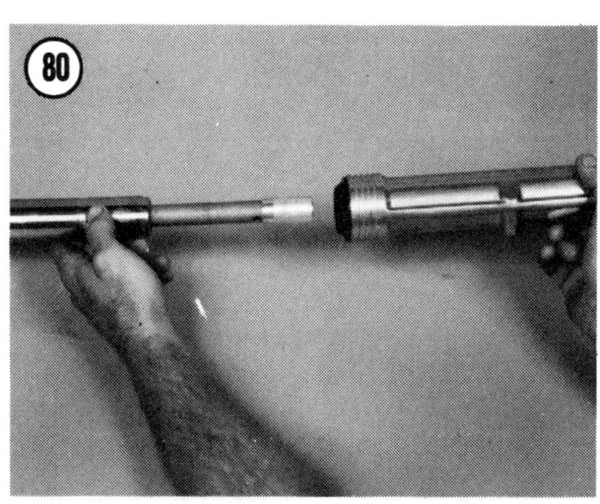

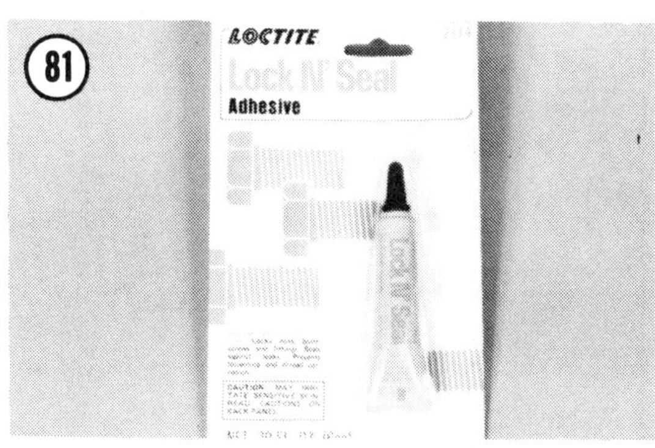

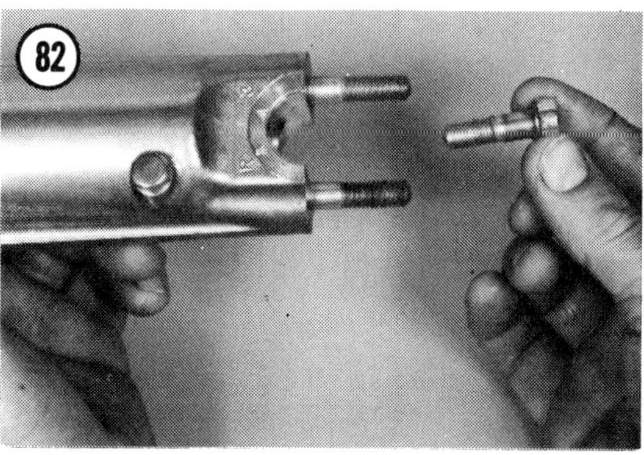

Assembly—1979-1980 Models

1. Coat all parts with fresh ATF (automatic transmission fluid) or fork oil prior to installation. If removed, install a new oil seal and circlip (**Figure 76**).
2. Install the rebound spring onto the damper rod (**Figure 77**).
3. Insert the rebound spring and damper rod into the fork tube (**Figure 78**).
4. Temporarily install the fork spring and top bolt to hold the damper rod in place.
5. Install the oil lock piece onto the damper rod (**Figure 79**) and install the upper fork assembly into the slider (**Figure 80**).
6. Make sure the gasket is on the Allen head screw.
7. Apply Loctite Lock N' Seal (**Figure 81**) to the threads of the Allen head screw prior to installation. Install it in the fork slider (**Figure 82**) and tighten to 6-9 ft.-lb. (8-12 N•m).
8. Remove the top bolt and fill the fork tube with Dexron ATF (automatic transmission fluid) or SAE 10W fork oil. Refer to **Table 3** for the specific quantity for each fork leg.

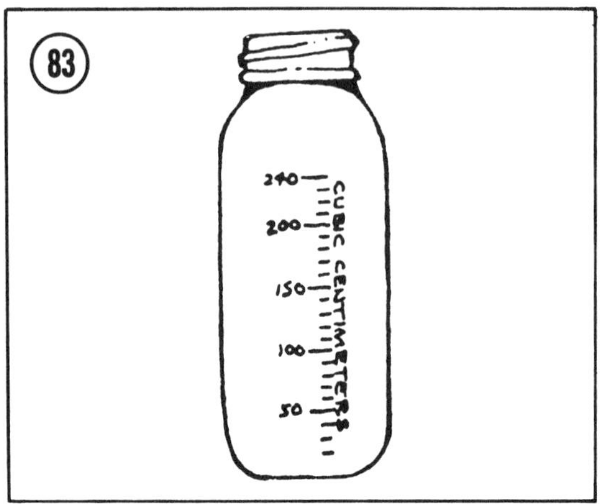

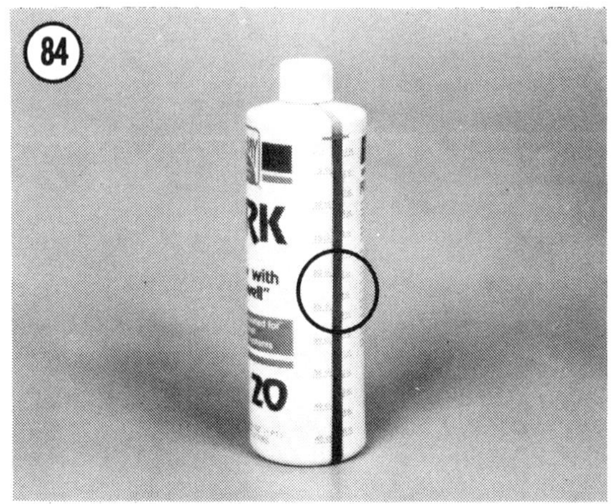

NOTE
*In order to measure the correct amount of fluid, use a plastic baby bottle. These have graduations in fluid ounces (oz.) and cubic centimeters (cc) on the side (**Figure 83**). Many fork oil containers have a semi-transparent strip (**Figure 84**) on the side of the bottle to aid in measuring.*

9. Inspect the condition of the O-ring seal on the top bolt (**Figure 85**); replace if necessary.
10. Install the fork spring with the tapered end (**Figure 86**) in first down toward the axle or with the closer wound coils up toward the handlebar (**Figure 87**).
11. Install the flat washer and top bolt (**Figure 88**). Tighten the top bolt to 22-29 ft.-lb. (30-40 N•m).
12. Repeat for the other fork assembly.
13. Install the fork assemblies as described under *Front Fork Removal/Installation—All Models* in this chapter.

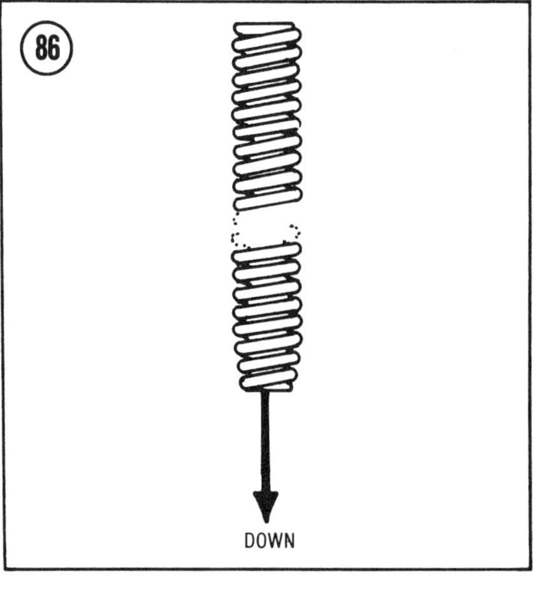

Disassembly/Assembly—Models Since 1981

Disassembly of this model's front fork should be entrusted to a Honda dealer. In order to disassemble the fork the oil seal in the slider must be removed with special Honda tools and a hydraulic press.

Do not try to disassemble the fork tube from the slider with force as many internal components will be damaged. A considerable amount of money can be saved by removing the fork assemblies yourself and taking them to a Honda dealer for repair.

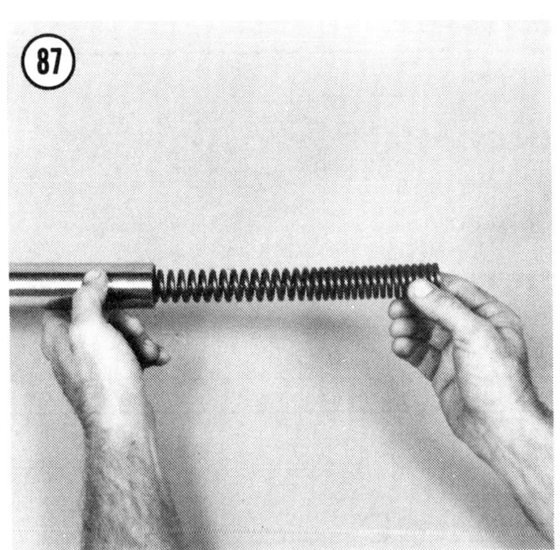

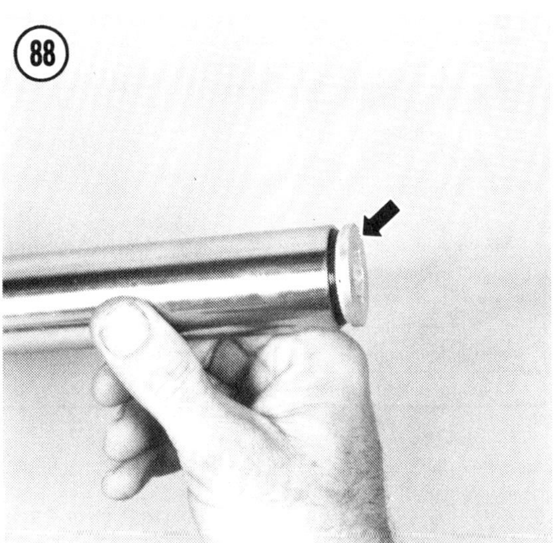

TABLE 1 FRONT SUSPENSION TORQUE SPECIFICATIONS

Item	Foot pounds	Newton meters
Front axle nut		
Standard model and 1980 Custom	40-48	55-65
Front axle clamp nuts	13-18	18-25
Front axle		
Custom since 1981	40-48	55-65
Caliper mounting bolts	22-29	30-40
Brake disc flange bolts	20-24	27-33
Brake system union bolts	18-25	25-35
Handlebar holder/fuse panel bolts	20-23	28-32
Fork bridge bolts		
Upper	7-9	9-13
Lower	22-29	30-40
Steering stem bolt	58-87	80-120
Fork cap bolt		
Non air assist	15-22	20-30
Air assist	11-22	15-30
Air assist forks air fittings		
Connector to right-hand fork leg cap bolt	3-5	4-7
Air hose to left-hand fork fork cap bolt	3-5	4-7
Air hose to right-hand connector	11-15	15-20

TABLE 2 TIRE INFLATION PRESSURE

Load	Air Pressure
Up to 200 lb. (90 kg)	
Front—all models	28 psi (2.0 kg/cm^2)
Rear	
Standard models	28 psi (2.0 kg/cm^2)
Custom models	28 psi (2.0 kg/cm^2)
Maximum load limit *	
Front—all models	28 psi (2.0 kg/cm^2)
Rear	
Standard models	36 psi (2.5 kg/cm^2)
Custom models	32 psi (2.25 kg/cm^2)

* Maximum load limit includes total weight of motorcycle with accessories, rider(s) and luggage.

TABLE 3 FRONT FORK OIL CAPACITY *

Year	Drain	Rebuild
1979	5.0 oz. (150 cc)	5.7 oz. (170 cc)
1980		
Standard	5.3 oz. (155 cc)	5.9 oz. (175 cc)
Custom	6.5 oz. (190 cc)	7.1 oz. (209 cc)
Since 1981		
Standard	6.4 oz. (190 cc)	7.1 oz. (210 cc)
Custom	7.6 oz. (225 cc)	8.3 oz. (245 cc)

* Capacity for each fork leg.

NOTE: If you own a 1982 model, first check the Supplement at the back of the book for any new service information.

CHAPTER NINE

REAR SUSPENSION

This chapter contains repair and replacement procedures for the rear wheel, rear hub and rear suspension components. Service to the rear suspension consists of periodically checking bolt tightness, replacing swing arm bushings and checking the condition of the shock absorbers and replacing them as necessary.

Refer to **Table 1** for rear suspension torque specifications. **Table 1** is at the end of the chapter.

REAR WHEEL

Removal/Installation

1. Place the bike on the centerstand or block up the engine or frame so that the rear wheel is off the ground.
2. Loosen the drive chain adjuster locknuts and adjuster bolts (**Figure 1**) on each side of the wheel.
3. Unscrew the rear brake adjust nut completely from the brake rod (A, **Figure 2**). Depress the brake pedal and withdraw the brake rod from the brake lever. Pivot the rod out of the way and reinstall the adjust nut to avoid misplacing it.
4. Remove the cotter pin then remove the nut and washer (B, **Figure 2**) securing the rear brake torque link. Let it pivot down out of the way.

5. Remove the cotter pin and axle nut (A, **Figure 3**). Discard the old cotter pin.
6. Pivot the chain adjusters down.
7. Push the wheel forward until there is slack in the drive chain. Remove the chain from the drive sprocket.
8. Withdraw the axle from the left-hand side of the wheel. Do not lose the spacer next to the brake panel (B, **Figure 3**).
9. Pull the wheel to the rear and remove it.
10. Leave the axle adjusters on the swing arm. If they are loose, remove them, tap the open end slightly with a hammer and reinstall the adjusters on the swing arm.
11. Install by reversing these removal steps; note the following.
12. Be sure to install the axle spacer on the brake panel side of the wheel (B, **Figure 3**).

CAUTION
Rear wheel spacers should be periodically replaced. Frequent tightening of the rear axle nut causes the spacers to compress slightly. A compressed spacer alters swing arm to rear wheel clearance.

NOTE
Make sure the axle adjusters are attached to the swing arm prior to installing the axle.

13. Install the axle from the left-hand side and install the axle nut finger-tight.
14. Make sure the drive chain adjuster stoppers are in place on the swing arm (**Figure 4**).
15. Adjust the drive chain tension as described under *Drive Chain Adjustment* in Chapter Three.
16. Tighten the axle nut and brake torque link nut to the torque values in **Table 1**.

NOTE
Install a new cotter pin on the axle nut and torque link nut; never reuse an old one as it may break and fall off. Bend the ends over completely.

17. After the wheel is completely installed, rotate it several times to make sure it rotates smoothly. Apply the brake several times to make sure it operates correctly.
18. Adjust the rear brake as described under *Rear Brake Pedal Adjustment* in Chapter Three.

Inspection—All Models

Measure the radial and axial runout of the wheel rim with a dial indicator as shown in **Figure 5**. The maximum radial and axial runout is 0.08 in. (2.0 mm) for both the wire spoke type and ComStar wheel. If the runout exceeds this dimension, check the condition of the wheel bearings.

On wire spoke type wheels, some of this condition can be corrected as described under *Spoke Inspection and Replacement* in Chapter Eight.

On models with ComStar wheels, if the runout exceeds this dimension the wheel will have to be replaced as it cannot be serviced.

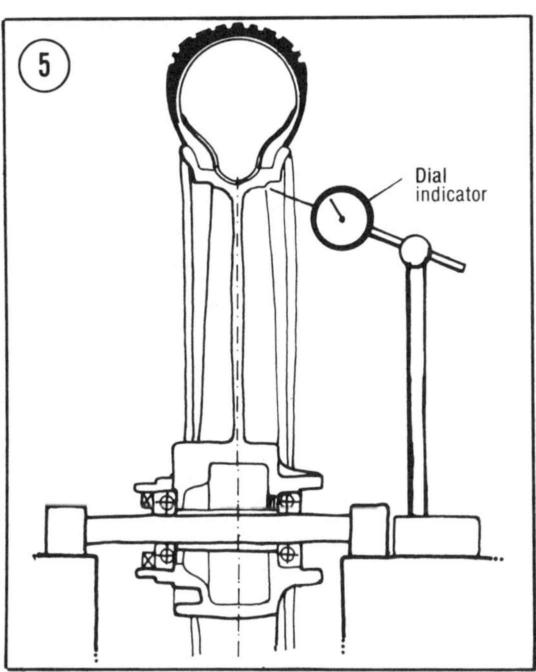

Inspect ComStar wheels for signs of cracks, fractures, dents or bends. If it is damaged in any way, it must be replaced.

WARNING

Do not try to repair any damage to a ComStar wheel as it will result in an unsafe riding condition.

Check axle runout as described under *Rear Hub Inspection* in this chapter.

REAR HUB

Refer to **Figure 6** for this procedure.

Removal of the bearing retainers can be accomplished with a small drift and hammer or with the use of special tools. These are available from a Honda dealer and are as follows:

a. Retainer wrench body (part No. 07710-0010401).
b. Retainer wrench "A" (part No. 07710-0010100)—wheel hub bearing.
c. Retainer wrench "C" (part No. 07710-0010300)—driven flange bearing.

Disassembly

1. Remove the rear wheel as described under *Rear Wheel Removal/Installation* in this chapter.
2. Remove the axle spacer from the wheel (**Figure 7**).
3. Pull the brake assembly straight up and out of the drum.
4. Use a small drift and hammer or special tool (part No.07710-0010100 and 07710-0010401) and unscrew the bearing retainer (A, **Figure 8**). Remove the dust seal from the driven flange.
5. Loosen the sprocket nuts (B, **Figure 8**).
6. Remove the driven flange assembly from the left-hand side of the wheel. Don't lose the spacer in the driven flange bearing.

NOTE

If it is difficult to remove, tap on the backside of the sprocket (from the opposite side of the wheel through the spokes) with the wooden handle of a hammer. Tap evenly around the perimeter of the sprocket until the assembly is free.

7. Use a small drift and hammer or special tools (part No. 07710-0010300 and 07710-0010401) and unscrew the bearing retainer on the left-hand side of the hub.
8. To remove the hub right- and left-hand bearings (**Figure 9**) and distance collar, insert a soft aluminum or brass drift into one side of the hub. Push the distance collar over to one side and place the drift on the inner race of the lower bearing. Tap the bearing out of the hub with a hammer, working around the perimeter of the inner race.
9. Remove the distance collar and tap out the opposite bearing.
10. If the bearing in the driven flange is to be replaced, tap it out using a soft aluminum or brass drift and a hammer. Work around the perimeter of the inner race.

Inspection

1. Thoroughly clean out the inside of the hub with solvent and dry with compressed air or a shop cloth.

NOTE

Avoid getting any greasy solvent residue on the brake drum during this procedure. If this happens, clean it off with a clean shop cloth and lacquer thinner.

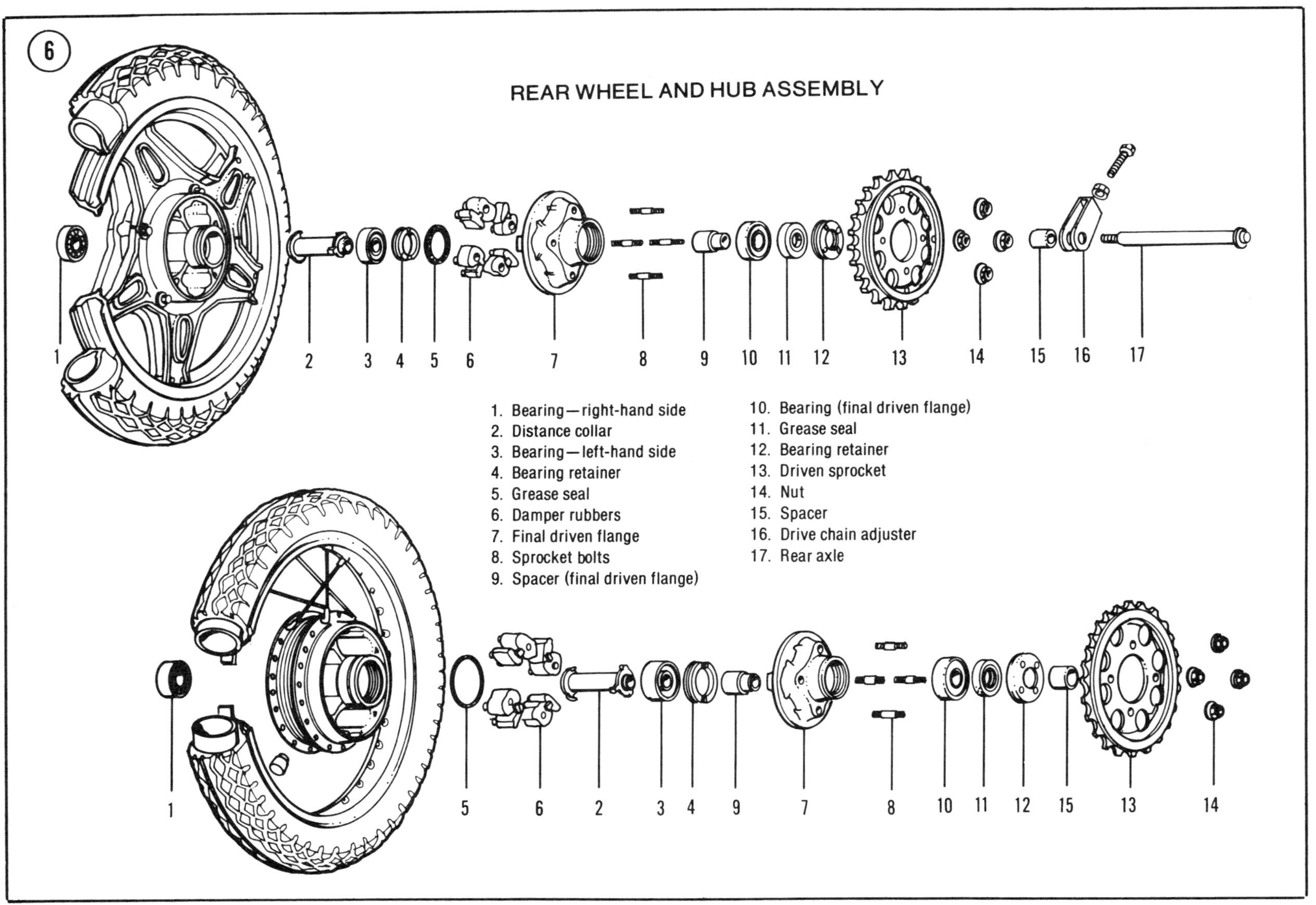
6
REAR WHEEL AND HUB ASSEMBLY
1 2 3 4 5 6 7 8 9 10 11 12 13 14 15 16 17
1. Bearing—right-hand side
2. Distance collar
3. Bearing—left-hand side
4. Bearing retainer
5. Grease seal
6. Damper rubbers
7. Final driven flange
8. Sprocket bolts
9. Spacer (final driven flange)
10. Bearing (final driven flange)
11. Grease seal
12. Bearing retainer
13. Driven sprocket
14. Nut
15. Spacer
16. Drive chain adjuster
17. Rear axle
1 5 6 2 3 4 9 7 8 10 11 12 15 13 14

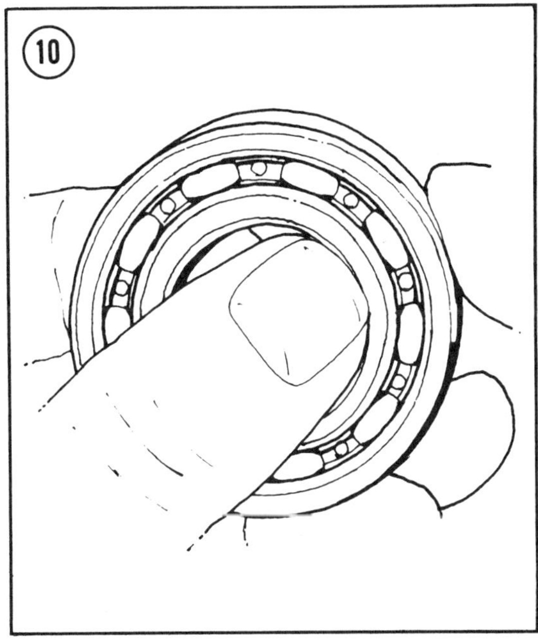

2. Do not clean sealed bearings. If non-sealed bearings are installed, thoroughly clean them in solvent and thoroughly dry with compressed air. Do not let the bearing spin while drying.

3. Turn each bearing by hand (**Figure 10**). Make sure the bearings turn smoothly.

4. On non-sealed bearings, check the balls (on the non-sealed side) for evidence of wear, pitting or excessive heat (bluish tint). Replace the bearings if necessary; always replace as a complete set. When replacing, be sure to take your old bearings along to ensure a perfect matchup.

NOTE

Fully sealed bearings are available from many good bearing specialty shops. Fully sealed bearings provide better protection from dirt and moisture that may get into the hub.

5. Check the axle for wear and straightness. Use V-blocks and a dial indicator as shown in **Figure 11**. If the runout is 0.008 in. (0.2 mm) or greater, the axle should be replaced.

Assembly

1. On non-sealed bearings, pack the bearings with a good quality bearing grease (**Figure 12**).

9

Work the grease in between the balls thoroughly. Turn the bearing by hand a couple of times to make sure the grease is distributed evenly inside the bearing.

2. Blow any dirt or foreign matter out of the hub prior to installing the bearings.

3. Pack the wheel hub with multipurpose grease.

4. Press the distance collar into the hub from the left-hand side.

CAUTION

*Install sealed bearings with the sealed side facing out. Tap the bearings squarely into place and tap on the outer race only. Use a socket **(Figure 13)** that matches the outer race diameter. Do not tap on the inner race or the bearing might be damaged. Be sure that the bearings are completely seated.*

5. Install the right-hand bearing into the hub.

6. Install the left-hand bearing into the hub.

7. Inspect the condition of the threads on the bearing retainer; replace if the threads are damaged. Screw the bearing retainer into the hub.

8. After the bearing retainer has been screwed in securely, lock it into place by staking it with a center punch and hammer.

9. Install the bearing into the driven flange.

10. Lubricate the new oil seal with fresh multipurpose grease and tap it gently into place.

11. On the backside of the driven flange, install the spacer into the driven flange bearing.

12. Install the driven flange into the wheel and tighten the sprocket nuts to 58-72 ft.-lb. (80-100 N•m).

13. Inspect the condition of the threads on the bearing retainer; replace if the threads are damaged. Screw the bearing retainer into place in the driven flange.

14. After the bearing retainer has been screwed in securely, lock it into place by staking it with a center punch and hammer.

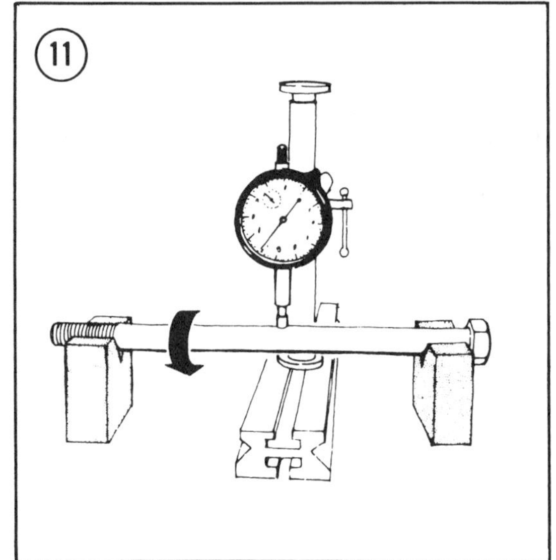

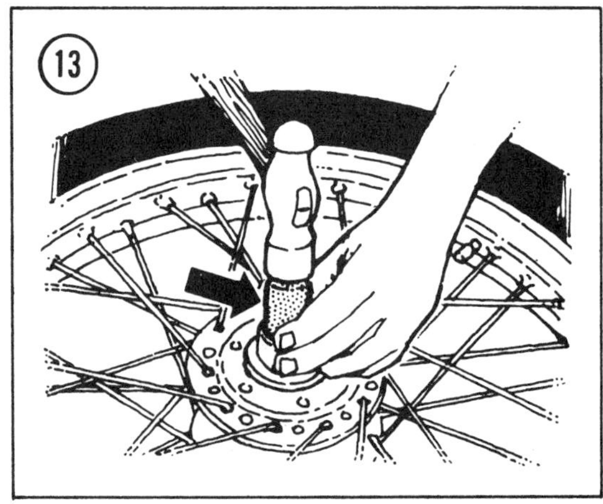

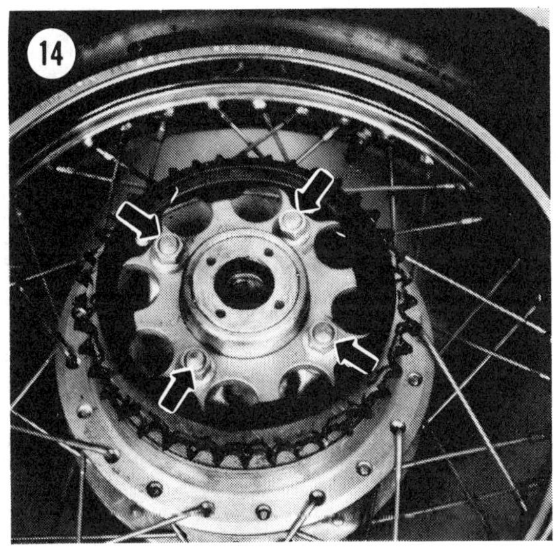

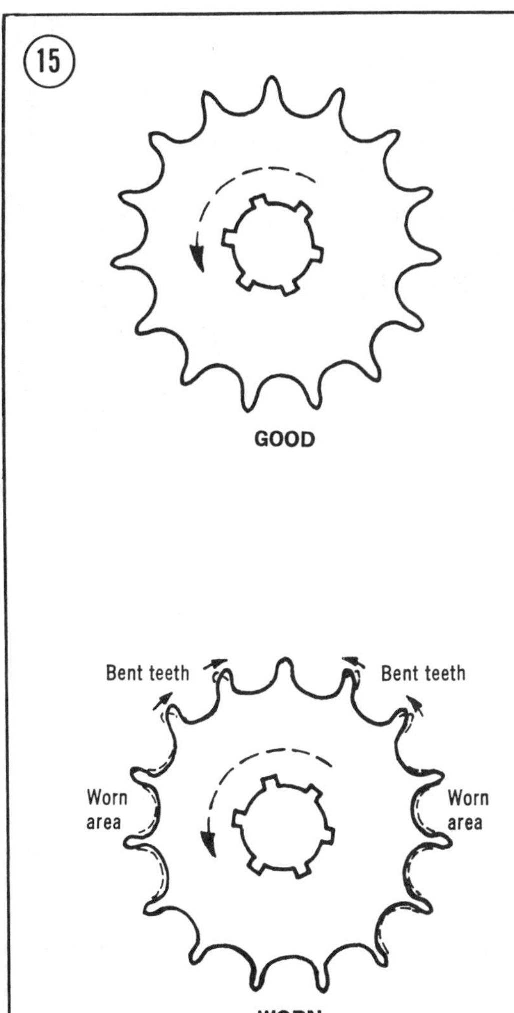

15. Install the rear wheel as described under *Rear Wheel Removal/Installation* in this chapter.

DRIVEN FLANGE ASSEMBLY

Disassembly/Assembly

1. Remove the rear wheel as described under *Rear Wheel Removal/Installation* in this chapter.

2. Loosen the sprocket nuts (**Figure 14**).

3. Remove the driven flange assembly from the left-hand side of the wheel. Don't lose the spacer in the driven flange bearing.

NOTE

If it is difficult to remove, tap on the backside of the sprocket (from the opposite side of the wheel through the spokes) with the wooden handle of a hammer. Tap evenly around the sprocket perimeter until the assembly is free.

4. If the bearing needs replacing, refer to Steps 4 and 10 of *Rear Hub Disassembly* in this chapter.

5. Assemble by reversing these disassembly steps, noting the following.

6. If the bearing was removed, refer to Steps 9-14 of *Rear Hub Assembly* in this chapter for new bearing installation.

7. If the bearing was not replaced, tighten the nuts to 58-72 ft.-lb. (80-100 N•m).

Inspection

1. Inspect the condition of the rubber dampers for signs of damage or deterioration. Replace as a complete set even though only one may require replacement.
2. Inspect the flange assembly housing for cracks or damage; replace if necessary.
3. Inspect the condition of the teeth on the sprocket. If they are visibly worn as shown in **Figure 15**, replace the sprocket.
4. If the sprocket requires replacement, the drive chain is probably worn also and may need replacement. Refer to *Drive Chain Adjustment* in Chapter Three.

DRIVE CHAIN

Removal/Installation

CAUTION
The drive chain is manufactured as a continuous closed loop with no master link. Do not cut it with a chain cutter as this will result in future chain failure and possible loss of control under riding conditions.

1. Remove the mufflers on the left-hand side as described under *Muffler Removal/Installation* in Chapter Six.
2. Remove the gearshift pedal (A, **Figure 16**).
3. Remove the bolts securing the left-hand crankcase cover (B, **Figure 16**) and remove it.
4. Remove the rear wheel and rear swing arm as described under *Rear Swing Arm Removal* in this chapter.
5. Remove the bolts (A, **Figure 17**) securing the drive sprocket.
6. Rotate the drive sprocket holding plate to align the tangs with the splines on the shaft (B, **Figure 17**) and slide it off the output shaft.
7. Remove the drive chain and drive sprocket.
8. Install by reversing these removal steps.

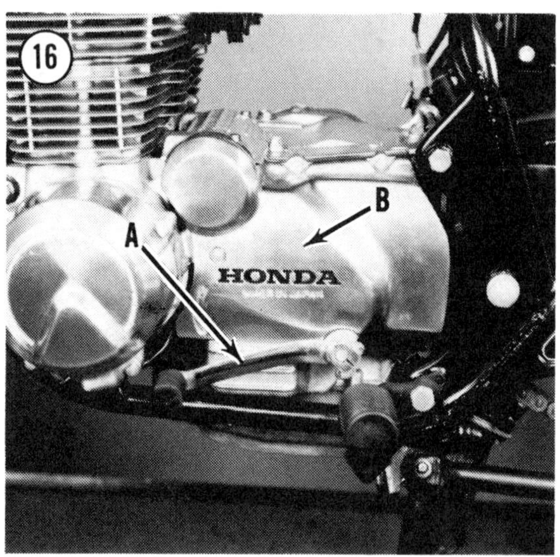

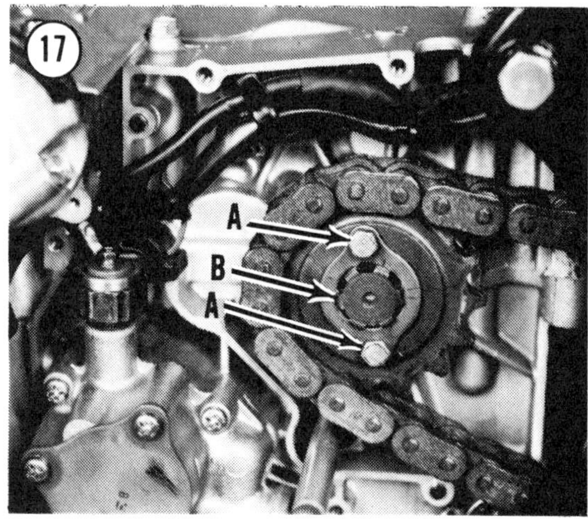

Lubrication and Adjustment

For lubrication and adjustment of the drive chain, refer to *Drive Chain Lubrication* and *Drive Chain Adjustment* in Chapter Three. This is an O-ring chain and requires special lubrication as described in this procedure in Chapter Three.

WHEEL BALANCING

Balance the rear wheel in the same manner as the front wheel. See *Wheel Balancing* in Chapter Eight.

TIRE CHANGING AND TIRE REPAIRS

Service the rear tire in the same manner as the front tire. See *Tire Changing* or *Tire Repairs* in Chapter Eight.

REAR SWING ARM

In time, the bushings or pivot collar will wear beyond the service limits and will have to be replaced. The condition of the bushings can greatly affect handling performance and if worn parts are not replaced they can produce erratic and dangerous handling. Common symptoms are wheel hop, pulling to one side during acceleration and pulling to the other side during braking.

Removal

1. Place the bike on the centerstand and remove the seat and both side covers.
2. Remove the mufflers as decribed under *Exhaust System Removal/Installation* in Chapter Six.
3. Remove the drive chain guard (**Figure 18**).
4. Remove the rear wheel as described under *Rear Wheel Removal/Installation* in this chapter.

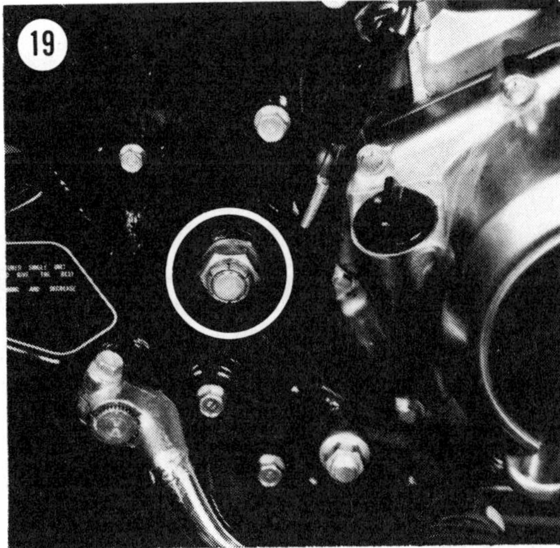

5. Remove the lower mounting bolts on both shock absorbers.

NOTE
It is not necessary to completely remove the shock absorbers.

6. Grasp the rear end of the swing arm and try to move it from side to side in a horizontal arc. There should be no noticeable side play. If play is evident, and the pivot bolt is tightened correctly, the bushings or pivot collar should be replaced.
7. Remove the self-locking nut and washer (**Figure 19**) and withdraw the pivot bolt from the left-hand side.
8. Pull back on the swing arm, free it from the drive chain and remove the swing arm from the frame.

NOTE
Don't lose the dust seal caps on each side of the pivot points; they will fall off when the swing arm is removed.

Disassembly/Inspection/Assembly

Refer to **Figure 20** for this procedure.
1. Remove the swing arm as described under *Swing Arm Removal* in this chapter.
2. Remove the rear brake torque link from the swing arm.
3. Remove both dust seal caps if they have not already fallen off during the removal sequence.
4. Withdraw the pivot collar, clean in solvent and dry it.
5. Measure the outside diameter of the collar with a micrometer at both ends. If the diameter is 0.843 in. (21.4 mm) or less at either end, the pivot collar must be replaced.

NOTE
If the pivot collar is replaced, the bushings at each end must be replaced at the same time.

6. Wipe off any excess grease from the bushings at each end of the swing arm. Measure the inside diameter of both bushings. If the diameter is 0.854 in. (21.7 mm) or greater, both bushings must be replaced.

NOTE
Always replace both bushings even though only one may be worn.

7. If the bushings need replacing, refer to *Rear Swing Arm Bushing Replacement* in this chapter.
8. Prior to installing the pivot collar, coat it throughly with multipurpose grease. Insert the pivot collar and both dust seal caps.
9. Install the brake torque link arm onto the swing arm.

Installation

1. Place the dust seal caps on each end of the pivot points.
2. Slip the left-hand end of the swing arm through the drive chain—the drive chain must be on the inside of the swing arm.

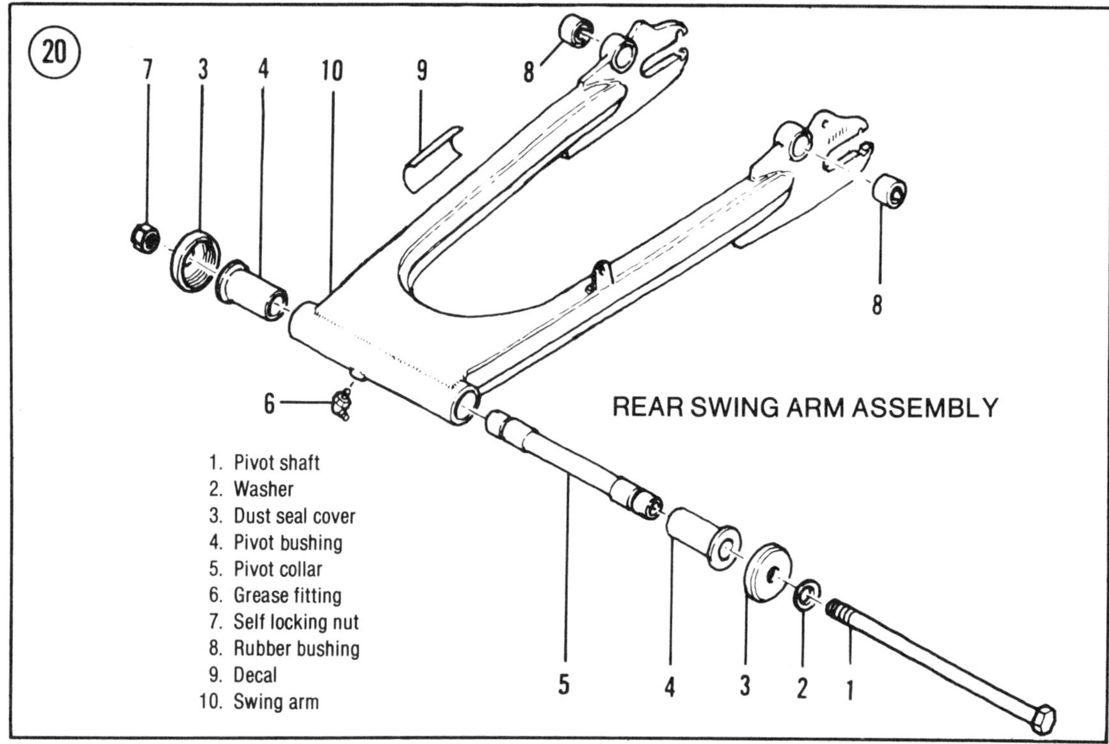

3. Position the swing arm into the mounting area. Align the holes in the swing arm with the holes in the frame. To help align the holes, insert a drift in from the right-hand side.
4. Apply a light coat of grease to the pivot bolt. After all holes are aligned, insert the pivot bolt from the left-hand side and install the washer and self-locking nut. Tighten the self-locking nut to 43-51 ft.-lb. (60-70 N•m).
5. Install the shock absorber lower mounting bolts and tighten to 22-29 ft.-lb. (30-40 N•m).
6. Install the drive chain guard.
7. Install the rear wheel as described under *Rear Wheel Removal/Installation* in this chapter.
8. Install the mufflers as described under *Exhaust System Removal/Installation* in Chapter Six.
9. Install the seat and side covers.

Rear Swing Arm Bushing Replacement

1. Remove the swing arm as described under *Rear Swing Arm Removal* in this chapter.
2. Secure the swing arm in a vise with soft jaws.
3. Carefully tap out the bushings. Use a suitable size drift or socket and extension and carefully drive them out from the opposite end (**Figure 21**).

CAUTION
Do not remove the bushings just for inspection as they are usually damaged during removal.

4. Repeat for the other end.
5. Wash all parts, including the inside of the swing arm pivot area, in solvent and thoroughly dry.
6. Apply a light coat of waterproof grease to all parts prior to installation.
7. Install the new bushings. Tap new bushings into place slowly and squarely with a block of wood and hammer (**Figure 22**). Make sure that they are not cocked and that they are completely seated.

CAUTION
Never reinstall a bushing that has been removed. Removal slightly damages it so that it is no longer true to alignment. If installed, it will damage the pivot collar and create an unsafe riding condition.

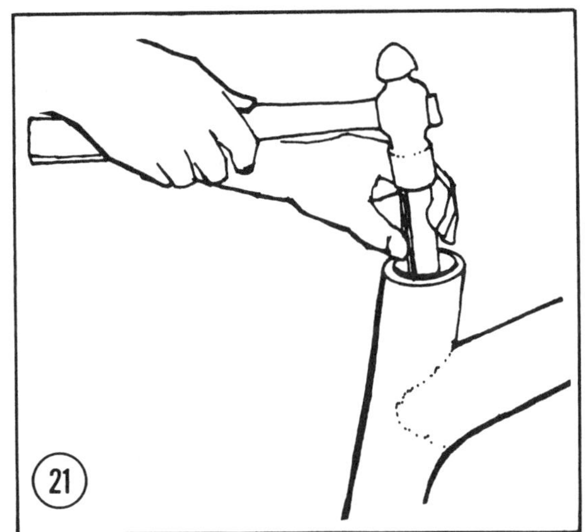

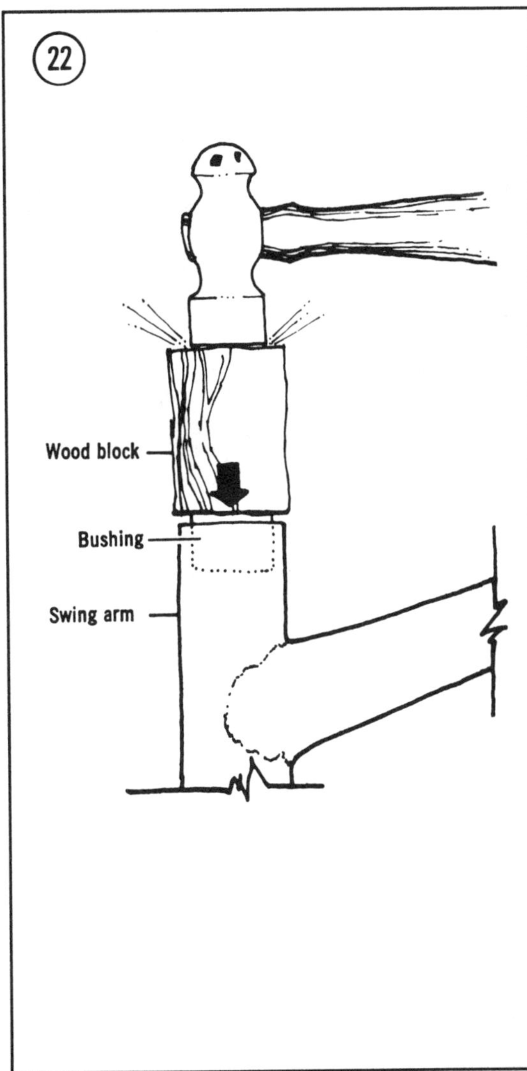

8. Install the rear swing arm as described under *Rear Swing Arm Installation* in this chapter.

SHOCK ABSORBERS

The rear shocks are spring controlled and hydraulically damped. The units are sealed and cannot be serviced. Service is limited to removal and replacement of the damper unit or the spring. If either fails to dampen adequately, replace them as a set.

9

Spring Pre-load Adjustment

Spring pre-load can be adjusted by rotating the cam ring at the base of the spring (**Figure 23**). Rotate it *clockwise* to increase pre-load or *counterclockwise* to decrease pre-load. Use the spanner wrench provided in the owner's tool kit for this adjustment.

Both cam rings must be indexed on the same detent.

Removal/Installation

Removal and installation of the rear shocks is easier if they are done separately. The remaining unit will support the rear of the bike and maintain the correct relationship between the top and bottom mounts.

1. Place a milk crate or wood block(s) under the engine or frame to lift the rear wheel off the ground.
2. Adjust both shocks to the softest setting, completely *counterclockwise.*

3. On standard models, remove the mufflers as described under *Exhaust System Removal/Installation* in Chapter Six. On Custom models the mufflers are short and do not have to be removed.
4. Remove the rear carrier/grab rail (A, **Figure 24**).
5. Remove the upper cap nut and washer (B, **Figure 24**).
6. Remove the lower mounting bolt and nut (C, **Figure 24**).
7. Pivot the lower end of the shock to the rear and pull the shock off of the upper stud. Do not remove the inner washer unless the washer is to be replaced.
8. Install by reversing these removal steps; note the following.
9. Make sure the upper inner washer is on the stud prior to installing the shock and that the rear carrier/grab rail is mounted outside of the shock (**Figure 25**).
10. Tighten the bolt and cap nut to 22-29 ft.-lb. (30-40 N•m).
11. Repeat Steps 5-10 for the other shock.
12. Adjust the shocks as previously described.

Disassembly/Inspection/Assembly

Refer to **Figure 26** for this procedure.

WARNING
Without the proper tool, this procedure can be dangerous. The spring can fly loose, causing injury. For a small bench fee, a dealer can do the job for you.

1. Install the spring compression tool as shown in **Figure 27**. This special tool is available from a Honda dealer. It is the shock absorber compressor tool (Honda part No. 07959-3290001).
2. Compress the spring just enough to remove the locknut.
3. Clamp the upper mount in a vise equipped with soft jaws.
4. Loosen the locknut and unscrew the upper mount.
5. Release the spring tension and remove the shock from the compression tool.
6. Slide off the spring.
7. Measure the spring free length (**Figure 28**). The spring must be replaced if it has sagged to the service limit of 8.7 in. (220.6 mm) or less.
8. Check the damper unit for leakage and make sure the damper rod is straight.

NOTE
The damper unit cannot be rebuilt; it must be replaced as a unit.

9. Assembly is the reverse of these disassembly steps, noting the following.
10. Note the order of the parts shown in **Figure 26**.
11. Apply Loctite Lock N' Seal to the threads prior to installing the upper mount.
12. Tighten the locknut to 15-25 ft.-lb. (20-35 N•m).

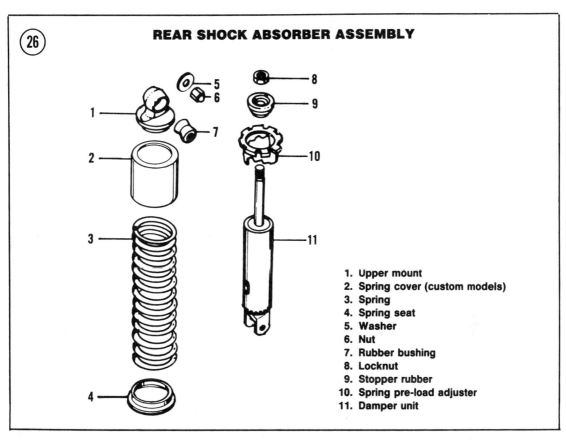

26

REAR SHOCK ABSORBER ASSEMBLY

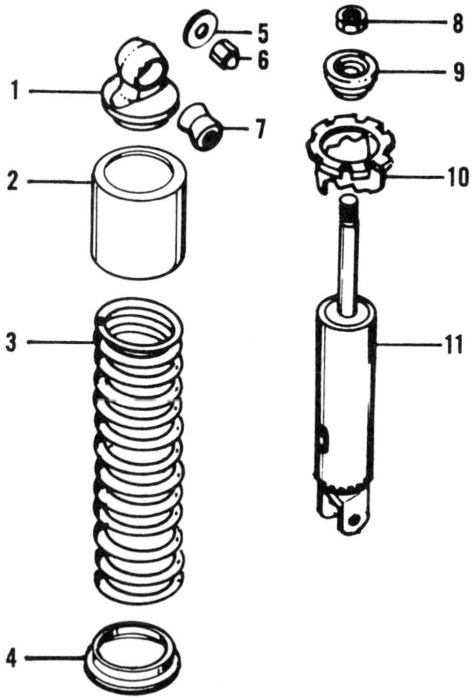

1. Upper mount
2. Spring cover (custom models)
3. Spring
4. Spring seat
5. Washer
6. Nut
7. Rubber bushing
8. Locknut
9. Stopper rubber
10. Spring pre-load adjuster
11. Damper unit

27

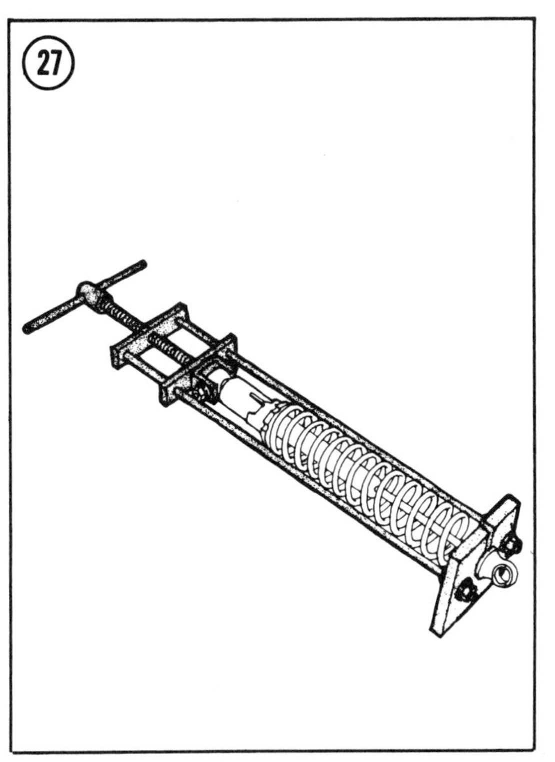

28

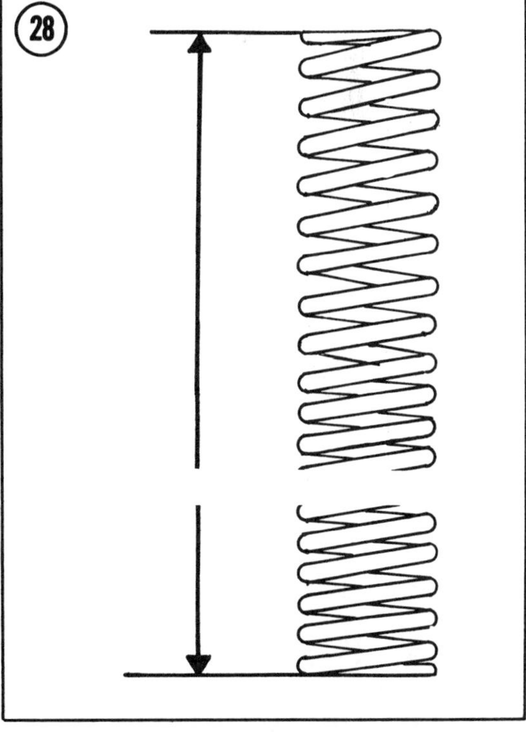

TABLE 1 REAR SUSPENSION TORQUE SPECIFICATIONS

Item	Foot pounds	Newton meters
Rear axle nut	58-72	80-100
Rear swing arm pivot bolt nut	43-51	60-70
Shock absorbers		
Upper and lower mounting nut and bolt	22-29	20-40
Brake torque link bolt	13-18	18-25
Driven sprocket nuts	58-72	80-100

NOTE: If you own a 1982 model, first check the Supplement at the back of the book for any new service information.

CHAPTER TEN

BRAKES

The brake system on the Honda CB650 consists of either a single or dual disc on the front (depending on model) and a drum type on the rear. Refer to **Table 1** for torque specifications and **Table 2** for specifications and wear limits on all brake components. These tables are located at the end of the chapter.

FRONT DISC BRAKE(S)

The front disc brake(s) is actuated by hydraulic fluid and is controlled by the hand lever on the right-hand side of the handlebar. As the brake pads wear, the hydraulic fluid level drops in the master cylinder reservoir and automatically adjusts for pad wear.

When working on a hydraulic brake system, it is necessary that the work area and all tools be absolutely clean. Any tiny particles of foreign matter or grit on the caliper assembly or the master cylinder can damage the components. Also, sharp tools must not be used inside the caliper or on the caliper piston. If there is any doubt about your ability to correctly and safely carry out major service on the brake components, take the job to a dealer, motorcycle repair shop or brake specialist.

When adding brake fluid use only a type clearly marked DOT-3 and use it from a sealed container. Brake fluid will draw moisture which greatly reduces its ability to perform correctly, so it is a good idea to purchase brake fluid in small containers and discard what is not used.

Whenever *any* component has been removed from the brake system the system is considered "opened" and must be bled to remove air bubbles. Also if the brake feels "spongy" this usually means there are air bubbles in the system and it must be bled. For safe brake operation, refer to *Bleeding the System* in this chapter for complete details.

FRONT MASTER CYLINDER

Removal/Installation

1. Remove the rear view mirror.

CAUTION

Cover the fuel tank, front fender and instrument cluster with a heavy cloth or plastic tarp to protect them from accidental brake fluid spills. Wash any spilled brake fluid off any painted or plated surfaces immediately, as it will destroy the finish. Use a soap solution and rinse thoroughly with fresh water.

2. Pull back the rubber boot and remove the union bolt securing the brake hose to the master cylinder. Refer to **Figure 1** for standard models or **Figure 2** for Custom models. Remove the brake hose and both sealing washers. Cover the hose end to prevent the entry of foreign matter and moisture. Tie the hose end up to the handlebar to prevent the loss of brake fluid.
3. Remove the 2 clamping bolts and clamp (A, **Figure 3**) securing the master cylinder to the handlebar and remove the master cylinder.
4. Install by reversing these removal steps, noting the following.
5. Install the clamp with the notch relief facing down. Align the clamp lug with the line on the switch housing (B, **Figure 3**) and tighten the upper bolt first, then the lower.
6. Install the brake hose onto the master cylinder. Be sure to place a sealing washer on each side of the hose fitting and install the union bolt. Tighten the union bolt to 18-25 ft.-lb. (25-35 N•m).
7. Bleed the brake system as described under *Bleeding the System* in this chapter.

Disassembly

Refer to **Figure 4** for this procedure.
1. Remove the master cylinder as described under *Front Master Cylinder Removal/ Installation* in this chapter.
2. Remove the bolt, washer and nut securing the hand lever and remove the lever.
3. Remove the screws securing the cover (**Figure 5**). Remove the cover, gasket and diaphragm; pour out the brake fluid and discard it. *Never reuse brake fluid.*
4. Remove the rubber boot from the area where the hand lever actuates the internal piston.
5. Using circlip pliers (**Figure 6**), remove the internal circlip from the cylinder in the master cylinder body.
6. Remove the stop plate, secondary cup and piston assembly.
7. Remove the primary cup and spring.

Inspection

1. Clean all parts in denatured alcohol or fresh brake fluid. Inspect the cylinder bore and

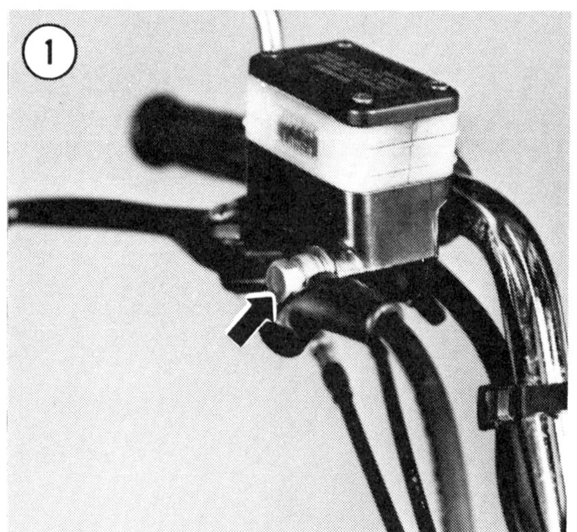

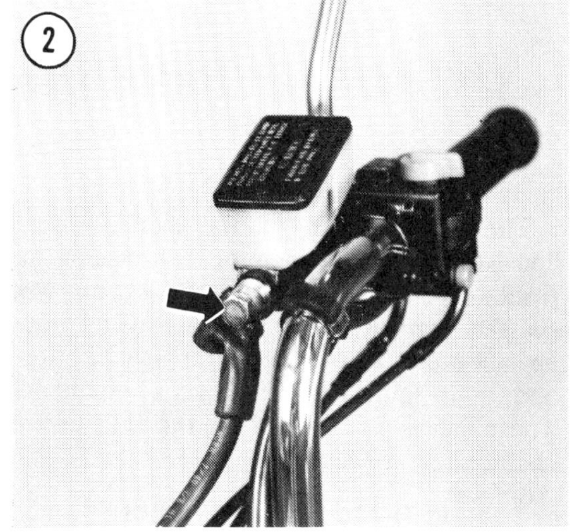

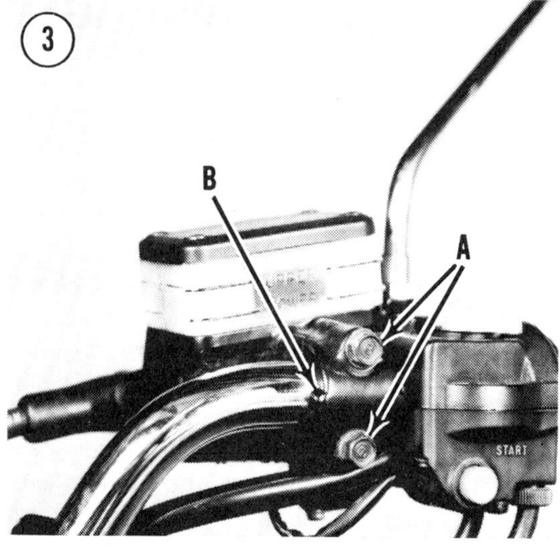

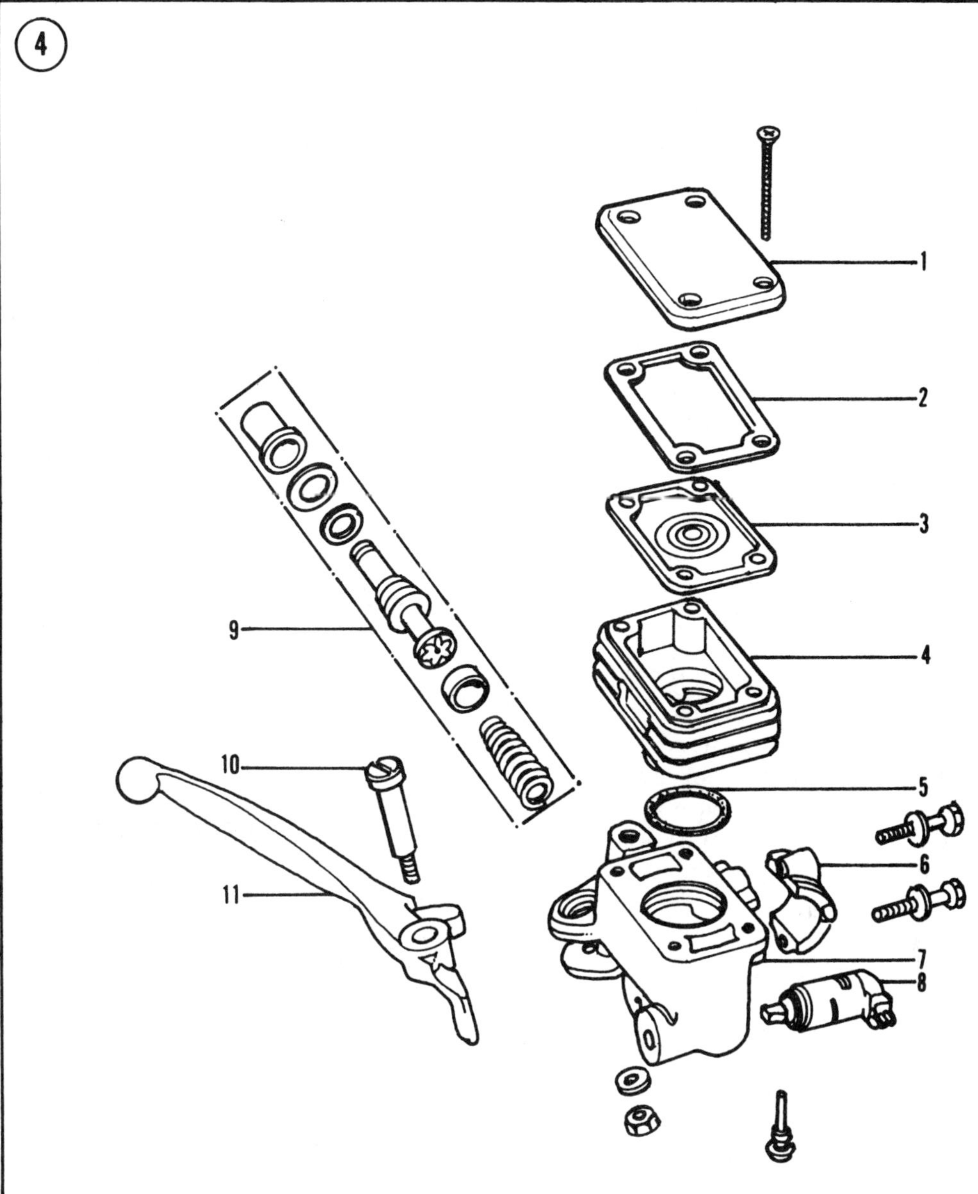

FRONT MASTER CYLINDER

1. Cover
2. Gasket
3. Diaphragm
4. Reservoir
5. Seal
6. Clamp
7. Master cylinder body
8. Brake light switch
9. Piston assembly
10. Lever bolt
11. Lever

piston contact surfaces for signs of wear and damage. If either part is less than perfect, replace it.

2. Check the end of the piston for wear caused by the hand lever. Replace the piston if the secondary cup requires replacement.

3. Inspect the pivot hole in the hand lever. If worn or elongated it must be replaced.

4. Make sure the passages in the bottom of the brake fluid reservoir are clear. Check the reservoir cap and diaphragm for damage and deterioration. Replace if necessary.

5. Inspect the condition of the threads in the master cylinder body where the brake hose union bolt screws in. If the threads are damaged or partially stripped, replace the master cylinder body.

6. Check the hand lever pivot lug on the master cylinder body for cracks. Replace the master cylinder body if necessary.

7. Measure the cylinder bore (**Figure 7**). The cylinder bore must not exceed 0.5533 in. (14.055 mm). Replace the master cylinder assembly if it exceeds this dimension.

8. Measure the outside diameter of the piston in both locations shown in **Figure 8**. If the dimension is 0.5490 in. (13.945 mm) or less at either location the piston assembly must be replaced.

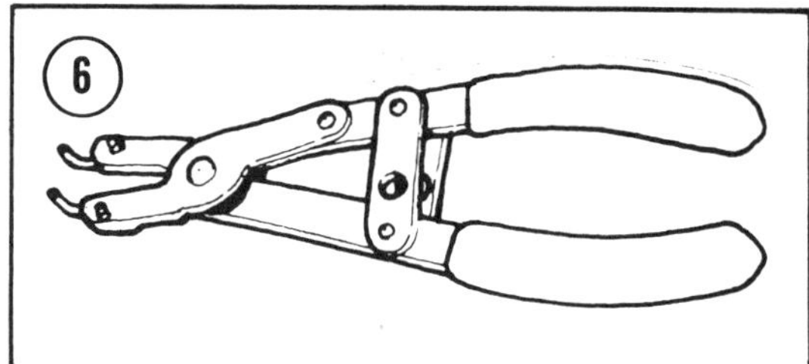

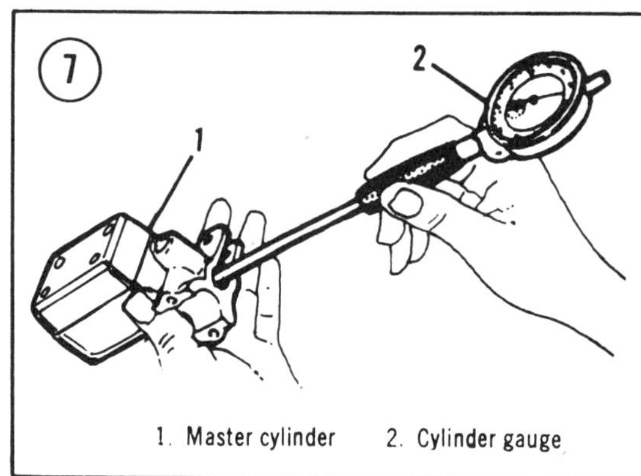

1. Master cylinder 2. Cylinder gauge

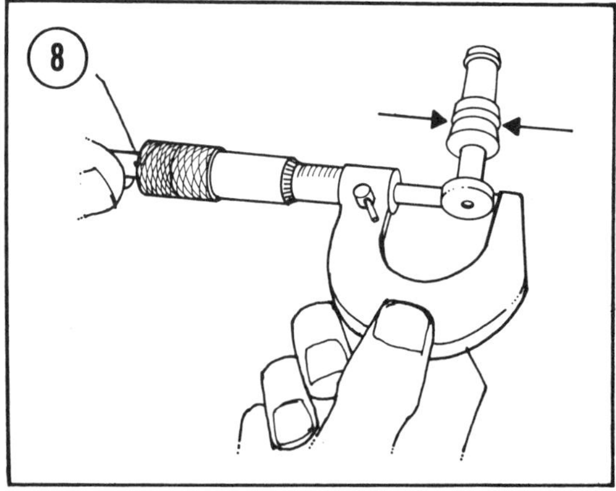

Assembly

1. Soak the new cups in fresh brake fluid for at least 15 minutes to make them pliable. Coat the inside of the cylinder with fresh brake fluid prior to the assembly of parts.

CAUTION

When installing the piston assembly, do not allow the cups to turn inside out as they will be damaged and allow brake fluid leakage within the cylinder bore.

2. Position the spring with the tapered end facing toward the primary cup. Position the primary cup so the open end will go in first (toward the spring). Install the spring, primary cup and piston assembly into the cylinder.

3. Install the stop plate and circlip. Make sure the circlip is firmly seated in the groove in the cylinder.

4. Slide in the rubber boot.

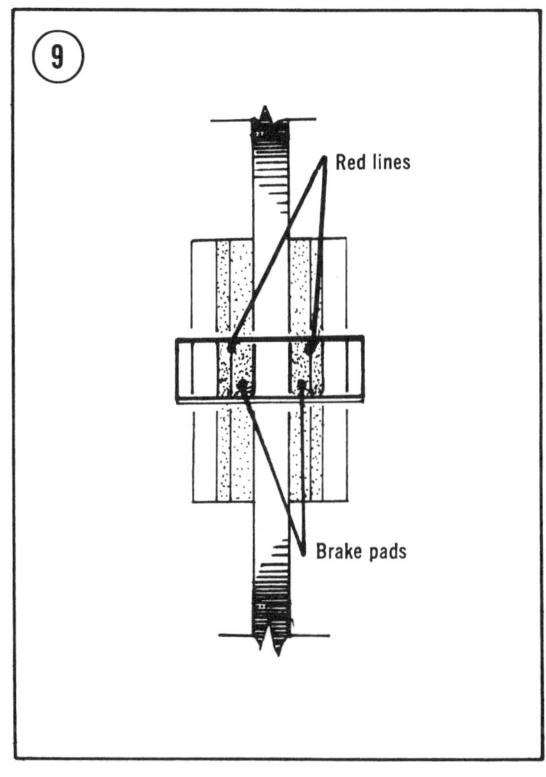

5. If the brake fluid reservoir was removed from the master cylinder body, inspect the condition of the O-ring seal between the 2 parts. Replace if necessary.
6. Install the diaphragm, gasket and cover. Do not tighten the screws at this time as fluid will have to be added later.
7. Install the brake lever onto the master cylinder body.
8. Install the master cylinder as described under *Front Master Cylinder Removal/ Installation* in this chapter.
9. Bleed the brake as described under *Bleeding the System* in this chapter.

FRONT BRAKE PAD REPLACEMENT

There is no recommended mileage interval for changing the friction pads on the disc brake. Pad wear depends greatly on riding habits and conditions. The pads should be checked for wear every 600 miles (1,000 km) and replaced when the red line wear indicators (**Figure 9**) reach the edge of the brake disc. Always replace both pads (2 per disc) at the same time.

CAUTION

Watch the pads more closely when the red line approaches the disc. On some pads the red line is very close to the pad's metal backing plate. If pad wear happens to be uneven for some reason the backing plate may come in contact with the disc and cause damage.

Refer to **Figure 10** for this procedure.

1. Remove the screw securing the caliper cover (**Figure 11**) and remove it. Pull up and remove the clip (**Figure 12**) and remove the 2 pins securing the pads in place (**Figure 13**). Remove the pads and discard them.
2. Clean the pad recess and end of the piston with a soft brush. Do not use solvent, a wire brush or any hard tool which would damage the cylinder or the piston.
3. Carefully remove any rust or corrosion from the disc.
4. Lightly coat the end of the piston and the backs of the new pads *(not the friction material)* with disc brake lubricant.

NOTE

When purchasing new pads, check with your dealer to make sure the friction compound of the new pad is compatible with the disc material. Remove any roughness from the backs of the new pads with a fine cut file; blow them clean with compressed air.

5. When new pads are installed in the caliper the master cylinder brake fluid level will rise as the caliper piston is repositioned. Clean the top of the master cylinder of all dirt and foreign matter. Remove the cap and diaphragm from the master cylinder and slowly push the caliper piston into the caliper. Constantly check the reservoir to make sure brake fluid does not overflow. Remove fluid, if necessary, prior to it overflowing. The piston should move freely. If it does not, and there is evidence of it sticking in the cylinder, the caliper should be removed and serviced as described under *Caliper Rebuilding* in this chapter.
6. Push the caliper in toward the wheel to allow room for the new pads.
7. Install the inboard brake pad (**Figure 14**).
8. Apply a light coat of silicone grease to both sides of the shim. Install the shim on the

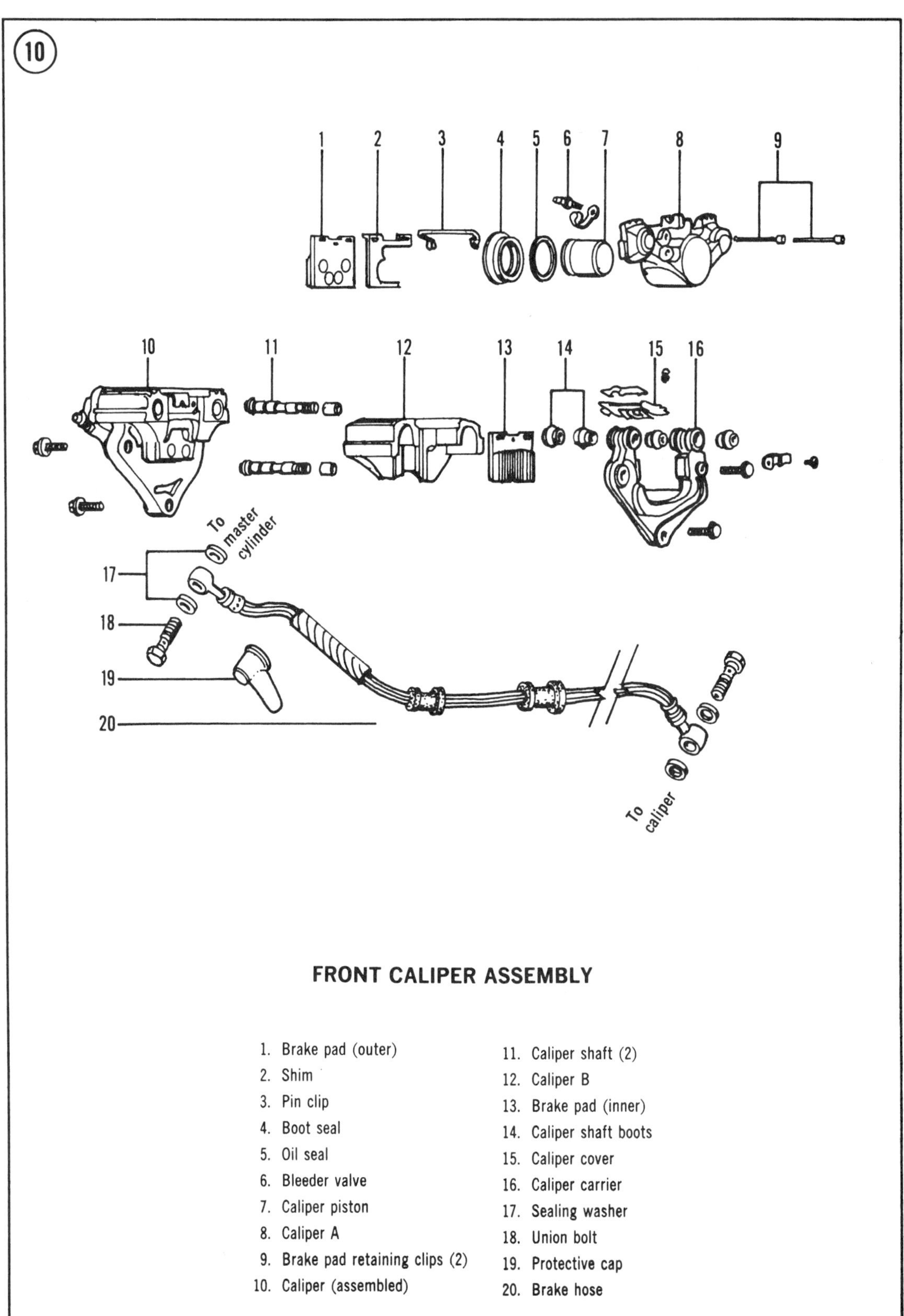

FRONT CALIPER ASSEMBLY

1. Brake pad (outer)
2. Shim
3. Pin clip
4. Boot seal
5. Oil seal
6. Bleeder valve
7. Caliper piston
8. Caliper A
9. Brake pad retaining clips (2)
10. Caliper (assembled)
11. Caliper shaft (2)
12. Caliper B
13. Brake pad (inner)
14. Caliper shaft boots
15. Caliper cover
16. Caliper carrier
17. Sealing washer
18. Union bolt
19. Protective cap
20. Brake hose

outboard pad next to the piston and install the outboard brake pad (**Figure 15**).

9. Install both pins (**Figure 13**) with the holes facing upward to allow the insertion of the clip.

10. Install the clip (**Figure 12**) and the caliper cover (**Figure 11**).

11. Place a milk crate or wood blocks under the engine or frame so that the front wheel is off the ground. Spin the front wheel and activate the brake lever as many times as it takes to refill the cylinder in the caliper and correctly locate the pads.

12. Refill the master cylinder reservoir, if necessary, to maintain the correct fluid level. Install the diaphragm and top cap.

WARNING
Use brake fluid clearly marked DOT-3 from a sealed container. Other types may vaporize and cause brake failure. Always use the same brand name; do not intermix as many brands are not compatible.

WARNING
Do not ride the motorcycle until you are sure the brake is operating correctly with full hydraulic advantage. If necessary, bleed the brake as described under ***Bleeding the System****.*

13. Bed the pads in gradually for the first 50 miles (80 km) by using only light pressure as much as possible. Immediate hard application will glaze the new friction pads and greatly reduce the effectiveness of the brake.

FRONT CALIPER(S)

Removal/Installation

Refer to **Figure 10** for this procedure.

It is not necessary to remove the front wheel in order to remove either or both caliper assemblies.

1. Remove the brake pads as described under *Brake Pad Replacement* in this chapter.
2. Remove the union bolt and 2 sealing washers attaching the brake hose to the caliper (A, **Figure 16**). To prevent the loss of brake fluid, cap the end of the brake hose and tie it up to the fork leg. Be sure to cap or tape the ends to prevent the entry of moisture and dirt.
3. Loosen the caliper "A" bolts (**Figure 17**) gradually in several steps. Push on the caliper while loosening these 2 bolts to push the piston back into the caliper. Remove caliper "A".
4. Remove the screw securing the speedometer cable clamp and remove the clamp (B, **Figure 16**).
5. Remove the 2 bolts (C, **Figure 16**) securing caliper "B" and the caliper carrier to the fork and remove both of them.
6. On models with dual disc brakes, repeat Steps 1-5 for the other caliper assembly.
7. Install by reversing these removal steps. Tighten the bolts securing both the caliper assemblies "A" and "B" to 22-29 ft.-lb. (30-40 N•m) on all models.

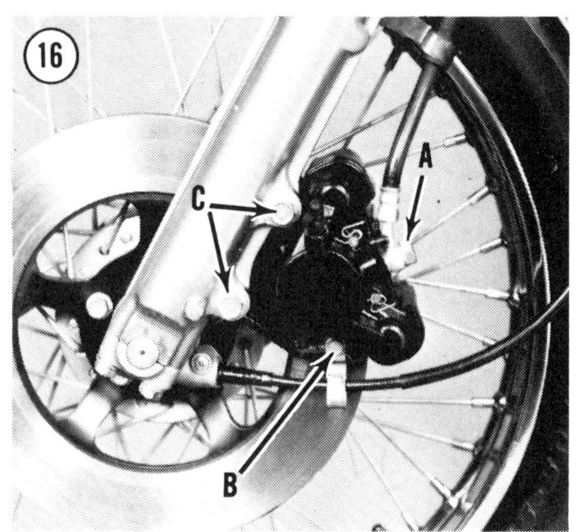

8. Install the brake hose, with a sealing washer on each side of the fitting, onto the caliper. Make sure the metal portion of the fitting is properly engaged into the recess on the caliper. Install the union bolt and tighten to 18-25 ft.-lb. (25-35 N•m).
9. Bleed the brake as described under *Bleeding the System* in this chapter.

WARNING
Do not ride the motorcycle until you are sure that the brakes are operating properly.

Caliper Rebuilding

If the caliper leaks, the caliper should be rebuilt. If the piston sticks in the cylinder, indicating severe wear or galling, the entire

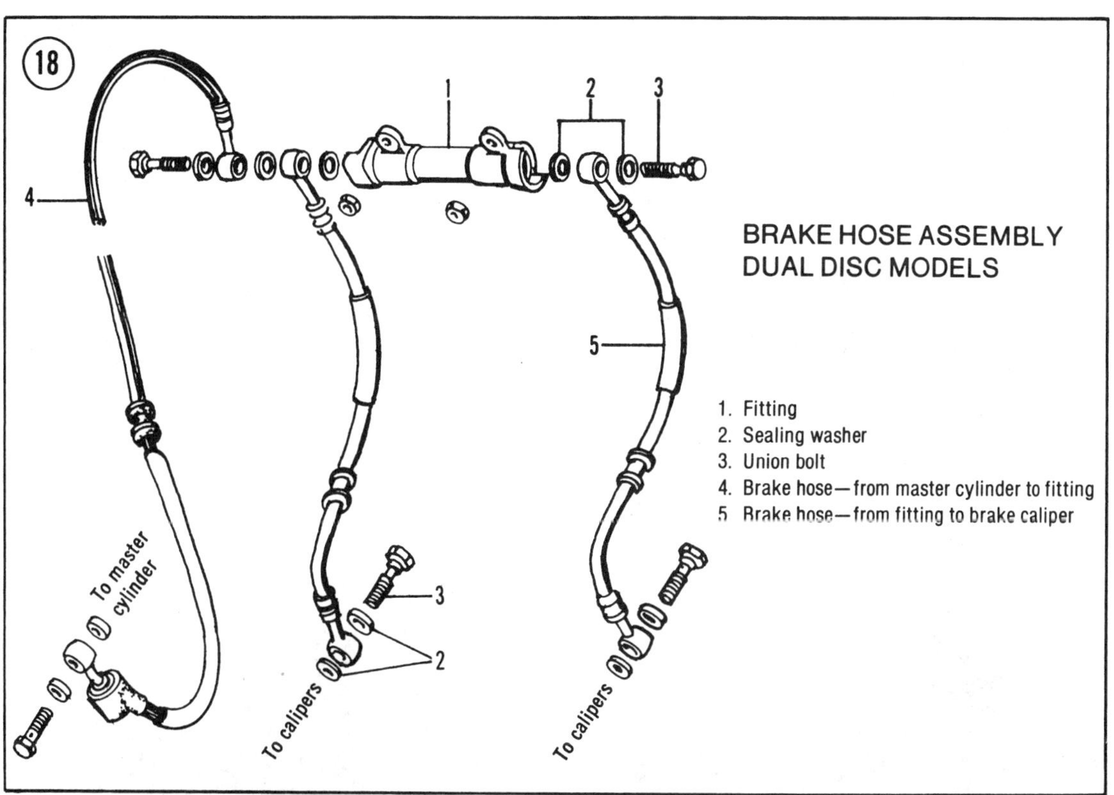

unit should be replaced. Rebuilding a leaky caliper requires special tools and experience.

Caliper service should be entrusted to a dealer, motorcycle repair shop or brake specialist. Considerable money can be saved by removing the caliper yourself and taking it in for repair.

FRONT BRAKE HOSE REPLACEMENT

There is no factory recommended brake hose replacement interval but it is a good idea to replace all brake hoses every 4 years or when they show signs of cracking, leakage or damage.

Refer to **Figure 10** for single disc models and **Figure 18** for dual disc models.

CAUTION

Cover the front wheel, fender and fuel tank with a heavy cloth or plastic tarp to protect it from the accidental spilling of brake fluid. Wash any spilled brake fluid off of any painted or plated surface immediately, as it will destroy the finish. Use soapy water and rinse completely.

1. Remove the union bolt and sealing washers (**Figure 19**) securing the brake hose to the caliper and remove it. Drain the brake fluid from the hose and discard it—***never reuse brake fluid.*** On models with dual front discs, repeat for the other side.
2. On models with a single disc, remove the union bolt and sealing washers (**Figure 20**) securing the brake hose to the master cylinder. Remove the hose from the clamps on the fork (**Figure 21**).
3. Remove the screws securing the nameplate (**Figure 22** or **Figure 23**) to the front forks and remove the nameplate.
4. On models with a single disc, remove the bolts securing the inner plate (**Figure 24**) and remove the brake hose from the inner plate.
5. On models with dual discs, remove the union bolt and sealing washers (A, **Figure 25**) securing the left-hand brake hose to the fitting and remove the left-hand brake hose. Remove the union bolt and sealing washers (B, **Figure 25**) securing the right-hand brake hose and upper brake hose to the fitting and remove the right-hand brake hose. Slide back the rubber

10

19

22

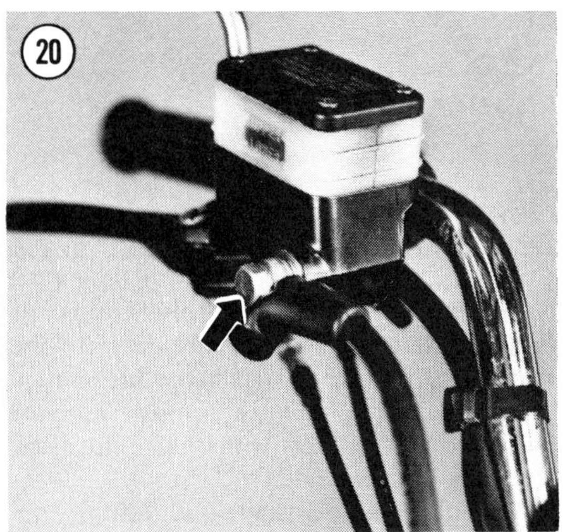
20

23

21

24

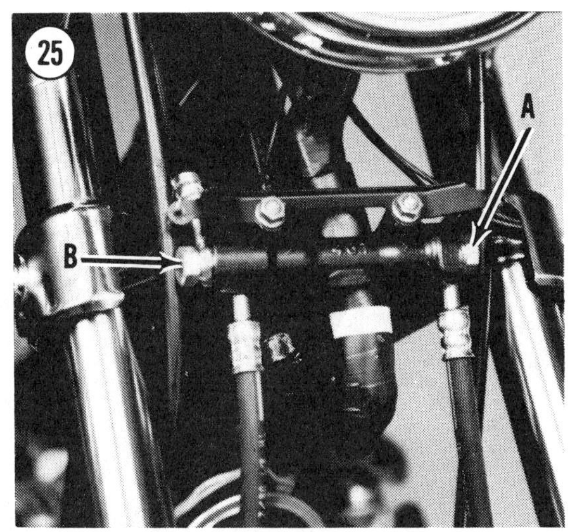

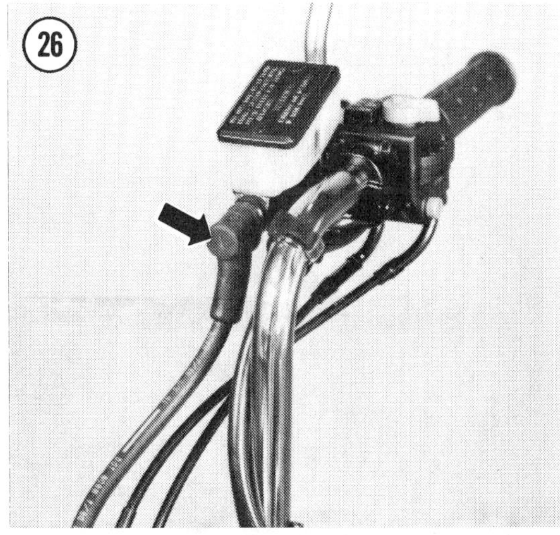

protective boot (**Figure 26**) and remove the union bolt and sealing washers securing the upper brake hose to the master cylinder and remove the upper brake hose.

6. Install new brake hoses, sealing washers and union bolts in the reverse order of removal. Be sure to install the new sealing washers in their correct positions; refer to **Figure 10** or **Figure 18**. Tighten all union bolts to 18-25 ft.-lb. (25-35 N•m).

7. Refill the master cylinder with fresh brake fluid clearly marked DOT-3. Bleed the brake as described under *Bleeding the System* in this chapter.

WARNING

Do not ride the motorcycle until you are sure that the brakes are operating properly.

FRONT BRAKE DISC

Removal/Installation

1. Remove the front wheel as described under *Front Wheel Removal/Installation* in Chapter Eight.

NOTE

Place a piece of wood in the caliper(s) in place of the disc(s). This way, if the brake lever is inadvertently squeezed the piston will not be forced out of the cylinder. If this does happen, the caliper might have to be disassembled to reseat the piston and the system will have to be bled. By using the wood, bleeding the system is not necessary when installing the wheel.

2. On single-disc models, remove the front axle (**Figure 27**).

3. Remove the speedometer drive housing (**Figure 28**).

4. On models with a single disc and wire wheels, remove the bolts (**Figure 29**) on the left-hand side and remove the disc.

5. On models with a single disc and ComStar wheels, remove the nuts on the right-hand side and withdraw the bolts from the left-hand side. Remove the disc and the cover on the right-hand side.

6. On models with dual discs, remove the nuts on the left-hand side and remove the bolts from the right-hand side. Remove both discs from the wheel.

28

29

7. Install by reversing these removal steps. Install the bolts from the correct side and tighten to 20-24 ft.-lb. (27-33 N•m) on all models.

Inspection

It is not necessary to remove the disc from the wheel to inspect it. Small marks on the disc are not important, but deep radial scratches, deep enough to snag a fingernail, reduce braking effectiveness and increase brake pad wear. If these grooves are found, the disc should be replaced.

1. Measure the thickness around the disc at several locations around the disc with vernier calipers or micrometer (**Figure 30**). The disc must be replaced if the thickness, at any point, is 0.24 in. (0.6 mm) or less.

2. Make sure the disc bolts and nuts are tight prior to running this check. Check the disc runout with a dial indicator as shown in **Figure 31**. Slowly rotate the wheel and watch the dial indicator. If the runout is 0.012 in. (0.3 mm) or greater the disc must be replaced.

3. Clean the disc of any rust or corrosion and wipe clean with lacquer thinner. Never use an oil based solvent that may leave an oil residue on the disc.

30

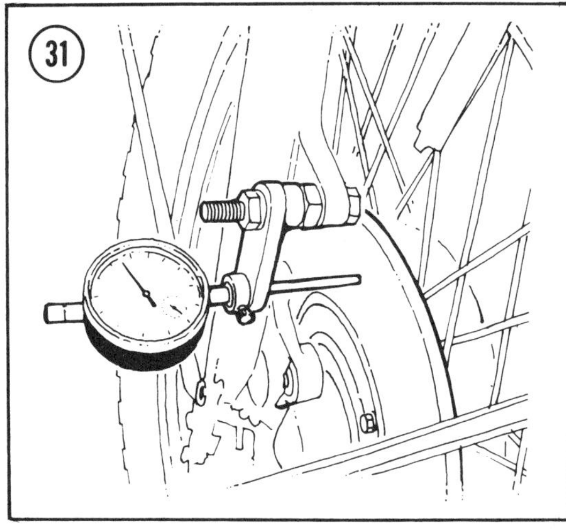

31

BLEEDING THE SYSTEM

This procedure is necessary only when the brakes feel spongy, there is a leak in the

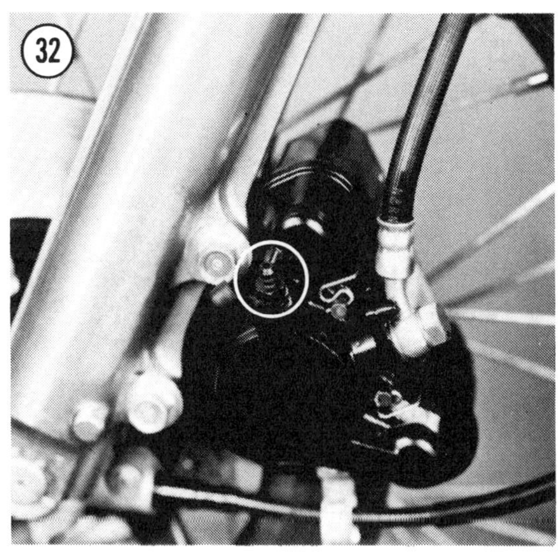

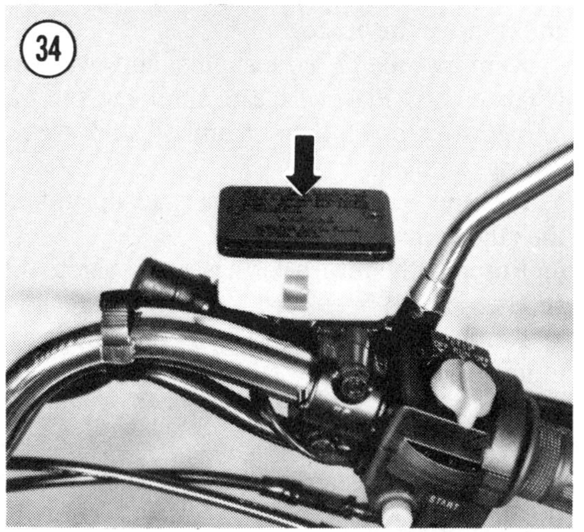

hydraulic system, a component has been replaced or the brake fluid has been replaced.

When bleeding the front system with dual discs, do one caliper at a time.

1. Flip off the dust cap from the brake bleed valve (**Figure 32**).
2. Connect a length of clear tubing to the bleed valve on the caliper (**Figure 33**). Place the other end of the tube into a clean container. Fill the container with enough fresh brake fluid to keep the end submerged. The tube should be long enough so that a loop can be made higher than the bleed valve to prevent air from being drawn into the caliper during bleeding.

CAUTION

Cover the front wheel, fender and fuel tank with a heavy cloth or plastic tarp to protect it from the accidental spilling of brake fluid. Wash any spilled brake fluid off of any painted or plated surface immediately, as it will destroy the finish. Use soapy water and rinse completely.

3. Clean the top of the master cylinder of all dirt and foreign matter. Remove the cap, diaphragm and gasket (**Figure 34**). Fill the reservoir up to about 3/8 in. (10 mm) from the top and insert the diaphragm. Leave the diaphragm in place during this procedure to prevent the entry of dirt.

10

WARNING

Use brake fluid clearly marked DOT-3 only. Others may vaporize and cause brake failure. Always use the same brand name; do not intermix as many brands are not compatible.

4. To prevent the overtravel of the caliper piston, place a 3/4 in. (20 mm) spacer between the brake lever and the throttle grip.
5. Slowly apply the brake lever several times. Hold the lever in the applied position and open the bleed valve about one-half turn. Allow the lever to travel to its limit (against the spacer). When this limit is reached, tighten the bleed screw. As the brake fluid enters the system, the level will drop on the master cylinder reservoir. Maintain the level at about 3/8 in.

(10 mm) from the top of the reservoir to prevent air from being drawn into the system.

6. Continue to pump the lever and fill the reservoir until the fluid emerging from the hose is completely free of air bubbles.

7. Hold the lever in the applied position and tighten the bleed valve. Remove the bleed tube and install the bleed valve dust cap.

8. If necessary, add fluid to correct the level in the master cylinder reservoir. It must be up to the upper level line (**Figure 35**).

9. Install the cap and tighten the screws securely.

10. Test the feel of the brake lever. It should feel firm and should offer the same resistance each time it's operated. If it feels spongy, it is likely that there still is air in the system and it must be bled again. When all air has been bled from the system, and the brake fluid level is correct in the reservoir, double check for leaks and tighten all fittings and connections.

WARNING

Before riding the motorcycle, make certain that the brakes are operating correctly by operating the lever several times. Then make the test ride a slow one at first to make sure the brake is operating correctly.

REAR DRUM BRAKE

The rear brake is a drum type; **Figure 36** illustrates the major components of the brake assembly. By pushing down on the brake foot pedal it pulls the rod which in turn rotates the camshaft. This forces the brake shoes out into contact with the brake drum.

Pedal free play must be maintained on the brake to minimize brake drag and premature brake wear and maximize braking effectiveness. Refer to *Rear Brake Pedal Free Play* in Chapter Three for complete adjustment procedures.

Disassembly

Refer to **Figure 37** for this procedure.

1. Remove the front wheel as described under *Front Wheel Removal/Installation* in Chapter Eight.

2. Pull the brake assembly straight up and out of the brake drum.

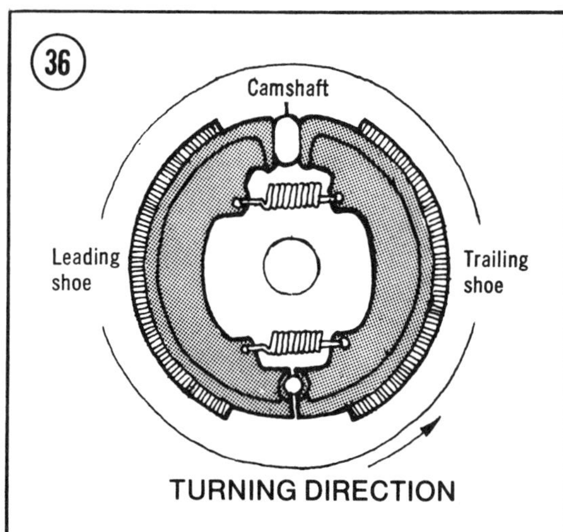

3. Loosen the clamping bolt (A, **Figure 38**) and remove the brake arm.

4. Remove the 2 cotter pins and washers (**Figure 39**). Place a clean shop rag on the linings to protect them from oil and grease during removal.

5. Pull the brake shoes and springs up and off the guide pins and camshaft.

6. Remove the return springs and separate the shoes.

7. Remove the camshaft, oil seal and wear indicator plate.

Inspection

1. Thoroughly clean and dry all parts except the linings.

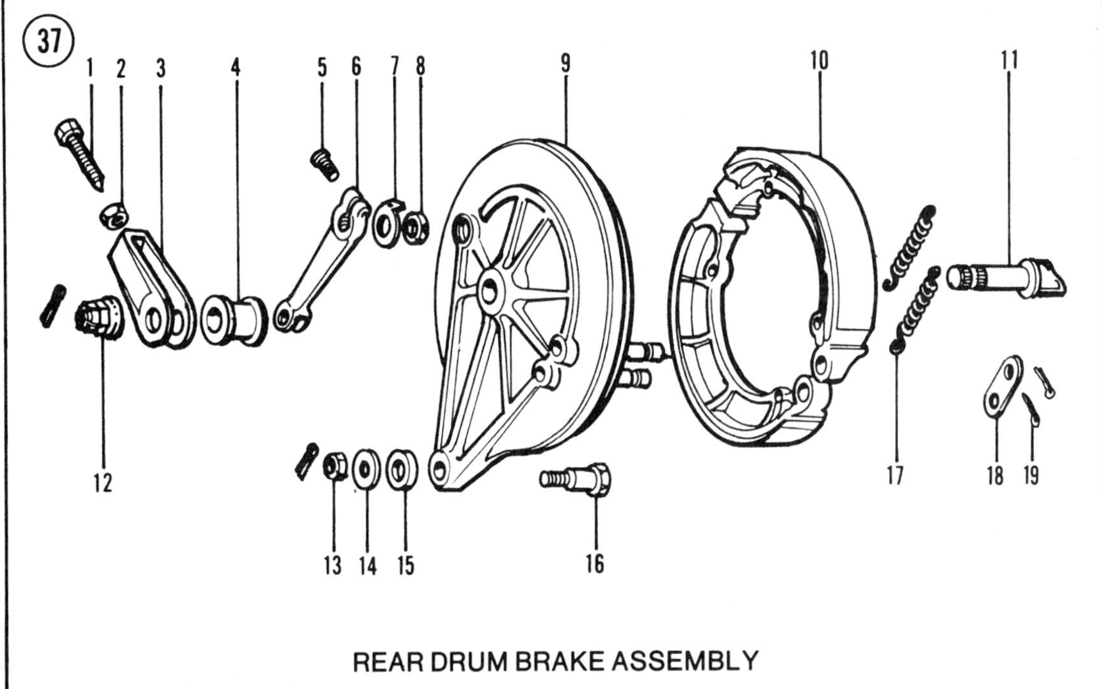

REAR DRUM BRAKE ASSEMBLY

1. Drive chain adjuster
2. Drive chain adjuster locknut
3. Drive chain adjuster bracket
4. Spacer
5. Bolt
6. Brake arm
7. Brake lining wear indicator
8. Oil seal
9. Brake panel
10. Brake shoe assembly
11. Camshaft
12. Nut
13. Nut
14. Washer
15. Rubber cushion pad
16. Bolt
17. Return spring
18. Anchor pin washer
19. Cotter pin

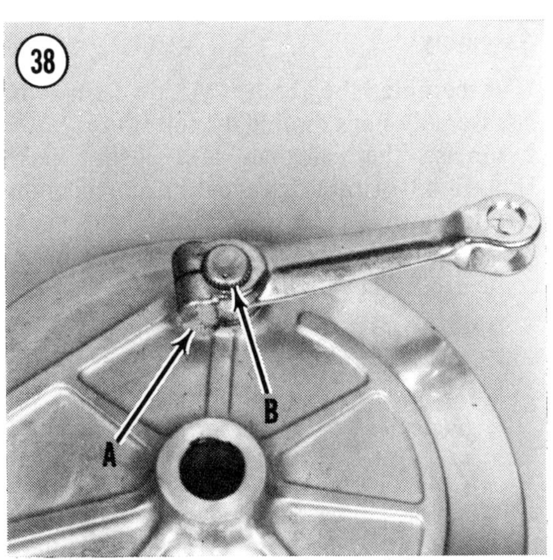

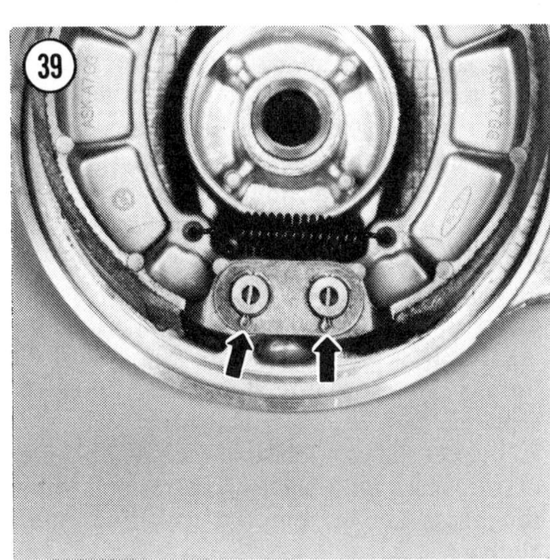

2. Check the contact surface of the drum (**Figure 40**) for scoring. If there are grooves deep enough to snag a fingernail, the drum should be reground and new shoes fitted. This type of wear can be avoided to a great extent if the brakes are disassembled and thoroughly cleaned after riding the motorcycle in water, mud or deep sand.

NOTE

If oil or grease is on the drum surface, clean it off with a clean rag soaked in lacquer thinner—do not use any solvent that may leave an oil residue.

3. Use vernier calipers (**Figure 41**) and measure the inside diameter of the drum for out-of-round or excessive wear. Refer to **Table 2** for brake specifications. Turn or replace the drum as necessary.
4. If the drum is turned, the linings will have to be replaced and the new linings arced to the new drum contour.
5. Check the brake linings. They should be replaced if worn within 0.08 in. (2.0 mm) of the metal shoe table (**Figure 42**).
6. Inspect the linings for embedded foreign material. Dirt can be removed with a stiff wire brush. Check for traces of oil or grease. If the linings are contaminated, they must be replaced.
7. Inspect the cam lobe and the pivot pin area of the shaft for wear and corrosion. Minor roughness can be removed with fine emery cloth.

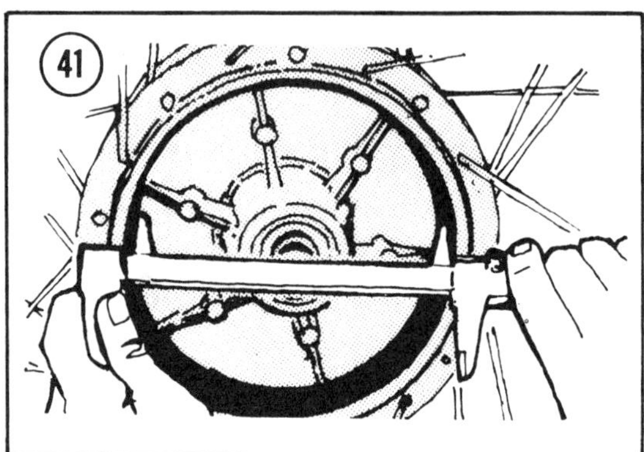

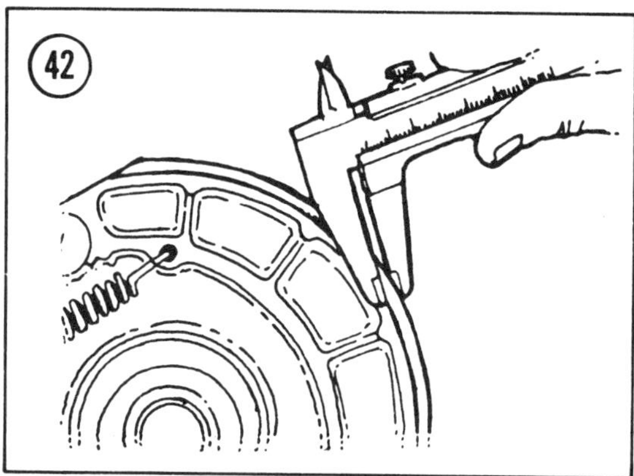

8. Inspect the brake shoe return springs for wear or distortion. If they are stretched, they will not fully retract the brake shoes from the drum, resulting in a power-robbing drag on the drums and premature wear of the linings. Replace as necessary and always replace as a pair.

Assembly

1. Assemble the brake by reversing the disassembly steps, noting the following.
2. Grease the camshaft and anchor posts (**Figure 43**) with a light coat of molybdenum disulfide grease (**Figure 44**); avoid getting any grease on the brake plate where the linings come in contact with it.

NOTE

*If new linings are being installed, file off the leading edge of each shoe a little (**Figure 45**) so that the brake will not grab when applied.*

3. When installing the brake lever onto the brake camshaft, be sure to align the punch

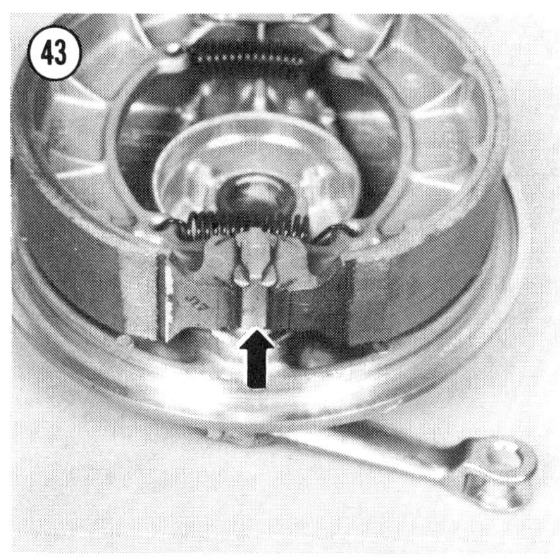
43

44

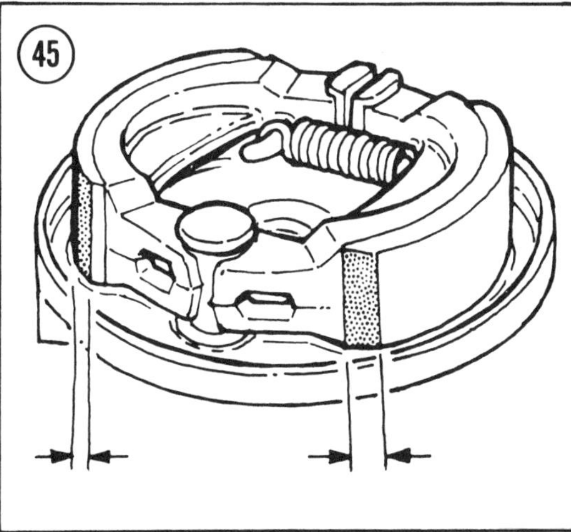
45

46

marks on the 2 parts (B, **Figure 38**) and tighten the nut securely.
4. Install the brake panel assembly into the brake drum.
5. Install the front wheel as described under *Front Wheel Removal/Installation* in Chapter Eight.
6. Adjust the rear brake as described under *Rear Brake Pedal Free Play* in Chapter Three.

REAR BRAKE PEDAL ASSEMBLY

Removal/Installation

1. Place the motorcycle on the centerstand.
2. Completely unscrew the adjustment nut and disconnect the rear of the brake actuating rod from the brake arm (**Figure 46**). Reinstall the adjustment nut to avoid losing it.
3. Unhook the rear brake light switch spring (**Figure 47**) from the brake pivot lever.
4. Disconnect the pedal return spring.
5. Loosen the clamping bolt (**Figure 48**) and remove the brake pedal.
6. Remove the cotter pin from the clevis pin and remove the brake actuating arm from the brake pivot lever.
7. Withdraw the brake pivot lever from the frame.
8. Install by reversing these removal steps, noting the following.
9. **Apply grease to the brake pivot lever prior to installing the assembly into the frame.**
10. Install a new cotter pin in the clevis pin and bend the ends over completely.
11. Adjust the rear brake as described under *Rear Brake Pedal Free Play* in Chapter Three.

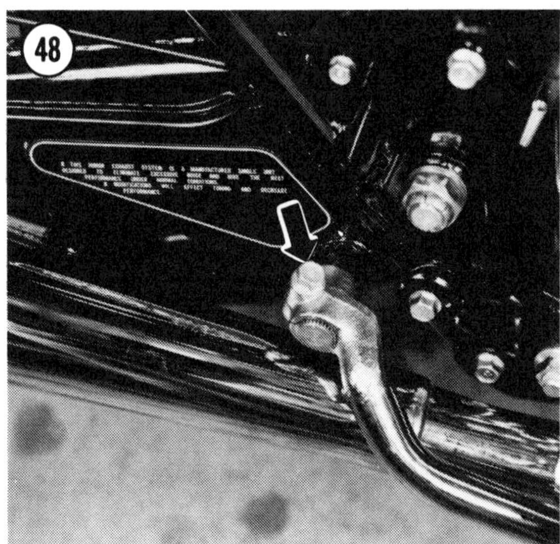

Table 1 BRAKE TORQUE SPECIFICATIONS

Item	Foot Pounds	Newton meters
Brake hose union bolts—all	18-25	25-35
Master cylinder cover screws	9-17 in.-lb.	1-2
Caliper mounting bolts	22-29	30-40
Caliper shaft bolts	22-29	30-40
Brake disc mounting bolts	20-24	27-33

TABLE 2 BRAKE SPECIFICATIONS

Item	Specifications	Wear Limit
Master cylinder		
Cylinder bore ID	0.5512-0.5529 in. (14.00-14.043 mm)	0.553 in. (14.005 mm)
Piston OD	0.5495-0.5506 in. (13.957-13.984 mm)	0.5490 in. (13.945 mm)
Caliper		
Cylinder bore ID	1.6870-1.6000 in. (42.850-42.926 mm)	1.6905 in. (42.940 mm)
Piston OD	1.6856-1.6858 in. (42.815-42.820 mm)	1.6850 in. (42.800 mm)
Brake disc		
Thickness	0.27-0.28 in. (6.9-7.1 mm)	0.24 in. (6.0 mm)
Runout	——	0.01 in. (0.3 mm)
Rear brake drum ID	7.09-7.10 in. (180-180.3 mm)	7.1 in. (181 mm)
Rear brake lining thickness	0.197 in. (5.0 mm)	0.08 in. (2.0 mm)

CHAPTER ELEVEN

FRAME AND REPAINTING

The frame does not require routine maintenance. However, it should be inspected immediately after any accident or spill.

This chapter describes procedures for completely stripping the frame. In addition, recommendations are provided for repainting the stripped frame.

This chapter also includes procedures for the kickstand, centerstand and footpegs.

KICKSTAND (SIDESTAND)

Removal/Installation

1. Place the bike on the centerstand.
2. Raise the kickstand and disconnect the return spring (A, **Figure 1**) from the pin on the frame with Vise Grips.

3. From under the frame, remove the cotter pin from the bolt.
4. Remove the bolt and nut (B, **Figure 1**) and remove the kickstand from the frame.
5. Install by reversing these removal steps. Apply a light coat of multipurpose grease to the pivot surfaces of the frame tab and the kickstand yoke prior to installation. Install a new cotter pin and bend it over completely.

CENTERSTAND

Removal/Installation

1. Place a milk crate or wood block(s) under the frame or engine to support the bike securely.
2. Remove the rear wheel as described under *Rear Wheel Removal/Installation* in Chapter Nine.
3. Remove the exhaust system as described under *Exhaust System Removal/Installation* in Chapter Six.
4. Place the centerstand in the raised position. Use Vise Grips and disconnect the return spring (A, **Figure 2**) from the C-shaped spring retainer on the pivot shaft.
5. Loosen the bolts and nuts on the clamps (B, **Figure 2**) securing the pivot tube. Remove the cotter pin on the left-hand side.
6. Withdraw the tube from the right-hand side and lower the centerstand.
7. Install by reversing these removal steps. Apply a light coat of multipurpose grease to all pivoting points prior to installation.

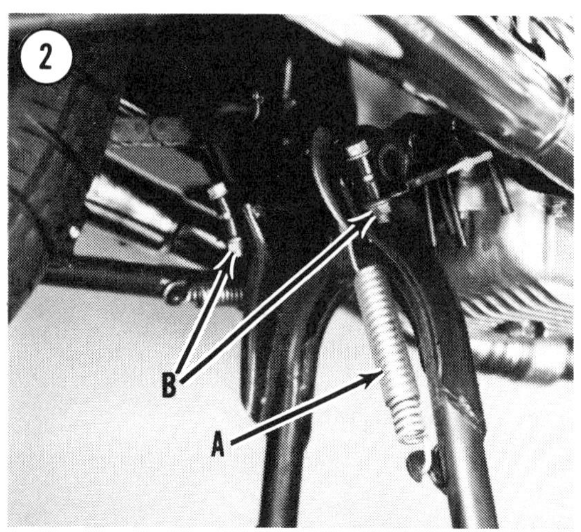

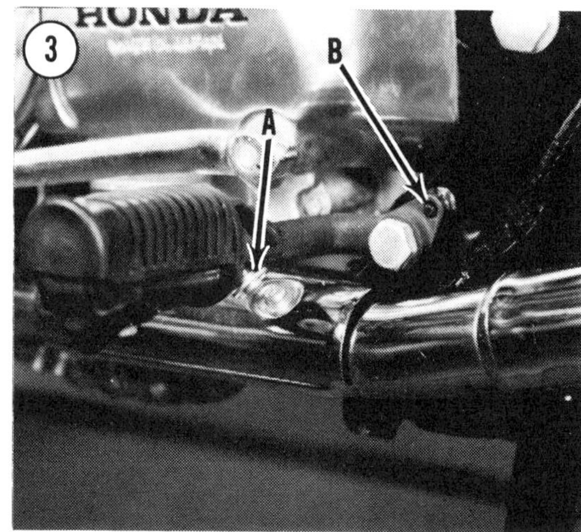

FOOTPEGS

Replacement

Remove the cotter pin (A, **Figure 3**) securing the footpeg to the bracket on the frame. Remove the pivot pin and footpeg.

Make sure the spring is in good condition and not broken. Replace as necessary.

Lubricate the pivot point and pivot pin prior to installation. Install a new cotter pin and bend it over completely.

To remove the entire rear foot peg assembly, remove the bolt and nut (**Figure 4**) securing the footpeg assembly to the frame and remove it.

NOTE

This bolt and nut also holds the rear portion of the exhaust system in place. Tie the muffler(s) up to the luggage rack with a Bungee cord.

The front footpegs are held in place with the rear lower engine mounting through bolt. Remove the rear brake pedal and remove the self-locking nut (**Figure 5**) on the bolt. Remove the through bolt and footpeg assembly.

When installing the footpeg assemblies, make sure the locating tabs are correctly positioned on the pins (B, **Figure 3**). On the front footpegs, tighten the through bolt and self-tightening nut to 58-72 ft.-lb. (80-100 N•m). Tighten the rear footpeg bolt and nut to 22-29 ft.-lb. (30-40 N•m).

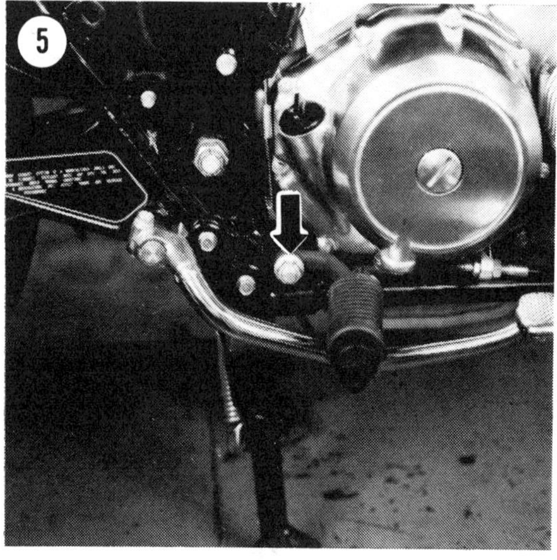

6

FRAME

Component Removal/Installation

1. Remove the seat, side cover panels and fuel tank.

2. Remove the engine as described in Chapter Four.

3. Remove the front wheel, steering and front forks as described in Chapter Eight.

4. Remove the rear wheel, fender, shock absorbers and rear swing arm as described in Chapter Nine.

5. Remove the battery, lighting and ignition equipment and wiring harness as described in Chapter Seven.

6. Remove the kickstand, centerstand and footpegs as described in this chapter.

7. Remove the steering head races from the steering head tube as described in Chapter Eight.

8. Inspect the frame for bends, cracks or other damage, especially around welded joints and areas that are rusted.

9. Assemble by reversing these removal steps.

Stripping and Painting

Remove all components from the frame. Thoroughly strip off all old paint. The best way is to have it sandblasted down to bare metal. If this is not possible, you can use a liquid paint remover and steel wool and a fine, hard wire brush.

CAUTION

*The side covers, air box and instrument cluster are molded plastic (**Figure 6**). If you wish to change the color of these parts, consult an automotive paint supplier for the proper procedure. Do not use any liquid paint remover on these components as it will damage the surface. The color is an integral part of some of these components and cannot be removed.*

When the frame is down to bare metal, have it inspected for hairline and internal cracks. Magnafluxing is the most common and complete process.

Make sure that the primer is compatible with the type of paint you are going to use for the final coat. Spray on one or two coats of primer as smoothly as possible. Let it dry thoroughly and use a fine grade of wet sandpaper (400-600 grit) to remove any flaws. Carefully wipe the surface clean and then spray the final coat. Use either lacquer or enamel base paint and follow the manufacturer's instructions.

11

A shop specializing in painting will probably do the best job. However, you can do a surprisingly good job with a good grade of spray paint. Spend a few extra dollars and get a good grade of paint as it will make a difference in how well it looks and how long it will stand up. It's a good idea to shake the can and make sure the ball inside the can is loose when you purchase the can of paint. Shake the can as long as is stated on the can. Then immerse the can *upright* in a pot or bucket of *warm water (not hot — not over 120° F).*

WARNING

*Higher temperatures could cause the can to burst. **Do not** place the can in direct contact with any flame or heat source.*

Leave the can in the water for several minutes. When thoroughly warmed, shake the can again and spray the frame. Be sure to get into all the crevices where there may be rust problems. Several light mist coats are better than one heavy coat. Spray painting is best done in temperatures of 70-80° F (21-26° C); any temperature above or below this will give you problems.

After the final coat has dried completely, at least 48 hours, any overspray or orange peel may be removed with a *light application* of Dupont rubbing compound (red color) and finished with Dupont polishing compound (white color). Be careful not to rub too hard or you will go through the finish.

Finish off with a couple coats of good wax prior to reassembling all the components.

It's a good idea to keep the frame touched up with fresh paint if any minor rust spots or scratches appear.

SUPPLEMENT

1982 SERVICE INFORMATION

The following supplement provides procedures unique to the 1982 CB650. All other service procedures are identical to earlier models.

The chapter headings in this supplement correspond to those in the main body of this book. If a change is not included in the supplement, there are no changes affecting 1982 models.

CHAPTER THREE

LUBRICATION, MAINTENANCE AND TUNE-UP

PERIODIC LUBRICATION

Front Fork Oil Change

The service procedure is the same as described in Chapter Three in the main body of this book. Fork oil capacity for 1982 models is listed in **Table 1**.

ENGINE TUNE-UP

Engine tune-up specifications are listed in **Table 2**.

Correct Spark Plug Heat Range

Spark plug service is the same as on previous models with the exception of the heat range. Refer to **Table 2** for correct spark plug heat range for 1982 models.

GENERAL SPECIFICATIONS

General information and specifications are covered in **Table 3**.

Table 1 FORK OIL CAPACITY*

Model	Drain	Rebuild
Standard	6.5 oz. (190 cc)	7.1 oz. (210 cc)
Nighthawk	10.2 oz. (300 cc)	10.8 oz. (320 cc)

* Capacity of each fork leg.

Table 2 TUNE-UP SUMMARY

Valve clearance (cold)	
Intake	0.002 in. (0.05 mm)
Exhaust	0.003 in. (0.08 mm)
Compression pressure (at sea level)	170 ±28 psi (12.0 ±2.0 kg/cm^2)
Spark plug type	
Standard heat range	ND X24ESR-U or NGK DR8ES-L
Cold weather*	ND X22ESR-U or NGK DR7ES
Extended high-speed riding	ND X27ESR-U or NGK DR8ES
Spark plug gap	0.024-0.028 in. (0.6-0.7 mm)
Spark plug torque	9-12 ft.-lb. (12-16 N•m)
Ignition timing	"1.4 F-1" @ 1,050 ±100 rpm
	Advance timing mark "II" @ 2,725 rpm
Idle speed	1,050 ±100 rpm
Firing order	1-2-4-3

* Cold weather climate: below 41° F (5° C).

Table 3 GENERAL SPECIFICATIONS

Engine type	Air-cooled, 4-stroke, SOHC, transverse mounted inline 4	
Bore and stroke	2.354 x 2.197 in. (59.8 x 55.8 mm)	
Displacement	38.2 cu. in. (627 cc)	
Compression ratio	9.0 to 1	
Carburetion	4 Keihin carburetors with accelerator pump on No. 2 carburetor only	
Standard	VB 44A constant velocity type	
Nighthawk	VB 44C constant velocity type	
Ignition	Capacitor discharge ignition (CDI)	
Lubrication	Wet-sump, filter, oil pump	
Clutch	Wet, multi-plate (7)	
Transmission	5-speed, constant mesh	
Transmission ratios	Standard	Nighthawk
1st	2.500	2.692
2nd	1.722	1.778
3rd	1.333	1.333
4th	1.074	1.042
5th	0.885	1.885
Final reduction ratio	2.500 (16/40)	2.294 (39/17)
Drive chain		
Standard	DID 50V or RK 50MO by 104 links	
Nighthawk	DID 50V or RK 50 MO by 106 links	
Starting system	Electric starter only	
Battery	12 volt, 12 amp/hour	
Alternator	Three phase, AC, 0.26 kw/5,000 rpm	
Firing order	1-2-4-3	
Wheelbase		
Standard	57.9 in. (1,470 mm)	
Nighthawk	59.4 in. (1,510 mm)	
Steering head angle		
Standard	26° 50'	
Nighthawk	29° 0'	
Trail		
Standard	4 in. (105 mm)	
Nighthawk	4.2 in. (106 mm)	
Front suspension travel	Telescopic forks	
Standard	5.6 in. (142 mm)	
Nighthawk	6.3 in. (160 mm)	
Rear suspension travel	Swing arm and shock absorbers	
Standard	3.6 in. (91 mm)	
Nighthawk	4.1 in. (105 mm)	
Front tire		
Standard	3.50 H19 4PR	
Nighthawk	3.50 S19 4PR	
Rear tire		
Standard	4.50 H17 4PR	
Nighthawk	130/90-16 x 67S	
Ground clearance		
Standard	6.1 in. (155 mm)	
Nighthawk	5.7 in. (145 mm)	
Overall height		
Standard	45.5 in. (1,155 mm)	
Nighthawk	46.1 in. (1,170 mm)	

(continued)

Table 3 GENERAL SPECIFICATIONS (continued)

Overall width (handlebar)	
Standard	34.1 in. (865 mm)
Nighthawk	31.5 in. (800 mm)
Overall length	
Standard	85.8 in. (2,180 mm)
Nighthawk	87.0 in. (2,210 mm)
Weight (dry)	
Standard	437 lb. (199 kg)
Nighthawk	452 lb. (205 kg)
Fuel capacity	3.5 U.S. gal. (13.5 liters, 3.0 Imp. gal.)
Oil capacity	
Oil and filter change	3.2 U.S. qt. (3.0 liters, 2.6 Imp. qt.)
At overhaul	3.7 U.S. qt. (3.5 liters, 3.0 Imp. qt.)
Front fork oil	Dexron automatic transmission fluid
Drain capacity*	
Standard	10.2 oz. (320 cc)
Nighthawk	6.5 oz. (190 cc)

* Capacity of each fork leg.

CHAPTER SIX

FUEL AND EXHAUST SYSTEMS

CARBURETOR SERVICE

Carburetor specifications for 1982 models are listed in **Table 4**.

Disassembly/Cleaning/Inspection

The slow jet on earlier models is pressed into place in the carburetor body and cannot be removed. On 1982 models, the slow jet can be removed.

1. Perform Steps 1-8 of *Carburetor Disassembly/Cleaning/Inspection/Assembly (Models Since 1981)* in Chapter Six in the main body of this book.
2. Remove the slow jet (**Figure 1**).
3. Perform Steps 9-30 of *Carburetor Disassembly/Cleaning/Inspection/Assembly (Models Since 1981)* in Chapter Six in the main body of this book.
4. Install the slow jet until it lightly seats, then tighten it approximately 3/4 of a turn.

Table 4 CARBURETOR SPECIFICATIONS

Carburetor model No.	
Standard	VB 44A
Nighthawk	VB 44C
Main jet No.	
Standard	120
Nighthawk	118
Jet needle clip setting	Non-adjustable
Float level	0.61 in. (15.5 mm)
Idle speed	1,050 ± 100 rpm
Fast idle speed	1,000-2,700 rpm

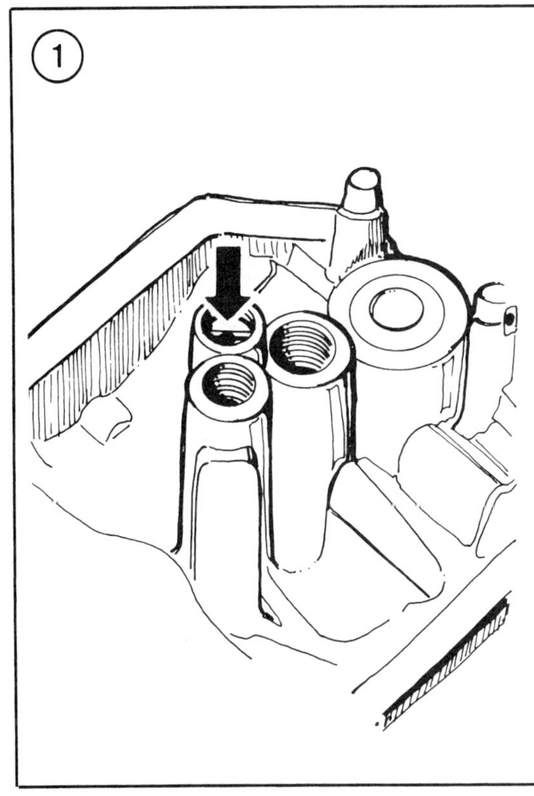

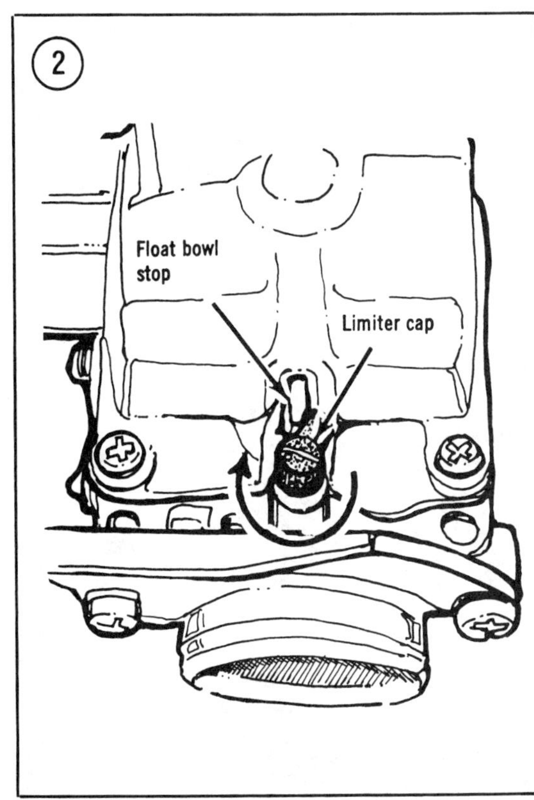

5. Perform Steps 31-35 of *Carburetor Disassembly/Cleaning/Inspection/Assembly (Models Since 1981)* in Chapter Six in the main body of this book.

CARBURETOR ADJUSTMENTS

High Altitude Adjustment

If the bike is going to be ridden for any sustained period of time at high elevation (above 5,000 ft./1,500 m), the pilot jet on each carburetor must be adjusted.

CAUTION
If the carburetors have been adjusted for high-altitude operation (pilot jet readjusted), they must be changed back to their original setting when ridden at altitudes below 5,000 ft./1,500 m. Engine overheating and piston seizure may occur from a too-lean mixture.

1. Start the engine and let it reach normal operating temperature.
2. Place the bike on the centerstand.
3. Turn each pilot screw and limiter cap (**Figure 2**) *clockwise* (looking up at the pilot screw) 1/2 turn away from the float bowl stop.
4. Readjust the idle speed to 1,050 ±100 rpm as described under *Idle Speed Adjustment* in Chapter Three in the main body of this book.

Choke Friction Adjustment (CB650SC)

Operate the choke lever and check for smooth operation of the cable and the choke mechanism. The choke lever should remain in any position to which it is set. If it will not stay in all positions, the friction on the lever must be adjusted.

1. To adjust the friction of the choke lever, remove the electrical wire band on the left-hand handlebar.
2. Move the left-hand switch electrical wires down and away. Disconnect the clutch switch wires and move them out of the way.
3. To increase friction on the choke lever, turn the adjust screw (**Figure 3**) clockwise. To decrease friction on the choke lever, turn the adjust screw counterclockwise.

4. Reposition the electrical wires and install the wire band on the electrical wires.

Choke Adjustment (CB650SC)

Operate the choke lever and check for smooth operation of the cable and the choke mechanism.

1. Push the choke lever all the way to the left to the fully closed position.
2. At the carburetor assembly, pull up on the choke lever to make sure that it is at the end of its travel (thus closing the choke valves). If you can move the choke lever an additional amount, it must be adjusted.
3. Remove both side covers (A, **Figure 4**).
4. Remove the Allen bolt (B, **Figure 4**) on each side and remove the seat/rear tail section.
5. Remove the bolt securing the fuel tank at the rear. Pull the fuel tank up slightly and prop it up. It is not necessary to completely remove the fuel tank.
6. To adjust, loosen the cable clamping screw (**Figure 5**) and move the cable sheath *up* until the choke lever is fully closed. Hold the choke lever in this position and tighten the cable clamping screw securely.
7. Push the choke lever all the way to the right to the fully open position.
8. At the carburetor assembly, check that the choke lever is fully open by checking for free play between the cable and the choke lever. The cable should move slightly, as there should be no tension on it.
9. If proper adjustment cannot be achieved using this procedure, the cable has stretched and must be replaced. Refer to *Choke Cable Replacement (CB650SC)* in this section of the supplement.
10. Reinstall the fuel tank rear mounting bolt. Tighten securely. Install the seat/rear tail section and both side covers.

Choke Cable Replacement (CB650SC)

1. Remove both side covers (A, **Figure 4**).
2. Remove the Allen bolt (B, **Figure 4**) on each side and remove the seat/rear tail section.

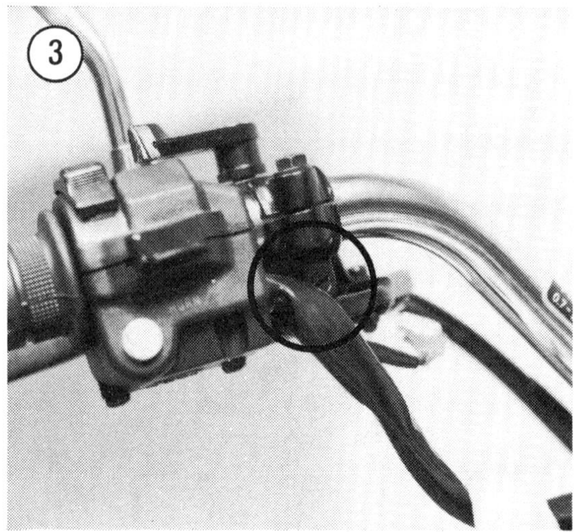

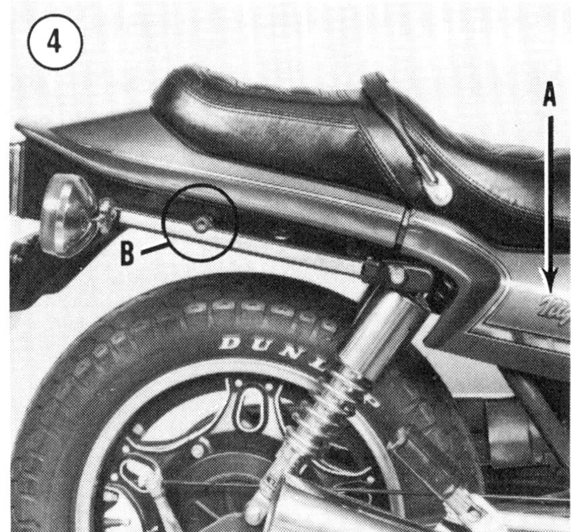

3. Remove the fuel tank as described under *Fuel Tank Removal/Installation* in Chapter Six in the main body of this book.
4. Remove the carburetor assembly as described under *Carburetor Removal/ Installation (Models Since 1981)* in Chapter Three in the main body of this book.

NOTE
It may not look like it, but it is practically impossible to remove the choke cable from the carburetors with the carburetor assembly in place. There is just not enough room for 2 hands within the area.

5. Loosen the choke cable clamp screw and remove the cable end from the choke linkage (**Figure 6**).

NOTE
The piece of string attached in the next step will be used to pull the new choke cable back through the frame so it will be routed in the same position as the old cable.

6. Tie a piece of heavy string or cord (approximately 6-8 ft./1.8-2.4 m long) to the carburetor end of the choke cable. Wrap this end with masking or duct tape. Do not use an excessive amount of tape as it will be pulled through the frame loop during removal. Tie the other end of the string to the frame or air box.
7. Remove the screw securing the choke cable clamp in place. Remove the clamp and remove the choke cable end from the choke lever.
8. At the choke lever end of the cable, carefully pull the cable (and attached string) out through the frame and from behind the headlight housing. Make sure the attached string follows the same path as the old cable.
9. Remove the tape and untie the string from the old cable.
10. Lubricate the new cable as described under *Control Cables* in Chapter Three in the main body of this book.
11. Tie the string to the carburetor assembly end of the new choke cable and wrap it with tape.
12. Carefully pull the string back through the frame routing the new cable through the same path as the old cable.
13. Remove the tape and untie the string from the cable and the frame.
14. Insert the cable end into the choke lever and install the cable clamp and the screw.
15. Attach the choke cable to the carburetor choke linkage as shown in **Figure 6**.
16. Operate the choke lever and make sure the carburetor choke linkage is operating correctly and with no binding. If operation is incorrect or there is binding carefully check that the cable is attached correctly and there are no tight bends in the cable.
17. Adjust the choke cable as described under *Choke Adjustment* in this section of the supplement.
18. Install the carburetor assembly.
19. Install the fuel tank, the seat/rear tail section and the side covers.

FUEL STRAINER

Removal/Cleaning/Installation

Refer to **Figure 7** for this procedure.
1. Turn the fuel shutoff valve to the OFF position.
2. Remove the fuel cup, O-ring seal and filter screen from the bottom of the fuel shutoff valve (**Figure 8**). Dispose of the fuel remaining in the fuel cup properly.
3. Clean the filter screen with a medium soft toothbrush and blow out with compressed air.

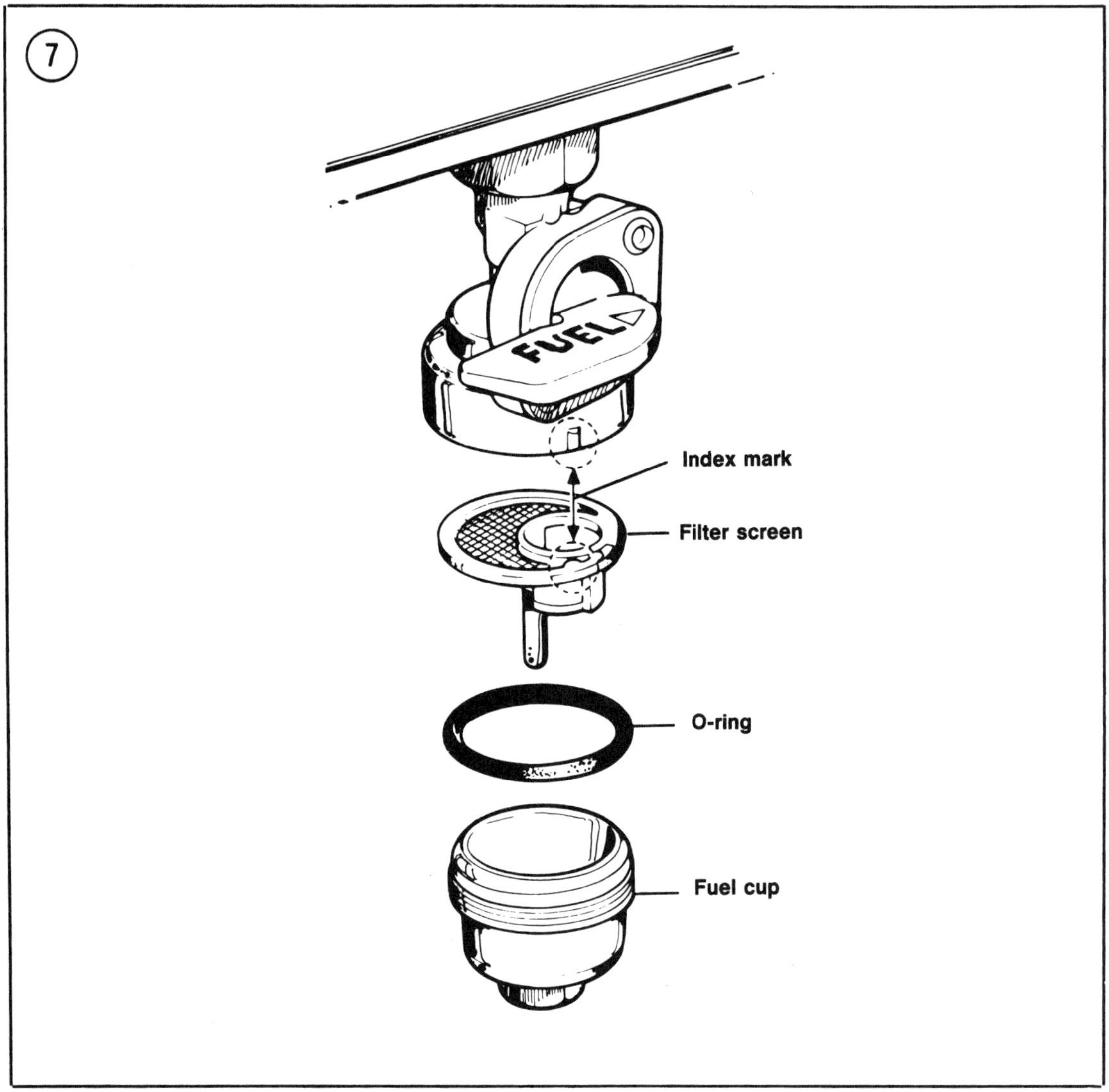

7

Index mark

Filter screen

O-ring

Fuel cup

Replace the filter screen if it is broken in any area.

4. Wash the fuel cup in kerosene to remove any residue or foreign matter. Thoroughly dry with compressed air.

5. Align the index marks on the filter screen and the fuel shutoff valve body.

6. Install the O-ring seal and screw on the fuel cup.

7. Hand tighten the fuel cup and then tighten to a final torque of 2-4 ft.-lb. (3-5 N•m). Do not overtighten the fuel cup, as it may be damaged.

8. Turn the fuel shutoff valve to the ON position and check for leaks.

CHAPTER SEVEN

ELECTRICAL SYSTEM

9

10

LIGHTING SYSTEM (CB6505C)

Taillight/Brakelight Replacement

Remove the screws securing the lens (**Figure 9**) and remove the lens. Wash the inside and the outside of the lens with a mild detergent and wipe dry. Wipe off the reflective base surrounding the bulbs with a soft cloth.

Inspect the lens gasket and replace if it is damaged or deteriorated.

Replace the bulb(s) and install the lens; do not overtighten the screws as the lens may crack.

Indicator Light Replacement

1. Unscrew both front side reflex reflectors from the side of the headlight.
2. Unscrew the headlight mounting bolts (**Figure 10**) on each side of the headlight housing. Pull the housing forward and down.
3. Remove the screws (**Figure 11**) securing the top of the instrument cluster. Remove the top of the cluster.
4. Remove the defective bulb(s) (**Figure 12**) and replace with new ones.
5. Make sure the meter perimeter chrome trim ring is positioned correctly onto the lower portion of the instrument cluster.
6. Push up on the lower trim panel. Make sure that the rubber base that holds the turn signal lamp sockets is correctly indexed into the lower trim panel.

7. Install the top of the instrument cluster and install the screws. Push up on the lower trim panel while carefully tightening the screws. Do not overtighten the screws as the screw thread bosses in the lower trim panel may either strip out or break off.
8. Reinstall the headlight assembly. Align the index mark on the headlight mounting bracket with the mark on the headlight housing (**Figure 13**). Install the front side reflex reflectors.

Instrument Cluster Removal/Installation

1. Unscrew both front side reflex reflectors from the side of the headlight.
2. Unscrew the headlight mounting bolts (**Figure 10**) on each side of the headlight housing. Pull the housing forward and down.
3. Disconnect the speedometer and the tachometer drive cables (A, **Figure 14**).
4. Remove the screw on each side of the headlight housing. Pull out on the bottom of the headlight assembly and disengage it from the locating tab on top of the headlight housing.
5. Disconnect the black electrical connector (containing 9 wires) within the headlight housing.
6. Unscrew the mounting nuts (B, **Figure 14**) securing the instrument cluster to the top fork bridge.
7. Carefully remove the electrical wires and connector from the backside of the headlight housing.
8. Install by reversing these removal steps.

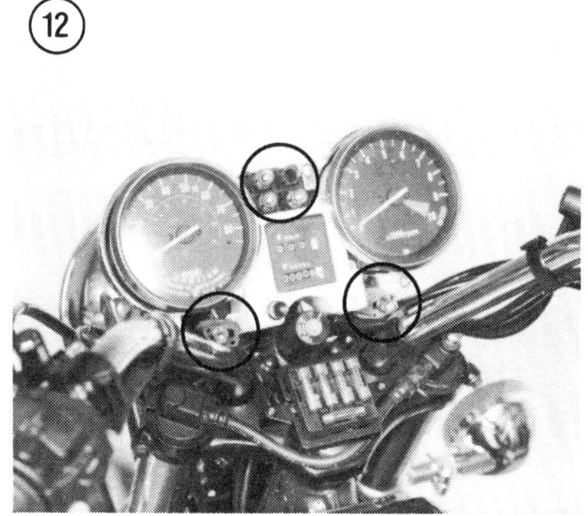

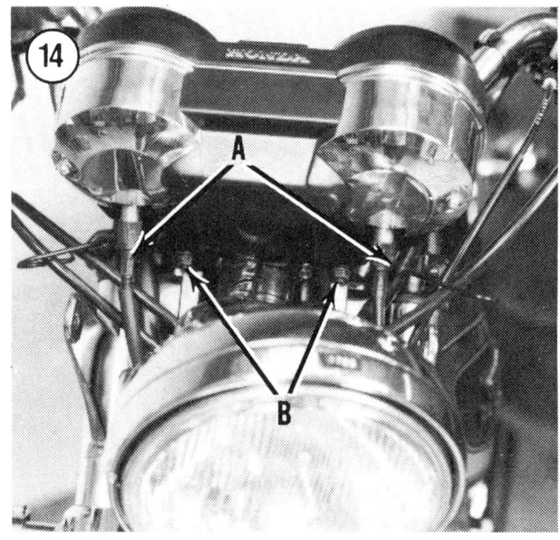

CAUTION
After the instrument cluster is removed, do not set it with the speedometer and tachometer faces down for an extended period of time, as the damping fluid will drain out onto the inside surface of the lens.

Fuse

There are 5 fuses used on the CB650SC. The main fuse (fusible link) is located next to

the starter solenoid and the remaining 4 are located in the fuse panel on the upper fork bridge.

If the main fusible link blows, disconnect the electrical connector (A, **Figure 15**). There is a spare link inside the panel (B, **Figure 15**). The remaining fuses are accessible by removing the screws (**Figure 16**) securing the fuse cover and removing the cover on the upper fork bridge. There is one spare fuse (**Figure 17**) here also; always carry spare fuses. Whenever a fuse blows, find out the reason for the failure before replacing the fuse. Usually the trouble is a short circuit in the wiring. This may be caused by worn-through insulation or a disconnected wire shorted to ground.

CAUTION
Never sustitute aluminum foil or wire for a blown fuse. Never use a higher amperage fuse than specified. An overload could cause a fire and complete loss of the motorcycle.

CHAPTER EIGHT

FRONT SUSPENSION AND STEERING

FRONT WHEEL

Removal

1. Place wood block(s) under the engine to support it securely with the front wheel off the ground.
2. Expand the speedometer cable set spring. Pull the speedometer cable (**Figure 18**) free from the hub.
3. On one side only, remove the bolts (**Figure 19**) securing the brake caliper assembly to the front fork and tie it up to the front fork. It is necessary to remove only one of the caliper assemblies, not both.
4. Remove the axle pinch bolt and nut (A, **Figure 20**).
5. Unscrew and withdraw the front axle (B, **Figure 20**).
6. Pull the wheel down and forward and remove it.

CAUTION
Do not set the wheel down on the disc surface as it may get scratched or warped. Set the sidewalls on 2 wood blocks.

NOTE
Insert a piece of vinyl tubing or wood in the caliper in place of the brake disc. That way if the brake lever is inadvertently squeezed, the piston will not be forced out of the cylinder. If this does happen, the caliper may have to be disassembled to reseat the piston and

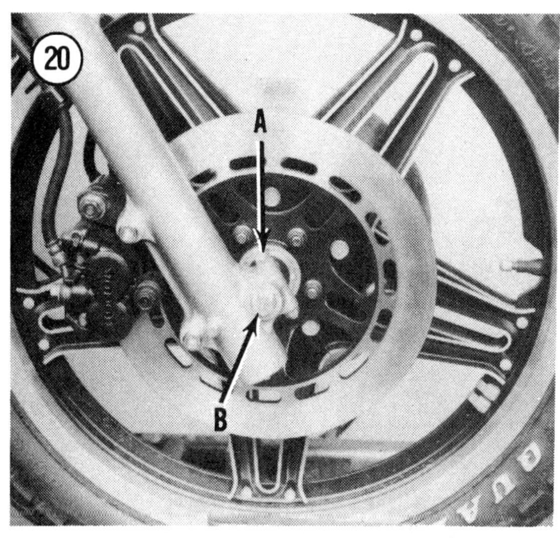

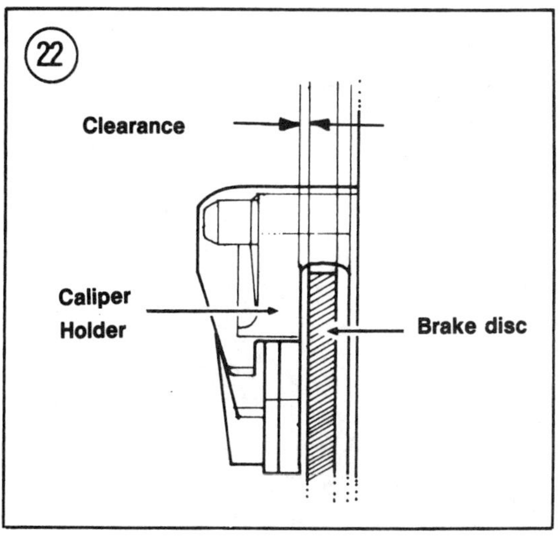

the system will have to be bled. By using the wood, bleeding the brake is not necessary when installing the wheel.

Installation

1. Make sure the axle bearing surfaces of the fork slider and axle are free from burrs and nicks.
2. Remove the vinyl tubing or pieces of wood from the brake caliper.
3. Position the wheel into place, carefully inserting the brake disc between the brake pads.
4. Position the speedometer housing so that it is perpendicular to the left-hand fork leg.
5. Insert the front axle from the right-hand side and screw it into the left-hand fork leg.
6. Tighten the front axle to 40-47 ft.-lb. (55-65 N•m).
7. Install the axle pinch bolt and nut. Tighten it finger-tight only.
8. Install the brake caliper assembly that was removed, being careful not to damage the brake pads.
9. Tighten the caliper mounting bolts to 22-29 ft.-lb. (30-40 N•m).
10. Slowly rotate the wheel and install the speedometer cable into the speedometer housing. Install the cable set spring.
11. With a flat feeler gauge (**Figure 21**), measure the distance between the outside surface of the right-hand brake disc and the caliper holder (**Figure 22**). The distance must be 0.028 in. (0.7 mm) or greater. If the clearance is insufficient, loosen the axle pinch bolt and pull the right-hand fork leg out until this dimension is achieved. Tighten the pinch bolt to 11-18 ft.-lb. (15-25 N•m).

CAUTION

If the specified clearance is not maintained, the brake disc will come in contact with the caliper holder and be damaged. Also brake effectiveness will be greatly reduced.

12. After the wheel is completely installed, rotate it several times and apply the brakes a couple of times to make sure that it rotates freely and that the brake pads are against the disc correctly.

HANDLEBAR (CB650SC)

The handlebar on the Nighthawk (CB650 SC) is the "clip-on" type. There is a separate handlebar on each side and they are removed separately.

Removal

1. Remove the Allen bolt on each side and remove the seat/rear tail section. Disconnect the battery negative lead.
2. Remove the right-hand rear view mirror (A, **Figure 23**).
3. Remove the screws securing the right-hand switch assembly (B, **Figure 23**) and remove the switch assembly and the throttle housing.

CAUTION
Cover the fuel tank and frame with a heavy cloth or plastic tarp to protect it from the accidental spilling of brake fluid. Wash any spilled brake fluid off any painted or plated surface immediately, as it will destroy the finish. Use soapy water and rinse thoroughly.

4. Remove the bolts (C, **Figure 23**) securing the front brake master cylinder and lay it over the fuel tank or front fender. Keep the reservoir in the upright position to keep air from entering into the brake system. It is not necessary to remove the hydraulic brake lines.
5. Remove the left-hand rear view mirror (A, **Figure 24**).
6. Remove the left-hand hand grip (B, **Figure 24**).
7. Slacken the clutch cable and remove the clutch cable from the hand lever.
8. Remove the screw and the clamp securing the choke lever cable. Remove the choke cable end from the choke lever.
9. Remove the screws securing the clutch lever/choke lever assembly (C, **Figure 24**) and slide the assembly off of the handlebar.
10. Loosen the Allen bolts (**Figure 25**) securing the handlebar holder in place.
11. Depress the limiter button (**Figure 26**) in the lower portion of the handlebar and

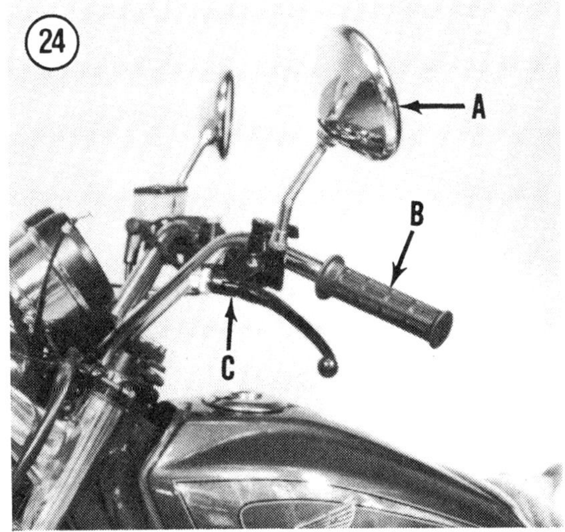

26

27

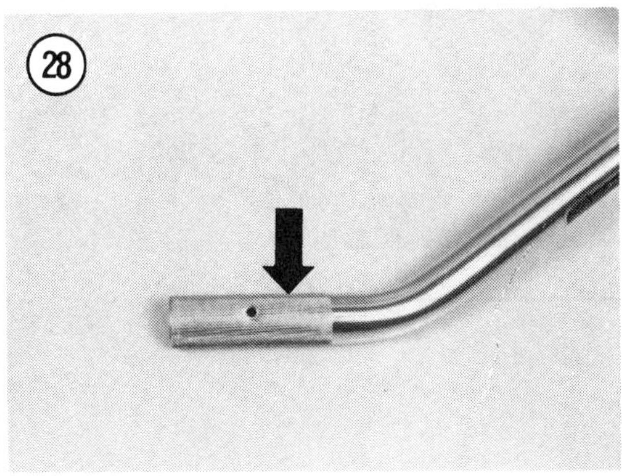
28

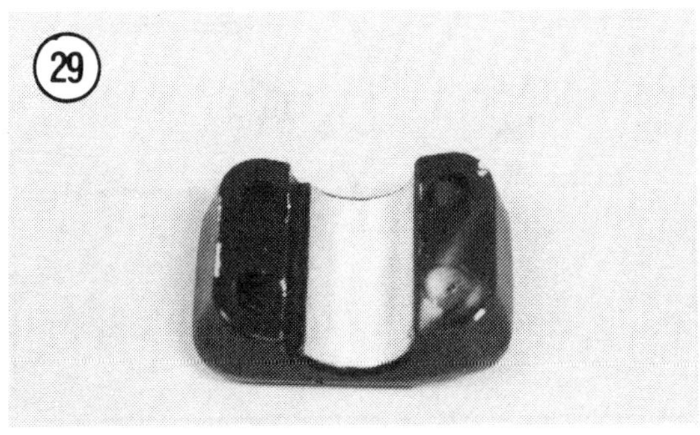
29

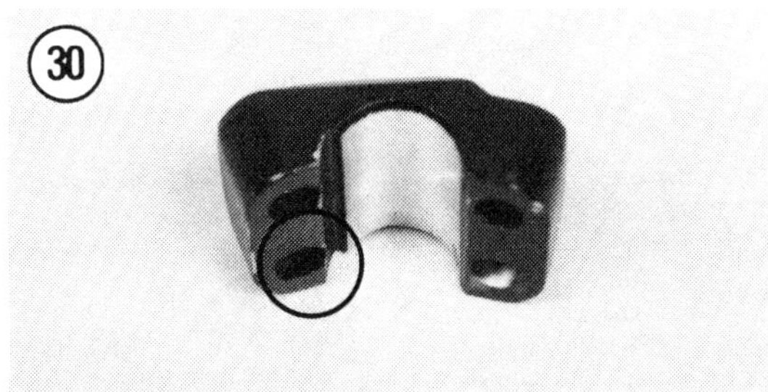
30

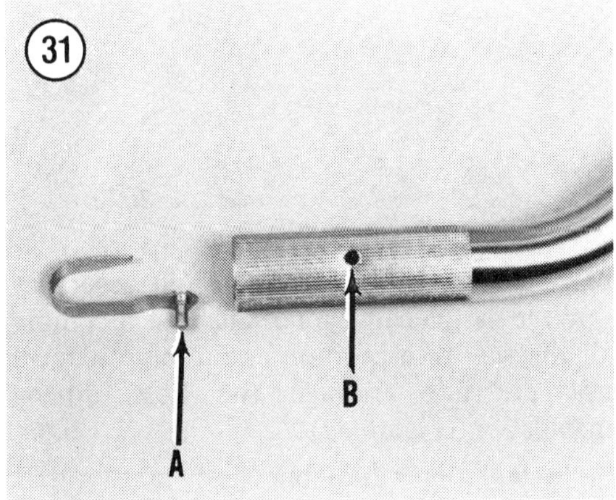

31

remove the limiter button assembly (**Figure 27**) from the bottom of the handlebar.

12. Pull the handlebar up and out of the upper fork bridge.

13. Repeat Steps 11 and 12 for the other handlebar.

14. If necessary, remove the Allen bolts and remove the handlebar holders from the upper fork bridge.

15. To maintain a good grip on the handlebar and to prevent it from slipping either up and down or sideways, clean the knurled section of each handlebar (**Figure 28**) with a wire brush. It should be kept clean and rough so it will be held in place securely by the holders. The holders (**Figure 29**) should also be kept clean and free of any metal that may have been gouged loose by handlebar slippage.

Installation

1. If removed, install the handlebar holders. Position the holder with the notch (**Figure 30**) toward the *rear* of the bike. Install the Allen bolts loosely.

2. Align the button (A, **Figure 31**) with the hole in the handlebar (B, **Figure 31**) and

partially push the limiter button assembly into the handlebar. Do not push the assembly all the way into position as the button must not protrude through the hole during installation (**Figure 32**).

3. Install the handlebar and temporarily tighten the Allen bolts to hold the handlebar in position.
4. Push the limiter button assembly (**Figure 33**) up until the button snaps through the hole in the handlebar (**Figure 34**).

WARNING
Always install each limiter button assembly. *This is a safety item that prevents the handlebar from coming completely out of its receptacle on the upper fork bridge if the Allen bolts should work loose.*

5. Repeat Steps 1-4 for the other handlebar.
6. Apply a light coat of multipurpose grease to the throttle grip area of the handlebar prior to installing the throttle grip assembly.

NOTE
*When installing all assemblies, align the punch mark on the handlebar with the slit on the mounting bracket (**Figure 35**).*

7. Install the throttle grip assembly and the right-hand switch assembly.
8. Install the master cylinder assembly onto the handlebar. Install the clamp with the

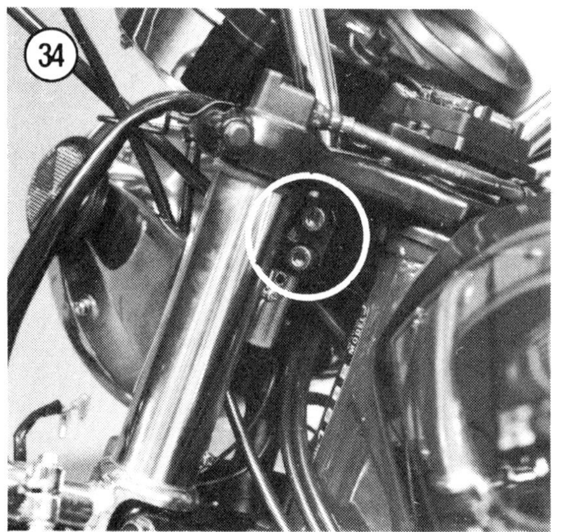

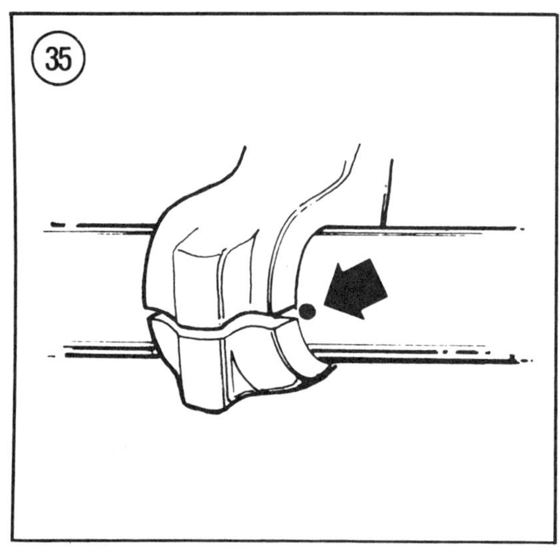

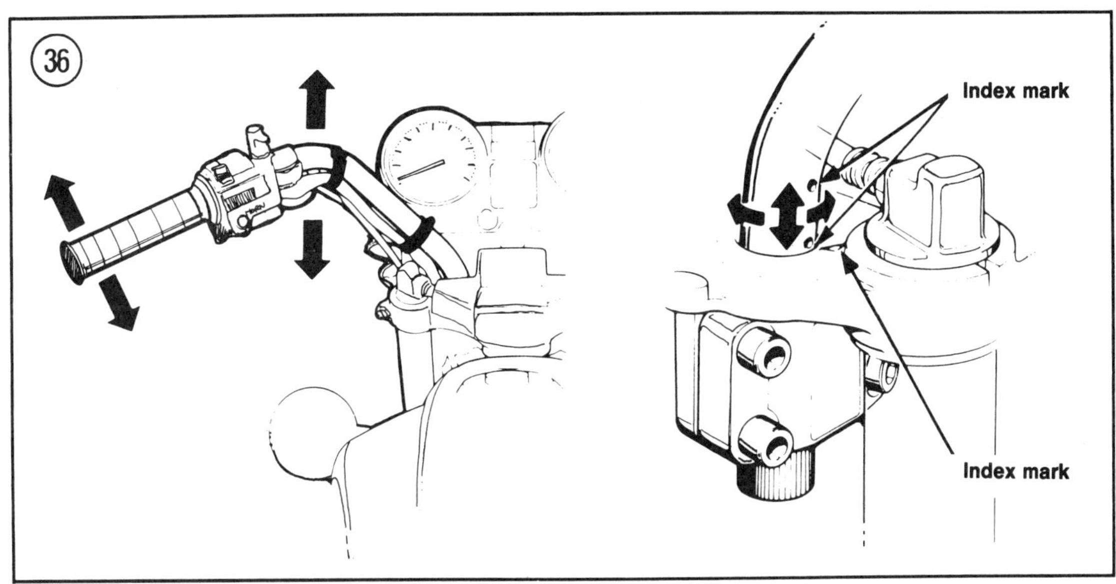

"UP" mark facing up and the wire relief facing down. Align the clamp mating surface with the punch mark on the bottom surface of the handlebar. Tighten the upper bolt first and then the lower bolt.

WARNING

After installation is complete, make sure the brake lever does not come in contact with the the throttle grip assembly when it is pulled on all the way.

9. Slide on the clutch lever/choke lever assembly and tighten the screws.
10. Install the left-hand handlebar switch assembly.
11. Connect the battery negative lead.
12. Install the seat/rear tail section.
13. Adjust the throttle and clutch as described in Chapter Three in the main body of this book.

Handlebar Adjustment

Refer to **Figure 36** for this procedure.

1. Loosen the Allen bolts (**Figure 25**) on each handlebar.
2. Rotate and slide the handlebars up or down to achieve a comfortable riding position.
3. Both handlebars should be in the same relative position. Use the punch marks (**Figure 37**) on the handlebar as a guide.
4. Tighten the front Allen bolts first and then the rear bolts. Tighten to 13-17 ft.-lb. (18-23 N•m).

WARNING

Push and pull on the handlebars with force to make sure they are held securely in place. You don't want one of the handlebars to work loose while riding. Also make sure that all electrical wires and cables are not kinked or pulled taut. They must be free during handlebar rotation from full right to full left.

CHAPTER NINE

REAR SUSPENSION

SHOCK ABSORBERS (CB650SC)

Disassembly/Inspection/Assembly

Disassembly and assembly of the shock absorber is exactly the same as on previous models. If the spring has sagged to 9.0 in. (229 mm) or less it must be replaced.

CHAPTER ELEVEN

BRAKES

FRONT DISC BRAKE

The standard CB650 has a single front disc brake while the CB650SC (Nighthawk) has dual front disc brakes. Both models have dual-piston calipers.

Service procedures are the same on all 1982 models. Caliper inspection specifications are covered in **Table 5**.

When working on hydraulic brake systems, it is necessary that the work area and all tools be absolutely clean. Any tiny particles of foreign matter and grit in the caliper assembly or the master cylinder can damage the components. Also, sharp tools must not be used inside the caliper or on the piston. If there is any doubt about your ability to correctly and safely carry out major service on the brake components, take the job to a dealer or brake specialist.

Brake Pad Replacement

There is no recommended mileage interval for changing the friction pads in the disc brake. Pad wear depends greatly on riding habits and conditions. The pads should be checked for wear every 600 miles (1,000 km) and replaced when the wear indicator reaches the edge of the brake disc. To maintain an even brake pressure on the disc always replace both pads in each caliper at the same time.

Table 5 BRAKE SPECIFICATIONS

Item	Standard	Wear limit
Caliper		
Cylinder bore ID		
Standard	1.1902-1.921 in. (30.230-30.280 mm)	1.193 in. (30.29 mm)
Nighthawk	1.0630-1.0660 in. (27.000-27.076 mm)	1.066 in. (27.076 mm)
Piston OD		
Standard	1.1869-1.1889 in. (30.148-30.198 mm)	1.187 in. (30.14 mm)
Nighthawk	1.0598-1.0618 in. (26.920-26.970 mm)	1.060 in. (26.912 mm)
Brake disc thickness		
Standard	0.27-0.28 in. (6.8-7.2 mm)	0.24 in. (6.0 mm)
Nighthawk	0.19-0.29 in. (4.8-5.2 mm)	0.16 in. (4.0 mm)

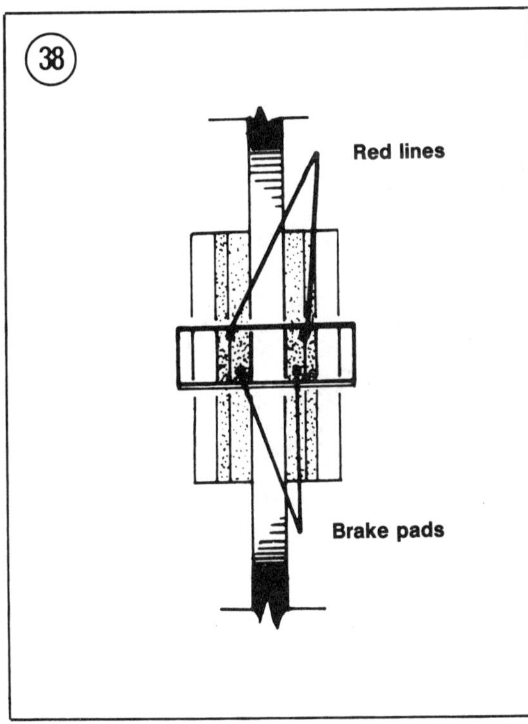

CAUTION
*Watch the pads more closely when the red line approaches the disc (**Figure 38**). On some pads the red line is very close to the pad's metal backing plate. If pad wear happens to be uneven for some reason the backing plate may come in contact with the disc and cause damage.*

Refer to **Figure 39** for this procedure.

1. Remove the bolts securing the caliper assembly to the front fork (**Figure 40**). Remove the caliper assembly from the disc.
2. Remove the bolt (A, **Figure 41**) securing the pin retainer to the caliper assembly and remove the pin retainer.
3. Remove the 2 pins (A, **Figure 42**) securing the pads in place.
4. Remove both brake pads.
5. Clean the pad recess and the end of the pistons with a soft brush. Do not use solvent, a wire brush or any hard tool which would damage the cylinders or pistons.
6. Carefully remove any rust or corrosion from the disc.
7. Lightly coat the end of the pistons and the backs of the new pads (*not the friction material*) with disc brake lubricant.

NOTE
When purchasing new pads, check with your dealer to make sure the friction compound of the new pad is compatible with the disc material. Remove any roughness from the backs of the new pads with a fine-cut file; blow them clean with compressed air.

8. When new pads are installed in the caliper the master cylinder brake fluid level will rise as the caliper pistons are repositioned. Clean the top of the master cylinder of all dirt and

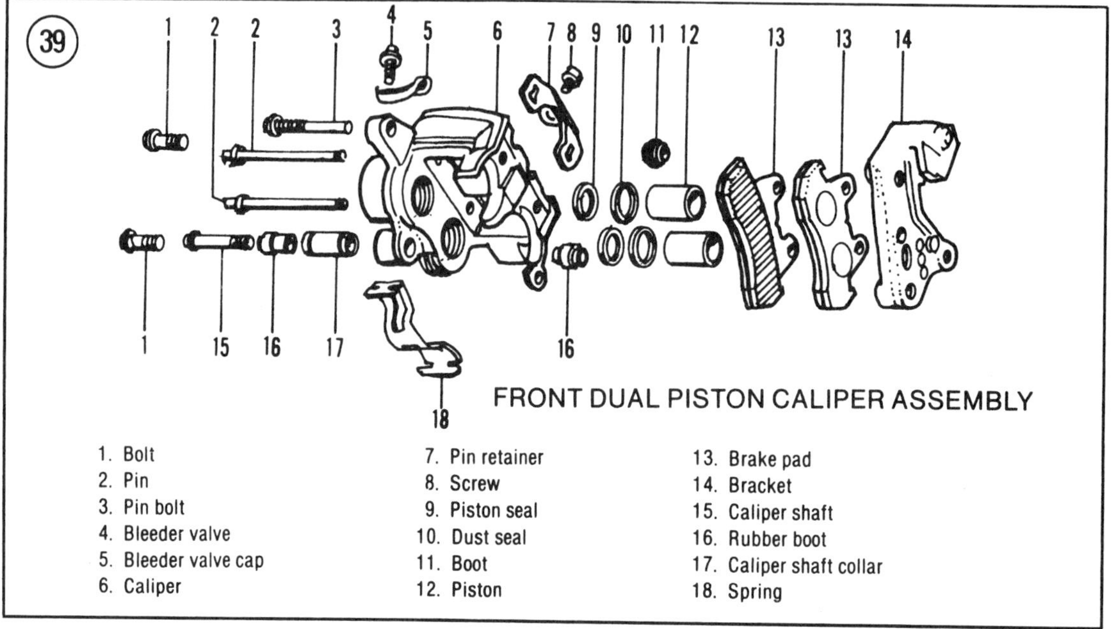

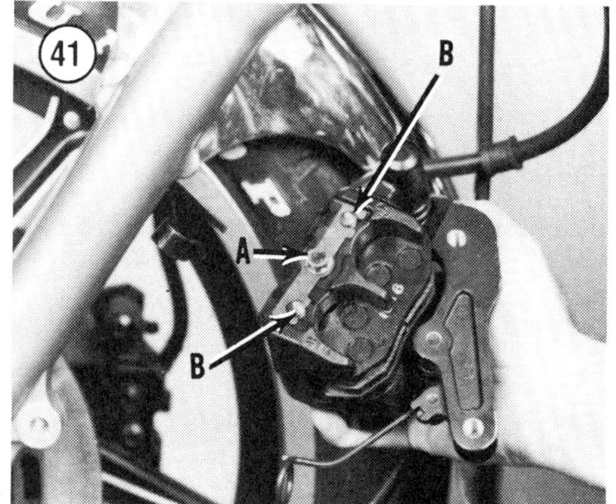

foreign matter. Remove the cap and diaphragm from the master cylinder and slowly push the caliper pistons into the caliper. Constantly check the reservoir to make sure brake fluid does not overflow. Remove fluid, if necessary, prior to it overflowing. The pistons should move freely. If they don't, and there is evidence of them sticking in the cylinder, the caliper should be removed and serviced as described under *Caliper Rebuilding* in this section of the supplement.

9. Push the caliper pistons in all the way (A, **Figure 43**) to allow room for the new pads.

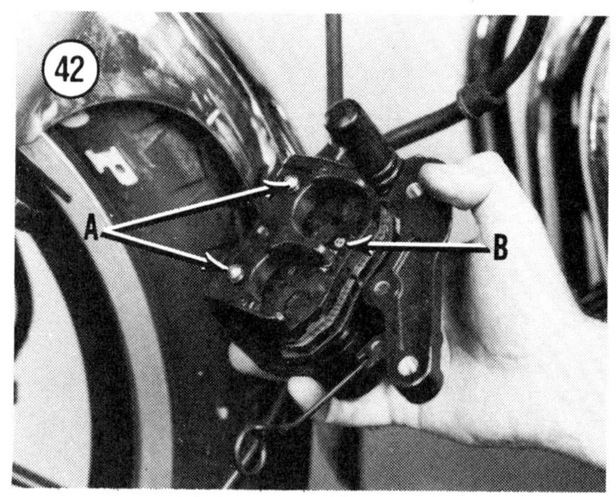

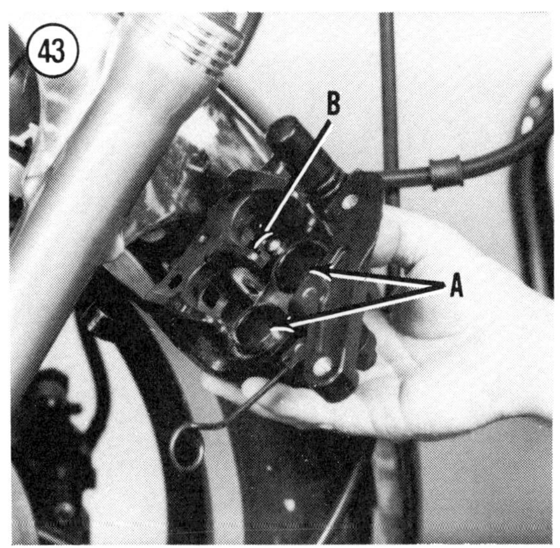

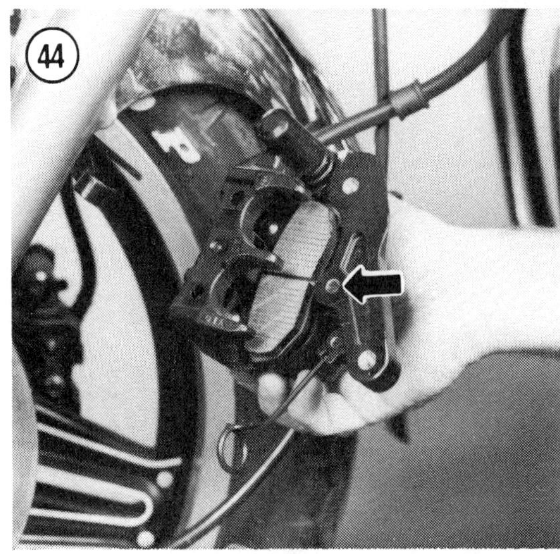

10. Install the anti-rattle spring (B, **Figure 43**).

11. Install the outboard pad (**Figure 44**) and push the pad down against the anti-rattle spring. Partially install the pins through that pad.

12. Install the inboard pad (B, **Figure 42**) and push the pins all the way through.

13. Install the pad pin retainer onto the ends of the pins. Push the pin retainer down and make sure it seats completely on the groove in each pin (B, **Figure 41**).

14. Install the pad pin retaining bolt (A, **Figure 41**).

15. Carefully install the caliper assembly onto the disc. Be careful not to damage the leading edge of the pads during installation.

16. Install the caliper mounting bolts and tighen to 22-29 ft.-lb. (30-40 N•m).

17. On models so equipped, repeat for the other caliper assembly.

18. Place wood blocks under the engine or frame so that the front wheel is off the ground. Spin the front wheel and activate the brake lever as many times as it takes to refill the cylinder in the caliper and correctly locate the pads.

19. Refill the master cylinder reservoir, if necessary, to maintain the correct fluid level. Install the diaphragm and top cap.

WARNING

Use brake fluid clearly marked DOT 3 from a sealed container. Other types may vaporize and cause brake failure. Always use the same brand name; do not intermix as many brands are not compatible.

WARNING

*Do not ride the motorcycle until you are sure the brake is operating correctly with full hydraulic advantage. If necessary, bleed the brake as described under **Bleeding the System** in Chapter Ten in the main body of this book.*

20. Bed the pads in gradually for the first 50 miles (80 km) by using only light pressure as much as possible. Immediate hard application will glaze the new friction pads and greatly reduce the effectiveness of the brake.

Caliper Removal/Installation

Refer to **Figure 39** for this procedure.

It is not necessary to remove the front wheel in order to remove either or both caliper assemblies.

CAUTION

Do not spill any brake fluid on the painted portion of the ComStar wheel. Wash off any spilled brake fluid immediately, as it will destroy the finish. Use soapy water and rinse completely.

1. Loosen the caliper bracket mounting bolts (**Figure 45**) gradually in several steps. Push on the caliper while loosening the bolts to push the pistons back into the caliper.
2. Place a container under the brake line at the caliper. Remove the union bolt and sealing washers (**Figure 46**) securing the brake line to the caliper assembly. Remove the brake line and let the brake fluid drain out into the container. Dispose of this brake fluid–never reuse brake fluid. To prevent the entry of moisture and dirt, cap the end of the brake line and tie the loose end up to the forks.
3. On models so equipped, repeat Steps 1-2 for the other caliper assembly.
4. Install by reversing these removal steps, noting the following.
5. Carefully install the caliper assembly onto the disc. Be careful not to damage the leading edge of the pads during installation.
6. Tighten the caliper mounting bolts to 22-29 ft.-lb. (30-40 N•m).
7. Install the brake hose, with a sealing washer on each side of the fitting, onto the caliper. Install the union bolt and tighten to 18-25 ft.-lb. (25-35 N•m).
8. Bleed the brake as described under *Bleeding the System* in Chapter Ten in the main body of this book.

WARNING

Do not ride the motorcycle until you are sure that the brakes are operating properly.

Caliper Rebuilding

If the caliper leaks, the caliper should be rebuilt. If the pistons stick in the cylinders, indicating severe wear or galling, the entire unit should be replaced. Rebuilding a leaky caliper requires special tools and experience.

Caliper service should be entrusted to a dealer, motorcycle repair shop or brake specialist. Considerable money can be saved by removing the caliper yourself and taking it in for repair.

Brake Disc Removal/Installation

1. Remove the front wheel as described in this supplement.

NOTE

Place a piece of wood or vinyl tube in the caliper(s) in place of the disc(s). This way, if the brake lever is inadvertently squeezed, the pistons will not be forced out of the cylinder. If this does happen, the caliper might have to be disassembled to reseat the piston and the system will have to be bled. By using the wood, bleeding the system is not necessary when installing the wheel.

2A. On standard axle fork models, remove the front axle and the speedometer housing.

47

48

2B. On leading axle fork models, remove the speedometer housing (**Figure 47**).

3A. On single-disc models, remove the bolts securing the brake disc to the hub and remove the disc.

3B. On dual-disc models, from the right-hand side remove the nuts and withdraw the bolts from the left-hand side (**Figure 48**). Remove both brake discs and the damping shim between each disc and the wheel hub.

4. Install by reversing these removal steps, noting the following.

5. On dual-disc models, be sure to install the damping shim between each disc and the wheel hub. Install the bolts from the left-hand side.

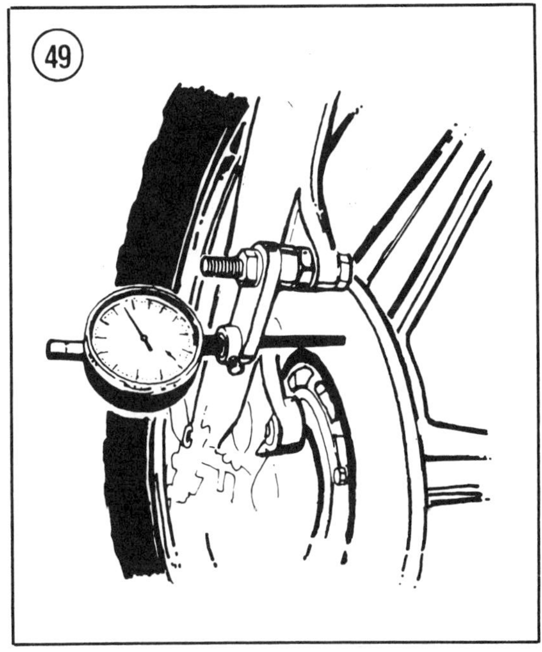

49

7. On all models, tighten the disc mounting bolts and nuts to 20-24 ft.-lb. (27-33 N•m).

Brake Disc Inspection

It is not necessary to remove the disc from the wheel to inspect it. Small marks on the disc are not important, but deep radial scratches, deep enough to snag a fingernail, reduce braking effectiveness and increase brake pad wear. If these grooves are found, the disc should be replaced.

1. Measure the thickness of the disc at several locations around the disc with vernier calipers or micrometer. The disc must be replaced if the thickness, in any area, is less than the following:
   a. CB650: 0.24 in. (6.0 mm).
   b. CB650SC: 0.16 in. (4.0 mm).
2. Make sure the disc bolts and nuts are tight prior to running this check. Check the disc runout with a dial indicator as shown in **Figure 49**. Slowly rotate the wheel and watch the dial indicator. On all models, if the runout is 0.012 in. (0.3 mm) or greater the disc must be replaced.
3. Clean the disc of any rust or corrosion and wipe clean with lacquer thinner. Never use an oil based solvent that may leave an oil residue on the disc.

INDEX

13

S

T

V

W

13

1979 CB650

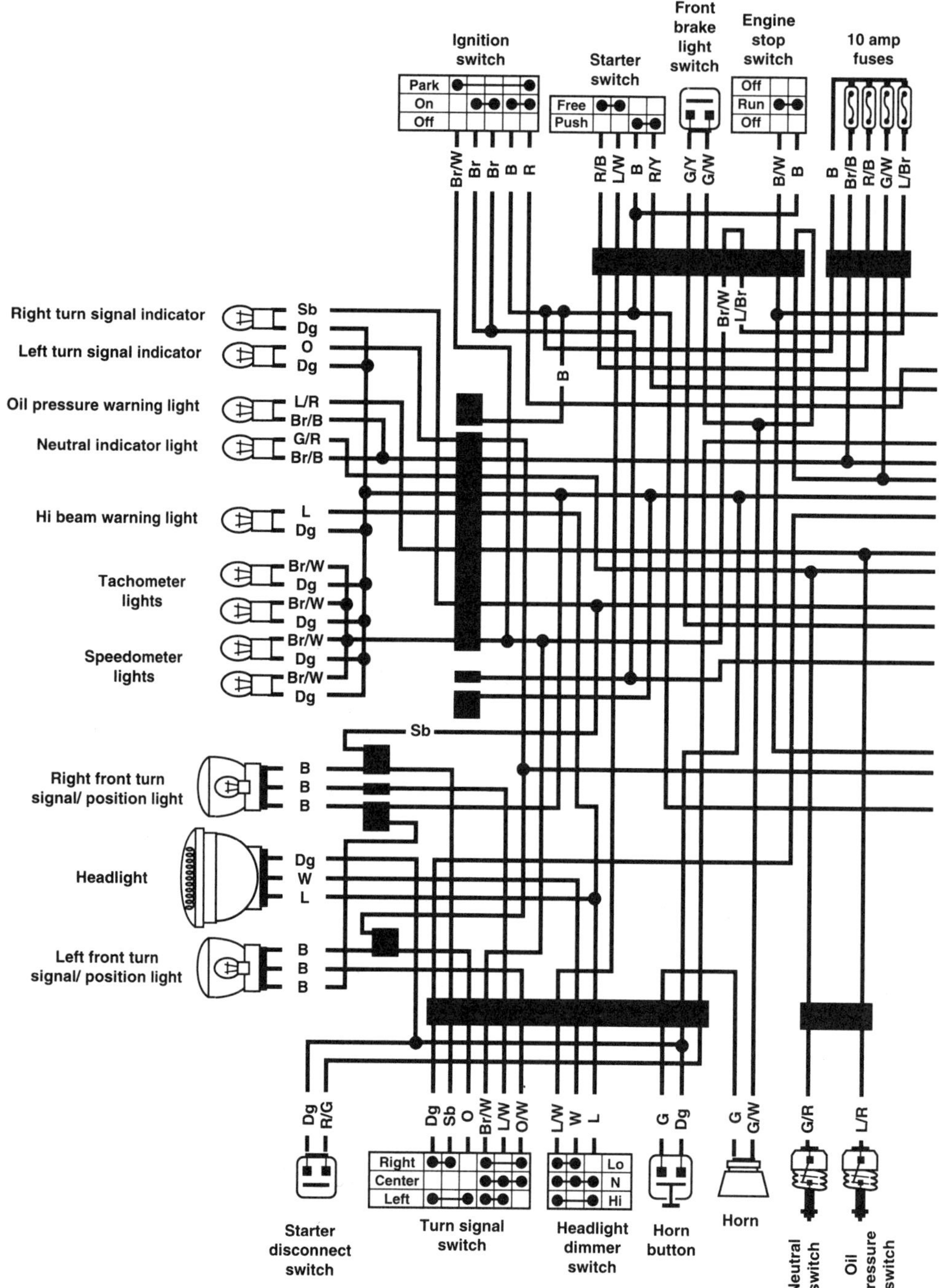

Ignition switch
Park
On
Off
Br/W
Br
Br
B
R
Starter switch
Free
Push
R/B
L/W
B
R/Y
Front brake light switch
G/Y
G/W
Engine stop switch
Off
Run
Off
B/W
B
10 amp fuses
B
Br/B
R/B
G/W
L/Br
Br/W
L/Br
B
Right turn signal indicator
Sb
Dg
Left turn signal indicator
O
Dg
Oil pressure warning light
L/R
Br/B
Neutral indicator light
G/R
Br/B
Hi beam warning light
L
Dg
Tachometer lights
Br/W
Dg
Br/W
Dg
Speedometer lights
Br/W
Dg
Br/W
Dg
Sb
Right front turn signal/ position light
B
B
B
Headlight
Dg
W
L
Left front turn signal/ position light
B
B
B
Dg
R/G
Starter disconnect switch
Dg
Sb
O
Br/W
L/W
O/W
Right
Center
Left
Turn signal switch
L/W
W
L
Lo
N
Hi
Headlight dimmer switch
G
Dg
Horn button
G
G/W
Horn
G/R
Neutral switch
L/R
Oil pressure switch

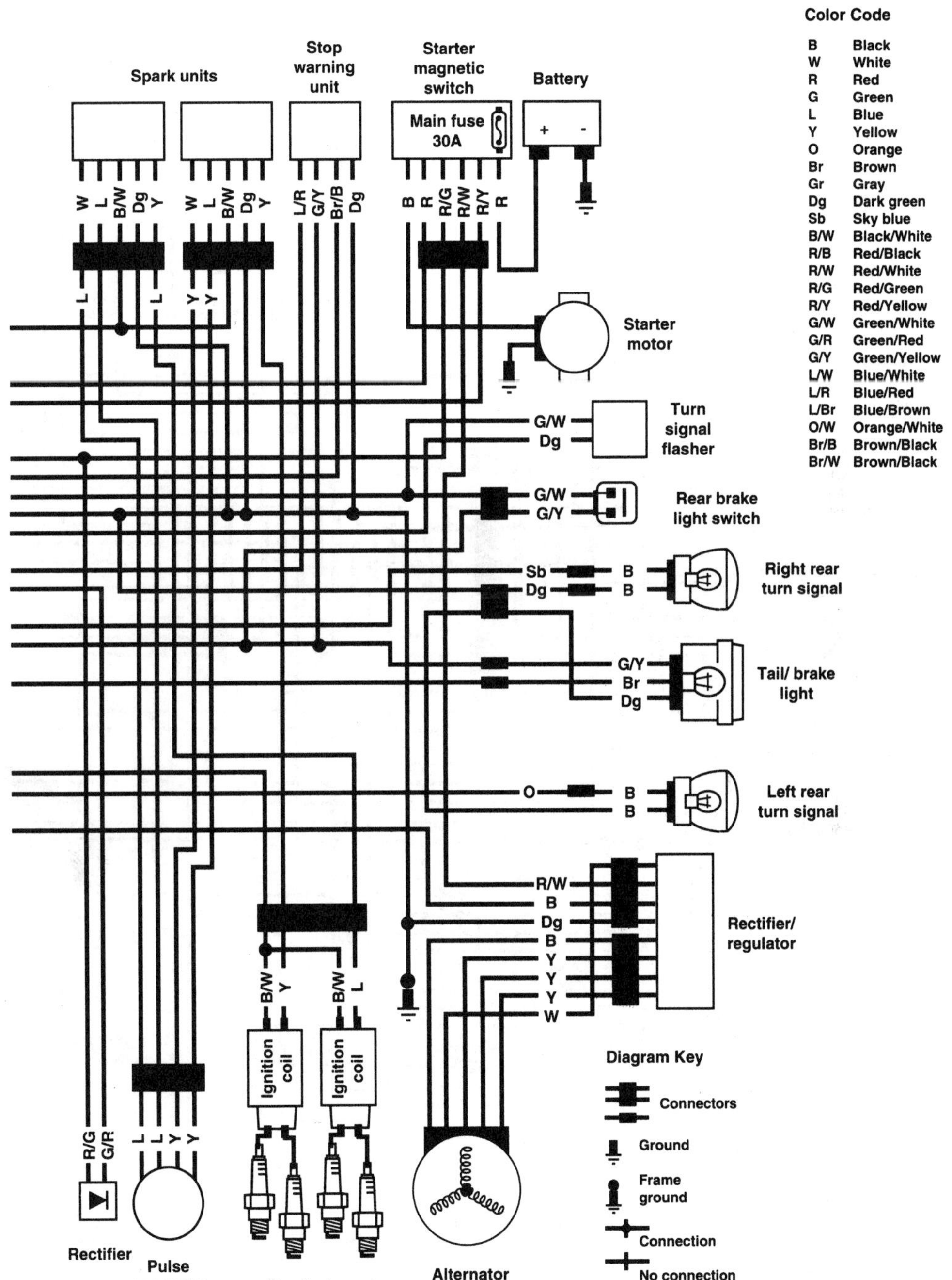
Spark units
Stop warning unit
Starter magnetic switch
Main fuse 30A
Battery
Starter motor
Turn signal flasher
Rear brake light switch
Right rear turn signal
Tail/ brake light
Left rear turn signal
Rectifier/ regulator
Rectifier
Pulse generator
Spark plugs
Ignition coil
Alternator
Color Code
B Black
W White
R Red
G Green
L Blue
Y Yellow
O Orange
Br Brown
Gr Gray
Dg Dark green
Sb Sky blue
B/W Black/White
R/B Red/Black
R/W Red/White
R/G Red/Green
R/Y Red/Yellow
G/W Green/White
G/R Green/Red
G/Y Green/Yellow
L/W Blue/White
L/R Blue/Red
L/Br Blue/Brown
O/W Orange/White
Br/B Brown/Black
Br/W Brown/Black
Diagram Key
Connectors
Ground
Frame ground
Connection
No connection

1980-1982 CB650 AND 1980-1981 CB650C CUSTOM

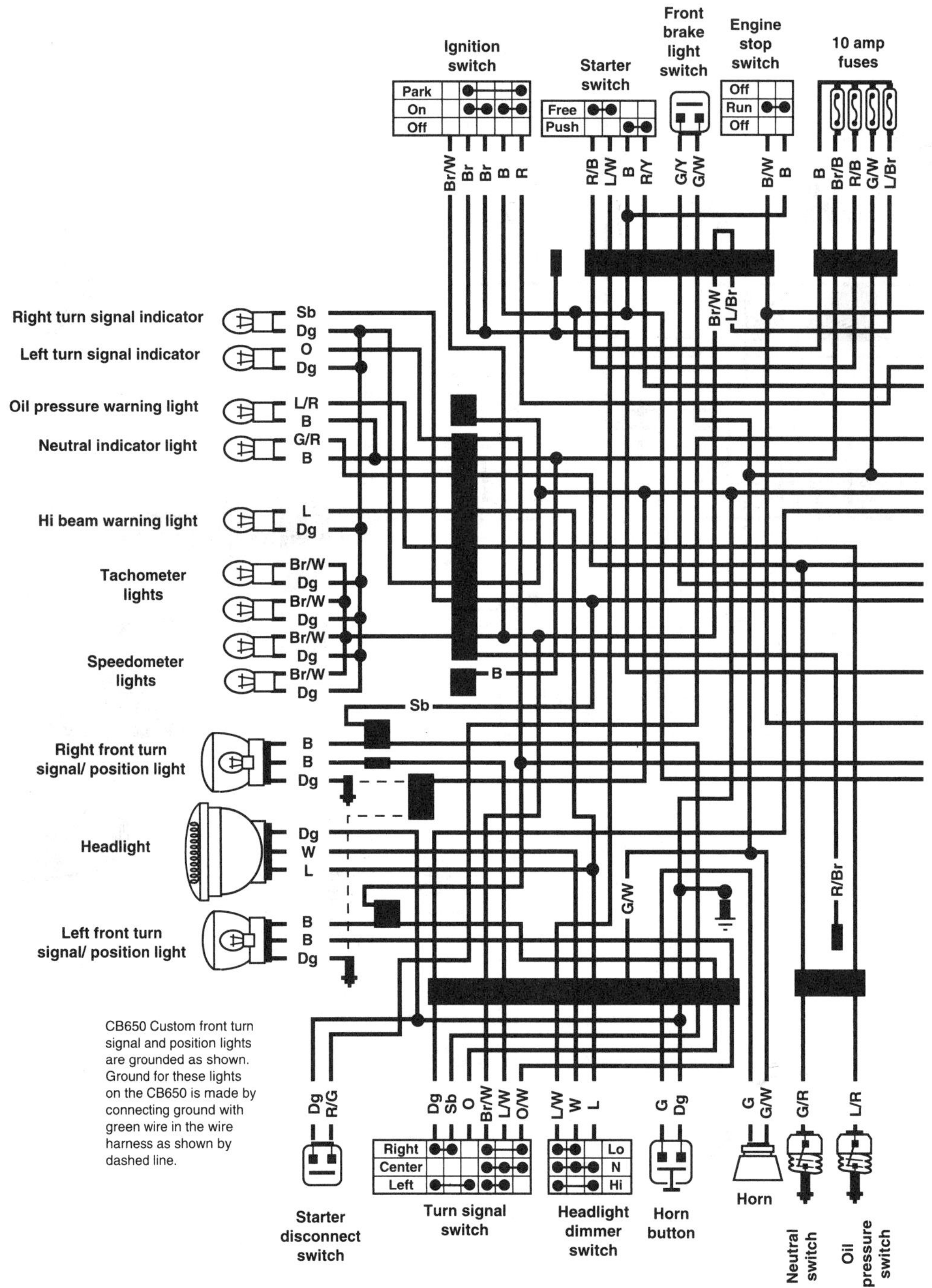

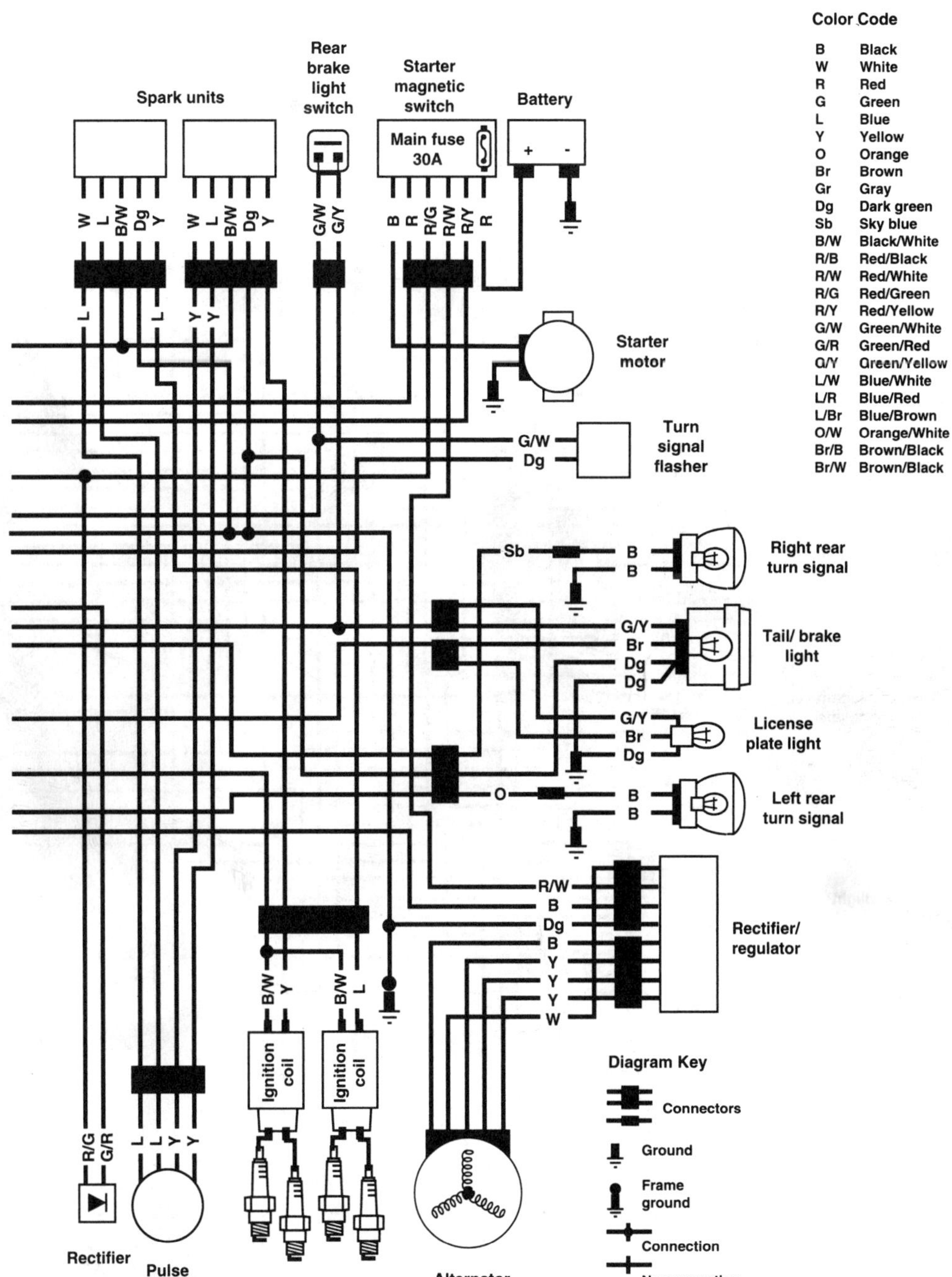
Color Code
B Black
W White
R Red
G Green
L Blue
Y Yellow
O Orange
Br Brown
Gr Gray
Dg Dark green
Sb Sky blue
B/W Black/White
R/B Red/Black
R/W Red/White
R/G Red/Green
R/Y Red/Yellow
G/W Green/White
G/R Green/Red
G/Y Green/Yellow
L/W Blue/White
L/R Blue/Red
L/Br Blue/Brown
O/W Orange/White
Br/B Brown/Black
Br/W Brown/Black
Spark units
Rear brake light switch
Starter magnetic switch
Main fuse 30A
Battery
Starter motor
Turn signal flasher
Right rear turn signal
Tail/ brake light
License plate light
Left rear turn signal
Rectifier/ regulator
Ignition coil
Ignition coil
Rectifier
Pulse generator
Spark plugs
Alternator
Diagram Key
Connectors
Ground
Frame ground
Connection
No connection

1982 CB650SC NIGHTHAWK

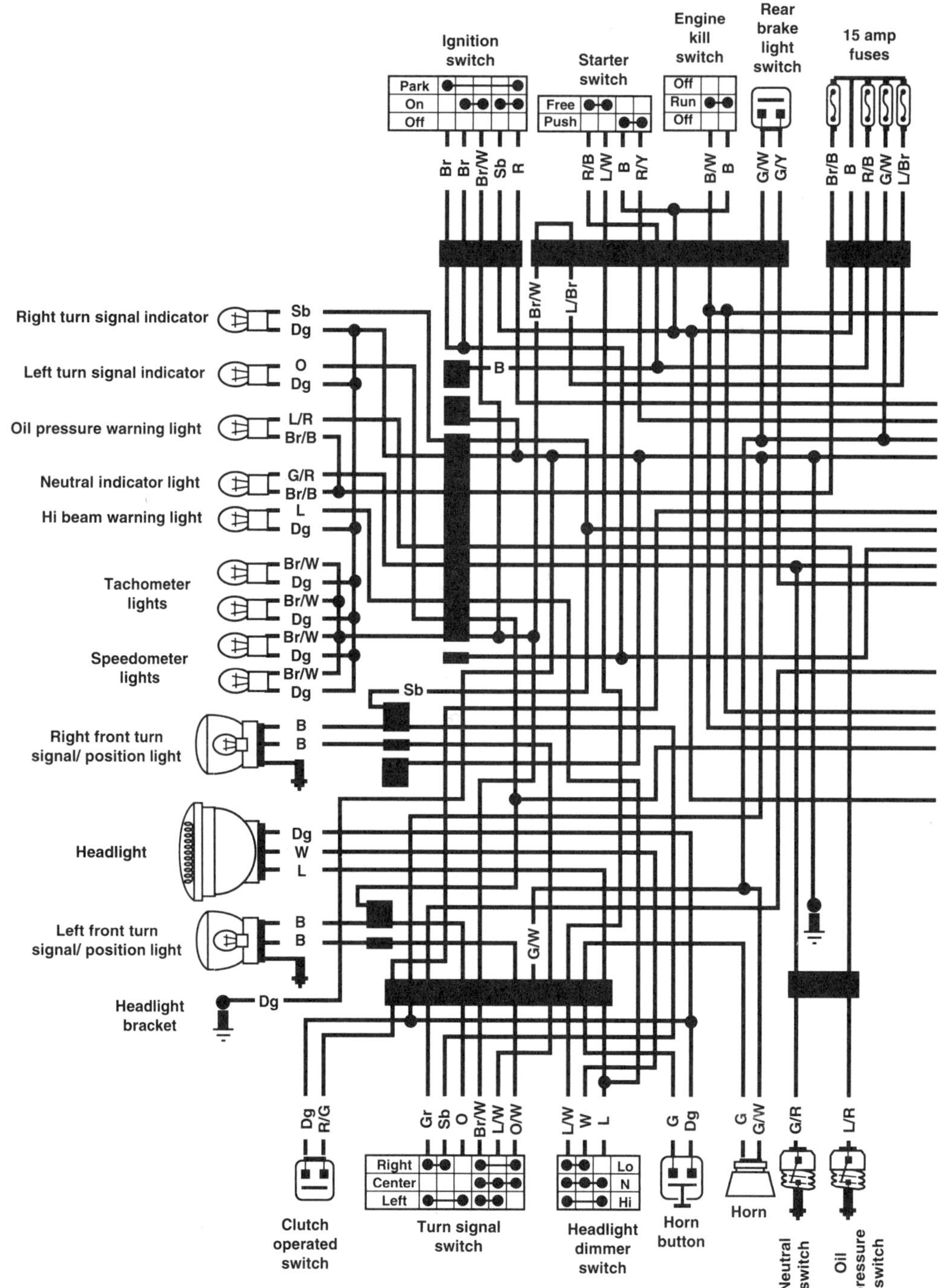

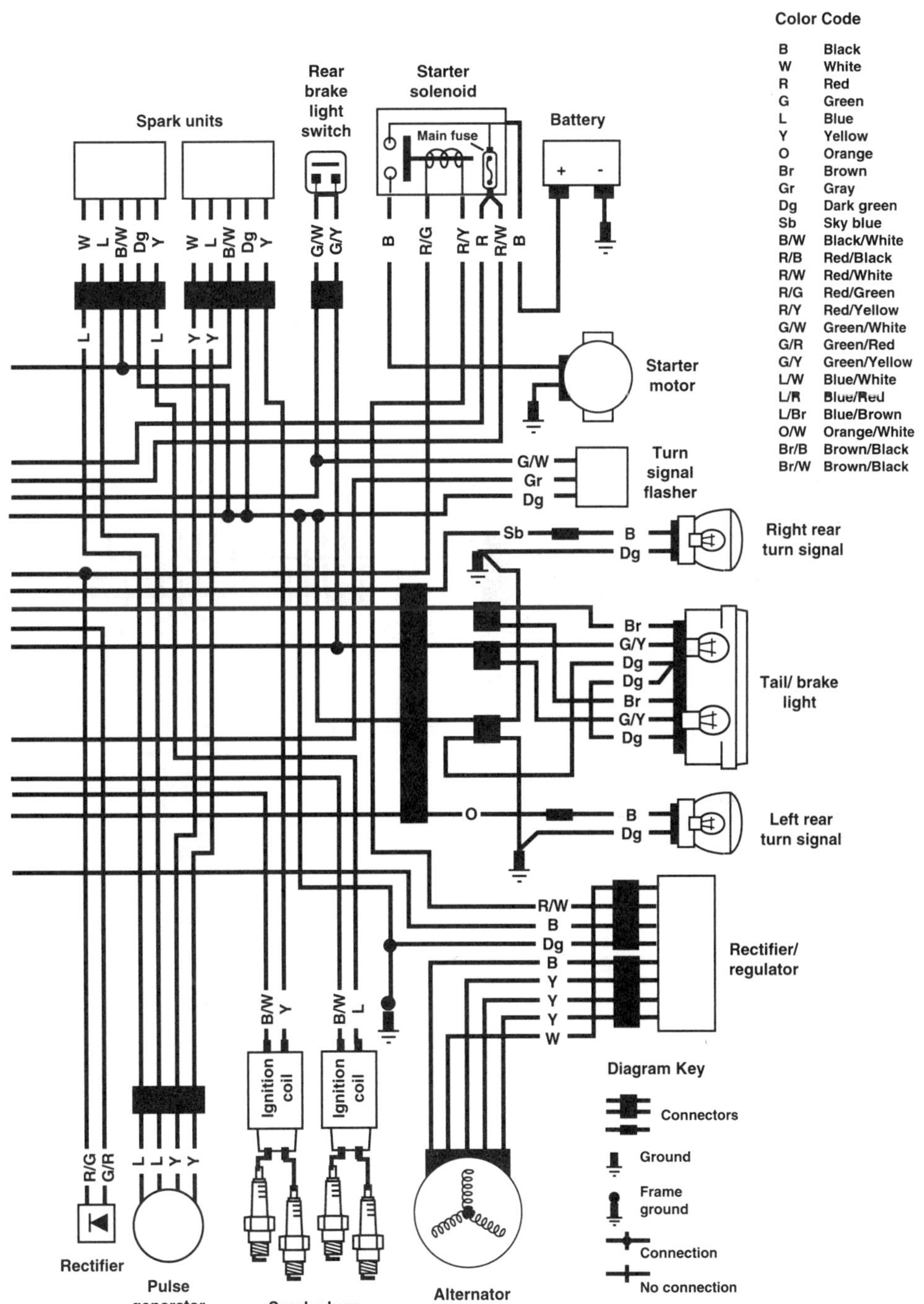
Color Code
B Black
W White
R Red
G Green
L Blue
Y Yellow
O Orange
Br Brown
Gr Gray
Dg Dark green
Sb Sky blue
B/W Black/White
R/B Red/Black
R/W Red/White
R/G Red/Green
R/Y Red/Yellow
G/W Green/White
G/R Green/Red
G/Y Green/Yellow
L/W Blue/White
L/R Blue/Red
L/Br Blue/Brown
O/W Orange/White
Br/B Brown/Black
Br/W Brown/Black
Spark units
Rear brake light switch
Starter solenoid
Main fuse
Battery
Starter motor
Turn signal flasher
Right rear turn signal
Tail/ brake light
Left rear turn signal
Rectifier/ regulator
Ignition coil
Ignition coil
Rectifier
Pulse generator
Spark plugs
Alternator
Diagram Key
Connectors
Ground
Frame ground
Connection
No connection

NOTES

NOTES

NOTES

NOTES

NOTES

MAINTENANCE LOG

Date	Miles	Type of Service